MW01353404

WHAT GROWS HERE?

May your garden be green,
your weeds be brown,
and your blisters be few!
Carol L. Young

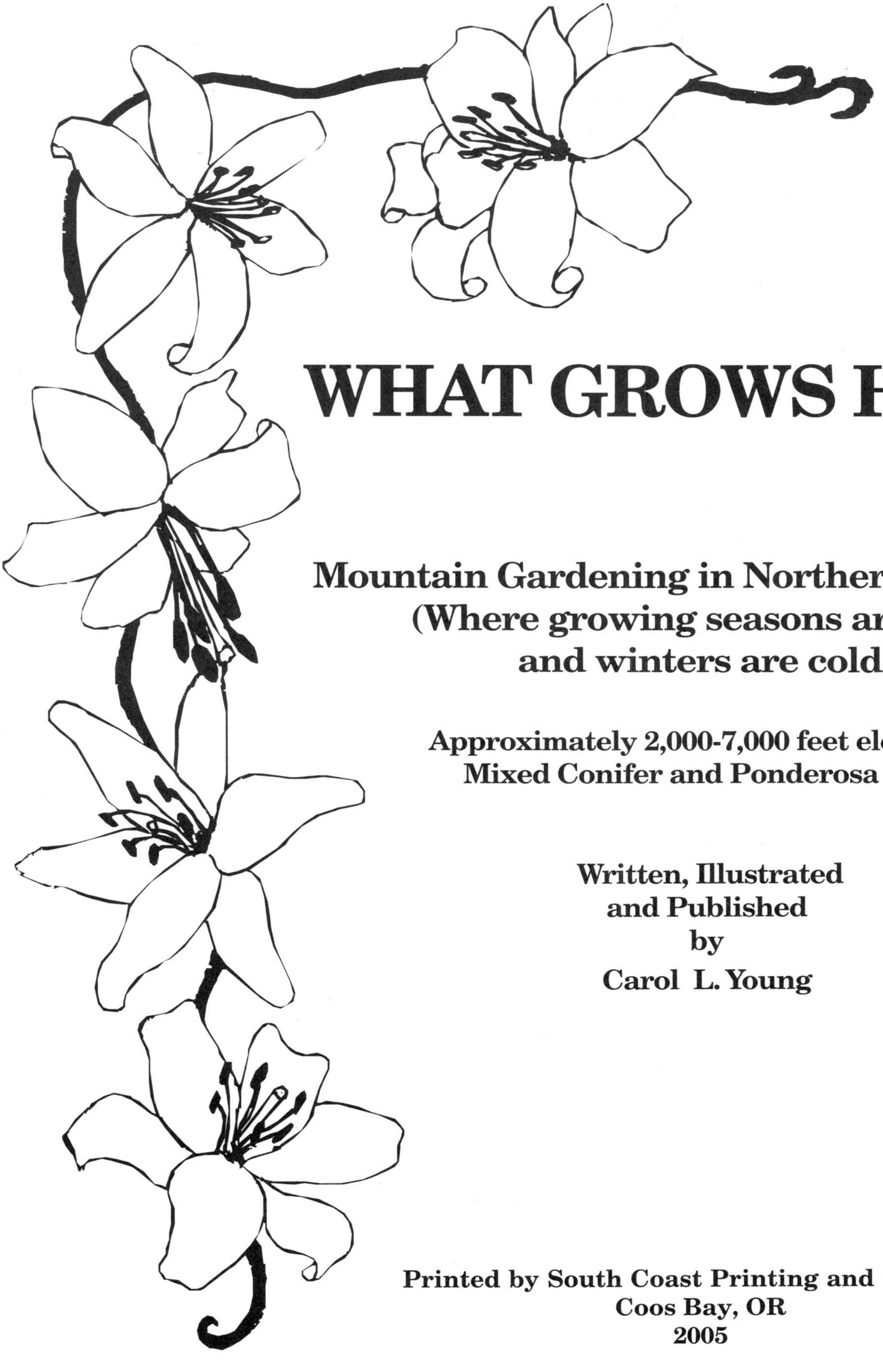

WHAT GROWS HERE?

Mountain Gardening in Northern California (Where growing seasons are short and winters are cold)

Approximately 2,000-7,000 feet elevation
Mixed Conifer and Ponderosa Pine

Written, Illustrated
and Published
by
Carol L. Young

Printed by South Coast Printing and Graphics
Coos Bay, OR
2005

BOOK REVIEWS

***The Chester Progressive* newspaper 9-17-86** said, "Gardeners here are constantly frustrated with the lack of information available on plants, and planting for this area. Our counties, with their varied mountain temperatures, altitudes, and irregular growing seasons do not seem to fit the maps of the popular gardening resource books. A Lake Almanor gardener and graduate in botany has solved the problem by forming the area's first complete gardening book and plant guide, What Grows Here? Local gardeners now have a resource book."

Dick Tracy, Master Gardener, from *Cal Life* Magazine of *Sacramento Bee* newspaper in Fall '87 and 5-9-87 said, "for up-country gardeners, finding the book is like having a garden friend right next door, full of free advice." "It's informative, factual and fun."

***Pacific Horticulture* magazine Fall '87** said, "This self-published volume recognizes the regional character of gardening as larger publishers seldom do."

***Sunset Magazine* May '88 page 279** said, "This book provides descriptive lists of adapted plants and helpful information on how to deal with problems common to mountain gardeners, such as protecting gardens from deer."

Lana Hekkala, in her Health & Environment column of the *North Tahoe/ Truckee Week* newspaper dated July 25-31, 1991 said "The guidelines and rules are compressed, yet clear and wrapped in enthusiasm and encouragement."

Jean Couzens, in her Bookmarks column, *Sierra Heritage* magazine Jan/Feb 1994 said, "If ever there was a tailor-made gardening book, this is it. With a wealth of research and experimentation behind her, the author has put together gardening guidelines for a unique segment of Northern California, --- mountain lands which lie between 2,000 and 7,000 feet elevation."

Dan Barnett at the *Chico Enterprise-Record* newspaper April 17, 1994 said, --- "Of special interest is the chapter on encouraging children to garden. Young is a mother of three, and she offers abundant practical advice. She says, 'A child's garden is not a place to say *no* to your child. It is a place for them to explore and experiment. Gardening can be creative, educational, imaginative, and a good way for families to spend time together.' "

Lydia in *Off The Shelf* newsletter, July 1997, representing Bookshelf stores at Tahoe City, and Truckee, and Kidshelf Bookstore in Truckee said, "Have you ever had your heart broken trying to grow something that you had no business trying to grow up here? Well, even if you haven't suffered the loss of a garden or favorite plant to deer, squirrel or blasting cold, **What Grows Here** is still an invaluable reference for gardeners at elevation 2000' to 7000'. This recently revised edition deserves a place on every mountain gardener's bookshelf."

Jean Couzens, in her Bookmarks Column, *Sierra Heritage* magazine, March/ April 1999 said, "A woman of many talents, Carol's love of gardening shines through all of her book. Both technical and freewheeling, her philosophy is well expressed in this quotation: 'If you would be happy for a week, get married. If you would be happy for a month, kill your pig. But to be happy for a lifetime, plant a garden. ---Old Chinese proverb'. While it's a piece of cake to write knowledgeably about gardening in valleys and foothills, it's definitely more challenging to cope with the problems of gardening between 2,000 and 7,000 feet elevation."

ACKNOWLEDGEMENTS

I wish to acknowledge the assistance of many people in the writing of this book. Thank you to the Chester Garden Club for sharing their years of knowledge and experience with me. Thanks to the following people for proofreading my manuscript: Karen Watson (Greenville Nursery owner), Meg Quiggle (Landscape Designer), Margaret Peak (good friend), Ruth Gibbs (my mother), and Steve Young (Hydrologist for U.S. Forest Service). Thanks to Allen Shellnut (the Art Teacher at Chester High School) for encouraging and helping me draw the illustrations. Thanks to Steve Young and my son Vance for helping me on the computer. And I want to give a special thank you to my children: Julie, Wendy, and Vance; my parents Dr. & Mrs. John Gibbs; and Karen Watson for their endless encouragement and patience.

I'm grateful to many people for permission granted to use information from their books, magazines, newspapers, maps, charts, pamphlets, handout sheets, and raw data. This often involved letters to both author of the article and editor of the book, plus many phone calls when letters weren't answered.

2nd edition (revised) 1987
3rd edition (revised) 1992
4th edition (revised with index) 1996
5th edition (revised) 2005

ISBN: 0-9638514-1-1

This book is available on my website: www.whatgrowshere.com, and will soon be in thirty Northern California stores. You may contact me on the website; at my mailing address of P.O. Box 208, Coos Bay, OR 97420; or my e-mail at carol@whatgrowshere.com. Discounts are available when you order five or more books.

DEDICATION

This book is dedicated to anyone who likes to plant seeds and watch them grow into colorful flowers and yummy vegetables that your neighbors will envy, ... and to the memory of Johnny Appleseed! John Chapman is Johnny Appleseed's real name. He once said, "I thank the Lord for the things that have been good to me: the sun, the rain and the apple tree." If people would think about sowing wildflower seeds like Penstemon, California Poppies, or apple seeds, along roadsides instead of throwing trash; America would be a more beautiful place to live!

TABLE OF CONTENTS

GARDENING

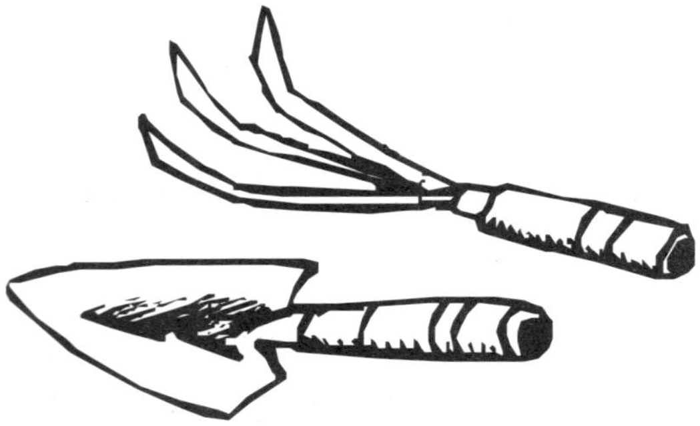

Why do people plant a garden? Gardening is one of the most popular activities in the world today; for some it is a hobby, for others a necessity. Some people plant flowers, while others prefer vegetables or fruits. A garden can satisfy your creative urge, or be an investment in recreation and good health. Landscaping your yard makes your house more attractive and increases its' value. People grow their own fruits and vegetables because they want more wholesome, fresh, chemical-free, delicious food. The price in a grocery store may be cheaper, but consider the value of gardening. Think of the wonderful outdoor exercise, the satisfaction of picking your own vitamin-packed vegetables, and the joy of sharing the garden's bounty with others. Gardening is worthwhile because it helps create health, happiness, and peace of mind.

After a day of stress you enter your quiet, happily growing garden, and almost immediately there is an easing of tension. Having your fingers in the dirt is relaxing. Its relaxing qualities can be compared to kneading bread or making mud pies; both are said to have therapeutic value. You see your problems in their proper perspective and soon you are at peace. One reason gardening appeals to me, is because when I am outdoors surrounded by growing things, I feel especially close to God. I love watching little seedlings grow! I also enjoy soaking up the warm rays of sunshine and absorbing my daily quota of sunshine vitamin D. This is all about the miracle of life.

There are many things to learn about gardening. Some topics are: improving the soil, planning a garden, selecting seeds, maintaining favorable growing conditions, dealing intelligently with insects and disease, harvesting the crops, and cooking and storing vegetables. Gardening can be both challenging and fun! If you like gardening and want to learn more about it, then this book is for you.

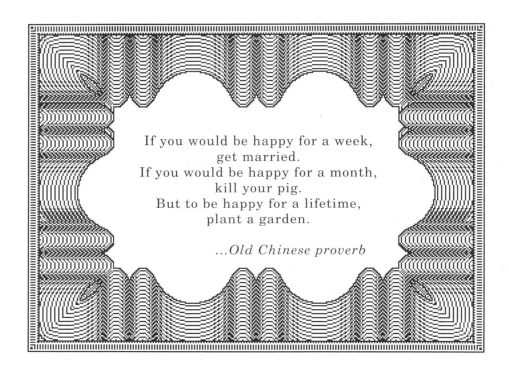

If you would be happy for a week,
get married.
If you would be happy for a month,
kill your pig.
But to be happy for a lifetime,
plant a garden.

...Old Chinese proverb

PLANTS THAT GROW HERE

Anyone who has lived where winters are cold and snowy can relate to the experience of venturing outdoors in early spring and having the joy of seeing the first crocus blooming next to a melting snowbank. Watching the tiny bright green leaves of shrubs and trees unfold and gradually grow larger and larger is particularly exciting to gardeners recovering from "cabin fever". These leaves are such a fresh, clean green color! We have been waiting for that green all winter! Green plants help us enjoy life and living.

Mountain gardeners, especially newcomers, are frustrated by the lack of gardening information on what plants will grow in their yards, and they can use planting tips on how to garden in mountain soils. When you find a plant you like, you need to know if it will grow in your climate zone. Short growing seasons, unexpected frosts, fluctuating temperatures, and irregular terrain (lots of ridges and valleys), make it difficult to assess your local climate zone. And many plants that grow at sea level will not grow in the mountains (higher elevation, colder climate) because they aren't frost resistant. Frosts can occur any day of the year at high elevations, and cold winters kill plants that are not specially adapted.

How do we choose hardy plants that can survive our climate? I wrote this gardening book to help people to garden in the mountains (and the foothills). Many people treat gardening "standards" such as the Sunset Western Garden Book like a "bible" on gardening; however, it doesn't tell people what grows here in the mountains. My book is the first comprehensive gardening book and plant guide for people living between approximately 2,000-7,000 foot elevations in Northern California. The main focus is on gardening in the Mixed Conifer and Ponderosa Pine zones up to the Red Fir zone, but this book may also be helpful for people in borderline areas such as the foothill Digger Pine type. Some areas are colder than others at the same elevation depending on latitude and local climatic conditions (see Climate chapters). This book includes many chapters of "how to" information for mountain gardeners and lists the plants that grow here.

The chapter on climate is an important one, since it discusses how to analyze the many climatic factors affecting your yard, and how to select plants that will grow there. Plants are listed in this book by "climate zones", and you must know what climate zone your garden is in to use the plant lists. After reading this chapter and carefully observing your yard, you should be able to estimate your climate zone. The Northern California mountains include USDA climate zones 4,5,6, and 7 (see map). Any plant that is known to grow in the colder USDA zones 1-4 will most likely grow here too.

Although this book was written as a guide to plants grown in the mountains of Northern California, it can also be applied in areas with similar cold climates and conditions such as is found in Colorado, Montana, the Dakotas, Wyoming, Idaho, Oregon, N. Nevada, Utah, etc. Generally, when you go north in latitude, the temperature decreases as though you were moving up in altitude. What grows at 4,000' in the Southern Cascades or Northern Sierra Nevada, may grow at about 5,000' in the Central Sierra Nevada, or at 6-7,000' in the Southern Sierra Nevada.

The "how to" information includes such topics as preparing the soil, planning the vegetable garden, using intensive gardening in raised beds, dividing perennials, pruning trees and shrubs, and planning a fern garden. It offers advice about easy maintenance by using proper tools, mulching, weeding, watering, composting, and handling garden pests. It offers ideas about how to prepare and preserve your crops of fruits and vegetables. Special interest chapters are included on subjects such as: forcing spring bulbs indoors, secrets of healthy house plants, and encouraging children to garden. There are many charts, maps, illustrations, and drawings; besides having lists of suppliers' catalogs, a bibliography, and an index.

This book includes extensive lists of plants (by category) which are suitable for California's mountain climates, based on local gardeners' experiences and on experts' recommendations. Plants listed in this book either have been successfully grown in the Chester-Lake Almanor (4,500'), the Lake Tahoe area (5,000-7,000'), or have been suggested by reference sources for these climate zones. While this is a fairly complete plant list for this area, just because a plant isn't listed here doesn't mean that it won't grow here. I may have missed some —or perhaps no one has tried it. There are also plant listings for problem situations such as: deer-resistant, fire-resistant, drought-tolerant, and shade-tolerant plants.

The most frequently used references were Sunset Western Garden Book (SWGB), Better Homes & Gardens (BH&G), Readers Digest: Basic, and The Garden Dictionary (Taylor). References cited in the text have a number in brackets like: [2]. The [2] is listed at end of chapter with the name of the article or book. References are fully cited in Reference List at end of book. Catalogs are fully cited in Suppliers' Catalog List.

Plants are either **woody** or **herbaceous**. Woody plants include trees, shrubs, roses, perennial vines, fruits & berries, and hardy ferns. Herbaceous plants include annuals, biennials, perennials, bulbs, ground covers (some are woody, but have a creeping habit), vegetables, and kitchen herbs. Annuals, biennials, and perennials are often called wildflowers or domesticated wildflowers.

An **annual** is a herbaceous plant that lives one year like its name says. A **biennial** is a herbaceous plant that lives two years as "bi" means two. A **perennial** is a herbaceous plant that lives more than two years but has to be divided after 2-5 years depending when the plants get too crowded. Trees and shrubs are woody plants. A **tree** usually has only one stem and is taller, while a **shrub** is usually multi-stemmed and shorter. Since annuals, biennials and perennials are man-made categories, there are often fuzzy lines between categories. For example, under optimal environmental conditions an annual may grow several years (like a biennial), while in extra cold climates some perennials have to be grown as annuals.

Most plants may be purchased from your local nursery or Suppliers' Catalog (see Suppliers' list at back of book). For the readers convenience I have marked with an asterisk * the wildflowers available from High Altitude Gardens Catalog, and a black dot • to denote unusual plants available from Nichols Garden Nursery. Some plants listed in my book are not available in California from out-of-state mail order catalogs because of certain diseases they might bring into California; however, they may be available from some specialized nurseries. References cited in text by number in square brackets, are fully cited in Reference chapter.

Because of the great variation in local microclimates, a plant listed in this book may grow in someones else's yard, but it may or may not grow in yours. Figuring out the climate zone and microclimates on your land is a challenge. Watching seeds and plants grow is an exciting experience. Good luck and happy planting !

UNDERSTANDING PLANT NAMES

We need a universal language for plant names. Common names are used by the general public, but they can be very frustrating. One popular plant may be referred to by hundreds of common names, besides being in many different languages. Common names are given indiscriminately to genera, species, or varieties. Often two or more unrelated plants are known by the same name (like Dusty Miller). Even in the same locality one plant may have more than one common name. Most plants have both a common and a scientific name.

Scientific or botanical plant names are based on a highly organized system used by botanists all over the world. Each kind of plant has one unique name. The scientific name (in Latin) may seem lengthy and difficult to pronounce, but they are the best way to identify a plant accurately. This name is often a concise description of some particular characteristic of the plant (e.g. alba= white), and usually reveals its relationship with other plants. It is the full name of the plant, just as we have a first and last name. A scientific name is made up of two or three words. The first word is the name of the **genus** (plants grouped together with the same characteristics). The following word or words is the **species** (specific plants within each genus). The first (genus) and second (species) names used together are the full botanical name of the species. The genus is always capitalized, while the species name starts with a small letter. For example, consider how we designate the name for a certain species of clover: white clover is Trifolium repens, and red clover is Trifolium pratense. The genus name Trifolium alone refers to all clovers, while the species name repens refers to a particular kind of clover. When you put the two words together (Trifolium repens), you refer to a distinct species, just as Trifolium pratense refers to another distinct species [1].

Taxonomists group the most similar genera (common ancestry) into families, naming the family after the most popular genus, and adding "aceae" on the end like Rose-aceae. Families are divided into genera, genera into species, species into botanical) varieties and (horticultural) cultivars. When you are learning to identify plants, it really helps to know the main characteristics of each family group.

For gardeners, the **species** is the unit of most interest, and they are also concerned with the variations within species. Slight variations of the species are indicated by "var" meaning variety (or subspecies), and a third or fourth word is added to the plant name. If the variation occurs in the wild it is called a **variety**, but if in a garden it is called a **cultivar**. A variety name is given in Latin, but a cultivar has a modern "fancy" name. According to Johnson [2], a maple from Asia, Acer ginnala, has a shrubby variety in Turkestan called Acer ginnalia var. semenoivii. But a purple form of the Norway maple, selected by a nurseryman, in a row of green ones (that he was growing from seed), has to be called Acer platanoides 'Crimson King' because it is a cultivar. A natural variety which occurs in the wild, can be grown from seed and be the same as its parents. A cultivar is usually the result of a chance mutation and has to be propagated by cuttings (because its' seed will produce plants like its' parents instead of like itself). Most modern roses are cultivars.

In the plants lists, the genus and species names are usually in parenthesis following the common name, like LILAC (Syringa albiflora var. repens). The genus name is always written out the first time it appears in a list, and after that it is abbreviated (S. albiflora var. repens). When buying a plant at a nursery, check its Latin name: genus, species, and variety or hybrid if it has one, like Vinca minor. Both common name and Latin names of the plants are listed in the index.

Species names are important because plants can vary widely within their genus. There can be wide differences among species and even varieties in any genus. Plants can vary by being evergreen or deciduous, in size, in hardiness, in flower color, in flowering time, and in other special requirements [3]. I'm using the most recent botanical names, but nurseries often are using older names, so be aware of this.

References cited:
[1] Botany, an introduction to plant science
[2] The Principles of Gardening
[3] Readers Digest: Success with House Plants

THE LANGUAGE OF BOTANY

A botanical description of a plant uses special terms that are an essential shorthand to prevent descriptions from being impossibly long-winded. Some typical terms are "solitary on pedicels", obovate leaves", and "margins irregularly toothed". When a gardener learns a few botanical terms, he can better use reference books and identifying keys. Glossaries of terms are often included in texts, but pictures really show what such words mean. These pictures were redrawn from Johnson's The Principles of Gardening, pp 248 and 254.

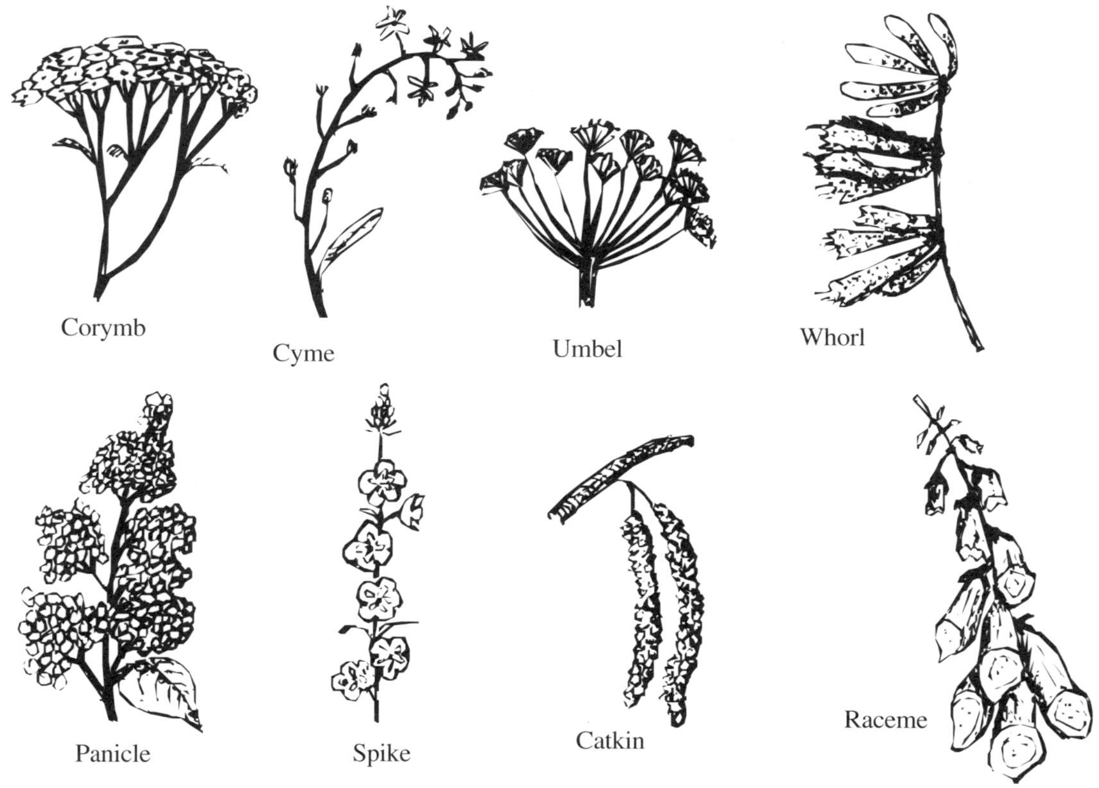

FLOWER FORMS

LEAF FORMS

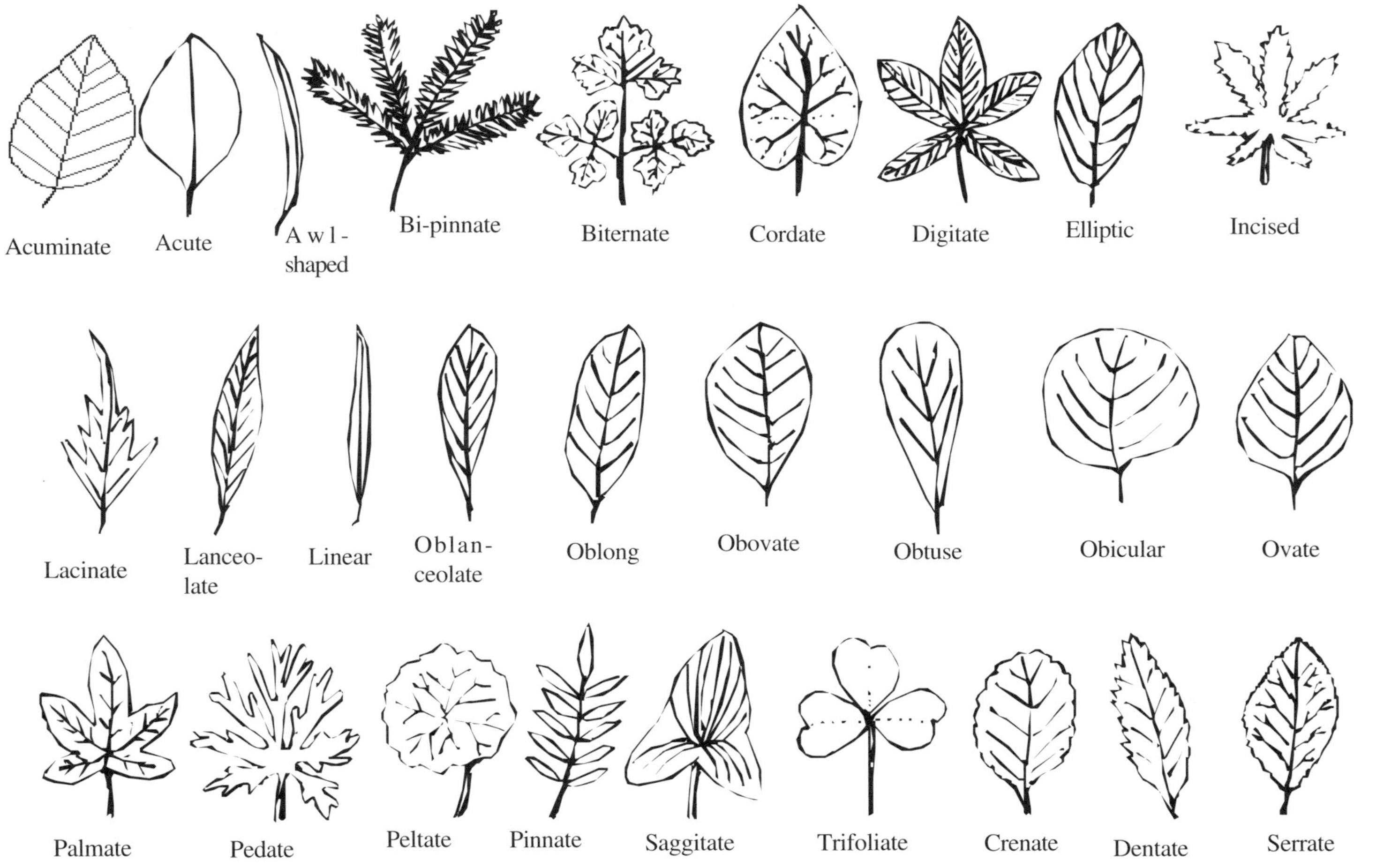

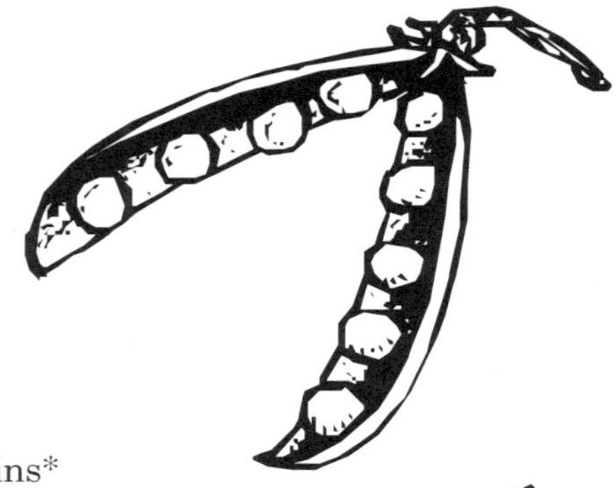

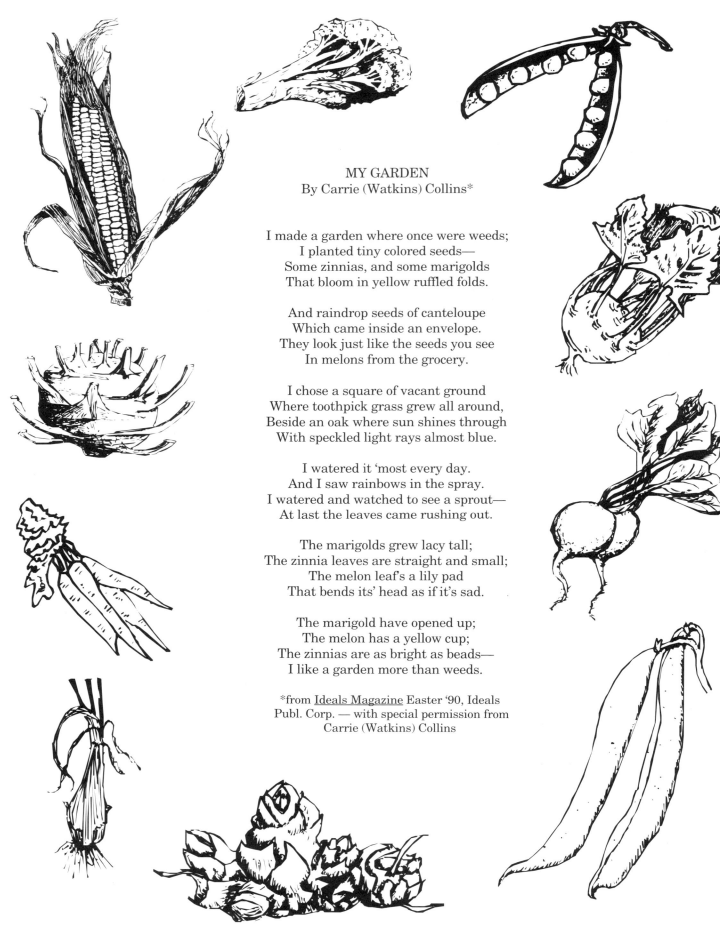

MY GARDEN
By Carrie (Watkins) Collins*

I made a garden where once were weeds;
I planted tiny colored seeds—
Some zinnias, and some marigolds
That bloom in yellow ruffled folds.

And raindrop seeds of canteloupe
Which came inside an envelope.
They look just like the seeds you see
In melons from the grocery.

I chose a square of vacant ground
Where toothpick grass grew all around,
Beside an oak where sun shines through
With speckled light rays almost blue.

I watered it 'most every day.
And I saw rainbows in the spray.
I watered and watched to see a sprout—
At last the leaves came rushing out.

The marigolds grew lacy tall;
The zinnia leaves are straight and small;
The melon leaf's a lily pad
That bends its' head as if it's sad.

The marigold have opened up;
The melon has a yellow cup;
The zinnias are as bright as beads—
I like a garden more than weeds.

*from Ideals Magazine Easter '90, Ideals Publ. Corp. — with special permission from Carrie (Watkins) Collins

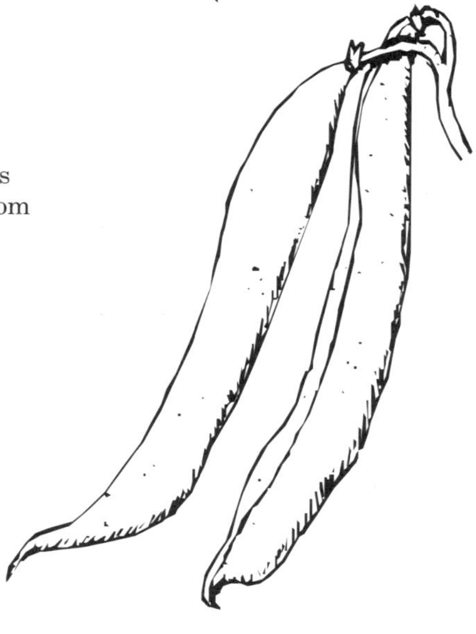

MICROCLIMATES ARE IMPORTANT

Are you a new gardener who has a great desire to have the best garden around? Every gardener who moves to a new climate goes through the same guessing game. You look at the plants growing around you and wonder what other ones will grow successfully there. If you live in the mountains, where frost can occur any day of the year, you need to select either native plants, or hardy plants able to withstand cold winters and summer occasional frosts. If you have a deer problem, you will also be checking to see if the plants are deer-resistant (see special chapter). By your own observations, by reading this book and other books on gardening, and by talking to local people, you will soon be selecting the plants you want to try in your own yard.

Analyze your climate

Gardening,—every aspect of it,—is related to climate. Learning gardening is a day-by-day process of observing plants and their responses to climate. First, study the overall climate zone characteristics for Northern California. Then become familiar with the more local (micro) climatic factors influencing your neighborhood and your yard. Ask questions like: how cold does your yard get in an average winter? How much winter rain, snow, and sun does it get? How much summer sun? Will I have to cut down a few trees to get more sun? Your local climate conditions determine the location of your ideal garden site and what plants will grow best there. Planting, watering, fertilizing, cultivating, and pruning are all things you must do so that the forces of climate can work with you to produce healthy plants. This book may help you find some of the answers.

What is a climate zone?

Climate zones illustrate where a plant is most hardy (where it is happy). The United States has been divided into major climatic zones. Most horticulturists, mail-order catalogs, and books use the USDA (U.S. Dept. of Agriculture) climate zones which are simply based on the average lowest winter temperature. The USDA system places the mountains of Northern California (approximately 2000' - 7000') in zone 4, 5, 6 or 7. The coldest zone where the plant is expected to grow is indicated. If Greenville is considered in zone 6,—this means that a plant suggested to grow in zone 6, —should grow in Greenville and in warmer areas (unless otherwise noted). The Sunset Western Garden Book [1] uses a different zoning system based on three major factors: length of growing season (the number of days between killing frosts), average lowest winter temperature, and average highest summer temperatures. Sunset's system places these same mountainous areas in the corresponding zones 1, 2 and 3.

How do you use climate zones?

This book will use USDA climate zones (based on minimum winter temperature) as a general reference base.

LOWEST WINTER TEMPERATURES (°F) 1973-1982

	1973	1974	1975	1976	1977	1978	1979	1980	1981	1982
Fort Jones R. Sta. (2725')	11	3	5	9	-6	8	—	10	14	—
Yreka (2625')	12	2	8	14	1	8	10	11	19	—
Mc Cloud (3300')	6	—	—	10	10	10	7	11	15	3
Weaverville R. Sta. (2050')	10	11	13	13	—	9	6	6	—	—
Alturus (4400')	-7	-21	-7	-5	-25	-14	-16	-1	-3	—
Hat Creek PH #1 (3015')	2	-8	5	9	-2	2	6	9	13	4
Burney (3127')	1	-18	1	4	-16	-4	-5	5	9	-9
Quincy (3409')	6	-2	—	6	4	—	9	—	—	8
Susanville Airport (4148')	3	-12	-8	5	-1	-5	-2	9	10	5
Chester (4525')	-4	0	2	5	-2	-4	-8	5	6	-2
Canyon Dam (4555')	-2	3	6	8	6	3	1	9	14	2
Mineral (4875')	0	1	3	5	3	0	-3	10	5	3
Sierraville R. Sta. (4975')	-9	-9	-19	3	0	-10	-11	6	-4	-2
Manzanita Lake (5850')	-1	-4	0	0	2	4	0	6	8	4
Tahoe City (6230')	2	5	3	1	-2	3	-3	6	8	-6

Data source: "Temperature Extremes & Freeze Data" sheets & microfiche. 1973-82 from National Climatic Data Center, Ashville, N. Carolina.

Then, consider other pertinent factors for your area, so you can better estimate which zone your garden is in. The **major factors** to consider are: minimum winter temperatures, length of growing season, and elevation (see maps and charts this chapter). **Minor factors** to consider are: slope exposure, cold air drainage, frost occurrence, soil characteristics, drainage, the nearness to a lake, the amount of native tree cover [2], seasonal rainfall distribution, amount of rainfall, humidity, average maximum summer temperatures, and duration & intensity of sunlight (i.e. shade), winter wind, and angle of slope. Depending on your area, minor factors listed here may be major factors in your garden, —so consider them all.

These climatic factors determine your garden's planting potential, but trying to capture ALL the factors on one map would just be a mess of exceptions. Climates tend to overlap, and lines of separation are not always as distinct as shown on a map [3]. So, when looking at these maps, use as a general guide only, because of local variation in microclimates.

Minimum winter temperatures has been charted, because the lowest temperature a plant can endure, can be the deciding factor of whether a plant can survive in your yard (providing it has adequate supplies of light, moisture, and nutrients). This is an average minimum temperature, because some winters are colder and some warmer. See USDA Climate Zone Map and my Zone Estimate Chart.

Consider more than just each zone's minimum temperature range; for example, temperatures of neighboring zones become similar near their boundaries. In fact there is a gradual change from one side of the zone to the other, except where terrain, such as a ridge line or elevation change makes a sharp boundary line. The USDA zone map trys to show this effect by dividing each zone into two parts (a & b) representing 5-degree differences in the higher 10-degree zones. The "a" represents the colder section; the "b" the warmer section. For example, Saucer Magnolia and Wisteria are suitable for zone 5b (warmer), but not for zone 5a (colder). Orchard peaches may be suitable in zone 6b (warmer), but will also succeed in the parts of zone 6a (colder) that don't have late frosts.

VARIATION IN GROWING SEASONS
(Frost-Free Days, 1973-1982)

	1973	1974	1975	1976	1977	1978	1979	1980	1981	1982
Fort Jones R. Sta (2725')	145	118	—	23	116	96	145	106	124	—
Yreka (2625')	156	139	161	164	136	119	166	147	141	—
Mc Cloud (3300')	105	—	—	138	132	116	145	143	114	107
Weaverville R. Sta. (2050')	130	131	120	131	—	119	145	104	141	—
Alturus (4400')	12	7	2*	5	37	49	58	13	20	—
Hat Creek PH #1 (3015')	76	114	111	120	117	125	143	138	139	124
Burney (3127')	56	54	6*	5	86	50	—	32	21	3
Quincy (3409')	60	113	93	25	—	63	—	—	27	85
Susanville Airport (4148')	100	117	140	17	116	75	119	100	101	—
Chester (4525')	99	80	5*	21	104	55	18	63	25	83
Canyon Dam (4555')	—	138	104	119	117	115	124	99	112	113
Mineral (4875')	66	15	3*	9	24	58	15	66	20	83
Sierraville R. Sta. (4975')	89	15	67	—	38	75	85	82	28	—
Manzanita Lake (5850')	69	50	5*	86	111	57	21	25	24	58
Tahoe City (6230')	67	15	3*	56	101	—	124	99	111	—

**Frost occurred in July at these stations.*

Note: "Growing season" is the number of days between killing frosts. It is the time (period in days) from the last 32°F of "spring" to the first 32°F of "fall" (or before).

Data source: "Temperature Extremes & Freeze Data" sheetss & microfiche. 1973-82 from National Climatic Data Center, Ashville, N.C.

Will the plant thrive, or merely survive?

The zone where a plant can survive may not be the zone where it can thrive. One plant may be miserably stunted in a colder area of zone 6 or even zone 5, but may develop normally in zone 7. So, that plant would grow best in zone 7 and warmer zones. Many plants recommended to grow in one zone will do well in the warmer part of the neighboring colder zone, as well as in the next warmer zone. However, many hardy fruit trees & bushes, perennials, lilacs, and bulbs require a cold-induced dormant season in order to produce flowers or fruit next season [3]. Tender plants can't survive temperatures below 32°F without some protection. Lettuce and carrots don't thrive in hot summers. A lot of weeds and bug pests (including fleas and mosquitos) can't survive cold winters. I survive shoveling snow and stacking firewood, but I thrive by applying a rule for me: for every hour I shovel or stack —I get at least equal time on the ski slope!

Some gardeners question a zone rating when a plant fails to survive its first winter. A single test may not be reliable. Young plants may be particularly tender, where an older plant might thrive. No winter is ever quite average because climate is always changing. Some winters may be severe, or warm, or there may be sudden unexpected frost. Today's climate isn't the same as even fifty years ago. The USDA climate zones, taken from the latest USDA Plant Hardiness Zone Map 1990 [4], are based on United States data averaged from 1974 to 1986. The minimum temperature information used on my charts is based on ten years of local data (1973-1982).

Can we alter some climatic factors?

Temperatures can seldom be changed by human effort, except at great expense. Rainfall, soil, and summer heat can be altered favorably by adding irrigation, soil correction, wind protection, partial shade, or humidity control. But frost dates, length of growing season, and minimum winter temperature are least controllable of the major factors that control the geographic adaptability of plants.

What are microclimates ?

The smaller local climates in each large zone category —and even in your yard —are called "microclimates". These smaller "island" climates may be considerably milder or colder than the zone average. These islands are especially common in hilly or mountainous areas. Since USDA climate zones are based on data from selected weather stations scattered across the country, the mountainous areas on the USDA map seem unexpectedly warm. This is because most of the weather stations are located in valleys where temperatures tend to be milder and where plants are most likely to be grown. Keep this in mind when considering temperature data. You can see why these zone maps can only be used as general guides for large areas.

Your yard's climate is unique

Compare your yard's microclimate with your neighbor's as you drive past on your daily rounds. You can observe whether you get frosts earlier or later, and whether the last cold spell damaged your plants more or less than it did the plants in a garden a block away. Often your garden's climate will differ from others in your neighborhood, and it can vary greatly from any mapped zone climate.

How do climatic factors affect my yard? Gardens with a south-facing orientation are warmer and thus have longer growing seasons. If your garden is in a cold air drainage area, you will get many more and harder frosts than your neighbor who doesn't get this cold air. A south-facing wall can be much warmer than that of a north-facing wall. A windbreak or trees' branches can shelter a less hardy plant. Our mountainous terrain has many microclimates on its' ridges and valleys. It

ELEVATION, PRECIPITATION and TEMPERATURE 1951-1980

			Average Annual Data		
County	**Station**	**Elev. (ft.)**	**Min.Temp. (°F)**	**Max.Temp. (°F)**	**Precip. (in.)**
SISKIYOU	Fort Jones R.S.	2725	23.7	91.5	22.48
	Yreka	2625	24.6	90.7	19.20
	Mc Cloud	3300	22.9	87.4	51.26
	Mt. Shasta	3544	25.5	85.1	37.0
TRINITY	Weaverville R.S.	2050	26.7	93.4	39.19
MODOC	Alturus	4400	16.0	88.2	12.45
SHASTA	Hat Creek	3015	21.5	91.1	18.87
	Burney	3127	19.1	86.9	28.06
	Manzanita Lake	5850	19.7	79.1	41.28
LASSEN	Susanville Airport	4148	19.9	89.9	14.29
TEHAMA	Mineral	4911	21.5	81.5	53.45
PLUMAS	Quincy	3409	23.1	91.0	41.04
	Greenville R.S.	3560	—	—	40.21
	Chester	4525	—	—	33.09
	Canyon Dam	4555	21.1	85.4	39.49
	Portola	4838	—	—	22.21
	Vinton	4950	—	—	13.06
SIERRA	Sierraville R. S.	4975	15.5	84.7	26.57
NEVADA	Truckee R. S.	5995	13.4	81.5	31.57
PLACER	Tahoe City	6230	19.4	77.0	31.50

Temperature can be estimated using a simple rule: for every 1000 feet rise in elevation, the temperature drops about 3°F.

Data Source: Climatography of the U.S. No. 81 (by State) Monthly Normals of temperature, precipitation, and heating & cooling degree days 1951-80 California (1982).

is colder at the top of a mountain than at its' base. The factor of elevation alone in Shasta County varies from Hat Creek at 3015', to Manzanita Lake at 5850'. Select the best possible site for your garden to take advantage of the most sun, so you can get the longest growing season.

What zone is your yard in?

My climate zone estimates on Chart #1 from the warmest (Zone 7) to the coolest (Zone 4), are based on the following observations:

McCloud, Mt. Shasta, Yreka, and Weaverville all are in Zone 7a. Their elevations vary from 2050' to 3544'. McCloud is near the town of Mt. Shasta, yet McCloud is colder in winter and warmer in summer than Mt Shasta. But Mt. Shasta gets 51" of rain/year, and McCloud only 37". Yreka and Mt. Shasta are both in the Shasta Valley, but Yreka gets only 19" rainfall/year while Mt Shasta gets 37". Though Weaverville is in the Trinity River Valley, and lies at a much lower elevation, it still is similar in climate to the other three towns in this zone 7 category. Many factors are at work here.

Though **Yreka and Fort Jones** are close neighbors and are similar in rainfall and temperature, Fort Jones has a shorter growing season and lower winter temperatures so it would be in a cooler zone.

CLIMATE ZONE ESTIMATES

	4b	5a	5b	6a	6b	7a	7b
Fort Jones					O	X	
Yreka						⊗	
Mc Cloud						⊗	
Weaverville						O	X
Alturus	O		X				
Hat Creek				X	O		
Burney			O		X		
Quincy				O	X		
Susanville			X		O		
Chester			O		X		
Canyon Dam					⊗		
Mineral			O				X
Sierraville	O			X			
Manzanita L.				O		X	
Tahoe City				OX			

X —based on USDA Climate Zones

O —the author's best estimate, considering many factors and 1972–1982 data

⊗ —when both estimates are the same

Fort Jones, Canyon Dam, Hat Creek and Susanville also have long growing seasons (averaging over 100 days) like the zone 7 stations, but because they have colder winters, they are in a slightly colder zone category (borderline between 6b/7a). Canyon Dam benefits from nearby Lake Almanor (discussed later under Almanor Basin, Banana Belt). Hat Creek will be discussed later, along with Burney. Although Susanville, located in the Honey Lake Valley, has one of the longest growing seasons, it is colder in winter and hotter in summer. And, since Susanville has the coldest winters of these towns, it lies basically in the colder zone (6b). However, some south-facing Susanville slopes do have a zone 7a climate.

Susanville (4148') is located on the East slope of the Sierras. It can grow fruit trees better than the West slope (i.e. **Lake Almanor area**), because Susanville has a 6-week longer growing season. Lake Almanor winters are wetter, but are harder on fruit trees, because unexpected spring frosts zap fruit blossoms, and heavy wet snow causes snow breakage (so we need to prune our trees in the fall).

Susanville has a much longer growing season than **Quincy** which is at a lower elevation of 3409'. Why? One would expect Quincy's lower elevation to create a longer growing season. Quincy is also in a valley (The American Valley), but it is nestled between mountain ridges and cold air drainage and pooling are probably two important factors.

Quincy, Manzanita Lake, and Tahoe City appear to be in zone 6a. These towns have similar growing seasons, with warmer winter temperatures than Chester and Mineral. In Quincy some south-facing exposures are zone 6b or warmer. Tahoe City has colder winter temperatures than Manzanita Lake, but Tahoe City has a longer growing season. **Truckee** (5995'), a neighbor of Tahoe City (6230'), should be in the same zone, but there is no official climate data on Truckee. In analyzing Truckee, consider that Tahoe City is at a higher elevation, located in the Lake Tahoe Basin, besides being by the West shore of Lake Tahoe. The West shore has colder temperatures and more snow than the North and East shores which are warmed by the moderating influence of the lake. As you drive around Lake Tahoe, the zones vary from 5-7.

Not far from Quincy is the Indian Valley which contains **Greenville, and Taylorsville** which are basically Zone 6, but likely zone 7 on some south-facing slopes (these two towns have no reported climate data).

Chester and Mineral have Zone 5b climates. Mineral is much warmer in winter, but has a shorter growing season than Chester, because of cold air drainage from nearby mountains.

Chester and Westwood are in the Almanor Basin, but they are not much affected by Lake Almanor's moderating influence. Though Westwood has no reported climate data, it is probably also in Zone 5. Only Chester's southern edge is influenced by the lake. In Chester the areas bordering meadows have later and heavier frosts in the spring and earlier frosts in the fall, as well as more damaging winds. The southern and central sections of Chester and the area along the river have a milder climate, and flowers will bloom earlier and longer there than in other areas of Chester. Chester has many microclimates, as does Lake Almanor Peninsula.

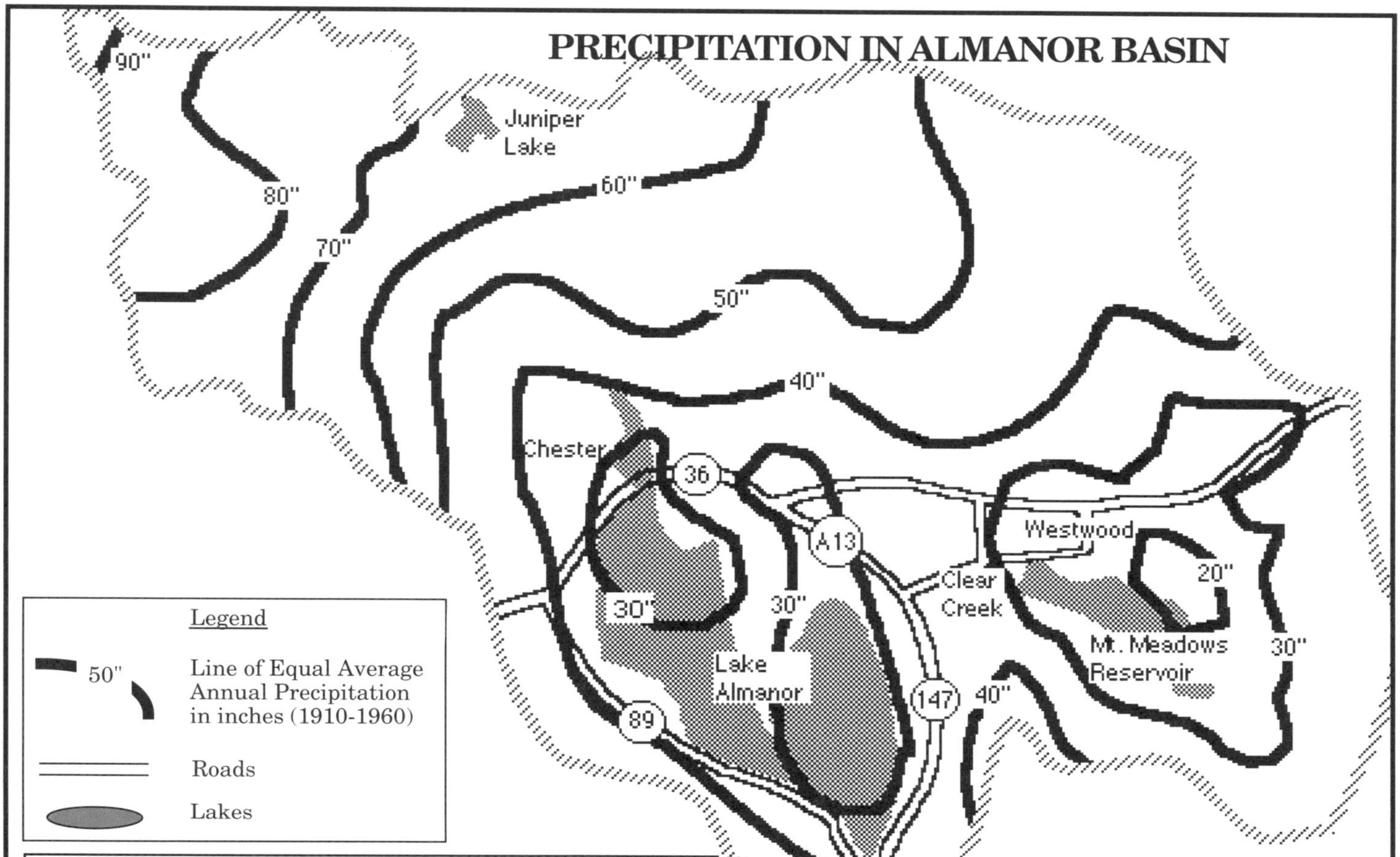

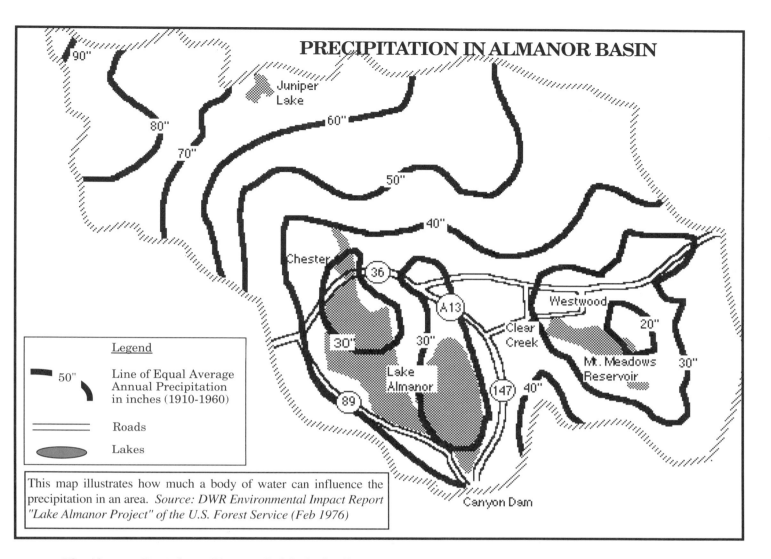

This map illustrates how much a body of water can influence the precipitation in an area. *Source: DWR Environmental Impact Report "Lake Almanor Project" of the U.S. Forest Service (Feb 1976)*

The Almanor Basin has a "Banana Belt" which affects areas near the lake by making them warmer than expected, due to the warming "influence of the lake" (Lake Almanor). **Canyon Dam, East Shore, Hamilton Branch, and the Lake Almanor Peninsula** lie in this local belt, and they have climates similar to Greenville's (zone 6) which is located at 1000 feet lower elevation.. This banana belt illustrates the major effect local factors can have on climate. The Lake's water temperature moderates nearby air temperatures making them more stable (less extreme). For example, the **Lake Almanor Peninsula** is surrounded on three sides by water. The peninsula's winter temperatures can be 10 degrees warmer than Chester, and summer temperatures 5-10 degrees cooler than Chester. Temperatures vary on the peninsula with changes in elevation and proximity to the lake. The tip of the peninsula varies from the beginning of the peninsula, and even the western and eastern sides of the peninsula vary from each other. Temperatures are cooler with increased elevation and/or distance from the lake. **Lake Almanor's East Shore**, like the peninsula, also has generally warmer temperatures than Chester. The East Shore, Hamilton Branch, the Peninsula, and Canyon Dam ("Banana Belt" areas) are generally warmer than Westwood, Chester and the West Shore of Lake Almanor. **The West Shore** generally gets more snow and has colder temperatures than the East Shore, because most storms arrive from the southwest and west, and winds are warmed somewhat by passing across the lake. **Canyon Dam** (4555') has higher elevation but longer growing seasons than Quincy (3409') because of the banana belt effect.

Mohawk Valley (zone 5) contains **Grayeagle, Blairsden, and Clio.** It is sheltered, but has some cold air settling in pockets. **Portola** (zone 5) is in a canyon surrounded by ridges, and nestled in the trees. Sierra Valley (zone 4b) contains **Sierraville, Vinton, Loyalton, and Beckworth** where the windchill factor is more important than the elevation. Of these towns, climate data are only available for Sierraville.

Sierraville (zone 4b) **and Burney** (zone 5a/5b) have similar growing seasons (less than 86 days), with many below zero winter temperatures. Burney's growing season is shorter than Chester's, and its winters are a little colder than Chester's; but it's not as cold as Alturus.

Burney (zone 5a/5b) **and Hat Creek** (zone 6b/7a) are neighbors with similar elevations, but Hat Creek has a much longer growing season, has warmer winter temperatures, gets 10 inches less rain/year, and is hotter in summer. Hat creek's more sheltered valley-bottom location makes for a warmer climate.

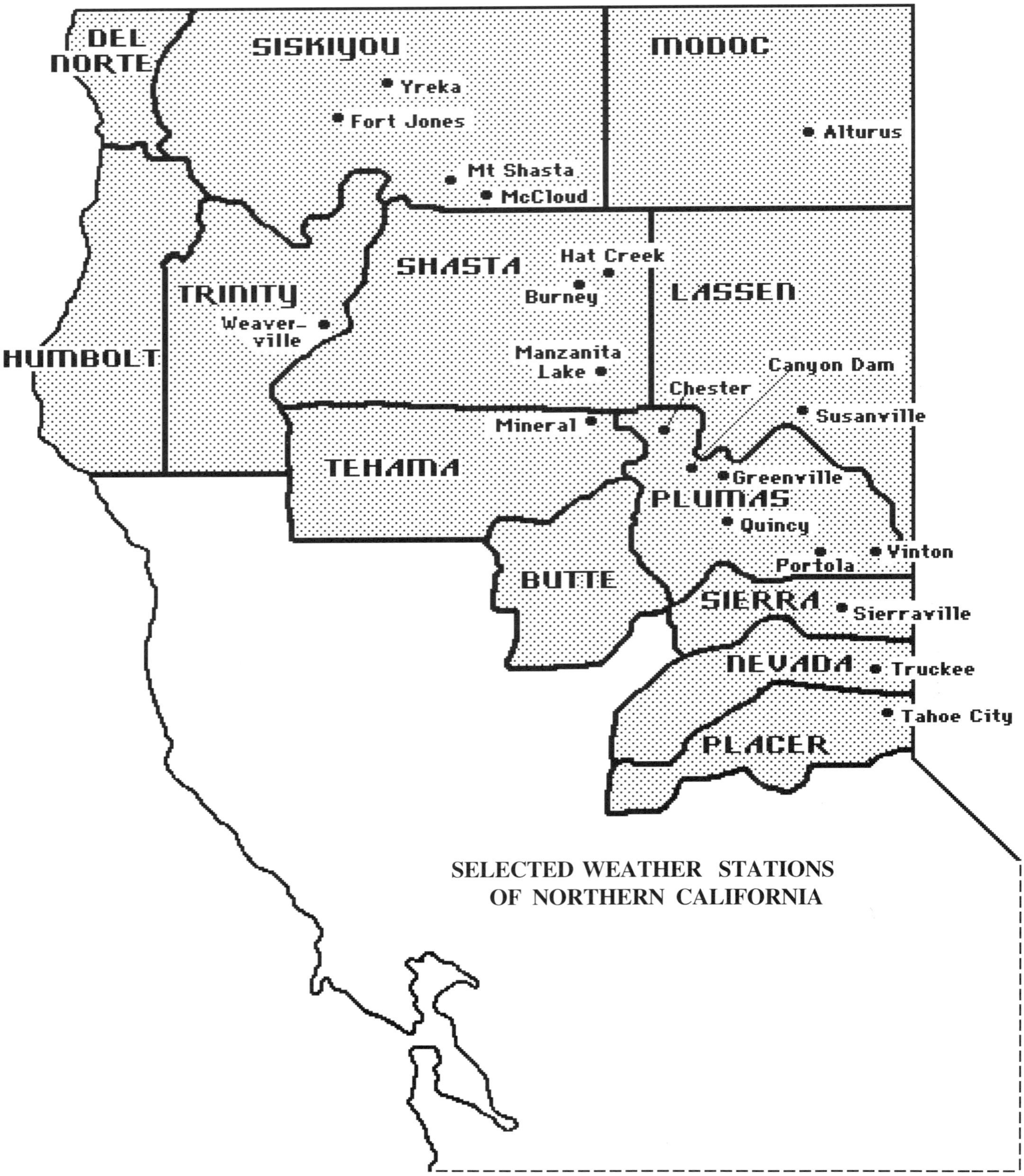

SELECTED WEATHER STATIONS OF NORTHERN CALIFORNIA

Alturus has the shortest growing season and coldest winters of the areas studied, and it is zone 4b. Alturus is out in the open flatlands (Madeline Plains) where cold winds shorten the growing season and make for colder winters, but the most important factor here is low humidity.

References cited:
[1] Sunset Western Garden Book {SWGB}
[2] Landscaping your mountain home
[3] Readers Digest: Basic
[4] USDA Plant Hardiness Zone Map, 1990.

EXTEND THE GROWING SEASON

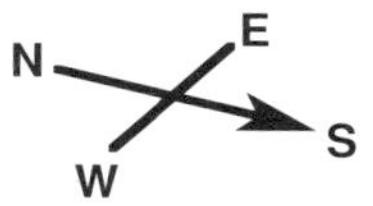

Cold frames must be facing South to South-West to take best advantage of the sun

Since our growing seasons are so short, many people are using special techniques to extend the season. Use protective devices to protect plants from snow breakage, wind, sunburn, and frost; to start seeds early indoors; to harden off seedlings, or to force vegetables to maturity. The chief fear is unexpected frost, so use hardy plants whenever possible. Choose your garden site carefully. Select early-maturing crops. And extend the harvest by storing and preserving crops. Gardening under glass or plastic is using "intensive gardening" and it gives you control over time [1].

Snow breakage, wind, and sunburn

Small trees, shrubs and roses should have some type of winter protection over them such as wooden tepees or A-frames to protect them from snow breakage. Some gardeners tie up branches in the fall, while others simply knock snow off with a broom [2]. Fences and trees make nice windbreaks for flowers and vegetable gardens, but smaller plants still need to get enough sun. Larger trees and shrubs can be staked against the wind. Use two stakes (one on either side of the trunk) held with a rope or an old bike inner tube around them loosely so it doesn't cut the tree. This loose tie encourages the plant to get strong on its own while still giving some wind protection. For sunburn protection and a partial bug and woodpecker retardant, paint the trunks of fruit trees with a water-base white paint (white reflects heat). Tree trunks can be wrapped with burlap to deter animals and birds, but plastic is undesirable because it can freeze or burn plants.

Use simple frost protective devices

Frosts that come in early fall or in spring after growth has started, can be much more damaging than when frosts come while plants are dormant or semi-dormant. Frost protective devices, ranging from inexpensive plastic containers to elaborate greenhouses, enable you to increase vegetable and fruit production by extending the growing season a month or two in both spring and fall. In some areas crops are grown under simple protective devices all year.

milk carton

Erect a temporary shelter over tender plants growing in the ground or in raised garden beds. Stretch protective material over stakes or frames, such as polyester, paper, burlap, any woven cloth, branches, Ross Garden Net, wire netting, or plastic film. Make sure the covering material doesn't touch the plant, and uncover the plant the next morning before the sun shines on it [3]. To use a waxed milk carton, first remove the top. Then cut three sides of the bottom to make a flap that can be opened in day and closed on cold nights. Then, set it over an individual plant. Or, cut off the top of plastic milk jugs or Clorox bottles and invert them over a plant. A plastic tunnel (bought or homemade) can be constructed by laying a sheet of plastic over wire supports. It protects seedlings from cold and from being washed away by heavy spring rains [4].

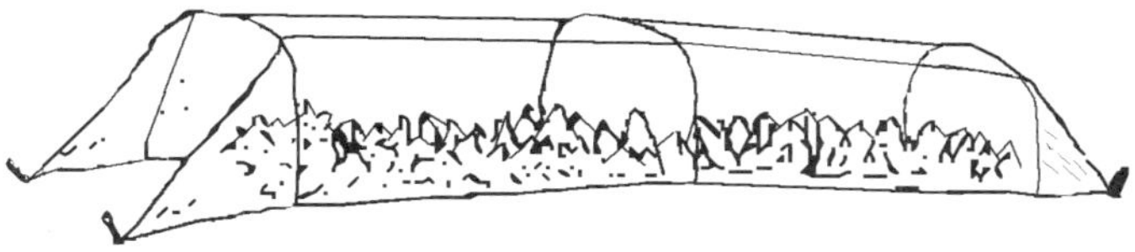

A plastic tunnel

Here are some different kinds of protective layers. Some plants such as roses can be buried under a mound of dirt over winter, while other plants like rhododendron can be sprayed with water to form an protective ice layer for winter, or an expected spring frost [2]. The best root protection against freezing temperatures is a good thick mulch around the base of roses (over the dirt mound), shrubs, and trees —but leave a couple inches clearance around the base of the trunk to prevent insect damage and rot. Pine needles make excellent protective mulch, as they don't seem to harbor as many bugs over winter. The simple devices discussed above are generally designed for short term use; while cold frames, hot beds, and greenhouses can be used year round.

Start seeds indoors to get a head start.

Many people start seed early in greenhouses, cold frames, hotbeds, or in a sunny window, to extend the season. A cold frame is a rigid box of wood outdoors approximately two feet high that can easily be covered at night and opened to the sun every morning. The top can be covered by plastic, an old door with windows, or just old windows. Some are made so side boards can be lifted off during the warmest part of the growing season, and replaced again when there is chance of frost. They can be designed simply, or very complex.

A cold frame protects seedlings so that seed can be planted several weeks before the safe planting date in the open garden [4]. It can also be used to "harden off" bedding plants started in a greenhouse, or to propagate plants from cuttings and seeds. A hot bed is a cold frame where some form of heat has been added, such as a heating cable or mat, incandescent bulbs, or fresh manure [1]. Hot beds can grow a wider variety of plants and can even protect tender plants over winter. Buy some seed starting equipment and experiment with different techniques of starting your own plants.

Greenhouses have many uses

Greenhouses are easier to maintain than cold frames and hot beds, but they still need a source of heating in winter and cooling in summer. A greenhouse can be a simple lean-to structure made out of plastic, a special bay window attachment on a house window, or a special separate structure with strict regulation of temperature, humidity, ventilation, watering and even day length. The size and style of greenhouse you choose depends on the need, the climate where you live, and the cost of construction. Greenhouses can be used to:

- grow tender plants that are not able to withstand cold outdoor temperatures.
- start seeds of annuals and vegetables early, and later transplant them to the garden after chance of frost is past.
- grow specialty plants such as orchids and tropical plants.
- start cuttings and special seeds requiring greenhouse controlled conditions.
- raise vegetables and flowers out of season [3].

It's fun to have a greenhouse in winter when it's snowing or raining outside. You can be warm and dry and still have your fingers in the dirt, with pretty flowers blooming all around you. The commonest problems in greenhouses are bugs, poor drainage, and lack of air circulation [5,6]. See also House plant chapter.

Use hardy plants, whenever possible

A "hardy" plant is one that is adapted to your garden's climate. If it can be killed or badly damaged in winter, or by a spring frost, it is called "half-hardy" or tender" [2]. Try to grow tender plants in containers, so you can move them to sheltered sites when the weather turns cold. Learn your garden microclimates. It takes time to discover which garden areas are warm and which are cool. For example, a constantly shady area is colder and moister, while a continually sunny area is drier and hotter. Don't have tender plants exposed to the sky on all sides, especially the north sky, —put in windbreaks of hedges, fences, shrubs, or trees, but not solid barriers that trap the air. Don't have plants in hollows or low areas where cold air is held motionless. The best area for tender plants are under overhangs of the house, tree branches, or lath structures. Slopes where cold air drains freely are safer than valley bottoms or canyons where the cold air is trapped. South-facing walls absorb heat during the day and warm the nearby plants. The warmest place is a south-facing wall with an overhanging roof [3].

Early blossoms can be zapped by frost

Minimum winter temperatures have nothing to do with unseasonal frosts. A plant that has survived a severe freeze while it is dormant, may be killed by having its new shoots or leaves killed by spring frost [2].

Some hardy plants, such as apple trees, have early blossoms that can be damaged by spring frosts; and if the blossoms are frosted at the wrong time, there will be no fruit that season. Some people try to delay blooming of these plants by planting them with a northern or shady exposure where you can hope to delay its bud break until warmer weather [3]. Another strategy is to time the pruning so it doesn't encourage growth at the wrong time. Another way is to plant later in the season [2]. If you get a warm spell in early spring, shovel some extra snow around those plants that might bloom too early, especially fruit trees and bulbs.

In the mountains of the west, the climate fluctuations are unpredictable. You might expect temperatures to warm up gradually in the spring, like each day getting one degree warmer. Instead, you might have a week of 60°F weather, then two days of 35°F, then 45°. Plants can withstand below 0°F temperatures if the gradual warming and cooling are predictable; so that when buds and flowers are produced, they aren't knocked off by a sudden hail storm, or frozen by unexpected frost or snow. Our nights are always cool (many plants need warmer nights). Our hardy plants would probably be happier in Siberia where temperatures of minus 30°F are common, but the temperatures are predictable in their gradual spring warming.

Choose your garden site carefully

The best general garden location for vegetables, flowers, and other plants that aren't harmed by early frost, is in the sunniest location of your yard, so they will mature quickly. A vegetable garden needs 6-8 hours of sun [7].

Note the path of the sun at different seasons of the year. The summer sun rises in the northeast and sets in the northwest —giving some light even to north-facing walls. The winter sun rises in the southeast and sets in the southwest, and the north wall is in permanent shade [2]. The north wall is best for shade-loving plants such as ferns, bleeding heart, etc.

Careful site selection, heat-absorbing back walls or fences, hedges, windbreaks, cold frames, and dark soil, can help to lengthen your growing season. But even with the best planning, our growing seasons are short, and frost dates are unpredictable.

When do frosts occur?

After studying ten years of Chester's climate records, I would say the last average hard SPRING frost is about May 15, and the first hard FALL frost about September 1-15. Thus, Chester's growing season can be 21-120 days long depending on the year, but remember frost or snow can occur any day of the year here. We have had snow on the forth of July at Lake Almanor!!! You can see from the climate records (in the maps and charts) that it is foolish to count on having a "normal" year. So, plant hardy plants!

A "hard frost" (about 26°F.) usually refers to a killing frost from which few plants can recover. A "frost" (32°F.) refers to temperatures that can kill some plants (like tomatoes and other frost-sensitive plants) while others can recover. "Growing season" is the number of days between killing frosts (using 26° or 32°F degrees as the frost figure). In this book, growing seasons will refer to mostly 32°F frosts.

For all their short-comings, the climate zone maps, frost maps, and planting guides (see Vegetable Planting Guide in Vegetable chapter) are still useful as references.

Select early-maturing vegetable and fruit varieties.

If your growing season is only two months long, plant beets that mature in 60 or less days and not peanuts that take 120 days, because late maturing varieties can be killed by fall frost before they mature. Plants that are "borderline" can be started indoors or put in a cold frame, and then transplanted into your garden after the last chance of frost is past; this is commonly done for tomatoes, corn, petunias, and marigolds [8].

The number of days to maturity is found in seed catalogs (see Suppliers' Catalog List), so plan on shopping by mail and starting your own seeds. You may feel your selection is limited, but you have the advantage of being able to grow spring or cool-season crops all summer. In the mountains, where the summers aren't as hot, your lettuce won't "bolt" [7].

Extend the harvest by storing crops

Store crops in a pantry, or preserve them by freezing, canning, or dehydrating. See Preparing & Preserving chapters.

References cited:
[1] Getting the Most from your Garden
[2] The Principles of Gardening
[3] Sunset Western Garden Book
[4] Readers Digest: Basic
[5] The Solar Greenhouse Book
[6] Growing Food in Solar Greenhouses
[7] Square Foot Gardening (MEL)
[8] Home Vegetable Garden

A JOYFUL WALK

I wasted an hour one morning beside a mountain stream,
I seized a cloud from the sky above and fashioned myself a dream,
In the hush of the early twilight, far from the
haunts of men,
I wasted a summer evening, and fashioned my
dream again.
Wasted? Perhaps. Folks say so who never have
walked with God,
When lanes are purple with lilacs or yellow with
goldenrod.
But I have found strength for my labors in that one
short evening hour.
I have found joy and contentment; I have found
peace and power.
My dreaming has left me a treasure, a hope that
is strong and true.
From wasted hours I have built my life and
found my faith anew.*

** As quoted by Tim Hansel in When I Relax I Feel Guilty, p. 67. Used with permission from David C. Cook Publishing Company.*

LANDSCAPING IS FUN !

Whether you live in the mountains or in the valley, plants help to cut down noise and improve privacy. Privacy in a sheltered spot where you can relax and enjoy your surroundings can be important to you. By using your land wisely you can create a retreat for yourself. Whenever possible, use existing, native trees and shrubs to advantage rather than removing them. Native plants grow naturally here and require very little care. They are adapted to the local climate and site, and usually no watering is needed after they are established. Think of a total plan for your house and lot where no space is wasted. Shape your outdoor space to fit your needs.

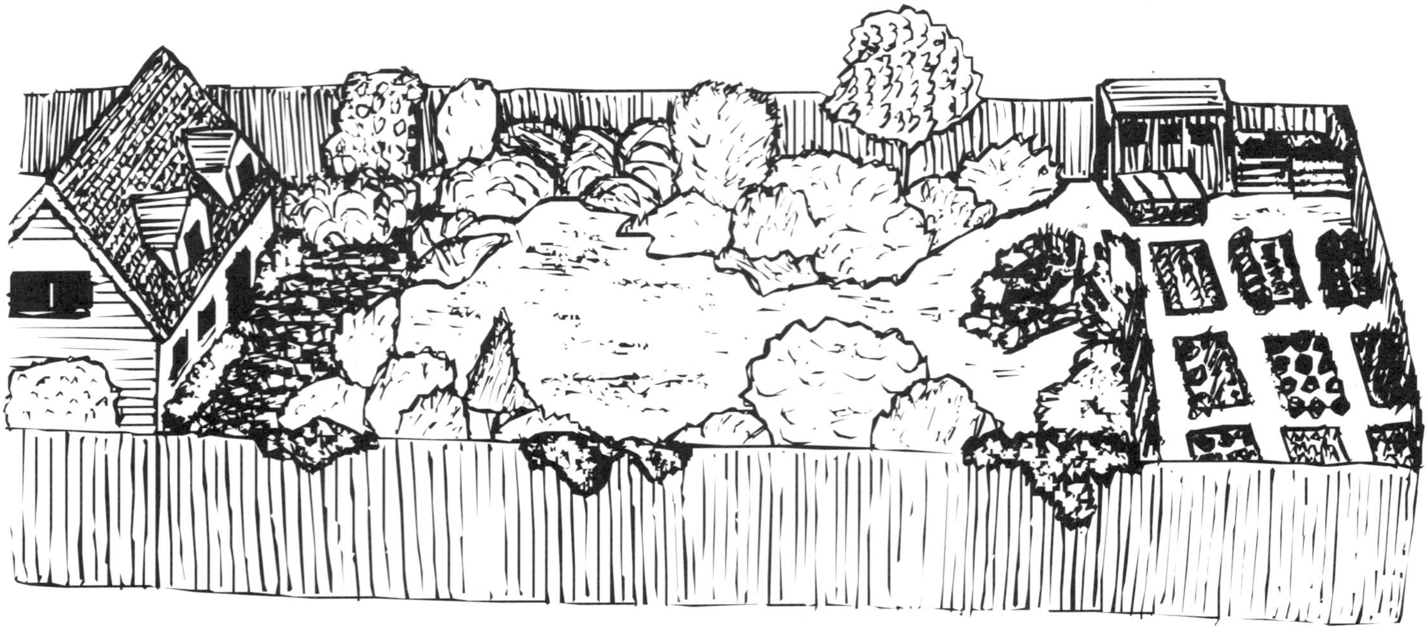

What is YOUR life style?

To begin planning your landscape, ask yourself some questions. Do I want my emphasis on recreation, children, or a vegetable garden? Do I eat outdoors a lot? Do I want to landscape only one part of my yard? How will I coordinate that area with other parts of my land? What materials are available for use (rock, brick, wood, or stone)? What kind of atmosphere do I want to create ? Should it be **formal** (fir, cedar, yew), **country** (birch, oak, weeping willow), **romantic** (magnolia, maple, beech), or **city** (flowering, cherry, Linden, honey locust, and some fir)?

What plants do you want to plant here?

Our summer season is short; will the plants I want, grow here? This garden book includes lists of plants that will probably grow here. When do I plant them? (see Planting chapter). There are many trees, shrubs, roses, perennials, annuals, biennials, vines, fruits, berries, ferns, ground covers, bulbs, vegetables, and herbs to choose from, but select ones that are hardy. Forget the cost for now, and list all the plants you might like to have.

Put your thoughts on paper before planting anything.

If you buy a tree on sale and rush right home and plant it, you may find a few months later that you want to build a garage at that location, and you'll have to move the tree. The first step is to plan ahead. Decide exactly what you want, and put it down on paper. Use a 50 or 100 foot tape measure. Plot on graph paper the actual property dimensions, building structures, all existing plants, and the contours of your land. Then place tracing paper over the graph paper, and draw in the plants that you want to plant. Design boldly. Use strong lines: a flower bed, a tree, focal points, etc.

Study your yard carefully.

Note the microclimates in your own yard. Observe the sun, wind, cold spots, and shade throughout the year. Where would you put a patio? The north-facing side of your house is always cool. What is the direction of the prevailing winds? Your house, a fence, tree, group of trees, tall shrubs, or even a lathe fence are all natural windbreaks. How close are you to your neighbors? Do you need a row of lilacs, or some kind of hedge to create a privacy wall between you and your neighbors? Where are your views? Don't block your view. What do you want to see out your windows? Look at a yard you admire and ask what they did. Find out what selected plants look like in flower, fruit and fall color (look in catalogs, nurseries, and neighbors' yards). Do you want evergreen or deciduous trees? Are you planting a tree for summer shade and winter sun? A deciduous tree provides summer shade, and drops its leaves in fall (the sun can heat your house all winter). What diseases do the trees get? Do you want hedges, fences, flower beds, a patio deck, walkways, wood, stone, ground cover, or a tool shed?

There are nine landscaping goals [1,2]:

- Privacy, especially in back yard (use hedges, fences, and shrubs). Dense trees such as incense cedar or sequoia can improve privacy or screening, and make a good windbreak.
- Comfort from shade in hot areas (plant shade trees, etc.).
- Beautify a house with trees and shrubs, and create a barrier against traffic noise. Consider an outdoor dining area or deck by the kitchen.
- Entertaining, meals, parties, for a dry outdoor play area on clear winter days, or for a quiet outdoor relaxing spot.
- Food production is economical these days (plant fruit trees, and a summer garden).
- Flexibility is important for the future. Swing sets give way to hot tubs or decks in some long range plans.
- Safety and convenience may require having steps leading to the front entryway lighted by low-voltage outdoor lights. Hand-rails and no skid outdoor carpet make outdoor steps safer, especially for older folks.
- Ease of maintenance is a gardeners dream. We appreciate the benefits of labor-saving ideas such as mulching, mowing strips, raised planting beds, and drip watering systems. We plant easy care shrubs, trees, and ground covers using native plants as much as possible.
- Recreation: swimming pool, tether ball, volleyball court, swing set, or just a grassy play area. (Sunset, and Color Form)

Remember four guidelines [1,2]:

When drawing your garden plan consider: unity, balance, proportion, and variety. **Unity** is important to avoid a chaotic overall picture. Try to avoid planting an array of unrelated plants. A sense that everything belongs together may be achieved by repeating common garden elements. **Balance** lies in creating the same visual weight on either side of a center of interest. The "weight" used to create the balance need not be mass; instead, it can be color, form, or interest. Choose plants and garden structures that are in **proportion** with the architectural lines of your home. Mature trees can get quite large. Check the mature heights of trees and shrubs, and allow for the shade that a mature plant will create. Mature heights are given: Height, Spread (i.e. Ht 20', S 10'). Don't put a huge tree by a small house, small lawn, or small yard (out of proportion). A large house needs a large tree. In a small yard or a patio, consider flowering plum (slow-growing), hawthorne, or flowering crabapple (matures at 20 feet). Ranch style homes and small lots need the horizontal spread of smaller trees (i.e. willow, Russian olive, or Amur maple). **Variety** is related to surprise, a welcome element in any landscape. It can lessen the monotony of a solid green mass, and will create a plant community having less disease and insect pests.

Choose the right tree or shrub for your yard [2]:

While you want some variety in your garden, try clustering some of the same types together. Group three trees together like three hawthorns, three birch, or three maple. The fruits, leaf shape, leaf color, flower color, or fall color can vary; for example, three hollies can be grouped together that have different colors of berries. Try placing three conifers together —some with golden leaves, or of varying shapes. Select evergreens with different foliage shape like golden, silver, or blue-green, and all green. Select characteristics you want:

form (what shape at maturity).
texture (size of twigs and leaves, open hedge or closed). Consider the different shapes and sizes of leaves like the fernlike delicate leaves of honey locusts. or the small attractive leaves of birch and Japanese maple.
four-season color (leaves, berries, twigs, and flowers).
size at maturity (plan ahead).
evergreen or deciduous, conifer or broadleaf.
hardiness (the plant's resistance to frost, disease, air pollution, smog, wind, and drought).
sun or shade (usually grow best in full sun, but some are specially adapted to grow in shade).
fast or slow growing (birch or aspen only live 20-30 years but grow fast, evergreens grow slower but live longer).
fragrance (sweet or pungent odor).
soil preference. Are soils wet or dry? For low, wet ground consider willow.
blooming season (see blooming time charts, this chapter).

Do you want to create shade?

Trees and shrubs once planted in your yard, require very little maintenance. They make an ideal backdrop for perennials and annuals, and can create shade for those needing shade. If shade is desired, don't plant tall columnar trees, plant instead the wide spreading or weeping trees like the traditional maple, birch, and willow. If you don't want shade use an "open" tree (i.e. paper birch, and honey locust). Trees are an expensive investment and they are permanent (unless you decide to move them). Buy small trees.

Color is VERY important in landscaping.

Plan four-seasonal color in shrubs and trees. Some have showy flowers in spring or summer. Some have beautiful fall color (leaves) i.e. red maple, hawthorne, sumac, sweet gum, euonymus, liquid amber, sugar maple, dogwood, ash, birch, or oak. Since fall color only lasts about 2-4 weeks, think what the tree looks like the rest of the year; and mix evergreen with deciduous trees to have interesting leaves present all year. For winter color select plants with bright colored berries or twigs such as: weeping birch, willow, dogwood, or tulip tree (mature tree has 40 foot crown).

To have a succession of beautiful flowers all summer, choose some plants that bloom in early spring, some in late spring, early summer, late summer, and fall. Consider each plant's flowering season, and choose a variety of colors in your yard that compliment each other. Try them as single masses of color, or mix colors. You can mix bulbs, shrubs, annuals, etc in the same bed or garden. As a general example, first to bloom in early spring is the crocus, then grape hyacinth and daffodils in mid-spring, tulips in late spring, and then Iris. Annuals and biennials generally bloom all summer. Listed below are some plants from the different time categories.

Bulb, Annual, & Perennial Blooming Time Chart

Perennials are winter hardy plants but only bloom 2-6 weeks. Annuals bloom continuously for one season and then die, but may return by seed the next season.

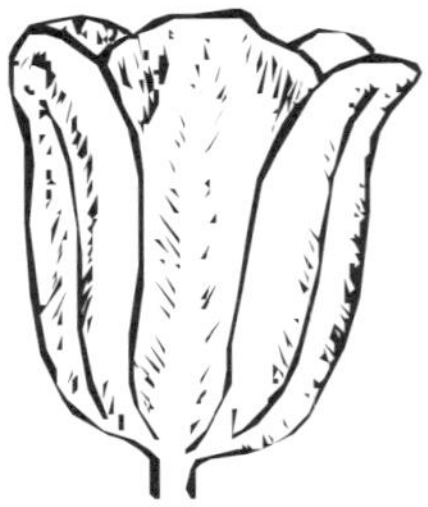

Tulip (bulb)

Very early spring: Star tulip, Narcissus, Iris (Little Dutch and Flag), crocus, snowdrops, winter aconites, squills, grape hyacinths, early daffodils, early tulips, violets, pansies, and candy tuft.

Spring: Daffodils, late squills, Star of Bethlehem, intermediate tulips, creeping phlox, candy tuft, Dutch and Bearded iris, roses, columbine, cornflower, primroses, Ajuga, Oriental Poppies (May), and Delphinium.

Buttercup (perennial)

Violets (annual)

Late spring: Pansies, Oriental Poppies, delphiniums, anemones, Buttercups (Ranunculus), Parrot tulips, wild strawberries, Painted Daisy, hybrid lupines, Coral Bells, Mulleon Pink, and Sedum.

Early summer: Allium, Canna lilies, Painted daisies, columbines, lupines, Gaillardia, California Poppies, and Creeping Buttercup.

Summer: Cornflower, Summer Phlox, Gloriosa Daisy, Snapdragons, Shasta Daisy, Gaillardia, Lavender, Golden Feather Feverfew, Gladiolas, and Chrysanthemums.

Early fall: Fall crocus, Dahlia, Chrysanthemums.

Winter: Indoor "forcing" of spring bulbs uses bulbs of Narcissus, crocus, daffodils, tulips, hyacinth, lily of the valley, and Gloxinia. For more information on "forcing" see chapter on Forcing Spring Bulbs Indoors.

Shrub Blooming Time Chart

Shrubs are woody plants varying from 6" to 15' high, and they occupy a relatively permanent spot in your yard (unless YOU decide to remove them).

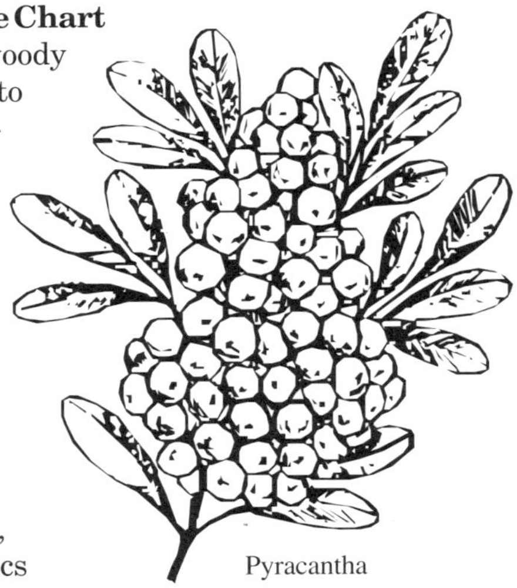

Pyracantha

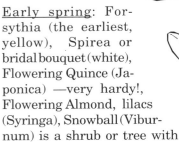

Early spring: Forsythia (the earliest, yellow), Spirea or bridal bouquet (white), Flowering Quince (Japonica) —very hardy!, Flowering Almond, lilacs (Syringa), Snowball (Viburnum) is a shrub or tree with very large white cluster of flowers), Serviceberry, Mollis (deciduous Azalia or Exbury), Peony, and Dogwood.

Early summer: Beauty Bush (small pink flowers, takes little water), Mock Orange (sweet odor), Minnesota Snowflake, Weigela (light pink and rose-pink).

Late summer: Honeysuckle, Tamarisk, Peegee Hydrangea, Rose of Sharon (Hibiscus type), and Chrysanthemum.

Early fall (berries or fall color): Virginia Creeper, Snowberry (native here), Choke Cherry (native here), dogwood, and Cotoneaster (leaves turn bright colors).

Late fall (foliage color): Oak leaf Hydrangea, Winged Eunoymus (turns bright red, is also called the burning bush), and Pyracantha.

Winter (berry or colored twigs): Amur Privet, Choke Cherry, Shiny Sumac, Willow, Siberian Dogwood, Dwarf European Cranberry, Snowberry (berries white), and Pyracantha (berries red).

References cited:

[1] Sunset Ideas for Landscaping & Garden Remodeling.
[2] Put Color, Form & Excitement in your Garden.

WATER GARDENS

Waterfalls, garden pools, fountains, and lily ponds have always fascinated me. Water in the garden pleases the eye and refreshes—even on the hottest summer day. Water adds an unusual and beautiful touch to any landscaping. A water garden—with water lilies floating on the surface, fish quietly gliding here and there, and the reflection of sky and clouds,—can give you a real sense of peace. Many birds, dragonflies, and damselflies are attracted to water gardens. Adding a few mosquito fish (Gambusia) to your pond will keep other pests under control.

Anyone can build a water garden.

All you need is some imagination, some time, money and a little space. The publication: Water Visions, the complete guide to water gardening, can provide all the materials and advice needed. Water Visions [1] is published annually by Van Ness Water Gardens, 2460 North Euclid Ave, Upland, CA 91786. Telephone: (714) 982-2425, cost $3. This booklet includes a "HOW TO" section on building waterfalls, fountains, and fish ponds. A "CATALOG" section includes descriptions and/or pictures of water lilies, bog plants, water snails, or ornamental grasses, flowering aquatic plants, and pond fish, as well as pumps, accessories, fountains, and lights. There is also a section on "EASY CARE MAINTENANCE" techniques. Water gardens need plenty of sun, and water of course. With the correct balance of plants and fish to keep your pool clear and healthy, you may only need to spend a few hours a year in maintenance. A LIST of books on water gardens and a description of each is included at the end of the booklet. For more design ideas, see Sunset: Garden Pools, Fountains, and Waterfalls [2].

Barrel

Tub

There are many types of ponds.

Some can be built from holes lined with vinyl or rubber fabric, with a natural looking edge of flat rocks. Fiberglas ponds can be custom built from modular sections; they are 1/4 the price of concrete ponds, while being much more durable. Bog gardens can be created by building an artificial "bog" around a dripping faucet or hose, with a buried plastic sheet "subsoil" layer to keep the first few inches of soil moist. The easiest water garden (for cold winter areas) would be an Indoor tub, near a South-facing window. Tub or barrel gardens are so simple that children can easily plant and care for one of their own. Mosquito fish (Gambusia) are better in tubs than goldfish, guppies or koi, as tubs are very susceptible to temperature extremes. Possible containers to use are: ceramic pots, old crocks, wash tubs, galvanized horse-troughs, or old bath tubs. If using a barrel, you should add a liner, as barrels usually contain bacteria harmful to fish and plants.

Can a water garden survive in our area?

If you really want one and are willing to go to a little more trouble, it is possible; however there are several important things to remember: Select hardy aquatic plants and water lilies that won't be killed by frost (dormant over winter).

Water Lily

Water lilies are easy to grow, and usually very fragrant. "Hardy" water lilies grow and flower beautifully in Alaska, Montana, and all cold winter areas North, South, East or West. They add an unusual dimension to the landscaping. And the more sun they get, the more flowers they will produce. ("tropical" water lily bulbs have to be stored indoors over winter.) Select hardy fish that are used to cold winters. If you have an outdoor pool, the fish could be moved indoors to a fish tank, or left outdoors if the water is deep enough (at least 3 feet),—or you could install a heater to keep part of the pool ice-free and open to the air. Select freeze-proof equipment (like waterfalls) that can be turned off, drained, and dismantled over winter.

There has to be an ecological balance.

You'll need to understand the ecological balance of the pond if you want a clear, healthy pond with reduced algae growth. Anacharis (Elodea canadensis) is a submerged aquatic plant which is essential for a balanced ecosystem. It improves water quality, prevents algae overgrowth, provides food and spawning niches for fish, produces oxygen for the fish and absorbs carbon dioxide. Water lilies are also needed, to cover the surface of the water with their pads, thus lessening oxygen loss through the water surface, and their shade helps keep the

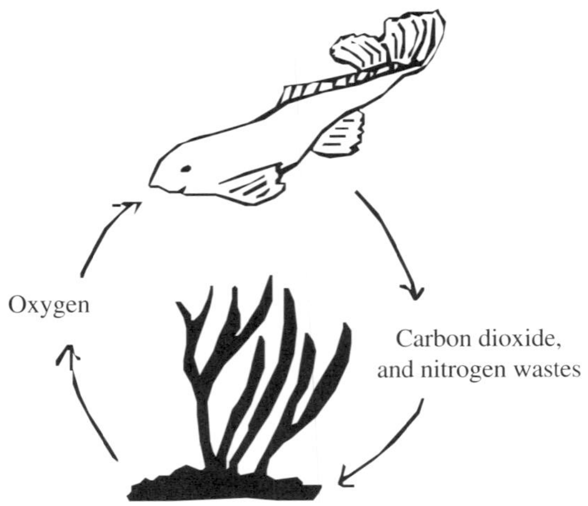

water cooler (the warmer the water, the more algae growth). Snails are important as they eat the algae, fish wastes (nitrogen products), and decaying matter that encourage algae growth. Fish are needed to eat aphids, flies, mosquito larvae and other insects as well as algae. At least four hours of sun daily is required to produce good lily blossoms, and to work as a balanced ecosystem. When you plan a pool, you must create a balanced ecosystem where plants, fish, and snails provide for one anothers needs in order for them to survive.

Some mountain gardeners share their experiences. Kitty Pippen, a resident of Lake Almanor, has an elaborate water fall made of concrete and rock. The water falls into several basins. She turns off the water for winter and drains the pipes. Kitty says to be sure to use a level when placing basins, to insure that the water flows in the direction you want.

Peter Moale of Lake Almanor has a Miniature Hydroelectric Plant that discharges water into two small childrens wading pools which have been placed at two different levels. In the summertime he adds some large shells to make a picturesque waterfall. This system (designed and built by Peter) requires a minimum flow (water pressure) of 40 gallons per minute when operating. When not operating, a small amount of water runs year round to keep the system from freezing. This was built for its landscaping attractiveness, but more basically for use in case the electric goes off. This Hydroelectric plant runs some lights and small appliances in case of emergency. Peter says he will "build to suit" a system of your desire. However, the Miniature Hydroelectric Plants that he makes, sell for $500. Simple waterfall pumps sell more in the range of $32. and up. To save water, get a waterfall pump that recirculates the water back through the pump. But for a hydroelectric plant, the water can only go ***one direction*** in order to ***make*** power (not use it).

Peter Moale's Miniature Hydroelectric plant

Eleanor Burns of Lake Almanor, built a water lily pond with goldfish that she leaves "as is" over winter. The surface of the pond freezes over, but the lilies and fish survive. This type of pond is ideal because you don't have to water it, feed it, fertilize it, or dismantle it for winter. Use hardy water lilies and regular goldfish. As long as the goldfish have a couple inches of water over them (that is not frozen) to cover them, it doesn't matter if there is a solid layer of ice over the pond. The fish hibernate. Their metabolic rate is so low that they barely move during winter. The Anacharis plants on the pond bottom give oxygen to the plants and fish, and the fish don't need to be fed as they have plenty of bugs. The Anacharis also protects the very young fish from being eaten by the parents. Every year the goldfish reproduce but the survival rate is low (Eleanor said that the parents probably eat most of them). The number and size of fish is determined by the size of the pond. A good number might be 10 small fish or 1-2 large fish. The fish grow to a bigger size in a bigger pond. (Trout do not survive in this type of pond, because they require more aeration from running water.)

Eleanor said that it is easy to build, and relatively inexpensive. The bottom and sides of her pond are cement. The size is 4' x 8' and 3' deep. (She said if she made it again, she would make it narrower so she could reach the other side better when picking off the water lily flowers.) After the cement is poured and has dried in the pond bottom, put in two redwood boxes filled with good fertile soil for the water lily bulbs and Anacharis plants. Plant the bulbs and Anacharis, and fill the pond with water. Let the cement cure at least several months before adding the fish, as cement gives off something toxic to the fish. Painting the cement may sound appealing, but the surface will soon be covered with algae, and the color won't show. Add rocks and plants around the edge of the pond as desired.

For a more elaborate water lily pond (depth 18") complete with water fall see Gardener's Supply Company Catalog [3]. It comes as a kit with a waterproof liner, a pump to recirculate the water through a bubbler or waterfall, oxygenating aquatic plants, water lilies and other plants (cost $249.). Then you can stock it with goldfish or other hardy pond fish.

References cited:
[1] Water Visions
[2] Sunset: Garden Pools, Fountains, & Waterfalls
[3] Gardener's Supply Company catalog (see Suppliers List).

Eleanor Burn's Lily pond

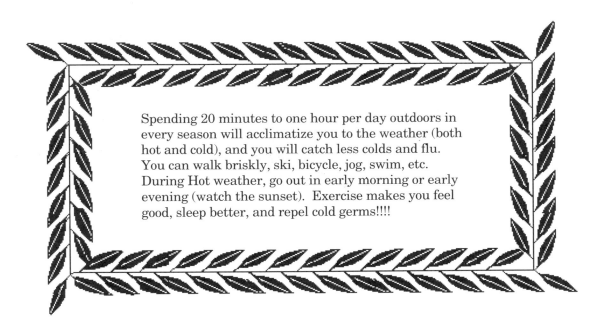

Spending 20 minutes to one hour per day outdoors in every season will acclimatize you to the weather (both hot and cold), and you will catch less colds and flu. You can walk briskly, ski, bicycle, jog, swim, etc. During Hot weather, go out in early morning or early evening (watch the sunset). Exercise makes you feel good, sleep better, and repel cold germs!!!!

INTENSIVE GARDENING IN RAISED BEDS

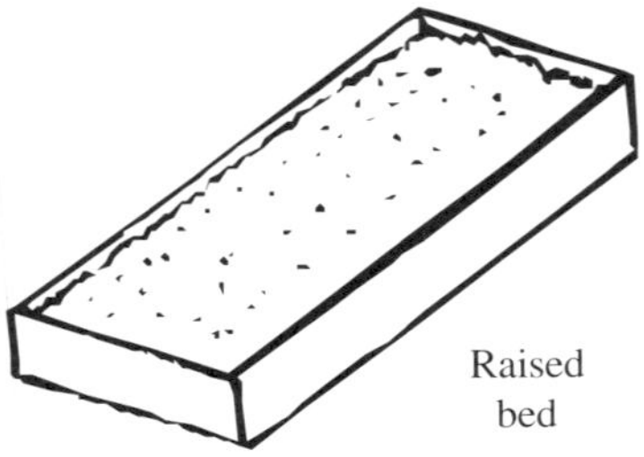

Raised bed

Raised growing beds, supporting close (intensive) interplanting of compatible plants, give maximum productivity in a garden. They can save time, labor, fertilizer, and water, while dramatically increasing garden yields [1]. Gardens with growing beds can be one fifth the size of conventional gardens for the same yields, so they automatically need eighty percent less water, space, and labor [2].

The conventional method of planting is one row of beans, one row of corn, etc., until there are 10-16 rows all paralleling one another on level ground (see Example 1). People often use a stick holding an empty seed packet at the end of each row to show what was planted there. When you walk between rows you compact the "soil" (the ideal soil is loose and airy). Compaction prevents air and water from getting to the roots. Your plants can't make good use of the space between rows, but the weeds like the space just fine!! However, you need to walk somewhere, to get access to the plants for weeding, thinning, and harvesting.

You might try planting five rows of vegetables very close together in a raised garden bed (see Example 2). This method is called **Intensive gardening in raised beds**. It doesn't compact soil near the plants, and few weeds grow in pathways between growing beds as this space isn't receiving water. In this intensive planting method, the seed can be sown across the entire bed instead of being planted in rows, to make better use of soil and to grow up to thirty times more vegetables than you could in a conventional garden on the same area.

Drip irrigation works great in raised growing beds, but other ways to water include: buckets, garden hose, mister, or bubbler. Overhead sprinklers are not efficient here, because you don't want to water the pathways.

When building growing beds, be sure they are not more than four feet wide, as you want to be able to reach the middle of the bed from both sides. Height and length of the boards aren't as critical (twelve inches high works fine). The beds can be as long as you like, but don't make them <u>too</u> long, since you have to walk around the end of the row to get to the next bed. In some narrow yards, you may want to sacrifice some bed space to "bridge" boards, so you can get around better. Any kind of board will work to make the beds, but most wood in contact with wet soil will rot in a few years. It would be wise to use more weather resistant wood such as redwood,

CONVENTIONAL VS RAISED BED GARDENS

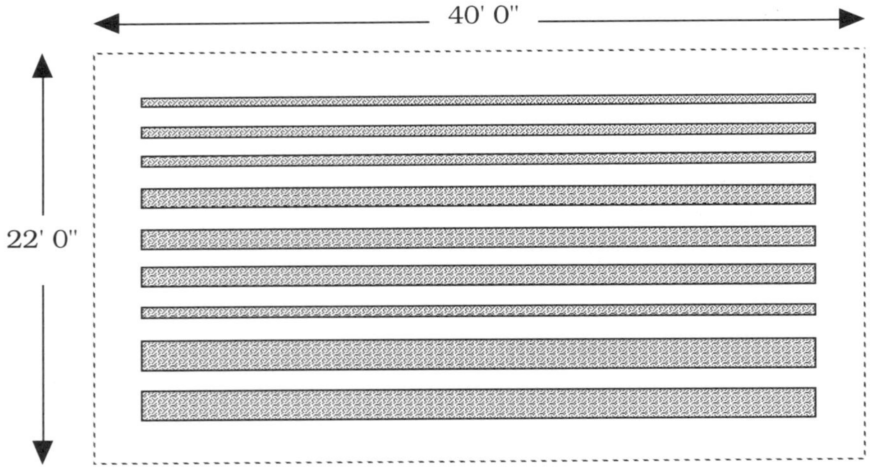

EXAMPLE 1– A Conventional Garden Layout with 6", 12" and 18" rows, with 12" spacing between rows. Total growing area used is 280 square feet.

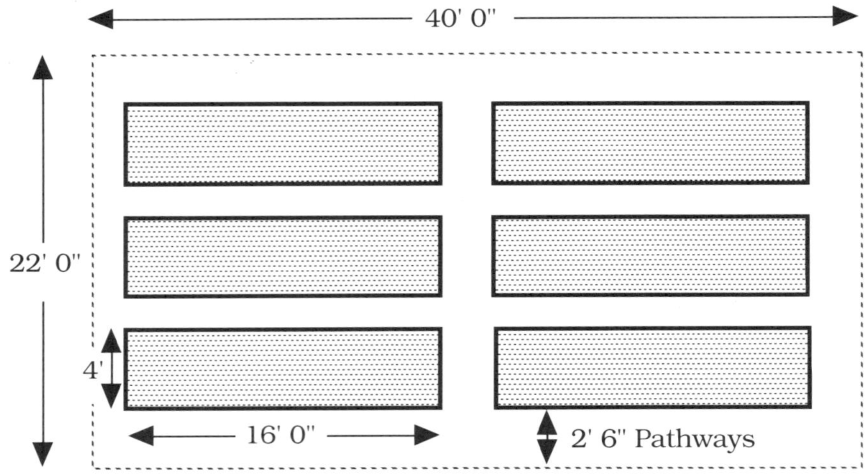

EXAMPLE 2 – Raised bed gardens, separated by walkways. Usable growing area is 390 square feet (a 30% greater growing space). Raised bed garden effectiveness is further increased by lessened compaction, better moisture control and improved soil management. The overall effect may result in doubled crop yields from the same garden area!

cedar, or cypress. I used 2 x 12 inch cedar (rough, unfinished), and made my beds 4 x 18 feet and 12 inches high. Railroad ties make effective, durable bed walls too.

In intensive gardening, when you plant seed across the whole bed, try interplanting four or more different crops to better use garden space. **Interplanting** is a sharing of growing space by two or more different types of plants, so that they have higher productivity, and often grow better than if they were grown alone on the same amount of space. This

Conventional garden with rows

benefit occurs because of mutual shading, confusion to insects, and the more uniform root networks.

An understanding of **Companion Species** (how plants relate to one other) is important in growing beds because plants are so close together. Be sure to interplant with some pest-deterring companion plants such as onion, garlic, or marigold; besides plants that are compatible with each other (see Companion Plant Chart in Insect pest chapter).

The rich, loose, deep soil in a growing bed allows vegetables to be planted closer together—the tall ones with short ones, long-season ones with short-season ones, deep-rooted ones with shallow-rooted ones, also leaf crops with root crops. Many more plants will fit in your garden at one time, and yield will be greater over the growing season than if you planted in the conventional way. To make sure plants harmonize the way they should, plan ahead. Before planting, make a map showing the location of the selected plants.

Since growing beds have more of a solid leaf canopy (like a "living" mulch), they have a more controlled microclimate. With complete shade, less water is lost, and fewer weeds can germinate. Water evaporating from the soil is trapped under the leaf canopy raising the microclimate's humidity. Plants grow better in higher humidity. Growing beds allow plants to act more as a complete environmental unit, while conventional row gardens treat each row as an individual group, thus minimizing the possible benefits of plants growing together [1].

John Jeavons [1] is a noted gardener, who uses raised growing beds with the intensive planting method. He has discovered a dramatic savings in water, fertilizer and labor. Jeavons has found that with careful soil preparation, lack of soil compaction, and the benefits of growing plants close together, —he can cut **WATER** use in his growing beds by 1/2 to 1/16th of the amount needed for conventional gardens, depending upon season and crop. Even better than his figures on saving water are his records for saving **FERTILIZER** in his growing beds, as he uses from 1/4 to as low as 1/62th of the fertilizer used in conventional plots, with no yield loss. Since raised growing beds take up such a small area, their preparation can all be **DONE BY HAND**, with very few tools. Using this method, Jeavons has estimated that his garden uses only 1/100 of the energy that commercial farmers use to produce similar yields. For those with limited space, growing beds are the only way to go; and for those with unlimited space, growing beds are still the the most productive and least wasteful way to garden.

Some advantages and disadvantages of raised growing beds are: In raised growing beds you don't have to de-rock the existing soil (usually 1/2 rock), but you do need truck loads of top soil, plus garden compost (commercially available at your local florist or nursery), peat moss, sand, fireplace ashes, organic matter (like grass and leaves, etc.) to fill the beds with a "supersoil". The basic tools required are a bucket, trowel and a shovel; —you don't have to have a drip irrigation system, expensive soil, or expensive boards. You don't need to rent a rototiller in fall and spring, but you do need to turn over the soil in the beds with a shovel or gardening fork (very important for aeration). The time consuming job of leveling, re-marking pathways, and de-rocking after rototilling is no longer necessary, but rotating of crops becomes particularly important. Plants in raised beds are a little more frost protected, as cold air tends to hug the ground. Best of all is easy access to the plants, a light airy soil, and FEWER weeds. Raised beds can also be more easily fenced, to keep deer or birds off your plants, or to create shade.

References cited:

[1] Getting the Most from Your Garden

[2] Square Foot Gardening, (Mel)

Every little
unfolding flower
Is a gentle reminder
of God's
great power.
...author unknown

TREES

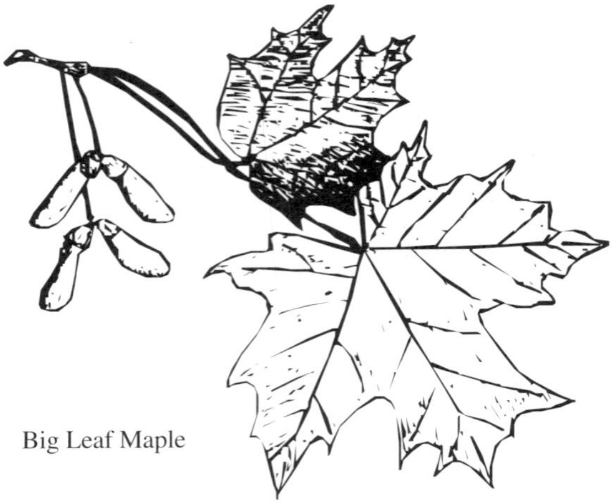

Big Leaf Maple

Many Californians now have permanent or summer homes in the high mountains. These gardeners often have problems landscaping their mountain homes particularly because of summer frosts. Many ornamentals are well adapted to cold winters, but not to summer frosts; so select frost hardy varieties from your local nursery. Plants used in coastal and valley landscapes seldom fit well into mountain settings, and may not adapt well to the climate change. And many trees normally 50-90 feet tall, don't grow as tall at the higher altitudes.

Snow breakage is a real problem for Hardwoods (protective shelters can be built of redwood), while Conifers (native to this area) are little affected. Trees overhanging paths, driveways, and house can be both a nuisance and a danger from broken branches.

Since cedar, birch, maple and popular (i.e. Aspen) trees seek out water, don't plant them too close to your house, pool, septic tank, or leach lines, or they can wreck sewage lines, clog drains, and uplift the house foundation. Never plant any tree closer than five feet from your house. As you can see, many things need to considered before planting a tree.

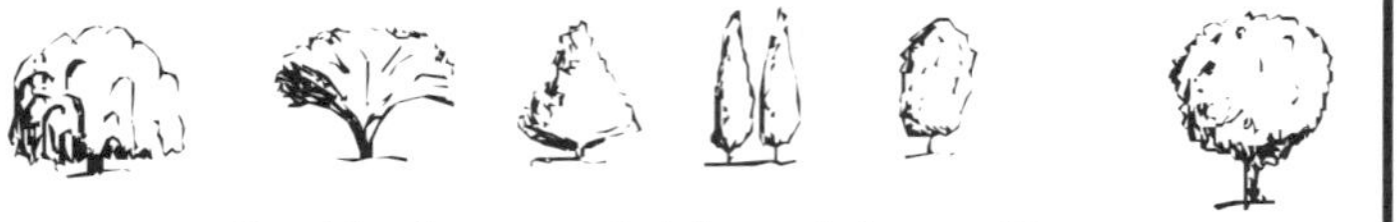

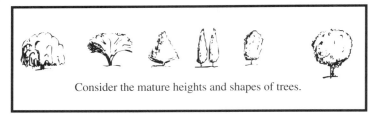

Consider the mature heights and shapes of trees.

Not only do trees have to be cold hardy these days, but it also helps if they are resistant to other problems. City trees have to be resistant against air pollution and smog (i.e. ash, cedar & cypress). Hawthorne and crabapple have to be small enough to grow under power lines. Many evergreens, especially conifers, are both wind and drought resistant once they get established. Medium to slow growing trees are more hardy to cold and storm damage and more disease resistant [1].

The Pacific mountain forests have been classified into four major zones: Yellow Pine 3-6000', Red Fir 6-8500', Subalpine 8-9000', and Alpine 9000'. and above. (These zones correspond to the four zones proposed by Merriam: Transition, Canadian, Hudsonian, and Arctic-alpine.) For example, the Lake Almanor area is classified in the Yellow Pine Zone. Trees characteristic of this zone are Ponderosa Pine, Jeffrey Pine, White Fir, Douglas Fir, Incense Cedar and Douglas Fir. In a little wider area including lower and higher elevation zones there are 5-6 pines, two firs, Mountain Hemlock, and Juniper trees. Trees from nearby zones can often adapt to a neighboring zone when planted in someone's yard. Some people have planted Juniper trees, White pines, and Colorado Blue Spruce in their yards in Chester.

Trees growing naturally in a forest make their own microclimate, which is a balanced environment between animals, plants, decaying organisms, insects, water, and nutrients. To a wild plant, our yard is an exotic place. Copy the plant's natural home as closely as possible when moving it to your yard. A dogwood tree in the wild is an understory tree with little sun or water. So plant it in a suitably shady spot in your yard—not in full sun! It is very easy to overwater a wild plant that is used to dry summer conditions in its natural home. The native dogwood that grow here (Pacific dogwood) are used to the shade, however the plant most commonly sold in nurseries is the Eastern Dogwood which requires more sun and water and is much easier to grow.

Plants that grow naturally (native plants) in the mountains can be arranged into a pleasing landscape of easy care. Young seedlings can be carefully transplanted if they aren't growing just where you want them. In most areas, the existing trees and shrubs need to be thinned out and trimmed to let in sun, open the view, improve growth, and reduce fire hazard. Manzanita, once the deadwood is removed, can be particularly beautiful when pruned artistically. Only in the high mountains can you have a beautiful Squawcarpet groundcover (and it is difficult to get a transplant to grow in your yard).

Transplanting a pine, fir or cedar from the wild into a selected place in your yard takes careful preparation. First, dig a hole and fill it with water. Then fill a bucket with water and set it next to your young plant. Carefully dig up the plant, disturbing the roots as little as possible. Place the roots immediately into the bucket. Timing is important and seconds count. Carry the bucket containing your young tree to the planting site. Place plant quickly into hole full of water. Gently fill in with dirt, packing the dirt, but be sure to leave a large depression around the base of the tree for watering (see chapter on Seeds about transplanting plants). Then, water with B1 solution to prevent transplant shock. Use B1 solution again in ten days.

Bonsai is a fascinating art form where very young trees are pruned and trained into artistic shapes. These plants add an Oriental touch to any patio, deck or yard. Mugo pine is a popular plant for this technique. Both the branches and the

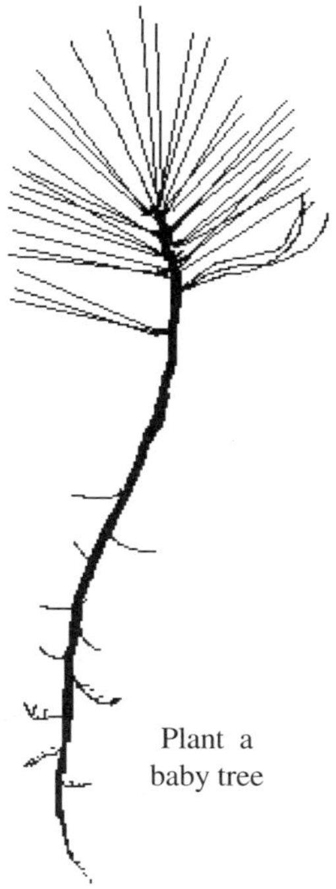

Plant a baby tree

roots are pruned to keep the plant small and growing into the desired shape.

Save a tree. When paving asphalt or concrete near a tree, allow space around the trunk. Don't pave inside the "drip line" of the tree's branches. The roots need to breathe and need water from rain or snow. Leave a space at least five feet from the trunk of larger trees (and those you expect to get large). If you are building a house, install a fence or some barrier around each existing tree at its' drip line. This fence will remind carpenters, etc., not to park under the tree and not to pile lumber or rocks there, because it compacts the soil, suffocating the tree, and can cause it to die in 1-2 years.

Plant a tree. Help yourself and help the world at the same time. You can make a difference! Planting a few deciduous trees strategically placed around your house can reduce your heating and cooling costs. If you are interested in planting a tree to help the environmental cause, contact one of these organizations. Global Releaf will plant a tree for you, if you call 800-740-TREE (phone call costs $5.00). In Penny Pines, one contribution of $68. will plant pine seedlings over one acre of National forest land. For each contribution they put up a special sign at the site, besides giving you a special certificate signed by the forest supervisor. This makes a nice living memorial gift for someone instead of sending flowers. Write to: Regional Penny Pines Coordinator, USDA Forest Service, Office of Information, 630 Sansome St., San Francisco, CA 94111.

Tree PLANT LIST

CONIFEROUS EVERGREEN TREES

ARBORVITAE (Thuja) (see shrub, conifer list)

CEDAR True cedars. Pinaceae family! One of the most widely grown conifers in the West. Needles in tufted clusters. Deep rooted and drought tolerant once established. Produces medium to dense shade. Single tree.

Atlas or Atlantic (Cedrus atlantica) Zone 6. Good for Oriental effect. Rich, well-drained soil. Ht 60', S 35'. Cones 2 x 3". Very resistant to pollution. Bark is gray, smooth and shiny. Branches get too long and heavy, so recommend trimming them back.

Deodar Cedar (Cedrus deodarus) Zone 7.(Borderline). Ht 100', S 40'. Rich, well-drained soil. Branches mostly horizontal with pendulous shoots.

Eastern Red (see Juniper)

Cedar of Lebanon (Cedrus libanotica) Zone 4. Most beautiful. Ht 100'. Leaves dark green, about 1" long. Cones 1-4" long. There is also a dwarf compact form, and another with bluish or silvery leaves.

CEDAR, CALIFORNIA INCENSE (Calocedrus decurrens) Not a true cedar. Native. Has scales, not needles. Used for firewood, fenceposts, shade tree, or privacy screen. Ht 50-125'. Beautiful tree.

FALSE CYPRESS (see shrub, conifer list)

FIR (Abies) Native. Produces dense shade. Firs have solitary needles (not in bundles). Needles smell good. Most particular of all conifers in requiring specific growing conditions. Dislike for dust, smoke, and hot dry climates. Prefers high altitudes with good air and light conditions, not scorching hot sun, dry winds, or drought. Needs moist, well-drained soil.

Alpine (A. lasiocarpa) Rocky Mountain Fir. Subalpine Zone. Ht 90'. Cones 3-4" long. Native to Alaska.

Red (A. magnifica) Indicator of Red Fir Zone (5700-8500 ft). Ht 60-175'. Cones grow upright on branches.

White (A. concolor) Smelly when wet as heartwood retains water. Occurs at 3,000 to 7,000' in Yellow Pine Zone Zone 4. Hardy. Fast growing for a conifer. Ht 75'. Fragrant 2" blue-green needles.

FIR, DOUGLAS (Pseudotsuga menziesii) Not a true fir. Beautiful. Shady moist, well-drained. Cones have pretty bracts. Zone 5. Native in Yellow Pine Zone. Hardy. Fast growing for a conifer. Ht 100'. Can be sheared for hedge, lawn tree, windbreaks, and backgrounds. Produces dense shade. One inch bluish-green, soft needles.

HEMLOCK, WESTERN or HEMLOCK SPRUCE (Tsuga heterophylla) Very hardy, dislikes open, windswept places. Zone 2. Produces dense shade. Moist, slightly acid soils. Ht 120'. Decorator lawn tree, hedge or screen. Native of Pacific Coast: Alaska through higher Sierra Nevadas. Likes moist, rich woods. Sensitive to dust and smoke (not good in cities). Small cones. In the East is T. canadensis, while in the West it is T. heterophylla.

HEMLOCK, MOUNTAIN (Tsuga mertensiana) Native of Pacific Coast: Alaska through higher Sierra Nevadas, at 7500-9200' in Red Fir and Subalpine Zones. Beautiful tiny cones, very hardy tree: withstands strong winds and snow. The top characteristically nods over. Ht 90'. Branches drooping. Resembles Western Hemlock, is often confused with it, and has the same climate requirements. Height smaller and slower in gardens, only 50'. Foliage blue-green with silvery cast. Good for bonsai, rock garden, containers.

JAPANESE BLACK (see Pine, not-native)

JUNIPER (Juniperus) Produces dense shade. Scale-like pointed leaves. Well-drained soil. (see also shrub, conifer list)

Chinese, or Twisted (J. chinensis) Zone 4. Ht 50'. Single tree. Other varieties in ground covers and shrubby forms.

Eastern red cedar (J. virginiana) Zone 3. Grows slow.

Single tree or windbreaks. Birds love the blue berries. Ht 80'.

LARCH, EUROPEAN (Larix decidua) Zone 2. Very unusual, a deciduous conifer! Ornamental. Pine family. Yellow fall foliage. Produces medium shade. Moist, slightly acid soil. Ht 60'. Cones stay on tree. Needle-like foliage. Branches slightly pendulous.

Western White Pine

PINE, Native (Pinus) Identified by number of needles in a bundle, and size and shape of cones. Produces dense shade. Must have well-drained soil. Very hardy, but damaged by winter sun and drying wind, so north-facing slopes are best.

Pinon or Nut Pine (P. monophylla) Needles (gray-green, stiff) solitary. Grows on East slope of Sierras towards Reno (3500-9000' elevation). Drought resistant. Ht 5-15'. Very slow growing. Brown cones 2" wide, roundish. Edible seeds (pine nuts). Mature tree crooked trunk, open and broad top. Bonsai, or rock garden.

Lodgepole or Tamarak (P. contorta var. murrayana) Slender, dark green needles in bundles of two. Yellow Pine Zone to Subalpine Zone (5000-9000'). Ht 80'. Usually low and bushy in cultivation. Cones, small (1 1/2 in), shiny brown, stay on tree until fire opens them. Easily adaptable, except in areas of drought and low humidity.

White Bark (P. albicaulis) Erect trees in protected places and at lower elevations, but gnarled, prostrate, and spreading at timberline. Ht only 1-30'. Indicator of Subalpine Zone: 8500-10,000'. Stout, dark green needles. Cones 3", roundish, purple. Good for rock gardens and bonsai. Very slow growing.

Western Yellow Pines—Native in N. CA. Long needles in bundles of three.

Ponderosa (P. ponderosa) Zone 6. Cone smaller (3-5 in.), spines sticking out (sharp!). "Prickly ponderosa". Needles yellow-green and long. Ht 60' (in 50 years grows to 150'). Moderate to rapid growth. Indicator of Yellow Pine Zone at 5000-6000'. Beautiful bark. Large garden, or bonsai. Does not like hot summers or wind.

Jeffrey (P. jeffreyi) Zone 4. Oval cone, larger (6-12" long), and smoother (spines sticking in). Ht 60-120'. Needles pale blue-green and long. Ponderosa and Jeffrey interbreed producing variations of both. Fragrant, vanilla-scented bark. Yellow Pine and Subalpine Zones 5000-8500'. Drought resistant. Slow growing. Natural bonsai tree.

White Pines—Native in N. CA. Short needles in bundles of five.

Sugar (P. lambertiana). Very large cylindrical cones (10-20" long). Ht 60-225'. Worlds tallest pine. Indicator of Yellow Pine Zone at 5500-6000'. Susceptible to White Pine Blister Rust; be sure no currant or gooseberry plants are nearby (alternate hosts of blister rust).

Western White or Silver Pine (P. monticola) Indicator of Red Fir Zone: 5900-9000'. A miniature Sugar Pine. Cones are smaller but look identical to those of Sugar Pine, and trees not get as tall. Ht 50-175'. Slender bluish-green needles.

PINES, Not-native (Pinus) Very hardy, desirable horticultural species. Well-drained soils. Differ in ways they react to sun, wind, and soil differences. Identified by number of needles in a bundle, and size and shape of cones.

Austrian (P. nigra) Zone 3. Cones 2-3" long. Ht 75'. Needles (4-6" long) dark green, in bundles of two. Soot resistant. Single tree or windbreak.

Red or Norway Pine. (P. resinosa) Zone 1. Needles (4-6" long) dark glossy green, in bundles of two. Single tree or windbreak. Pyramid shape. Fast growing. Ht 75-100'. Cones 2" long.

Scotch (P. sylvestris) Zone 2. Ht 75'. Needles (2-3" long), bluish-green, stiff and twisted, in bundles of two. Easily sheared to shapes. Produces dense shade. Fast growing. Tolerates seashore or city. Drought resistant. Cones 2", grayish to red-brown

White (P. strobus) Zone 2. Ht 100'. Needles (4-5" long), soft blue-green, in bundles of five. Several varieties. Not like strong winds. Gets White Pine Blister Rust (see Sugar Pine). Beautiful tree. Cones 3-8", slender, often curved.

Japanese Black (P. thunbergii) Zone 3. Grows fast. Ht 100'. Broad, cone-shaped tree. Evergreen shade tree, pruned, in planters, or as bonsai. Oval cones 3" long. Needles (3-4 1/2" long) in bundles of two, stiff, bright green.

Mugo Pine (see shrub, conifer list).

REDWOOD, DAWN (Metasequoia glyptostroboides) Zone 6. Very unusual, a deciduous conifer! Leaves turn bronze in the fall and then drop off. Produces medium-dense shade. Ht 100'. Moist, well-drained soil. Very fast growing. Good in large yards. (Same family as Sequoia) Best effect when planted in small groves. From China.

SEQUOIA, GIANT or BIG TREE (Sequoia gigantea) This is the mountain variety. Too big for small gardens. (Coast redwood do not grow here).

SPRUCE A dense shade tree. Very hardy. Zone 3.

Colorado Blue or Green (Picea pungens) Best in sun, well-drained soil. Tolerates light shade. Needs regular watering. Ht 70-100'. Needles sharp!, bluish-green. Cones 3-4" long. Native to Rocky Mountains. Susceptible to Spruce gall (pest). Blue spruce come in all shades so pick tree by color of foliage, and don't let anyone tell you green trees turn blue when they get older!

Norway (Picea abies) Probably the most widely cultivated evergreen tree in America. Ht 150'. Bark reddish brown. Branches pendulous at ends. Cones 5-7 in. long. Beautiful deep green foliage. Many varieties.

White (Picea glauca) Ornamental or windbreak. Ht 75'. Cones 1 1/2—2" long. Bluish-green needles. Tolerates drought and heat. Varieties include one dwarf and several compact forms.

DECIDUOUS TREES

ALDER (Alnus) A shade tree. Brown fall foliage. Tolerant, takes wet soil conditions (normally grows along stream banks). Needs constant moisture in a lawn or garden. Yellow flower catkins in winter. Nitrogen-fixing. Produces medium-light shade. Fast growing. Ht 40-90'.

Mountain (A. incana) Native. Ht 10-20'. Mostly shrubby, but can be pruned to multiple trunked tree.

European (A. glutinosa) Zone 4. Ht 75', S 40'.

Italian (A. cordata) Zone 6. Ht 60', S 25'.

Sierra White (A. rhombifolia) Ht 50-75'. Sun. Wet soil. Nice bark. Good for firewood.

Red (A. oregona) Good for firewood. Ht 60-90'.

ALMOND, FLOWERING (Prunus dulcis 'dulcis') See shrub plant list.

APRICOT, FLOWERING (Prunus armeniaca) Zone 6 (borderline). Yellow fall foliage, produces medium shade. Snow breakage. Frost kills blossoms. Early flowers, tasty fruit. Better in warmer areas. Ht 30', S 20'. Moist, well-drained soil.

ASH (Fraxinus) Yellow-lavender fall foliage. Shade, lawn, patio or street tree. All soils. Little care. Produces light shade. Fast growing. Tolerant of hot summer and cold winter. Leaves medium-green, divided into leaflets. Some species have male and female flowers on same tree, some on separate trees. When on separate trees, will get fruit on female tree only if it grows near male tree. When have both sexes, winged fruit and seedlings can become problem.

Green (F. pennsylvanica) Zone 2. Ht 30-40'. Dense, compact oval crown. Gray-brown bark. Male and female flowers on separate trees. Not like hot windy areas, but can tolerate wet soil or severe cold.

White (F. americana) Zone 4. Ht 90', S 45'. Straight trunk, oval shaped crown. Needs some watering. Not like hot windy areas.

Flowering (F. ornus) Zone 7. Ht 40', S 20'. Beautiful fluffy, white fragrant flowers in dense terminal clusters. Broad round crown. Ugly seed clusters.

ASH, MOUNTAIN (Sorbus) All zones. Small lawn or street tree, but berries can be messy on pavement. Sunny, well-drained soil. Grown for beautiful fern-like foliage, clustered white flowers in spring, bright orange-red berries in fall, and fall foliage. Birds love the berries. Tolerates winter cold, strong winds, low humidity, or extreme heat. Need average gardening watering. Susceptible to cankers and fireblight. Produces light-medium shade.

European (S. aucuparia) Zone 3. Bright orange-red or yellow fall foliage. Ht 25', S 20'. Hardy to -40°F. Fast growing. Dense oval to round crown.

Korean (S. alnifolia) Zone 5. Orange-scarlet fall foliage. Ht 50', S 30'.

ASPEN (see populus)

BEECH (Fagus) Yellow-gold fall foliage. Tolerant, but prefers acid soil. Produces dense shade. Lower branches sweep the ground. Smooth gray bark contrasts with dark glossy leaves for beautiful winter effect. Leaves turn red-brown in fall. Best in full sun; moderate watering needed. Roots near surface of ground (don't disturb them with digging) makes lawn maintenance difficult.

American, red, or white beech (F. grandifolia) Zone 4. Ht 40', S 60'. Leaves longer (to 5") and narrower, turning yellow before the red brown phase. Not as popular as European. Lower branches drop off.

European (F. sylvatica) Zone 5. Ht 90', S 50'. Leaves to 4" long, Seeds attract birds. Many varieties.

BIRCH (Betula) Yellow fall foliage. Produces medium.shade. All soils. White bark, finely toothed leaves. Needs plenty of water. Short lived. Not good in lawn.

White, Paper or Canoe (B. papyrifera) Zone 3. Tolerant but prefers moist soils. Ht 100', S 40'. Beautiful creamy white bark, peels by itself. Grows in clumps of 2-4 trunks. Taller than European, more open, less weeping, and leaves are longer. Since they are more susceptible to borers, and less hardy— they are less popular. The leaves oval, coarsely double-toothed. Will not grow in shade. Leaves brilliant yellow in fall. Indians used it to make canoes. Plant near evergreens for beautiful color contrast.

Gray (B. populifolia) Zone 4. Ht 25', S 10'. Not as showy as other varieties. White bark with black spots. Good choice for poor soil. Short lived.

European White (B. pendula) Zone 2 (hardy to -40°F). Delicate and lacy. Often grown in clumps of three. Ht 30-60', S 20'. Short lived (20 years). Good patio tree. Easily susceptible to borer. Gets name from drooping habit of young branches, but is not a weeping birch. Most popular birch! Three varieties.

BLACK LOCUST (Robinia pseudoacacia) A shade tree. Ugly thorns. Fast growing. Deer resistant. Clusters of pink to purplish-pink blossoms have effect similar to wisteria. Often trained upright to show off blossoms to best effect. Bright red bristles cover fruits and twigs. Seedpods 3" long. Messy. Makes excellent firewood. Grows rapidly to 75' tall.

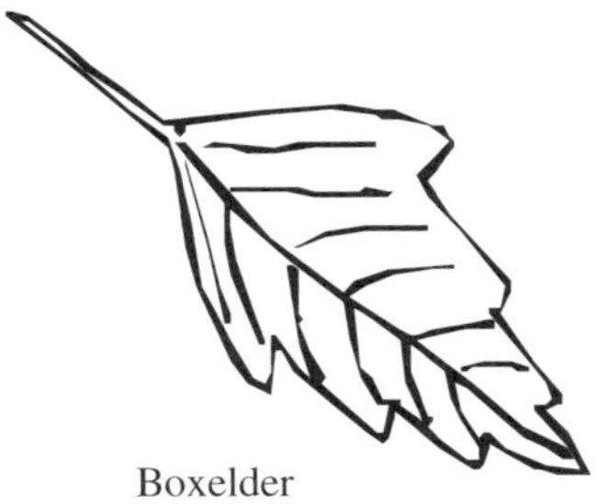

Boxelder

BOXELDER (Acer negundo) Zone 2. Native in California along stream valleys. Small tree Ht 60', S 30'. All soils. Drought, heat, and frost-resistant. VERY HARDY. Yellow-brown fall foliage. Branches break easily. Produces medium shade. Gets pests easily. Also a variegated variety (a striking green and white small tree)

BUCKEYE, OHIO (Aesculus glabra) Zone 4. Bright orange fall foliage. Ht 30', S 30'. Moist, well-drained soil. Greenish-white flower in spring. Nuts not edible. Produces medium shade.

CASTOR ARALIA (Kalopanax pictus) Zone 5. Red-brown fall foliage. Resists disease. Ht 80', S 60'. Produces medium-dense shade. Rich, moist soil. Half inch rounded leaves. Black fruits in late summer. Don't confuse with shrub Five-Leaved Aralia (Acanthopanax).

CATALPA (Catalpa speciosa) Zone 5. Brown fall foliage. Beautiful white flowers (panicles) in mid-summer. Curved pencil-like seedpods. Fast growing. Produces medium-dense shade. Ht 60', S 35'. All soils. About 1 out of every 10 years, it gets killed back by frost. Often messy. Beautiful large leaves. Resists disease

CHERRY, FLOWERING (Prunus) Produces light-medium shade. Moist, well-drained soil. Snow breakage. Frost kills blossoms.

Higan (P. subhirtella) Zone 6. Yellow fall foliage. Ht 30', S 30'. Pink flowers, early spring.

Oriental (P. serrulata) Zone 6. Yellow fall foliage. Ht 23', S 23'. Pink or white flowers in early spring.

Sargent (P. sargenti) Zone 5. Red fall foliage Ht 50', S 50'. Pink flowers in spring.

Joshino (P. yedoensis) Zone 6. Yellow fall foliage. Ht 40', S 40'. Pink or white flowers in early spring.

CHESTNUT, CHINESE (Castanea mollissima) Zone 5. Yellow-gold fall foliage. Produces dense shade. Ht 50', S 50'. Rich, well-drained soil. White flowers in early summer, then edible nuts. Not self-pollinating. Single tree or in open grove.

COTINUS (see smoke tree)

COTTONWOOD (see populus)

CRABAPPLE, FLOWERING (Malus) All zones. Yellow, orange, and brown fall foliage. Produces light-medium shade. Sunny, rich, moist well-drained soil. Apples good for jelly, and for birds. Flowers vary white to red in spring; fruits (apples) are yellow, green, or red. Ht 15', S 15'. Hardy varieties: Hopa and Betchel. Betchel has double pink blossoms, is non-fruiting, and is nice for patios. There are also some weeping varieties. Fruiting varieties are beautiful but very messy.

DOGWOOD Tree or shrub. Beautiful orange, brown and red fall foliage. Produces light shade. Well-drained soil. Red inedible berries loved by birds. (See also shrub, decid. list.)

Eastern or Flowering (Cornus florida) Zone 5. Tree. Easiest dogwood to grow in gardens. An East coast variety with pink and white flowers. Very hardy. Single tree. Ht 15-30'. Slow growing, open bush. Performs best in light shade, but tolerates full sun in Chico!

Japanese (Cornus kousa) Zone 6. Smaller tree. Ht 20'. Produces light shade. Well-drained soil. White flowers; inedible fruits, loved by birds.

Pacific (Cornus nuttalii) Tree, Native to Pacific Northwest (grows wild in Deer Creek Canyon. White flower (bracts) showy on bare branches in April-May. Easy to overwater and over-fertilize. Much taller tree than Cornus florida. Zone 6. Ht 50', S 20. Plant under high branching trees.

Siberian (Cornus alba 'sibirica') Tree. Less rampant than Cornus alba. Tolerates shade. Ht 7', S 5'. Coral red branches in winter. Cut back in spring to force new growth, because new wood is brighter red and beautiful.

Dogwood
Cornus florida

ELM (Ulmus) A shade tree. All soils. Fast growing. Produces medium shade. All have yellow and brown fall foliage, except Chinese which also has red.

American (U. americana) Zone 2. Large, long-lived. Ht 110', S, 40'. Produces medium shade. Susceptible to Dutch Elm disease.

Chinese (U. parvifolia) Zone 5. Ht 50', S 40'. Fast growing. Attractive gray peeling bark. Single tree or screen. Self sows and can become a problem. Produces medium shade. Evergreen in warmer areas.

Siberian (U. x pumila) Zone 4. Resistant to Elm diseases. Easily damaged in storms. Good for privacy screen. Ht 65', S 50' wide.

Smooth-leaf (U. carpinifolia) Zone 5. Ht 80', S 70' (there are smaller varieties). Disease resistant. Single tree in lawn, along street, or accent in foundation plantings. Produces medium-dense shade. Fastest growing and most disease resistant of the Elms.

FRINGE TREE (Chionanthus virginicus) Zone 5. Yellow-gold fall foliage. Lawn tree. Produces light shade. Ht 30', S 20'. Moist, well-drained soil. Leaves appear before fleecy white flowers (clusters). Slow growing.

GINKGO or MAIDENHAIR TREE (Ginkgo biloba) Zone 5. Will grow here, but is subject to snow damage, so it does much better in a warmer climate. Striking golden fall foliage. Produces medium-dense shade. Ht 90', S 40'. All soils. Slow growing. Insect, disease, and smog resistant. All leaves fall off at same time. Buy the non-fruiting varieties because the fruit smells terrible.

GOLDENCHAIN TREE (Laburnum x watereri) A patio tree, slow-growing. Zone 5. Yellow-brown fall foliage. Hardy to -20°F. Produces light shade. Ht 30', S 15'. Moist, well-drained soil. A hybrid. Disease resistant. Fantastic, prolific 20" hanging clusters of yellow flowers in mid-spring (clusters like that of Wisteria). Flowers are sweet-pea shaped. Remove brown seedpods because they are poisonous and because they drain the tree's strength. Buds often get frozen in spring.

GOLDENRAIN TREE (Koelreuteria paniculata) Zone 6. Will grow here as a beautiful ornamental, but doesn't bloom in the cold climates. Yellow-brown fall foliage. Produces light-medium shade. Ht 30', S 15'. Well-drained soil. Easily damaged in storms. Use as single tree. Pretty 15" hanging clusters of small yellow flowers in early summer. Tolerates soot, heat, cold, drought, wind, or alkaline soil.

GUM, AMERICAN SWEET or LIQUIDAMBAR (Liquidambar styraciflua) Zone 5. Fast growing in moist, well-drained soil. Produces medium-dense shade. Ht 70', S 50'. Disease and insect resistant. Deer love to eat it. Beautiful silver-grey bark. Leaves are dark green, turning purple, yellow or red in fall. Even young seedling trees give gorgeous fall color.

GUM, SOUR (see pepperidge)

HACKBERRY (Celtis occidentalis) Zone 4. Yellow-brown fall foliage. Produces medium-dense shade. Ht 75', S 50'. Moist, well-drained soil. Susceptible to fungus disease called "witches broom". Good in cities. Soot resistant. Warty bark.

HAWTHORN, THORNAPPLE, or HAW (Crataegus) All soils. Known for pretty spring flowers and showy red fruits (like small apple). Produces light-medium shade. Thorny branches need some pruning, makes nice barrier, but not like being clipped as hedge. Gets aphids, and Fire Blight. Rose family. Attract bees, birds. All very hardy. Like dry soil.

Downy (C. mollis) Zone 5. White flowers. Stiff thorns. Ht 25', S 15'. Fruit good for making jelly. Looks like a mature apple tree. Red-gold fall foliage.

English (C. laevigata) Zone 5. White flowers. Ht 25', S 15'. Scarlet fruits in fall. Slow growing. Best known through its varieties: **Crimson Cloud** Red flowers with white center. **Paul's Scarlet**-clusters of double rose to red flowers. Scarlet fruits in fall.

Single-seed (C. monogyna) Zone 5. White flowers. Stiff thorns. Ht 30', S 20'. Red gold fall foliage.

Washington (C. phaenopyrum) Ht 25', S 20'. Small white flowers. More graceful and delicate than other Hawthorns. Street or lawn tree. Orange and red fall foliage. Leaves have 3-5 sharp pointed lobes (like maples).

HICKORY, SHAGBARK (Carya ovata) Zone 5. Gold-brown fall foliage. Produces light-medium shade. Ht 90', S 50'. All soils. Good edible fruits. Slate-gray, loosely flaking bark.

HONEY LOCUST, THORNLESS (Gleditsia triacanthos) Zone 5. This is the most popular of the honey locust varieties. A shade tree. Yellow fall foliage. No thorns or seedpods. Ht 40-70' (varieties vary). Produces light-medium shade. Hardy in cities. Fernlike dainty foliage. All soils. Leafs out late and goes dormant early, so is good as a lawn tree.

HORNBEAM, EUROPEAN (Carpinus betulus) Zone 6. Yellow fall foliage. Produces medium shade. Ht 40', S 40'. All soils. Hedges, windbreaks.

HORSE CHESTNUT (Aesculus) Yellow-brown fall foliage. Moist, well-drained soils. Produces medium-dense shade. Soot tolerant.

Common (A. hippocastanum) Zone 3. Pretty 15" spikes of white flowers in spring. Messy. Ht 75', S 40'. Fruit not edible.

Red (A. x camea) Zone 4. Pretty 5-8" spikes of red flowers in spring. More hardy and less messy than the Common Horse Chestnut. Ht 40', S 35'.

JAPANESE PAGODA TREE (Sophora japonica) Zone 5. Red-gold fall foliage. Produces medium shade. Ht 75', S 60'. Moist, well-drained soil. Pest, disease, and soot resistant. Fast-growing. Pretty 10-15" clusters of tiny white flowers. Spreading habit. Shade tree for lawn or patio.

KATSURA TREE (Cercidiphyllum japonicum) Zone 4. Yellow-orange fall foliage. Produces medium-dense shade. Ht 60', S 40'. Moist, well-drained soils. Insect and disease resistant. Attractive peeling bark.

LINDEN (Tilia) Yellow fall foliage. Moist, well-drained soil. Tiny white flowers mid-summer; blue berries. Use as single tree.

American (T. americana) Zone 2. Not soot tolerant. Produces medium shade. Ht 70', S 40'. Flowers not fragrant.

Small-leaved European (T. cordata) Zone 4. Fast, hardy growth. Soot-tolerant. Produces medium-dense shade. Ht 70', S 30'. Flowers fragrant.

LIQUID AMBER (see gum, sweet)

MAGNOLIA (Magnolia) Brown fall foliage. Needs well-drained soil.

Cucumber tree (M. acuminata) Zone 5. Ht 85', S 30'. Produces dense shade. Rich, well-drained soil. Colorful seedpods. Beautiful, fast growing. Inconspicuous flowers.

Saucer (M. x soulangiana) Zone 6. Produces light shade. Ht 25'. S 25'. Moist, well-drained soil. Large 5-10" white-purple flowers in early spring appear before the leaves. Beautiful slate-grey bark. Several varieties, some hardier than others.

MAPLE (Acer) A shade tree. Subject to snow breakage, but some are stronger. The slower growers are damaged less by snow (e.g. Sugar and Red maple). Spectacular FAll COLOR! All maples grow here. Strong roots invasive to septic tanks, and can lift concrete.

Amur (A. ginnala) Zone 2. Striking scarlet fall color. Produces medium-dense shade. Ht 20', S 20'. All soils. HARDY. Small tree or multiple-trunked tall shrub. Toothed leaves 3x 2" wide.

Big leaf (A. macrophyllum) Ht 50-70'. Broad top, dense shade. Yellow flower clusters. Spectacular yellow fall foliage in cool areas. Native to stream banks and moist canyons. Large leaves 6-15" wide, with 3-5 lobes.

Japanese (A. palmatum) Several varieties. Zone 6. Scarlet fall foliage, produces medium-light shade. Ht 20', S 20'. Moist, well-drained soil in partial shade. Hardy, but still considered Borderline because it is EASILY BROKEN BY STORMS AND SNOW. Protect from heavy snow. Leaves finely divided. Very striking when kept dwarfed as potted plants for patios, etc.

Japanese Maple

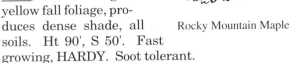

Rocky Mountain (A. glabrum) Native. Ht 5-10'. Leaves: opposite; simple; 3 lobes (often with 2 smaller ones near base), toothed margins.

Rocky Mountain Maple

Norway (A. platanoides) Zone 4. Bright yellow fall foliage, produces dense shade, all soils. Ht 90', S 50'. Fast growing, HARDY. Soot tolerant. Shallow root system.

Paperbark (A. griseum) Zone 6. Red-orange fall foliage, produces medium shade. Ht 25', S 20'. All soils. Peeling, cinnamon-brown bark.

Red (A. rubrum) Zone 4. Red-orange fall foliage, produces medium shade. Ht 70', S 50'. Any soils if kept moist. Moderate to slow growing. Pretty red flowers and seeds. Easily damaged by storms and snow.

Silver (A. saccharinum) Zone 3. Yellow-orange fall foliage, produces medium shade. Fast growing. Ht 100', S 80'. Any soils if kept moist. Finely divided leaves, silver underside. Easily damaged by wind and snow. Roots lift pavement.

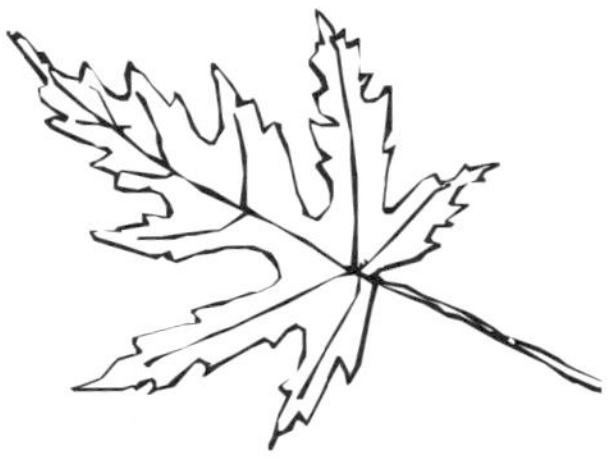

Silver Maple

Sugar (A. saccharum) Zone 3. Yellow, orange, or red fall foliage. Produces medium-dense shade. Ht 75', S 50'. Moist, well-drained soils. Grows slower than other maples. Not soot tolerant. Storm hardy. Source of maple syrup.

Vine (A. circinatum) Zone 4. Orange, yellow or scarlet fall color. Beautiful airy and delicate appearance. In shade (shade tolerant), it is a crooked, sprawling, vine-like shrub, but in full sun is a single-trunked small tree 5-35' tall. Native to moist woods, streambanks.

MULBERRY, FRUITLESS WHITE (Morus alba 'fruitless') Brittle, easily damaged by storms. Ht 50'. From China. Hardy all zones. The leaves of the Far Eastern variety are used as food for silkworms. Fruitless varieties are better for home gardens! Many varieties. The var. tatarica is Russian mulberry which is smaller, more hardy, and usually has red fruit. There also is a weeping variety.

OAK (Quercus) A shade tree. Generally, it must drop its leaves in fall or gets too much snow breakage. Fall color is best in the warmer areas . Produces medium shade. Well-drained, slightly acid soils. The species Red, Scarlet and Shingle prefer light sandy soil, while White and Willow like heavy damp clay soils. Fruit: acorns. Most are drought tolerant, meaning not need much water after once established after (1-2 seasons).

Pin (Q. palustris) Zone 5. Hardy, storm-sturdy. Fast growing, keeps leaves through winter. Scarlet fall foliage. Ht 75', S 40'. Native to Eastern U.S.

Red (Q. rubra) Zone 5. Beautiful red fall foliage. Ht 75', S 50'. Hardy. Fastest growing oak. Soot resistant.

Ornamental. Needs plenty water (deep roots).

Scarlet (Q. coccinea) Zone 4. Scarlet fall foliage. Ht 75', S 60'. Fast growing. Shade or single tree. Native to Eastern USA. Likes deep rich soil.

Pin Oak

Shingle (Q. imbricaria) Zone 5. Yellow-red fall foliage. Ht 75', S 60'. Hedge, windbreak. Leaves cling to tree into winter.

White (Q. garryana) Zone 4. Native from British Columbia to Santa Cruz Mts of Calif. Violet, purple-red fall foliage. Ht 90', S 80'. Slow-growing, majestic. Wide, rounded crown, branches often twisted. Bark grayish, scaly, checked. Leaves with rounded lobes.

Willow (Q. phellos) Zone 6. Yellow fall foliage. Ht 60', S 40'. Fast-growing. Shallow roots. Willow-like leaves. Gray smooth bark. Hardy. Native to Eastern USA.

California or Western Black (Q. kelloggii) Native. Ht 60-75'. Dark furrows in checkered bark. Pretty foliage.

OSAGE ORANGE (Maclura pomifera) Zone 3. Fast growing. Ht. 50'. Mulberry family. Leaves alternate, pointed, up to 5 inches long, shiny above. Both male and female flowers (dioecious). Female flowers greenish and in dense heads. Very unusual fruit 2-5 inches across, looks similar to an orange, but inedible. Flowers May -June; fruits Aug-Sept. Hedge or open-headed tree with spreading, thorny branches and furrowed orange-brown bark. Good windbreak. Can stand heat, cold, wind, drought, poor soil, and moderate alkalinity. Easily propagated by seed, cuttings, root cuttings, and easily transplanted. Needs water until established.

PEACH, FLOWERING (Prunus persica) Zone 6. Yellow fall foliage. Snow breakage. Frost often kills blossoms. Full sun. Produces light-medium shade. Ht 25', S 20'. Moist, well-drained soil. Pink or red flowers; good edible fruit. Susceptible to insects and diseases.

PECAN (Carya illinoensis) Zone 3. Yellow fall foliage. Lawn tree or ornamental. Produces light-medium shade. Ht 100', S 75'. Deep, well-drained soil. Some hardy varieties can withstand -20°F, but also need summer heat to produce nuts.

PEPPERIDGE, BLACK TUPELO, SOUR GUM (Nyssa sylvatica) Zone 5. Scarlet or orange fall foliage. Ht 70', S 50'. Produces medium shade. Likes wet, slightly acid, well-drained soil. Insect and disease resistant. Inedible black fruits loved by birds.

PLUM, FLOWERING (Prunus) Snow breakage, Frost often kills blossoms.

Pissard (P. cerasifera 'atropurpurea') Zone 4. Purple fall foliage. Produces light-medium shade. Full sun. Ht 25', S 20'. Moist, well-drained soil. Early spring pink flowers that cover the tree. Needs occasional pruning. Single tree fine for small yards.

'Thundercloud' variety has dark copper-colored leaves, white to pink flowers, and red fruits. Ht 20, S20'.

Wild Plum (P. americana) Zone 4-6. Extremely tough and hardy. Shrubby or small tree 15-20 feet tall. Forms thickets. Dark green leaves. One inch clusters of white flowers. Yellow-red sour fruit (but makes good jelly.)

POPULUS (Populus) Fast growing: good for reforestation, for preventing soil erosion, for windbreaks, and for low maintenance. Well-drained soil. Willow family. All have invasive roots and are not recommended for city streets, lawns or small gardens. Trees drip sap. Known for beautiful leaves, bark, and fall color. Leaves quaking in the slightest breeze.

Aspen, Quaking (P. tremuloides) Best planted in groups. Golden fall color. Native. A shade tree. Sends up shoots from roots and can become a PEST. Leaves quaking. Ht 50-70'. The most popular! Hardy all zones. White bark.

Balm of Gilead or Balsam poplar (P. balsamifera, P. candicans) Leaves not quaking. Ht 30-60'. Toothed leaves with hairy underside. Leaves more than 6" long. Canada and far Northwest. Broad topped. Hardy all zones.

Black Cottonwood or Calif. Popular. (P. trichocarpa) Ht 90'. Native along mountain streams and wet lowlands, CA to Alaska. Zones 4-7, growing above 2,000', while Fremont Cottonwood grows only below 2,000'. Leaves quaking. Messy cotton in season. A popular shade tree.

Lombardy Poplar (P. nigra 'italica') Zone 3. Yellow fall foliage. Produces light shade. Ht 90', S 15'. Short-lived. Screens, windbreaks. Susceptible to canker disease. Hardy all zones.

White Poplar (P. alba) Zone 3. Red-brown fall foliage. Produces light-medium shade. Ht 30-60', S 50'. Canker resistant, lives longer. Leaves not quaking. White or silver leaves. All soils. Hardy all zones.

PRUNUS (see almond, apricot, cherry, peach, plum)

PURPLE FRINGE TREE (see smoke tree)

REDBUD (see shrub plant list)

RUSSIAN OLIVE (see shrub plant list).

SARVIS TREE (Amelanchier arborea or A. laevis) Beautiful ornamental tree. Masses of white blossoms in early spring, small edible fruit. Fantastic reddish-orange fall foliage. Beautiful smooth, satiny bark has gray stripes with a touch of pink. Ht 30'. Fruit, similar to a plum but with large seed, has more Vitamin C than oranges. George Washington must have loved Sarvis trees, as he planted about 20 of them at his mansion at Mt. Vernon. Very hardy to disease and frost! Self-pollinating. Available from Raymond Nelson Nursery, Dept. OGF, Dubois, PA 15801. A clean tree as it doesn't drop fruit until it is dried (if there are any left from the birds!) It is the fifth hardest wood that grows in the United States, so it is resistant to breakage by ice, snow, or winds. Loved by more than 50 bird species! The

Sarvis tree is one of the few American trees which have been singled out for the "Award of Garden Merit" by the British Royal Horticultural Society. This outstanding award is one of the highest that can be given plants after trial in the garden of the Royal Society in Surrey, England. I have a Sarvis tree in my back yard, and I highly recommend it (it flowers but doesn't produce fruit here).

SERVICEBERRY (Amelanchier) Shrub or tree, Moist, well-drained soil. Rose family. White flowers in spring. Fruit like a small apple.

Western (A. pallida, A. alnifolia) Many stemmed shrub. Native grows at 5-6000' in Yellow Pine Zone. Fall color. Bark: tight, dark, with low, vertical ridges. Ht 3-12'. Leaves: alternate; simple 3/4—1 1/4" long, roundish, margins either toothed at tip or smooth.

Shadblow (A. canadensis) Zone 4. Yellow and red fall foliage. Produces medium shade. Ht 25-45'. Fruits: edible reddish-purple berries loved by birds. Flowers: many white, mid or late spring when or just before leaves open. Grayish bark beautiful in winter.

Apple (A. x grandiflora) Zone 5. Yellow and orange fall foliage. Produces dense shade. Ht 18-30'. Fruits: edible red-black berries loved by birds. Has largest flowers of these 3 species. Flowers: many white or pale pink open in late spring before leaves open.

SILK TREE, MIMOSA TREE (Albizia julibrissin) Zone 7 (in warmer areas only). Yellow fall foliage. Produces light shade. Ht 35', S 25'. Feathery, fern-like, compound leaves. Feathery pink and white flowers through summer. Patios, porches, lawns. Easily broken by storms and snow. All soils, but prefers dry gravelly soil of low fertility.

SMOKE TREE, PURPLE FRINGE TREE (Cotinus obovatus) Zone 6. Any soil, sun. Beautiful scarlet-red fall foliage. Ht 25', S 20'. Produces medium shade. Lawn or ornamental. DEER RESISTANT.

SOUR GUM (see gum, sour)

SYCAMORE (Plantanus) A shade tree, Zone 5. Yellow-brown fall foliage, produces medium-dense shade. Moist, well-drained soil. Maple-like leaves.

Buttonwood (P. occidentalis) All zones. Peeling, pretty variegated colors of creamy bark. Ht 100, S 80'. Messy. Subject to fungal blight. Round 1". seedball. Does not like city climate. Largest deciduous tree in the USA.

London Plane tree (P. x acerifolia) Good in abuse situations like: smog, soot, dust, or reflected heat. Round l" seedball. Ht 80, S 40'. Watch for spider mite and scale. This one is the most common at nurseries. Do not plant in the fall in areas colder than Zone 5. Best all-round street tree. Very weak wood; damages easily by snow or wind. Roots invasive, and tree drips sap.

TREE OF HEAVEN (Ailanthus altissima) Zone 5. Yellow-gold fall foliage. Produces light-medium shade. Ht 50', S 50'. All soils. Fast growing. Insect and disease resistant. Male trees have bad-smelling flowers. Soot tolerant. Breakage in storm and snow.

TULIP TREE, YELLOW POPULAR (Liriodendron tulipifera) Zone 5. Yellow fall foliage. Attractive leaves shaped like a tulip. Produces dense shade. Ht 100', S 50'. Wet, well-drained soil. Insect and disease resistant. Impressive massive tree if given plenty of space. Two inch size greenish-yellow flowers appear after leaves open.

WALNUT (Juglans) Yellow fall foliage. Snow breakage. Frost kills young leaves. Warmer areas only. Well-drained soil. Slow growing.

Black (J. nigra) Zone 5. Produces medium shade. Ht 100', S 50'. Tasty nuts in fall. Roots give off toxic chemicals that kill nearby trees. Plant two trees for better nut production. Not good for lawns or along streets.

Butternut (Juglans cinerea) Zone 2. Yellow fall foliage. Ht 80', S 50'. Moist, well-drained soil. Edible nuts in fall. Short lived. Produces medium shade. Use as single tree. Resembles Black Walnut but is smaller tree, leaves have fewer leaflets, nut shells are thick and hard. Native to Eastern U.S.

English (J. regia) Zone 6. Produces medium-dense shade. Ht 60', S 30'. Tasty nuts. Plant two trees to get more nuts.

Carpathian (J. regia var. carpathian) has thinner shells which are easier to crack, milder flavor, lower and more spreading trees, and greater tenderness in the fruit buds. Hardy to -30°F. (Most English Walnut varieties are hardy only to -10°F.) However, the early spring leaves can be killed many times by early frosts. I have had two of these trees in my yard for 18 years; they flower but don't produce nuts here. It could be because I prune them every year; maybe they produce on second year wood.

WILLOW (Salix) Yellow fall foliage, produces medium shade. Wet, well-drained soil. Fast-growing. Prune often.

Babylon weeping (S. babylonica) Zone 6. Pendulous branches touch ground. Ht 40', S 40'. Easily damaged by storms and insects.

White (S. alba) Zone 2. More upright than other willows. Ht 30-60', S 60'

Niobe weeping or Wisconsin (S. x blanda) Zone 4. Hybrid. Pendulous branches touch ground. Ht 40', S 40'. Easily damaged by storms and insects. Niobe is hardier than Babylon.

YELLOWWOOD (Cladrastis lutea) Zone 3. Orange and yellow fall foliage. Produces medium-dense shade. Ht 50', S 40'. Moist, well-drained soil. White flowers clusters 12-15" long! Pretty light gray bark.

References cited:
[1] Better Homes & Gardens

Carol L. Young

SHRUBS

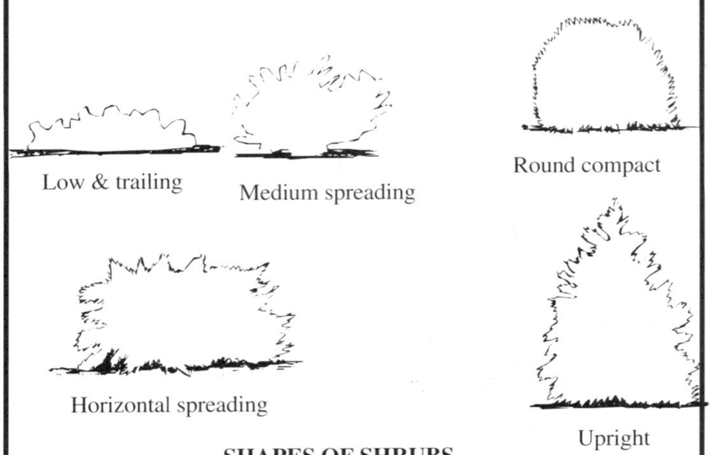

SHAPES OF SHRUBS (Evergreen & Conifers)

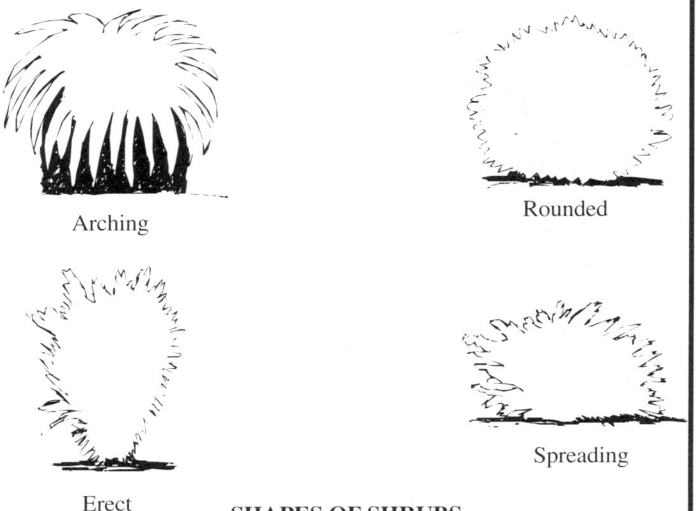

SHAPES OF SHRUBS (Deciduous)

A **shrub** is a low, usually multi-stemmed woody perennial plant that is shorter than a tree. The category of "shrub" refers basically to the size and growth habit of a shrub compared to a tree, as there are so many different kinds of shrubs and they vary greatly in shape and size. Basically, shrubs average from six inches to fifteen feet high, and occupy a relatively permanent spot in your yard (until YOU decide to remove them). Shrubs are a popular answer to landscaping questions as they have many uses, kinds, and shapes.

They may be used to dress up, cover up, or accent. They grow fast to fill an area, often bloom the first season, besides being easy care. They can be the basis of foundation plantings (around the base of the house), and they can bring out the best features of your house, besides blending it in with the surrounding landscape.

There are three basic kinds: **deciduous** (drop leaves for winter), **coniferous** (narrow-leaf evergreen), and **broad-leaved evergreen** shrubs. Deciduous plants lose all their leaves once a year and many are flowering (Forsythia, Dogwood). Conifers drop some (but not all) needles, have cones, and many are shaped like a pyramid (Pines, yews, and junipers). Broad-leaved evergreens usually retain their leaves (Rhododendrons, hollies, mahonias).

Shapes for narrow-leaved evergreen or coniferous shrubs may be low and trailing, medium spreading, horizontal spreading, round compact, or upright. In contrast, the shapes of deciduous flowering shrubs can have arching branches (Beautybush, Vanhoutte spirea), or forms that are erect (Common Lilac, Highbush Cranberry), rounded (Flowering Quince, Weigela), or spreading (Spreading Cotoneaster, Morrow Honeysuckle).

Other important shrub features to consider are: the great variation in texture, size, shape, and color of LEAVES; the height and shape of the plant; flower color, fall foliage color, decorative fruit, and colorful bark. The characteristics of the leaves are more important than the flowers, because the leaves are present longer. Each variation in leaves can create a different atmosphere [1].

Size, color, shape and texture of leaves are more important than flowers in creating atmosphere.

Shrub PLANT LIST

(Divided into three parts: conifers, broad-leaved evergreen, and deciduous shrubs)

CONIFEROUS EVERGREEN SHRUBS:

ARBORVITAE (Thuja) In the wild they are trees, but when planted at high altitudes are more shrub-like. Their horticultural varieties are also lower, shrubby or even dwarf. These varieties are among the most widely planted evergreens in the country. Many handsome shapes and colors. Sheared for foundation planting, hedges, or as accent plant on lawn. Dense foliage. Tiny scalelike needles in fan formation. Easily damaged in storms. They can be bound to protect from snow breakage. They do not like heat, wind, dust or smoke. Hardy to -40°F. Slow growing. (Thujopsis is a false arborvitae.) Rich, moist, well-drained soil. Prune when dormant.

American (T. occidentalis) Zone 3. Needles green or blue-green. Prune early spring while dormant. Average Ht 7-10' but varieties vary. Horticultural forms are shrubby, or dwarf (globular or columnar). Can't tolerate heat.

Oriental (T. orientalis, Platycladus orientalis) Zone 4. Needles bright green. Low, bushy tree, often branching near the base, the bark reddish-brown and scaly. Evergreen, but turns brown in winter. Sun. Ht 8-15'. Damaged by severe cold.

CEPHALOTAXUS, JAPANESE PLUM YEW (Cephalotaxus harringtonia) Multi-stemmed, spreading. Zone 6. (For columnar shape try variety 'fastigiata'). Dark green needles. Moist, well-drained acid soil. Sun or partial shade. Resembles yews but leaves are longer and show two bluish gray lines on underside, and not as dense as other yews. Hedges or screens. Purple-green fruits. Shear in spring before new growth appears. Ht 30'. Protect from high temperatures and dry conditions.

CRYPTOMERIA, JAPANESE CEDAR (Cryptomeria japonica 'nana') Zone 5. There is also a dwarf variety. Dark green needle-like foliage. Ht 3'. Forms broad mounds. Moist, well-drained soil. Foundations or patio tubs.

CUPRESSOCYPARIS (Cupressocyparis leylandi) Zone 5. Narrow, columnar shape. Scalelike foliage. Moist, well-drained soil. Very fast growing. Easily sheared. Ht 50'. Height variable with shearing. A hybrid between Monterey cypress and Nootka cypress. Prune in early spring before new growth starts. Good full hedge. Susceptible to snow damage.

FALSE CYPRESS (Chamaecyparis) Zone 4. Tree, shrub, or shrublet. Moist, well-drained, slightly acid soil. Red-brown bark. Dense foliage. Slow growing. Heights vary with shearing. Use taller ones as single plant; shorter ones for foundation or bonsai. Cone 1/2 in. long. Must keep pruned or get unsightly. Prune any time. Broad, flat, fan-shaped, scalelike leaves. Five basic plants with many varieties.

Bird Nest (C. lawsoniana 'nidiformis') Ht 5', S 3-5'. Dark green foliage. Spreading, flat-topped form with branches reaching outward with lower "nest at top center. Screen, hedge, or single unusual plant.

Golden Dwarf Hinoki (C. obtusa 'nana aurea') Zone 5. Ht 4', S 3'. Rock garden, foundation. New leaves yellow, old: dark green. Flat-sided sprays.

Lawson (C. lawsoniana) Blue-green variable color foliage. Native to extreme N. CA. Very adaptable in mild western climates (Better in warmer areas). Foliage burns in dry cold or hot sun in Zones 5-7. Ht 60', S 30'. Hedge, screen, background plant, or windbreak. Yellow-leaved varieties burn in CA.

Sawara (C. pisifera) Spine-tipped, conical, feathery soft, scalelike foliage. Ht 30', S 20'. Dark green above, lighter beneath. Loose, open growth.

Plume (C. pisifera 'plumosa') Fluffy, feathery green scalelike foliage. One variety is gold. Ht 20-30', S10-12' Upright branches, compact, cone shaped.

Thread leaf (C. pisifera 'filifera') Dark green, long, threadlike foliage. Some varieties are yellow. Ht 6-8', S 8'. Unusual foundation or single plant.

JUNIPER (Juniperus) Many varieties, blue to gold foliage. Form: ground huggers to trees. Easy care. Well-drained soil. Very hardy (-10 to-30°F). Snow breakage of taller varieties. All varieties are deer resistant except Shore (foliage too soft).

Bar Harbor (J. horizontalis 'Bar Harbor') Zone 3. Spreading prostrate form with attractive blue-gray foliage. A beautiful ground cover if planted in groups.

Creeping (J. horizontalis) Zone 3. Dense growth, low spreading. Ht 12". Blue-green or gray-blue needles. Excellent ground cover, especially on slopes. Showy blue berries in fall.

Chinese or Twisted (see tree, conifer list)

Dwarf Common (J. communis 'compressa') Zone 3. Broadly spreading Ht 4'. Needles gray-green. Foundation plants, rock gardens. Prune any time.

Hollywood (J. chinensis 'torulosa') Zone 3. Broadly cone shaped. Ht 20'. Tufted needles and scales. Use as single plant. Unusual branching. DO NOT prune. Also a variegated form.

Japanese garden (J. chinensis 'procumbens') Zone 4. Dense growth, low spreading. Ht 2'. Blue-green needle-like foliage. Foundation plantings, rock gardens. Prune any time.

Meyer singleseed (J. squamata 'meyeri') Ht 6-8', S 2-3'. Upright. Stiff branches at odd angle. Blend of green, gray, and reddish foliage.

Pfitzer (J. chinensis 'pfitzerana') Zone 4. Ht 6'. Dense growth, broad and flat-topped. Feathery, scalelike needles Fast growing. Can grow in partial shade. Needs constant pruning. Foundation plant. Snow breakage.

San Jose (J. chinensis 'San Jose') Zone 4. Ht 12". Dense growth, short and spreading. Needle and scalelike foliage. Popular ground cover. Prune any time.

Savin (J. sabina 'tamariscifolia') Zone 3. Ht 2'. Dense growth, low spreading. Blue-green, needle-like foliage. Branches grow slightly upwards. Rock gardens, foundation plantings, or beside walkways. Prune any time.

Shore (J. conferta) Zone 6. Dense low spreading. Ht 12". Green needles. Prefers sandy seashore. Good ground cover in sandy soil. Prune any time.

Tam or Tamarix Juniper (J. tamariscifolia) Dense, blue green. Widely used. Ht 18", S 10-20', spreads symmetrically. Not recommended. If planted too close together or next to a house it grow up! It too quickly over grows an area.

Utah (J. osteosperma, J. utahensis) Native. No cone, but has berries. Grows naturally at lower altitudes by Susanville. Very durable. Good for fence posts.

PINE (Pinus) Well-drained soil. Slow growing. Prune after spring growth starts.

Bristle-cone, Hickory (P. aristata) Zone 6. Single tree or accent, good in patio tubs. Picturesque branching. Ht 10-40'. Variable shape. Dark blue-green needles 1-1 3/4' long, in bundles of 5.

Dwarf white (P. strobus 'nana') Zone 4. Foundation plantings or rock gardens. Ht 6'. Soft green needles 4 in. long, in bundles of 5.

Mugo, Mountain or Swiss Mountain (P. mugo) Zone 4. Needs snow breakage protection. Any soil, full sun. Dense, rounded shrubby, symmetrical. Bonsai, or foundation plantings. Hardy to -40°F. Bright green needles (1 1/2 to 3 in. long), in bundles of 2. Gets scale(pest). DEER RESISTANT.

SPRUCE, DWARF WHITE (Picea glauca 'conica') Zone 5. Dense pyramidal growth. One trunk. Light green needles. Well-drained soil. Slow growing. Use with low-growing shrubs, or as single plant. No pruning. Ht 8'. Varieties: Bird Nest Spruce (P. abies 'Nidiformis'), and P. abies 'Pendula' which cascades over walls.

YEW (Taxus) Well-drained, slightly alkaline soil. Dark green, shiny, narrow (1-in. long) needles. Hardy to -30°F. Seeds and leaves are poisonous. Red fleshy berries in fall. Beautiful. All these species closely related.

Japanese (T. cuspidata) Zone 5. Bushy shrub. Shade density depends on variety. Columnar form. Foundation, hedge, screen or single plant. Protect from weight of snow! Ht 20'. Prune after spring growth has started. (For Japanese plum yew -see Cephalotaxus.) Far more hardy than English yew and faster growing. Most important of yews horticulturally and the best for hedges. Variety 'nana' is a popular fine shrubby form.

Spreading English (T. baccata 'repandens') Zones 5-10. Beautiful, dense, prostrate form with wide spreading branches. Foundation plantings or ground cover. Sun or shade. Rich, moist soil. Not happy where there are dry hot summers.

Western (T. brevifolia) Beautiful, slow-growing, evergreen shrubs and trees with reddish-brown bark. According to Taylor [2], the plant usually sold under this name is actually T. cuspidata nana (Japanese Yew—a fine shrubby form), while the true T. brevifolia of Western N.A. is rare in cultivation.

BROAD-LEAVED EVERGREEN SHRUBS:

ABELIA, GLOSSY (Abelia x grandiflora). Zone 6. Pink flowers in midsummer until frost. Bronze fall foliage. Full sun or partial shade. Well-drained soil. Dense rounded shape. Ht 6'. Loses leaves in winter in colder areas. Prune in early spring. Foundation plantings or small hedges.

ANDROMEDA (Pieris) Full sun or partial shade. Well-drained, slightly acid soil. Needs winter protection against cold. Young leaves are bronze, then bright green. Prune after flowers fade. Nice with ferns, hosta and other shade lovers. Related to azaleas.

Mt. Fetterbush (P. floribunda) Zone 5. White fragrant flowers in early spring. Attractive all seasons. VERY showy. Borders, foundations. Ht. 6'.

Japanese Lily of the Valley Bush (P. japonica) Zone 6. White fragrant flowers in mid-spring. Showy. Borders, foundation planting, or single plant Ht 10'.

APACHE PLUME (Fallugia paradoxa) Zone 6. Partially evergreen shrub. Ht 3-8'. Straw-colored branches and flaky bark. Small clustered, lobed leaves, dark green on top, rusty beneath. Flowers look like single white roses (1 1/2 inches wide), blooms April-May. Large clusters of feathery fruit. Full sun, very tolerant of heat and drought. Excellent for erosion control. Common with Pinion Juniper in rocky dry places.

AZALEAS (Rhododendron indicum) is the only broadleaf variety that grows here, and it is borderline. Zone 6. Partial shade. Well-drained, acid soil. Pink to violet flowers in early summer. Leaves glossy green. Dense and spreading. Foundation plantings, shrub borders, or in mass plantings. Keep faded flowers cut off. Keep mulched. (see also deciduous shrub list).

BARBERRY (Berberis) Full sun or partial shade. Moist, well-drained soil. Stems have sharp thorns. Needs little pruning. Dense branching habit. (see also deciduous shrub list). DEER RESISTANT !

Black (B. gagnepaini) Zone 6. Small yellow flowers in late spring, blue-black berries. Showy all seasons. Ht 6'. Hedges or shrub borders.

Darwin (B. darwinii) Hardy to 10°F. Showiest barberry. Fountain-like growth.
Ht 5-10', S 4-7'. Small (1 in.) leaves, crisp, dark green, holly-like. Orange-yellow flowers cover foliage. Many dark blue berries, loved by birds. Spreads by underground runners. Wonderful as background for Oregon grape.

Dwarf magellan (B. buxifolia 'nana') Zone 6. Ht 1 1/2—2'. Low hedges or borders. Yellow bloom. (Dwarf variety even smaller B. buxifolia 'Pygmaea').

Mentor (B. x mentorensis) Zone 6. Tiny yellow flowers in mid-spring; red berries. Cold and heat resistant. Ht 3'. Screens, hedges, or shrub borders. Good fall color. Drought tolerant.

Threespine (B. wisleyensis) Zone 6. Small white flowers mid-spring, blue-black berries. Hardy and vigorous. Ht 4'. Hedges or shrub borders. Three-parted spines instead of thorns.

Warty (B. verruculosa) Zone 6. Small yellow flowers in late spring; blue-black berries remain through winter. Showy all seasons. Ht 3'. Hedges or shrub borders. Leaf underside is white.

Wintergreen (B. julianae) Zone 6. Tiny yellow flowers in mid-spring; blue-black berries. Hardy and vigorous. Ht 7'. Hedges or shrub borders.

BOXWOOD (Buxus) Full sun or partial shade. Moist, well-drained soil. Small glossy green leaves. Ht 15'. Many varieties. DEER RESISTANT !

Common Box (B. sempervirens) Zone 7. Many varieties. Single plant or shrub borders. Needs winter protection against cold.

Little Box (B. microphylla) Zone 6. More cold hardy than Common Box. Ht 3' Hedge plants. Some varieties turn brown in winter, turn green again in spring.

CHINQUAPIN, BUSH or SIERRA EVERGREEN (Castanopsis sempervirens). Spreading shrub. Brown smooth bark. Beech family. Native plant at 5500-9000 ft in N. CA. Ht 1-8'. Fruit an unusual spiny burr. (The cultivated variety is C. chrysopylla called Giant or Golden Chinquapin. Tree 100 ft tall, leaves green above, golden beneath. Flowers in catkins, leaves oblong 4-6 in. long.)

COTONEASTER (Cotoneaster) Well-drained, slightly alkaline soil, kept slightly dry. Full sun. Flat horizontal spreading branches. Prune in early spring. (see also deciduous shrub list).

Rock (C. horizontalis) Zone 6. Pink flowers in early summer; showy bright red berries. Orange fall foliage. Semi-evergreen shrub Ht 2-3'. Hardy to -30°F. Popular! Train on wire, narrow hedge, rock gardens, or as ground cover on hard-to-plant slopes. Beautiful FALL COLOR!! A low, fast growing ground cover.

Small-leaved (C. microphyllus) Zone 7. White flowers in early summer, red berries. Rock gardens or along walls. Ht 3'.

DAPHNE (Daphne) Partial shade. Moist, well-drained soil. Poisonous berries, bark, and leaves. Particular about growing conditions. Little pruning. DEER RESISTANT !

Burkwood (D. x burkwoodi) Zone 6. White fragrant flowers in mid-spring, red berries. Leaves gray-green. Doesn't like wet soil. Single plant or shrub border. Dense mound. Ht 4'.

Rose, Garland flower (D. cneorum) Zone 5. Pink flowers in mid-spring. Leaves gray-green. Many varieties. Creeping, dense mat-like growth. Ht 12". Not like wet soil. Beds, borders, rock gardens, or ground covers. Needs winter protection in Zone 4. Grown for its' pretty flower clusters.

EUONYMUS (Euonymus) Full sun or partial shade. Any soils. Tiny flowers in spring; pink seed capsules with orange berries inside. Prune anytime. Variegated varieties also good. (see also deciduous shrub list).

Big leaf winter creeper (E. fortunei 'Sarcoxie') Zone 6. Train on walls, or use as ground cover, foundation plantings, or in rock gardens. Rambling shrub. Loses leaves in cold areas in winter. Ht 4'.

Spreading (E. kiautschovica) Zone 7 (borderline). Foundation plants, shrub borders, or single plants. Ht 10'.

FIRETHORN (see pyracantha)

FREMONTODENDRON or FLANNEL BUSH (Fremontia californicum) Zone 7. Evergreen shrub. Fast growing. Ht 6-20'. Native to foothills of the Sierra Nevadas, CA Coast Ranges and S. CA mountains. Dry granitic slopes 3000-6000 ft; in Chaparral, Yellow Pine F., and Pinyon-Juniper stands. Lemon-yellow, saucer-like flowers in great showy masses bloom all at once in May-June. Leaves, leathery, roundish, one inch long, unlobed or 3-lobed, dark-green above and felt-like beneath. Cone-like seed capsules covered with bristly, rusty hairs. Needs excellent drainage, prefers a hillside. Completely drought resistant; needs very little summer water.

GERMANDER (Teucrium chamaedrys) All zones. Low growing. Ht 12", S 2'. Many upright stems, woody at base. Leaves 3/4 inches long, toothed, and form a dark-green mass. Red, purple, or white flowers 3/4 inches wide in loose spikes, bloom in summer. Attract bees. Edging, foreground, low trimmed hedge, or small area ground cover. Shear twice a year to force side branching. Fire-retardant plant if well watered.

HEATH (Erica) Full sun. Moist, well-drained, acid soil. Beds, borders, or rock gardens. Use mulch for best results. Foliage needlelike. Many varieties.

Cornish Heath (E. vagans) Zone 7. Ht 2-3'. Robust and hardy. Bright green foliage. Bushy, open. Purplish-pink flowers, July-Sept.

Cross-leaved (E. tetralix) Zone 4. Small rose-colored flowers June-Oct. Foliage hairy, dark green above, silvery beneath. Hardiest of the varieties. Prune in early spring. Ht 1-2'. Prefers moist peaty soil, afternoon shade. New growth yellow, orange, or red.

Darley (E. x darleyensis) Zone 6. Small lilac-colored flowers in late fall-spring. Foliage bright green. Prune fading flowers. Most vigorous of varieties. Ht 2'.

Spring (E. carnea) Zone 6. Small rose, pink, or white flower, early spring. Foliage medium green. Prune after flowering to encourage more vigorous growth. Ht 1 ft. Upright branches rise from prostrate main branches.

Twisted (E. cinerea) Zone 6. Small rose, pink, white, or purple flowers in early summer. Foliage dark green and dainty. Not as hardy as other varieties. Prune after flowering. Ht 12". Spreading mound. Good ground cover.

HEATHER (Calluna vulgaris) Zone 5. Small rose, purple, pink, white, or coral flowers in midsummer. Many varieties. Leaves green or yellow, turning bronze in fall. Full sun, prefers slightly acid soil. Beds, foundation plantings, rock gardens, or ground cover. Mulch. Prune in early spring before new growth starts.

HOLLY GRAPE (see oregon grape)

HOLLY (Ilex) Shrub or tree. Full sun, or partial shade. Well-drained soil, slightly acid soil. Deer Resistant. Tiny inconspicuous flowers.

Holly

Chinese (I. cornuta) Zone 7. (borderline). Bright red berries in fall and winter. Female plant can produce berries without pollen. Pruning: little —in early spring. Needs cold protection. Ht 9'.

English (I. aquifolium, 'balkans') Zone 4. Shrub, tree or hedge. Ht 20-40'. (Balkans is the hardiest variety). Leaves: smooth upright, dark green. Needs protection from sun in hot areas. Male plants have no berries. If you wish to have bright red berries, buy a grafted plant. Slow growth. Sharply pointed, green leaves. A favorite for Christmas decor.

Japanese (I. crenata) Zone 6. Black berries in fall. Sexes are separate. Prune in early spring. Hedges, shrub borders, screens. Needs cold protection. Ht 15'. Many varieties and hybrids:

Blue Girl (I. crenata meserveae 'Blue Girl') Very hardy hybrid with glossy blue-green spiny leaves, purple stems, and red berries early fall through winter. This is the hardiest of the hollies that have a true holly look. Dense, bushy plant Ht 6-7'. **Blue Angel** variety has crinkly foliage, large berries.

Blue Prince is male plant for pollination. **Blue Princess** has deep green Christmas holly type leaves with many berry clusters along stems.

Long Stalk (I. pedunculosa) Zone 6. Bright red drooping berries. Sexes are separate. Fruit very showy. Single plants or shrub borders. More cold resistant than other varieties. Ht 15'. (Sounds best of the above varieties.) Leaves glossy green and spineless.

HUCKLEBERRY OAK (Quercus vaccinifolia) Native at 5500-6000 ft. in Yellow Pine Zone on dry rocky slopes. Oak family. Sprawling stems. Ht 2-4'. Leaves: smooth-edged, gray-green, 3/4 to 1-1/4 in. long. Popular in wild gardens, large rock gardens, mountain summer home gardens. Fruit: acorn.

LAUREL, MOUNTAIN or CALICO BUSH (Kalmia latifolia) Zone 5. Partial shade. Moist, acid soil. Ht 3-10' (depend on variety). White, pink or rose flowers in early summer. Very hardy (to -30°F). Glossy leathery leaves. Shrub borders or mass plantings. Little pruning—after flowering. Remove seed capsules for more vigorous growth. New cultivars available: Bullseye, Carousel, Elf, Freckles, Goodrich, Pink Surprise, Sarah, and Silver Dollar.

LAURELCHERRY or ENGLISH LAUREL (Prunus laurocerasus) Large shrub, small tree, or clipped hedge. As tree, fast-growing to Ht 30', S 30'. Leaves: leathery, glossy dark green, 3-7 in. long, 1 1/2—2 in. wide. Flowers: creamy white in 3-5 in. long spikes in summer, often hidden by leaves. Difficult to garden under or around. Hardiest varieties are: Schipka or Zabel. Select hardy varieties!

LEUCOTHOE, DROOPING (Leucothoe fontanesiana) Zone 5. Small white flowers in early summer. Bronze fall foliage. Partial or deep shade. Moist well-drained acid soil. Shrub borders, foundation plantings. Ht 6'. Cut off old canes in spring. Leaves drop off in cold winter areas.

OREGON GRAPE, HOLLY GRAPE (Mahonia aquifolium) Zone 6. Native. Recommended varieties: Leatherleaf Mahonia (M. bealei) is taller, nice against a wall; Creeping Mahonia (M. repens) is good ground cover, shady area. Bright yellow clusters of flowers in mid-spring; blue-black edible berries in midsummer. Holly-like leaves turn bronze in fall. Ht 3-5'. (dwarf var. 12 in. high). Partial shade. Moist, well-drained soil. Hardy to -20°F. Shrub borders, foundation plantings, or tall ground cover. Needs protection from winter winds or foliage will discolor or fall off. Prune in early spring. Invasive. Reproduces by underground runners. Seeds spread by birds. Often substituted for English holly because Mahonia is hardier. Ajuga ground cover is pretty growing under it. DEER RESISTANT.

PYRACANTHA or FIRETHORN (Pyracantha coccinea) Any soil, full sun. Espalier against wall or fence. Orange-red berries in fall. Berries produced on second year wood. Closely related to Cotoneaster and needs same care. Evergreen thorny shrub of rose family. Known for fine foliage and ornamental fruits. Recommend Lalandii and Scarlet varieties. Red berried varieties will not survive in cold winter areas.

RHODODENDRON (Rhododendron) Rich, moist, well-drained, acid soil. Showy flowers. Foundation plantings, beds, shrub borders, mass plantings. Protect against winter cold. Keep mulched. Keep faded flowers picked. DEER RESISTANT !

Carolina (R. carolinianum) Zone 6. Full sun, partial shade. Leaves green above, brown below. Rose-violet flowers in mid-spring. Dense mound shape. Blooms earlier than other varieties. Ht 6'.

Catawba (R. catawbiense) Zone 5. Partial shade. Flowers in early summer. Hardy hybrids (to -25°F), many colors. Large leaf, large flowers, fairly large size. Ht 10'. Likes protected areas under trees. Dense and spreading. Large border or mass bank planting. Easiest to grow and hardiest of the species.

Fortune's (R. fortunei) Zone 6. Partial shade. Rose-violet flowers in late spring. Hybrid varieties in red and pink. Very showy. Ht 12'.

Rosebay, Great laurel (R. maximum) Zone 4. Partial to deep shade. Not need rich soil. Red-violet (spotted with green) flowers in late spring. Not as showy. Use as background plant, shrub border, or mass planting. Ht 15'.

Smirnow (R. smirnowi) Zone 6. Rose-pink flowers (often frilled) in late spring. Leaves green above, fuzzy white beneath. Not need rich soil. Hardy. Ht 10'. Dense branches.

Rhododendron spp.

Blue Peter. One of hardiest varieties (Hardy to -10°F). Ht 4'. Broad sprawling growth. Needs pruning. Large trusses of lavender blue-purple flowers in May.

SNOWBUSH (Ceanothus cordulatus) Native at 5800-7000 ft. N. CA. Buckthorn family. Spreading shrub wider than high. Ht 1-4 ft. Whitish bark. Dry soil. Flowers: tiny white, growing in broad oblong clusters, 1/2 to 1/1/4 in. long. Leaves: alternate, simple, 1/4 to 3/4 in. long, egg shaped or elliptical with blunt tip, 3 prominent veins, light green above, pale beneath. Fruit: 3 lobed sticky capsules.

TOBACCO BRUSH (Ceanothus velutinus) Native at 5800-8000 ft. in N. CA. Buckthorn family. Forms thickets on dry, open slopes. Ht. 2-7'. Leaves: alternate, simple, 1 1/2—3 in. long, egg-shaped to elliptical, dark green and shiny above, pale beneath with short dense hair and sticky, finely-toothed margins, cinnamon odor. Flowers: tiny white in oblong clusters 2-3 in. long. Fruit: 3 lobed sticky capsules.

TOYON, CHRISTMAS-BERRY, RED BERRY, or CALIFORNIA HOLLY (Heteromeles arbutifolia). Another genus name is Photinia. Zone 7. Beautiful evergreen tree-like shrub with gray bark. Native in foothills of Sierra Nevada on semi-dry brushy slope and canyons below 4,000 feet elevation. Rose family. Ht 15'. Leaves alternate, thick, leathery, oblong, sharply toothed, abruptly pointed, 2-4 inches long. Tiny white flowers in dense clusters (panicles). Bees love the beautiful, bright-red berries. Berries used in Christmas decor.

VIBURNUM, LEATHERLEAF (Viburnum rhytidophyllum) Zone 6. Small yellow flowers in spring; red-black berries. Partial shade. Rich, moist, well-drained soil. Shrub borders, screens, single plant. Berries loved by birds. Keep mulched. Keep plants dry after mid-summer. Protect from winter winds. Prune in early spring while still dormant. Ht 10'. (see also deciduous shrub list).

DECIDUOUS SHRUBS

ALDER, BLACK (see winterberry)

ALDER, SITKA (Alnus sinuata) Shrub or small tree Ht 4-9'. Brown or grayish bark, twigs shiny. Leaves thin, ovate, shiny above, paler beneath. Likes wet places up to 7,000 ft. Very Hardy.

ALMOND, DWARF FLOWERING (Prunus glandulosa) Zone 4. White or pink flowers in mid-spring. No fruits. Well-drained soil. Full sun. Ht 3-5'. Showy. Use as low borders or single plants.

ALMOND, FLOWERING (Prunus triloba) Yellow fall foliage. Zone 3. Pink flowers in mid-spring (early May). No fruits. Ht 8-10'. Moist, well-drained soil. Full sun. Showy. Single plant or shrub border. Snow breakage. Slow growing. Frost kills blossoms. Produces medium shade. Pruning: light-after blooming.

ARALIA, FIVE LEAVED (Acanthopana x sieboldianus) Zone 5. Yellow fall foliage. Sharp spines. Sun or shade, any soils. Foliage plant,hedges. Soot-tolerant. Ht 3-6'.

AZALEAS (Rhododendron) Full sun or partial shade. Moist, acid soil. (see also broadleaf shrub list). Bright fall color: orange, red to maroon. Beautiful flowers cover the plant. Choose the hardiest varieties you can find (usually the hybrids).

Albrecht (R. albrechti) Zone 6. Rose-colored flowers in spring. Hardy and fragrant. Ht 5'.

Coast, dwarf (R. atlanticum) Zone 6. White (tinged with red) flowers in spring. Hardy and fragrant. Ht 2'.

Flame, yellow (R. calendulaceum) Zone 5. Orange to scarlet flowers. Hardy. Bright colors. Blooms later than other varieties, but holds flowers longer. Ht 10'.

Gable hybrids Zone 5.

Ghent hybrids Extremely hardy (Many -25°F). Upright growth. Height varies. Flowers (smaller than Mollis hybrids) yellow, orange, umber, pink, red, in May.

Knap Hill-Exbury hybrids. Zone 5. Plants vary from spreading to upright. Ht 4-6'. Large flowers (3-5 in. across), ruffles or fragrant. Flower colors: white- pink, yellow through orange and red, often with contrasting blotches. Good fall color.

Mollis hybrids Zone 6. Flower colors: yellow through red. Blooms in May. Foundation plantings, beds, or accent. Vigorous, showy. Ht 5'. Nice fall color.

Royal (R. schlippenbachi) Zone 5. Freckled, pink flowers in spring. Tall, slender Ht 15'. Beds, foundation plantings, accent plants. Red fall color. Hardy -20°F.

Sweet, smooth (R. arborescens) Zone 5. Very fragrant, white or rose-tinged flowers in early summer. Scarlet fall color. Ht 10'. Blooms later than others.

BARBERRY (Berberis) Full sun, partial shade. Loses some color in shade. Any soils. (see also broadleaf shrub list)

Japanese (B. thunbergi) Zone 5. Hardy to -20°F. Red berries and leaves in fall. Dense foliage, very thorny. Ht 3-6', (dwarf varieties Ht 1-2'). Yellow flowers bordered with red appear in early spring; bright red berries loved by birds. Some varieties have red leaves. Use for color accent, contrast with grey foliage, barrier, hedge or single plant. Light pruning anytime. Popular. Needs good watering.

Korean (B. koreana) Zone 6. Yellow flowers in spring; bright red berries. Thorny twigs. Use as a barrier, hedge, or single plant. Ht 4'.

BEAUTYBERRY, AMERICAN (Callicarpa americana) Zone 6. Verbenaceae family. Ht 4-5'. Sometimes called French Mulberry, though it is neither French nor a mulberry. Leaves: blunt toothed, 4-6 in. long, green above and rusty beneath. Flowers bluish in short stalked cluster (cyme) about 1/8 in. long. Easily propagated by seed, mature wood cuttings, or by root divisions. Full sun. Winter may kill it to ground, but new growth appears next spring, then flower and fruit.

BEAUTY BUSH (Kolkwitzia amabilis) Zone 6. Pink and white flowers in May-June; brown seedpods. Red fall foliage. Attractive peeling bark. Easy to grow. Full sun or partial shade. Moist, well-drained soil. Grow as single plants. Pruning: light-after blooming. Graceful upright, arching branches. Ht 15'.

BLUEBEARD (Caryopteris x clandonensis) Zone 7. Small blue flowers in fall. Full sun. Light, well-drained soil. Accent plant. Protect from frost. Prune severely in early spring to promote more flowers. Ht 3'.

BLUEBERRY, HIGHBUSH (Vaccinium corymbosum) Zone 3. Full sun or light shade. White or pink flowers in late spring; edible blue-black berries.Ht Fall foliage and twigs stay bright scarlet all winter. Well-drained, moist, acid soil. Single plant, or hedge, Shallow root system; keep mulched. Prune the old and dead wood in spring. Ht 15'.

BROOM (Cytisus) Fast growing. Well-drained soil, full sun. Showy, bright color.

Kew (C. x kewensis) Zone 6. Yellow flowers in early spring. Rock gardens or slopes. Ht 1', S 6'. Spreading mat.

Scotch (C. scoparius) Zone 6. Low mound to shrub Ht 10'. (dwarf var Ht 1-2'). Many colored varieties. Beautiful, sweet-scented, yellow flowers in June. Spreads and is VERY difficult to get rid of, besides uplifting pavement. Prune after flowering. DEER RESISTANT ! Considered a pest if overtaking native shrubs. Has nearly ruined Mt. Tamalpius in the Bay Area.

Spike (C. nigricans) Zone 5. Hardy. Yellow flowers on spikes 6-12 in. long in midsummer. Ht 6'.

BROOM, SPANISH (Genista) Zone 6. Deciduous shrubs but have green branches. Mass of spiny stems with half inch long leaves. Ht 1-2' tall and wide. Bright golden yellow flowers in clusters at tip of stem, bloom May -June. Less aggressive than other brooms (Cytisus, Spartium). Need sun, and good drainage. Tolerate rocky or infertile soil, drought, and sea-shore conditions.

BUCKEYE, DWARF HORSE CHESTNUT (Aesculus parviflora) Zone 5. Beautiful white flowers in spike 10-15" long in midsummer. Yellow fall foliage. Full sun. Moist, well-drained soil. Vigorous and showy. Dense mound. Reproduces by underground suckers. Shiny brown inedible nuts. Ht 15'.

BUCKTHORN, ALDER (Rhamnus frangula 'tallhedge') Zone 3. Berries red to black. Smooth branches. Full sun or partial shade. Moist, well-drained soil. Hedges, screens. Pest-resistant, vigorous. Ht 12'.

BURNING BUSH (see euonymus, strawberry bush)

BUSH CLOVER (Lespedeza bicolor) Zone 5. Light purple flowers in midsummer to early fall. Well-drained soil, full sun. Cut back to ground each season without hindering blooming. Ht 10'.

BUTTERFLY BUSH (Buddleia) Well-drained soil, full sun. Vigorous and hardy. Leaves are a pretty gray-green. DEER RESISTANT !

Fountain (B. alternifolia) Zone 6. Lilac flowers on long spikes in early summer. Arching branches. Ht 12'. Accent plant in large yard. Needs lots of room to be showy. Prune back after flowering. Branches not die-back in winter.

Orange-eye, Summer lilac (B. davidi) Zone 5. Purple flowers (long spikes). Open shaggy appearance. Plants die back to ground each winter. Ht 15'.

CALIFORNIA ALLSPICE (see sweet shrub)

CASCARA SAGRADA (Rhamnus purshiana) Zone 4. Tall shrub or small tree 20-40'. Leaves dark green, 6-8 inches long, finely toothed, and tufted at ends of branches. Flowers in small hairy umbels (clusters), bloom May-June. Round, purplish-black fruit attracts birds. Dense shade or full sun (shade tolerant). Needs plenty of water. Native. Smooth (gray or brownish) bark has medicinal properties. Yellow fall color. Beautiful branching pattern.

CHERRY, NANKING (Prunus tomentosa) Zone 3. Whitish pink flowers in early spring; red edible berries. Well-drained soil, full sun. Hardy, showy. Use fruits raw or in jams. Borders, or as a single plant. Ht 5'.

CHERRY, PURPLE-LEAF SAND (Prunus x cistena) Zone 3. White or pink flowers in mid-spring; blackish-blue edible berries. Berries used in preserves, and are loved by birds. Leaves red-brown all season. Well-drained soil. Full sun. Hardy. Shrub borders or as a single plant. Ht 7'.

CHERRY, SAND (Prunus besseyi) Zone 3. White flowers in mid-spring; prolific, edible blue-black berries (jams and preserves), loved by birds. Full sun. Light, well-drained soil. Ht 7'. Hardy, and drought resistant.

CHOKEBERRY (Aronia) Full sun or partial shade. Well-drained soil. Hardy and pest-resistant. Berries are not edible, and not attractive to birds. Red fall foliage.

Black (A. melanocarpa) Zone 4. White flowers in spring; purple-black berries. Does better in drier conditions than other varieties. Low borders. Ht 3'.
Purple (A. prunifolia) Zone 5. White or pink flowers; purple berries. Upright growth form. Screens or windbreaks. Ht 12'.
Red (A. arbutifolia) Zone 6. White or pink flowers; bright red berries. Upright growth form. Ht 12'. Use for shrub borders.

Cotoneaster

CHOKECHERRY, Western (Prunus virginiana 'demissa') Native N. CA. Bush, or trained to tree form. Branches trailing in beautiful, graceful shape. Ht 6-20'. Red fall foliage. White flowers; black berries good for jelly. Spreads by suckers. There are two species in this area (red & black berries). Very invasive. Poisonous juice in leaves.

CINQUEFOIL, SHRUBBY (Potentilla fruticosa) Zone 2. Yellow-white flowers midsummer until fall. Well-drained soil, full sun. Hardy and pest-resistant. Low growing and dense. Foundations plants, low borders. Ht 4'. Little pruning required. Valued for long blooming period.

COTONEASTER (Cotoneaster) Well-drained soil. Full sun, partial shade. (see also broadleaf shrub list). Flowers in spring. Birds love the berries!

Cranberry (C. apiculatus) Zone 5. Tiny red-violet flowers; orange-red berries. Ht 4'. Spreading, horizontal branches. Slopes, foundations, or walls.
Creeping (C. adpressus) Zone 5. (see ground cover list)
Diel's (C. dielsianus) Zone 6. Pink flowers; red berries. Red fall foliage. Widely spreading branches. Forms dense mound Ht 7', S 14'.
Many Flowered (C. multiflorus) Zone 6. White flowers; large red berries. Arching branches. Ht 12'. VERY showy all seasons! Accent plant.
Peking (C. acutifolius) Zone 3. Tiny pink flowers; black berries. Dense, upright growth. Shrub borders, screens, or hedges. No pruning needed.
Spreading (C. divaricatus) Zone 5. Small pink-violet flowers; red berries. Red fall foliage. Widely spreading branches on upright plants. Ht 3-6'. Hedge, single plant or shrub border. Hardy to -10°F.
Sungari (C. racemiflorus) Zone 4. White flowers in spring; red berries. Leaves gray-green. Hardy, vigorous. VERY showy all seasons. Long arching branches. Accent plant.

CRANBERRY (see Viburnum)

DEUTZIA (Deutzia) Full sun or partial shade. Any soils. Prune off old wood every year, and new wood after flowering. Blooms completely cover the branches !

Fuzzy (D. scabra) Zone 6. White or pink flowers in early spring. Varieties have other colors. VERY showy, use as single plants. Ht 7'.
Slender (D. gracilis) Zone 5. White flowers in early spring. Wide-spreading arching branches. Ht 4-6'. Beds, borders, or single plants.

DOGWOOD (Cornus) Hardy. Red fall foliage. Full sun, partial shade. Any soils. Berries loved by birds. Attractive foliage and flowers. (see also deciduous tree list).

Canadian or Bunchberry (C. canadensis) Native under trees, by lakes, and streams in Northwest. Creeping rootstocks send up shoots with leaves. Yellow fall color. Plant dies back in winter. Tiny white flowers bloom

May-June; bright red fruit Aug-Sept. Prefers cool, moist acid soil and lots of humus (shade tolerant).

Cornelian cherry (C. mas) Zone 5. Shrub or tree. Small yellow flowers in very early spring (Feb-March); edible red berries (good in preserves). Pest resistant. Good color all seasons. Hedge, screen, or single plant. Ht 20'.

Japanese (C. kousa) Zone 5. Big shrub or small tree. Dense horizontal growth habit. White flowers in June or July, gradually turning pink; red fruits. Blooms later than other dogwoods. VERY showy. Ht 20'.

Red-osier (C. stolonifera) Zone 2. Big multi-stemmed shrub. Ht 15'. White flowers in late spring-midsummer; inedible white berries. Twigs a beautiful bright red in winter. Vigorous. Prefers moist areas. Reproduces by underground stolons so give it large area. Hedge, screen, or on moist bank near pond.

Tatarian (C. alba) Zone 3. White flowers in late spring; inedible bluish-white berries. Twigs also bright red in winter. Grown mostly for winter color of twigs. Pest resistant. Informal hedge, screen, or as single plant. Tolerant of wet areas. Prune before new growth in early spring. Ht 10'.

ELAEAGNUS (Elaeagnus) Well-drained soil. Full sun. Vigorous and hardy. Hedges, screens. Requires little care. Fragrant flowers.

Autumn olive (E. umbellata) Zone 2. Tiny, yellow-white flowers in spring; red inedible berries in fall. Leaves dark green above and silvery below. Ht 18'.

Cherry (E. multiflora) Zone 5. Flowers (3/4 in.) in late spring; red edible berries loved by birds Leaves dark green above, silvery below. Ht 6'. Soot resistant.

Silverberry (E. commutata) Zone 2. Tiny silvery-yellow flowers in spring; silver berries. Leaves silver on both sides. Ht 10-12'. Prefer slightly alkaline soil.

ELDERBERRY, AMERICAN SWEET (Sambucus canadensis) Zone 4. Tiny white flowers in midsummer; edible red berries used in wines and preserves, and loved by birds. Rich, moist, well-drained soil. Vigorous. Ht 8'. Large spreading plant. Prefers wet areas. Deer resistant. All parts of plant are poisonous except the berries.

EUONYMUS (Euonymus) Full sun or partial shade. Any soils. Very hardy.

European spindle tree: (E. europaea) Zone 4. Tiny flowers in spring, pink seed capsules with orange berries inside. Bright pink seed capsules in fall (orange seeds inside). Red fall foliage. Ht 20'. Susceptible to scale (pest). Vigorous.

Strawberry bush, Burning bush, Cork bush: (E. americana) Zone 7 (borderline). Native shrub. Peculiar cork-like bark. Ht 8-10'. (Dwarf varieties Ht 4-5'). Sun. Tiny pinkish-purple flowers in spring, pinkish-red ornamental seed pods, dark red fall foliage. Pruning: light in early spring. Use in hard-to-plant (moist) areas.

Winged: (E. alata) Zone 4. Crimson fall foliage. Ht 4-8'. Rounded form. Hedges, screens, or as single plants. Very showy all seasons.

FORSYTHIA (Forsythia) Sun or partial shade. Any soils. Prune after flowering. Easy to start from cuttings (may even root if trailing branch touches ground). Easy to grow. One of earliest shrubs to bloom (Feb.-April). Deer love to eat it. Fountain-shaped shrubs. Screen, espalier, bank cover, or shrub border. Many hybrids.

Arnold dwarf (F. intermedia 'Arnold dwarf') Zone 5. Greenish-yellow flowers (not many) in early spring. Ht 2-3', S 6'. Low growing with arching branches. Dense mat. Fast growing ground cover to hold soil on slopes.

Border (F. x intermedia) Zone 5. Yellow-gold flowers in early spring (before the leaves), graceful arching branches, Ht 10'. Many varieties. Vigorous and hardy.

Goldenbells (F. 'Suspensa') a weeping variety. Ht 8-10', S 6-8'. Dense upright growth. Drooping vinelike branches root where they touch moist soil. Golden-yellow flowers. Can be trained as vine if support main branches, let others hang.

Korean goldenbell, Early (F. ovata) Zone 5. Yellow-gold flowers in early spring. Ht 5'. The most cold hardy of forsythias, and blooms earliest.

Lynwood Gold (F. intermedia 'Lynwood Gold') Ht 7', S 46'. Grows stiffly upright. Profuse dark yellow blooms survive spring storms.

FOTHERGILLA (Fothergilla) Dark green leaves. Prefers light shade, moist well drained soil. Foundation plantings or single plants. Unusual white thimble-like flowers on spikes, before leaves appear. Grown for fall color.

Alabama (F. monticola) Zone 6. Yellow to scarlet fall foliage. Ht 6'.

Large (F. major) Zone 5. Yellow, orange, or red fall foliage. Ht 10'.

FRANKLIN TREE (Franklinia alatamaha) Zone 6. Full sun. In the fall, fragrant white flowers with yellow centers cover plant, while leaves turn bright orange-scarlet. Moist, rich, well-drained, acid soil. Use as single plant. Will die back in colder areas. Mound soil around stem for winter cold protection. Ht 10-30'.

HAZELNUT (Corylus) Any soil; catkins all winter; edible nuts; hardy; spreading.

European, Filbert (C. avellana) Zone 5. Sun or shade. Ht 25'. Large green leaves. Reproduces by suckers, needs room to spread. Showy in winter months.

Purple-leaved (C. maxima 'purpurea') Zone 5. Needs full sun. Large purple leaves. Ht 30'. Use as single plant. Colorful all seasons.

HIBISCUS, ROSE OF SHARON (Hibiscus syriacus) Zone 6. White, pink, red, blue, and violet bicolored flowers in late summer. Some varieties have variegated leaves. Ht 6-10'. Full sun or partial shade. Moist, well-drained soil. Soot resistant. Put in hard to plant narrow areas like hedges, screens, or as single plants. Need winter protection from frost, and snow breakage. Valued for late blooming color.

HONEYSUCKLE (Lonicera) Hardy. Many flower colors. Full sun or partial shade. Well-drained soil. Birds love the berries. (for vines see perennial vine list)

Amur (L. maacki) Zone 3. Whitish-yellow fragrant flowers in late spring; scarlet inedible berries through winter. Ht 15'. Cold resistant. More upright and later flowering than other honeysuckles. Hedges, screens, or single plants.

Blueleaf (L. korolkowi) Zone 5. Rose flowers in late spring; red-orange inedible berries. Spreading dense mound shaped. Grown for attractive blue-green leaves. Looks best in a large area. Hard to get started. Ht 12'.

Clavey's dwarf (L. x xylosteoides 'Clavey's dwarf') Zone 4. Yellow flowers in late spring; tiny red berries. Foliage gray-green. Dense and compact, excellent hedge plant (clipped or unclipped) Ht 3'.

Hall's (L. japonica 'Halls') see perennial vine list.

Morrow (L. morrowi) Zone 4. Whitish-yellow flowers in late spring; deep red-purple inedible berries. Spreading dense mound. Ht 8'. Hedge, screen, single plant.

Tatarian (L. tatarica) Zone 5. Flowers scarlet, rose, pink, white, or bicolored in late spring; red berries later. Foliage blue-green. Ht 10'. (dwarfs Ht 2-3'). Insect and disease resistant. Very vigorous. Showy. Upright growth, rounded form. Hedges, screens, or single plants. Looser and more attractive in partial shade.

Winter, Fragrant (L. fragrantissima) Zone 6. White fragrant flowers in early spring; red inedible berries. One of earliest blooming woody shrubs. Spreads, needs large area. Hedge, screen, or single plant. Prune after flowering. Ht 8'.

HYDRANGEA (Hydrangea) Large leaves and large showy flower clusters cover plant in midsummer. Rounded form. Full sun or partial shade. Rich, moist, well-drained soil. Prune to encourage more vigorous growth, and to control size and form. Needs heavy watering. Fast growing. Cut out stems that have flowered.

Hills of Snow, or Smooth (H. arborescens 'grandiflora') Zone 4. Best of the varieties. Ht 4'. Six-inch clusters of tiny white flowers. Dense globular shape. Foundation plantings, or low informal hedges. Prune in early spring while dormant. Large bright-green leaves. Long lasting flowers.

Peegee (H. paniculata 'grandiflora') Zone 4. Upright form. Best as shrub (Ht 10-15'), or can be pruned to tree form (Ht 30'). Twelve-inch clusters of tiny white flowers gradually turning pink or purple and remain into winter. Needs large yard. Good for dried bouquets.

Hydrangea

Bronze fall foliage.

Oak-leaved (H. quercifolia) Zone 5. Six-inch clusters of tiny creamy-white flowers. Oak-like leaves turn red in fall. Showy all seasons. Ht 3-6'. Very spreading, best planted alone. Prune after flowering and thin out the branches.

KERRIA or JAPANESE ROSE (Kerria japonica) Zone 5. Yellow flowers in May. Rounded form. Ht 6-8'. Showy green twigs in winter. Shrub border or single plant. Prune after flowering. May die back in winter, cut off deadwood in spring. Full sun or partial shade. Well-drained soil. Deer resistant!

LILAC (Syringa) Well-drained soil, full sun. Fragrant flowers clusters in late spring (May) sometimes killed by late frosts. Buy young plants. Remove faded blooms and seed clusters. NEVER prune in fall or no flowers next year.

Chinese (S. x chinensis) Zone 3. Red-purple flowers. Upright spreading. Accent plant. Ht 10-15'. More graceful than common lilac, and with finer textured, small leaves. Profuse blooms.

Common (S. vulgaris) Zone 4. Violet, blue, pink, white, yellow or magenta flowers. Many hybrids. Dense, vigorous, erect. Ht 20', S 20'. Single plant, hedge or screen. Cold resistant. Smaller blossoms. Very hardy. Dark green leaves.

French This hybrid has larger flowers (some even double), and it blooms later. There are many varieties and colors.

Hungarian (S. josikaea) Zone 4. Red-purple flowers. Single plant, hedge, or screen. Ht 12'. Dense upright growth. Dark green foliage. Slightly fragrant.

Late (S. villosa) Zone 2. Rose to white flowers with different fragrance than other varieties. Ht 10'. Cold resistant, vigorous. Dense, spreading. Hedge, screen, or windbreak.

Littleleaf (S. microphylla) Zone 4. Red-violet flowers. Broad growth habit (2x as wide as high). Ht 6-10'. Use as single plant.

Meyer's (S. meyeri) Zone 6. Violet flowers. Ht 6'. Low compact growth form. Informal hedges, borders.

Persian (S. x persica) Zone 5. Lilac flowers. Rounded form. Ht 6-10'. Small leaves. Valued for small size. Single plant or accent.

Preston (S. x prestoniae) Zone 2. Pink flowers. Plant is large and dense. Ht 8'. Windbreak or screen.

MOCK ORANGE or MINNESOTA SNOWFLAKE (Philadelphus) Propagated by cutting, seed, layering, or sucker. Prune immediately after flowering. Full sun or partial shade. Fragrant white flowers in early summer. Little pruning except deadwood. Single plants or shrub border.

Lemoine: (P. x lemoinei) Zone 5. Erect form Ht 6'. Moist rich well-drained soil.

Minnesota snowflake is the hardiest type. Sun or light shade. Ht 6-12'. Needs fertile soil. Hardy to -20°F.

Sweet: (P. coronarius) Zone 5. Very fragrant flowers. Any soils. Yellow fall foliage. Tolerates drier conditions.

Virginalis: (P. x virginalis) Zone 5. Moist, rich, well-drained soil. Very showy dainty flowers. Ht 5-9' (Dwarf varieties Ht 2-3').

MOLLIS (see rhododendron, azalia)

MOUNTAIN MAHOGANY (Cercocarpus) All zones. Evergreen or deciduous. Native to Western mountains and foothills. Very drought-tolerant. Beautiful open branching pattern. In fall has a small characteristic fruit topped with a long twisted feathery plume. Sun or light shade.

C. ledifolius Evergreen native on dry mountain slopes at 4,000-9,000 ft. elevation throughout Western States. Excellent hedge or small tree. Leaves leathery 1/2 - 1 inch long, resinous, dark green above, white below, with edges rolled under.

C. montanus Deciduous shrub 4-6' tall and wide. Leaves 1-2 inches long and white underside. Likes dry places in the coldest climates. Does best in zones 5 & 6.

NINEBARK (Physocarpus opulifolius) Zone 2. Whitish-pink flowers in early spring; green-brown seed capsules that remain through winter. Ht 10'. (a spreading variety is Ht 4'.) Full sun or partial shade. Well-drained soil. Very dense. Cold hardy. No pruning. Screens, borders, or windbreaks. Not very showy.

PEARLBUSH (Exochorda) Full sun. Any soils. Use as single plant in large yards. Strings of white flowers in mid-spring, open from many pearl-like buds.

Common (E. racemosa) Zone 5. Ht 12', S 12'. More hardy, less flowers than Wilson. Loose, open, slender shrub. Blooms in April.

The Bride (E. x macrantha) Zone 6. Single plant or low shrub border. Compact shrub. Ht 4', S 4'. Plant it beneath south or west-facing windows.

Wilson (E. giraldi 'wilsoni') Zone 5. Ht 10'. Prune after flowering. Upright form.

PEONY, TREE (descendents of Paeonia suffruticosa) Zone 5. Very showy flowers up to 12" across, bloom in late spring. Leaves gray-green. Prefers partial shade, but full sun okay. Rich, moist, well-drained soil. Single plants or in beds. Ht 7'. Protect from winter cold. Hardier than they look! May need staking.

PHOTINIA, ORIENTAL (Photinia villosa) Zone 5. Shrub or small tree. Related to hawthorn, pyracantha. Showy all seasons. Red fall foliage. Small white flowers in late spring; red berries loved by birds. Full sun or partial shade. Well-drained soil. Prune to shape. Screens, background, unusual accent plant. Ht 15'. In the Northwest stop watering in late summer to improve growth, and lessen frost damage.

PIERIS. (Pieris, or Andromeda) Heath family. Leathery leaves and clusters of small urn-shaped flowers. Flower buds look like strings of pink beads. Related to rhododendron and azalia; have same needs and make good companion plants. Full sun in humid areas, but part shade normally (shade tolerant).

Mountain Pieris (P. floribunda) Zones 6-9, but needs wind protection. Compact shrub 3-6' tall. Leaves alternate, toothed, dull green, and 1 1/2—3 inches long. White flowers in upright terminal clusters (panicles). Very hardy to cold, and can also take hotter, dryer air than other Pieris species. Fairly rare.

Lily-of-the-valley shrub (P. japonica) All zones, but in zones 5-7 needs protection from sun and wind, and needs generous watering. Upright dense growth up to 9-10'. New leaf growth bronzy-pink to red, with leaves maturing to shiny dark green. Beautiful clusters of drooping white, pink or red flowers bloom Feb-May. Many horticultural varieties. Rock garden or accent plant.

PLUM, BEACH (Prunus maritima) Zone 3. Tiny white flowers in mid-spring, red edible berries. Ht 10'. Well-drained soil. Full sun. Showy. Use fruits raw or in jams. Hardy. Borders or single plants.

POTENTILLA (see cinquefoil)

PRIVET (Ligustrum) Quick growing. Full sun or partial shade. Leathery green foliage. Berries loved by birds. White flowers in early summer; black berries in fall. Very dense growth. Clipped or unclipped hedges, screens, or single plant. All soils.

Amur (L. amurense) Zone 4. Hardy to -30°F. Very dense. If you want flowers, don't trim your hedge. Soot-tolerant. Various heights: Ht 3-15'.

Border (L. obtusifolium) Zone 4. Soot-tolerant. Ht 9'.

California (L. ovalifolium) Zone 6. Variegated varieties not as hardy. Ht 15'. Can grow in dry shade. Semi-deciduous. Hedges, shear to any height. Dark green leaves. Tolerates heat. Greedy roots (for food and water).

Common (L. vulgare) Zone 5. Hedges must be clipped. Susceptible to blight. Ht 15'. Light green leaves (less glossy than Calif. Privet). Clusters of black fruit.

Ibolium (L. x ibolium) Zone 4. Soot-tolerant. Ht 12'.

PRUNUS, shrubby (see almond, cherry, chokecherry, and plum)

PUSSY WILLOW (Salix) Full sun. Moist, well-drained soil. Quick growing. Catkins in early spring, later turn yellow with pollen. Prune after catkins disappear.

French pussy willow (S. caprea) Zone 5. Silver-pink catkins. Leaves gray-green. Screen, single plant. Ht 25'.

Rose gold (S. gracilistyla) Zone 6. Rose catkins. Bushier form; blooms earlier than others. Screen, shrub border, single plant. Ht 10'.

Purple osier (S. purpurea) Zone 5. Gray catkins. Tall and short varieties. Good in wet areas. Ht 9'. Border, bed, hedge, or screen.

Pussy willow (S. discolor) Zone 2. White catkins. Smaller, hardier, and flowers later than French. Screen or single plant. Ht 20'.

QUINCE (Chaenomeles Full sun, well-drained soil. Among first to bloom in spring. Easy to grow. Hardy! Hedge or barrier. Bright, beautiful colors.

Flowering (C. speciosa) Zone 5. Pink, red, bicolor or white flowers in mid-spring; yellow-green fruits. Ht 6'. Very showy. Fruits used in jellies and jams. Rounded form. Pruning: light after blooming. Very hardy. Blooms before leaves develop. Some varieties spreading, some upright. Looks beautiful on a fence, or use as border, hedge or single plant.

Japanese (C. japonica) Zone 5. Reddish-orange flowers in mid-spring. Ht 3-4.' Low borders or foundation plantings. Little pruning. Spreading form.

Stanford Red is good variety for low plant in front of Forsythia.

REDBUD or JUDAS TREE (Cercis) Shrub or small tree. Very showy flowers. Blooms before leaves appear.

American or Eastern Redbud (C. canadensis) Zone 5-7. Yellow fall foliage. Produces light-medium shade. Moist, well-drained soil. Rosy-pink or purple-pink flowers in early spring. White and pink varieties also available. Small, round headed tree. Ht 15'. Taller, hardier, and easier to grow than Western. Native in N.Y., Ontario, to Florida and Texas.

Western Redbud (C. occidentalis) Zone 6. Large shrub to small tree. Native to N. CA below 4,500 ft. elevation. Hard to get started. More shrub-like than Eastern, and best for screening. Red-purple flowers. Will grow here but does best below 2500 ft.

ROSE (see special plant list on roses)

ROSE ACACIA, MOSS LOCUST (Robinia hispida) Zone 6. Well-drained soil, full sun. Pink flowers in early summer; red-brown seed pods. Twigs have red-brown bristles. Reproduces by underground stolons, can become pest. Keep height at 7 ft. Prune after flowers fade. Use on hard-to-plant slopes.

ROSE OF SHARON (see hibiscus)

RUSSIAN OLIVE or Oleaster (Elaeagnus angustifolia) Zone 4. Tree or shrub. Yellow-brown fall foliage. Produces medium shade. Ht 20', S 20'. All soils. Pretty silver-grey foliage (willow-like). Yellow-green flowers in spring; berry-like fruit resembles olives. Hardy, pest-resistant, and soot tolerant. Beautiful peeling brown bark. Often has gnarled trunk. Good background plant, barrier, screen or hedge.

SALTBUSH (Atriplex) Unusually tolerant of seashore environment and highly alkaline soils. Grown for its' silvery-gray foliage. Birds attracted to flowers and seed. Fire-resistant, drought-tolerant, and good erosion control. Dry hillsides or rock garden. Buy at desert nurseries.

Four-wing Saltbush (A. canescens) Zone 6. Native in the arid West. Dense growth. Ht 3-6', S 4-8'. Mass plantings and hedges. Space plants at least 4 feet apart.

Desert Holly (A. hymenelytra) Zone 7. Native to Western deserts. Compact shrub. Ht 1-3'. White branches and silver, toothed, round leaves up to 1 1/2 inches long. Looks like Christmas holly, but is white. Common in Christmas decor. Needs excellent, fast drainage. Water heavy only during blooming (Feb-May). Short life span [1].

SERVICEBERRY (see tree list)

SCOTCH BROOM (see broom)

SIBERIAN PEA TREE (Caragana arborescens) Zone 2. Full sun, any soil. Yellow flowers in late spring; yellow-green seedpods. Very hardy and vigorous. Windbreak, screen, or tall hedge. Ht 20'. Drought and cold resistant. Use weeping variety as single plant. Prune after flowers fade.

SNOWBALL (see viburnum)

SNOWBERRY (see symphoricarpos)

SPICEBUSH (Lindera benzoin) Zone 5. Fragrant yellow flowers in early spring; red berries. Yellow-gold fall foliage. Needs partial shade. Moist, well-drained, acid soil. Single plant, or mixed shrub border. Ht 6-15'. Both sexes are needed for berry production. Leaves used in tea. Prune after flowers fade.

SPIREA (Spiraea) Spirea is preferred spelling for the common name of genus Spiraea [2]. Rose family. Full sun or partial shade, any soil. Varies in form, height, and flowering season. Prune spring-flowering kinds when they finish blooming; and prune summer-flowering ones in late winter or early spring while still dormant. On plants with loose graceful branching, remove old wood that has produced flowers, cutting back to the ground. The shrubby types require less severe pruning. Other plants "resembling" Spirea are Caryopteris and Sorbaria (False Spirea).

Anthony Waterer or Dwarf Red Spiraea (S. x bumalda 'Anthony Waterer') Tiny, deep pink flowers June to fall. Dwarf to 2 1/2 ft. Low hedge, or border. Full sun. Very hardy. Prune when dormant. Zone 5.

Big Nippon (S. nipponica 'rotundifolia') Tiny white flowers in late spring (June). Leaves blue-green. Single plant or shrub border. More upright growth than other varieties. Ht 5-8'. Prune after flowering. Zone 5

Billiard (S. x billiardi) Tiny pink-red flowers July-August. Borders, mass plantings. Reproduce by underground stems. Dense mound. Ht 6'. Prune when dormant. Leaves green above, gray-green beneath. Zone 5.

Bridal-wreath (S. prunifolia) White flowers in mid-spring (April-May). Red-orange fall foliage. Fast growing. Very popular. Showy. Long arching branching. Single plant or shrub border. Ht 6'. Very hardy. Prune after flowering. Zone 5.

Garland (S. x arguta) Tiny white flowers in mid-spring (April-May). Showy arching branches. Single plant, shrub borders. Use dwarf varieties in foundation plantings or beds. Prune after flowering. Ht 3-6'. Zone 5.

Japanese, Mikado (S. japonica 'atrosanguinea') Zone 6. Tiny red flowers in early summer (July). Single plants, shrub borders. Dwarf forms in rock gardens and edgings. Prune when dormant. Ht 6'.

Reeves (S. cantoniensis) Zone 7. White flowers in late spring (June, July). Red-brown fall foliage. Showy arching branches. Ht 5-6'. Single plants or shrub border. Prune after flowering.

Snowmound (S. nipponica tosaensis 'Snowmound') Round clusters of white flowers in June (late spring). Low mound. Ht 2-3'. Dense foliage. Small blue-green leaves. Prune after flowering.

Thunberg (S. thunbergii) Zone 5. White flowers in mid-spring (April-May). Yellow fall foliage. Very showy. Blooms earlier than other varieties. Ht 5'. Prune after flowering.

Vanhoutte, Bridal-wreath (S. x vanhouttei) Zone 5. Most popular. White flowers in late spring(June-July). Red-orange fall foliage. Very hardy, showy. Single plant, border. Long, arching branches. Ht 4-6'. Prune after flowering. Blue-green leaves.

SPIRAEA, FALSE (Sorbaria or Spiraea) Small white flowers in summer.

Kashmir (S. aitchisoni) Zone 6. Partial shade. Any moist soil. Single plant in large yards, or mass planting. Good on slopes for erosion control. Cut off fading flowers, and severely prune branches every 2-3 years. Ht 10'.

Ural (S. sorbifolia) Zone 2. Full sun or partial shade. Any soil. Must prune often, or becomes pest. Use in large yards, shrub borders, or on slopes. Ht 6'.

STEPHANANDRA, LACE SHRUB (Stephanandra incisa) Zone 5. Very tiny white flowers in early summer. Red-purple fall foliage. Twigs dense and contorted. Ht 8'. Full sun or partial shade. Any moist soil. Showy foliage. Shrub borders, informal hedges. Dwarf forms in beds, edgings, rock gardens. Prune when dormant.

SUMAC (Rhus) Full sun, any soil. Outstanding red fall foliage. Quick growing. Pruning encourages more stems to grow. Plant both sexes to get fruit. Smooth and Staghorn take extreme heat and cold, and will grow in any soil. The evergreen kinds are fire resistant if they are fairly well watered. Poison Oak is in this genus. Poison Oak grows on this side of the Rocky Mountains, and Poison Ivy on the other side. Poison Oak and Poison Sumac are the only serious contact poisons in our native flora, but they are not garden plants. **Poison Sumac** has white-gray berries and it found only in Eastern N. America along water or in swamps. **Poison Oak** has white berries and leaves with 3 leaflets (shape varies) containing no thorns or stickers. The leaves, berries, sticks in winter, and smoke when any part of plant is burned — all are poisonous (usually cause hives). Poison Oak is often confused with Virginia Creeper which has 5 leaflets [2,3].

Fragrant (R. aromatica) Zone 3. Light, well-drained soil. Tiny yellow flowers in midsummer; red berries. Yellow and red fall foliage. Foundation plantings, or ground cover on hard-to-plant slopes. Ht 8'.

Shining, Dwarf (R. copallina) Zone 5. Tiny green-yellow flowers; red berries. Scarlet fall foliage. Single tree, or back -of -shrub border. Ht 20'.

Smooth (R. glabra) Zone 2. Tiny green-yellow flowers in midsummer; bright red berries. Bright red fall foliage. Background, screen. Can become a pest! Ht 20'.

Staghorn (R. typhina) Zone 3. Green-yellow flowers in early summer; bright red berries. Bright red fall foliage. Background plant in large yards. Spreads by underground runners. Can become a pest. Ht 30'.

SUMMER-SWEET (Clethra alnifolia) Zone 5. Fragrant white or pink flowers in summer. Yellow fall foliage. Full sun or partial shade. Any moist soil. Shrub borders, informal hedges. Spreads by underground runners. Ht 10'.

SWEET SHRUB or CALIFORNIA ALLSPICE (Calycanthus floridus) All zones. Maroon (red-brown) flowers May-July. Fragrant: flowers, leaves and bark all smell like fresh strawberries. Yellow fall foliage. Prefers partial shade, can tolerate full sun. Shade tolerant. Rich, moist, well-drained soil. Single plant, shrub border. Ht 10', S 5-8'. Stiff branches. Oval, shiny leaves —dark green above, gray-green underside.

SYMPHORICARPOS (Symphoricarpos) Flowers inconspicuous. Any soil. Full sun or partial shade (shade tolerant). Berries make showy fall color, and birds love them. Prune while plant is dormant. Fruit persists, so branches are good for arrangements. Good for erosion control.

Chenault coralberry (S. x chenaulti) Zone 5. Pink flowers in midsummer; red berries. Shrub border; dwarf forms in ground covers. Graceful arching branches. Spreads by underground runners. Ht 3'.

Indian currant, Coralberry (S. orbiculatus) Zone 3. Green-white flowers midsummer; red-violet berries. Use on hard to plant slopes. Spreads by under-ground runners. Ht 7'

Snowberry (S. albus 'laevigatus') Zone 3. Native. Tiny pink or whitish flowers; white berries. Single plant, hedges, shrub borders. Upright arching branches. Ht 3'. Hard to find in nurseries.

TAMARISK (Tamarix) Thrives in dry areas. Well-drained soil, and full sun. Single plant or shrub border. Prune back severely when plant dormant. Pink flowers in late summer. Foliage light green and scalelike creating a feathery appearance. Try varieties Odessa (Ht 18'), and Small-flowered (Ht 9'). Zone 5.

VIBURNUM (Viburnum) Full sun or partial shade. Well-drained soil. Birds love the berries. Red fall foliage. Little pruning needed. "Red-black" berries refers to being red first, gradually turning black. (See also broadleaf shrub list.)

Arrowwood (V. dentatum) Zone 3. Tiny white flowers in early summer; blue berries. Single plant or shrub border. Ht 15'.

Burkwood (V. x burkwoodi) Zone 5. Fragrant tiny pink or white flowers in late spring; red-black berries. Shrub border, foundation plant. Ht 6'. Sometimes called Fragrant Snowball. Semi-deciduous (holds leaves until Dec). Grown for its flowers!
Black haw (V. prunifolium) Zone 3. Tiny white flowers in spring; blue-black edible berries (Jams &Jellies). Shrub backdrop or screen. Ht 15'.
European cranberry bush, or Common Snowball (V. opulus) Zone 3. Tiny white flowers in late spring; red berries. Dense and vigorous. Tall forms (Ht 12') good for shrub border or screen. Low forms used for edging or rock garden. Gets aphids (pest).
Fragrant (V. farreri) Zone 6. Fragrant white flowers in early spring; red-black berries. Single plant or shrub border. Earliest blooming varieties. Not very cold hardy. Ht 10'.
Highbush cranberry (V. trilobum) Zone 2. Tiny white flowers in late spring; red berries (edible, jams & jellies). Vigorous and hardy. Shrub border, screen. Erect form (Ht 12'). Sometimes called American Cranberry Bush.
Korean spice (V. carlesi) Zone 5. Hardiest variety (-30°F). Small, fragrant pink flowers in mid-spring; black berries. Single plant or shrub border. Ht 5-8'.
Linden (V. dilatatum) Zone 5. Tiny white flowers in early summer; red berries. Vigorous. Ht 10'. Single plant, screen in large yards. Foliage red-brown in fall.
Nannyberry, Sheepberry (V. lentago) Zone 3. Tiny white flowers in late spring; black berries. Shrub background or screen. Ht 30'. Dense, arching branches. Vigorous and hardy. Foliage red-purple in fall.
Sargent cranberry bush (V. sargenti) Zone 6. Tiny white flowers mid-spring; red berries. Similar to European cranberry bush. Very vigorous and hardy. Shrub border, screen, or single plant. Ht 12'.
Siebold (V. sieboldi) Zone 5. Tiny white flowers; bright red-black berries. Very showy all seasons. Vigorous and hardy. Single plant, shrub border. Ht 10'.
Snowball:
Common (V. roseum) Best of snowballs. Bonus: nice fall color.
Fragrant (V. x carlcephalum) Zone 5. Fragrant small white flowers; red-black berries. Single plant or shrub border. Ht 9'. Hardier than European.
Japanese (V. plicatum) Zone 5. Tiny white flowers in late spring. Single plant or shrub border. Ht 10'.
Wayfaring tree (V. lantana) Zone 3. Tiny white flowers in mid-spring; red-black berries. Ht 15'. Single plant in large yards, shrub backdrop. Hardy and drought resistant.
Withe-rod (V. cassinoides) Zone 4. Tiny white flowers in early summer; red-black berries. Mass plantings or beds. Ht 12'.

WEIGELA (Weigela) Full sun or partial shade. Any soils. Graceful, arching branches. Single plant, or shrub border. Needs winter protection as flowers will bloom on one-year-old wood. If frozen back will send up new shoots. Prune after flowering. Dark green leaves.
Old-fashioned (W. florida) Zone 5. White or Pink flowers, late spring. Ht 8-10'.
Weigela hybrids (W. hybrids) Zone 6. White, pink, red, magenta flowers in late spring. Very showy. Dies back in particularly cold areas. Ht 9-12'.
Bristol Ruby (W. 'bristol ruby') Ht 6-7',S 6'. Ruby-red flowers in late spring, some repeat bloom midsummer and again in fall.

WILLOW (see pussywillow)

WINTERBERRY, BLACK ALDER (Ilex verticillata) Zone 4. Tiny white flowers in early summer; red berries. Yellow fall foliage. Full sun or partial shade. Moist, well-drained, slightly acid soil. Plant both sexes for fruit production. Borders or single plant. Good in wet area. Upright growth. Winter twigs good for Christmas decorations. Ht 15'. (Dwarf varieties Ht 2- 3'.)

WITCH HAZEL (Hamamelis) Zone 5. Yellow ribbon-like flowers. Full sun, or partial shade. Rich, moist, well-drained soil. Needs little pruning. Fragrant yellow flowers with narrow, ribbon-like, crumpled-looking petals in flowers clusters.
Arnold promise (H. x intermedia) Flowers in early spring. Grown for very early blooms. Single plant, shrub borders. Ht 15'. Red-brown fall foliage.
Chinese (H. mollis) Flowers in early spring. Grown for early bloom and scent. Dense, rounded form. Single plant, shrub borders. Ht 30'. Yellow fall foliage.
Common (H. virginiana) Flowers in late fall, same time as yellow fall foliage. Grown for late bloom. Shrub backdrop. Open, loose growth. Soot-tolerant. Ht 15'.
Vernal (H. vernalis) Flowers in late winter or early spring. Blooms on sunny days only. Yellow fall foliage. Grown for early bloom and scent. Vigorous and dense growth. Single plant, shrub border. Ht 6'.

References cited:
[1] The Principles of Gardening (Johnson)
[2] The Garden Dictionary (Taylor)
[3] Sunset Western Garden Book

Peace in a beautiful garden
Is like peace no where else
On this Earth.
...Old gardening saying

ROSES

Roses demand more attention than other plants. Roses can survive with only minimal care,—watering; but if you want beautiful, healthy roses, they also need proper fertilizing, pruning, pest and disease control, and winter protection. They require good drainage, a deep fertile soil (slightly acid), and at least six hours of full sun (preferably in the morning). Types vary from three inch miniatures to twenty foot high climbers that cover walls, fences or arbors; and shrub roses that vary from ground covers to hedges and screens. All types of roses grow in cold winter areas (Sunset zones 1-3, USDA zones 4-7) except the tree or standard, but some varieties are not as tolerant of extreme cold as others. A winter mulch is highly recommended, with a lesser mulch of 2-3 inches the rest of the year. Roses require a lot of tender loving care, but rose growers say it's worth all the effort when they see the beautiful flowers.

Good drainage and watering techniqe are both critical for roses. Roses can't sit in water constantly—even during winter dormancy—or they will rot [1]. Drip irrigation is ideal for outdoor plants because the bed is soaked slowly and thoroughly to a depth of 5-6 inches. If you use other methods of watering, roses must be watered in the morning, so their leaves can dry and not get mildew, and you have to be sure to water to 5-6 inches depth.

Select the hardiest and most disese-resistant varieties. Buy the highest quality stock available. The American Rose Society (ARS) rates modern roses on a scale of 1-10, and the higher the rating, the most likely it will perform well in most climates. Look around you in neighbor's gardens, in public and private rose gardens, and see which varieties perform well. The common non-patented varieties tend to be hardier. Keep track of the rose varieties you plant. If you leave the name tag on the plant, be sure the wire isn't so tight that it cuts off circulation in the branch.

What characteristics do you look for in a rose? Roses are grown for their petal count, fragrance, long stems, color, vigor, hardiness, disease resistance, foliage, flower production, bud and flower form, opening and final color, overall value, and special effect. Based on these traits there is an All-American rose award (AARS) given each year to roses worthy of recommendation to the public. They have to be grown outdoors under normal gardening care for two years, and only the top scoring roses are given an AARS tag. Bloom color varies according to season (spring or fall); weather (warm & wet, vs cool & dry); and new plants vs old plants [2].

Propagation of roses is not recommended for two reasons. First, roses are grafted on very sturdy root stock, and when you propagate from a cane you get a less hardy plant. Secondly, it is illegal to propagate any patented plant material, and many roses are patented, especially the newer varieties. Most modern roses are hybrids of hybrids, or mutations from the old wild roses. They can be planted from seed, bought in nurseries, or purchased from catalogs.

Types of roses:

Two main types of roses according to their growth habit are: bush roses and climbing roses. Bush roses are 1-6 feet tall and need no support, while climbing roses produce long canes that must be supported.

A cross between a Hybrid perpetual and Rosa Foetida

<u>BUSH TYPES</u>: hybrid tea, floribunda, grandiflora, polyantha, hybrid perpetual, shrub, old fashioned, tree or standard, and miniature. All bush types do well here except the standard or tree form (it's the least cold hardy). If the one cane (or stem) on the tree type should die the plant dies, so it is not recommended here.

Hybrid teas, floribundas, grandifloras, and miniatures are generally hardy to 20°F, but should have soil mounded over the canes. Miniatures need to have mulch piled over the entire plant.

a shrub rose

Shrub, hybrid perpetuals, polyanthas, and old fashioned are all hardy. A deep layer of snow makes a nice blanket protecting and insulating them all winter, so they usually have little winter damage. Rugosas (<u>Rosa</u> <u>rugosa</u>) are an old fashioned rose type that is ideal for hedges or ground cover because of their dense foliage. They have a long flowering period, are extremely hardy, disease resistant, large size, and easy care. These are available by catalog.

<u>CLIMBER TYPES:</u> the hardy <u>old garden climbers</u>, and <u>climbing sports</u>. The old garden climbers include the ramblers, large-blossomed, everblooming, and trailing roses. The large-blossomed climbers that either are "repeat-blooming", or "ever-blooming", are now more popular than the older type having only one period of bloom. The sports are mutations most commonly from hybrid teas, grandifloras, floribundas, and polyanthas. These modern sports have flowers identical to their parents but are on longer canes; and they are less hardy [3], thus needing winter protection.

Climbers are usually sold by variety name, rather than types. Some popular varieties are 'Blaze' (crimson), 'Paul Scarlet' (bright scarlet), and 'Climbing America' which is a vigorous grower 6x 6 feet with fragrant coral flowers —and deer love it!

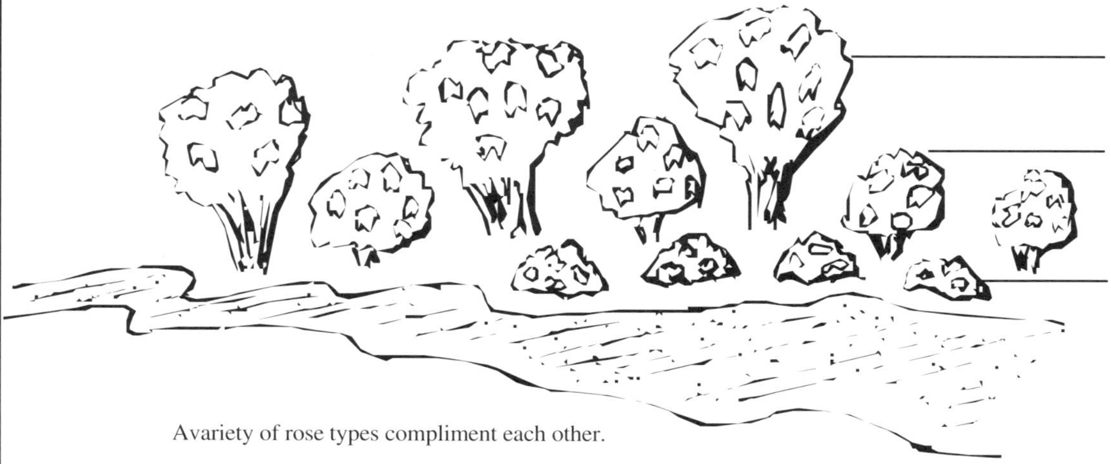

Avariety of rose types compliment each other.

Most popular types of roses

Hybrid tea, floribunda, grandiflora, miniatures, and modern climbers are all relatively recent developments, and they are the most popular roses sold today in nurseries. The other types can be ordered from catalogs.

Hybrid Tea

Hybrid tea Noted for the long stem, large long pointed buds, double flowers, and long blooming period. Grown for flower arranging; the perfect flower for a vase. The most popular selling rose type today. They are a hybrid cross between the ever-blooming old tea roses, and the hardy hybrid perpetual. They flower intermittently, and have a wider range of colors to choose from. Plant low growing perennials and annuals around base of hybrid tea plants to hide the scraggly stems. Ht 3-5' tall.

Floribunda- Noted for the clusters of 15-25 flowers per stem. Comes in single, and double flowers. Blooms continuously from June to frost. Disease-resistant. They are hardier, shorter stem, lower growing, have a looser flower form, and are bushier than most hybrid teas. For a fuller flower cluster remove the center bud as soon as it appears. Grow 2-4 feet tall.

A Floribunda

Floribundas make good hedges

Grandiflora A tall stately bush with great vigor. Since it is a cross between hybrid tea and floribunda, its appearance is half-way between. It has individual flowers on a long stem from the hybrid tea; but gets the hardiness, continuous flowering, and flowers in clusters from the floribundas. Grows 5-8 feet tall.

Grandiflora

Miniatures. Only 10-15 inches tall, with tiny semi-double or double flowers 1-2 inches across! Some flowers are identical to hybrid tea, but smaller. Use in containers, window boxes, hanging baskets, low hedge, hardy ground cover, to fill any small space; or hang from tree limbs, posts, gutters, overhangs, or brackets attached to fences or house. If planted outdoors in the ground (plant twelve inches apart), they like partial shade, but not too much competition with roots of shrubs or trees. If in window boxes, try filling box with individual flower pots, instead of planting directly in the soil, so you can bring them in the house when cold weather comes. Indoors, the miniatures need lots of light; try a south window or high intensity fluorescent lights 10-14 hours/day. Set them

Miniature

Miniatures in window boxes

on a tray of pebbles to keep up the humidity. Spider mite is a problem in indoor miniatures, so keep leaves and stems clean. **Climbers**. Most of their blooms are on lateral branches that grow on the long canes. For the most and best blooms, train canes horizontally along a fence or wall. When a long upright cane is arched over or bent down to a horizontal position, the terminal bud at the tip no longer functions, and all the "growth eyes" along the cane will begin to grow upward ("growth eyes", "growth buds" and "lateral buds" are interchangeable terms). These lateral shoots produce the flowers. Since they don't have tendrils, each new leader must be tied to a support with plastic twisters, twine, rags, or other soft material. The leaders can also be woven through the trellis. Frame climbers around a doorway, decorate a pole, spread on a fence or wall, or use as a good ground cover on banks. Height 20' tall.

Train climber along a fence.

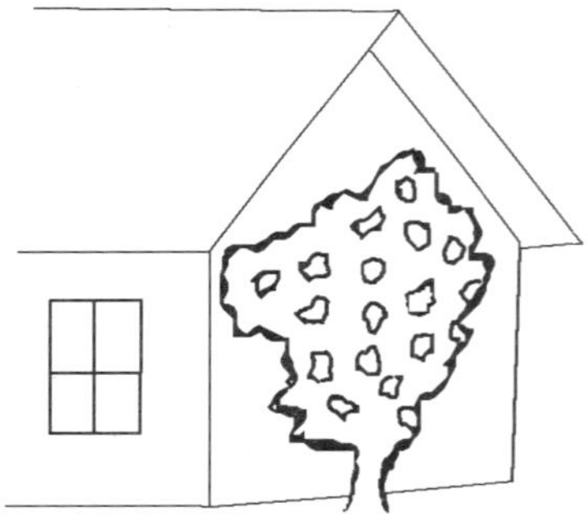

On a wall

Up a pole

Over a doorway

CLIMBERS

Spacing

Roses need to be planted in an open area, so air can circulate freely around them to help prevent disease. Don't plant too close to trees or shrubs or they will compete with the roses for sun, nutrients and water. Don't plant near the vegetable garden as roses attract bugs to the garden—and the garden attracts bugs that like roses.

Don't plant too close to any wall or building. Plant bush roses 18-24 inches away from any wall, or they will grow leggy, lean away from the wall, and the blooms get sunburn spots from reflected sunlight off light-colored walls. Climbers should be at least 12-15 inches away from any solid structure, as this gives good air circulation and gives you room to prune and spray; but to cover a trellis or wood fence, the climbers can be planted closer [4].

Spacing between climber plnts should be 4-5 feet apart, unless you plan to espalier on a trellis or fence, then plan on climber covering 6-8 feet area. In cold winter areas where winter temperatures reach 20°F and below, space the hybrid teas 24-30 inches apart, floribundas 18-24 inches, and grandifloras 21-27 inches apart. Floribundas make nice hedges when planted 18 inches apart [4].

Special planting instructions.

Roses are available bare-root, Balled & Burlaped (B&B) or container-grown from nurseries and mail order catalogs. In cold winter areas, plant bare-root and B&B roses only in early spring [2], approximately April 1-April 20. Containerized roses can be planted anytime except winter. See planting chapter (nursery stock) for more details.

Just before planting a bare-root rose, remove the nursery wrapping. Cut any broken canes or roots back to below the breaks. Cut off the very tips of the roots, then immerse whole plant in a bucket of water 6-24 hours. Make planting hole at least eighteen inches deep; large enough to spread out roots without bending or cutting back. Enrich the soil with the usual organic matter such as leaf mold, compost, and peat moss before planting. Then add a half cup superphosphate or bone meal to the organic matter. Add sand or vermiculite if necessary to provide good drainage. Then mix 1/3 of the organic matter with 2/3 of the garden soil. Make a soil mound in middle of hole and firm it. Place roots over mound. Add soil as necessary to mound until the bud union is located about 1 1/2 inches above soil level. Then fill hole 2/3 full of the soil mixture, and firm it with your foot. Water well and let soak in. Fill hole with soil mixture and firm gently. Make a depression around the plant including a raised ridge to catch water. Water well. Mound the rest of the soil mixture up over the plant (about 6-12 inches) and water well again. This mound protects the plant from drying out as it starts to grow. When buds start to swell in the spring, remove the soil mound.

Right after planting (before mounding), prune all rose canes back by 1/3, make cut just above an outside facing bud (this will create a stronger bush with larger blooms). Balled and Burlaped plants are planted in the same way and placed on the soil cone (see Planting chapter).

Plant Bareroot ROSES in early spring in cold climates.

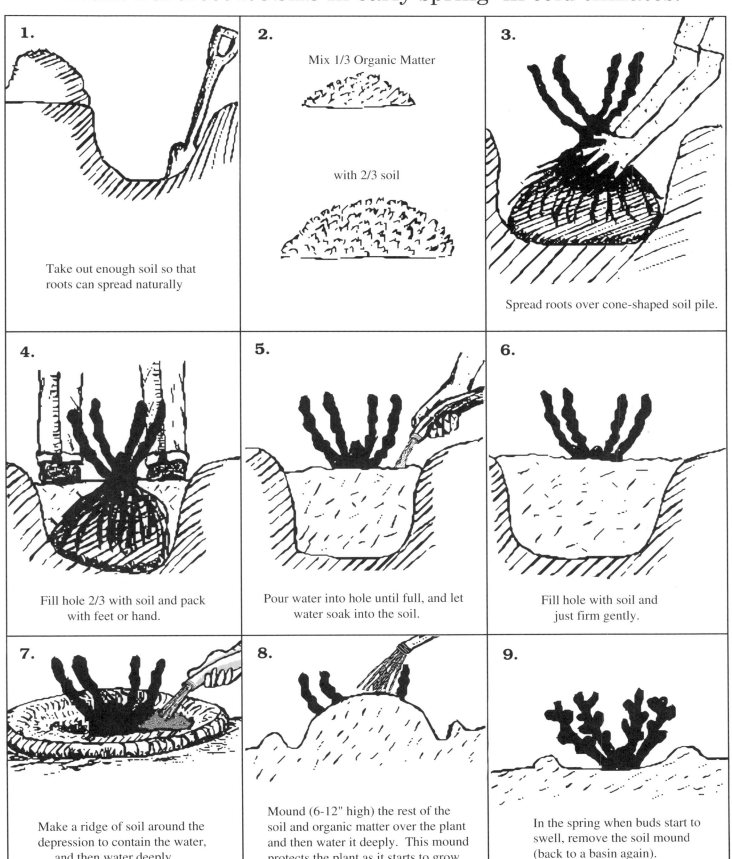

1.

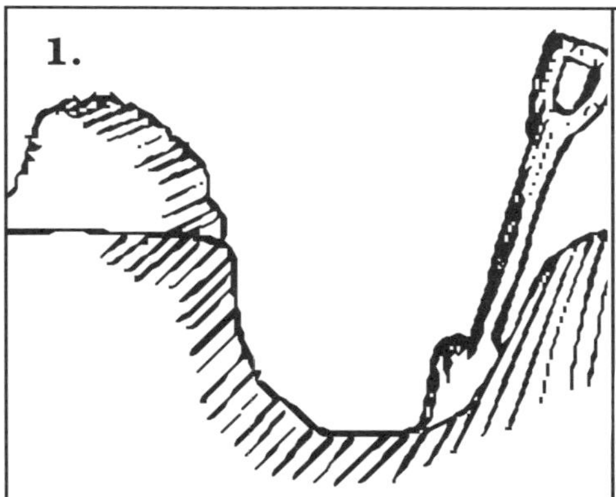

Take out enough soil so that roots can spread naturally

2.

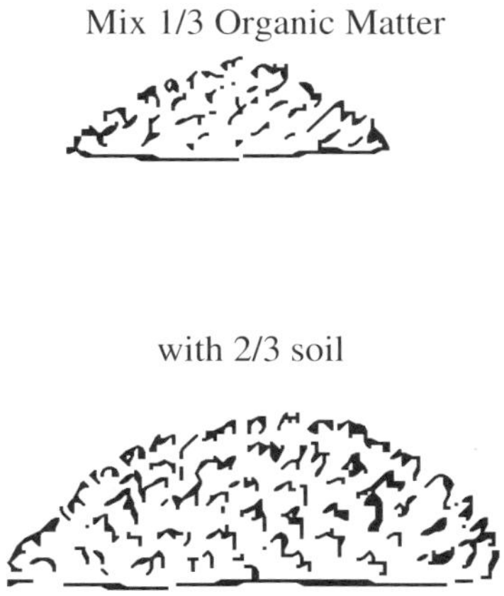

3.

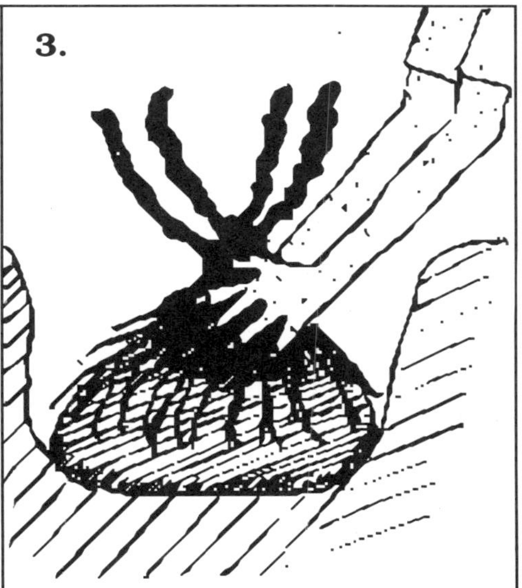

Spread roots over cone-shaped soil pile.

4.

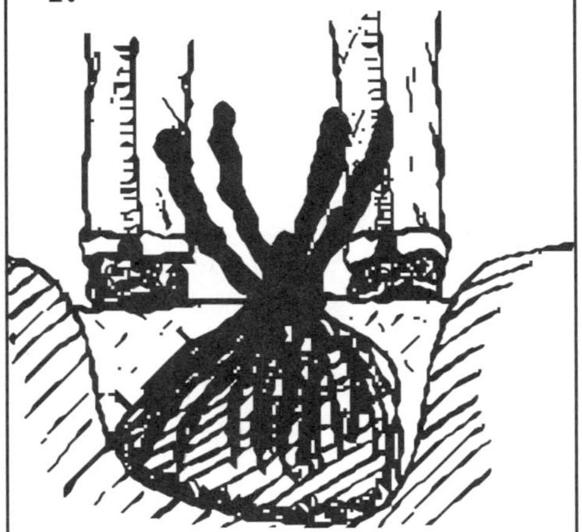

Fill hole 2/3 with soil and pack with feet or hand.

5.

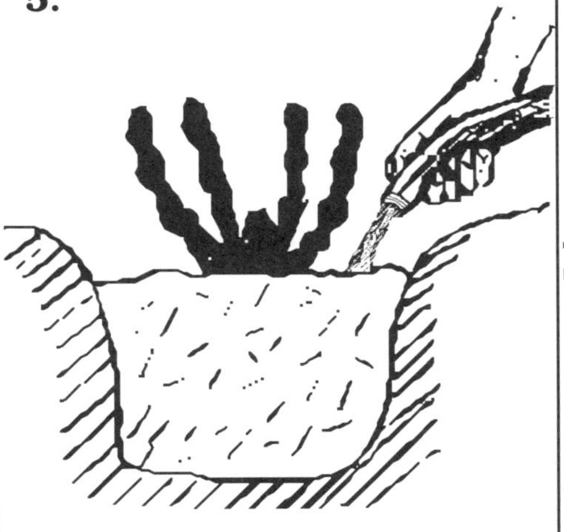

Pour water into hole until full, and let water soak into the soil.

6.

Fill hole with soil and just firm gently.

7.

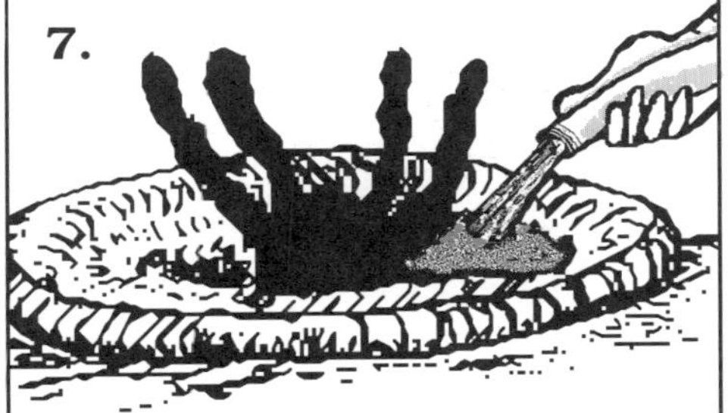

Make a ridge of soil around the depression to contain the water, and then water deeply.

8.

Mound (6-12" high) the rest of the soil and organic matter over the plant and then water it deeply. This mound protects the plant as it starts to grow.

9.

In the spring when buds start to swell, remove the soil mound (back to a basin again).

Roses in <u>containers</u> for terrace decor. Floribunda, polyanthas, and miniatures make bushy plants with many flowers, so they look nice in containers, tubs, pots, and boxes for terrace decoration. The best general container size for roses is 20x20x20 inches, but miniatures need only 12x12x12 inches. Buy container plants in at least a two gallon pot, but preferably a 3-5 gallon size. A small container can mean that roots may have been pruned or broken to fit into the pot. Containerized plants need watering more often than those planted in the ground; never let soil dry out completely. A plastic pot is recommended as it keeps the moisture better than clay pots. Clay pots freeze and break, so don't leave them out over winter. Check moisture daily during heat of summer; use mulch on a planter box or container to keep plant moist. Water till drops run out the drainage hole. Control insects and diseases with a regular spraying program and apply either a dry or liquid fertilizer once a month; or use a rose fertilizer containing a systemic pesticide. If you use commercial potting soil (it is sterilized) in your containers, it can be used in the house or outdoors. See also House plant chapter.

Winter protection

Healthy roses in general aren't hurt by winter temperatures that drop occasionally below 20°F, but the combination of low winter temperatures, fluctuating temperatures, and drying winds, can cause cane dieback or kill the plant [5]. Most of the time, the dieback can be pruned away in the spring. Some rose varieties that are hardy in extremely cold climates like Siberia, are injured in warmer areas where temperatures constantly fluctuate, like at Lake Almanor. And since cold air seeks the lowest level, don't plant roses in a low area of the terrain.

So, in cold winter areas use winter protection (a soil mound) around canes of both bush and climbing roses. And tie all canes together to protect from wind damage. A general rule of thumb for soil mound depth: add one inch of soil for every 10° below freezing (32°F). Use a five-inch soil mound down to -20°F; but where there is no snow and winters are cold, a deeper soil mound is recommended. Susanville (USDA Zone 5) often has a winter low of -18 or -20°F. Susanville is classified as the high desert which is a more severe climate, as it has low winter temperatures, no humidity, and much less snow. Don't add

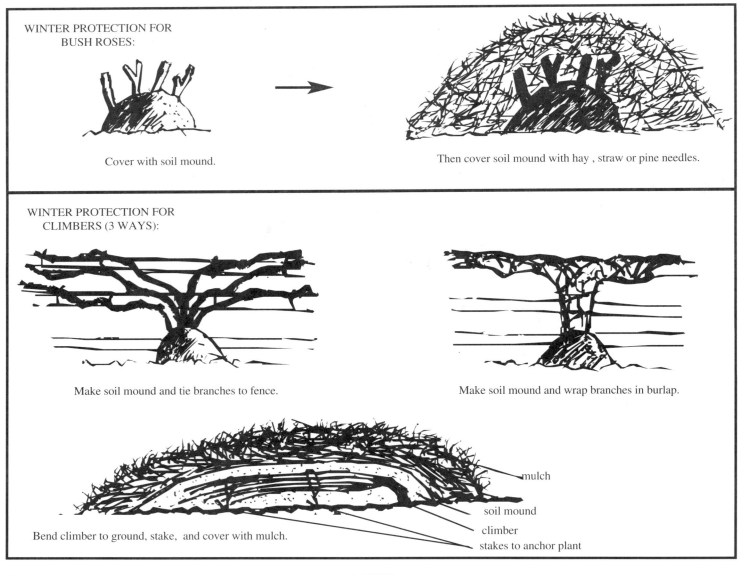

WINTER PROTECTION FOR BUSH ROSES:

Cover with soil mound.

Then cover soil mound with hay , straw or pine needles.

WINTER PROTECTION FOR CLIMBERS (3 WAYS):

Make soil mound and tie branches to fence.

Make soil mound and wrap branches in burlap.

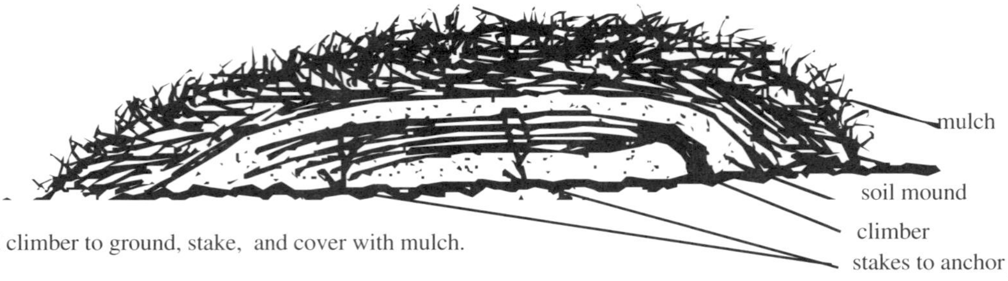

Bend climber to ground, stake, and cover with mulch.

the winter protection until after first hard frost, as this prevents disease caused by poor circulation.

Adjust your care of roses so they are mature when the first frost occurs, not still actively growing and blooming — because actively growing plants are more susceptible to frost damage. Help your roses prepare for winter. Do not apply nitrogen fertilizers after August 1st in cold winter areas (six weeks before expected frost). Allow the last blooms of the season to stay on the plants to form rose hips (seed pods), because cutting off blooms stimulates more growth [6]. "Rose hips" are what's left of the flower when the petals fall off; the round base between flower and stem swells and turns red. They are pretty berries packed with vitamin C.

Bush roses. In cold winter areas where temperatures can drop below 10°F, you need to prune back and winterize bush roses (hybrid teas, floribundas, and grandifloras) in the fall. After the first hard frost, **prune** bush roses back to about eighteen inches from the ground [4]. Apply Tree Seal or Pruning Paint to the cut branch ends. Burn the pruned branches and leaves to destroy insect eggs and diseases so they won't overwinter. Spray the remaining plant and soil surface with **dormant spray**. Cover each plant with a **soil mound** 6-8 inches high. The soil for the soil mound must be brought in from another area of the garden (don't disturb the shallow rose roots). Then cover the entire plant and soil mound with a **mulch** of hay, straw, or pine needles (after the first hard frost). Put a few shovels full of dirt on top to hold the straw in place or use a cylinder of wire mesh stuffed with straw around each bush. This mulch helps prevent freezing and thawing of the soil around the canes, and also protects against the drying wind. In spring when the buds start to swell, is the time to remove the winter protection because poor circulation now can cause disease. (The bud swelling usually occurs after danger of severe frost is past.) Use a garden hose to wash away the soil mound (so you won't damage the new buds or roots).

Climbing roses can usually survive 20°F temperatures, but if you have fluctuating temperatures or if your coldest winter temperature can dip below 0°F —you must provide winter protection:

- In less cold areas (+5° to 15°F), mound dirt around base as with other roses, and tie canes to prevent wind whipping.
- Where lows are -10°F to +5°F, leave canes in place and insulate with straw wrapped in burlap.
- In coldest climates (colder than -10°F), take climbers off their supports, lay the canes on the ground, and cover with soil. Then mulch with straw, hay or pine needles. In early spring, remove mulch and tie climbers back up. Modern varieties need deeper winter mulch.

Roses in containers or pots must over-winter where temperatures range between 28-40°F. Place in an unheated shed, garage, or root cellar and protect roots with mulch. Water only lightly during winter storage so that soil does not completely dry out, and don't use fertilizer. If the garage is separate from the house, or if you anticipate an extra cold winter, keep them in a cool part of your house (they were raised in a greenhouse). If brought into the house for the winter, they have to be "hardened off" (see Propagation chapter) gradually before planting outdoors or leaving pot outdoors in spring. Or you can just wait till temperatures warm up, and take them out in late spring.

Plastic foam cones should only be used where winters are colder than USDA Zone 5, and then only for the most tender rose types, —which you shouldn't be planting anyway! The cone can become a hot house if you get some warm winter days due to fluctuating temperatures, and the plant will cook. It may be a good way to protect plants during a very cold spell, but uncover when cold spell is over.

General pruning of roses.

Pruning promotes strong new growth and stimulates production of more blooms. Wear heavy gloves, a long sleeved shirt, and old clothes; as rose thorns can rip anything! Be careful not to damage the tender new shoots coming off the bud union when raking, pruning, or using any tools near the rose bush. Use sharp pruning shears, as mashed torn twigs result from using dull shears. Cut above an outside bud at a 45° angle, slanting the cut downward toward the inside of the plant, as this makes the leaves grow away from the center of the bush and leaves the center open for good air circulation. Cut about 1/4 inch above the bud; not closer or the bud will die, and not too long a stump or it will rot. Blooms are produced on the new growth on bush roses, but on the second year wood on climbers, so the pruning rules differ.

Remove any shoots coming from below the bud union (suckers), as these take energy from plants with bud unions. Leave all shoots starting above the bud union as these will form your plant. If in doubt, wait till leaves develop, because there is a distinct difference in leaf size and shape. PULL the suckers down and off the plant; if you CUT them off they will grow back. Don't remove suckers on miniature, old garden, and shrub roses,—as they are grown on their own roots, and are made denser by the new sucker growth.

Pruning Bush roses.

In spring after danger of severe frost is past, remove the winter soil mound and mulch. Cut deadwood back to living green stem just above the nearest live leaf bud —a reddish purple swelling on the cane. Where there are cold winters, you may have to prune to ground level (the level of the mulch). Remove completely any weak or diseased canes. Plus, do the usual pruning of branches such as dead, crossing over, rubbing, or too dense in center of bush (see Pruning chapter). As rose becomes established, you can remove old canes as new ones become established. Prune to shape when needed so plant isn't scraggly (out of bounds). Floribundas in hedge form can be sheared to uniform height.

On bush roses, for a "cut flower", cut stem above first 5-leaflet leaf. Leave two 5-leaflet leaves remaining on the stem.

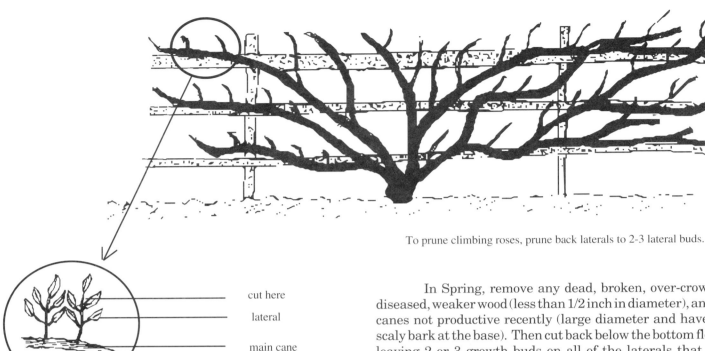

To prune climbing roses, prune back laterals to 2-3 lateral buds.

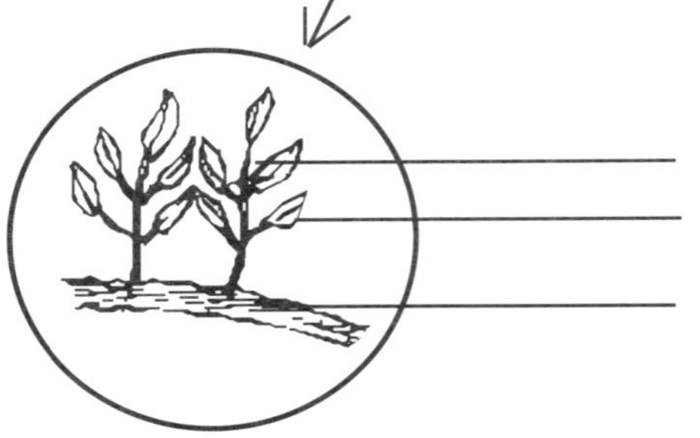

During the blooming season on bush roses, as soon as a flower fades (or when you cut a rose for a vase), cut the stem down to the first leaf containing 5 leaflets, but be sure to leave at least two 5-leaflet leaves remaining on the stem to maintain vigor. Cut, do not tear or twist stem off, as clean cuts heal quickly and do not invite disease and insects. When you cut just above a leaf, a new bud will form in the leaf axil. Many types of roses will bloom again, but shrub, old garden, and some climbing roses only bloom once.

Disbudding (as on hybrid tea and grandiflora), is a method of pinching off any lateral buds, so the main bloom will have more energy to produce a larger bloom. Not really necessary unless you are preparing blooms for a show.

Pruning climbers

There are two kinds of climbing roses: those that bloom in spring; and those that bloom off and on, spring through fall (the repeat-flower-climbers). Those that bloom in spring should be pruned right after blooming (removing the oldest growth). Repeat-flower-climbers (they are the climbing sports of bush varieties) are pruned the same time as bush roses-(during dormant season).

All climbers should be left unpruned for the first 2-3 years after planting so they can get established [6]. During this time only remove dead, too dense, or weak twiggy growth, and trim any scraggly branches reaching beyond the shape you want. Since most climbers bloom on second year and older wood, don't expect blooms the first year.

Once climbers are established, prune them in early spring and again after they bloom. They should be thinned by only about 10% per year. Climbers don't grow much from the base of the plant; so don't remove any main canes unless they grow too long for the space.

In Spring, remove any dead, broken, over-crowded, diseased, weaker wood (less than 1/2 inch in diameter), and old canes not productive recently (large diameter and have dry scaly bark at the base). Then cut back below the bottom flower leaving 2 or 3 growth buds on all of the laterals that bore flowers during the last year. Note that climbers are pruned in a different manner than bush roses.

Some say that removing faded blooms on climbers during the summer is not necessary, but removing them will stimulate more vigorous blooming.

Pruning miniatures.

At the end of the dormant period, prune back to the lowest outward facing growth eye on previous seasons wood [7]. This is severe pruning but it encourages strong growth for the new seasons flower production. Remove also all weak and twiggy growth.

Insect pests and disease in roses

Watch garden plants for signs of insects and disease. Buy only healthy plants and keep weeds pulled. The earlier you detect a pest problem, the easier it is to handle. Insect pests affecting roses are aphids, spider mites, and thrips. Try home made sprays and remedies first, but if these methods don't work try systemic granules, pesticide sprays or dusts.

The main diseases affecting roses are mildew, rust, and black spot. The best prevention is a good fall clean up with burning of all rose leaves and any diseased or insect-infested canes. Then spray with dormant spray of lime sulfur. To prevent disease from spreading —after each pruning cut, dip shears into a 50:50 solution of water to Clorox. If your watering method gets rose leaves wet, water only in the morning so leaves won't get mildew. Daily washing (in the morning) also helps keep leaves healthy. There are commercial bug and disease sprays available, but preventative maintenance works wonders.

Fertilizing

Add a half cup of superphosphate or bone meal to the organic matter when planting [4]. Then add a balanced fertilizer when plant is fully leafed out. Fertilize again about

Roses have a "special" fragrance.

If you love roses

Jackson and Perkins highly recommend becoming a member of the American Rose Society. For information write to: The American Rose Society, P.O. box 30,000, Shreveport, Louisiana 71130.

References cited:
[1] Landscaping With Roses J&P [B]
[2] Readers Digest: [Basic] p 204-221
[3] BH & G p 306-335
[4] Home Garden Guide, J&P [A]
[5] Roses for the Home
[6] SWGB p 450-455
[7] Sunset: Roses

Suggested References:
The Principles of Gardening
Roses of Today and Yesterday

every six weeks during growing season or each time a new cycle of blooms start. The last feeding in cold winter areas, should be no later than August 1st, which is about six weeks before the earliest normal hard frost [6]. (One time bloomers need only one application of fertilizer,—in early spring.)

Dry fertilizer such as 5-10-5 is the most popular, or use a prepared rose food. A variation of dry fertilizer is the slow-release fertilizer. If you use it for the second feeding (about a month after applying the 5-10-5), it will provide nutrients only when the soil is warm, so you don't have to fertilize again that season.

Cut Flowers

When cutting flowers, bring a sharp knife and a bucket of warm water with you. and plan to quickly immerse the cut stem in the water. Select a rose that has the outside petals just starting to open. Always cut the stem down to the first leaf containing 5 leaflets (and leave at least two sets of 5 leaflets remaining on the plant to maintain vigor.) Remove all thorns and leaves that will be below water level in the vase. Then in the house, cut rose stem again at a 45° angle. Put roses back in the warm water and leave them there until the water cools, then refrigerate (in water) for 2-3 hours before arranging in vase [4]. Here are some things you can add to the water to make your cut flowers last longer:

- A commercial floral preservative (follow directions on package);
- An Asprin, or 1 drop of Clorox, to keep bacteria level down;
- Or try adding a 1:4 ratio of lemon-lime soda to water, to keep the flower's waterways open and active.

Display roses in a cool place. Add fresh water daily and make sure stems have plenty of water. "Cut roses" can last 3-7 days, depending on the variety. Cut the roses (and most all other flowers) in late afternoon or very early morning when their sugar content is highest.

The artistic quality of a single rose in a vase.

PERENNIAL VINES

An arbor

A vine is a general term for all woody or herbaceous plants that twine or cling and require some support. Annual vines (herbaceous) aren't recommended where there are frequent summer frosts. A Perennial vine is a woody plant producing showy prolific flowers year after year with little care. Most are winter hardy in very cold climates. The tops may die back in winter, but new growth comes back every spring. Some are twining, some clinging, some have tendrils, and some must be tied. Vines are perfect for disguising pillars and porch supports, or they can transform a brick wall, fence, trellis, or side of house into a fantastic wall of color. And many are excellent ground covers. Training climbing plants to grow up chicken wire, an arbor, a trellis, or a string support (tied to upright posts set into the ground), enables them to get more sunlight and bear earlier [1]. And many make wonderful ground covers.

The only maintenance they need is some annual pruning. Some massive plants need pruning to maintain shape (prune while dormant). Some very slow growers need only a few inches trimmed at the ends to encourage dense growth (prune while dormant). But those that flower profusely should be pruned right after blooming to give next years' flower buds maximum time to develop. (Dormant pruning encourages growth, while summer pruning controls growth.)

Perennial Vines PLANT LIST

ACTINIDIA, BOWER (Actinidia arguta) Zone 5. Greenish-white flowers, berries edible. Sun or shade. Dense foliage ideal for screens. Grows fast.

BITTERSWEET (Celastrus sp.) Deciduous. Good ground covers, sun or shade. Likes poor soil. Hardy all zones but adapted only where winters are cold. Grown most for clusters of bright fruit. Birds not interested in the fruit. The vigorous, twining rope-like branches need support. Need constant pruning or will become tangled mass. Cut out fruiting branches in winter, and pinch out tips of vigorous branches in summer.

American Yellow capsules crack in fall to show red berry. Sun. Wall or fence.
Oriental Red and yellow berries. One of best twining vines.

CLEMATIS (Clematis sp.) All will grow in shade.
Armand Zone 7, white flowers in spring.
Big-petal Zone 6, blue flowers in spring.
Curly Zone 6, purple flowers all summer.
Duchess of Edinburgh Zone 6, white flowers.
Durand Zone 6, dark blue flowers midsummer. Dies to ground in winter.
Fragrant tube Zone 4-5, blue flowers late summer. Sun or partial shade.
Golden Zone 5, yellow flowers late spring.
Henryi Zone 5, ivory flowers. A showy climbing vine.
Jackmani Zone 6, purple flowers in midsummer.
Jouin Zone 5, white or purple flowers in midsummer. Vigorous climber.
Nelly Moser Zone 6, mauve flowers.
Pink anemone: Zone 6, red or pink flowers in late spring.
Scarlet Zone 6, scarlet flowers in midsummer. Ornamental native.
Solitary Zone 6, white, blue, or purple flowers in midsummer.
Sweet autumn Zone 5, white flowers in late summer. Dense foliage. Resistant to insects or disease. Good for a bank or slope.
Traveler's joy Zone 5, white flowers in late summer. Good for bank or slope.
Virgin's bower Zone 5, white flowers. in late summer. Native wildflower. **White** Zone 5, white flowers 2nd year, June-July. Drought tolerant.Wildflower.*

Trellis or string support

CROSS VINE (Bignonia capreolata) Zone 6. Red-orange flowers in late spring. Sun or part shade. Evergreen or semi-evergreen. Good for privacy screen.

FIVE-LEAF AKEBIA (see ground cover list)

GRAPE (Vitis sp.) Sun or shade, good for bank plantings.
- **Amur** (V. amurensis) Zone 5. Black grapes in fall, very hardy. Purple fall color.
- **Glory vine** (V. coignetiae) Zone 5. Red fall color. Ideal for privacy screen.
- **River-bank** (V. riparia) Zone 3. Tiny fragrant flowers, purple or black grapes in fall.

GREENBRIER, COMMON or **HORSEBRIAR** (Smilax rotundifolia) Zone 5. Black berries in fall, good for bank plantings, sun or light shade.

HARDENBERGIA (Hardenbergia) Zone 7. An Australian woody vine. Pea family. Compound leaves with 3-5 leaflets. Small, pea-like flowers in long showy clusters (racemes). Fruit is a flat, slightly swollen pod.

HONEYSUCKLE (Lonicera sp.) Sun or shade. For other honeysuckles see shrub list. Halls is the most vigorous and popular.
- **Chinese woodbine:** Zone 6. Bright yellow flowers all summer; fall, red berries.
- **Everblooming:** Zone 4. Purple and yellow flowers all summer.
- **Hall's Japanese:** Zone 5-9. White flowers in late spring through summer, black berries in fall, any soil, sun or shade, also a good ground cover, turns bronze in fall. Ht 18-24'. Vine must be contained by shearing, or it will choke out any shrubs or trees in the area.
- **Henry**: Zone 6. Red, purple, or yellow flowers early summer, black berries in fall, also good as ground cover.
- **Sweet, Italian woodbine:** Zone 6. Fragrant ivory flowers in late spring, orange-red berries in late summer.
- **Trumpet:** Zone 4. Orange-scarlet flowers all summer, red berries in fall.

HYDRANGEA, CLIMBING (Hydrangea anomala 'petiolaris') Zone 5. White flowers in early summer. Will grow in shade but blooms best in sun.

IVY, BOSTON, or JAPANESE CREEPER (Parthenocissus tricuspidata) Zone 5. Dark blue berries in fall, turns scarlet in fall, clings to stones.

IVY, ENGLISH (Hedera helix) Zone 5. Black berries. Clings to walls and stone, or ground cover. Most popular ground cover in CA; dependable, uniform, and neat. Prevents soil erosion. Drought resistant. Thick, leathery, lobed leaves. Many hardy varieties. Evergreen. Sun or shade (shade tolerant). Very susceptible to salt damage. Very slow growing in coldest areas. DEER RESISTANT !

IVY, BALTIC (Hedera helix 'baltica') Zone 5-10. Sun or shade, rich moist soil. Lobed leaves. Hardiest of the English ivies. Good ground cover.

JAPANESE HOP (Humulus scandens) Fast growing. Spreads, pest! Screens, fences, or trellis.

MATRIMONY VINE, COMMON (Lycium halimifolium) Zone 5. Light purple flowers in early summer, orange to red berries in fall. A rambling shrub, must be pruned. Good for bank planting in sun.

RAMBLER ROSE (Rosa sp.) Zone 4. Red, pink and white flowers in late spring. Needs support. Prune old canes right after flowering. Protect in winter. Good for bank plantings in sun. See also Rose list.

ROSE DAPHNE (see daphne, BLE on shrub list)

SILVER LACE (Polygonum auberti) Zone 4. Fragrant white or greenish flowers in long drooping clusters in late summer. Sun, tolerates dry soil.

TRUMPET VINE or TRUMPET CREEPER (Campsis spp.) All zones. Deciduous vines. Vigorous climbers with aerial rootlets that cling tightly to wood, brick and stucco surfaces. Spreads by root suckers; can become a pest. If you dig up the suckers—don't leave even one root or it will grow another plant. Train as large shrub, flowering hedge, or privacy screen. Beautiful arching sprays of orange, yellow, or scarlet trumpet-shaped flowers, bloom Aug-Sept. Dry or wet soil, sun, average water. Fire-resistant.

Trumpet Vine

VIRGINIA CREEPER, WOODBINE (see ground cover list)

WINTERCREEPER (Euonymus fortunei) Zone 5-10. Evergreen vine. Walls, stone, or ground cover for steep banks. Forms dense mat only 6 in. high. Purple variety turns purple-red in fall. Sun or shade. Vegeta variety has orange berries.

WISTERIA (Wisteria sp.) Very hardy in the North.
- **Chinese** (W. sinensis) Zone 5. Blue or purple flowers in spring. Fast growing. Sun, light shade.
- **Japanese** (W. floribunda) Zone 5. Violet, pink, red, or white flowers in spring, many varieties available, grows fast in sun.

References cited:
[1] Readers Digest: Basic

FRUITS, NUTS, and BERRIES

Strawberries

Only the hardiest varieties of fruits, nuts, and berries can grow here, and even then they may not bear fruit every year. A fruit tree described as very hardy and able to grow in Siberia at temperatures of -50°F, may still not be able to endure our changeable spring temperatures. Maybe in Siberia they have a gradual spring warming trend from April to June, but here the weather is not predictable. One day we might have a high of 80°F with a night low of 40°, and the very next day might be a high of 60° with night low of 26° and icy cold north winds. Sometimes we have a week of 75-80° temperatures in April or May, and the fruit trees respond as if it was spring. Their flowers or delicate new leaves are often killed by the next frost.

I had four Manchurian Apricot trees (hardy to -30°F), and Joe Martin in Chester also had some. They bloomed several times in five years, but never set fruit because of freak spring snowstorms, rain, hail, or frost, so we took them out. I have two Carpathian Walnut trees (hardy to -30°F) that have their delicate new spring leaves zapped by frost 2-4 times every spring. Much energy is lost when new leaves are killed so many times. The above two types will probably never set fruit here at Lake Almanor (for nut trees see Tree chapter). Apple trees, raspberries, and strawberries are the most dependable here for producing every year, but when the season is unusually hot or cold they may not produce as well. Warmer areas have the best results with fruit crops: The "Banana Belt" of Lake Almanor's East Shore and Peninsula, plus some areas in Susanville, Greenville, American Valley, Indian Valley, and Honey Lake Valley.

Advantages of Dwarf Trees

Dwarf or semi-dwarf fruit trees have several advantages for the home gardener. These dwarfs can be tended without such expensive equipment like tall ladders. They can be pruned, fertilized, mulched, and harvested with much less effort, time, or expense. They have less trouble with limb breakage, wind damage, or loss of fruit. On a small lot they take up less room. Semi-dwarf apple trees can be planted 12-15 feet apart, while giving the grower more trees and more fruit for the available space, and they have the same size fruit as the larger trees. The short life span is not a disadvantage, since bearing starts much sooner, and care and costs are much less per tree. The biggest disadvantage is its weaker root system, and the more dwarf they are, the weaker the root system is. A rock mulch of stones about 1 1/2 inches (and not smaller) helps to anchor and hold roots and actually helps dwarf apple trees [1]. One disadvantage is deer can reach them better too.

Do You Need to Plant in Pairs ?

Some fruit, nut and berry producing plants have to be planted in pairs to insure fruit production. Some of these are: apples, blueberries, sweet cherries, cherry-plums, elderberries, pears, plums, and native chokecherries.

Even self-pollinating varieties often are more productive with a cross pollinator nearby. Some that are self-pollinating are sour cherries, grapes, peaches, nut trees, quince, small fruits such as: strawberries, gooseberries, raspberries, currants, blackberries, loganberries, boysenberries, and dewberries,

Do They Need Special Soils?

Fruit trees prefer deep, enriched, well-drained soils, but will grow in most soils. Apples, quince, and pears can grow on wet, heavy soils better than most other fruit trees. Plant to same depth as they were in the nursery.

COMPARING apples And Apples

Characteristics	Dwarfted or Semi-Dwarfted tree	Standard tree
Mature size	7-12 feet	20-25 feet
First fruits	2-4 years	4-6 years
Life expectancy	10-15 years	15-20 years
Crop at 3 years*	1/2 bushel (30 lbs.)	none
Crop at 5-6 years	1-2 bushels	0-2 bushels
Crop at 10 years	3-5 bushels	5-15 bushels

**The fruits are all standard size apples. A 1/2 bushel is roughly enough for a family of 4 to eat fresh fruit all year —if the "orchard" includes summer, fall, & winter apples.*

Reprinted from Gardening & Houseplants, 1983 issue of Family Circle Great Ideas, copyright 1983 The Family circle, Inc. Permission granted by Marian Harrison. Article "Two Trees an Orchard Make", p 24, by James F. Gauss.

Planting Distance

How far apart should fruit trees be planted? ***Apple trees*** should be set 30' apart, while ***Peach, apricot, cherry, plum, and pear*** should be planted 15' apart [2]. Some people prefer to set apple trees 40' apart, and set smaller trees such as peaches, plums and cherries in among the apple trees as fillers. Plan your landscaping before you plant, not after!

Pruning techniques

Prune fruit trees before planting, trimming both roots and tops equally. Always prune just above a strong, healthy bud. When properly pruned, fruit trees should not have more than 3-4 main branches. As the tree grows, prune out the crossed branches, bad crotches, and limbs and branches which rub against each other. (See chapter on Pruning.)

Protection from snow -breakage and sunburn.

Snow protection is necessary for young trees, and sunburn protection is necessary for all fruit trees. The tree trunk should be painted with water-base white paint, as white paint reduces the heat by reflecting it away from the tree. This helps prevent trees from blooming too early in Spring only to get their tender new leaves "zapped" by frost. Sunburn causes bark to peel away and crack, reducing the vigor of the tree and opening wounds for pests to enter. See also Microclimates chapter.

Pest Prevention

A regular spraying program is the best way to combat pests and disease in home gardens or orchards (see Insect Pest chapter). Many people think this is too complicated or too much trouble. Spraying on a regular basis will stop problem insects before they have time to do damage, and will make a big difference in quality and quantity of fruit produced. Home Garden sprayers and chemicals are available in catalogs and hardware stores. For more information see Garden Pest chapter.

Fruits, Nuts, and Berries PLANT LIST:

APPLE TREE (Malus pumila). Very hardy. The cultivated apple tree. Many varieties:

EARLY: Lodi, Arkansas Black, Beacon, Yellow Transparent, Red Gravenstein, Tydeman Red, Earliblaze, Paula Red. ("Very early" varieties will likely bloom too early in most locations and be killed by frost).

MEDIUM:

Jonathan types: Blackjon, Jonared, Nured, Idared, Melrose, MacIntosh. Yellow Delicious types: Smoothee, Golden Delicious.

Red Delicious types: Miller Sturdeespur, Redspur, Royal, Starkcrimson, Topred, Wellspur, and Red King.

LATE: Newtown Pippin, Ruby, Melrose. Rome Beauty types: Gallia Beauty, Red Rome, Nero, Nured, Seeando 262, Stayman Winesap. ("Late" varieties may not have long enough growing season for fruit to mature).

DWARF: East Malling VII, Malling 26 (M26)— Support must be provided.

SEMI-DWARF: Malling Merton 106 (MM106).

Some apple varieties need a pollenizer (another tree), and some are self-fruitful. If a pollenizing variety grows in your neighborhood, you don't need to plant one in your yard. Golden Delicious is an excellent pollenizer for other varieties. Frank Rice in Chester grows about 7-8 apple varieties in his yard. The colder the weather, the stronger the buds and the better the apples. Golden Delicious produces fruit without a pollenizer, starts bearing earlier, and keeps well; in contrast to Red Delicious which becomes mealy if not stored below 50°F. The Golden D. is good for eating and cooking, but Red D. is best used for eating only [3].

APRICOT TREE (Prunus armenica) Zone 7. Varieties: Manchurian (good to -30°F.), Moongold and Sungold are good to -25° or -30°F. Fragrant pink blossoms bloom in spring. Good for fruit and as a shade tree. Manchurian bush varieties are even hardier; fruits form on very young plants, and they need little space. These plants are available from Lakeland Nurseries Sales, Hanover, PA 17331.

BLACKBERRY (Rubus). Very hardy. Varieties: Boysenberry, Logan, Nectar, Ollalie. The Ebony King brand do well here. They like rich, well drained, moist soil. Soak roots in bucket before planting. Plant 4' apart, in rows 6' apart, and about 2" deeper than at the nursery. Spread roots well and pack soil. After planting, prune to within a few inches of the ground, and mulch to prevent weeds. Plants don't need trellis the first season.

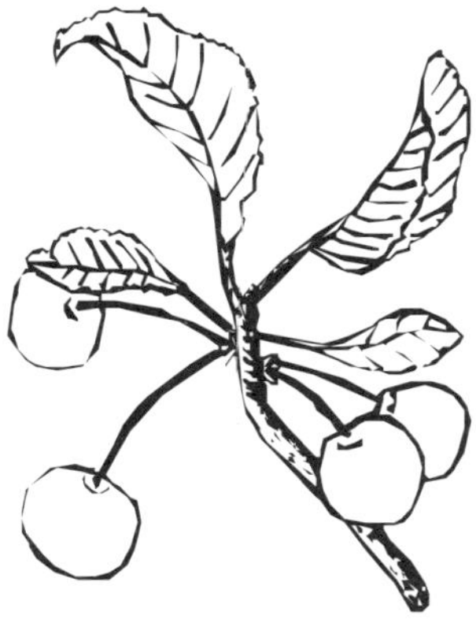

Cherry

When new growth is 2' tall, pinch off tips to encourage branching. In the fall after growth has stopped, prune back half of all the new growth and cover plants with about 2" of straw or similar mulch just before ground freezes. Early next spring trim the canes back to 10", and when vines begin to bud, build a 3-wire trellis with the top wire 5' high and bottom wire 2' high.

Weave vines carefully in a fan shape on these wires. They don't need much pruning. Remove the smaller, weaker canes, and shorten the longer ones at the time you put canes on trellis wires. After harvest, remove canes that bore fruit, and dig out sick-looking bushes. Propagate from root cuttings. Plant a few extra vines if you want to share the fruit with local birds. Thornless varieties are recommended for the small gardener, unless you are purposely planting a barrier [4] or plant them at the far end of your yard.

BLUEBERRY (Vaccinium corymbosum) Zone 7. Varieties: Blueray, Corvelle, Berkeley. Those maturing mid-season (as opposed to early or late) do best here. In the coldest areas, must have an acid, well-drained, humus-rich, moist soil. For best pollination, plant two varieties. Choose a mixture of varieties with some: early, mid-season and late to extend the harvest season. Shade tolerant. Plant in early spring, spacing about 4' apart and rows 6' apart. Prune only to thin, cutting 1/3 of the old canes off at ground level. Leave 6-8 canes on a mature plant. Mulch in fall with peat moss or leaves. Joe Martin grows blueberries in Chester. Use Ross Garden Net over them, unless you want to feed hungry birds. Deciduous shrub.

BOYSENBERRY - see blackberry.

CHERRY TREE (Prunus) Hardy. Varieties: Sour Cherry: English Morello, Montmorency, and North Star (makes good pies). Sweet Cherry: Bing, Black Giant, Black Tartarian, Chinook, Hardy Giant, Lambert, North Star, Royal Ann, Sam, and Van. Use Van as a pollinator for the others. The root stock of Mahaleb and Mazzard may be used. Don't prune cherry trees except to remove broken or decayed wood, and for shaping. Bush Cherries are low growing. Cherries cover the bush from the ground up, are excellent eating when fresh, or preserved in jams and jellies. The Cherries are loved by 49 species of birds.

COWBERRY (Vaccinium vitis-idaea). Hardy. Evergreen shrub, slow grower to 12 inches tall. Spreads by underground runners until is about 3 feet wide. Leaves shiny dark green; new growth brightly tipped with red or orange. White or pink flowers in clusters, bloom in May. Edible but sour berries, good in preserves. Small scale ground cover, informal edging. Full sun in cool-summer areas. Shade tolerant.

CRABAPPLE TREE (Malus). Hardy. Ornamental, flowering tree, beautiful all seasons. Many species. Varieties: Hyslop, Transcendant, Whitney. Small to medium size tree 10-30' tall. I have two of these trees in my yard. Leaves vary from deep green to nearly purple. White to pink flowers in spring. Small round fruits in red, purple, orange, or yellow; used for jam. The crabapples are loved by 29 species of birds.

CRANBERRY (Vaccinium macrocarpon) Zones 2-5. Hardy. Prostrate creeping vine. Evergreen, blunt leaves. Long stems. Fruit bright red, 3/4 inch in diameter. Commercial source of our cranberry.

CURRANT (Ribes) Hardy. Varieties: Red Lake, Perfection, and Cascade. Rich, moist soil. Sun or partial shade. Plant in spring or fall (if winters are severely cold, plant in spring). Set plants 4-6' apart. Trim tops back to 6-12" after planting, and mulch to reduce weeds. Plant in area where plants won't be disturbed. All very hardy.

GOOSEBERRY (Ribes) Hardy. Varieties: Champion, Welcome, and Pickwell. The latter two varieties are grown by Joe Martin in Chester. Culture is the same as for currants. I have gooseberries growing wild in my front yard, but the wild variety has long thorns on the fruit. Also gooseberries can host one life stage of the blister rust fungus that attacks young Sugar pines. So don't grow it near Sugar pines.

GRAPE, American (Vitis labrusca) Deciduous vine. Grow hardest varieties: Concord, Niagara, Catawba, Golden Muscat, Pierce, and Niabell. Frank Brown of the Lake Almanor Peninsula grows grapes. These grow best in warmer areas. Choose hardiest variety. For best results plant two or more varieties. For wind protection, tie it to a trellis. Full sun. Soil enriched with well-aged manure or compost.

Before planting, trim tops and roots leaving only two buds above ground surface. Set plants 5' apart in rows 10' apart. For the first summer only let the main stems grow without support.

DO NOT PRUNE GRAPES IN SUMMER! Prune in winter, while plants are dormant, but before it gets too cold. Cut out all old wood which has borne fruit. Train up on trellises, stakes, fences, arbors, porches or to cover side of building. Of the new canes (just started last spring), remove all but four canes from each clump, training two in each direction on the trellis wires (or other support). Cut these four back to 3-4 buds each. From these buds (found at the joints) come new shoots that bear leaves and grapes the following summer. Four of the new shoots will be used the next winter in the same way.

Grapes

Some variety of grape may be grown in every soil or climate where tree, bush, or bramble fruits are planted [5]. Some grapes can withstand down to -20°F. See also Perennial vine list. Dust grapes with sulfur powder if they get mildew.

HUCKLEBERRY, RED (Vaccinium parvifolium) Zone 6. Deciduous shrub. Often mistaken for the blueberry, and similar to red currant. Native. Used for jam or to attract birds (robins, sapsuckers, waxwigs, and bluebirds). Beautiful pri

Pruning of grape vines.

vacy screen for outdoor living areas. Requires little care. Partial shade and acid soil. Most of the fruit sold in markets is collected from wild plants, not cultivated ones. The ornamental species G. brachycera is a ground cover in shaded, peaty areas [6].

NECTARINE TREE (Prunus persica nucipersica) Zone 7. A smooth-skinned, hairless peach. Their culture is same as for the peach. Some say the nectarine flavor is richer and sweeter than the peach. The variety most recommended is Fantasia, although less hardy varieties: Flavortop, Independence, Late La Grande, Le Grand, Regal Grand, and Red Grand are also recommended [7].

PEACH TREE (Prunus persica) Zone 7. Varieties: Reliance, Alamar, Indian Blood, Fay, Red Haven, Elberta, Rio Oso Gem, Red Glove, Suncrest, Regina, and Redtop. Do best in warmer areas where late frosts aren't a problem, but you can get a successful crop once every 3-4 years in marginal climates. Pruning: Cut back the leader and all branches very short so they grow low.

PEAR TREE (Pyrus) Zone 7. Varieties: Bartlett, Max-Red Bartlett, Bosc, Anjou, Comice, El Dorado, Seckel, Winter Nelis and Kiefer. Bosc is a long neck, yellow russet ripening two weeks after the Bartlett, and will store until Christmas. The Bartlett will ripen in August and is excellent for canning or fresh use. Kiefer is fire blight resistant, but only fair in quality. Grow pears in protected warmer areas. Cornell Kurtz (East Shore) and Frank Brown (L.A. Peninsula) have pear trees (both live in The Banana Belt). Some pear tree varieties can survive down to -20°F.

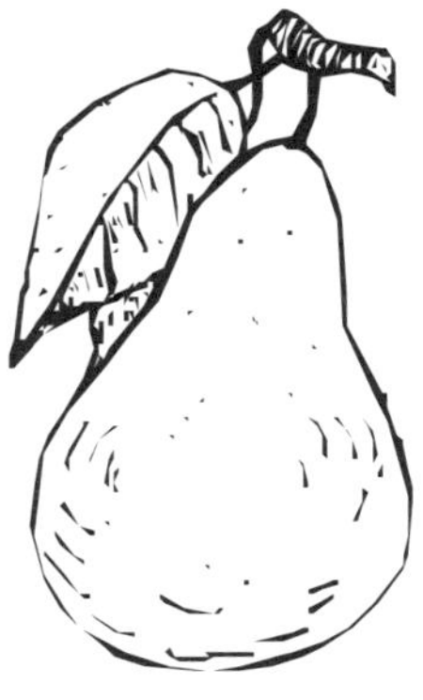

Pear

PLUM TREE (Prunus) Zone 7. Varieties: Italian, Stanley, French and Damson. Two root stocks are available for plums: Marianna 2624 and Myro 29C. Two or more plants are needed for pollination. They do best in warmer areas where late frosts aren't a problem. Don't prune Plum trees except to remove broken or decayed wood, and for shaping. Plum trees tend to get many bug pests, so a strict spraying "preventative maintenance" program is very important.

RASPBERRY (Rubus) Hardy. Varieties: Willamette, Washington, Ranier, September and Indian Summer. The latter two are known as everbearing and produce fruit all summer. Raspberries need lots of water. Don't plant near vegetable gardens as they roots spread and can take over.

Planting and culture is similar to blackberries (Plant 3' apart, in rows 6' apart). Trellis: 2 posts, 2 cross arms 18" long on each post, with wires stretched from end of cross arms. The lower wire and cross arms should be 2' above the ground, top wires about 3' up.

In August after berry crop is harvested, cut out old fruiting canes (when their leaves turn yellow and curl, and fruit production has almost stopped). This assures a good crop on the new canes next year. Keep only the healthiest 3-4 of the new canes per clump and they will be more productive, have better air circulation —thus get less mildew. To protect from wind, bind together and tie to one of top wires on the trellis. —and cut back to 5' tall. Cut laterals back to 2-3 buds. If you plant closer together than 3' they will be less productive and get mildew.

STRAWBERRY (Fragaria) Choose hardy varieties: Washington, Tioga, Sequoia, Mastadon, Shasta, Northwest, Quinalt, Improved Rockhill, and Red Rich Everbearing. Everbearing varieties are best for severe winter, high altitude climates with late frosts. Strawberries are perennials that bear 2-3 summers, then become too crowded and need to be divided.

Keep runners cut off unless you want to start new plants. Baby plants are attached to the parent by runners or stolons (like an umbilical cord). Cut the runner, throw away (or give away) the parent plant, and transplant the baby plant into a different, enriched bed, because strawberry plants are heavy feeders (need lots of nutrients). If you can't put them in a different bed, refresh their bed with organic matter and a 10-10-10 fertilizer before replanting. Select babies having the most and healthiest roots. Planting and transplanting are best done in the fall. Strawberry plants planted in the fall will bloom the next summer, but those planted in the spring will probably not bloom the same year. See Planting chapter.

In the spring after plants start to grow, work some 5-10-5 fertilizer into the soil. Pale new leaves indicate need for nitrogen fertilizer, while dark green indicates an adequate supply. Don't use high nitrogen fertilizers during fruit production, or you get too much leaf growth, and too few strawberries. Mulch around plants in spring to conserve moisture, reduce weeds, and keep berries clean. Since strawberries don't hybridize, many varieties can be planted in one bed, extending the fruit season. If winter gets very cold without snow to act as a blanket, put a 3-5" mulch of pine needles over the strawberry plants for a winter protection. Many local gardeners have extra strawberry thinnings in the fall that can be yours for the asking.

WALNUT TREE —See Deciduous trees chapter.

References cited:
[1] Best Methods for Growing Fruits & Berries
[2] Gurney's Grow-it-Guide
[3] Sunset Western Garden Book [SWGB]
[4] Growing Berries & Grapes at Home (Clarke).
[5] How to Grow Vegetables & Fruits BOM
[6] The Garden Dictionary (Taylor)
[7] Growing Fruits & Nuts in L P & S C

HARDY FERNS

Growing hardy ferns is amazingly easy. Since ferns occur all over the world with majority found in the tropics, be sure to choose hardy ferns. Ferns are valued for their fresh green color and the natural effect they create. They die back in fall to reappear in the spring. "Height" is usually the same as the "spread", because you are measuring the length of the frond (fern leaf). Height ranges from the tiny maidenhair spleenwort (only 5 inches) to the majestic royal fern (6 feet tall). Plant them about 12 inches apart for best effect. Many are evergreen such as shield ferns, and asplenium.

Ferns need light soil, with peat moss or leaf-mold added to keep the soil loose and crumbly, as well as plenty of moisture. Most will grow in any soil, but have to have good drainage, be shaded from midday sun, and be protected from wind (i.e. at the north side of house or fence, or in shade of a tree). A shady or partially shady area is usually preferable (ferns require more sun in the north and partial shade in warmer areas); with the exception of hay scented fern which can grow in almost full sun. Mix ferns in varying sizes, shapes of fronds, and shades of green to form a fern border; nice background for shade-loving flowering plants (i.e. bleeding heart, astilbe, viola, columbine, primrose, or lilies); as a wall or foundation plant; in bare spots under trees; or as a good ground cover.

Weed by hand so as not to disturb the fern's shallow root system. Use three inches of fresh mulch (leaf mold, peat moss or compost) around the ferns in the fall and again in the spring. In the spring, sprinkle fertilizer (10-10-10) around the fern before applying the mulch. Also in spring, cut off all dead fronds down to crown to make room for the new shoots.

Dryopteris (the shield ferns) are drought resistant, and are hardy ferns for the outdoor garden. Some shield ferns are put under the genus Polystichum, while others are still called Aspidium or Thelypteris by dealers [1].

One source for ordering ferns is Wayside Gardens Catalog [2]. Plant names were based on SWGB, Reader's Digest: Basic, BH &G, and Taylor.

Fern PLANT LIST:

ALASKA; or Old English Hedge Fern (Polystichum setiferum 'Angulare') Zones 5-9. Very hardy. Usually damp shade. Prefers sun in the north, partial shade in warmer areas. Dark green fronds. Ht 1-2'. Propagate by rhizomes.

BRACKEN (Pteridium aquilinum 'lanuginosus') Ht 16-32". Shade. Well-drained, moist or dry soil. Large coarse fern. Good for background plantings. Very common native in Foothill and Yellow Pine Zones, especially on acid soils. Propagate by rhizomes (see Transplanting wild ferns, above).

CHRISTMAS FERN; or Dagger Fern (Polystichum acrostichoides) Zones 3-9. Any well-drained soil. Likes dry shade or moist sunny places. Ht 12-30". Deep green fronds.

Very popular. Evergreen. Excellent for cutting. Often listed under Dryopteris. Propagate by rhizomes.

CINNAMON FERN (Osmunda cinnamomea) Zones 3-8. Light shade. In wet swampy land will grow 72" tall, but also thrives in dry shade. Average height 30-60". Prefers well-drained, damp, acid soil. Fronds turn cinnamon brown. Deciduous. Very hardy. New fronds are white-woolly. First fern up in the spring.

CLIFF BRAKE FERN (Pellaea atropurpurea) Ht 12". Fronds tough, leathery. Native. Good in hardy fern garden, preferably on a dry limestone rock wall.

CLIMBING FERN; or Hartford Fern (Lygodium palmatum) A vine-like fern, climbing or sprawling. Requires shade, an acid soil of 4—4.5 pH, and needs heavy mulch. Prefers growing among mountain laurel or blueberry bushes or other high acid loving plants. Feathery foliage.

DEER FERN (Blechnum spicant) Very Hardy. Evergreen. Shade. Moist, acid soil. Suitable anywhere except in alkaline soils. Ht 12".

DRYOPTERIS—no common name (Dryopteris erythrosora) Very hardy all zones. Variation in color: young fronds are first red, then deep green in late spring and summer. Shade. Spreading form. Ht 18-24".

FANCY FERN (Dryopteris intermedia) Very hardy. Evergreen. Ht 24". Shade. Neutral to acid soil. Chosen for dark blue-green fronds.

FRAGILE FERN (Cystopteris fragilis) Very hardy. Deciduous. Ht 8". Shade. Neutral soil. Grows on soil or in rocks. Called fragile because of its appearance.

GOLDIE'S FERN (Dryopteris goldieana) Shade. Neutral soil. Ht 4'. Evergreen. Hardy. Large, impressive. One of finest of our native ferns (Eastern N.A.). Fronds in dense crown

HAY SCENTED FERN (Dennstaedtia punctilobula) Zones 3-8. Sword-shaped lacy fronds. Light shade, or almost full sun. Any well-drained soil or moisture. Ht 16-36". Quick spreading ground cover, useful on slopes. Hardy. Deciduous.

HOLLY FERN, GIANT; or Sword Fern (Polystichum munitum) Rare. Damp shade. Native in Yellow Pine and Red Fir forests to 7000 ft. elevation. (Pacific Coast). Found in canyons, and in dry rock crevices. Ht 1-4'. Smaller varieties to 15" tall on some talus slopes. Hardy. Evergreen. Beautiful plant with glossy dark-green leaves. Propagated by rhizomes. Grows well in Northwest. Prefers acid soil.

Bracken fern

Deer fern

Fragile fern

Hayscented fern

HOLLY FERN, MOUNTAIN (Polystichum lonchitis) Damp shade. Hardy. Evergreen. Ht 2'. Fronds stiff and leathery. Native to North America.

INTERRUPTED FERN (Osmunda claytonia) Zones 4-8. Shade or partial sun. Well-drained, damp, acid soil. Ht 2-4'. Graceful, large fronds in clusters. Grows slowly. Very young wooly fronds (fiddles) are edible. Plant 2 feet apart.

LACE FERN (Cheilanthus gracillima) A tufted small fern with fronds only 4" long. Dry rocky slopes and rock crevices. Native in Red Fir and Subalpine Zones 6700-7800 ft. Western U.S. Use in fern gardens.

LADY FERN, CALIFORNIA (Athyrium felix-femina) Zones 3-8. Shade. Delicate lacy fronds. Any well-drained, moist soil. Any exposure. A good background for smaller ferns, and effective with azaleas and dogwoods. Ht 16-32". Wide fronds. Most common native fern in Yellow Pine and Red Fir Zones 5500-6800 feet. (Pacific Coast). Transplants easily.

MAIDENHAIR FERN, AMERICAN; Five Finger; or Western Maidenhair (Adiantum pedatum) Zones 3-8. Very popular. Light shade. Moist, stony banks. Well-drained, soil. Tolerates dry shade but grows taller with more moisture. Ht 1-2'. Lacy fronds on black wiry stems. Very hardy. Deciduous. Native to Pacific Coast. Excellent in containers or shaded garden beds.

MAIDENHAIR FERN, CALIFORNIA (Adiantum jordani) Ht 2'. Native in central Sierra at 2000 to 3000 ft in moist sites. More common in Coastal Ranges.

MALE FERN (Dryopteris filix-mas) Shade. Toughest and suitable for driest, most hopeless spots. Ht 12-30". Well-drained, moist, rocky soil. Beautiful under trees. Fronds, almost 1 ft. wide, in dense crowns. Nearly evergreen. Very popular garden plant. Offered also in crested and in dwarf forms.

NEW YORK FERN (Thelypteris noveboracensis) Zone 2. Grey-green fronds. Ht 6-36". Many varieties. Shady side of walls, or

Maidenhair fern, American

Ostrich fern

Royal fern

Shield fern, Crested

quick spreading ground cover. Well-drained, slightly acid, rich soil. Deciduous. Hardy. Light shade. Formerly called Dryopteris noveboracensis.

OSTRICH FERN (Matteuccia struthiopteris, Pteretis struthiopteris) Zones 2-8. Ostrich plume-like fronds. Shade or partial sun. Needs well-drained, moist to wet (boggy), rich soil. Ht 2-5'. Impressive tall and stately fern. Propagated by rhizomes. Use in backgrounds. Likes mixture of swamp muck and fine loam. It soon forms a dense growth. Mulch until plants are established. Dimorphic fronds. Hardy. Deciduous.

ROYAL FERN (Osmunda regalis) Zones 3-9. Prefers wet ground (i.e. lake borders, bogs, meadowland). Open shade. Well-drained, moist to wet, acid soil. Hardy. Deciduous. Tall dramatic clumps. Ht 4-6'. Young growth is wine red changing to green as it matures. Brown spore clusters look like flowers. Nice contrast with other plants.

SHIELD FERN (Polystichum. scopulinum) Damp shade. Native to rocky places in Red Fir Zone, 7200-7900 ft. (Pacific Coast). Rare.

SHIELD FERN, CRESTED (Dryopteris cristata) Hardy. Evergreen. Shade. Acid, boggy soil. Ht 2-3'. Leaflets look like steps. Beautiful feathery erect fronds. Edgings for walks in damp woodlands. North temperate zone.

SHIELD FERN, PRICKLY; or Braun's Holly Fern (Polystichum brauni) Damp shade. Thick root stock. Needs rich, neutral to acid soil. Evergreen. Hardy. Beautiful glossy, dark green leaves. Ht. 2'.

Shield fern, Prickly

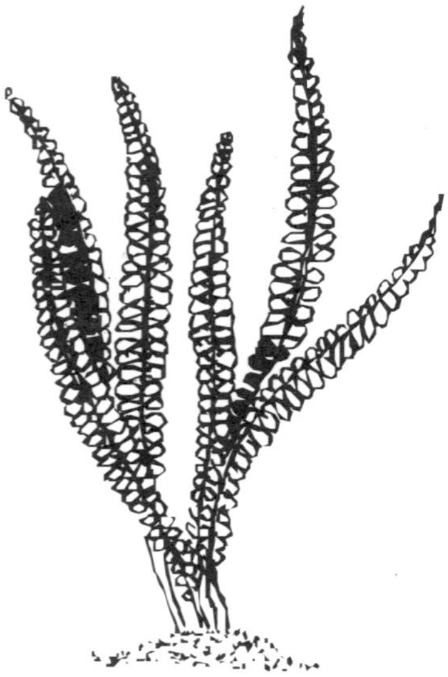

Spleenwort, Maidenhair

SPLEENWORT, EBONY (Asplenium platyneuron) Zones 3-8. Light shade. Extremely hardy. Evergreen. Very unusual variegated effect caused by two types of foliage: one low and sterile (only 6" tall). and the other erect fertile fronds almost 2 ft tall. Prefers well-drained moist soil but will tolerate some dryness. Plant in rocks.

SPLEENWORT, MAIDENHAIR (Asplenium trichomanes) Ht 3-6". Shade. Well-drained, dry, neutral to acid soil. Hardy. Evergreen. Best in rock crevices.

WOOD FERN; or Shield Fern (Dryopteris arguta) Dark green, finely cut fronds. Hardy. Evergreen. Avoid overwatering! Ht 2'. Native to Yellow Pine Zone 2,000-6,000 ft., under logs or overhanging rocks.

WOOD FERN, EVERGREEN; or Marginal Shield Fern (Dryopteris marginalis) Shade. Likes rocks and stones. Prefers neutral or acid, well-drained, dry soil. Makes good ground cover. Has gray-green, thick fronds. Ht 2-3'. Fronds in dense crown. Nearly evergreen. Easy to cultivate. Popular with Florists.

WOOD FERN, SIERRA (Thelypteris nevadensis) Grows on wet slopes in deep shade. Native in Butterfly Valley near Quincy, CA.

WOOD FERN, TOOTHED (Dryopteris spinulosa) Zones 4-9. Shade. Very similar to the evergreen wood fern but requires more moisture. Strong clumps. Ht 30". Beautiful lacy fronds. Easy to grow.

WOODSIA (Woodsia scopulina) Dry rocky ledges and rock gardens. A low growing background or ground cover. Needs little moisture. Lance shaped, dark green fronds. Native from 4,000 to 12,000 ft. in rocky places. Rare.

References cited:

[1] The Garden Dictionary (Taylor)
[2] Wayside Gardens Catalog

ANNUALS

California Poppy

Many perennials able to be grown in other parts of the country, may have to grown as summer annuals in cold winter areas —if they aren't frost hardy. **Annuals** are herbaceous plants that grow, flower, and die within one year. Easy to grow. Grown for long blooming season. Keep faded flowers picked to insure continuous blooming all season till frost. Most will reseed themselves (i.e. cosmos, marigold, and kitchen herbs). "Half-hardy" (not frost tolerant) annual seed must be planted indoors (or buy transplants), and transplanted outdoors later when all chance of frost is past,—around June 1st (see Propagation chapter). Seed for "Hardy" annuals can be sown outdoors in spring,—around June 1st. "Super-hardy" annuals are called **biennials** because they can live overwinter into a second season. After the first hard frost, remove all dead plant material (or bugs will lay their eggs in it). Plant names were based on The Garden Dictionary (Taylor) and Better Homes & Gardens.

Annual PLANT LIST

ACROCLINIUM (see helipterum)

AFRICAN DAISY or CAPE DAISY (Dimorphotheca, Arctotis or Osteospermum) Half hardy. Daisy-like flowers on stems 2' tall. Mixed colors, some bicolors. Full sun. Light sandy soil. Cut flowers. Drought resistant.*

AGERATUM or FLOSSFLOWER (Ageratum houstonianum) Half hardy. Sun or partial shade. Borders, edgings, rock gardens, small beds, and indoor pot plants. Ht 3-6". Blue, white or pink.

ALYSSUM, annual (see sweet alyssum)

AMARANTH or TASSEL FLOWER (Amaranthus caudatus) Half Hardy. Ht 3-6'. Red tassel-like flowers. Full sun, any soil. Background plant in mass planting or against a wall. Drought resistant. Likes long hot growing season.

AMETHYST (Browallia spp) All zones. Hardy annual, able to over- winter as perennial in warmer areas. Known for its' blue flowers. Clusters of bright blue, violet or white flowers 1/2 -2 inches long and wide. Prefers warm shade or filtered sunlight (shade tolerant). Hanging baskets, pots, cut flowers. Order seed from mail order. Sow seeds indoors in early spring, plant outdoors for summer, then cut back and put in pots as house plant for winter, and it will continue producing flowers.

AMMOBIUM or WINGED EVERLASTING (Ammobium) Half hardy. White flowers, yellow center. Dried flowers. In everlasting group, Composite fam.. Ht 2'. Full sun, sandy soil.

ASTER, CHINA (Callistephus chinensis) Half hardy. Cut flowers. Blooms July till the first hard frost. Varieties vary Ht 8" to 3'. Sun or light shade. Rich, well-drained soil. Shallow roots need mulch. Gets fungus diseases. Heavy feeder.

ASTER, WILD (Aster tanacetifolius) Daisy-like bright purple flowers, yellow centers, bloom July-Oct. Good for cut flowers. Ht 1-3'. Full sun. Very well drained, gravelly or sandy, soil. Drought tolerant after established. Plant seeds in fall.*

BABY BLUE-EYES (Nemophila menziesii) Hardy. Blue flowers with white centers. Plants in mounds 6-8" diameter. Ground cover, cut flowers, edging plant, or with flowering bulbs. Prefers cool, lightly shaded area.

BABY'S BREATH (Gypsophila elegans) Hardy. Ht 15-24". Much-branched stem. White or pink flowers. Use for fresh or dried flowers. Easy to grow. Full sun. Does best in poor soil.

BABY'S BREATH, NEW (Gypsophila muralis) New variety. Very quick to flower. Good in garden and as cut flower. Has larger flowers on smaller 2' plant than perennial G. paniculata.

BACHELOR'S BUTTON or CORNFLOWER, annual (see dusty miller on perennial list)

BARTONIA (Bartonia aurea or Mentzelia lindleyi) Hardy annual. Ht 1-4'. Flowers bright yellow, very fragrant. Open in evenings, close in morning.

BEGONIA, WAX (Semperflorens) Half hardy. Grown as an annual. Sun or light shade. Start seed in January and transplant in early summer. Continuous bloom. Beds, borders, and boxes.

BELLS OF IRELAND or SHELL FLOWER (Molucella laevis) Half hardy. Ht 2". Tiny, white, bell-shaped flowers. Sunny, well-drained, moist soil. Cut or dried flowers. Bell-shaped bracts.

BISHOPS'S FLOWER (Ammi majus) White lacy flowers in beautiful, large, 6" umbels. Blooms Aug.-Sept. Fresh or dried flower arrangements. Looks like Queen Anne's Lace. Leaves finely divided. Easy to grow. Ht 2-3'. Full sun. Any soil, including clay. Requires little water. Plant seeds in spring.*

BLANKET FLOWER (see gaillardia on perennial list)

BLAZING STAR (Mentzelia lindleyi) All zones. Large, showy, star-shaped, bright, yellow flowers with orange or reddish center ring, and big brush of yellow stamens. Blooms April-June. Full sun. Ht 1-4'. Leaves light green, rough with short hairs. Any site. Drought tolerant. Water until established, then stop watering. Plant seed in fall.

BLUE MARGUERITE (see felicia on perennial list)

BLUE BELLS, CALIFORNIA or Desert Blue Bells (Phacelia campanularia) Very early. Popular. Bright blue, bell-shaped flowers, bloom July-Aug. Grayish-green foliage. Ht 1-3'. Very adaptable. Prefers rocky soils. Tolerates hot, dry conditions. Regular watering. Plant seeds early spring.*

BLACK-EYED SUSAN (Thunbergia alata) Tropical vine, tender annual. Daisy-like flowers in yellow, orange or white, bloom all summer. Sun or shade. Temperatures below 50°F may kill. Needs long growing season. Sold in Susanville Nursery. Only grown in warmer microclimates or Zone 7.

BLACK-EYED SUSAN (Rudbeckia hirta)—see biennial list.

BROWN-EYED SUSAN (Rudbeckia triloba) not grow here,—grows in the South).

CALENDULA or POT MARIGOLD (Calendula officinalis) Half hardy. Garden accent or cut flowers. Well-drained soil. Orange-yellow flowers bloom spring till frost. (see marigold).

CALIFORNIA POPPY (Eschscholzia californica) Hardy. Easy to grow. Any soil, full sun. Blooms early. Ht 1-2'. Likes cool weather. Reseeds itself. Also a charming, pale-yellow dwarf species (E. caespitosa). Both bloom July-Sept.*

CALLIOPSIS (see coreopsis on perennial list)

CANDYTUFT (see ground cover list)

CANTERBURY BELLS (see biennial list)

CAPE DAISY (see dimorphotheca)

CARNATIONS or CLOVE PINK (see dianthus)

CATCHFLY (Silene armeria) Clusters of bright, pink flowers, bloom June-Aug. Bushy plants. Easy to grow. Ht 2-3'. Partial to full sun. Any soil. Survives on lesser amounts of water. Plant seeds in spring. Reseeds nicely.*

CELOSIA (see cockscomb)

CENTAUREA, annuals (see dusty miller on perennial list)

CHINESE HOUSES (Collinsia heterophylla) Purple and white snap-dragon-like blossoms, bloom Aug.-Sept. Ht 1-2'. Partial to full sun. Any soil, but does best in moist, loamy soil. Plant seeds in spring*.

CHRYSANTHEMUM (see painted daisy on perennial list)

CHRYSANTHEMUM, GARLAND (Chrysanthemum coronarium) Young green leaves are delicious steamed. Prolific, beautiful, golden daisies on 2-4' stems, bloom Aug.-Sept. Prefer full sun. Well-drained soil. Tolerates dry conditions, but thrives with regular watering. Plant seeds in spring. *

CLARKIA, FAREWELL-TO-SPRING or GODETIA (Clarkia amoena, Godetia amoena, or G. grandiflora) Beautiful clusters of bright-pink, red, white, crimson, or carmine flowers, bloom July-Sept. Easy to grow. Ht 2-3'. Full sun or partial shade. Cool, light, moist sandy soil. Drought tolerant once established. Will survive mid-summer frosts. Plant seeds in spring. Borders, beds, and cut flowers.

CLARKIA or MOUNTAIN GARLAND (Clarkia unguiculata, or Clarkia elegans.) Hardy. Flowers vary from salmon-pink to purple, bloom July-Sept. Cut flowers. Easy to grow. Blooms better when crowded. Ht 18-36". Prefers semi-shade and dry soil. Tolerates wider range of conditions than C. amoena, including partial sun and heavier soils. Will survive harsh, mid-summer frosts. Plant seeds in spring.*

CLEOME (Cleome spinosa) Half hardy. Ht 3-6'. Pink, rose, or white flowers. Full sun, dry soil. Screen or patio tub plant. Unusual seedpods for dried arrangements.

COCKSCOMB (Celosia) Half hardy. Striking flowers in tall plumes or fan-like clusters. Mixed colors. Any soil. Drought tolerant. They keep color well as dried flowers. Dwarfs for edgings and borders; tall ones for mass plantings.

CONVOLVULUS (see morning-glory on ground cover list)

COREOPSIS or TICKSEED (see perennial list)

CORNFLOWER, annual (see dusty miller on perennial list)

COSMOS (Cosmos bipinnatus) Half hardy. Sow seed outdoors after frost danger has past. Summer and fall blooming varieties. Any soil (slightly dry). Sun or partial shade. Daisy-like flowers in many colors. Shrub-like. Ht 4-6'. Background plant, temporary hedge, and cut flowers. Reseeds itself.*

DAHLIA (Dahlia) Half hardy annual. Ht 12-20". Taller varieties are grown as perennials. Full sun. Rich, moist, well-drained soil. Bedding plants and cut flowers. Don't confuse this with the bulb Dahlia.

DELPHINIUM or LARKSPUR (see perennial list)

DIANTHUS or PINK (Dianthus) Generally hardy annuals. Keep trimmed for continuous bloom.

- **Sweet William or Bunch Pink** (D. barbatus) see biennial list.
- **Carnation or Clove Pink**, (D. caryophullus) Half hardy. Pick hardest varieties.
- **China Pink or Indian Pink** (D. chinensis) Ht 12-18". Red, white or lilac flowers.
- **Maiden Pink or Meadow Pink** (D. deltoides) Ht 4-12". Turf-forming mat. Red, pink flowers.
- **Grass or Scotch Pink** (D. plumerius) Mat forming, Ht 9-18". Fragrant rose-pink to purplish, or white with variegated colored. Petals fringed.

DUSTY MILLER (see perennial list)

EUPHORBIA (see snow-on-the-mountain, on gr. cover list)

EVERLASTING (see helipterum)

FELICIA or BLUE MARGUERITE DAISY (see peren. list)

FEVERFEW or MATRICARIA (see perennial list)

FLAX, SCARLET (Linum grandiflorum rubrum) Beautiful burgundy-red flowers, bloom July-Sept. Similar to Lewis flax, but flowers later (see perennial list).*

FLOSSFLOWER (see ageratum)

FLOWERING TOBACCO (see nicotiana)

FORGET ME NOT (see biennial list)

FOUR O' CLOCK (Mirabilis) Hardy. Shrubs with dense foliage. Ht 2-3'. Red, pink, white, salmon, yellow, and bicolored flowers. Blooms mid-summer through fall. Flowers open late in the day. Full sun. Well-drained soil.

GAILLARDIA or INDIAN BLANKET (Gaillardia grandiflora, G. pulchella) Red daisies with bright yellow on the petal tips, blooms July-Sept. Excellent as cut flower. Ht 18-24". Easy to grow. Full sun. Prefers will-drained, not too rich soil. Plant seeds in early spring.* (see also perennial list.)

GAZANIA (Gazania splendens) Half hardy. Ht 6-12". Daisy-like flowers in cream, red, bronze, orange, yellow, pink (with contrasting centers). Full sun. Sandy, dry soil. Use in hot areas. Takes tough conditions.

GERANIUM (Pelargonium) Half hardy. Ht 4" dwarfs to 5' trees. Scented leaves. White, pink, red, and bicolor. Full sun or partial shade. Well-drained soil. Bedding and pot plants. Ivy and scented varieties in hanging baskets and patio tubs.

GLORIOSA DAISY (see biennial list)

GODETIA (see clarkia)

GYPSOPHILA (see baby's breath)

HELICHRYSUM or STRAWFLOWER (Helichrysum) Half hardy. Yellow, red, orange or white papery flowers. Fresh cut or dried. In everlasting group, Composite family. Ht 2-3'.

HELIPTERUM or EVERLASTING (Helipterum) Half hardy. Yellow flowers. Any soil, full sun. Dried flowers. In everlasting group, Composite family. Varieties vary Ht 8-20". Often confused with the genera Xeranthemum or Acroclinium.

HELIANTHUS or SUNFLOWER (see perennial list)

HELIOTROPE (Heliotropium peruvianum) Half hardy. Ht 1-2'. Very fragrant, lilac-like clusters of flowers. Full sun or light shade. Rich, well-drained soil. Borders, patio tubs, or window boxes.

HOLLYHOCK (see biennial list)

ICE PLANT (Mesembryanthemum criniflorum) Half hardy. Ht only 6". Daisy-like flowers in pink, white, yellow, and lavender. Silver-flecked leaves. Full sun, sandy soil. Dry rocky banks, rock gardens, window boxes.

IMPATIENS

Impatiens glandulifera. IMPATIENS. Hardy summer annual. Mounded plants 6-8" in diameter. Flowers blue with white centers. Sun or partial shade (in hot areas), well-drained soil. Ground cover, bedding, hanging baskets, edging plant, or mix with flowering bulbs. Nice color in shade. Flowers attract birds.

Impatiens wallerana. BUSY LIZZIE. A perennial usually grown as a summer annual. Rapid, vigorous growth. Tall, dwarf, and semi-dwarf varieties. Leaves are dark green, shiny and narrow (1-3 inches long). Bright flowers can be scarlet, pink, rose, violet, orange or white. Partial shade (shade tolerant), and rich, moist soil. Grow from seed, cuttings, or buy nursery flats.

JOB'S TEARS (Coix) Half hardy. An ornamental grass. Ht 24-30". Dried for bouquets. Large gray, bead-like seeds. Beads are easily strung. Full sun, any soil.

JOHNNY JUMP-UPS (see viola)

LARKSPUR (see delphinium on perennial list)

LIMNANTHES, MEADOW FOAM, or MARSH FLOWER (Limnanthes douglasii) Hardy sprawling. Ht 4-8". Fragrant white or yellow flowers. Needs very moist soil. Said to be almost extinct as a wildflower—a few still found in pastureland.

LINARIA or BABY SNAPDRAGON (Linaria) Hardy. Borders and beds. Looks like tiny snapdragons, in many colors. Full sun, any soil. Not heat resistant. Rock gardens, borders, mass plantings. Ht 12". Bicolor varieties with reds, yellows, and lavenders.

LOBELIA (Lobelia erinus) Half hardy. Ground covers, beds, borders, edgings, and rock gardens. Trailing varieties used in hanging baskets and pots. Partial shade. Not heat resistant. Only 6" tall. Vines up to 2 feet long. Blue, white, and pink flowers. Moist, well-drained soil. Keep trimmed for continuous blooming. Recommended varieties: Crystal Palace (dark blue), Cambridge (light blue), and Sapphire (dark blue) have trailing habit.

LUPINE, ARROYO (Lupinus succulentus) Easy to grow. Bright blue/violet flowers, bloom July-Aug. Good as cut flower. Ht 2-4'. Full sun. Needs moderate water. Tolerates most soils, including clay. Plant seeds in early spring.* (see also perennial list.)

LUPINE, GOLDEN (Lupinus densiflorus var. aureus) Golden yellow flowers on 2' spikes, bloom Aug.-Sept. Similar to L. succulentus. Mix with other lupine colors.*

MALLOW, ROSE (Lavatera trimestris) Mallow family. Hollyhock-like blossoms. Wildflower. Hardy annual. Ht 3-6'. Very showy flowers in red, rose-pink or white on 2' spikes, bloom Aug.-Oct. Full sun; will tolerate partial sun. Well-drained, rich soil with consistent watering. Plant in early spring as soon as soil can be worked.*

MARIGOLD (Tagetes) Half hardy. Various heights, habits, and colors. Pungent scent repels insects. Good companion for tomatoes. Edgings, beds, borders, window boxes, cut flowers. Full sun (shade in hot areas). Not heat resistant. Also dwarf varieties. Any rich, well-drained soil.

MARSH FLOWER or MEADOW FOAM (see limnanthes)

MEXICAN SUNFLOWER (Tithonia rotundifolia) All zones. Family Compositae. A perennial grown in colder zones as an annual. Rapid growing to 6'. Fantastic large flower heads 3-4 inches across, have scarlet rays, and raised yellow centers, bloom July to frost. Velvet green leaves. Sow seed in garden in spring. Full sun. Drought and heat resistant. Rock gardens.

MIGNONETTE (Reseda odorata) Half hardy. Sun (or partial shade where summers are hot). Ht 12-18". Drab looking greenish brown flowers on 6-12" spikes. Moist soil. Planted for strong pleasant odor, so plant near house. Plant some every two weeks for continuous blooming all season.

Petunias

MORNING GLORY (see ground cover list)

MYOSOTIS or WOODLAND FORGET ME NOT (see forget-me-not, on biennial list)

NASTURTIUM (Tropaeolum majus) Half hardy. Sow seed in garden after chance of frost is past (don't transplant). Ht 8-15". Climbing and trailing plants. Well-drained dry soil. Prefers poorer soils. Deters aphids from vine crops such as melons, squash and cucumbers. Mixed colors and bicolors. Full sun. Thrives on neglect !

NEMESIA (Nemesia strumosa) Half hardy. Ht 10". Mixed bright colors. Full sun (or shade in hot areas). Plants fold up in hot weather. Any moist soil. Keep trimmed for continuous blooming. Ground cover, edging, or with flowering bulbs.

NEMOPHILA (see baby blue-eyes)

NICOTIANA or FLOWERING TOBACCO (Nicotiana affinis) Half hardy. Sweet scent. Blooms are best in evening. Prefers rich soil, full sun. Ht 1-3'. Crimson, rose, lavender, pink, and white flowers. Full sun (some shade in warm areas). Any soils. Heat resistant. Use with border plants.

NIGELLA or FENNEL FLOWER (Nigella damascena) Hardy. Ht 12". Fernlike leaves. Blue, white, rose, pink, or purple flowers. Full sun, any soil. Cut flowers. Attractive seedpods.

PAINTED DAISY (see perennial list)

PANSY (see viola)

PERIWINKLE (see ground cover list)

PETUNIA (Petunia hybrida) Half hardy. Beds, borders, pots, tubs, hanging baskets and window boxes. Some with double ruffles. Annuals and perennials. Ht 1-2'. Not like overhead watering. Full sun to partial shade. Rich, well-drained moist soil. Keep trimmed to encourage continuous blooming.

PHLOX, MOUNTAIN (Linanthus grandiflorus) Dark ever-green-like foliage. White to pale-lavender blossoms, bloom July-Sept. With plenty of water will bloom all summer. Easy to grow. Ht 1-2'. Full sun. Well-drained soil. Plant seeds in early spring.*

PHACELIA or CALIFORNIA BLUEBELL (Phacelia campanularia) Full sun. Hardy. Flowers deep blue and bell-shaped on rolled, one-sided racemes, the raceme unrolling as the flowers open. Plant in masses. Important plants for bees. Ht 8". Common native in desert of Southern California.

PINKS: Clove, China, Maiden, Grass, Scotch (see dianthus)

POOR MAN'S ORCHID or BUTTERFLY FLOWER (Schizanthus pinnatus). Perennial grown as annual in zones 4-9. Ht 18 inches tall. Profuse, small, showy orchid-like flowers decorated with varicolored markings. Flower background colors are pink, rose, lilac, purple, or white. Fern-like foliage. Sensitive to frost and heat; prefers cool coastal regions. Grows in filtered shade (shade tolerant). Good in greenhouses and pots. Start seed indoors early (germination is slow).

POOR MAN'S WEATHERGLASS (Anagallis arvensis var. coerulea) Blue, star-shaped, delicate flowers, bloom July-August. Low spreading. Rock gardens and borders. Max Ht only 10". Easy to grow. partial to full sun. Any soils. Tolerates dry conditions. Plant seeds in spring.*

POPPY (see perennial list)

PORTULACA, ROSE MOSS, MOSS ROSE, or SUN PLANT (Portulaca grandiflora) Half hardy. Creeping plants, max Ht 7". White, red, rose, yellow-orange, lavender flowers. Full sun, any well-drained soil. Use in problem areas, beds, and rock gardens. Easy to grow from seed. Very colorful.

PRIMROSE, WHITE EVENING (Oenothera pallida) Beautiful, fragrant, 3" wide, white (sometimes tinged with lavender) flowers, bloom July till first frost. Annual. Even does well in very sandy soil (has been used to control sand dunes). Easy to grow. Only 14" tall. Plant seeds anytime. May be invasive.*

RUDBECKIA (see gloriosa daisy on biennial list)

SALPIGLOSSIS, VELVET FLOWER, PAINTED TONGUE (Salpiglossis sinuata) Half hardy. Ht 2-3'. Petuna-like flowers: purple, pink, yellow, orange, and red; all intricately veined with contrasting colors. Full sun. Rich, well-drained soil (moist for young plants, dry or older ones). Use back of borders or cut flowers. Keep trimmed to encourage continuous flowering.

SALVIA or SAGE (Salvia) Half hardy. Ht 14-20", dwarf to 12". Bedding plants, in beds and tubs. Showy, VERY BRIGHT flowers in deep scarlet, pink, blue, and white. (S. splendens = Half hardy, and S. horminum = hardy). Full sun or partial shade. Rich, well-drained soil. Annuals and perennials.

SCHIZANTHUS (Schizanthus pinnatus) Half hardy. Ht 18-24". Leaves fernlike. Bicolors in pink, red, yellow, white, and purple. Prefers some shade. Moist, rich, well-drained soil. Window boxes or beds. Prefers cool summers. Greenhouse plant.

SEA LAVENDER or SEA PINK (Limonium) Half hardy. Ht 16-20". Blue, lavender, rose, and white flowers. Full sun. Prefers dry, well-drained soil. Annual or perennial. Dried flowers; in everlasting group. Name often confused with Statice.

SNAPDRAGON (Antirrhinum majus) Half hardy. Ht varies 6" to 3'. Garden color, cut flowers. Rich soil. Full sun or semi-shade. Rich, well-drained soil. Often comes up again from roots. Mixed colors. Dwarfs in rock gardens or borders; tall ones in bed backgrounds. Keep trimmed (pinching back) to encourage flowering. Likes hot sun at Lake Almanor (4,500' elevation).

SNOW-ON-THE-MOUNTAIN (see ground cover list)

STOCK (Matthiola bicornis) Hardy. Ht 1-2". Cut flowers, beds and borders. Rich, moist, well-drained soil. Full sun (partial shade in hot areas). Deep blue, white, and pink.

Violets

STRAWFLOWER (see helichrysum)

SUNFLOWER, WILD (Helianthus annuus) Annual. Typical sunflower. Bright yellow flowers, 3-4" across, bloom Aug.-Oct. Easy to grow. Full sun. Well-drained, even disturbed soil. Drought tolerant once established. Although small, the seeds are edible. Plant seeds in fall or early spring. (see also helianthus on perennial list). Native wildflower.*

SWEET ALYSSUM (Lobularia maritima) Hardy. Ht 2-6". Low growing for borders, edgings, rock gardens, beds, pots, and window boxes. White, rose, and blue flowers. Fast growing. Blooms early summer till frost. Fragrant. Well-drained soil, full sun. Keep trimmed to encourage new growth. Don't confuse with perennial Alyssum (Basket of Gold). Easy to grow from seed.

SWEET PEA (see lathyrus on perennial list)

SWEET SULTAN (Centaurea moschata) Hardy. Thistle-like flowers in lilac, pink, purple, white, red, yellow. Ht 2-3'. Leaves finely cut. Full sun, any soils. Mixed beds, or cut flowers. Often confused with Dusty Miller and Cornflower (see Dusty Miller for details).

SWEET WILLIAM (see biennial list)

TIDY TIPS (Layia platyglossa) Yellow daisies, with white tips on broad petals, bloom August (late)-October. Easy to grow. Only 12" tall. Requires dry, sunny site. Not do well in shade or soggy soil. Plant seeds in spring*. Often grows in pastureland.

SWEET WILLIAM CATCHFLY (Silene armeria). Silene is closely related to Lychnis. Spectacular pink flowers on bushy plants. Ht 2-3'. Partial to full sun. Any soil. Needs little water. Blooms July-Aug. Plant seeds in spring, reseeds nicely.*

VERBENA or VERVAIN (Verbena hybrida) Half hardy. Ht 6-10", spreading to 2' wide. Many fragrant bicolors with white centers. Edgings, beds, ground cover, rock gardens, window boxes, cut flowers. Full sun. Prefers rich well-drained moist soil, but tolerates poor soil and drought conditions. Heat resistant. In warmer climates acts as perennial.

VIOLA is the Latin name for Violet. Keep faded flowers picked off to encourage continual blooming. Rich, moist, well-drained soil with humus. Sun or partial shade. Edgings, borders, window boxes, or rock gardens. Annuals, biennials, perennials. Basically zones 3-5, depending on variety. Not like long hot summers. Many books are confusing on terminology here.

Horned Violet or Tufted Pansy (Viola cornuta) Annual, but perennial in warmer regions. Have smaller flowers than pansies, require cooler conditions. Ht 6-8". MANY COLORS. Good in rock gardens. Start by seed.
Johnny Jump up (Viola tricolor hortensis) Flowers blue, white, yellow, or bicolor. Reseeds readily; lives about 3 years. Annual-perennial. A miniature pansy with a sprawling habit to 1 ft or more.
Pansy (Viola tricolor) Zone 4. Ht 8". Blooms spring to fall in purple, blue, white, yellow, and bicolors. Edges of flower beds, borders, or in rock gardens. Usually biennial.
Sweet, Florist's, or Garden Violet (Viola odorata) Hardy. Cut flowers. Stemless plants with bold heart-shaped leaves. EXTREMELY FRAGRANT. Much grown for perfumes. Propagated by plant divisions, offsets, and runners. Hardy perennials. Zones 4. Dark violet or white flowers, a source of perfume. Must be kept contained. Needs rich soil and winter mulch. Great in rock gardens.

XERANTHEMUM (Xeranthemum) Hardy. Daisy-like flowers in pink, red, rose, purple. Full sun. Ht 30-36". Any soil. Cut (fresh) and dried arrangements. In everlasting group (hold dried color for long time).

ZINNIA (Zinnia) Half hardy. Ht 2-3'. Full sun, any soil. Blooms till frost. Mixed colors and bicolors. Use dwarfs in borders, rock gardens, or window boxes. Tall ones in mixed beds or as single plants. Also good for cut flowers, or in gardens to repel insects.

BIENNIALS

Wallflower

A ***biennial*** is a herbaceous plant that takes two years to complete its life cycle, producing leaves the first year and flowering and fruiting the second. Most are able to reseed themselves (i.e. Sweet William), and come back year after year. Start in flat or cold frame and plant seedlings outdoors after all danger of frost is past. Keep all faded flowers picked off to encourage continuous bloom. After the first hard frost, remove any dead plants, and trim stems and stalks to within four inches of the ground. Mulch for winter protection in the colder areas. For planting and propagation information see appropriate chapter.

Biennial PLANT LIST

BLACK-EYED SUSAN or GLORIOSA DAISY (Rudbeckia hirta) Wildflower. Hardy all zones. Flowers have brown centers with shades of yellow, orange, russet, mahogany or bronze petals, often zoned or banded. Blooms July-August. Well-drained soil. Sun or partial shade. Rough hairy stems. Ht 18-24". Annuals, perennials and biennials, but most often the latter. Propagate by seed; reseeds itself, almost acts like a perennial. Keep trimmed to encourage continuous blooming. Nice for cut flowers. Many varieties. Don't confuse with Black-eyed Susan (Thunbergia) which doesn't grow here.*

Gloriosa Daisy

CANTERBURY-BELLS (Campanula medium) Zone 4. Many varieties: height varies from 8-24". Blooms May to July in blue, rose, white, yellow, and pastels. Plant in mid-border of bed. Likes sun, keep moist. A perennial best grown as biennial. Great for cut flowers.

ENGLISH DAISY (Bellis perennis) Zone 4. Ht 4-8". Blooms May-Aug. in rose, lavender, red, and white. Rock gardens or edging plants. Needs sun but not like long, hot summers. Likes rich, moist soil.

PRIMROSE, EVENING (Oenothera hookeri) Western native wildflower. All zones. Ht 2-6'. Blooms June-Aug. Prefers dry, sunny site. Not too rich soil. Rock gardens or front-of-border. Lemon scented, bright yellow flowers. Blooms in late afternoon and stays open till sunrise. Has succession of flowers going up the stem. Hairy elliptical leaves. Plant seed, use nursery stock, or divide clumps (in early spring).*

FORGET-ME-NOT, ALPINE or WOODLAND (Myosotis sylvatica or alpestris) Zone 3-10 (Depending on variety). Ht 8-24". Hardy annuals and biennials. Blooms early spring till late August if in moist, shaded, cool place. Flowers: blue, white, and pink. Spreads quickly to make good ground cover. Rock gardens, beds, borders, edgings. Likes rich soil. Good for planting over bulbs.

Sweet William

FOXGLOVE (Digitalis purpurea) Zone 4. Ht 3-6'. Wildflower. Blooms June to July in white, cream, yellow, rose, red, and lavender. Staking needed. Sun or part sun. Any soil. Leaves poisonous, as they act as heart stimulants. A perennial best grown as a biennial. DEER RESISTANT !*

HOLLYHOCK (Alcea rosea) Zone 3. Ht 4-8'. Blooms July-Sept. in red, pink, rose, and yellow. Back of the border, or along fences. Rich, well-drained soil. Sun or semi-shade. Gets caterpillars, beetles, and rusts. Choose hardiest varieties as some are frost tender.

Hollyhock

HONESTY or SILVER DOLLAR PLANT (Lunaria annua) Zone 4. Ht to 3'. Blooms June-July in white or blue flowers, but grown for unusual coin-like seed capsules (good in dried arrangements). Sun or partial shade, any soil. Also a perennial variety.

PANSY (see viola on annual list)

SCARLET GILIA or SKYROCKET (Gilia aggregata, or Ipomopsis aggregata). Wildflower. Bright red trumpets encircle spikes! Found on dry summer hillsides in sagebrush country. Easy to grow. Prefers full sun. Any soil. Height to 30". Drought tolerant, yet responds to moderate watering. Plant seeds in spring or fall, reseeds easily. New seedlings can be transplanted in spring or fall. Blooms June -August.*

SWEET WILLIAM (Dianthus barbatus) Zone 4. Many varieties, heights vary 5-20". Blooms May-July in purple, red, rose, white, or bicolor. Mixed border or rock garden. Full sun, well-drained, alkaline soil. A perennial best grown as a biennial.

WALLFLOWER (Cheiranthus cheiri) Zone 3. Ht 18-24". Blooms early spring in yellow, russet, and mahogany. Pinch tips back if get too tall. Morning sun, slightly alkaline soil. Fragrant! Winter protection not needed.

PERENNIALS

Iceland Poppy

A **perennial** is a herbaceous plant which lasts up to five years (under ideal conditions), not dying after flowering and fruiting (i.e. Lupine, Shasta Daisy, and Phlox). They live longer, but might not bloom the first year (or more). Perennials produce flowers every year once they get started. When selecting a perennial look up information on season of bloom (Chart #5), what climate zone they grow in (Chart #1), mature plant height, sun or shade, soil preference, colors available, and special comments. Usually prefer rich soil. For "starting" information see Propagation and Planting chapters.

Keep all faded flowers picked off to encourage continuous bloom. After the first hard frost, remove any dead plants, and trim stems and stalks to within four inches of the ground. Divide and replant overgrown clumps. Before replanting, turn under some bone meal or superphosphate. Apply a protective winter mulch of straw, peat moss, or pine needles to fall-planted perennials to avoid alternate freezing and thawing of the ground which can damage the roots. Then remove the mulch the following spring.

Perennial PLANT LIST

ADONIS, or SPRING ADONIS (Adonis vernalis) Zone 3. Ht 12". Blooms March to April. Sun, any moist soil. Rock gardens, borders, in masses, or mixed with wild flowers. Propagate from seed or root division.

AGERATUM, HARDY or MIST FLOWER (Eupatorium coelestinum) Zone 3. Ht 2-3'. Bright blue flowers, bloom Aug. to Sept. Prefers slight shade. Very showy in mass plantings or borders. Propagate by root cuttings.

AJUGA (see bugleweed on ground cover list)

ALUM ROOT (see coral bells)

ALYSSUM or BASKET OF GOLD (Aurinia saxatilis) Zone 3. Sun. Ht 8-15". Bright gold flowers, bloom April-May. Low growing. Edging, rock gardens, and on slopes. Often confused with the annual Sweet Alyssum. Easy care, sun or shade. Propagate from seed, or stem cuttings (in summer).

ANCHUSA or ALKANET (Anchusa azurea) Zone 3. Ht 1-4'. Deep blue flowers, bloom all summer. Slight shade. Propagate by root cuttings (in spring or fall) or let reseed themselves.

ANTHEMIS or GOLDEN MARGUERITE (Anthemis tinctoria) Zone 3. Ht 30-36". Yellow or white flowers, bloom June to frost. Any soil. Sun. Foliage aromatic and finely cut. Propagate by seed or divide rootstock. Mid-border plant.

AQUILEGIA (see columbine)

ARMERIA (see thrift on ground cover list)

ARNICA (Arnica cordifolia) Large, yellow, daisy-like flowers surrounded by two opposite, soft, green, heart-shaped leaves. Blooms June-July. Ht 12". Prefers partial shade under pine and fir trees, but tolerates full sun. Needs well drained, slightly acid soil. Plant seeds in fall. Does not transplant easily. Nice border plant.*

ARROWLEAF BALSAMROOT (Balsamorrihiza sagittata) Yellow, 2-3" flowers, bloom second or third year, May-July. Leaves light-green, large, arrowhead-shaped. Needs full sun. Well-drained, slightly alkaline soil. Drought tolerant after germination. Plant seeds in fall, as they will not transplant.*

ARTEMISIA (see dusty miller)

ASPEN DAISY (Erigeron speciosus) Dainty, lilac-colored daisy with yellow center. Woody roots. Ht 1-2'. Each stem has 12 or more 1" flowers. Very adaptable to harsh conditions. Easy to grow.*

ASTER, HARDY, or MICHAELMAS DAISY (Aster) Zone 4. Ht to 4'. Tall with small flowers, bloom late summer to fall. Taller varieties may need staking. Well-drained rich soil. Sun. Divide plants in early spring every 3-4 years, being sure to remove the woody center of the plant. To encourage bushiness, pinch back in mid-June.

ASTER, STOKES (see stokesia)

ASTILBE, or FALSE SPIREA (Astilbe x arendsi) Saxifrage family. Resembles and often mistakenly sold as Spirea. Ht 15-30". Popular border perennial. Zone 4. White, pink, red, or salmon flowers, bloom June-July. Sun or shade. Any moist, rich soil. Propagate by seed or root division. Likes mulch. See Spirea on shrub list.

AVENS (see geum)

BABY'S BREATH (Gypsophila paniculata) Zone 3. Full sun. White or pink flowers, bloom June-Sept. Ht 1-4'. Alkaline soil. Needs considerable space for branching habit. Mass plantings, dried and fresh bouquets. Popular! Divide clumps every 2 years. (G. repens is a creeping variety for rock gardens.) Propagate from root cuttings or seed.* (See also annual list.)

BACHELOR'S BUTTON, or MOUNTAIN BLUET, CORNFLOWER, Centaurea montana (see dusty miller)

BALLOON FLOWER (Platycodon grandiflorus) Zone 3. Ht 20". Star-shaped blue, pink, or white flowers, bloom July to Aug. Sun or shade, well-drained soil. Propagate by seeds or root cuttings. Mid-borders.

BAPTISIA, FALSE INDIGO, or BLUE INDIGO (Baptisia australis) Zone 3. Ht 4-5'. Lupine-like flowers usually blue; white (B. alba); or yellow (B. tinctoria), bloom in June. Back of the border locations. Native to N. America. Full sun or partial shade. Any soil. Survives periods of drought. May need staking. Spreads quickly. Great ground cover on problem slopes. Start from seed or root divisions.

BARRENWORT (Epimedium spp.) Zone 4. Prostrate. Creeping underground stems. Heart-shaped, leathery leaflets 3 inches long on thin wiry stems. Leaves are bronzy-pink in spring, green in summer, and bronze in fall. Flowers: pink, red, cream-yellow or white, in loose spikes, bloom in spring. Good ground cover under trees, in rock gardens, and in containers. Shade tolerant. Needs more than average water. Foliage lasts in arrangements. Cut off old leaves in spring.

BERGENIA (Bergenia spp.) Zone 4. Evergreen except in coldest areas. Saxifrage family. Native to Himalayas and mountains of China. Thick root stalks. Large shiny green leaves, mostly basal. Grown for ornamental foliage. Grows in dense clumps 12-18 inches high. Dainty nodding clusters of tiny white, pink, or rose flowers. Foreground, borders, under trees, ground cover, nice with ferns. Cut back annually to keep shape. Divide crowded clumps. Light shade (shade tolerant).

BASKET OF GOLD (see alyssum)

BEARGRASS (Xerophyllum tenax) Tall white flower plumes. Lily family. Native wildflower. Long, shiny-green leaves are in tufted clumps (used by Florists). Blooms second or third year, July-Aug. Ht 2-3'.*

BEE BALM, or BERGAMOT (Monarda didyma) Zone 4. Ht 2-3'. White, pink, red, or purple flowers, bloom July-Aug. Quick growing. Mid to back-of-the-border location. Drought & insect resistant. Divide clumps every 1-2 years. Sun or partial shade. Keep mulched. Attract bees & hummingbirds.

BELLFLOWER (see canterbury bells on biennial list)

BERGAMOT (see Beebalm)

BETONY (see lamb's ears on ground cover list)

BLANKET FLOWER (see gaillardia)

BLEEDING HEART, COMMON (Dicentra spectabilis) Zone 4. Ht 2'. Pink heart-shaped flowers, bloom early spring. Moist, partial shade. Bulb gardens. Variety "Fernleaf" blooms May-June, Ht 1', and "Old Fashioned" blooms June-Sept., Ht 2'.

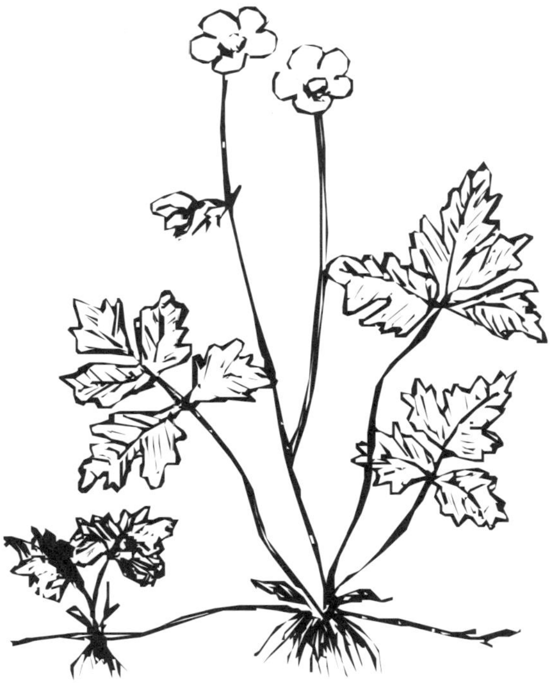

Buttercup (Ranunculus sp.)

BLOODROOT (Sanguinaria canadensis) Zone 4. Poppy family. Red roots with orange-red sap. Large, deeply lobed, grayish leaves. White or pink 1 1/2 inch flowers solitary on 8 inch stalks, bloom early spring. Damp, shaded rock garden or beneath trees and open shrubs. Shade-tolerant.

BLUEBELLS, VIRGINIA (see virginia bluebells)

BLUE DAISY or BLUE MARGUERITE (see felicia)

BLUET, MOUNTAIN (see dusty miller)

BRUNNERA, SIBERIAN FORGET ME NOT, or SIBERIAN BUGLOSS (Brunnera macrophylla) Perennial, all zones. Ht 8-18". Moist, well-drained soil. Full sun, half-shade or shade depends on variety. Blue forget-me-not like flowers with yellow centers, bloom May-July. Dark green, heart shaped leaves 3-6" across. Nice addition to bulb garden. Self-sows freely after once established. Start by division of clumps in the fall. Sometimes confused with Anchusa, but Brunnera blooms earlier.

BUCKWHEAT, SULPHUR (Eriogonum umbellatum) Bright sulphur-yellow flowers on 12" stalks, blooms second year, July-Sept. Glossy, dark-green leaves. Thick beautiful ground cover 3-6" tall. Dried flower arrangements. Full sun, well-drained soil. Drought tolerant after germination. Plant seeds in fall. *

BUTTERCUP (Ranunculus spp.) Zone 4. Ht 12-18". Sun. Golden flowers, bloom May-June (spring). General term for many in the Ranunculus family. Rock gardens or mixed with blue bearded iris and bleeding-hearts.

BUTTERFLY WEED or MILKWEED (Asclepias tuberosa) Zone 4. Ht 2-3'. Bright orange umbel flowers, bloom all summer. Close relative of milkweed. Any soil. Sun. Insect and disease resistant. Attractive seed pods. Seed or nursery plants. Long taproot.

CALCEOLARIA (Calceolaria 'John Innes') All zones. Figwort family. Loose clusters of slipper-shaped, showy, golden-yellow flowers with purple spots, bloom June-July. Dark green crinkly leaves 3 inches long. Bedding plant or rock garden. 8 inches high. Spreads easily. Shady, rich moist soil. Shade tolerant.

CALIFORNIA CONEFLOWER (see coneflower)

CAMAS (Camassia quamash) Bright sky-blue flowers, bloom in June. Germination can take up to 6 months. Won' t flower until second or third year after planting seed, but it is worth the wait! Full sun, well-drained, rich soil. Needs plenty of moisture. Native wildflower.*

CAMPANULA, BELLFLOWER or CANTERBURY BELLS (see canterbury bells on biennial list)

CANDY TUFT (see ground cover list)

CANTERBURY BELLS (see biennial list)

CARDINAL FLOWER (see lobelia)

CAROLINA LUPINE (see thermopsis)

CATANANCHE (see cupid's dart)

CATCHFLY (see lychnis, or sweet william catchfly on annual list)

CENTAUREA (see dusty miller)

CENTRANTHUS (see jupiter's beard)

CERASTIUM (see snow-in-summer, on ground cover list)

CERATOSTIGMA (see leadwort)

CHILE AVENS (see geum)

Columbine

CHINESE LANTERN PLANT (Physalis alkekengi) Zone 3. Bright orange seed pods used for dried arrangements. Sun. Any soil. Blooms July-August. Ht 1-2'. Not recommended for borders because of its spreading habits. Propagate from seed or by dividing established clumps.

CHRISTMAS ROSE (see helleborus)

CHRYSANTHEMUM means golden flower. A general term refering to Pyrethum, Shasta daisy, Marguerite daisy, Feverfew, Oxeye, Painted Daisy. Those underlined are the only ones in genus Chrysanthemum. Ht 1 to 3'. Sun. Well-drained soil. Start from seeds, root divisions, and stem cuttings. Mulch summer and winter. Choose hardiest varieties. Some start blooming at time of frost and then die, but do well in house pots for 6 weeks. (Composite family). Refer to common names.

CINQUEFOIL, or POTENTILLA (Potentilla fruticosa) Zones 4-5. Ht 3-18". Low-growing shrub. Bright edging for border or walkway. Native. Bright yellow, cerise, or orange flowers, bloom June to frost. Very hardy. Propagate by seed, root divisions. Sun, good drainage. DEER RESISTANT.

CINQUEFOIL, SPRING (Potentilla tabernaemontanii). All zones. Evergreen perennial. Fast growing ground cover and border. Leaves bright-green or gray-green, divided into 5 leaflets, on a creeping plant 2-6 inches high. Small bright-yellow flowers 1/4 inch wide, forming clusters 3-5 inches wide, bloom spring-summer. Plant can turn brown in cold winters. May need shade if summers are hot and dry. Makes a good ground cover over bulbs, or lawn substitute where there is no foot traffic. Fire-resistant.

COLUMBINE (Aquilegia spp.) Zone 3. Ht 20-30". Sun or partial shade. Flowers in pastels, deeper shades, or white, bloom May-June in the second year. Good for cut flowers. Start by seed. Keep old flowers picked for continual bloom. At end of season cut foliage back to 4". DEER RESISTANT ! Native wildflower.*

COMPHREY (Symphytum officinale) All zones. Clump-forming. Leaves covered with stiff hairs; basal leaves 8 inches long, upper leaves smaller. Deep roots. Ht 3'. Flowers inconspicuous 1/2 inch long (white, cream, or purple). Leaves are used as feed for stock animals, but are poisonous to people as they contain pyrrolizidine [2] so don't eat them. The leaves can be dried as medicinal tea. Full sun or partial shade (shade tolerant). Average watering. Plants go dormant over winter in cold areas. To keep plant producing leaves, cut out flowering stalks and enrich soil with compost each spring. Grow from root cuttings.

CONEFLOWER, CALIFORNIA (Rudbeckia californica) Zone 3. Ht to 30". Many varieties. Yellow or orange flowers, bloom July-Sept. Sun, any soil. Tolerate summer droughts, but need watering. Disease and insect resistant. Divide mature clumps in the fall when they are too large. Native wildflower.

CONEFLOWER, PURPLE (Echinacea purpurea) Orange cone in center of flower surrounded by purple petals, bloom second year, June-Aug. Excellent border plant. Ht 2-4'. Prefers full sun. Any soil (including clay), but must be well-drained. Drought tolerant once established. Plant seeds in spring. Plant seeds near surface as they need light to germinate.*

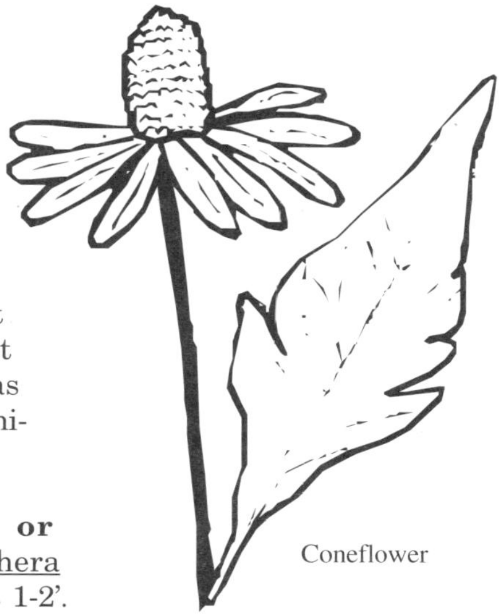
Coneflower

CORAL BELLS or ALUMROOT (Heuchera saguinea) Zone 3. Ht 1-2'. Borders, rock gardens, cut flowers. Sun or partial shade. Any moist well-drained soil. Coral, pink, white, red, or chartreuse flowers, bloom June-Sept. Propagate by seed, or divide clumps in Spring or Fall.

COREOPSIS or TICKSEED (Coreopsis) Zone 4. Hardy. Ht 16-30". Sun. Any soil. Showy, 2-tone, daisy-like, yellow flowers, bloom June-frost (Sept). Backgrounds and borders. Propagate by seed or root divisions in early spring. Also annual varieties.

CORNFLOWER (see Centaurea montana under DUSTY MILLER)

CRANESBILL GERANIUM (see geranium)

Coreopsis

CREEPING PHLOX (see ground cover list)

CUPID'S DART or CATANANCHE (Catananche caerulea) Zone 4. Ht 15-18". Start from seed, or divide clumps in spring. Sun. Well-drained soil. Blue or white flowers, bloom July to Sept. Mid-border, and dried flowers.

DAISY. The traditional daisy is *Bellis perennis* or English Daisy. Daisy is a general term also applied to *Chrysanthemum, Townsendia, Arctotis, Aster, and Rudbeckia*, plus many more in the Composite family. Most all daisies do well here: Ester Reed, Painted, Shasta, Oxeye, Blue, English (biennial), except Transvaal Daisy (Zone 8). Refer to common names.

DAY LILIES (Hemerocallis) Deciduous, evergreen. Hardy all zones, any soils, easy care. Insect and disease resistant Filtered shade or full sun. Plant in fall, feed in spring. Ht 18" to 5'. Flowers yellow, orange to reds. Water during dry spells. Root divisions in spring or fall. Arching, sword-shaped leaves.

DEAD NETTLE (Lamium maculatum) All zones. Many varieties, including the favorite 'Beacon silver'. Stems trail on ground or hang from wall or container; stems can be 6 feet long. Heart-shaped leaves 1 1/2 inches long, in pairs, bluntly toothed at the edges, green with silver and white markings. Flowers vary pink to white. Hanging baskets, or ground cover in shade (shade tolerant). Requires rich soil, and plenty of water. Deciduous in cold winters. Where winters are mild, it is partially evergreen, so cut off old stems to make room for new growth. Can be invasive.

DELPHINIUM or LARKSPUR (Delphinium) Zone 3. Perennials. Many species. Ht 1-8'. Sun or part shade. Blue, red, pink, lavender, purple, white, or yellow flowers, bloom June-July. Beautiful leaves are lobed and fanlike. Borders, backgrounds, and cut flowers. Heavy feeders. Rich, moist, alkaline soil. Staking required. Flowers on spikes. Plants have poisonous sap. (Annual varieties are 1-2' tall.) DEER RESISTANT ! Attracts birds. poisonous to livestock.*

DIANTHUS, or PINK (Dianthus) Zones 3-7. Flowers pink, white, red, or bicolor, bloom all summer. Hardy perennial. Ht 3-24". Sunny, rich sandy, well-drained soil. Slightly alkaline or neutral soil. Propagate from seeds, stem cuttings or root divisions. Not like hot, dry weather. Also are annual varieties.

DORONICUM or LEOPARD'S BANE (Doronicum cordatum) Zone 4. Hardy. Bright yellow daisy-like flower, bloom in spring. Ht 24". Front or mid-border. Sun or partial sun. Rich, fertile soil. Mulch in summer. Divide clumps every 2-3 years.

DRAGON HEAD (see physostegia)

DROPWORT (see meadowsweet)

DUSTY MILLER has small insignificant daisy-like flowers, white hairy leaves, commonly used for color contrast. According to Taylor [1], Dusty Miller is an old plant name of wide usage but confusing application, as it has been used as another name for all of the following plants, but probably should be only applied to *Artemisia or Senecio.*

Annuals:

Centaurea moschata Sweet sultan —many colors.
Centaurea cyanus Cornflower or Batchelor Buttons. Pale blue flowers (other colors available). Ht 1-2'. Sprawling habit. Borders, beds, dried arrangements, cut flowers, and nice when naturalized with California Poppies.*

Biennials or Perennials:

Centaurea montana Mountain Bluet, Batchelor's Buttons, or Cornflower. Blue flowers summer-fall. Zone 4. Sun. Ht 1-2'. Seeds or root cuttings. Mid-border, cut flowers. Self-sows & can become pest. Divide mature plants every 2-3 years.
Centaurea cineraria Yellow or purple fl. Ht 12-18".
Centaurea gymnocarpa Rose-purple flowers.
Senecio cineraria Yellow or cream flowers. Ht 30".
Lychnis coronaria Mullein Pink and Rose Campion. Ht

18-30". Crimson flowers. Spreads, very aggressive and invasive. Don't confuse with L. chalcedonica (Maltese cross).

Artemisia stelleriana Beach Wormwood. Zone 3. Height varies with variety. Yellow flowers bloom spring-summer. Grown for attractive gray-green foliage and delicate scent. Propagate by seed, root divisions or stem cuttings. Sun.

ECHINACEA (Echinacea angustifolia) Used as an antibiotic. Flower is similar to purple coneflower, but has shorter stem. Blooms second year, June-Aug. Ht 1-2'. Plant from seed.*

ECHINOPS (see globe thistle)

ELEPHANT HEAD (Pedicularis groenlandica) Many pink flowers, each looking like an elephant head, encircling a 12-18" spike. Spikes occur in clusters. Blooms second or third year, May-July. Prefers full sun. Likes moist meadows and wetlands. Plant seeds in fall. Native wildflower.*

ENGLISH DAISY (see biennial list)

ESTER REED DAISY (see shasta daisy)

EUPATORIUM (see ageratum)

EUPHORBIA (see spurge)

EVENING PRIMROSE (see oenothera)

FALSE DRAGONHEAD (see physostegia)

FALSE SPIREA, saxifrage family (see astilbe)

Fleabane Daisy

FALSE SPIREA, rose family (see spirea, false on shrub list)

FALSE SUNFLOWER (see helenium)

FELICIA, BLUE MARGUERITE, or BLUE DAISY (Felicia amelloides) Zone 5. *Best treated as an annual* in areas with cold winters. Good in greenhouses. Ht 1-3'. Sky-blue flowers bloom early summer to frost. Cut flowers. Sun. After blooming cut plant back to 4-6". Propagate from seed, or cuttings. Will self sow. (F. bergeriana is a hardy annual.)

FEVERFEW, GOLDEN FEATHER FEVERFEW, or MATRICARIA (Chrysanthemum parthenium) Zone 3. Small cream-colored daisy flowers, bloom all summer. Spreads easily, carpets large area. A pest near lawns. Sun or light shade, rich soil. Cut flowers. Grow with brighter perennials. A dwarf perennial or annual. Cuttings or nursery stock. Divide clumps every 3-4 years. Cut off faded flowers. Perennials to 30", (half-hardy annuals 10-24").

FILIPENDULA (see meadowsweet)

FIREWEED (Epilobium angustifolium) Bright pink flowers mid-summer (late June-Sept.). Borders or backgrounds. Both flowers and young leaves are edible. Often the first flower to come in after a fire (thus its' name). Full sun. Prefers well-drained, moist loam. Plant seeds in spring or fall, or propagate by root division. Native wildflower.*

FLAX, LEWIS (Linum perenne lewisii) Zone 3. Perennial. Ht 1-2'. Beautiful blue flowers, bloom June-Aug. Full sun, easy care. Divide established clumps every 1-2 years. Beds and borders. Difficult to transplant. Light, or well-drained sandy soil. Drought-tolerant once established. Reseeds freely, but is not invasive. See also annual list.*

FLEABANE DAISY (Erigeron) Zone 3. Ht 10-36". Daisy-like flowers in pink, lavender, white, orange, or blue, bloom all summer. Propagate from seed or by division. Borders, edgings, or rock gardens. Resemble wild asters.

FORGET ME NOT, SIBERIAN (see brunnera)

FORGET ME NOT, ALPINE or WOODLAND (see biennial list)

FOUNTAIN GRASS (Pennisetum setaceum). All zones. Perennial grass. Forms large round clump up to 4' high and wide. Narrow arching leaves up to 2' long. Stem tips have fuzzy, showy, copper-pink flower spikes. Nice accent in a ground cover bed. Likes dry site, any soil, full sun. Drought resistant. Winter dormant period. Cut stems before flowers go to seed, or it will spread (pest).

FOXGLOVE (see biennial list)

GAILLARDIA, or INDIAN BLANKET (Gaillardia aristata) Zone 3. Perennial. Any soil. Sun or shade. Ht 12-30". Two-tone flowers in gold, red, and brown, bloom all summer. Likes hot areas. Mass or mid-border plantings, and cut flowers. Keep trimmed for continuous bloom. Divide clumps every 1-2 years. Propagate by seed.* (Hardy annual varieties in red, yellow, cream and bicolor 14-18" tall.)

Gaillardia

GAS PLANT (Dictamnus) Zone 3. Sun. White flowers with prominent green stamens, bloom all summer. Ht 2-3'. Borders. Easy care. On a hot night with no breeze, you can get a small burst of flame by holding a lighted match over the blooms. Buy nursery stock (takes 3 years to get blooms from seed). Back of the border, and cut flowers. Almost impossible to transplant once established. Leaves have lemon fragrance.

GAY FEATHER (see liatris)

GENTIAN, MOUNTAIN (Gentiana affinis) Zone 4. Ht 6". Blue, tubular flowers, bloom July to Sept. Rock gardens. Low growing. Dislikes hot weather. Buy nursery stock (plants from seed not bloom for two years). Light shade, well-drained soil. Wild gentians are endangered species.*

GERANIUM, WILD (Geranium viscosissum) Pink flowers with deeper pink veins (are edible), bloom second or third year, May-Aug., and is well worth the wait! Shiny dark green leaves. Ht 1-3'. Partial to full sun. Rich, well-drained, slightly acid soil. Water moderately. Plant seeds in fall, or propagate by dividing rhizomes. Native wildflower.*

GERANIUM, CRANESBILL (Geranium) Zone 4. From dwarfs to 10" tall. This true geranium is a hardy perennial; often confused with genus Pelargonium (also commonly called geranium). Flowers in pink, red, white, or purple, bloom summer-fall. Edging plants, or rock gardens. Upright or trailing. Sun or partial shade. Prefers poor soil. Divide clumps every 4-5 years. Easy care. Flowers single or in clusters.

GEUM or CHILE AVENS (Geum chiloense) Zone 5. Low growing up to 2 feet. Cut flowers. Sensitive to extreme heat and cold, so use mulch both summer and winter. Yellow, orange, or scarlet flowers, bloom all summer. Full sun. Needs soil high in organic matter. Buy nursery stock (from seed it does not produce flowers for three years).

GLOBEFLOWER (Trollius europaeus) Zone 3. Ht 30". Yellow or orange flowers, bloom May-June. Part shade. Moist soil, plus plenty of organic matter. Seed, or buy nursery stock.

GLOBEMALLOW, ORANGE (Sphaeralcea munroana) Bright orange flowers, bloom July-August! Bush-like plant Ht 6-12". Full sun. Prefers well-drained soil, but tolerated poor, disturbed, even clay soil. Drought resistant. Plant seeds in spring or fall.*

GLOBE THISTLE (Echinops exaltatus) Zone 4. Ht 2-4'. Sun. Metallic-blue flowers, bloom July-Sept. Attractive, unusual back-of-the-border plant. White wooly leaves. Seeds or root divisions. Any soil. Sun, partial shade. Dried flowers. Great with late flowering yellow daylilies.

GLORIOSA DAISY (see black eyed susan on biennial list)

GOLDEN GLOW (Rudbeckia hortensia) Sun, moist soil. Easy care. Ht 6-7'. Backgrounds. Yellow double flowers, bloom summer-fall. Popular. (Composite family). Spreads by underground stems, sometimes aggressively. Tolerates heat.

GOLDENROD (see solidago)

Sunflower
(Helianthus)

GRASS OF PARNASSUS (Parnassia fimbriata) Very beautiful, dark green heart-shaped leaves. Ht 8-10". Grow along alpine stream banks. One fringed white flower per stem. Plant seeds in the fall. Blooms July-Aug. Native wildflower.*

GREEK VALERIAN (see jacob's ladder)

GYPSOPHILA (see baby's breath)

HAREBELL (Campanula rotundifolia) All zones. Bell-shaped, lavender-blue flowers rise above ground-hugging green leaves. Blooms profusely June-Sept, until first hard frost. Rock gardens. Extremely adaptable. Full sun to full shade. Prefers rich, well-drained, moist soil. Ht 6-20". Plant seeds in fall. Reseeds freely, but is not invasive.*

HELENIUM, FALSE SUNFLOWER, or COMMON SNEEZEWEED (Helenium autumnale) Zone 3. Ht 3-4'. Daisy-like flowers in yellow, red, bronze, bloom late summer. Good fall color. Shorter varieties preferred. Tolerates extremes in temperature and soil types, but prefers rich, organic soil. Divide clumps every other year. Sun. New plants from seeds, division, or root cuttings. Back-of-the-border, small hedge, and cut flowers.

Hosta

HELIANTHUS or SUNFLOWER (Helianthus decapetalus 'multiflorus') Zone 4. Perennial. Ht to 3'. Any sunny dry spot. Flowers range from pale yellow to deep orange, bloom July to frost. Seeds or root divisions. Back of border, and tasty seeds. Spreads rapidly so use as single plants. Many annual varieties 15" to 10' tall, see also Veg. and Herb list.

HELLEBORE (Helleborus) Zone 4. Ht 12". Partial shade or full shade. Rich, woodsy soil. Flowers in purple, white, pink, and green. Must be protected from killing frosts (like in a cold frame). Mulch with couple inches of straw. Not like to be transplanted. DEER RESISTANT !

Christmas Rose (Helleborus niger) Blooms Dec.- April. Often opens its flowers through bare spots in the snow.

Lenten Rose (H. orientalis) Blooms later: between March and May.

HEMEROCALLIS (see day lily)

HOLLYHOCK (see biennial list)

HONESTY (see silver dollar plant)

HOSTAS or PLANTAIN LILY (Hosta) Zone 3. Partial shade. Popular. Great variety of heights (4" to 3 ft.), leaf textures, and leaf shapes. White or blue flowers, bloom in August. Grow from seeds (slow growing) or from started crowns. Early and late flowering varieties. Prefer rich moist soil, but tolerate poor soil. Clumps are easy to divide. Ground covers, edgings, or separate beds of mixed varieties. Nice with ferns. Grown for interesting foliage, not blossom.

HYPERICUM or ST. JOHN'S WORT (Hypericum patulum) Zone 5. Ht 2-3'. Bright yellow flowers, bloom May to Aug. Any soil, even sand. Many varieties, mostly shrubs. Will survive in Zone 4 if given winter protection. Propagate from stem cuttings, divisions, or nursery stock. Another species used as ground cover.

IBERIS (see candy tuft, on ground cover list)

ICELAND POPPY (see poppy)

INDIAN PAINTBRUSH (Castillega spp.) Brilliant red, to orange, to yellow flowers, blooms second or third year, June-August. Full sun. Prefers well-drained soil and occasional watering. Adaptable once established. Difficult to start from seed, but well worth the effort! It helps to sow seed in with other wildflowers and grasses. Native wildflower.*

INDIGO, BLUE (see baptisia)

IRIS (see bulb list)

JACOB'S LADDER or GREEK VALERIAN (Polemonium caeruleum) Zone 4. Ht to 2'. Bright blue flowers, bloom in spring. In bulb garden or shrub border. Attractive fern-like foliage. Shade, partial shade, cool area. Any moist soil. Divide clumps or let plants self-sow.

JERUSALEM SAGE (Phlomis fruticosa). Shrubby perennial. All zones. Rugged, woody garden plant. Wrinkled, coarse, wooly, gray-green leaves. Pretty yellow flowers in tight whorls above each set of opposite leaves. Blooms early summer. Likes poor soil on dry slopes, full sun. Resistant to Oak root fungus. Ht 4'. Prune in fall to keep its shape. Cut back after each flowering and it will flower again.

JUPITER'S BEARD or RED VALERIAN (Centranthus ruber) Zone 4. Ht 3'. Mid or back-of-the-border. Rose or white flowers, bloom in summer. Sun or partial shade. Cut flowers. Any soil. Easy care. Propagate by dividing clumps, or dig up young seedlings around mother plants. Self-sows and can become a pest.

KNIPHOFIA (see poker plant)

LAMB'S EARS (see ground cover list)

LARKSPUR (see delphinium)

LATHYRUS or SWEET PEA (Lathyrus) Vigorous climber. Annuals and perennials. Many colors, bloom July-Aug. Cut flowers. Sun or shade. Vines and bushes. Rich, moist deep soil. Sow seed outdoors as early as possible. Ht 2-5'. Does not like hot summers. Screens, borders, window boxes, beds, or cut flowers.

LAVENDER & LAVENDER COTTON (see gr. cover list)

LEADWORT or PLUMBAGO (see ground cover list)

LEMON BALM (Melissa officinalis). All zones. Ht 2'. Leaves light green, many veins, lemon scent. White flowers not showy. Shear plant to keep compact form. Spreads quickly. Prefers rich, moist soil, sun or partial shade (shade tolerant). Very hardy. Start from seed or root divisions. Self sows. Fresh leaves used in drinks, fruit cups, salads, or with fish. Dried leaves give lemon scent to sachets and potpourris. Cut branches keep well in flower arrangements.

LENTEN ROSE (see hellebore)

LEOPARD'S BANE (see doronicum)

LIATRIS or GAY-FEATHER (Liatris spicata) Zone 3. Ht 18-72". Rose, purple or white flowers, bloom June-Sept. Opens its' flower from the top down! Sun or partial shade. Any well-drained soil. Borders, mass plantings, cut (fresh) and dried flowers. Propagate by dividing clumps every 3-4 years, or by seeds.

LILY OF THE VALLEY (see ground cover list)

LINUM (see flax)

LOBELIA or CARDINAL FLOWER (Lobelia cardinalis) Zone 2. Ht 24-30". Bright red flowers, bloom June-Sept. Shade or semi-shade. Rich, moist cool soil (prefers woodland setting). Beautiful trailing plant, good in pots. Best planted in groups like back of the border. Propagate by seeds or root divisions.

LONDON PRIDE (Saxifraga umbrosa). Zone 4. Leaves are shiny green, tongue-shaped, 1 1/2 inches long, and in rosettes. Pink flowers occur in open clusters on red flower stalk, bloom in May. Prefers shade (shade tolerant). Good ground cover for small areas, near rocks, or stream beds. Needs average watering.

LOOSESTRIFE (Lythrum) Zone 3. Ht 3-4'. Sun. Any moist soil. Mid- to back-of-border locations. Pink, purple or red flowers, bloom July-Aug. In hot dry areas need summer mulch. Divide plants every 3-4 years (in spring).

LUNARIA (see silver dollar plant)

LUNGWORT (Pulmonaria) Zone 3. Ht 10-15". Shady, moist soil. Low-growing. Place with wildflowers or bulbs. Flowers first are pink then turn blue or purple, bloom April to May. Can propagate from seed, but clump divisions (late summer) or nursery stock is better. Grows quickly and spreads, forming a carpet. Foliage attractive all summer.

LUPINE (Lupinus) Many species! Zone 4-7. Ht 3-5 ft. Well-drained sandy or woods soil. Part shade. Recommend Russell hybrids. These have blue, pink, red, yellow, purple, and bicolored flowers, bloom May-Aug. Foliage is deeply cut and attractive. Buy nursery stock or plant seed in early spring. Not like long hot summers. Plant as mass in back-of-the-border location. Needs staking in windy areas. Cut flowers. Trim old flower spikes for continuous blooming. Also hardy annual varieties. Deer Resistant ! Lupinus often confused with Delphinium.

LUPINE, CAROLINA (Thermopsis caroliniana) Zone 3. Ht 3-4'. Yellow, pea-like flowers, bloom June to July. Finely cut, dark green foliage. Showy. Hardy even in long hot summers. Insect and disease resistant. Clumps 4 ft wide. Propagate by root divisions of established clumps, nursery stock, or seeds (plant in early fall). Keep mulched.

LUPINE, SILKY (Lupinus sericeus) Blue, sweet pea-like flowers on erect spikes, blooms second year, June-Aug. Leaves and flowers are poisonous to livestock. Native wildflower.*

LYCHNIS, CATCHFLY, or MALTESE CROSS (Lychnis chalcedonica) Zone 3. Hairy perennial herb. Ht 12-36". Scarlet flowers, bloom May-July. Beds, borders, and cut flowers. Full sun. Grows quickly from seed, or clump divisions (in early spring). Well-drained soil. Divide clumps every 3-4 years. Closely related to Silene.

LYCHNIS, MULLEIN PINK, ROSE CAMPION, Lychnis coronaria (see dusty miller)

LYTHRUM (see loosestrife)

MALTESE CROSS (see lychnis chalcedonica)

MARGUERITE, BLUE (see felicia)

MARGUERITE, GOLDEN (see anthemis)

MATRICARIA (see feverfew)

MEADOW RUE (see thalictrum)

MEADOWSWEET or DROPWORT (Filipendula vulgaris) Zone 4. Ht 18". Prefers moist, partial shade, but can grow in full sun and poor dry soil. Wet woodsy gardens, borders. White flowers with a pink blush, bloom July-Aug. Attractive finely cut leaves. Propagate from seeds or divisions (taken in early spring). Multiplys quickly.

MERTENSIA (see virginia bluebells)

MICHAELMAS DAISY (see aster, hardy)

MIMULUS (see monkey flower)

MINT (see herb list)

MIST FLOWER (see ageratum)

MONARDA (see bee balm)

MONKEY FLOWER (Mimulus spp.) Semi-shade. Moist soil. Showy bright flowers in yellow, red, rose-purple, or white, bloom late spring-summer. Perennials, but usually treated as annuals. Figwort family. Native wildflower.

MONKSHOOD (Aconitum) Zone 3. Ht 3-5'. Low maintenance border. Blue, white, yellow, or purple flowers in spike-like clusters, bloom July-Sept. Spreads slowly. Sun or partial sun. Moist, well-drained soil. All parts of plant are poisonous. Propagate from seed.

MULE'S EAR (Wyethia amplexicaulis) Bright, yellow, daisy-like flowers, bloom second year, May-June. Dark-green, mule's ear-shaped leaves. Native wildflower.*

MULLEIN (see verbascum)

MULLEIN PINK (see lychnis coronaria)

OBEDIENCE or OBEDIENT PLANT (see physostegia)

ORIENTAL POPPIES (see poppy)

OXEYE DAISY (Heliopsis helianthoides, or Chrysanthemum leucanthemum) Zone 3. Ht to 5'. Orange-yellow flowers, bloom all summer. Hardy in almost any location. Full sun. Storm-resistant. Mid and back-of-the-border locations.*

PAINTED DAISY or PYRETHUM (Chrysanthemum coccineum, or Pyrethum roseum) Zone 4. Winter hardy to -20°F. Ht 14-24". Bright white, pink, red daisy-like flowers, bloom second year, in June-July. Bright, finely cut foliage. Bushy clumps. Full sun. Rich, moist soil. Divide mature plants every 2-3 years (in late summer). Plant seeds in spring as soon as soil is warm. Keep watered during drought. Edgings, mid-border. backgrounds, or cut flowers. (Also hardy annuals, many colors, 10-24" tall.) Soak dried flowers for several days in warm water to make a powerful insecticide*

PENSTEMON or BEARD TONGUE (Penstemon). Many species! Ht 12-20". Red, rose, blue, lavender-blue, pale pink, or purple flowers. Front-of-the-border. Sun or partial sun. Well-drained, sandy soil. Infrequent watering. Propagate from seed, stem cutting, or clump division. Attract hummingbirds. Native wildflower.*

PEONIES (Paeonia hybrids) Zone 4. All are herbaceous except tree peony (for tree peony see Tree chapter). Fragrant flowers in all colors but blue, bloom May-June. Extend blooming season by mixing early, mid-season and late-blooming varieties. some flowers up to 10 inches across! Rich, deep soil. They grow best in the cold zones 1-7 where they thrive in full sun. Very hardy. (Hardier than tree peonies). Spreads. Long lived. Divide clumps in fall (every 2-3 years), and plant in fall. After dividing plants, cut back all stems to about 4 inches. Be sure eyes on tubers are no deeper than 2 inches or they won't bloom. Provide support for heavy flowers. Heavy feeder. Easy care. Ht 2-4'. Beautiful cut flowers or perennial borders. Tuberous roots.

PERIWINKLE (see ground cover list)

PHLOX, SUMMER (Phlox) Many species, annual and perennial types. Blooms July-August. Full sun, or part shade. Rich moist soil (or sandy soil with humus added). Propagate from stem cuttings (mid-summer), root divisions, or nursery stock. Ht 6" to 4 ft. Plant in a mass in rock gardens, and borders. Will get mold if planted too close together. When plant matures, thin to only 4-5 main stalks per plant. Divide roots every 3 years. Keep faded flowers picked to encourage continuous blooming. Needs winter mulch. (Creeping phlox is a ground cover.)

PHYSALIS (see chinese lantern)

PHYSOSTEGIA, OBEDIENCE, or FALSE DRAGON-HEAD (Physostegia) Zone 3. Part shade. Ht 30" to 5'. Spreading habit. White or pink flowers on tall spikes, bloom July-Sept. Easily confused with Foxglove. Propagate by seed, or by clump division every 2-3 years (Spring or Fall). Full sun. Any soil. Mid-border, or woodland setting.

PINCUSHION FLOWER (see scabiosa)

PINK (see dianthus)

PLANTAIN LILY (see hostas)

PLATYCODON (see balloon flower)

PLUMBAGO (see leadwort on ground cover list)

POLEMONIUM (see jacob's ladder)

POKER PLANT, TORCH LILY, or RED HOT POKER PLANT (Kniphofia) Zone 5. Needs winter mulch. Ht 3-5'. Flowers white, bright yellow, red, and several pastel shades on tall cigar-shaped spike, bloom mid-summer through fall. After blooming, cut off flower spike. Full sun, protected from wind. Fertile, well-drained soil. In fall, cut entire plant to 1-2" above ground. Single plants, back-of-border, cut flowers. Often sold as Tritoma. Slow growers. Buy nursery stock. Divide mature plants every 5 years. DEER RESISTANT.

POPPY (Papaver) Blooms May -June. Many varieties.

California (see california poppy on annual list)

Iceland (P. nudicaule) Zones 2-5. Ht 12". Hates long hot dry summers. Rock garden or borders. Sun. Propagate by seed. Perfect accent for spring bulbs.*

Oriental (P. orientale) Ht 10" to 3 ft. Many bright colors. Full sun, well-drained soil. Crimson solitary flowers. Get poppy roots from nursery. Likes a thick winter mulch and light summer mulch. Any well-drained rich soil. Pick hardiest varieties.

Shirley or Flanders (P. rhoeas) Bright red, crinkled flower on a slender, hairy stem. Blooms July-Aug. Easy to grow. Competes well with grass. Ht 18-24".*

POPPY, HIMALAYAN (Meconopsis betonicifolia) Zone 4. Spectacular, 3-4 inch wide, silky flowers of light-blue or rosy-lavender, with yellow stamens. Requires shade (shade-tolerant), humid air, cool temperatures, loose acid soil, summer watering. 2-4' tall, short-lived. Hairy, alternate leaves.

PRIMROSE (Primula x polyantha) Zones 3. Hardy. Large blossoms. Ht to 12". Flowers bright pinks, reds, yellows, scarlets, purples, and whites, bloom early spring. Cool shade, moist rich soil. Stays green even under snow. Propagate from seed, or clump divisions. Watch for red spider (pest).

PRIMROSE, EVENING (see biennial list)

PYRETHRUM (see painted daisy)

RAMONDIA (Ramondia myconi) Also spelled Ramonda [1]. Delicate little perennial herb. Hardy. Gesneriaceae family. Basal leaves, almost stemless, are covered with soft red hairs. Flowers purple or bluish-lavender, flat bell-shaped, sit on top of a leafless stalk. Fruit is an oblong pointed capsule. Shade-tolerant.

RED HOT POKER PLANT (see poker plant)

RUDBECKIA. A group of plants (composite family.) that like dry soil, mid or back of border, grow from seed, and bloom all summer.

Coneflower (perennial) Rudbeckia californica Wildflower.

Black-eyed Susan or Gloriosa Daisy (annual) Rudbeckia hirta

Black-eyed Susan (biennial) Thunbergia alata—BORDERLINE.

Brown-eyed Susan (annual) Rudbeckia triloba—NOT GROW HERE.

SAGE (see salvia)

SALVIA or SAGE (Salvia spp.) Many varieties of annuals, perennials, and shrubs bloom July-Sept. Zone 4. Ht to 4 ft. Perennials have blue or blue-violet flowers on tall spikes (annual varieties have scarlet). Full sun, any soil. Mid-border or back-of-the-border. Keep faded flowers picked off for continuous bloom. Propagate by seed, division, cuttings or nursery stock. Spreads quickly. Divide mature clumps in 3-4 years. Use 2-3" winter mulch where winters are cold. (see also Kitchen Herb list.)

SCABIOSA or PINCUSHION FLOWER (Scabiosa) Zone 5. Ht to 30". Blue or white flowers, bloom all summer. Mingle with other plants, or in small clumps of their own. Sun, any soil. Propagate from seeds or root divisions. Dwarf varieties grow to 18". Divide plants in spring if get too crowded. Keep faded blooms picked to encourage continuous bloom. Cut flowers. Attractive silver-gray foliage.

SEA PINK (see sea lavender on annual list)

SEA THRIFT (see thrift on ground cover list)

SEDUM or STONECROP (see stonecrop on gr. cover list)

SHASTA DAISY or ESTER REED DAISY (Chrysanthemum maximum) Zone 4. Full sun. Extremely hardy! White flowers, bloom Aug-Sept. Ht 2-3'. Bush and taller varieties need support. Cut flowers. Propagate by seed or root divisions. Mulch both summer and winter.

SHOOTING STAR (Dodocatheon pulchellum) Dainty purple and yellow flowers with reflexed petals, bloom May-June. No leaves on stalk. Ht 6-18". Impossible to transplant.*

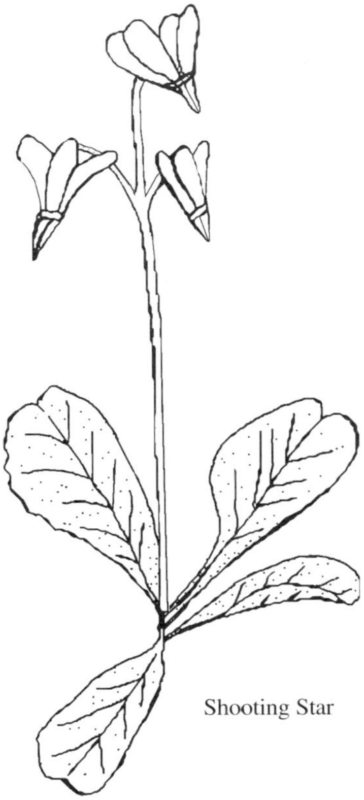

Shooting Star

SHORTIA (Shortia spp) Zone 4. Beautiful evergreen plant that spreads slowly by underground stems. Needs shade and moisture (shade tolerant). Acid soil with peat or compost. Nice with azaleas or rhododendrons. Shiny, rounded leaves with toothed edges, forming clumps. White, pink, or rose flowers are bell-shaped and solitary, on top of the many 4-6 inches tall stems, bloom March-April.

SIBERIAN FORGET-ME -NOT (see brunnera)

SILVER DOLLAR PLANT or HONESTY (Lunaria rediviva) Outstanding pods look like silver dollars, good in dried arrangements. Flowers violet-purple or white, bloom May-June. Also a biennial variety.

Squirrel

SNEEZEWEED (see helenium)

SNOW IN SUMMER (see ground cover list)

SOLIDAGO or HYBRID GOLDENROD (Solidago) Zone 3. Native. Ht 3'. Blooms Aug-Sept. Has been blamed for causing hay fever, but its timetable coincides with ragweed pollen which is the true villian; Goldenrod is harmless. Very showy fall color especially when mingled with patches of hardy asters. Informal borders. Propagate by root divisions, clumps, or nursery stock. Sun, any soil. Very insect and disease resistant. Divide mature plants every 3-4 years.

SOLOMON'S SEAL (Polygonatum multiflorum) Zone 4. Herbaceous. Tall, arching, leafy stems grow from underground rhizomes. Slow spreading. Beautiful white, bell-shaped flowers hang down, sharply contrasted against bright green leaves. Bloom in spring. Dies back over winter. Nice with ferns & hosta. Needs shade (shade tolerant); and loose, moist, woodsy soil; average water. Nice in pots.

SOLOMON'S SEAL, FALSE (Smilacina racemosa). Zone 4. Ht 1-3'. Leaves 3-10 inches long (with hairy undersides). Cluster of fragrant, small, creamy-white flowers at tip of stem, bloom March-May —followed by red, purple-spotted berries. Common in shaded wood —CA to British Columbia, and east to the Rockies. Sun or shade (shade tolerant). Water while growing in spring. Let it go dry in summer if in shade.

SPEEDWELL (see veronica)

SPIDERWORT, COMMON (Tradescantia andersoniana or T. virginiana) Sun or partial shade (shade tolerant). Well-drained moist soil. Ht 1-2'. Grows quickly. Mid-border, or ground cover for shaded areas. Deep, green grass-like foliage. Blue or white flowers, bloom all summer. Propagate by stem cuttings, or seeds. Many flower colors.

SPIREA, FALSE (see astilbe)

SPRING ADONIS (see adonis)

SPURGE (Euphorbia myrsinites.) Zone 3-9. Prostrate perennial. Ht 12-15". Easy care. Hot, dry, sunny slopes. Small yellow flowers (floral bracts), bloom April-May. Leaves: blue-gray or gray-green attractive foliage on fleshy stems. Use in Rock or wall gardens, single plants, ground cover, or accent plant in a mixed border. Propagate in late spring from clump divisions, seed, cuttings. or buy nursery stock. Sun, any well-drained soil.

ST. JOHN'S WORT (see hypericum)

STACHYS (see lamb's ears, on ground cover list)

STOKESIA or STOKES' ASTER (Stokesia laevis) Zone 5. Ht 12-15". Blue and blue-lavender flowers, bloom July-Sept. Grown for late summer bloom. Easy care. Sunny, well-drained soil. Grows quickly. Divide mature plants every 4-5 years; propagate by root divisions (fall or early spring). Use as single plants, or small clumps in front or mid-border.

STONECROP (see ground cover list)

SUMMER PHLOX (see phlox, summer)

SWEET PEA, PERENNIAL (see lathyrus)

SUN DROPS (see oenothera)

SUNFLOWER, PERENNIAL (see helianthus)

SWEET WILLIAM (see biennial list)

TANSY (see vegetables & kitchen herbs list)

THALICTRUM, or MEADOW RUE (Thalictrum) Zone 3. Ht 3-4'. Delicate yellow, white, or lavender flowers, bloom June-July. Good mixed with daylilies. (T. minus is sold by nurseries, a green-tinged yellow flower, blooms July).

THRIFT (see ground cover list)

TICKSEED (see coreopsis)

TORCH LILY or TRITOMA (see poker plant)

TRANSVAAL DAISY (Gerbera) Zone 8. Not grow here (not frost hardy).

TROLLIUS (see globeflower)

VALERIAN, TRUE (Valeriana capitata ssp. californica). According to Taylor [1], the name Valerian is sometimes applied to Centranthus, Fedia, and Polemonium (Jacobs' Ladder, or Greek Valerian). Perennial herbaceous plant. Thickened strong-scented roots or rhizomes with leafy stems. Leaves opposite, lance-shaped, sometimes cut into lobes, margins sometimes toothed. Native. Moist or dryer places 5,000-10,000 ft; Red Fir F. to Subalpine F.; Sierra Nevada. Small white or rose flowers in compact clusters at end of branches. Nice border plant. Propagated by seed or divisions of rootstocks. Drought resistant.

Yarrow

VALERIAN, RED (see jupiter's beard)

VERBASCUM or MULLEIN (Verbascum) Zone 5. Yellow, white, pink or salmon flowers, bloom June-Oct. Ht 30" to 5' Once only a roadside weed, now some forms available as excellent choices for hot, dry, sunny spots requiring tall background color. Furry, gray foliage once used by the Indians for toilet paper. Propagate by root division or seeds. Biennial in nature, but plants usually self-sow.

VERONICA or SPEEDWELL (Veronica) Zone 3. Ht 6-36". Blue, pink, or white flowers, bloom June-Sept. Plant in small masses in rock gardens, low edgings, mid or back-of-the-border. Sunny, well-drained soil. Divide mature clumps every 4-5 years. Keep faded flowers picked to encourage longer bloom season. This genus includes shrubs and perennials, but shrub forms are hardy only in warmer zones.

VIOLA or VIOLET (see annual list)

VIRGINIA BLUEBELLS or MERTENSIA (Mertensia virginica) Zone 3. Sky-blue flowers, blooms March-April. Ht 18-24". Informal borders. Semi-shade. Needs well-composted soil. Spreads rapidly. Propagate from seed, or buy nursery stock. Dies down in midsummer.

WAKE ROBIN (Trillium spp.) Choose hardy species. Lily family. Blooms early spring. Whorl of three leaves at top of each stem, and where they meet is a single flower with three maroon or white petals. Thick, deep growing, fleshy rhizome. Prefers shady woods (shade tolerant). Never let the plants completely dry out.

WALLFLOWER, SIBERIAN (Cheiranthus allionii) VERY fragrant, its aroma compared with roses. Bright orange flowers on a bushy plant, blooms late June-July. Ht 18". Prefers cool summers. Full sun, but will grow in partial shade. Dry or moist soil. Plant seeds in late spring, or start indoors for transplant.*

WALL ROCKCRESS (Arabis albida) All zones. Ht 6-12". White or purple flowers, almost cover plant in early spring. Sunny dry spot with sandy or poor soil. Ground cover, wall, rock garden or open border. Propagate by dividing root clumps in spring or fall. Easy care. Whitish-gray hairy leaves. (A. caucasica grows at Lake Tahoe.)

YARROW (Achillea millefolium) Zone 3. White, red, or yellow flowers, bloom June-Sept. Tall plants (6-36") used in mixed border, single, or in small groups. Dwarfs (4-6") used in rock or wall gardens. Beautiful fernlike foliage. Sunny, dry spot. Any soil. See Ground Cover chapter for ground cover species.*

YUCCA (Yucca) Zone 4. Ht 3-6'. Flowers white, bloom all summer Many heavily scented. Full sun, any dry soil. Seed, root divisions, or offsets. Space plants 3 or 4' apart!

References cited:
[1] The Garden Dictionary (Taylor)
[2] Sunset Western Garden Book (SWGB)
[*] High Altitude Gardens Catalog

Lorquin's Butterfly
(a California butterfly)

BULBS and Bulb-like plants

Fritillaria

A **bulb** is a mass of overlapping (membranous or fleshy) leaves on a short stem base enclosing one or more buds able to develop into new plants. The bulb is the dormant or resting stage of a plant. A bulb is really a tiny flower, wrapped in leaves, enclosed with enough food to enable it to survive for months without soil or moisture. Add warm spring sunshine and water, and these little brown lumps come to life with a bright burst of color, and they have enough food to get them safely through their flowering cycle. (They remind me very much of caterpillars in their cocoons.) Bulbs are easy to grow, but to have them produce beautiful blooms year after year requires a certain amount of know-how — and a little work.

Many bulbs that are called "bulbs", are not truly bulbs at all. The general term bulb includes the following types of plant structures:

•**True bulbs** (i.e. tulip, daffodil, and hyacinth) have a flower bud surrounded by layers of food supply.
•**Corms** (ie: crocus and gladiolus) have a solid mass of stored food with roots growing at bottom and small buds on top.
•**Tubers** (Tuberous begonia and Buttercup) are an enlarged round food-storing part of the stem, and the flower doesn't develop inside until after planting.
•**Tuberous roots** (ie: dahlia) are a food storing enlargement of the root.
•**Rhizomes** (i.e. Iris and Calla Lily) are underground stem tissue with eyes, similar to tubers, but are longer and often form a "V".
•**Pips** (Lily of the Valley) are the raised crown or individual rootstock of a plant, as distinguished from a mass of rootstocks. A "rootstock" is a rhizomatous underground part of a plant, or a stock for grafting consisting of a root or piece of a root.

Selecting the right bulb.

Select bulbs for their mature height, flower color, and time of blooming. (Refer to Suppliers's Catalog list.) Try them as single masses of color, or mix colors. Plan arrangements on paper first. You might try a drift pattern where you throw bulbs and plant them where they fall, as this gives a natural look. The larger more expensive bulbs result in larger, showier, healthier flowers in spring.

Consider selecting some bulbs for "forcing". This is a trick that makes bulbs bloom early, during winter, inside your house. For this technique, see Forcing Spring Bulbs chapter.

Do you leave bulbs in ground over winter?

Hardy bulbs thrive where there are cold winters, because they need to undergo a cold period in order to bloom in the spring; but where there are mild winters (i.e. Los Angeles), the tulips or daffodils have to be dug up in fall, kept in the refrigerator for a while, and then planted in spring in order to have spring flowers.

Hardy bulbs need cold winters, but a few frost tender bulbs (such as Gladiolus, Dahlias, Ranunculus, Tuberous begonia, Montbretia, and Canna lilies) must be dug up and stored indoors over winter, then planted outdoors the next spring. Stored bulbs should be dusted with fungicide and packed either in a paper sack or in a box with dry sawdust, vermiculite, or perlite. Don't use plastic bags because they trap moisture, causing mold. Bulbs must be kept in a dry, indoor location that has no extremes in temperature. None of the stored bulbs should touch each other or they will rot.

Care and feeding of bulbs

Before planting, enrich the soil with peat moss, steer manure, or organic compost. Then put a half teaspoon of bone meal in bottom of hole. Bone meal only travels 1/4 inch per year through soil; so if it is "top dressed" only, it will take years to reach the root zone where it is needed most. Fertilize with 5-10-5 (encourages blooms) in the spring before buds open, and after blooming work in some 10-10-10 fertilizer, and water well. This after blooming care is particularly important, or you may have NO flowers next season. Cut off flower stalks before seed capsules form, but let leaves remain to make food for the plant. Continue watering plants until foliage turns yellow and dies. Both hardy and tender bulbs are easy to grow and produce beautiful flowers year after year. For planting and propagation see Planting chapter. Those in list marked with asterisk are available from High Altitude Gardens Catalog.

<u>Bulb PLANT LIST</u>

ALLIUM, GIANT (<u>Allium sp.</u>.) Purple 4" globe flowers growing on 2-4' stems. Sun or shade. Well-drained soil. Easy care. Insect, pest, and disease resistant. Fresh or dried arrangements. Zone 4. Also is a Dwarf Allium. (Onion family)

ALLIUM, WILD (<u>Allium sp.</u>) Native wildflower. Elegant, edible flower! Use in salads, or sprinkle on grilled foods. Easy to grow. Ht 3-10". Prefers full sun. Well-drained, sandy loam. Water moderately until blossoms dry. Plant seeds in fall. Delicate, pink umbels, bloom second or third year, May-June.*

ALPINE ROSY BELLS (<u>Allium ostrowskianum</u>) Multi-flowered, rosy pink clusters bloom spring through summer. Easy to grow. Multiply rapidly. Border, or rock garden. Pleasing fragrance. Ht 14". Available from Breck'sCatalog.

ANEMONE or WINDFLOWER (<u>Anemone blanda</u>) Hardy, tuberous roots. Plant in fall. Blooms very early spring. Flowers: pink, rose, deep blue, lavender. Plant twelve bulbs

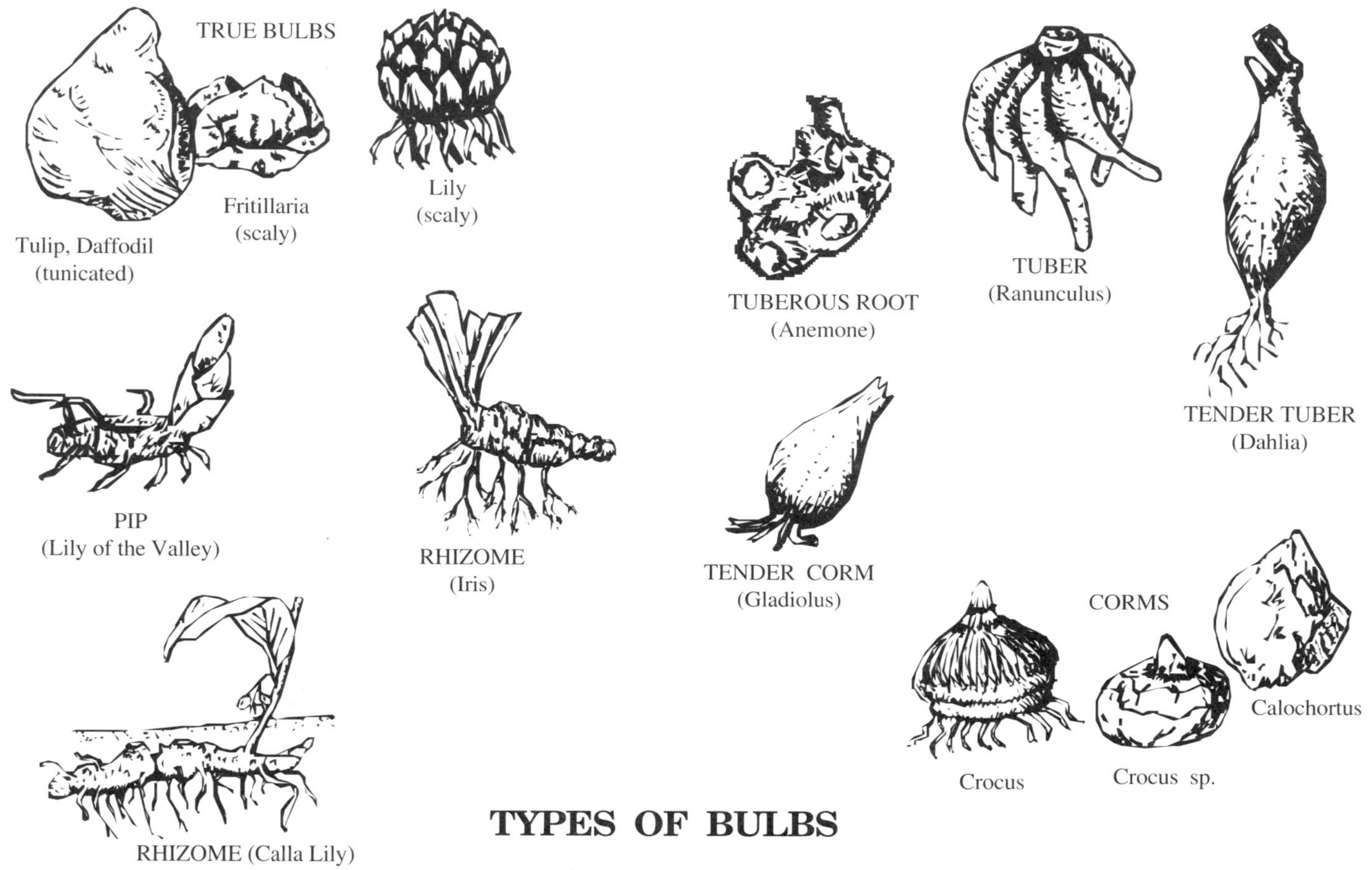

TYPES OF BULBS

together of same color for effect. Low growing (max Ht only 8"). Rock gardens, along a garden path, or in front of shrub plantings. Likes rich, well-drained soil and some shade. Zone 6. Consider as an annual.

CANNA LILY (Canna) Tender, rhizome. Flowers: apricot, orange, white, red, pink, or yellow. Leaves: bronze or green. Rich soil. Full sun. Don't divide roots until spring planting and then cut into pieces with 2-3 eyes or buds per tuber. Keep weeded. After fall frost kills the tops, dig and store in DRY & COOL (but not freezing) basement or garage. Don't clean off dirt, and leave 14" of tops attached. Dust with fungicide and store in dry sand or sawdust with their tops down.

CASCADE BELLS (Allium neapolitanum) Multi-flowered, white clusters bloom early summer with a sweet fragrance. Ht 14". Available from Breck's Catalog.

COLCHICUM (Colchicum) Hardy, corms. Zone 4. Likes a SHADY, cool, moist location. Rock gardens, flower beds, and under shrubs. Foliage starts growing early, becomes dormant during July heat, and then blooms in fall with 5-9" flower stalks. Blooms till cold weather forces it to become dormant again. Looks like crocus but not related !

CROCUS, FALL (Crocus) Goes dormant twice a year (like Colchicum), once in July heat and again in cold of winter. Reproduces quickly and carpets an area in few years. Flower colors: orange-scarlet, bright red, white, blue, and lavender. Stamen are used to make saffron. Zone 4. Plant in August.

CROCUS, SPRING (Crocus) Hardy, corms. Very early bulbs, first welcome sight of spring. Sun, any soil. Low growing. Flowers bloom before leaves appear. Flowers last a little over a week, so mix species and hybrids for the longest season of color. Multiplies rapidly. Thin every three years. Zone 4. Plant in fall.

DAFFODIL (see narcissus).

DAHLIA (Dahlia) Tender, tubers. Blooms mid-summer till frost. All shapes and types, even dwarfs (to 6' tall). Most are about 4' tall and need staking. When plants are about 12" tall, pinch out tops to encourage side branches. Keep faded flowers picked off. Divide only in spring, have at least one bud or "eye" on each tuber. Sunny, rich soil. (Family Compositae) In fall, after frost kills tops, cut plants back to 6" stems. Dig carefully, hose off dirt, cut away any broken roots. Let tubers dry in shade for a week before storing them, tops down, in box of dry sawdust, vermiculite or sphagnum moss. If roots start to shrivel, add some moisture.

DOG-TOOTH VIOLET, TROUT LILY, FAWN LILY, ADDER'S TONGUE, AVALANCHE LILY, or ALPINE LILY (Erythronium spp.) Corm. Zone 4. Small lily-shaped flower, 1—1 1/2 inches across on stems 12 inches high. Each plant has two broad, tongue-shaped, basal leaves. Native to the West. Shade or partial shade (shade tolerant). In groups under trees, in rock gardens, beside pools or streams. Plant in fall in rich, porous soil.

ENGLISH BLUEBELLS or WOOD HYACINTH (Endymion non-scriptus) Bulb. All zones. Most dealers still sell it as Scilla. Look like hyacinth, but are taller and have looser clusters of flowers, and less but broader leaves. Full sun or partial shade (shade tolerant). Mix in with tall shrubs, under open trees, and among low-growing perennials. In dry-winter areas, they need water from October on. Everywhere, let them dry out through summer. Potted or for cut flowers.

FRITILLARIA (Fritillaria) Native. Plant in fall. Zone 5. Slightly acid soil. Fall mulch. Need watering in dry weather.

Crown Imperial (F. imperiallis) Blooms mid-season. Ht 2'. Has drooping, bell-shaped flowers of red, orange, yellow, or bronze. Has unpleasant smell that is said to repel moles and rodents from your garden.

Snake's head fritillaria, Checkered lily, Guinea-hen tulip (F. meleagris). Purple & white flowers. Ht 12".

GALANTHUS (see snowdrop)

GLADIOLUS (Gladiolus) Tender, corms. Likes deep, well-enriched soil. Full sun. In fall, when foliage has died (either naturally or from frost damage) dig bulbs immediately. Cut tops off close to bulb, and remove old withered bulb at bottom. Store in cool, moist, frost-free location. If too warm and dry, bulbs shrivel. Plant in late spring in rows or clumps of four, eight or more. It blooms 65-100 days after planting. To stretch season, plant some every two weeks until mid-July. Each planting will bloom about two weeks. Showy flowers: all colors but blue. Some with ruffles, some miniatures. Need staking. Mulch to keep roots cool. Keep beds weeded. Flowers can be cut when lowest buds start to open (leave at least four leaves remaining on stalk). Mini-Gladiolus come back in spring without digging them up for the winter. (Iris family).

GLORY-OF-THE-SNOW (Chionodoxa) Star-shaped, blue flowers bloom very early spring. Ht only 6". Extremely hardy bulb, likes cold winters. Good in border, at base of deciduous trees, or around shrubs. Any soil, full sun. Flowers more glamorous the second year. When plants get too crowded, thin them, but wait till foliage turns yellow. Zone 5.

GRAPE HYACINTH (Muscari armeniacum) Hardy, bulb. Not a true hyacinth, but when seen at a distance, appears to be a miniature of one. Sun or shade, well-drained soil. Blooms mid-spring with white or blue flowers. Some varieties early, some later. Multiply rapidly and need thinning every three years. Rock gardens, edges, borders.

HYACINTHS (Hyacinthus) Edges and borders. Flowers: rose pink, white, yellow, and blues. Blue variety contrasts well with yellow daffodils or tulips. Refreshing smell. Less hardy than other bulbs, and needs winter mulch. Plant in dense clumps. Blooms about three years, before needs dividing. Nice in front of taller Iris, between lawn and dark green shrubs, or at corners of foundation plantings.

Iris cultivar
Iris pseudacorus

IRIS (Iris) Popular, easy care. Types: Bulbous, tall bearded, dwarf bearded, Dutch, spuria, Japanese, and Siberian. Many colors and sizes. Lengthen bloom season by mixing the early-blooming bearded and Siberian with the later-blooming spuria and Japanese. Divide roots when clumps become too large. DEER RESISTANT !

Bearded, Dwarf is only 12" tall. Rock garden or border. Many colors.

Bearded, Tall are good in borders. Many colors. Winter hardy in Zones 3 and 4 if given protection. If planted too deep, no blooms. Soil must be well drained. Divide clumps every 4-5 years.

Bulbous (I. reticulata) Ht 6-8". Zone 4. This iris grows from bulb, while other iris grow from rhizomes or tubers. Winter mulch. Mixed border or rock garden. Alkaline soil.

Crested. Choose hardy varieties. Dainty plant, closely related to bearded iris. Flowers have small narrow crest at base of outer petals. Shade-tolerant.

Dutch are grown from bulbs, hardy to Zone 5. Yellow, blue, violet, white and bicolors. Cut flowers. Alkaline soil. Need winter mulch.

Gladwin (I. foetidissima) A beardless iris. All zones. Hardy iris with evergreen leaves up to 2' long. Ht 1 — 1 1/2'. Spring flowers not showy. Grown for unusual large seed capsules with round, scarlet seeds. Used in flower arrangements. Sun or deep shade (shade tolerant). Needs little care. Very drought-resistant.

Japanese like wet conditions. Ht 4-5'. Slightly acid soil. June blooming. Sun.

Rocky Mountain have blue-purple, delicately sculptured Ht 2'. Blooms second or third year, May-July.*

Siberian bloom same time as tall bearded group, but flowers last longer. Rich, moist soil. Division rarely needed.

Spuria is the hardiest. Ht 36-50". Sunny, well-drained soil, rich in organic matter. Spuria start blooming when Tall bearded Iris finish blooming.

LEUCOJUM (see snowflake)

LILY OF THE VALLEY (see ground cover list)

MADONNA LILIES (Lilium candidum) Plant in fall and mulch well. Full sun. Well-drained soil. Add 2" of sand to the hole before planting. Don't fertilize with manure. Plant looks similar to Washington Lily. Ht 4'. Flowers large, very fragrant, white trumpets. Deer love to eat them.

MONTBRETIAS or BLAZING STARS (Tritonia) Tender, corm. Flowers look like Gladiolus. Blooms July to frost. Each stem 22" tall with 10-12 buds that flower in succession. Plant at least a dozen per group. Plant orange, yellow, apricot, and scarlet separately or together, as colors are compatible. Likes full sun. In fall, dig corms and let dry in a warm place for two weeks. Then store like Gladiolus at 35-45°F. Cut flowers.

NARCISSUS (Narcissus spp.) Daffodils, jonquils, and narcissus. Hardy early, mid-season, and later bulbs. Narcissus are short-cupped members of this family, while Daffodils have long trumpets. Plant in fall, immediately after dividing. One spectacular variety: Fortissimo has bright yellow flower 5 1/4 inches across, with a trumpet of orange. Plant 6 of a variety in one clump. Likes plenty of water, well-drained soil, full sun, and light mulch in winter.
DEER RESISTANT !

RANUNCULUS (Ranunculus asiaticus) Tender, tubers. Blooms 4 months, in many colors. Long lasting in bouquets. Ht 15-18". Requires sunny, well-drained soil. Dig in fall after leaves die back. Store over winter in dry peat or perlite at 50-55°F. Soak tubers in warm water for several hours before planting in the spring. Consider as an annual.

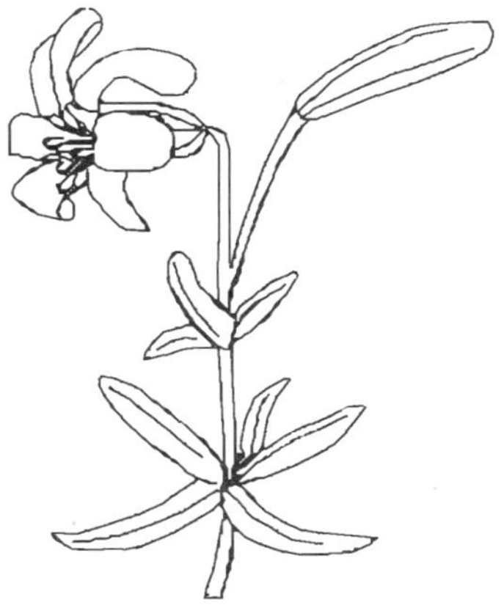

Washington Lily

ROYAL or REGAL LILY (Lilium regale) Ht 4-5. Showy, fragrant flowers that are lilac or purplish outside, white inside, and yellow at base.

SEGO LILY (Calochortus spp.) Native wildflower. Beautiful silky-white petals with touches of deep-purple, blooms third or fourth year, June-Aug. Bulbs can be eaten. Prefers full sun. Well-drained soil. Ht 12". Plant seeds in fall.*

SIERRA LILY (Lilium kelleyanum) Rhizomatous bulb, stems 2-6' tall, leaves in whorls of 3-8. Clusters of small (1 1/2" long), nodding, fragrant flowers are orange toward the tips or yellow throughout, with small maroon dots. Blooms July-Aug. Native on wet banks and in boggy places at 4,000-10,500' elevation from Tulare to Siskiyou and Trinity counties.

SNOWDROP (Galanthus) Family Amaryllidaceae. Very early bulb. Hardy, likes cold climates. Plant has basal leaves, and bell-shaped, nodding white flowers tipped with green solitary flowers on 12-18" stalk. Divide plants just after flowering and try not to disturb the roots. Zone 4. Often confused with Snowflake.

SNOWFLAKE (Leucojum) Family: Amaryllidaceae. Very early bulb (blooms March). Hardy. Basal leaves. Bell-shaped, nodding white flowers with green tips. Flowers in clusters of 3-5, on 12-18" stalk. Plant in groups in the fall with other bulbs. Blooms early March. Often confused with Snowdrop.

SQUILL, SIBERIAN (Scilla siberica) Early and late varieties. Flowers: blue, white or pink nodding bells. Ht only 5". Place beneath shrubs, or at edge of flower border. Multiply rapidly, cover like a carpet. Sun or partial shade. Also have petite squills. Zone 4.

SQUILL, STRIPED (Puschkinia scilloides) Creamy white flowers touched with blue, blooming in March or April. Plants up to one foot tall. Rock gardens. Shade or sun. Zone 4.

STAR OF BETHLEHEM, STAR LILY, SAND LILY, or MOUNTAIN LILY (Leucocrinum) Clusters of 5-6 star-shaped, white flowers. Multiplies. Easy care. Blooms in May. Ht only 6".

STAR TULIP, SIERRA (Calochortus nudus) Corm. All zones. Native in Mts of N. CA. Blooms early. Flowers: white to lavender, 1 to 1 1/2 in. wide on 4-10 in. stems. Moist soil.

SUNNY TWINKLES (Allium moly luteum) Multi-flowered, bright yellow clusters bloom in spring (mid June - mid July). Ht 14". Prefer light shade. Easy to grow. Multiplies rapidly. Very popular! Available from Breck's Catalog.

TIGER LILY, COLUMBIA LILY, or OREGON LILY (Lilium tigrinum) Ht 4-6'. Flowers drooping, nearly 5" wide, orange-red or salmon-red, and black spotted. The tips of the petals are recurved. Likes moist shade. Very popular!

TRITONIA (see montbretias)

TULIP (Tulipa) Many varieties: Early, mid, and late bloomers. Rich, well-drained soil. Sun or light shade. Plant in fall. In colder climates bulbs last longer if planted 10-12" deep. For longer blooming season, mix varieties. DEER RESISTANT !

Tiger Lily

WASHINGTON LILY, CASCADE LILY or WHITE LILY (Lilium washingtonianum) Large showy, white, often purple-spotted, sweet-smelling flowers. Blooms in July. Native. Ht 4-6'. Deer eat the flowers.

WINTER ACONITES (Eranthis) Hardy tubers. Dainty gold buttercups. Plant in late summer. Light shade or full sun. Zone 4.

GROUND COVERS

Clover

Ground covers are low or creeping, herbaceous or woody plants, often used where it is difficult to grow grass. They are excellent for preventing erosion on steep slopes, for those bare shady spots, for poor soil conditions, and they also grow on level ground. Select the cover that best fits the sun, soil, and climate of your area. Generally ground covers require much less water than grass.

These plants usually spread quickly by creeping stems rooting as they grow, or by underground stolons. Check planting instructions for each type of plant, as the spacing of individual plants can vary from 6 inches to 5 feet apart. Clumps spread faster than individual plants. Most vines will not take foot traffic. Propagation from clump or root division, seed, layering, or cuttings. See also Propagation chapter.

Ground covers are easy to care for, pretty, and most need no mowing. They require little maintenance once established, but do need occasional watering, weeding, mulching, and pruning. Quite resistant to diseases and pests. Ground covers can slow down water loss by crowding out unwanted bushes and weeds that have deeper root systems. Many plants die back in winter to reappear in spring. Many advantages when used as a living mulch. See Mulching chapter.

Applying fertilizer to ground cover plants, can often do more harm than good. Prepare soil as you would for a lawn. For most ground covers work in a good balanced fertilizer and peat moss; but for alpine ground covers which naturally grow in poor soils, be light on the fertilizer [1].

Some examples are: For shade use Pachysandra, Lily of the Valley, Creeping Charlie, or Vinca minor. On steep banks with northern exposures use Vinca minor, Snow-on-the-mountain, or Hall's Honeysuckle. On steep slopes with southern exposures use Hall's Honeysuckle or Crown Vetch.

Ground Cover PLANT LIST

AJUGA (see bugleweed)

AARON'S BEARD (Hypericum calycinum) Yellow flower, blooms July-Sept. Yellow-green leaves. Part shade. Covers large areas: slopes or flat areas. Evergreen low shrub. Ht only 12". Zone 4. Sandy soil. Also a perennial variety. Mow in Spring, then fertilize.

ARTEMISIA, SILVER MOUND (see silver mound artem.)

BARREN STRAWBERRY (Waldsteinia fragarioides). Zone 6. Evergreen strawberry-like ground cover, but with dry, hairy fruits. Ht 2-3", S 6-8". Shiny green leaves with three leaflets. Yellow flowers in spring. Bronze fall color. Full sun to light shade (shade tolerant).

BEARBERRY COTONEASTER (Cotoneaster dammeri) Zone 5-10. Sun or light shade. White flowers; red berries. Any well-drained soil (even rocky). Good variety: Lowfast.

BEARBERRY, KINNIKINNICK (Arctostaphylos uva-ursi) Zone 2-10. Sun, shade. Sandy acid soil. White flowers; bright red berries attract birds. Slow growing, evergreen. Slopes, under trees.

BIRD'S-FOOT TREFOIL (Lotus corniculatus) Zone 3-10. Sun, light shade. Large areas. Ht 1-2'. Yellow flowers. Any well-drained soil. Mow to keep growth even.

BISHOP'S WEED, GOUTWEED (Aegopodium podagraria 'variegatum') Zone 3-10. Shade, part sun. Ht 8-10". White flowers, mid-summer. Any soil. Grow under trees and shrubs. Attractive green and white leaves.

BLUE FESCUE (Festuca ovina 'glauca') Zone 3-9. Shade or part sun, any soil (prefer drier sites). Creates compact mounds of whitish blue.

BUGLEWEED, CARPET BUGLE (Ajuga reptans) Zone 3-10. Mint family. Sun, light shade. Hardy to -30°F. Rich moist soil. Creeping evergreen perennial. Blue flowers in Spring. Popular! DEER RESISTANT !

CANDYTUFT (Iberis) Zone 3. Sun. Perennial evergreen shrub. Ht 8-12". White flowers in early spring lasting 4-6 weeks. Small areas edging, good for cut flowers. Also are hardy annuals in dwarf to tall forms (see annual plant list).

CERASTIUM (see snow in summer)

CLOVER, RED (Trifolium pratense) Pink flowers, bloom spring-summer Ground cover and soil conditioner (has nitrogen-fixing bacteria in the roots that feed the plant nitrogen). Easy to grow. Ht 1-2'. Partial to full sun. Any soils. Drought tolerant, yet consistent watering is necessary. Plant seeds any time of year. Can be invasive.*

CLOVER, YELLOW SWEET (Melilotus officinalis) Bright yellow and white flowers, bloom Aug.-Sept. Excellent soil conditioner (adds nitrogen to the soil). Easy to grow. Ht 3-5'. Prefers full sun. Any soil, including clay. Drought tolerant. Plant seeds any time of year. Can become invasive.*

CORSICAN or CREEPING MINT (Mentha requieni) Zone 6-10. Sun or light shade. Max Ht 2" green cushion. Crushed leaves smell like peppermint. Tiny pale lavender flowers in late spring. Needs lots of water and rich soil. Use between stepping stones, will tolerate light traffic.

CORSICAN PEARLWORT, IRISH MOSS (Sagina subulata) Zone 4-10. Light shade. Mossy evergreen mat 4 in. tall, tiny white flowers in summer. Use between stepping stones or in rock gardens. Well-drained rich, moist, soil.

COTONEASTER (see bearberry c. or creeping cotoneaster)

CREEPING BUTTERCUP (Ranunculus repens) Widely adapted. Filtered shade (mildews in heavy shade), hardy prostrate perennial. Yellow flowers late spring-summer. Can become a vigorous weed in lawns.

CREEPING CHARLIE, MONEYWORT, or CREEPING JENNIE (Lysimachia nummularia) Shade. Zone 2-10. Native plant. Mint family. Not the house plant variety. One inch thick carpet with bright yellow flowers all summer. Only light traffic. Contain by pruning or borders. Deer Resistant !

CREEPING COTONEASTER (Cotoneaster adpressus) Any soil and all climates (hardy to -30°F). Sun or shade. Lowfast and Dammeri are good varieties. Deciduous vine. Slow growing. Pink flowers in spring; bright red berries. Cascades over wall, fence, covers ground, or rock gardens.

CREEPING LILYTURF (Liriope spicata) Zone 4-10. Sun or shade. Forms mounds, Ht 6-12". Grass-like leaves. Lavender-white flowers in summer. No foot traffic. Use for beds, borders, slopes, and under trees and shrubs.

CREEPING MAHONIA, or DWARF HOLLY-GRAPE (Mahonia repens) Zone 5-10. Sun or shade. Evergreen shrub, leaflets have holly-like spines. Yellow flowers in spring; grape-like fruit. Add organic matter to the soil.

CREEPING MAZUS (Mazus reptans) Zone 5-10. Sun or shade. 1 in. high. Lavender flowers. Needs moist, rich, soil.

CREEPING PHLOX, MOSS PHLOX, GROUND PINK, or MOSS PINK (Phlox subulata) Zone 2-10. Forms carpet, Ht 4-6". Pink, white, violet, or red flowers early spring-summer. Slopes, borders, slopes, rock gardens. After flowering, trim stems. Hardy to -40°F. Sun. See also dianthus or thrift.

CREEPING SPEEDWELL (Veronica repens) Zone 5-10. Sun. Forms mat 4 in. high. Pink, blue, or white flowers in spring. Likes organic matter. Keep away from lawns.

CREEPING THYME (Thymus serpyllum) Zone 3-10. Aromatic perennial, long lived and very persistent. Ideal for hot and dry areas, easy care, takes traffic. Sun. Flowers red, pink, white, rose-purple in summer. Can be mowed. Used as a dried aromatic herb. Attracts bees. Another species is kit. herb.

CROWN VETCH (Coronilla varia) Zone 3-10. Sun. Creeping Ht 1-2". Pink and white flowers spring till early fall. Hardy vine, good along freeways, once established it maintains itself. Drought tolerant. Good in ravines, steep slopes or level ground. Difficult to eliminate. It thrives in the poorest growing conditions and actually enriches the soil (legume family). DEER LOVE TO EAT IT.

CYPRESS SPURGE (Euphorbia cyparissias) Zone 3-9. Ht 12". Yellow-orange flowers in spring. Hot sunny slopes. Grey-green leaves.

DIANTHUS, MAIDEN PINK, or GARDEN PINK (Dianthus deltoides) Zone 2-10. Full sun. Grass-like leaves. Spicy fragrant flowers in red, pink, or white in late Spring. Prune back after flowering. Keep weeds out. See also Dianthus, thrift, or creeping phlox on annual list.

EUONYMUS (see winter creeper on perennial vine list)

EUPHORBIA, see:
Snow-on-the-mountain;
Cypress spurge;
Spurge (on perennial plant list); or
Japanese spurge (not Euphorbia) —see pachysandra

FIVE-LEAF AKEBIA (Akebia quinata) Zone 4-10. Sun or light shade. Fragrant purple flowers in early spring. Grows too fast in rich soil. Invasive. Banks, slopes, or ground cover. Semi-evergreen. Start by seeds, root cuttings, or divisions.

FORGET-ME-NOT or MYOSOTIS (see biennial list)

GALAX, GALAXY, or BEETLEWEED (Galax urceolata) Zone 3-8. Shady, cool, moist soil, high in humus. Grow under rhododendrons. White flowers in mid-summer. Cut leaves used by florists.

GERMANDER, or CHAMAEDRYS GERMANDER (Teucrium chamaedrys) Zone 5-10. Small shrub to 18 in. tall. Tiny rose-colored flowers. Needs pruning.

GINGER, WILD (Ascarum canadense) Zone 4-10. Sun-deep shade. Ht 6-10". Red-purple flowers in late spring. Rich soil. Grows under taller plants. When dried, is a good flavoring.

HONEYSUCKLE (see perennial vines list)

HYPERICUM (see aaron's beard and st. john's wort)

IBERIS (see candy tuft)

JAPANESE SPURGE (see pachysandra)

KNOTWEED (Polygonum cuspidatum compactum). All zones. Perennial. Fast growing with creeping roots (invasive). 10-24 inches tall. Red, stiff, wiry stems. Pale-green, heart-shaped leaves with a red vein. Red fall color (leaves). Plants die back to ground in winter. Small flowers in dense, showy clusters. Buds are red, turning to pale-pink when open in late summer. Sunny, dry banks. Controls erosion on hillsides.

LAMB'S EARS, BETONY (Stachys byzantina) Zone 3-10. Soft, silvery, woolly-looking leaves. Grown for color contrast. Ht 12-18". Tiny purple flowers in summer. Hardy in hot, sunny well-drained soil. Needs little water. Root divisions (in early spring), or buy from mail order nurseries. Annuals and perennials (both about same height). Easy care.

LAVENDER (Lavandula angustifolia) Zones 5-9. Dwarf shrubby perennial. Lavender or pink flowers. Silvery-grey leaves. Ht 15-30". EXTREMELY FRAGRANT. Blooms July-

Aug. Prune right after flowering. Divisions or cuttings. Hedges, herb gardens, edgings, or ground covers on banks. Warm dry sunny soil. Not frost hardy. Use 2-3" winter mulch. To dry, hang upside down in a shady, well-ventilated area until dry. Often confused with Lavender Cotton.

English (true lavender) used in potpourris and sachets (for drawers), has showiest and most fragrant flowers.

Spike lavender has larger, more fragrant leaves.

French lavender grown mainly as bath scent.

Super-Hardy (L. officinalis) has the "old English" fragrance, blooms the first season, easy to grow, sun or part-shade, blue-violet (lavender) flowering spires blooming June to fall. Silver-green foliage. Ht 18". An improved Northern, Sub-Zero variety. For sweet-scented linens, sachets. Along paths, borders, rock gardens, or hedges.

LAVENDER COTTON (Santolina chamaecyparissus) Zone 6. Sun, sandy soil. Grown for attractive silver-grey leaves (pungent odor). Evergreen perennial. Prune to ground level or will grow 2' tall with uneven ragged growth, and yellow flowers. Blooms June-July. Yellow flowers dried are used for fragrance in drawers and closets. Also a moth deterrent. Propagate every 4 years by root divisions or stem cuttings (spring or fall). Edgings, borders, to divide bright colors in patterned beds, single in rock gardens, or as ground cover. Not winter hardy in zones colder than Zone 6, so use in a cold frame, or overwinter as house plant on a sunny windowsill.

LEADWORT (Ceratostigma plumbaginoides) Zone 6-10. Partial shade. Hates hot locations. Bright cobalt-blue flowers, bloom Aug.-Sept. Semi-evergreen. Leaves red-bronze in fall. Ht 9-12".. Under shrubs, on slopes or banks, in small beds, rock gardens, edgings, or shrub borders. Spreads rapidly by underground roots. Confine or will overrun area. Well-drained rich soil. Pruning. Needs winter mulch in Zone 6. Propagate by stem cuttings (mid-summer), or dividing clumps.

LILY OF THE VALLEY, FALSE (Maianthemum dilatatum) Spreads by underground roots. Tiny white flowers in early spring, heart-shaped leaves. Often confused with Convallaria.

LILY OF THE VALLEY, true (Convallaria majalis) Zones 2-7. Grown from pips. Shade (even dense shade). Fragrant white or pale pink flowers! Moist, organically enriched soil. Perennial herb. Best in cold climates. Spreads easily.

LYCHNIS, Mullein Pink, Rose Campion, Lychnis coronaria (see dusty miller on perennial list)

MAX GRAF ROSE (Rosa rugosa x Rosa wichuraiana) Zone 5-10. Sun. Bright pink, white, or red-purple flowers with yellow centers all summer. Ht 3-4'. Colorful fruits. Rugged slopes or banks. Prune for denser growth. (see rose chapter).

MORNING GLORY VINE (Convolvulus) Grey-green prostrate hardy annuals or perennials. Spreading to 3 ft across. Lavender-blue flowers June-Nov. (or frost). Sunny, well-drained soil. Easy care. Fences, posts, ground cover, hanging baskets.

MOSS PINK (see creeping phlox)

MOSS SANDWORT, IRISH MOSS, LAZY-MAN'S LAWN (Arenaria verna) Zone 2-10. Sun or light shade. Looks like moss. Tiny white flowers. Small areas, slope, or between stepping stones. Moist, well-drained soil. In hot areas, grow in light shade.

PAXISTIMA (Paxistima canbyi) Zone 5-8. Sun or shade. Ht 12". Leaves turn bronze in fall. Tiny white flowers in spring. Well-drained, moist, rich, acid soil (good in front of rhododendrons). In hot areas, grow in the shade only.

PACHYSANDRA, JAPANESE SPURGE (Pachysandra terminalis) Zone 4-9. Light to deep shade. Moist, rich soil. Evergreen. White flowers in spring. Level ground, slope, borders. Very popular! Easy care.

PERIWINKLE or COMMON DWARF PERIWINKLE (Vinca) Evergreen perennial, very popular! 6" high creeping mat, rooting as it spreads. Prefers full sun in zones 4-7, but shade in hotter areas. The more sun it gets, the more water it needs. Sometimes called Creeping myrtle, but be aware that another less hardy ground cover also goes by that name.

V. minor is hardy to -30°F. White or blue flowers in early spring and fall. Tolerates light foot traffic. Resists insects and disease. Any soil. Slopes or flat. Requires more care, more water, and more fertilizer than V. major.

V. major has a larger flower and larger leaves. Flowers are blue or hot pink. A little less hardy but a tougher plant and easier to grow. Mow occasionally.

PINKS (see dianthus, thrift, or creeping phlox)

SCOTCH HEATHER (Calluna vulgaris) Zone 4-10. Sun, light shade. Small bushy shrubs, 4" to 2'. Tiny pink, lavender, purple, and white flowers midsummer-fall. Highly organic moist soil. Plant in early spring. Prune old plants back by 1/2 of growth each year to make compact mats.

SEDUM or STONECROP (Sedum) Succulent perennials or subshrubs. Choose hardy varieties. Some tiny and trailing, others are upright. Fleshy leaves are highly variable in size, shape, and color. Usually evergreen. Flowers tiny, starlike, in large clusters, sometimes brightly colored. Small plants used in rock gardens, ground or bank cover, pot or dish garden; while larger ones used as borders, in containers, or as shrubs.

SILVER MOUND ARTEMISIA, or SATINY WORMWOOD (Artemisia schmidtinana) Zone 3-10. Sun. Unusual silver-grey foliage, Ht only 12". Very tiny yellow flowers late summer-early fall. Any well-drained soil, resists drought. Little care. Prune back to keep mound effect.

SNOW-IN-SUMMER (Cerastium tomentosum) Zone 2-10. Sun. Quick spreading, evergreen, perennial that forms dense tufty mats of silvery grey leaves. Tiny white flowers bloom all summer. Ht only 3-6". Any well-drained soil (desert, mountain, or coast). Hardy cover for large areas, rock gardens, steep slopes, sandy areas. New plants by division, seeds, or cuttings. Pruning keeps plants from getting scraggly. Invasive.

SNOW-ON-THE-MOUNTAIN (Euphorbia marginata) Ht 2'. Full sun. Steep banks with northern exposure, borders, foundation, and group plantings. Leaf margins white, upper leaves almost all white. Hardy annual. Poor soil okay. Stems contain poisonous sap.

SPRING HEATH (Erica carnea) Full sun needed in Zomes 5-8. Prefers acid soil. Ht 7-15". Well-drained banks and slopes. Many varieties, many colors. Early spring flowers bloom 4 months. Cut off faded blooms. Keep watered. Tolerates wind.

SPURGE, see
Pachysandra, Japanese spurge (Pachysandra);
Cypress spurge (Euphorbia); or
Spurge (Euphorbia) on perennial list

SQUAW CARPET (Ceanothus prostratus) Native prostrate shrub in Lassen Park at 5600-7000 ft. Ht 1-4". Tiny blue flowers. Forms mats in open woods, on slopes, and flats. Almost impossible to transplant,—try growing in a container till is root-bound and then transplant into final location.

ST. JOHN'S WORT (Hypericum repens) Zone 5. Sun. Tall thick prostrate carpet. Perennial herb. Tiny yellow flowers. Good substitute for lawn.

STRAWBERRY, INDIAN MOCK (Duchesnea indica) Zones 5-10. Sun or shade. Mat 2-3" high. Yellow flowers; inedible red berries. Semi-evergreen. Large areas. Any soil. Can be used in hanging baskets. DEER RESISTANT !

STRAWBERRY, WILD or SAND STRAWBERRY (Fragaria chiloensis) Zone 3-10. Sun, light shade. No foot traffic. Mat 6-12" high. White flowers in spring; edible red berries. Moist areas. Mow (with setting on 2 in.) in early spring and apply complete fertilizer. To encourage spreading (produce runners), remove blooms on the new plants.

STONECROP SEDUM (Sedum) Zone 3-10. Succulent thick fleshy leaves. Herbaceous, hardy evergreen perennial only 2-3" high. Flowers red, pink, cream, white, orange, yellow, or rust brown. Blooms May-frost. Any soil (even poor), sun or shade, drought resistant. No foot traffic. Rock gardens, edgings, stony areas, ground covers on difficult banks and slopes. Little care, but needs winter protection. Root divisions. Popular variety: Dragon's Blood (for a small area) has green to reddish-bronze foliage, with red flowers in July-Sept.

SWEET WOODRUFF (Galium odoratum) Zone 4-10. Evergreen perennial. Shade. Ht 6-8". Tiny white flowers spring-summer. Fragrant green leaves. Flavoring and perfume. Good under rhododendrons and high branched conifers. Moist, acid, organically rich soil.

THRIFT, SEA PINK, COMMON THRIFT (Statice armeria, or Armeria maritima) Zone 2-10. Grass-like, evergreen, perennial only 6" high. White, pink, red, or lilac flowers spring-summer in cool areas; intermittent blooming in warmer areas. Beds, edgings, or rock gardens. Any well-drained soil in full sun. Divide and replant when centers of old plants die (makes hundreds of starts). Root divisions or nursery stock. Latin names Statice, Limonium and Armeria are often used interchangeably; but Armeria is old name for Statice, and Limonium is name of different plant: Sea pinks or Sea lavenders [2,3]. Difference between Statice and Limonium is that the latter has an open, branching flower cluster [3].

THYME (see creeping thyme)

TRAILING ARBUTUS (Epigaea repens) Zone 4. Very fragrant pink or white flowers cluster at branch tips. Creeping or prostrate, evergreen, woody shrublet. Excellent woodland ground cover. Spreading—each plant 12-24 inches wide, stems rooting as they grow. Oval leaves. Very hardy, but not easy to grow. Prefers acid soil; mulch with leaf mold or peat moss. Do not fertilize. Needs excellent drainage, and shade from summer sun (shade tolerant). Keepmoist all summer.

TWINFLOWER (Linnaea borealis) Hardy to -40°F. Dainty shiny evergreen. Fragrant pale pink fl. Shade or semi-shade.

VIOLET, SWEET (see viola on annual list)

VIRGINIA CREEPER, WOODBINE, AMERICAN IVY (Parthenocissus quinquefolia) Zone 3-10. Sun, light shade. Ht 10-12". Deciduous vine, leaves bright red in fall. Rocky ground, ravines, or slopes. Little care in rich, moist soil. Tiny greenish flowers, blue-black berries.

WILTON CARPET JUNIPER (Juniperus horizontalis 'wiltoni') Zone 2-10. Sun. Very hardy creeping evergreen only 4" high. Leaves blue-green. Dry soil okay.

WINTERCREEPER or EUONYMUS (see peren.vine list)

YARROW, SILVERY (Achillea argentea) Sun. Yellow flower, silver-grey leaves. Covers small area. Ht only 3-6".

YARROW, WOOLY (Achillea tomentosa) Zone 2-10. Sunny sandy, dry soil. Yellow flowers spring to fall. Pungent silvery-green evergreen herb or perennial mat 6-12" high. Hardy ground cover in sandy or rocky areas. Mow to maintain even height. See also Perennial list.

YELLOW-ROOT (Xanthorhiza simplicissima) Zones 4-10. Sun or shade. Low-creeping shrub, Ht 24". Leaves turn orange in fall. Purple flowers in early spring. Moist, areas along banks and streams. Likes soil with peat moss.

YEW, SPREADING ENGLISH (see shrub list)

References cited:
[1] Better Homes & Gardens [BH&G]
[2] A Calif. Flora [Munz}
[3] The Garden Dict. [Taylor]

LAWNS

a sod lawn

Having a lawn by your house can raise humidity, reduce the amount of dust, and make the house cooler in summer. If you choose to have a lawn instead of a ground cover, there are some important rules to remember for a healthy, happy, disease-free lawn.

Starting a lawn from seed

Select a grass type adapted to your climate. Select "cool-season" grasses in areas with cold winters. These contain a mixture of mostly bluegrass, some fine fescue, bentgrass, and a portion of perennial ryegrass. You also need to select for sun or shade. Remember that growing lawn in the shade needs more fertilizer to provide plant food for both the tree roots and the grass!

Plant lawns or sod in early spring or fall—preferably not during the summer! Optimum temperatures for lawn growth are about 70-75°F. If you plant in early fall, when there are still several weeks of cool weather before freezing, the grass roots will grow all winter and usually will be well established by spring. If you feel you have to plant a lawn in summer, you will have to water about 5 times/day, or whatever it takes to keep the soil surface moist.

Before planting, prepare your soil properly. First, use rototiller to break up dirt clods, aerate the soil, and remove stones and debris. Then add layer of peat moss, and well-aged steer manure evenly over the area. Use a mechanical spreader to add fertilizer and lime. Then cultivate using a rotary tiller. Level the area with backside of metal rake.

Stir the seeds in the package or hopper so that the different kinds of seeds are evenly distributed, and then use a mechanical spreader to broadcast the seeds evenly. Follow the package directions for correct amount of seed per 1,000 square feet. Set the spreader at the correct setting for seed, fertilizer, or lime; as this regulates particle size and the density you want to spread it. Make sure the seed isn't planted too deep or it won't grow at all. Spreaders, rototillers, and rollers can be rented at most hardware stores.

After broadcasting the seed, use a roller on the lawn to level and firm the seed in place,—but only go over the area once. After rolling the lawn, apply mulch of straw or peat moss in a thick layer (approximately a half inch deep) to protect the seed from being dried out, washed off, or blown away. Then water immediately with a fan attachment on your hose, or use sprinklers for a short time, but stop when the water starts to run off. Keep the soil surface moist until the seedlings get established by watering lightly and often. (This may mean 4-5 times a day if the weather is hot!)

When the new grass is two inches high, mow it carefully or you will pull it up by the roots. Then start watering deeper and less often until you have a nice deep root system and a beautiful lawn. It may seem a little thin at first, but it thickens with time. If you don't think it's thick enough by next spring you can spread more seed. This time you won't need to add mulch, as the existing grass will protect the new seed. Rake it gently into the surface and add topsoil as needed to cover the seed. All new lawns will produce a healthy crop of weeds at first. The weed seeds are brought to the surface with cultivation. Be prepared to weed the first year.

Some lawn clippings can be left where cut, since they supply some food, but too many clippings left in place can suffocate the lawn. (Grass clippings are a good addition to your compost pile, but only add in THIN layers, and put a soil layer in between grass layers.

A variation of the seeded lawn is to plant grass and clover seed together. The clover feeds the lawn nitrogen and keeps it a healthy green.

The sod alternative for an "instant" lawn

Sod or turf grass (rolls of already growing grass) is easy to apply and grows well here, but it is expensive. It depends what your time is worth. Sod is often used when a quick lawn is desired (as in making a house more saleable). Many lawns in Lassen and Plumas Counties were first grown at Green Valley Turf Farm in Sierra Valley.

There are slightly different watering needs to establish and support sod lawns. Prepare a level surface of enriched soil and add complete fertilizer (same as for seeding a lawn), but have the prepared surface be 3/4 inch lower than the surrounding area. SOAK the enriched soil thoroughly before unrolling the sod strips. Lay strips parallel to each other, but stagger the strip ends so they don't all end at the same place (i.e like laying out a brick wall). Press each strip closely against the last strip so there is no gap. If you need to cut one, cut it with a sharp knife and at the correct angle for fitting. Roll with roller half full of water [1]. Then water regularly to a depth of six inches (usually daily) until roots are well established. If on a hill, you may have to drive in some stakes to hold the sod in place until the roots are established [2]. At least with sod lawn you don't have to worry about the seed washing away. See also Watering chapter.

How do you keep lawn healthy?

• **Mow to proper height**. Proper grass heights are suggested on seed packet. Leaving the grass longer is healthier for the lawn, and shades weeds out. See watering chapter for lawn types and heights.

• **Aerate and thatch** established lawns every spring before enriching or fertilizing. Use a special tool for aerating that you step on (see illustration). For large lawns a power aerator may be rented. When aerating be sure the soil beneath the lawn is damp before you start or it will be like trying to push through a board! A thatching blade can be attached to a power mover, or you can pull hard when raking with a metal rake. Thatching loosens and removes old cut grass and dead stems that choke out or slow the growth of new grass.

•**Enrich lawns every spring** with peat moss, steer or chicken manure, and 10-10-10 fertilizer. Spread the enrichments evenly over the lawn surface and work in with a metal rake or mow with mower set at 2" to get the "stuff" down to ground level. Fertilize according to package directions for your type of grass.

A complete or balanced fertilizer of 10-10-10 is better than 21-0-0 (nitrogen alone) or 27-3-3 (nitrogen too high for our high acid soils). See also chapter on Soils. Nitrogen alone promotes fast top growth and greens it up fast, but doesn't promote equal growth of tops and roots. Feed the roots too for a healthy lawn! Ortho Grow Lawn food 22-4-4 contains iron which is helpful, but also has sulfur,—which makes the soil more acid (okay for alkaline soil areas). Our soils are already very acid. Read ingredients carefully on any fertilizer packages you buy.

Lawns need fertilizer when they are growing the most. In cold winter areas, lawns have their most active growth period during the cool seasons of spring and fall. That is why we call them "cool season" grasses. Fertilize these only in spring (May). If you fertilize also in fall, the lawn would not slow its growth going into winter.

Be sparing on the manures, but generous on the peat moss. I have a fairly large lawn and I add 1 large bale peat moss, 1 steer manure, 2 chicken manure, and a small bag of 10-10-10. If your lawn "needs help", apply peat moss up to 3 times a year. Adding organic matter usually helps any "growing" problem.

•**Water deeply and infrequently**, and only when the lawn needs it (not every day!). This will promote growth of deep healthy roots (see chapter on Watering). I live at 4,500' and water lawns every third day for 20 minutes, except for hot spells when I extend the time to 30 minutes. Let your plants be your guide, watch them for indication of wilting.

•**Do you have a problem with Lawn Moths?** As soon as you see the first one on the lawn in the spring, spray with Diazinon. Then spray again 10 days later to kill the eggs it laid. If lawn moths are not controlled, they can kill your grass. and also can spread into your house!

References cited:
[1] Sunset Western Garden Book
[2] Time-Life Books: LAWN & GARDEN.

Other References:
RD: Practical Guide to Home Landscaping
Sunset Ideas for Landsc & Garden Remodeling
Put Color, Form & Excitement
Natures Design

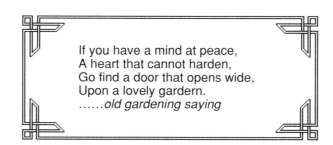

If you have a mind at peace,
A heart that cannot harden,
Go find a door that opens wide,
Upon a lovely gardern.
......*old gardening saying*

VEGETABLES

A productive vegetable garden, just like landscaping, takes lots of planning. Select a sunny location, preferably one with a south-facing exposure, and away from low ground, where cold air drains. Do you need fencing to keep animals out? Will you be planting on raised beds or on flat ground? Will you be watering using sprinklers, furrows, or drip irrigation? What kind of mulch will you use? What kind of soil do you have? Do you need to improve it? How much organic matter should you add, and what kind? Should you add manure? What kind? How do I keep bugs out of my garden? Do I plant in March, April, May, or June? Seeds or seedlings? Many of these questions will be answered in this book.

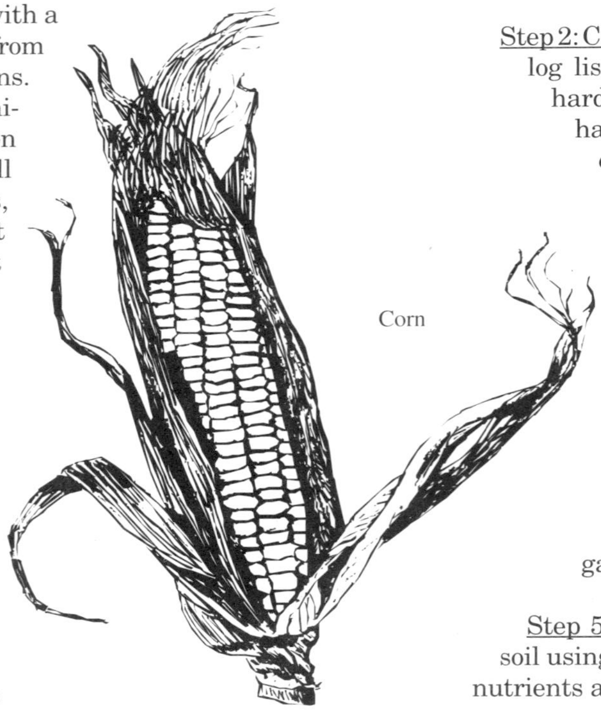

Corn

Every year you will plant fewer seeds (give away less produce), and understand your garden and your family's needs better. If you continue enriching your soil with organic matter and nutrients, and rotating your crops (heavy feeders one year should be followed by light feeders the next year), your soil will get better each year instead of worn out and you will be able to plant closer together.

Select vegetables that are hardy and early maturing, preferably in sixty days. All root vegetable crops do exceptionally well here, especially those designed to grow in cool or cold weather. Vegetables requiring hot temperatures and long growing seasons need to be grown in a greenhouse, cold frame or patiently covered every night when frost is expected. Green pepper, squash, melons, pumpkins, cucumbers, okra, and tomatoes have been grown successfully in cold frames and greenhouses, and in some "Banana Belt" gardens or protected spots, but as these plants are very "frost sensitive", they are killed by frost. Some plants tried in gardens at Lake Almanor (4,500' elevation.) without success include sweet potato, watermelon, cantaloupe, red pepper, Lima beans, Butternut and Acorn squash, and soybean. These either will not grow, or never reach maturity because of frost. They might be successful in a greenhouse or in a warmer site.

Try to change location of your vegetables every year, especially corn which is a heavy feeder and potatoes which tend to collect wireworms if left more than one season in the same bed. Most vegetables do well with drip irrigation because it applies water at ground level and their dry leaves don't get mildew or sunburn (from wet drops acting like magnifying glasses).

Planning a Vegetable Garden:

Step 1: Plan your garden. Draw garden dimensions to scale. Draw in your raised beds or rows. Draw in pathways. Locate internal and external fencing. Decide what plants you want to plant and how many of each.

Step 2: Consult seed catalogs (see Suppliers' Catalog list). Order the earliest maturing, most hardy, and disease resistant varieties. You have more selection in a seed catalog than enough time to order by mail.

Step 3: Create your planting timetable on paper (See Vegetable Planting Guide in this chapter). When will you plant seeds? Seedlings? Consider also how your garden varies from the local climate zone (See Microclimate chapter). In a particularly cold area you will have to plant later or provide frost protection at night.

Step 4: Begin indoor planting (see Propagation chapter).

Step 5: Make your "supersoil". Analyze your soil using a soil test kit. Add organic matter and nutrients as needed. (See Soils chapter).

Step 6: Plant your seeds and seedlings the intensive way (see Intensive Gardening chapter) using dates on planting timetable (step 3).

Step 7: Use protective, season-stretching devices to get an early start or to provide optimum growing conditions i.e. broccoli or tomatoes (See Extending Season chapter).

Step 8: Remove protective devices as the weather warms up.

Step 9: Harvest, add fertilizer, manure, etc., to make your gardening beds ready for the next planting (see Soils chapter).

Some Planning Tips:

Put tall plants like corn, or peas on a trellis, at the north end of your garden so they don't shade other crops. Put spreading plants like squash on a trellis or in a garden corner. If your garden is on a slope, place rows parallel with the slope to prevent erosion. Stagger the plants in a row (the rows may be closer together but the plants should be evenly-spaced). Make frequent small plantings of carrots, radishes and lettuce (instead of planting them all at once in one long row), to assure a steady supply for the whole season.

Succession planting (planting another row of vegetables to replace a row just finished bearing) is very limited here because our growing season is short. Instead, you can interplant different kinds of plants that grow well together, and these plants complement each other because when one is harvested early in the season it leaves room for the other to spread. Good interplanting can include radishes with squash, lettuce with tomatoes, lettuce with radishes, and early peas with squash (squash vines take over when peas are finished).

Planting By The Moon

A planting method called "Planting by the Moon" is based on the dates of the full and new moon. Consult a current Farmers' Almanac for these dates, for example:

May 3 full moon
"dark of the moon"
May 17 new moon
"light of the moon"
June 1 full moon
"dark of the moon"
June 16 new moon

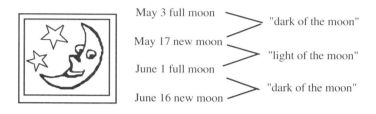

The "dark of the moon" is the period of time between the full moon and the next new moon. It is the time to plant flowers and vegetables which bear crops BELOW ground (root crops). An easy way to remember this, is that roots are underground where it is dark. So, plant root crops by the dark of the moon.

The "light of the moon" refers to the period of time between the new moon and the full moon. Plant flowers and vegetables which bear crops ABOVE ground during this time.

"Barren days" are certain days on which you do NOT plant. These occur in both the light and dark periods of the moon. These dates also need to be looked up in a Farmers Almanac every year.

Farmers Almanac lists the different weather regions of the United States such as Pacific Northwest, or Southwest, etc. Find the area chart for where you live, and all flowers and vegetables have planting dates listed according to the moon.

Some farmers swear by this method and assure you that it works, but basically as long as you also keep in mind the last frost-free date and how hardy your plants are (very important at higher elevations), I can't see that it makes any difference whether you plant on a "barren" day or a favorable day. Two years I planted by this method and couldn't see any significant difference. I planted some things on barren days and some on favorable days, as controls, to see if there was a difference. This experiment was just done for fun, but was hardly enough testing to prove anything. Try it yourself some summer. Consider the planting dates given in the following chart as being flexible (set in rubber!); they should be stretched to fit the weather as it varies from year to year.

VEGETABLE PLANTING GUIDE
(Based on last frost date in spring)

Cool Season vegetable		Warm-Season Vegetable	
Very hardy. Plant 4-6 weeks before frost- free date: Mar 30-Apr 15.		NOT cold hardy. Plant ON frost-free date: May 15+/-	Requires hot weather. Plant 1 week or more after frost-free date: June 1+
carrots	asparagus crowns	cucumbers	beans
kale, kohlrabi	beets	peppers	asparagus seed
radishes	broccoli (pl)	pumpkins	tomato (pl)
spinach	brussels sprouts	squash	okra
turnip	cabbage	sweet corn (pl)	parsnips
swiss chard	cauliflower	watermelon	sunflower
potatoes	lettuce		
rhubarb (pl)	onion, garlic & shallot sets		
strawberries	peas		

The last group may or may not reach maturity, depending on the timing of the first, fall frost. The onion family, peas, and spinach can be planted as soon as the ground can be made ready in spring. pl= started plants.

Vegetable PLANT LIST

Refer to Vegetable Planting Guide as you read this list.

ALFALFA (Medicago sativa) Grows well here, and when turned under as a green manure crop, it enriches the soil (legume family). Usually grown for livestock, or seed.

ALFALFA SPROUTS. Sprout alfalfa seeds in your kitchen! They are delicious, high in nutrition, and add a delicious crunchy taste to salads, sandwiches, and tacos. Use a wide-mouthed mayonnaise jar, and special sprout lid or make your own lid with cheesecloth and a rubberband. Soak the seed for eight hours in just enough warm water to cover. Then drain well. Rinse seed every morning and evening until the sprouts turn green (about five days), then enjoy. Buy untreated seed for sprouting.•

During the rinsing phase, to keep the jar at a 45° angle, use a dish drainer or place jar on a "cut" milk carton lying on its' side. To prepare the milk carton, make cut at back higher than cut at front. This is to

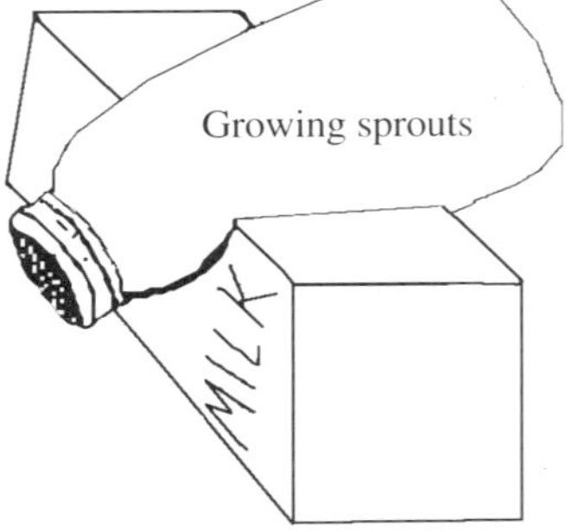

insure that all rinse water drains out, and sprouts don't mildew.

ASPARAGUS, Garden (Asparagus officinalis) A perennial vegetable. Frost hardy (will stand freezing). Plant one year old crowns in March or April, or plant seeds in May or June. Maturity is one year from crowns, and two years from seeds. Use lots of well-rotted manure, fertilizer, and rich top soil, as it is a heavy feeder. Don't cut stalks until second or third year after planting. In Fall, as soon as tops turn yellow, cut close to ground, then fertilize and mulch for winter. Needs a large area in which to grow. Name often confused with the "Smilax" of the florists, and the asparagus fern, —both are completely different species of Asparagus [1].*

BEANS (Phaseolus vulgaris) Bush beans are very prolific and recover well from a slight frost, but pole beans are killed by any frost. Don't plant beans outdoors until all chance of frost is past, and plant in warm soil. Moisten soil thoroughly BEFORE planting, and don't water again until seedlings have emerged. Snap beans are most popular. Harvest while pods are still smooth.*•

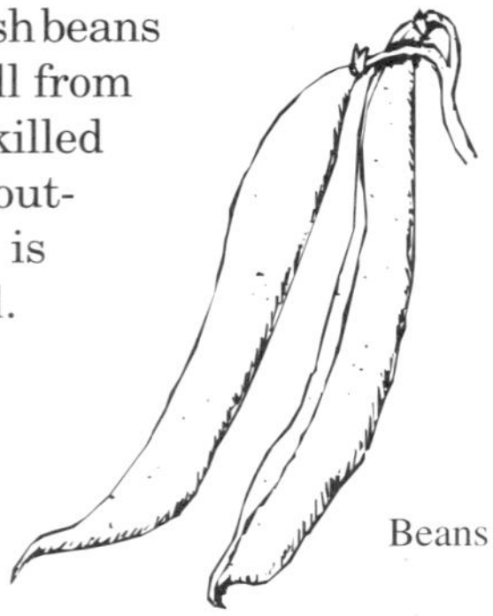
Beans

BEETS (Beta vulgaris) Family: Chenopodiaceae. Frost hardy, will stand light freezes. Delicious root crop that grows well here. (Red and golden varieties). Young leaves are delicious in salad when mixed with lettuce. Don't plant whole package; place selected seeds about 2 inches apart. To avoid woodiness, harvest beets young, at about 1 1/2 to 2 inches diameter. Use 5-10-5 fertilizer at 3-4 week intervals so they will grow fast and but won't become woody. You can store them in the freezer but they must be fully cooked or will turn black during storage.*•

BROCCOLI (Brassica oleracea botrytis). Family Cruciferae (cabbage). Frost hardy. After cutting off main head, it continues to produce little broccoli flowerlets. Feed a high nitrogen fertilizer when heads start to form. Start seed indoors. Plant seedlings outdoors instead of seeds to get a head start on the bugs. Harvest before flowers show yellow color, and while buds are still tight*•

Broccoli

BRUSSEL SPROUTS (Brassica oleracea gemmifera) Family: Cruciferae (cabbage). Frost hardy, resistant to light freezes. Care is similar to broccoli but brussel sprouts take longer to mature. Taste is similar to cabbage.*•

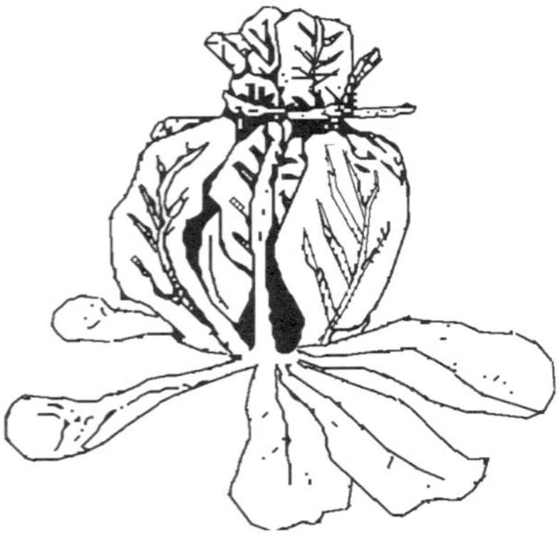
Tie up cabbage leaves

CABBAGE (Brassica oleracea capitata) Family: Cruciferae (cabbage). Mature heads may be injured by frost but young plants will stand light freezes. Keep it growing with fertilizer, as any stop in its growth will cause tiny heads. It can develop brown spots from too much direct sun. May have to cover heads with the longer leaves and tie them in place. Harvest when head is firm and heavy. After main head is harvested, small heads will form on the stalk.*•

CARROTS (Daucus carota) Family Umbelliferae. Frost hardy. Fernlike leaves. Must keep seeds wet, especially when young. Need loose, rock-free soil 12 inches deep. Drying out can cause roots to fork, besides causing a strong, unpleasant flavor. Fresh manure can also cause forking. Broadcasting seed instead of using rows works great (see Intensive Gardening chapter). Harvest anytime that the roots are firm and brittle. Delicious root vegetable, well worth the trouble!

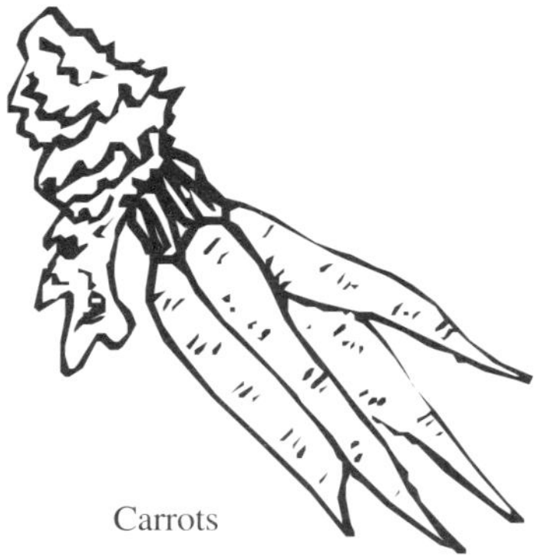
Carrots

You can have whole fresh carrots from your garden all winter if you cut the tops off, layer them in the garden soil, and heap mulch over them. But they must be buried below the frost level! Pauline Vogan of Chester said she has overwintered carrots layered in damp sand in an old wash tub (keep container covered so cats don't use it). Disadvantages of having carrots over wintered growing in your garden soil: 1) the moisture can be drawn out by frost heaving and carrots become dry and woody. 2) then you can't spread fertilizer and organic matter and rototil the garden, —because they are in the way. And 3) if you have lots of snow and ice, you need to mark the location in the fall with a stick. Once located, you need to dig away the snow and break the ice (often several inches thick) to get the carrots out. The ice is COLD and so are the carrots; a few cold carrots may not be worth that much work! I usually microwave carrots (blanch) and then put them in my freezer.*•

CAULIFLOWER (Brassica oleracea botrytis) Family: Cruciferae (cabbage). Frost hardy. Growth similar to cabbage. Any stop in growth will cause tiny heads. Must cover developing heads, same as cabbage, to protect from sunburn as will develop brown spots (harmless, but not appetizing). To protect them, gather the leaves together at the top and tie loosely. Harvest before curd loosens and discolors. After removing head, discard the plant. It doesn't form baby heads like Broccoli.*•

Don't use sprinklers or hoses while leaves are tied together, because if the head stays wet, the plant will rot. IF you must water this way (or if it rains), untie the leaves every day and tie up again during heat of day.

CORN, Sweet (Zea mays) Buy "Sweet córn". ("Field corn" is not desirable for home garden, and "dried corn" used for chicken feed can be bought cheaper than you can grow it.) Choose early maturing, hardy varieties. Nichols Garden Nursery Catalog sells Early Sunglow hybrid, 62 days to maturity, grows about 4 feet tall —and Tokay White Hybrid, 65 days to maturity, grows anywhere. Start it indoors. Sensitive to frost, may stand light freeze and recover. Harvest when kernel juice is milky, silk begins to dry, and kernels are full all the way to the end (usually picked 3-4 weeks after silks appear). It takes practice to know when to harvest.*•

CHINESE CELERY (Apium) Very adaptable to harsh mountain climates. similar to common celery, having slim dark-green stems and celery-flavored leaves. Delicious in soup, stew or stir-fry. Easy to grow. Only 60 days to maturity.*

CUCUMBERS (Cucumis sativus). Easily injured by frost. Should be protected by cold frame or greenhouse. Don't plant outdoors until all chance of frost is past. Plant on hills for better drainage. Train on fence or trellis to conserve space !! (Squash, melon, watermelon, pumpkin, gourds, and several ornamental vines all belong to the cucumber family.)*•

FORAGE BEETS Only the ROOTS are used as animal feed, as the leaves are a laxative. The beets grow huge and goats love them (I don't know about other animals). Thin the beets as needed but don't give the goats more than one pound at a time until the beets are mature (when the tips die down in the fall). DO NOT REFRIGERATE OR FREEZE THEM or they will turn black! Flesh is yellow gold.•

JERUSALEM ARTICHOKES (Helianthus tuberosus) A perennial vegetable. The edible part is underground like a potato. Eat it raw for a delicious, crunchy, nut-like flavor! Dig tubers for eating when tops are killed by frost (or when leaves turn yellow in late fall); or they can be left in the ground for storing since freezing won't hurt them. If heavily mulched with straw or pine needles, you may be able to dig them all winter. It spreads fast and remains for the next season. Grows tall. Has a crunchy taste similar to jicama. It is not an artichoke and it doesn't come from Jerusalem. Originally cultivated by North American Indians. Grow all by itself in one corner; invasive.•

Jerusalem Artichoke

KALE (Brassica oleracea acephala) Family Cruciferae (cabbage). Frost hardy. Tastes similar to cabbage (but very mild), looks like very curly dark green lettuce. Keep leaves picked because older ones get bitter. A type of cabbage that doesn't produce a head. Nice accent in a salad bowl.*•

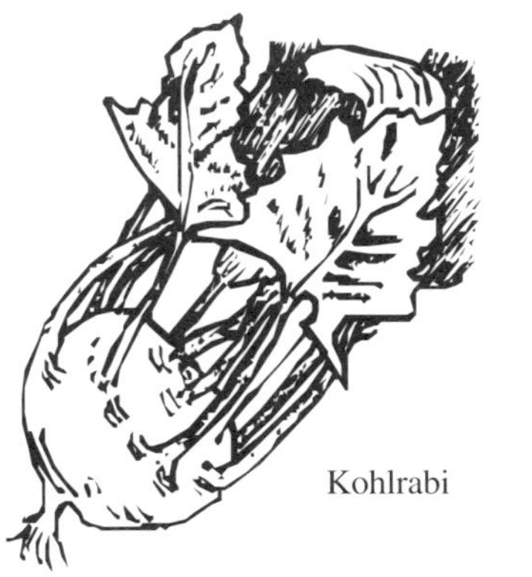

Kohlrabi

KOHLRABI (Brassica caulorapa) Family: Cruciferae (cabbage). Frost hardy. Tastes similar to cabbage. The part you eat looks like an above-ground turnip. It's great raw, in salads, or stir fried. Harvest when bulbs reach 2 inches diameter.•

LEEK (Allium porrum) Frost tolerant. (onion family).*•

LETTUCE (Lactuca sativa and varieties) Family: Compositae. Hardy, will stand light freezes. Leaf lettuce is easy to grow and, if outer leaves are kept picked, will provide new leaves all summer. Some head lettuce also does well, but harvest when heads are good size. Don't wait too long or lettuce will become bitter and go to seed. Be sure to thin them (leaf 3-4" apart, and head 6-7" apart), because if you don't, they will grow VERY slowly. Choose a variety that doesn't "bolt" in hot weather. Bolting is premature rapid growth to the flowering stage (in annuals and vegetables) during hot weather. Pick while tender and mild flavored, before seedstalk begins to form.*•

Lettuce

NEW ZEALAND SPINACH (Tetragonia expansa) Excellent flavor (slightly different from Spinach). Wonderful raw in salad or cooked like spinach, freezes well. It takes more summer heat (without bolting) than regular spinach.•

ONIONS (Allium cepa) NEVER let onions get dry while they are growing. They do well both as young green onions or mature for dried onions in winter. Usually started from sets. If you peel or chop onions while frozen, they won't make your eyes water. Fresh, or as Dried Onion powder, adds a delicious

onions

onion flavor to meats, stews, soups, sauces, fish, salads, and eggs. When storing for winter use, pull them after the tops have died down in fall. Egyptian onions remain in the ground year after year but get HUGE (new plants are started from babies formed on top of plant). The Yellow Bermuda is probably the mildest onion for slicing and eating fresh.*• See Bulb chapter for some of the onion family that are grown for their flowers.

PARSNIPS (Pastinaca sativa) Family Umbelliferae. Delicious sweet, nutty flavored root vegetable that looks like a white carrot. Pick after first fall frost when tops are lying on the ground. Don't peel skins off. Delicious raw, cooked, or in soups.*•

PEAS (Pisum sativum). Family Leguminosae (legume) Young plants are hardy to frost, but blossoms and pods are injured easily. Peas do well here and may be planted very early in spring (April). Moisten ground thoroughly BEFORE planting 1/2 to one inch deep. Planting many varieties will assure having peas over a longer season. I like Sugar Snap Peas best as you can eat pod and all, and often the fleshy pod is better than the peas inside! Keep peas picked or they will stop producing. Do not water by sprinkler as leaves get mildew very easily. Likes alkaline soil so add fireplace ashes and lime. Harvest after pods form, but before they turn yellow (taste awful!).*•

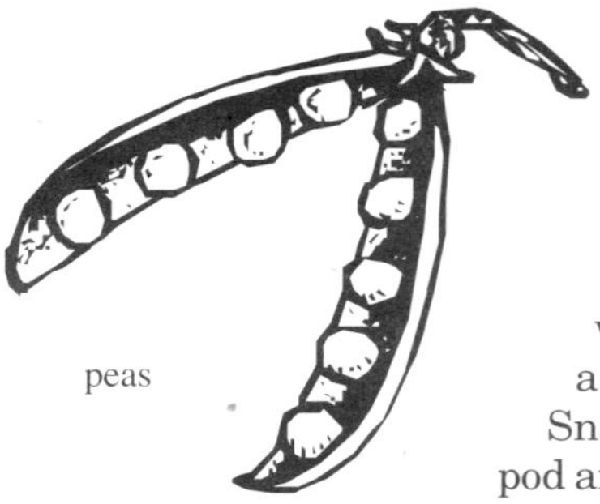

peas

PEPPERS (Capsicum annuum) Needs frost protection (like tomatoes). Does best in greenhouse or cold frame. Start seed indoors to plant seedlings outdoors. This genus includes the red, Cayenne, green, and other fleshy-fruited peppers, but not the spice pepper. Likes Basil as companion plant.*•

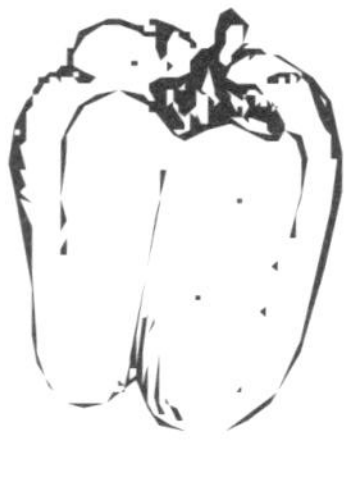

pepper

POTATOES (Solanum tuberosum) Family Solanaceae. Great root crop, requires large area. When tops are killed by frost, new shoots soon appear. Plant as soon as heavy frosts are over. Plant in an area with beans or by itself. Planting beans as companion species confuses most bugs, but watch out for white flies. Plant 4 inches deep, about 18 inches apart in mostly dry soil. To take less growing space, try growing in an old tire. Add tires as tops grow, —up to three tires high.

potatoes

Too much water causes black rot inside; they prefer less water than most other vegetables. Soak occasionally after shoots appear. Needs a well-drained, rich, acid soil (so don't add fireplaces ashes or lime there). Must rotate crops as potatoes get wire worm if in one place more than one year, besides the fact they are heavy feeders. Keep weeds pulled. Butte potato from Gurney's Catalog is an especially good type.

What is poisonous? Sprouts of potato are poisonous! Potatoes will get sunburn (turn green) if they aren't covered well with a thick straw, pine needle mulch, or dirt. Green potatoes are NOT poisonous after they are COOKED.

Digging for potatoes is like digging for buried treasure! Let the kids help. When tops begin to dry at end of season and fall over, the potatoes are ready to dig. For long storage be careful not to bruise them. Eat bruised ones right away as sliced or mashed potatoes. Use your hands to dig them, and when you are sure you have them all, then dig the area with a garden fork (and you will find more). Don't store apples near potatoes, as apples give off ethylene gas that causes potatoes to sprout, and most fruits to ripen faster.

Potatoes are VERY easy to grow, easy care, delicious, and good for you. Home grown potatoes are so delicious you don't need salt or butter. Most of the calories of the potato comes from the butter you add to eat it! Happy hunting!

RADISHES (Raphanus sativus) Family: Cruciferae (cabbage). Frost hardy, will stand light frost. Successive plantings (a small amount) every two weeks are recommended, so they don't all ripen at same time. Both red and white varieties. Must keep wet, because if they dry out even once, they will have a HOT taste! Since carrots are slow to come up, it helps to scatter some radish seeds in carrot rows to show where they are. If you wait too long to pick them, they will be too woody to eat. Once they have gone to seed they aren't good to eat.*•

radishes

RHUBARB (Rheum) A hardy perennial preferring rich, well-drained soil with lots of organic matter, fertilizer and heavy mulch. Harvest stalks lightly the second year. After that, they can be pulled (don't cut them off) from early spring until early summer. Plants can be dug, divided, and moved in fall or spring. Well established clumps require little attention and continue producing for many years. Leaves are poisonous, so fence them if you have kids. Remove seed stalks as they appear. DEER RESISTANT !

RUTABAGAS (Brassica napobrassica) Family: Cruciferae (cabbage). Looks like a yellow turnip, but is sweeter. Delicious and easy to grow. They take longer to mature than turnips.•

Shallots

SHALLOTS (Allium ascalonicum). A French vegetable. Has small, pointed, grayish bulbs, sometimes called cloves. Used in cooking or for flavoring and are milder than onions. A cross between onion and garlic. Growing season is 120 days, but can stay in ground over winter. Multiply rapidly. Onion family. Smell discourages the bad bugs.•

SPINACH (Spinacea oleracea) Family Chenopodiaceae. Like lettuce, be sure to choose a variety that doesn't "bolt" in heat of summer. A good leaf crop doing best in spring and early summer. Harvest while leaves are crisp and dark green. (See also New Zealand Spinach.)*•

squash

SQUASH, CROOKNECK (Cucurbita) A summer squash. Very sensitive to frost, but has been grown successfully when we have a long growing season; give protection when you expect frost. Keep stems and leaves as dry as possible (they can get moldy), but water roots regularly; so don't use overhead sprinklers. Two main types of squash: winter and summer. The rind color does not always tell you if it is ripe, and in summer squashes the rind should be picked when it is soft enough to dent with a finger nail [1].*•

SUNFLOWER (Helianthus) Sensitive to frost. Choose early maturing varieties or seeds will get moldy before they ripen. Be sure the seeds are mature before picking, and thoroughly dried before storing. (Composite family). See also Helianthus on perennial list.•

SWISS CHARD (Beta vulgaris var. Cicla) Family Chenopodiaceae. Frost hardy, will stand light freezes. Good for greens, and if outer leaves are kept picked, it will produce all summer (older leaves get bitter). Plants can last two years. Taste similar to spinach but a little stronger. Small leaves great in salad. Harvest while leaves are crisp and dark green.*•

tomatoes

TOMATOES (Lycopersicum esculentum) Family Solanaceae. Will produce tomatoes if protected from ALL frosts. Start indoors and plant seedlings outdoors after all chance of frost is past (June 1- 15+/-). Try Cherry Tomatoes, as they are small, mature fast, and taste delicious! Best planted in containers or apart from garden for two reasons: you can take it in at night if expecting a frost, and they easily get bugs and disease. Train vines on a trellis, as on the ground they easily mildew. Don't water them the last three weeks before harvest. Harvest when fully colored but still firm.

If frost kills the plants, take the tomatoes indoors. Place on a cookie sheet with an edge around it (to keep them from rolling off). Place several thicknesses of newspaper above and below the tomatoes. The sulfur in the newspaper will ripen them after several days to several weeks. Check them once every day, take out the red ones, and watch others for rotting.

Serve them warm, not from refrigerator and they will have much more flavor. Basil bring out the flavor better than salt.*•

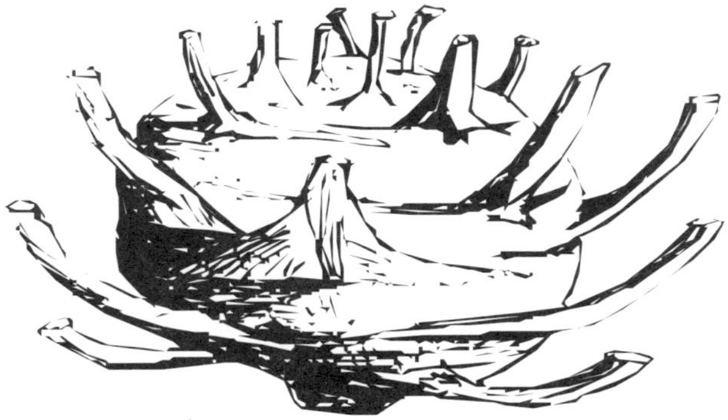

turnip

TURNIPS (Brassica rapa) Family: Cruciferae (cabbage). Frost hardy. Good root crop. Delicious raw, but can be cooked. Greens also are used. Likes acid soil (don't add ashes or lime).*•

ZUCCHINI Produces summer crop, but VERY sensitive to frost. Plant several at different locations in your garden, as some areas get frost when other areas seem more protected.

References cited:
[1] The Garden Dict. [Taylor]
* High Alt. Gardens Catalog.
• Nichols Garden Nursery Catalog.

KITCHEN HERBS

Spearmint

Herb gardens are beautiful, magic, require little care, and spread naturally. They can be planted formally, informally, mixed in with the vegetable garden, or scattered here and there in the main garden. They are easy to grow and tolerate poor soils. Vegetables, herbs, and annuals are often planted together in the same garden bed, because the whole bed has to be dug up at the end of the season. The leaves, stems, blossoms, roots, and stalks all can be used.

By botanical definition, a **herb** is any plant that dies back to the root each year. By horticultural or culinary definition, a herb is an edible plant that can be dried and used for its flavor, its healing properties, or its perfume. As a food it is rarely eaten alone, but is usually eaten with other foods [1].

There are three basic kinds: **kitchen herbs** used in cooking (for flavor or fragrance), **food herbs** (for health and well-being), and **medicinal herbs** (stronger effect). Herbs fresh from the garden add that gourmet touch to any meal. For a list of flavorings see herb chart at end of this chapter. Fragrances can be sweet or sour, subtle or strong. Herbs are also good for teas, potpourri, and dried arrangements [2].

Herbs and spices get their strong, distinctive flavors from volatile aromatic oils which may occur in leaves, seeds, flowers, or roots, sometimes in all of them in the same plant, sometimes in only one or two plant parts. When herbs are dried properly, the oils become more concentrated, so that much less of the dried product than of the fresh herb is needed for flavor [1]. These volatile oils in herbs can act as insect and animal repellents in your garden (see Deer-Resistant Plant Chapter). Most herbs belong to four large plant families: Labiatae (mint family), Compositae, (daisy family), Umbelliferae, (carrot family), and Cruciferae (mustard family).

The herbs mentioned in this chapter are tolerant to cold (even frost) except basil and rosemary, and most will "come back" year after year. Rosemary will come back if winters are not too cold. (Don't confuse this herb Rosemary with the shrub). Many Kitchen herbs can be grown outdoors in summer and potted as house plants during the winter. To order seed or plants see Suppliers list. References used to supplement the plant list were: (*) High Altitude Gardens Catalog, (•) Nichols Garden Nursery Catalog, The Garden Dict. (Taylor), SWGB, and BH&G.

Kitchen Herbs PLANT LIST

BORAGE (Borago officinalis) Annual. Purple-blue, star-shaped flowers. The blossoms taste like cucumbers, and the young tender leaves garnish iced teas, salads, cold soups and fruit plates.*

CALENDULA (Calendula officinalis) Annual. Bright, orange-yellow flowers repel insects. Petals are delicious in salads, soups, on top of canapes, or use for teas.*

CATNIP (Nepeta cateria) Perennial. Garden border, to delight cats, or discourage mice. Leaves and flowers make good tea, and repel insects. Ht 5'. Gray-green leaves. Can be grown in pots in the house to distract cats from eating house plants.*

CHAMOMILE (Chamaemelum recutia) Zone 3-10. Ht only 3-6". Sun or partial shade. Herbaceous, evergreen, annual Tiny yellow, daisy-like, flowers, bright green leaves. Resists drought. Excellent ground cover, can be mowed and walked on. Looks like moss. Aromatic when stepped on. Hardy to -30°F. Flowers make a soothing tea, insect repellent, and a fungicide solution to prevent "damping off" in new seedlings.*

CHICORY, Endive or Curly Endive. (Cichorium intybus) All zones. Dried ground roots can be used as a substitute for coffee, or mixed 50:50 with coffee to lessen acid taste. Pretty sky-blue flowers grow wild along roadsides. Ht 3-6'. Perennial.•

CHIVES (Allium schoenoprasum) Hardy perennial. Leaves have mild onion flavor, freezes well. Lavender flower globes, blooms all summer. Long-lasting bouquets. Use in salads, cottage cheese, eggs and sauces, and egg dishes and greens. Blend with cream cheese or use like parsley. Sun or shade. Use flower globes, or separated petals to add color to salads.* (onion family)

CILANTRO (Coriandrum sativum) Annual. Very fragrant, shiny, bright-green leaves make our mouths water! Often called Coriander. Used in Mexican, Thai and Chinese cooking.*

COMFREY A common (perennial) herb in Europe, related to borage. Frost hardy. Grows best in rich, moist alkaline soil. Keep moist, and shade from hot direct sun. Grows 3' tall with large leaves. Tips of new growth can be picked and used for tea, or for a soothing poultice for a wound. A good animal feed. Goats eat it like candy.

DILL (Anethum graveolens) Annual. Grown for seeds and leaves. Leaves are lacy, gray-green and may be dried for winter use. Dill Seed is used to flavor soups, fish, sauces, eggs, salads, potatoes, creamed dishes, and famous for pickling. Yellow, umbel-shaped flowers, bloom late summer.*

GARLIC chives (Allium tuberosum) Perennial. Extremely hardy. Sets grow into bulbs containing a number of cloves. Plant cloves in fall before ground freezes. Bulbs will keep over winter for cooking purposes if kept in cool dry place. Can be grown in pots indoors during winter. Also called Chinese Leeks. Garlic powder is used in soups, sauces, potato recipes, for meat, in stews, salad dressings. Beautiful, white flower globes. Shiny, flat, green leaves have a mild garlic flavor.*

HOREHOUND or HOARHOUND (Marrubium vulgare). All zones. Native CA perennial herb. Wrinkled, white woolly, oval-shaped, aromatic, gray-green leaves. Mint family (square stem). Flowers profuse in leaf axils. Ht 1-3'. Grows in poor, sandy, dry soil, full sun. Used for medicinal purposes, for candy, and for its aromatic oil. Bitter flavor. Foliage is pretty in bouquets.

LAVENDER and **LAVENDER COTTON** (see gr. cover list.)

LEMON BALM (Melissa officinalis) Perennial. Fresh lemon flavor and fragrance when growing in the garden, or used in Oriental recipes, cakes, cookies, and potpourris, or to make a delicious tea. Use bright-green, heart-shaped leaves in salads. Mint family.*

MINTS (Mentha) Perennial herbs and ground cover. Spread rapidly by underground stems and can be invasive; so contain in pot or box. Once established, very drought tolerant. Prefers light, medium-rich moist soil. Partial shade. Propagate from runners. Keep flowers cut off. Replant every 3 years. Hardy all zones. Many kinds available•. Square stems (mint family) with aromatic leaves [3].

Golden Apple mint (M. gentilis) Ht 2'. Smooth, deep green leaves, variegated yellow. Tiny flowers. Used to flavor foods. Foliage is excellent in bouquets.

Peppermint (M. piperita) Ht 3'. Strong-scented, toothed, long leaves, good to make tea. Small purple flowers in spikes. Used for flavoring sweets, ice tea, or hot drinks.

Spearmint (M. spicata) Dark green leaves, slightly smaller than peppermint, used fresh or dried. Used in mint and apple jelly or sauce, cooked with vegetables, in soups, fruit salad, iced drinks, fresh fruit deserts, or anywhere an aromatic mint flavor is desired. Ht 18-24" Purple flowers on small spikes. Propagated by seed, cuttings, or by division.

Apple Mint (M. suaveolens, or M. rotundifolia) Stiff stems 20-30" tall. Slightly hairy, gray-green, rounded leaves have an apple-mint fragrance. Purplish white flowers in small spikes.

MINT, SAWTOOTH MOUNTAIN (Agastache urticifolia). Perennial herb and native wildflower. Large pink flowers, bloom July-August. Dried flowers and leaves make an excellent herbal tea. Easy to grow. Ht 3'. Prefers full sun. Well-drained soil. Drought tolerant, yet prefers regular watering. Extra hardy. Plant seeds in fall.*

MINT, CREEPING or CORSICAN (see corsican on ground cover list)

MOLEPLANT (Euphorbia lathyris) Biennial. Foliage forms natural boundary above ground, while below ground the volatile oils in the roots repel pesty rodents. Plant 20" apart.*

OREGANO, True Greek (Origanum spp.) Perennial. Soft, fragrant, gray-green leaves dried for use in cooking, and also makes an excellent ground cover. Pinkish-white flowers used in dried-flower arrangements.*

PARSLEY, ITALIAN (Petroselinum neopolitanum) Biennial. Feathery dark green leaves, resembles carrot tops. Survives mountain winters and provides us with early spring greens. Small plant may be potted for use in winter. Used on salads, vegetables, meat, cheese, eggs, soups, baked fish, potatoes, and also as a garnish. Can be frozen in bunches and cut off as needed.*

ROSEMARY (Rosmarinus officinalis) Zone 8. Not hardy here, but can be grown in pots in sheltered place in summer and indoors in winter. Leaves add flavor to meats, soups, stews, fish, salads, and sauces. Rugged, picturesque, evergreen shrub. Flowers attract birds, bees. Once established, little watering needed.

SAGE (Salvia officinalis) Perennial. Both the silver-green leaves and purple flowers are fragrant. Kitchen herb and attractive ornamental. Leaves dried and used to season sausage, poultry stuffings, and many meats. Zones 3-9. Attracts bees. Use in rock gardens, containers, as a border plant, or unusual edging.*

SWEET BASIL (Ocimum basillicum) Annual. Grown for its aromatic leaves. Freeze or dry the leaves for winter use, and keep tightly sealed in a dark, cool place. Mint family. Delicious in soup, salads, or on vegetables (especially tomatoes). Protect from frost.*

TANSY (Tanacetum vulgare) Grown to flavor beef, fish, lamb, pork, or omelets. Some people find tansy too bitter. Also used in dried flower arrangements. Divide clumps in early spring. Roots are invasive so plant in containers.

THYME (Thymus vulgaris) Perennial. German, English or winter thyme. Tiny, fragrant leaves with small flower spikes, create a beautiful, sweet-smelling ground cover. A very popular seasoning.*

WINTERGREEN, CREEPING (Gaultheria procumbens) All zones (hardy to -40°F). Shady, acid soil. Evergreen. White flowers; red fruits are a source of oil.

WORMWOOD (Artemesia absinthium) Perennial. Feathery, silver leaves have a strong odor that repels dogs, cats, and insects pests. Forms ornamental two inch clumps.*

References cited:

[1] How to Grow Fruits & Vegetables By The Org. Method
[2] Better Homes & Gardens
[3] Sunset Western Garden Book
[4] Basic Herb Cookery & Herb Recipies

Cooking Hints for Herbs & Spices

Use plenty of herbs and spices to flavor your food, and you won't miss using salt. Use three times more fresh herbs than you would dried herbs. Add herbs sparingly at first. Taste the food as you cook it and add more herbs as needed. It is easy to add too much flavoring! Use herbs only to accent the flavor —not to overpower the taste of the food! Try adding a dash of lemon or lime juice to liven up any dish or salad.

BEVERAGES - ***Chocolate & Cocoa:*** cinnamon, cloves, nut-meg. ***Coffee:*** cloves, cinnamon stick, cardamon seeds. ***China Tea:*** rose geranium, mint. ***Lemonade:*** lemon balm, rose geranium, rosemary, borage leaves. ***Herb Teas:*** sage, anise seeds, mint, catnip, chamomile blossoms.

BREAD & CAKES - caraway, coriander, sesame, anise.

DESSERTS - marjoram, mint, anise seeds.

FRUIT-Apples baked & in pies: seeds of cardamon, dill, fennel, cloves, cinnamon. ***Apricots cooked & pies:*** cinnamon, cloves, hyssop foliage. ***Cherries in pie etc:*** allspice, cinnamon, cloves, nutmeg. ***Currants:*** cinnamon. ***Peach:*** allspice, cinnamon, nutmeg.

CHEESE ***Hot dishes:*** basil, oregano, caraway seeds. ***Cottage Cheese:*** chives, chervil.

EGGS ***Creamed & deviled:*** cayenne, celery seeds, chives, curry powder, tarragon, dry mustard, paprika, summer savory. ***Scrambled Eggs & Omelettes:*** basil, chives, parsley, summer savory, rosemary. ***Eggs Souffle:*** dill, thyme.

MEATS -***Beef:*** rosemary, basil, marjoram, summer savory, chervil, garlic.
Pork *(chops, roasts)*: thyme, marjoram, sage. ***Baked Ham:*** whole cloves, mustard. ***Ham Croquettes:*** cayenne, dry mustard. ***Lamb Broiled:*** oregano, rosemary, cumin. ***Roast Lamb:*** chervil, lemon balm, thyme, parsley.
Veal Roast: Basil, celery seeds, oregano, lemon balm, ginger. ***Veal Stew:*** marjoram, rosemary, thyme.
Veal Hungarian style: paprika.

POULTRY - ***Chicken & Turkey*** (broiled, roasted): marjoram, tarragon, savory, thyme. ***Creamed Chicken*** *or* ***Turkey:*** Celery salt, curry powder, nutmeg. ***Croquettes:*** same as roasted poultry. ***Fricassees:*** marjoram, rosemary, savory. ***Roast Duck:*** Anise, cinnamon, curry powder, ginger. ***Goose:*** caraway seeds, oregano, sage, thyme, savory.
Pheasant: Like chicken with oregano added.

POULTRY STUFFING - Marjoram, sage, thyme, lemon balm, summer savory.

GAME (Wild) - ***Venison etc:*** basil, juniper berries, oregano, summer savory, thyme.

SPECIALTY MEATS - ***Brains:*** basil, thyme. ***Liver:*** ginger, margoram. ***Kidneys:*** garlic, hyssop, dry mustard. ***Tongue:*** bay leaf, peppercorns, tarragon.

SEAFOODS - ***Clams:*** celery seed, marjoram, sage, savory, oregano, thyme. ***Crab:*** dill seed, fennel seed, chervil, oregano, rosemary. ***Fish:*** basil, chives, dill seed, tarragon, marjoram, oregano, rosemary, bacon, paprika.
Shrimp: basil, celery seed, oregano, parsley, thyme, garlic. ***Lobster:*** marjoram, oregano, thyme, garlic.
Oysters: Marjoram, savory, mace.

VEGETABLES - ***Asparagus:*** basil, caraway seeds, tarragon. ***Avocado:*** dill leaf. ***Beets:*** basil, caraway seed, dill seed, chervil, onion, cloves, thyme. ***Broccoli:*** basil, caraway seeds, nutmeg, parsley, dill seed, onion, curry.
Cabbage & Brussels Sprouts: basil, caraway seeds, dill seeds, cumin, marjoram. ***Cauliflower:*** dill seed, mace, paprika. ***Celery:*** basil, thyme, tarragon, oregano. ***Cucumber:*** basil, borage leaf, thyme, tarragon, chervil.
Carrots: basil, chives, dill seed, fennel seed, mint, thyme, caraway. ***Lettuce:*** chervil, dill seed, marjoram, mint, tarragon.
Peas: basil, chives, dill seed, marjoram, rosemary, oregano, onion. ***Potatoes:*** basil, chives, dill seed, parsley, chervil.
Mashed: orange juice or bouillon. ***Green Beans:*** basil, dill seed, parsley, onion, rosemary, oregano, tarragon.
Spinach: thyme, rosemary, oregano, marjoram. ***Mushrooms:*** coriander seeds. ***Sauerkraut:*** crushed peppercorns, caraway seed, dill seed. ***Squash*** (winter): crushed peppercorns, caraway seed, cloves, ginger, mace, nutmeg.
Squash (summer): basil, caraway seeds, chives, fennel seed, marjoram, thyme. ***Tomatoes:*** basil, chervil, chives, dill seed, oregano, thyme, tarragon, parsley. ***Sweet Potatoes:*** allspice, cinnamon, cloves, mace, nutmeg.
Turnips: allspice, basil, celery seed, dill seed, onion.

SALAD DRESSINGS: dill leaf, dill seed, tarragon, chervil, parsley, garlic.

HERB VINEGARS: tarragon, salad burnet, dill, basil, mint, lemon balm, and marjoram.

*Information on this page was reprinted from Basic Herb Cookery & Herb Recipies, a handout sheet produced by N.P. Nichols of Nichols Garden Nursery, Albany, OR. Used with permission from Better Walker.

GARDEN TOOLS

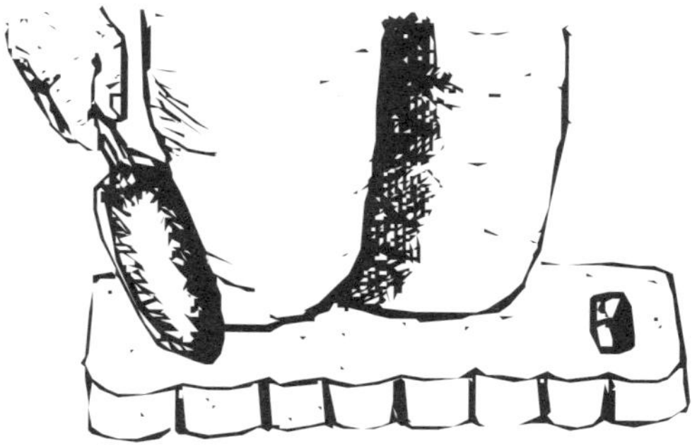

Kneeling pad

Whether you are landscaping your whole property, or just starting a lawn or garden, ease of maintenance is often the gardener's goal. Methods such as drip irrigation, intensive gardening with raised growing beds, and mulching can take a lot of the "work" out of gardening. These methods particularly save water, reduce evaporation loss, and discourage weeds, thus saving money and labor. For special pruning tools see Pruning chapter. Using the proper tools for a particular job really makes a difference.

Gardening carts are not a "new" invention but they are much more useful than wheelbarrows, better balanced, and are easier on

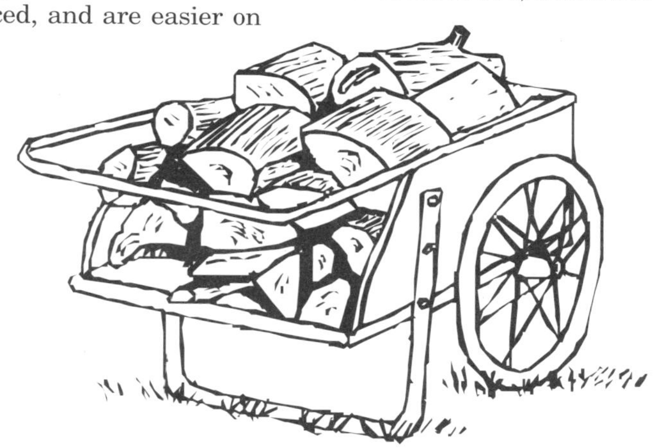

Gardening carts have many uses.

your back. They can haul firewood, brush, pruned branches, pine needles, buckets of rocks, or bags of weeds.

You can use **blowers** for fall cleanup when a lot of leaves need to be moved, but the rest of the time use a rake or your fingers to remove leaves around your plants. Leaf blowers are often advertised as a labor-saving tool, but they can create problems while saving "work". Blowers often create a wind so strong it is comparable to a gale or hurricane. Blowers can strip leaves, damage tender new growth and developing flowers, blow away valuable topsoil, dehydrate plants, "burn" leaves, and spread disease spores all over the area. Regular use of blowers can actually retard plant growth [1]. Many people hate the blowers because they are noisy, raise dust clouds, and burn gasoline. In the cities almost all the gardeners do is mow, blow, and go.

World's Best Edging can be installed around trees, along paths, and surrounding flower or vegetable beds to create an almost invisible weed barrier. It can be walked on and mowed over. In cold climates, the extreme cold cracks and heaves most cement edgings within a year or two, but this special, sturdy plastic, ribbed edging is long lasting, won't crack, and is low maintenance. The ribbed sides form dirt-locking pockets that hold the edging upright, and a T-shaped bottom keep it from lifting out of the ground. It even carries a 20 year guarantee. When buried in the g round, all you see is the top part that looks like a hose. It is sold by the roll from Gardener's Supply Company Catalog (See Suppliers list).

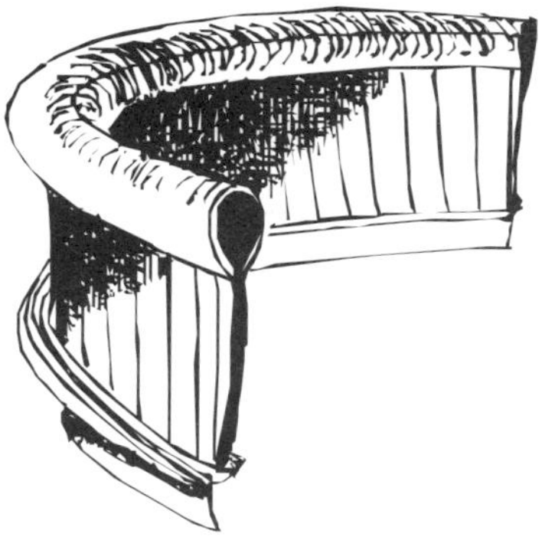

World's Best Edging

Try a **Pressure sprayer** to spray water, homemade spray, pesticides, or fertilizer. Tank size varies from 1 1/2 - 3 gallons. Dilute the chemicals to proper proportion inside the tank. Use shoulder strap and wand to reach tall trees or hard to reach areas up to 30 feet away. Nozzle can be adjusted to create a high pressure stream or a fine mist. Great for misting or watering house plants. Easy to use and portable.

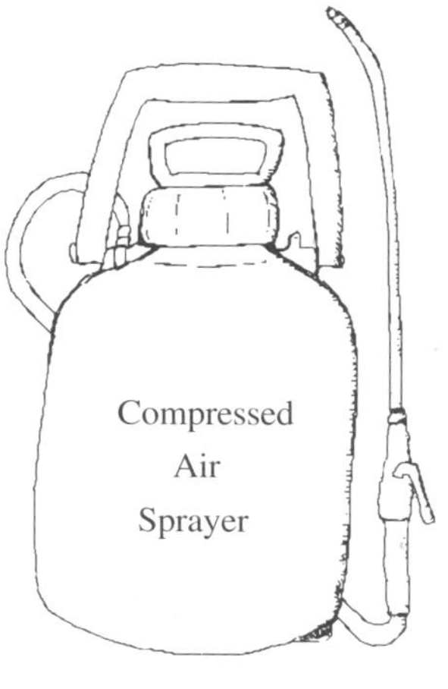

The **Hose-end sprayer** mounts on end of garden hose to spray fertilizer or pesticide, etc. It controls the dilution ratio of <u>water</u> (from garden hose) to <u>liquid chemical</u> (stored in sprayer container). Has no adjustable nozzle.

<u>References cited</u>:

[1]"What Bugging You"

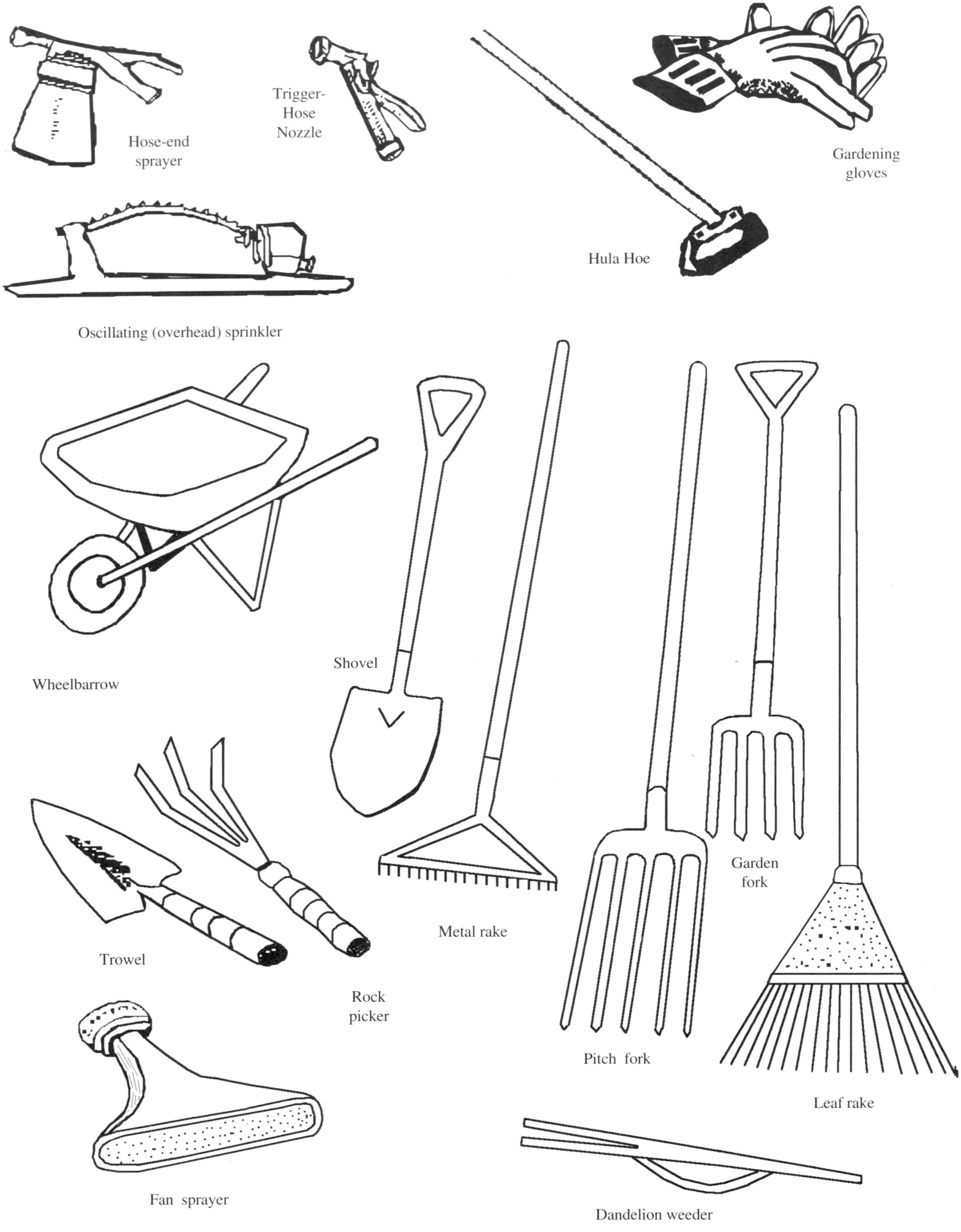

GARDEN TOOLS

PLANTING INSTRUCTIONS

BASIC TECHNIQUES

This chapter first describes those planting techniques basic to most plants, including shrubs, trees, perennials, and bulbs; then how to plant nursery stock, and other planting situations. For planting of seeds see Propagation chapter.

Planting

When do you plant?

Fall planting (October) is recommended in cold winter areas for all plants, except the tender (not frost-hardy) plants, such as annuals, roses, vegetables, herbs, and a few bulbs. Tender plants are planted in spring after last chance of frost is past. Plants are dormant when they drop their leaves, but many roots do grow all winter, and by spring roots are often well established. An apple tree planted in the fall is a whole years growth ahead of one planted the following spring. That might be important to you if you are waiting for those first apples. Strawberry plants planted in the fall will produce berries the next summer, but those planted in spring probably won't bear until the next year.

Deciduous trees and shrubs can be planted anytime fall through spring while the plant is dormant, but not when the soil is waterlogged or frozen. Broad-leaved plants are planted earlier in fall, or late spring when soil is warm and moist. Conifers are planted mid-spring. Keep roots moist to prevent leaves or needles from shedding.

Choose the best planting site.

Drainage is very important; avoid swampy or low-lying land. (If you have to use a swampy area, choose plants adapted to this habitat.) Fill the planting hole with water, and if it takes more than an hour for the water to sink in, you may have a drainage problem. If it drains too slowly: add sand, gravel, and plenty of organic matter. If it drains too fast (which is common in mountain soils), just add plenty of organic matter (see Soil chapter). For more site selection info see Climate and Landscaping chapters.

Prepare the soil by loosening and enriching it.

For general plantings such as lawns, annuals, perennials, and vegetables, pull any existing weeds, and turn the soil with a shovel to at least one foot depth. Spread organic matter (garden compost, peat moss, well-aged manure), and fertilizer in an even layer across top of the soil. Then turn the added layer into the soil with a shovel, and level the area with the back of a metal rake. If planting in the fall, add 10-10-10 fertilizer; if planting in the spring, add 5-10-5 (to encourage bloom).

DO NOT put fertilizer in the hole before you plant any seedling. People take this literally and dump some fertilizer in the hole, then drop the plant in the hole. When the roots touch the concentrated fertilizer, it kills them. You can add bone meal, superphosphate, enriched soil, or compost to the hole before adding the plant.

Fertilizer can be worked into the soil before planting, or added later after plant is well established. For trees, shrubs, and roses don't add any fertilizer to the soil till plant leafs out after planting, and then work some fertilizer into the soil around the plant (called "top dressing"). Later you can use slow-release fertilizer tablets, sticks or spikes inserted into ground at the "drip line" of the tree branches. Or dig holes twelve inches deep with a soil auger or shovel, 18-24 inches apart evenly over the root area and put fertilizer into the holes. Then water thoroughly to carry fertilizer down to the deep roots.

Use as much organic matter as you can, as it holds the water available for the plants, and they will grow faster and bloom much better than if you depend on fertilizer alone. You can't get too much organic matter, but it is easy to get too much fertilizer. See also Soils chapter.

You are now ready to plant.

Plant in the evening after the sun is off that area for the day, and don't let the sun shine on the seedling's roots while seedling is waiting to be planted. Prepare the new hole

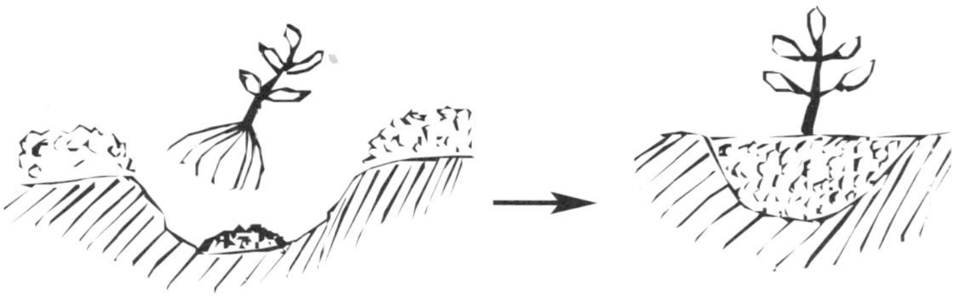

When seedling has two pair of leaves, it is ready to transplant into a larger pot or into the garden [1].

before you dig up or move the plant that is to be transplanted. Dig the hole plenty large and fill it with water. If you don't have wet soil in the hole, the fine roots will be killed on contact with the dry soil. Then dig up, unpack, or lift the selected plant. When picking up the plant, try not to disturb the roots by leaving as much soil around them as possible. If it is a larger

Firm the soil. Water deeply & thoroughly

plant, trim off some of the leaves and some of the roots. Make a cone of damp soil in planting hole. Place seedling gently over soil cone, while carefully spreading out the roots. Push the soil in around it and firm the soil. Firming settles the soil, eliminating the air pockets around the roots. Water thoroughly with water containing B1 solution to reduce transplant shock. Water daily until plant gets established. Fertilize with 5-10-5 in the spring before buds open and once a month till blooming period is over.

CHART # 9. BULB & PERENNIAL PLANTING CHART

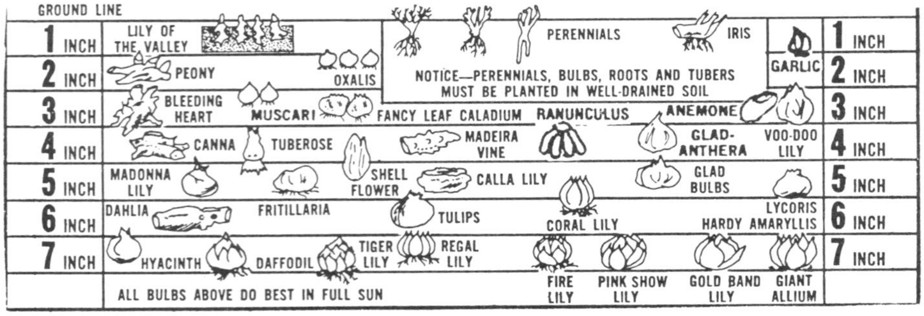

BULB & PERENNIAL PLANTING CHART
Source: Gurney's Seed & Nursery Company: Gurney's Grow-it-guide,

Water new transplants frequently.
Keep fall plantings well watered, not just at the time of planting, but weekly and even after hard frosts, until the ground is actually frozen! Whether or not you put a basin around the plant, depends on your watering method, and the type of plant. If you use drip irrigation or

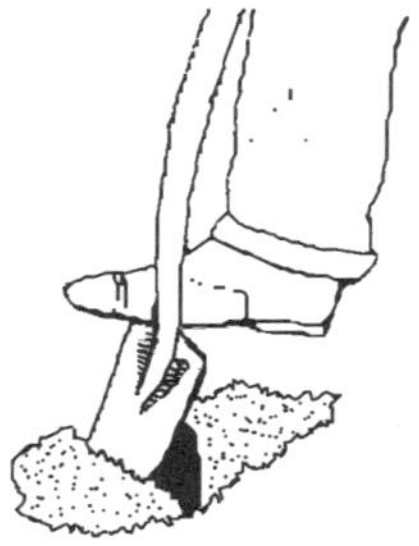

Dig a hole.

Make a basin around baby trees.

canvas soaker hoses, you usually don't need a basin; however for individual trees and shrubs, it helps to have a basin. Deep water other trees and shrubs already established if the season has been dry.

How deep do you usually plant ?

The "crown" is the point where the stem and roots meet, usually at the soil line. Most plants should be transplanted with the crown at the same depth it was previously planted (i.e. strawberry plants). Place strawberry plants with

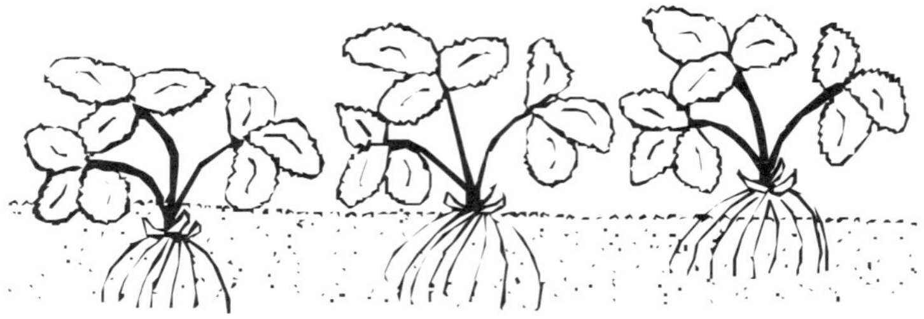

Too low Proper depth Too high

TRANSPLANTING STRAWBERRY PLANTS

their crown just at the surface of the soil. Set the baby plants 10-12 inches apart in all directions. DO NOT COVER CROWN with dirt. Spread roots well in a large hole. Remove any dead or bruised leaves, leaving only three new leaves on plant. If the crown is planted too deep it will rot, and if the crown is planted too high it will dry out and die.

Some plants are more particular.

To figure proper planting depth, measure the height of the bulb, and then plant them at a depth equal to three times their height. There are exceptions, like the Iris, which is planted with the top half of the rhizome exposed, and tulips which will last longer if you set them even deeper —up to twelve inches deep. See Bulb and Perennial Planting Chart. After planting the bulbs, pack the soil down firmly, and then soak the ground well. Leave them alone after planting until spring unless fall season is very dry, in which case you would water the bulbs until ground freezes. The soil must be well-drained or bulbs will rot. Bulbs usually do best when grown in full sun. If the plants seem to wilt in mid-summer, —provide them some shade.

Shade protection.

Don't plant seedlings in summer without some shade protection. Make a temporary shelter using pieces from a large cardboard box, old lumber, or a piece of fencing, but allow plenty of ventilation or you will cook the plants. See also shade cloth in Watering chapter.

Stake tall plants.

If you know you are planting a tall-growing plant, install the stakes while planting or just before planting. If you put in the stakes later, it is too easy to stab the bulb or roots. Tie plants loosely so you don't cut off their water and food circulation.

Mulch around new transplants.

Use 2-3 inches of mulch around new transplants, but keep wet mulch at least two inches away from tree trunks to reduce risk of decay and insect damage. Mulch prevents rapid soil temperatures changes that can cause frost heaving of soil,—this can break roots, lift up, or even kill the plant. Mulching also inhibits weed growth, preserves soil moisture, and encourages organisms like earthworms that aerate and enrich the soil. Use straw, hay, pine needles, etc. See Mulching chapter.

Potted

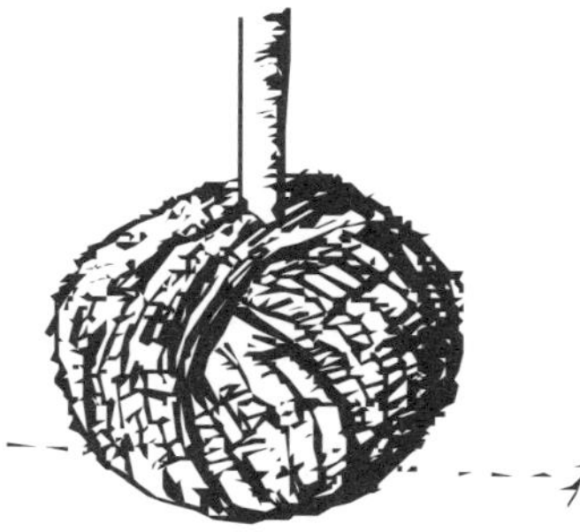

Balled & Burlapped (B &B)

Bareroot

PLANTING NURSERY STOCK, and trees

Nursery stock can be bought from your local nursery or favorite mail order catalog. See Suppliers' Catalog list. Ask your neighbors which plants are successful where your live. Check the plant lists in this book to see if it is hardy enough to grow here. Trees and shrubs can be expensive, so select the right ones the first time.

Many trees, shrubs, and roses bought at nurseries now have **bud unions**, as they have been grafted to hardier stock. The "bud union" is usually a little knob located at the base of the shrub or tree, where the hybrid variety has been budded (grafted) to the rootstock. Place this tender bud union about 1 1/2 inches above ground level and facing north, because the bud union is sensitive to hot summer sun. In extremely cold winter areas like North Dakota where temperatures often drop to -10°F, the bud union should be planted 1-2 inches below ground level. However, it tends to rot when placed below ground.

Nursery stock is available with roots: **Balled and Burlaped (B & B)**; as **bare-root** stock; or grown in a nursery **container** or tub. Balled and Burlaped means they have been dug with a ball of soil left around the roots, then wrapped in burlap. Bare-root stock costs half as much, but feeder roots aren't established yet, so sometimes they take longer to get established. Container plants have roots that are well developed and least disturbed. With container stock, you often can see the plant in flower and/or in fruit, but these are the most expensive plants.

Bare-root plants are available late winter through spring while plant is dormant), but don't plant them when soil is soggy or frozen. In cold winter areas (USDA zones 4-7) you plant in spring after the ground has thawed. B&B can be planted earlier in fall and later in spring while soil is still warm and damp. Container plants can be planted anytime except mid-winter, but if planted in summer keep them well watered and shaded for a couple weeks. If the sun is very hot, mulch the soil surface and shade pot in some way, but be sure the leaves are exposed to the sun. You could wrap the pot in white butcher paper (reflects the sun). You could set pot in a larger white container, but keep bottom open for drainage. Or you could sink pot into the ground (so top of pot is at ground level). Nurseries often sink their pots into raised beds full of sawdust.

Plants bought in supermarkets and department stores may be somewhat dried out after long storage and warm temperatures, so try to buy them when they first appear in the store (and they might be incorrectly named).

Don't buy deciduous bare-root plants after they leaf out; they must be dormant. Nurseries try to plant bare-root stock into containers (in spring) as soon as they start to leaf out. Bare-root roses are graded by the number and thickness of canes; buy only the best grade, No. 1 or 1 1/2. Bare-root trees are rated only by trunk diameter, and larger is not always better —choose a healthy one.

If you buy flowering plants in containers during the summer growing season, you will pay a higher price, but you get to see what the bloom looks like. Try to buy plants that were put in containers that spring. Choose a healthy-looking one. A bare-root plant that has been placed in a container must have been growing in container at least 1-3 months (then the feeder roots are established). This assures the roots are sufficient to hold a soil ball together. There is now a type of paper container that can be planted into the soil without disturbing the plant, and it decomposes into the soil. Be sure to tear holes in side and bottom to let the roots grow out. Some pulp containers do not decompose. Ask at the nursery if you don't know.

Sunset [1] says bare-root is best, while Better Homes & Gardens [2] says container and B & B are best. I don't think it matters as long as you plant during the proper season, dig the hole plenty big, and enrich the soil for the hole with plenty of organic matter (peat moss, leaf mold, and/or compost), as these soil amendments make up for any soil deficiencies.

Plant as soon as possible after it arrives.

When planting bare-root trees, shrubs, or roses in the fall or spring, soak the roots in water for a few hours (but don't soak perennials or strawberries). Remember the plant is living, so handle it carefully. While preparing the hole, don't expose roots to air, sun, or wind, any more than is absolutely necessary; put the roots in a wet paper bag.

If planting is delayed several days, keep roots and top moist with wet burlap, damp leaves or a waterproof plastic. If you can't plant for 2-3 weeks and ground isn't frozen, you can

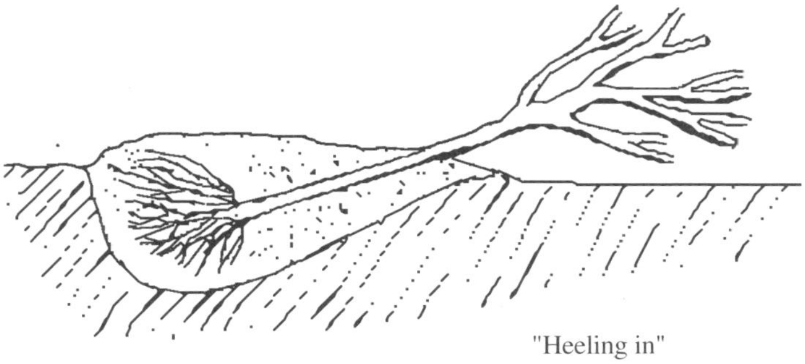

"Heeling in"

"heel in" the plant. Dig a sloping trench for the roots, resting the tree against the sloping side, cover roots with loose soil, and keep moist. If the plant is very dehydrated or if you are expecting severe cold, just bury the whole plant (top and all) in moist soil or sand. (Evergreens should be heeled in upright and placed close together if more than one). When nurseries receive bare-root stock in the spring, they plant them in a raised bed with damp sand or sawdust, and they remain there until sold.

What do you do if the ground is frozen, and someone gives you a Christmas present of some bare-root fruit trees or roses with roots wrapped in burlap (B&B)? What do you do with the plants until the ground thaws? Pot both the bare-root and B&B plants in extra large containers with potting soil, sand, or wet sawdust. If the bare-root plants are hardy, it won't matter whether they are put temporarily outdoors or in your garage. B&B plants are less hardy, so keep them in your garage or a cool place in your house. For either type, do not let the roots dry out (but not soggy either), and make sure container has a drainage hole.

How to plant bare-root stock

Just before planting, immerse roots in a bucket of water for several hours or overnight. (For roses, immerse whole plant—see Roses chapter). Dig hole large enough to spread out but not bend the roots (at least two times the size of root mass). Put water in hole and let it soak in. Just before planting, remove damaged or dead roots to prevent fungus diseases, cutting the roots back into healthy tissue. Add soil to hole till you have a six inch high soil mound in center for roots to rest on. Place tree on soil mound, spreading out roots carefully on all sides. Set plant deep enough so tree when planted is slightly higher than before being dug up (you'll see the old soil line stained on the trunk). Fill in soil to about 2/3 of top of hole, and tread on it firmly. Water with 1-2 buckets of water (preferably containing B1 solution). Let water sink in, giving tree some time to settle. Then hold onto trunk and gently tug the tree a little to the right and then left. This action helps fill in the soil around the roots. Then finish filling hole with soil, but don't firm soil this time. Leave a depression around tree to catch the water, then water thoroughly [1].

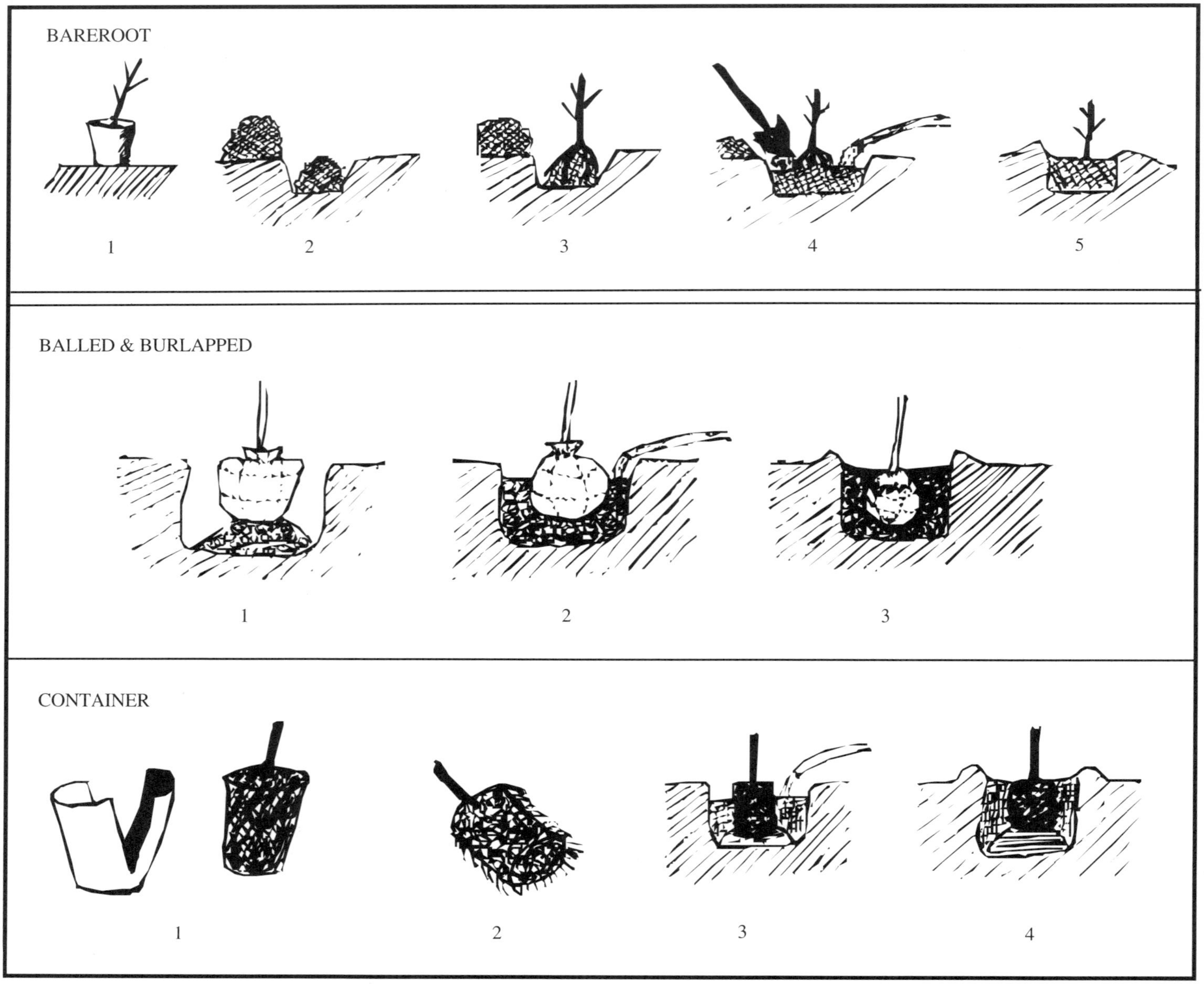

Planting B&B and Container-grown stock.

This method is similar to that used for bare-root. Fill hole with water. Set tree in hole on six inch soil mound. If root ball came in burlap, cut and loosen the binding of the burlap at the trunk, but leave burlap in place, as it will disintegrate in time. If root ball came in plastic, gently cut plastic off without damaging roots. If in a container, remove container (cut if necessary); then cut off any outer roots that circle the root mass, and loosen any tangled roots.

Planting trees and shrubs is much easier when two people work together.

One person holds the tree trunk in upright position at the proper level, while the other person adds enriched soil with the shovel. To find the proper level, put broom stick or ruler across hole at approximately the soil line on the tree. When finished planting, the soil level of surrounding soil should be even with the old soil mark on tree (just visible at soil level).

All trees should be staked for the first 1-3 years.

Bare-root trees need one pole 2x2 inches wide and about 5-6 feet long. Stake the tree before you fill in the dirt, to prevent stabbing a root. To attach stake to tree, run a wire through a piece of old bike inner tube, an old garden hose section, or use pieces of burlap or old sheet; but don't use wire or string! As the tree grows, loosen ties so as not to girdle or cut the tree trunk.

B&B plants need much more support, because the root ball acts like a ball and socket, rocking back and forth when the wind blows. Pound 2-3 short sturdy stakes into ground equally spaced around the tree. Run hose-protected wires from about 2/3 way up on the tree trunk to each stake. Adjust the pull of wires so it is even. Then paint tree trunks (see Insect disease chapter). Adjust wires as tree grows. After tree is well established (about 2-3 years), remove the stakes.

Pruning.

Prune back branches about one third to balance loss of roots when tree was first moved. Prune for shape, to make a basic scaffolding for survival (snow breakage), and to take out crossed, diseased branches etc. See Pruning chapter. Evergreens often do not need branch pruning because their root ball was wrapped and roots were not injured.

Transplanting shrub or small tree (not from a nursery).

Move transplants during cool weather when plant is dormant. Deciduous plants like lilac, or roses can be moved bare-root. Prepare the new planting hole before you dig up the plant, in order to transplant as quickly as possible so the roots won't dry out. To move evergreen plants (both broadleaf and conifer) or deciduous plants not dormant, dig them up with a ball of soil around the roots. Bigger plants are more difficult to move. Wrap the soil ball of larger plants with chicken wire to prevent the soil from falling off the roots. If the plant is too large, get a professional to move it for you. Some professional equipment can handle huge root balls of older trees.

References cited:
[1] Sunset Western Garden Book [SWGB]
[2] Better Homes & Gardens [BH&G]

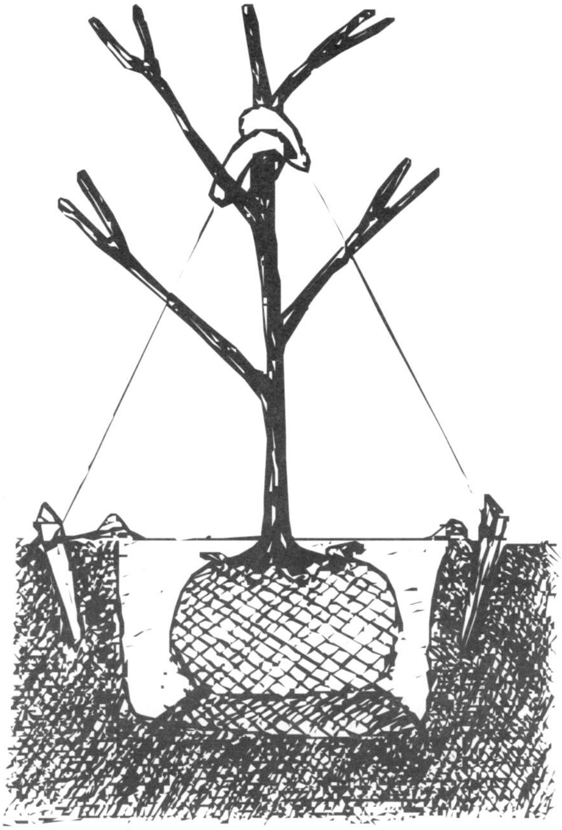

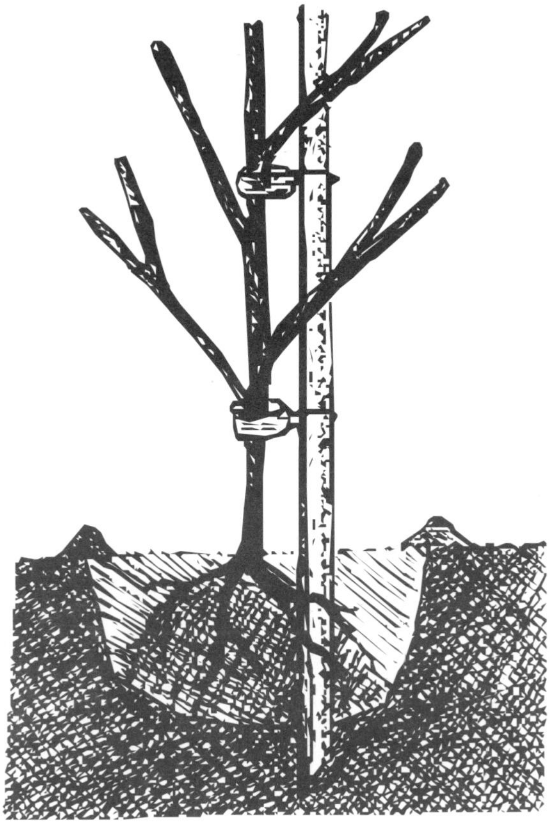

PROPAGATION TECHNIQUES, or STARTING NEW PLANTS

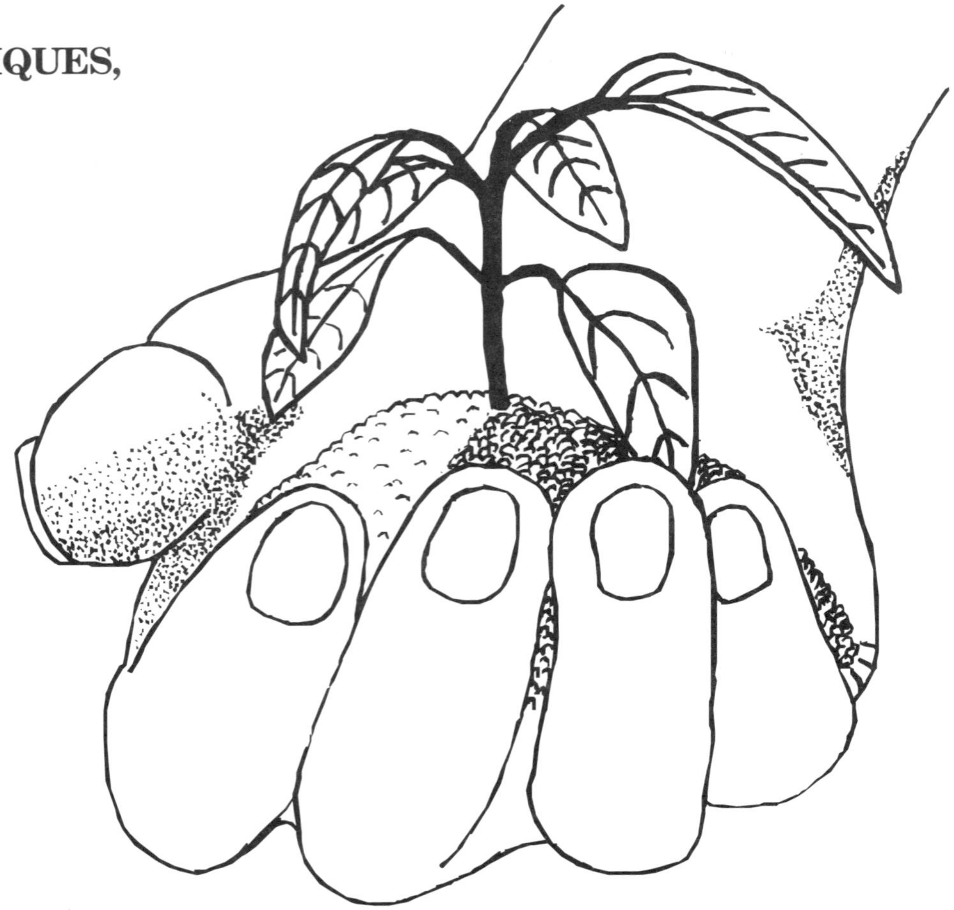

Where do you get the plants for your garden? There are basically four choices: you can buy from nurseries or mail order catalogs; get some from a friend; start them yourself from seed (seed propagation); or start them from divisions, cuttings, layering, budding, or grafting from a plant (vegetative propagation). Where you get your plants will depend on your time, patience, and available money. For basic planting instructions and how to plant nursery stock see Planting chapter.

"Propagation" refers to all the ways of starting new plants. The two main types: **planting seed** (new plant may vary because it is the product of the union of two separate individuals), and **vegetative propagation** (new plant will be identical to the plant from which it came). Seeds are used to breed new plants that are prettier, hardier, more disease resistant, or selected for some special trait. Vegetative propagation makes it possible to keep a favorite plant, and make many more of them (uniform population).

Plants can be propagated anytime during the growth season, from late spring to early autumn, but the new plants get a faster start at the beginning of the growth season. And keep the new plants in a warm, shaded location for 2-3 weeks.

It is illegal to propagate any "patented" plant material. Mostly newer varieties and hybrids are patented, especially roses. Besides, roses are grafted on a very sturdy root stock, and when you propagate from a cane, you get a less hardy plant.

Trees and shrubs are usually bought in a nursery and are relatively permanent. Biennial and annuals can be bought as seed or seedlings. Biennials bloom the second year and then die. Annuals bloom the first year and die in winter. Perennials last 2-5 years, and in order to have a continuous supply of healthy blooming ones, you need to know how to propagate them. Some perennials are started from seed, some from stem cuttings, and some increased only by clump division. Other types of plants can be started these ways too. House plants can be started by division, tip cuttings, seed (annuals), offsets, plantlets, leaf cuttings, ground layering and air layering. Seed propagation is the most popular method of increasing plants in general.

PLANTS FROM SEEDS

In the wild, seeds are scattered from the parent plant by wind, gravity, animals, and birds. You can scatter seeds at random ("broadcasting") when you plant lawns or wildflowers; or you can carefully plant seeds where you want them, such as vegetables, flowers, and kitchen herbs. You can either plant seeds directly in the garden, or into flats and containers (to be transplanted later into the garden).

Selecting Seeds.

Seeds come in packets, in pellets (with each seed having special coating like a pill), and seed tapes (seeds properly spaced and sealed in soil-degradable plastic). You just plant tape in furrow and cover with soil. Instruction for each method are on the package. The seed packet is the cheapest technique and most commonly used.

When selecting seed, check several seed catalogs (see Suppliers list). If you buy seed from a feed store, ask for untreated, unpoisoned seed, as some seeds contain mercury to prevent pests from eating the planted seeds (seeds that are dyed pink are treated and poisonous). Seed catalogs have more varieties than nurseries and stores. When you intend to store the seed you buy, choose standard varieties of seeds that have been dependable for years. For our climate zones, be sure

STORAGE LIFE OF SEEDS

Good for ( ) years	
2	corn, onion, parsnip, rue, salsify, & hop
3	bean, leek, parsley, pea, & most herbs
4	carrots, mustard, pepper, pumpkin, & tomato.
5	cabbage, broccoli, cauliflower, lettuce, radish, spinach, New Zealand spinach, turnip, & muskmelon.
6	beet, eggplant, squash, & watermelon
7	cardoon & purselane
8	chicory & borage
10	cucumber & endive

Not all of the above plants grow here. Reprinted with permission from editor: Peggy MacDonald of Let's Live Mag. (Jan '74 issue), and from author, Bargyla Rateaver, of seed article page 61.

to get seeds that are frost hardy and disease resistant. Take good care of your seed packets. When you buy the seed, write the year on the packet with a permanent ink marking pen. When you finish planting, seal the seed packet with magic scotch tape. Place all seed packets in a plastic bread bag or air tight container, and store in a COOL, DRY place like a closet, pantry, or root cellar. The following chart was reprinted with permission from editor Peggy MacDonald of Let's Live Magazine [1] (Jan 1974 issue), and from Bargyla Rateaver, author of the seed article page 6l.

The storage life of seeds noted in this chart is only an estimate. Under the best conditions seeds can last longer and still grow, but for best possible germination use within the charted times. First year germination is usually 100% under the best conditions, and declines after that. Some wildflower seeds have germinated after 100 years! However hybrid seeds generally have much shorter shelf-life.

To test seed viability before sowing, place a few seeds between sheets of moist paper towels. If most sprout in 1-2 weeks, then the seeds are worth planting. Do this for each variety of saved seed that you want to plant. However, some seed need to be treated first by scratching, soaking, heating or chilling, before they will germinate (see Children's Gardening chapter). Some seed that are particularly hard to get started, may be wrapped in compost, securely sealed in plastic, then frozen and thawed several times prior to planting.

You can choose the best all around plant from your garden to be a parent plant. Save seed from lettuce, celery, pepper, carrot, all of the tomato family (i.e.tomato, eggplant, potato), and legumes (peas, beans, sweet peas). DO NOT SAVE seed that can hybridize like corn, most of squash family (melon, pumpkin, and cucumber), and cabbage family (kale, brussel sprouts, collards, kohlrabi, swiss chard, beets, mustard, radish, and turnip). For example, if you have more than one variety, say of hot and sweet pepper —they will hybridize. Seeds that are wet when gathered must be dried before being stored or they will get moldy.

Unless you want to collect seed from a plant, cut off all flowers after they finish blooming. Letting a plant go to seed wastes the plants' energy, and can make more work for you pulling up many seedlings later.

Planting Seeds Outdoors (in the garden).

Don't plant seeds until soil is warm in the spring, since seeds need warmth and moisture to germinate. Draw a garden plan before planting seeds. Enrich the soil (see planting chapter) and moisten it well. When ready to plant seeds, cut the seed packet straight across the top, and only use the amount of seed you need for your family. The larger seeds can be planted individually, in rows, or in groups (see Intensive gardening chapter). Pour a little seed in one hand and plant one seed at a time. Poke it in the hole with your finger (see illustration), and then fill hole with vermiculite to help keep seeds moist [2]. Cover seeds only as deep as twice their diameter [3]. The tiniest seeds i.e. lettuce, carrots can be mixed with dry sand (to help distribute them evenly), and broadcast over the soil surface. Then cover the seed with vermiculite, potting soil, or peat moss, to keep them moist. If the weather turns cold after planting seeds, cover with black plastic to keep them warm and moist. If you use black plastic, you only have to water them once (right after planting). But you must keep checking the seeds, because as soon as they sprout the plastic must be removed. Some seeds need light to germinate while others need only darkness [4].

Firm the soil, and then water well using a watering can, or attachments on your garden hose i.e. fan sprayer or hose nozzle, so as not to wash away the seeds. Keep watering 2-3 times a day if necessary to keep the soil around the seeds moist, for about 2 weeks or until they sprout: then water more conservatively, only about every 3 days depending on weather. If you don't keep the seeds moist (about 2 inches deep) till they germinate, they will die. Sprouted seeds will grow slowly if they have competition with other plants or weeds. So, only put one seed per hole and keep weeds pulled as they appear. If you plant in these ways, you won't spend hours thinning plants, and you will save money as well as seed. Seed is more expensive every year, and saved seed keeps well.

Keep a diary of all you do in your garden.

Write down what was done, when, where, how and why. What plants and date you planted; what fertilizer used and date applied; type of garden spray used on your fruit trees and date applied. Include a layout plan of your garden and what seeds were planted where (each year). If the seeds don't come up,— you will know if it was the zinnia or parsnips; and you won't plant carrot seed on top of where you already planted beets. You will know what you planted last year in a particular area, so you won't place a heavy feeder this year where a heavy feeder was last year (i.e. tomatoes, strawberries, corn take a lot of nutrients from the soil). Also keep track of the type of organic matter added, how much, and date applied. You will learn a lot from your written observations of what works and what doesn't.

Starting Seed Indoors (in flats or containers).

Start seeds indoors and give your garden a head start. Seed catalogs have a greater selection of plant varieties to choose from, and it's cheaper than buying the plants from a licensed nursery. You'll need seed, a "sterile" soil mix (not garden soil), sterile containers, and a liquid or water soluble fertilizer.

Both commercial potting soil and special seed starting mixes have been sterilized to destroy pests, disease, damping off fungi, and weed seeds. These soil mixes contain either peat moss or potting soil (to retain moisture), and clean sand, perlite or vermiculite (for good drainage). You can buy these soil mixes, or you can make your own <u>Seed Starting Mix</u> using equal amounts of vermiculite or perlite, peat moss, and potting

Start seed indoors in a seed flat.

soil. Some plant types require special soils. Seeds and plant cuttings start faster in soil-less mixtures (i.e. peat moss with perlite), but when they grow big enough to transplant, put them into individual pots with potting soil. If you use perlite, wear a mask so you don't inhale it.

Use only sterile components if you make your own mix. All bought ingredients are sterilized except leaf mold. Never use ordinary garden soil or used potting soil for growing plants or seeds in containers, unless you first sterilize it. Soil can be sterilized in your oven between 160-180°F in a shallow pan for two hours [3]. DO NOT sterilize anything containing fertilizer [5]. So, sterilize what you need to, and <u>then</u> add the peat moss, perlite, and fertilizer, etc. Don't use leaf mold when starting plants indoors in containers; since it can't be oven sterilized, just use it outdoors.

Starting containers can vary from peat pots to flower pots, egg or milk cartons, shallow wooden trays or boxes, and styrofoam cups or meat trays. If they don't have a drainage hole, make one. Without a drainage hole, the plant will rot sitting in water. This applies to any container plant or house plant. If you use containers that have held plants before, be sure to scrub them thoroughly with soapy water and 1:10 solution of Clorox to water. And scrape off any residues. Plastic containers stay clean longer, are easier to clean, and require less watering.

Collect all items needed. Fill the selected container with potting soil to within an inch of the top. Slightly moisten the soil. Pack the soil lightly. Use pencil or similar object to make depressions on the soil surface. Drop one seed into each hole. Slightly cover seeds with soil mix (the smaller the seed the less soil you put over it). Pack down gently on entire soil surface using a flat object such as a small box or plate. Water gently so as not to dislodge the seeds, either with a spray watering can or soak container in a tub for 2 hours to absorb the needed water. Place this container in a clear plastic bag, and store in a warm room 70-80°F. The plastic bag retains the moisture so you don't have to add water. Check container daily. When seedlings emerge, remove plastic cover and move container to a cool, sunny room. Most failures are due to lack of light. Add water when soil feels dry just below the surface, but don't overwater as the seedlings will rot.

Transplanting Seedlings into Larger Containers.

When new seedlings have their second pair of leaves, it is time to transplant to a larger container. Do this so they will develop a healthy root system, lessening transplant shock when planted into the garden. Have ready a milk carton, styrofoam cup, or similar container (with hole) filled half way with damp potting soil. Make a hole (plenty large) in the container's soil for the seedling with your finger or a table knife. When ready to transplant, carefully lift a clump of seedlings supported in a spoon, trowel, or your hand. Gently pull the roots apart, leaving as much soil on the roots as possible. Cut any intertwined roots with a knife. Do not <u>pull</u> the little seedling out of the soil. Instead, carefully lift the seedling out by its leaves (not the fragile stem), and place roots in the prepared container. Add more soil till it is a half inch from top of container, gently firming soil around the plant. Water it right away, then continue planting rest of transplants. Water with B1 solution, fish emulsion liquid fertilizer, or other very diluted liquid fertilizer like VF-11. KEEP PLANTS OUT OF DIRECT SUN FOR 2-5 DAYS AFTER TRANSPLANTING, and water as needed. Use a shade shelter for about 5 days, made with shade cloth or cheese cloth stretched over a wood or fencing frame (see watering chapter); or be creative with whatever you have on hand i.e. cardboard or boards. Water new transplants daily at first, then about every 3-5 days depending on the weather and plants needs. Let grow 2-4 weeks in these containers and then plant in your garden (after hardening off).

Hardening Off.

In a few weeks seedlings can be "hardened off" which means gradually adjusting them to the extreme temperatures of the outside world. When you place them outside (still in the container), remember they need sun but protection from wind. For several days bring them in at night, and later leave them outdoors day and night. Putting plants in cold frames outdoors also works well at this stage. Gradually open the cold frame more and more each night until finally you can put the

Original container

Cold frame

plant outdoors all night. "Tender" plants such as tomatoes and marigold do not harden off—they freeze!

Transplanting Seedlings outdoors.

This final transplanting of seedlings is best done on a cloudy or drizzly day, or in evening. Dig the hole and fill with water. Gently remove seedling from container, keeping the soil on the roots, and place in hole in your garden. If plant is in a peat pot, just place entire peat pot into the hole. If roots have grown into a thick mat at the bottom of the container, gently pull them apart. This will allow new roots to grow out of the root-bound-ball. Water right after transplanting with B1 solution to help prevent transplant shock. Then water every third day. When they start growing again, water less often. If they are frost sensitive plants, be sure to time their planting after all chance of frost is past.

PLANTS FROM VEGETATIVE PROP.

Methods of starting new plants from vegetative propagation are: **division, cuttings** (from stem, leaf, or root), **layering** (ground and air), **budding** and **grafting**. Only the most popular methods: division, cuttings, and ground layering will be discussed here.

DIVISION

Division is a fast, easy, inexpensive way to get many new plants from perennials, bulbs, shrubs, and house plants. To divide or split a plant, it has to have two or more stems coming from below ground level, and each stem must have an independent, well-developed root system and some leaves. Some house plants suitable for division are: Asparagus ferns, Baby's tears, Maiden ferns, Snake plants, and Spider plants. These types of plants: clump-forming perennials, strawberry plants, bulbs, plants with rhizomes, plants with tubers, and ferns —all need to be divided every 2-5 years, depending on how crowded they are. Crowded plants have too much competition for nutrients, water, and space, so they don't flower. Even if you don't wish to make more plants, they need to be divided when they need more space. (Perennials with a taproot and only a single crown, are best propagated by cuttings of side branches, or by planting seed.)

Use simple division (vertically between 2 pairs of leaves).

• **Clump-forming perennials** should be divided in early fall (in cold winter areas). Cut back the stems of deciduous and semi-deciduous perennials to 4 inches from the ground. (Never cut back evergreen perennials, just keep the dead leaves removed). Lift the clumps out of the ground. Pull the plants apart carefully trying not to damage the roots. Some can be easily pulled apart, some have to be pried apart using two garden forks back to back (see illustration), and many require a sharp knife or shovel for cutting through the thick mass.

Some clumps of perennials and ferns have to be cut or pried apart.

Since you cut some off the stems, now cut some off the roots, so the plant is balanced. Take off any dead leaves and cut off older portions of the plant or root. For example, on Shasta

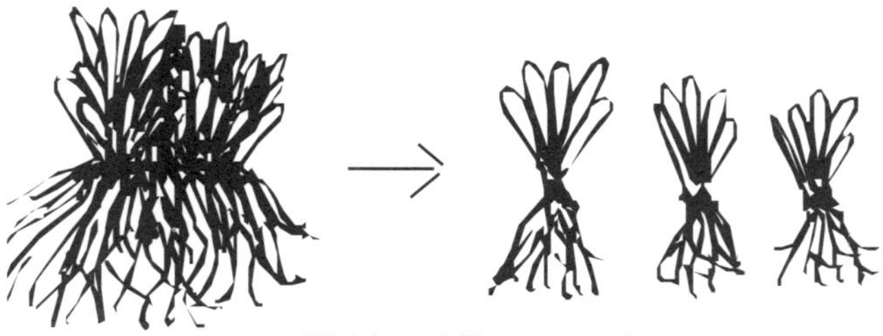

Division of fibrous roots

Daisy, cut the whole clump in half (from the top of the stems to the bottom of the roots) with a sharp shovel or knife, and then cut again if it is a big clump. Be sure each division retains enough healthy roots. Plant right after dividing and water well. If you have to wait a few hours, keep roots moist or they will die.

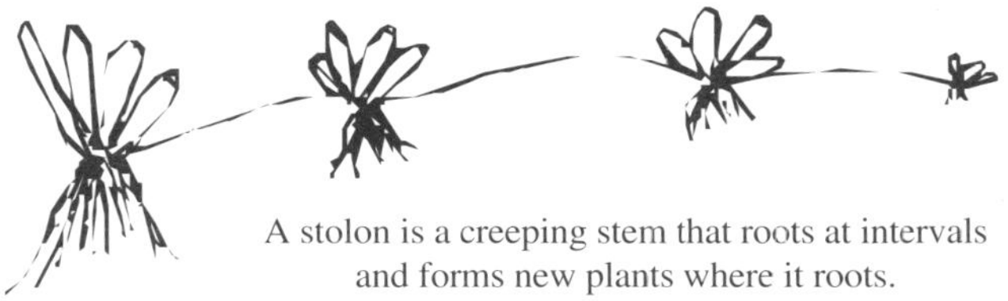

A stolon is a creeping stem that roots at intervals and forms new plants where it roots.

• **Strawberry plants** as perennials are a little different. The baby plants are attached to the parent by runners or stolons. Cut the runner (umbilical cord), throw away the old woody parent plant, and save the baby strawberry plants. Select the babies that have the most and healthiest roots.

• **Plantlets.** Some house plants grow plantlets which are small replicas of themselves on flowering spikes, on leaves, at the end of runners, or as miniature bulbs. In some cases (i.e. strawberry begonia) cut the runner both from the parent plant and from the plantlet. Put vermiculite or potting soil in a pot, make a small depression on the surface, set the plantlet in the depression, and firm the soil around the base of the plantlet.

Spider plants have babies called plantlets.

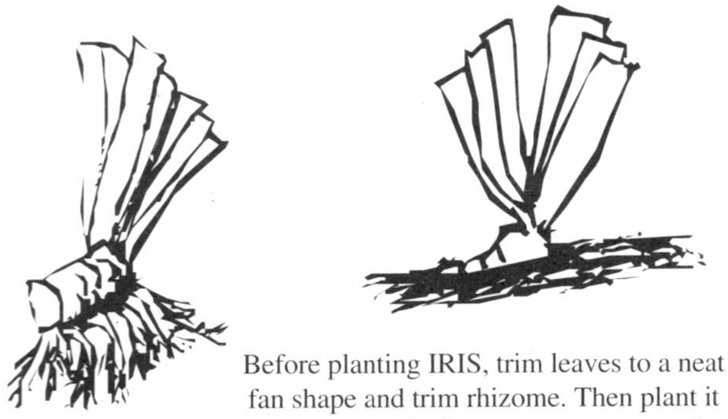

Before planting IRIS, trim leaves to a neat fan shape and trim rhizome. Then plant it so top part of rhizome is above ground.

Put a plastic bag over plantlet in pot until it gets roots. Keep soil moist and warm, but no direct sun. A single leaf containing a plantlet (i.e. Piggyback, Bryophyllum, or Asplenium) can be planted in the same way, laying leaf in soil depression. Put a pot of soil under the plantlet of a Spider plant, cover the base lightly with soil, and in about 3 weeks the plant will be rooted.

• **Offsets or suckers** occur on most Bromeliads, some Cacti, Amaryllises, Aglaonemas, and plants with a bulb. Offsets are small plants which develop either close to the base of the parent plant, or a short distance away from it, and may eventually over-crowd a pot. Wait till offsets are half the height of the parent before you remove them and pot separately [5]. Carefully cut or pull them away from parent.

Offsets

• **Bulbs** that stay in the ground should be divided when they get too crowded or when they stop producing flowers. Dig after foliage dies back (early fall) and pull bulbs apart. Replant in enriched soil. Gladiolas, Dahlias, and other plants (frost tender) that have to be dug up every fall, divided, and stored till time to replant (see individual plant instruction in Bulb chapter).

• **Plants with tubers**. Peonies and Day lilies only need divided every 5 years or more, in early fall. Peonies have growth buds in the crown, where the tubers join together. Cut the rootstock so that each piece contains several tubers and several growth buds to assure successful planting [5]. Trim off any rotten stumps. Peonies seldom require division so disturb them as little as possible. Day lilies need to have clumps pried apart with garden forks; then separated into individual fans.

• **Plants with rhizomes** are divided in early spring. The rootstalk is a swollen underground stem called a rhizome that grows at, or just below the soil surface, and has many thin fibrous roots. Examples are Bearded Iris, Solomon seal, some lilies, some ferns, and Bergenia. Cut a 2-3 inch long piece of rhizome that contains at least 2 growth buds (or shoots) and healthy thin fibrous roots [5]. When planting these plants, the rhizomes are completely covered with soil, except Bearded Iris which is planted with upper third of rhizome above soil level. For Iris, keep dead foliage trimmed or pulled off so as not to form a home for bugs. Plant all fans facing same way. Cut tops every fall to 4 inches from ground. When transplanting, also cut roots to same length as tops.

• **Bulbs with rhizomes.** Lilies with rhizomes should be divided every 3-4 years and separated with a sharp knife. Each scale can also be planted to make new plants, but you have to wait 2-3 years to get flowers on these.

Lily is a bulb with a rhizome.

• **Ferns**. The easiest way to start new fern plants is by division. Cut the fronds off down to the crown or base of plant in mid-spring and then divide the plant. There are three types of ferns: crown-forming, those with rhizome-like roots, and rock ferns. A "rhizome" is a modified stem that grows horizontally along or under the soil surface. The rhizome might be long and slender (i.e. some grasses), or thick and fleshy (i.e. many irises).

A "crown-forming" fern (i.e. shield ferns, and ostrich ferns) has fronds emerging from a stout rhizome in a crown shape. The crowns are divided by pulling apart and/or cutting the clump in half (see illustration under clump-forming perennial). If the clump is large, cut each clump in half again, and then plant each portion as a new plant. Prepare the soil by loosening it to 1 foot depth. Add fertilizer (10-10-10), add a 3 inch layer of leaf mold or garden compost, and then work it in. Dig hole as deep as the root system, fill with water, place fern in hole, fill with soil, firm soil around plant with your foot, and water well.

A "rhizomatous" fern (i.e. hay scented fern) produces fronds along the rhizome without forming a crown. Dig up roots carefully in the spring. Cut off portions of the rhizomes into sections,—each with at least one new shoot emerging (see illustration). Each section will make a new plant. To plant it,

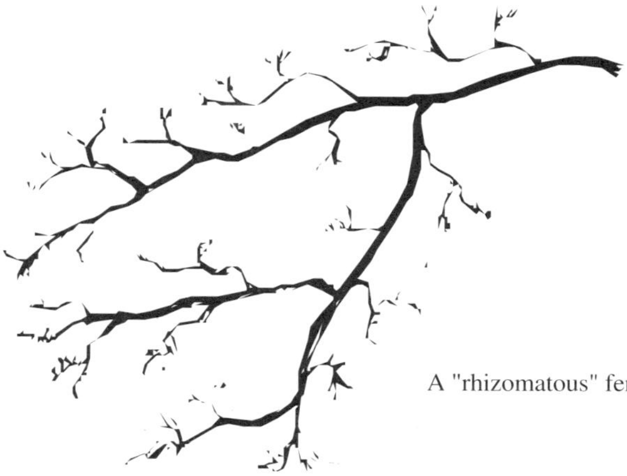

A "rhizomatous" fern

prepare the soil as above but instead of making a hole, only make a shallow depression with a trowel. Fill depression with water. Lay rhizome in hole, fill hole with soil, firm soil with your fingers, and water well.

A "rock fern" is ideal in rock gardens or on dry stone walls, especially if lightly shaded (i.e. maidenhair spleenwort,

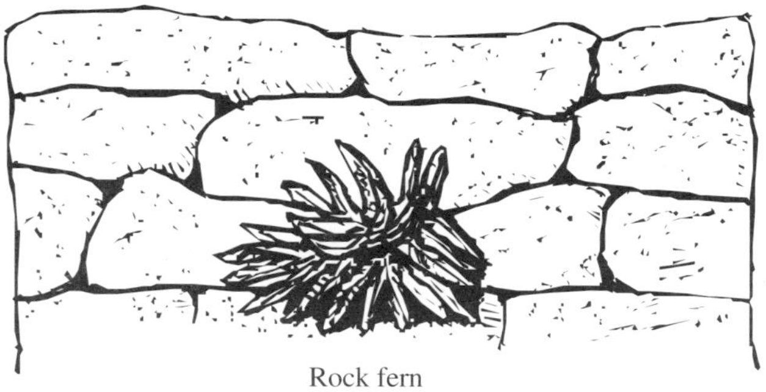

Rock fern

and woodsia). To plant, remove a stone from wall or rock garden, place fern on its side with roots in the hole, cover its roots with lots of leaf mold, firm the soil, water well, and then replace the stone.

Try transplanting native ferns into your garden (i.e. Bracken Fern). Select a piece of the rhizome (horizontal underground stem) with roots, because a fern frond alone won't root. Dig up plant in early spring while fronds are tiny. Bring bucket of water with you. Dig carefully to get enough of the rhizome, and place roots quickly into bucket of water. Bring bucket (with fern) to planting site, dig hole, fill with water, pop roots into hole, fill in dirt, and water well. Leave a depression around the plant for future waterings. I have Bracken fern, Bleeding heart, and viola as a foundation planting on the shady north-side of my house.

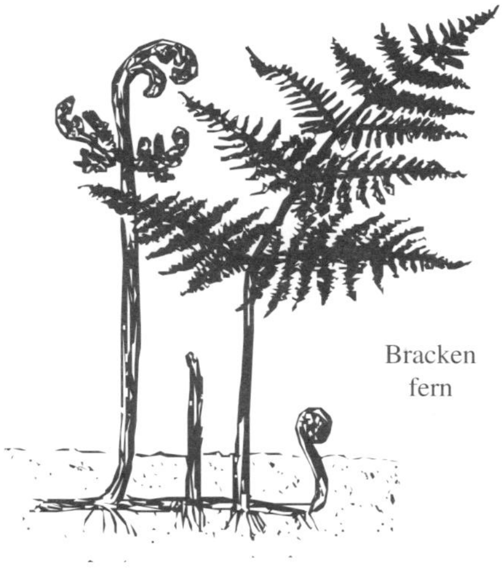

Bracken fern

CUTTINGS

• **Stem tip cuttings** (both softwood and semi-hardwood) are easy to take any time except winter, but spring is best. And they give quick results. The following plants can be started by tip cuttings: deciduous and evergreen shrubs and trees, and many herbaceous or evergreen perennials. This includes low growing shrubby plants like Phlox, Penstemon, and Sedum; and foliage perennials such as Anthemis and Rue. It is also a popular way to start house plants such as Ivies, Impatiens, Wandering Jew, and other plants that are easy to root.

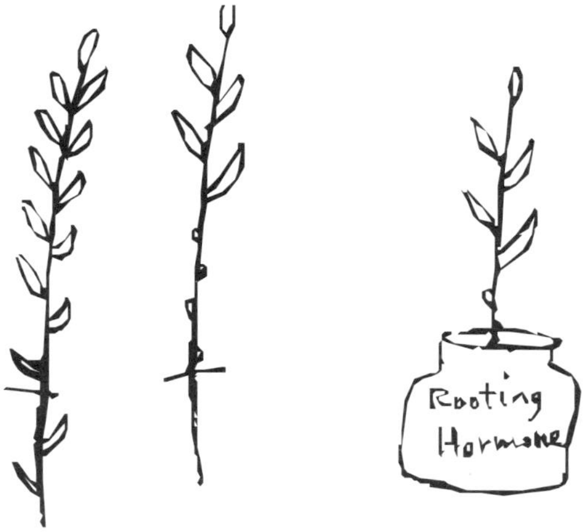

Stem tip cuttings

Select a healthy, non-flowering, side branch. (1) With a sharp knife, cut off about six inches of the branch tip, cutting just below a leaf. Even the thick, older stems can be cut into several short lengths, and the pieces with two or more nodes can be rooted (see two illustrations). (2) Gently pull off the lower half of the leaves. (3) If base of each cutting is dipped in hormone rooting powder before planting, rooting will be faster, but it isn't essential. (4,5) Place cuttings either in 2-inch pots of damp rooting medium (50 % vermiculite & 50% potting soil) or in a jar of water. If you root cuttings in water, either change the water once a week or add a piece of charcoal to the water to keep cuttings from getting moldy.

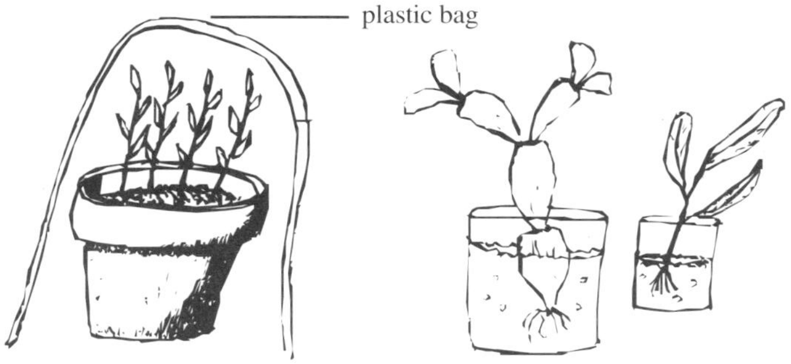

Start cutting in soil ---or in water

Thick old piece of stem

Insert half the stem into the soil (or water) and cover with a plastic bag, but don't seal it (see illustration). Set container (with drainage hole) in a warm room with indirect light. Allow no direct sunlight during rooting, whether container is exposed or covered in plastic. When you see new growth forming on the cuttings, you will know they have rooted (usually takes 2-5 weeks), so take off the plastic bag. Wait a little longer to be sure they are well established, then transplant to individual containers of potting soil. If they are outdoor plants, transplant them to the garden (after hardening off). Later, when set out in the garden, pinch off growing tip to encourage strong roots. Protect in cold frame for first winter.

Thick old pieces of stem can be cut into short pieces having a minimum of two nodes. Plant in horizontal position.

• **Hardwood cuttings** are made during the fall-spring (dormant season). They take much longer to get started, and do not grow from a branch tip, but require cutting a section from farther back on the branch. This method is used for many deciduous shrubs and trees i.e. Deutzia, Forsythia, grape, Kolkwitzia, Philadelphus, rose, and Weigela. Make top cut just above a leaf bud, and bottom cut just below a leaf bud (see illustration). Then plant the stem cutting halfway into the soil [3]. Be sure to cut the stub that remains on plant back to a bud. Cuttings must be planted top side up. One way to remember which way is up, is to slant the top cut, but make the bottom cut straight across.

Hardwood stem cutting

Sunset [3] states that most nut and fruit trees, and the large hardwood shade trees (beech, birch, maple, and oak) will not root easily from cuttings, so are propagated by grafting, budding, or from seed.

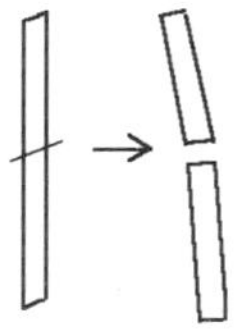

Cut thin roots into 2" pieces.

• **Root cuttings** can be taken in the spring from any plant that sprouts from the roots (i.e. Oriental Poppy, Trumpet Creeper, blackberry, raspberry.). These plants have no well-defined vegetative shoots and have thick or fleshy roots. Take the plant out of the soil and wash soil off the roots. Select a healthy root and cut into 3 inch sections. (Then replant the plant.) These root cuttings don't have to have visible growth buds, since buds develop after the root cutting is planted. Set root cuttings horizontally in flat, box or other shallow container (with a drainage hole). Cover with half inch of soil, and water well. Place plastic or pane of glass over container, and take off glass when seedlings appear. Allow NO direct sun on them until seedlings appear.

• **Basal shoot cuttings** (or suckers) can be taken from maple, lilac, aspen, and <u>most clump-forming perennials</u> that are propagated by division. Normally you remove young shoots or suckers growing from tree bases or roots (unless you want to start some new plants). Use a sharp knife to cut some basal shoots that are 4-6 inches long, and plant in seed starting mix. Then you can transplant the newly rooted plants directly into your yard.

Best way to "get rid" of suckers: Dig to where the sucker joins the stem or root, then pull down and break it off.

• **Leaf cuttings** are taken from house plants with thick, fleshy leaves often growing in rosettes, i.e. Gloxinias, African violet, Peperomias, most rhizomatous plants, Begonias, and many fleshy-leaved succulents like Crassulas and Echeverias. First choose a healthy, mature leaf with a sturdy leaf stalk. Long-stalked leaves can be rooted in water, the others in soil. Add a small piece of charcoal to a water-filled jar. Lay a piece of plastic across the top of the water-filled jar, and secure the plastic with a rubber band. Insert the long leaf stalk through

Start leaf cuttings in soil

---or in water

a hole punched in the plastic. When roots and leaves appear underwater, transplant to a pot, and cut off the parent leaf. Short-leaf-stalks are placed directly in rooting mixture, with the stalk at an angle of 45° for support [6]. Some plants root easily from a leaf or even a portion of a leaf.

GROUND LAYERING (A & B METHODS)

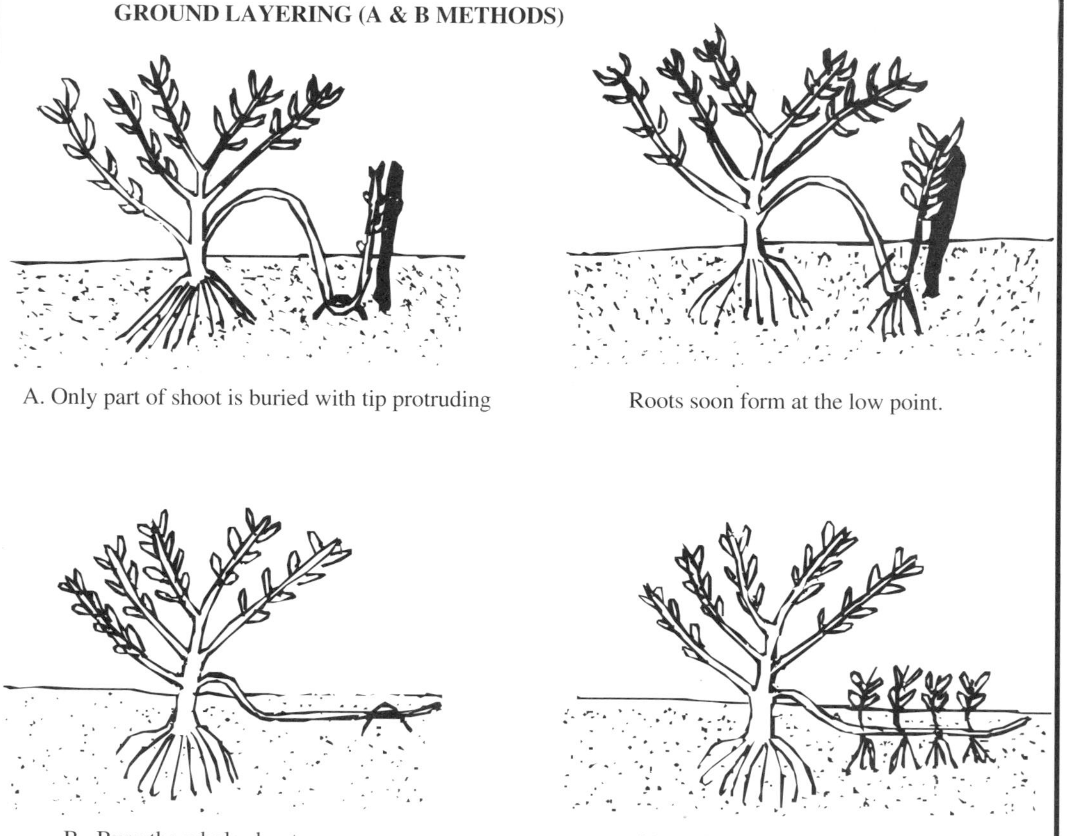

A. Only part of shoot is buried with tip protruding

Roots soon form at the low point.

B. Bury the whole shoot.

New plants form at each bud.

LAYERING

There are two ways to layer: air layering and ground layering. Layering is a very slow method, but with some hard-to-root plants it is more successful than with cuttings. This is because you don't separate branch from parent plant until branch has formed roots.

• **Ground layering** is a natural method to increase many prostrate ground covers or shrubs that have trailing branches, but the soil has to be rich enough (you can enrich it) to promote new root growth. Select a low-growing branch that can be easily bent to the ground. Dig a shallow hole. Strip away leaves where branch will be inserted in the hole. With sharp knife, make small nick in underside of branch where it touches soil in bottom of hole. (Use of rooting hormone in nicked opening is optional.) Then fill in the hole. Anchor branch if necessary with rock, stick, brick or bent wire, and keep soil moist. Six to twelve months later, when you see new growth coming from end of branch, you will know roots have formed. Now you can cut new plant from parent plant. Then dig up new plant and move to different location. Use this method also on climbing or trailing house plants such as Ivies and Philodendrons.

• **Air layering** is similar to ground layering but applies to branches higher on the plant. It is most commonly used on large, upright house plants that have stiff or woody stems such as aging Rubber plants, Codiaeum, or Dracena that have become unattractive after losing many lower leaves [6]. Attach the stem securely to a stake. Make an upward cut into the stem, separating the bark by inserting a small stick. Cover the cut area with a ball of moist, but not soggy, sphagnum moss. Then cover the moss with polyethylene film and seal it with tape at each end to trap the humidity. Continue to grow the mother plant in the usual way. When you can see the roots in the moss, cut the top off the mother plant above the roots, and put in a pot. Cut the parent plant off again about two inches above soil level and in a few weeks it will sprout new leaves. You can air layer the same mother plant many times [7].

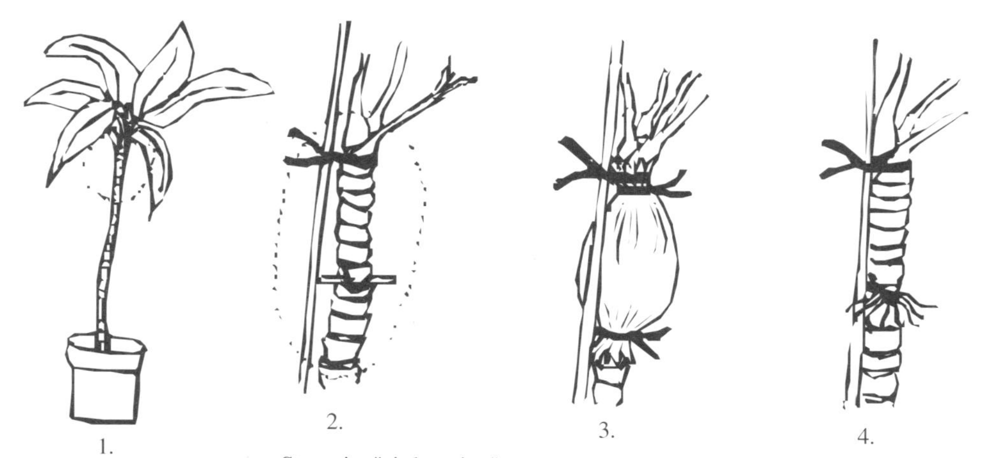

Steps in "air layering".

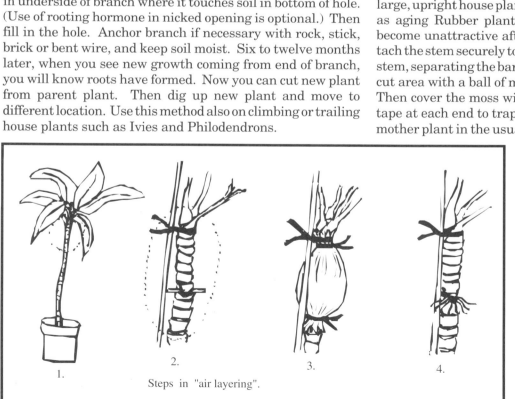

References cited:
[1] Let's Live Magazine
[2] Square foot gardening (Mel)
[3] Sunset Western Garden Book [SWGB]
[4] Parks Seed Catalog
[5] Readers Digest, Basic
[6] RD: Success with House Plants
[7] Indoor gardens for decorative plants

WATER WISELY

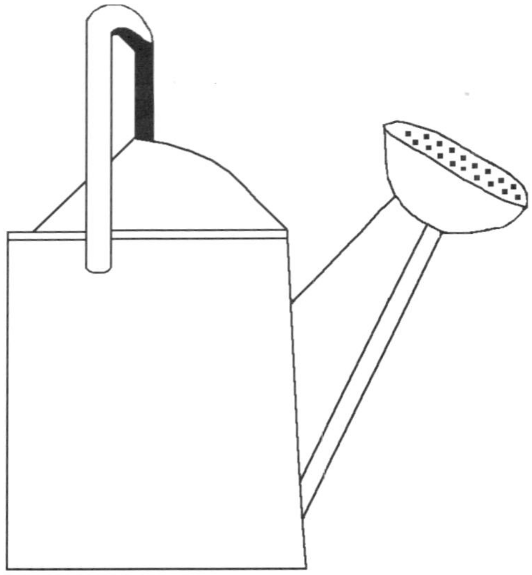

Watering can

Conserving water is necessary in California during recurring droughts, and where water is scarce or expensive. Improved watering techniques save more water, save money, create fewer weeds, promote less disease, and make gardening easier. The best way to "stretch" your water is to enrich the soil with compost, mulch to conserve moisture, and use drip irrigation to water efficiently. Water less frequently, but deeply, before 10 AM. Choose drought-tolerant plants, and plant them in groups. Turn off sprinklers when runoff starts; don't waste water. Cut lawns to a longer length; and aerate and dethatch them when necessary. Keep weeds pulled to eliminate competition. Keep container plants mulched and in the shade during the hot summer. Less fertilizer means less growth, and fewer leaves use less water.

Amount of water needed depends on many factors.

Consider size and age of the plant, type of plant, season of the year, weather (temperature, humidity, and amount of wind), nature of the soil, nature of the water, and method of water application [1]. Young plants need more water, because they are more susceptible to stress than older established ones. Also, drought stress increases plants' susceptibility to insect and disease attack. If you ignore these factors and water by calendar or clock only, you will either kill your plants by lack of water or drown them [1].

Most people either over-water or under-water.

Well-meaning gardeners can do the most harm by poor watering techniques on hot summer days. If, as a daily practice, you hold the hose and walk around the garden splashing plants, you will only be wetting the top inch of soil at most, and the hot sun will evaporate most of it before the plants can use it [1]. Light waterings are least effective and can harm your plants or lawn. With frequent shallow watering, roots respond by forming a shallow root system, and if you forget to water one day the roots will die. Shallow roots make your lawn less drought resistant in summer and more prone to winter kill.

Daily soakings, on the other extreme, are almost as dangerous, since plants drown when the soil's pore spaces are continually full of water (they can't breathe). More plants die from well-intended over-watering, than from scanty watering.

What is the ideal situation?

If watered every two weeks, some plants would barely survive. If watered once a week, they would grow to normal size, flower and do well. But if they are watered every three days, they would grow lush and twice as tall. The medium situation is satisfactory. The weather is also important on how often to water. If weather is hot and windy, watering may be necessary every three or four days. Having well-drained, enriched, mulched soil will be very important in this situation, so the soil will have good moisture storage.

Water thoroughly, but less frequently

For the most efficient irrigation, water thoroughly, but less frequently, soaking deeply for longer lengths of time. Try to extend the number of days between waterings. Soils should be watered deeply enough to encourage plant roots to grow deep, firm, and solid. To keep your plants growing well, you should water to their whole rooting depth. Let your beds dry out to the point where plant roots can no longer take moisture from the soil, then water again. Do not wait till plants wilt; occasionally check soil near plants to a depth of about four inches to see if the soil is dry and powdery [2]. Keep watering periods as many days apart as you can and yet avoid wilting plants, maybe only three days for a lawn, but possibly ten days for tomatoes. Water for as long a time period (half an hour or longer for example) as you can and still avoid runoff.

A simple test for lawns is to step on a patch of lawn briefly and see if the grass blades spring back up (no water necessary), or if the blades tend to stay flat (time to water deeply again). Gardeners with a more scientific bent sometimes install moisture meters or tensiometers to measure available moisture situation at preset soil depths. Hardware stores, nurseries or scientific supply companies may have catalogs listing such specialized equipment.

Should you water every day?

The only time to provide daily shallow watering is when you start seeds in a lawn or garden, since you have to keep the soil surface wet. Use a sprinkling can or garden hose with fan sprayer attachment to avoid washing the seeds away. When starting a lawn, cover grass seed with a layer of peat moss and/or vermiculite to protect seeds from being washed away and to help keep soil surface and seeds moist. When plants are tiny they have shallow roots and need frequent irrigation. When they get older their roots are longer and need deeper irrigation. When plants mature, their growth slows and they'll need less water, so readjust the timing of their irrigation. Water them to the length of their root zone, but less often. Learn how to stretch the time between waterings safely.

How do you know when you have watered enough?

You can save gallons of water, if you learn how long your lawn irrigation system takes to deliver one inch of water. First, make sure all sprinklers are functioning properly. Let sprinklers run fifteen minutes. Then dig several slits in the lawn and measure the depth of water penetration. If water penetration is a half inch, then it would takes thirty minutes to deliver one inch of water. The water needs to penetrate to the bottom of the root zone. If the root zone is only one inch deep, then this is the ideal amount to apply at one time providing there is no runoff. If there is runoff, stop and wait an hour, then resume watering until runoff starts again or until the full time is used. Each week in the summer your lawn loses about two inches of water by evaporation from the soil and transpiration from the grass leaves. So water twice a week, or every four days at the rate of one inch at each irrigation. The evaporation and transpiration are greater on days that are unusually hot or windy; you may have to water every other day during such hot spells.

Once you've established how long to water, you can do it without checking in the future. But, don't depend entirely on a watering schedule, because if the weather gets cool and humid, you need less frequent watering than in hot, dry weather. And just because you are on water restrictions and are only supposed to water every other day, doesn't mean you have to water every other day if your plants don't need it. Experiment to see what method of watering, and what length of time, works for your particular situation. Remember to consider all factors!

Use drip irrigation whenever possible.

Common watering methods are the use of: drip irrigation, sprinklers, or garden hose. However, the most efficient way to apply water is to use drip irrigation. This method drips water just above a plant's roots, because you (or an automatic timer) can strictly control the distribution: where, how long, and how much is delivered to each plant for drip irrigation. Small, flexible, polyethylene, dripper hoses containing special "emitters" allow water to be distributed evenly drop by drop, under low pressure, over a long period of time. The water is slowly put exactly where it is needed (and no where else), giving deep penetration without evaporation. Drip irrigation is usually worth its expense, because it saves both water and your time. Evaporation can be further reduced if the dripper hoses are buried under 2-3 inches of mulch.

Drip irrigation can be used for growing vegetables, ornamental and fruit trees, shrubs, and vines on ground level and in raised beds, as well as for plants growing in containers both indoors and out. It is easy for the average homeowner to install; no glue is needed as the pieces just snap together using hot water. Drip does NOT work as well with solid plantings of numerous, widespread, shallow-rooted plants, such as grass and some ground covers, unless the drip system includes "misting" emitters [3]. Some drip systems also allow for small sprinkler attachments.

Sprinklers, or overhead watering, is the most widely used method but the least efficient. Sprinklers may be rotary, oscillating, or fan types. They waste more water by evaporation, while germinating every weed seed, spreading plant diseases, attracting undesirable insects, requiring long watering times to deliver enough water for adequate soil penetration. Sometimes they can actually cause scald or "burn" damage on leaves. This "burn" is caused by the "magnifying glass" effect of hot sunlight hitting water droplets left on leaves. However, it is still the easiest method of watering large gardens. If you do use overhead watering, be sure to water in early morning, so the foliage won't get sunburn or fungus disease.

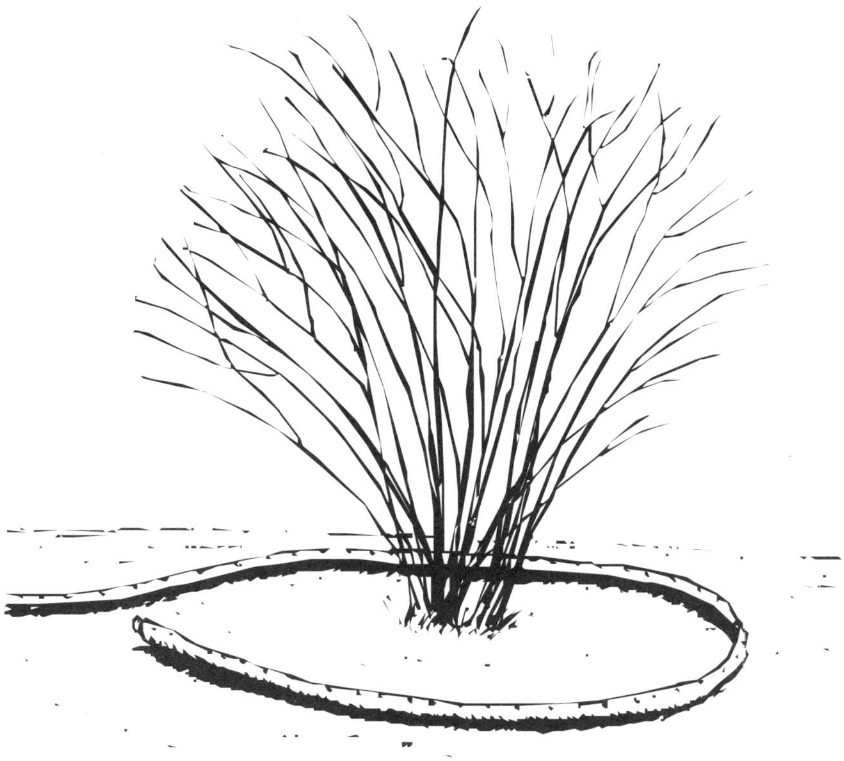

Place soaker hose at drip line of the plant.

If you don't have drip irrigation equipment, try deep soaking using a garden hose. Rubber garden hoses are more expensive (than plastic) but last longer and have a life time guarantee —at Sears. There are three popular techniques used: furrow, earth basin, and soaker hose. Lay the garden hose down in a furrow or an earth basin, and let the water flow slowly (till basin or furrow is filled) so it soaks down to wet the roots. Furrow irrigation (see Intensive gardening chapter) can be used for row crops such as corn. Soaker hoses are used to drip water slowly around drip lines of mature trees and shrubs, and near flower and vegetable roots. The "drip line" is the circle beneath the outer leaves of a plant where most rainwater drips to the ground.

Earth basins are used around young trees and shrubs, and large vegetable plants such as tomatoes and squash. The feeder roots are usually at the drip line, so if the plant is four feet in diameter, make the basin that size. Usually one inch of water standing in the basin will soak down one foot. "An earth basin" is a mechanical means of creating a water reservoir around the base of each plant by mounding earth in a circle around the plant at the drip line. Put 3-4 inches of mulch in the earth basin. When the rainy season starts, open the mound to let water escape so the plant won't drown [2]. A combination of drip, and water basins works best in my yard.

Earth basin

Water only in the early morning

Water before 10 AM, especially during the summer, to reduce evaporation loss, prevent disease, and leaf burn. Water pressure is usually stronger in the morning, and plants have a chance to dry off before fungus diseases take hold. Afternoon watering is wasteful because of the high evaporation rate.

Enrich the soil before planting.

The ideal lawn is fairly level, underlain by 6-8 inches of topsoil with good water retention. But if you have thin topsoil, compacted soil, or are on a slope, you may have water absorption problems. Your soil type also affects how often you need to water. Water quickly penetrates sandy soil, but it is held in clay soils; and sandy soil needs watered twice as often as clay soil. Adding decayed organic matter will increase any soil's ability to hold water. Enrich the soil to 8-12 inches depth. If only planting one plant, dig compost into the individual planting holes about twelve inches deep.

Improve aeration and water penetration.

In the spring, consider spiking or aerating lawns (makes tiny holes in the lawns) or use soil penetration chemicals. If thatch is present, use a dethatching attachment on your power mower (or use a metal garden rake). Then spread a thin layer of aged (or bagged) manure over your lawn to enrich it. These methods are particularly important if you have compacted soils or lawns. In non-lawn areas, cultivate or loosen soil around plants to aerate it.

Mulch all the plants

Use mulch in the yard everywhere except on lawns, and don't forget to mulch outdoor containers. Mulch is the best protection for plants in summer because it keeps the soil cool, while reducing water loss from evaporation, so you can water less often. Always mulch immediately after planting. Natural or organic mulches are best, because eventually they break down to improve soil texture and drainage.

Cut lawns to proper height

In areas with cold winters, grow "cool season" grasses. They usually are sold as a mixture of Kentucky bluegrass, perennial ryegrass and fescues. Gradually let lawns reach 3-4 inches high. Set lawn mower to cut grass at two and a half inches tall. Mowing grass too short increases water evaporation from the soil. Higher grass can go 3-4 days longer between waterings.

Keep weeds pulled

Weeds compete with your plants for water and nutrients. Mulch helps control weed growth. Remove weeds as they appear (don't let them go to seed or you'll have a million more to pull).

Use drought-tolerant plants

They need less water to survive. That doesn't mean just using cactus. Use plants that do well under your local weather conditions (see Drought-tolerant plant list). They can be native or hybrid, sun-loving or shade-loving, preferring humid or dry conditions, or be flowering or non-flowering. Don't put a shade loving plant in the sun. Use good common sense and plant them where they will grow best.

Group plants together

Plants that have similar sun, air and water requirements should be planted together [4]. A dry site planting might include cactus with other succulents. Plants needing wetter conditions include cottonwood, alder, and willow. Shady plant groups might include fern, bleeding heart, and viola. Become familiar with your plants needs. Some ferns do well in dry, sunny spots, while others prefer shade. Deep rooted vegetables such as tomatoes need a longer watering period. Shallow-rooted vegetables include potatoes, onions, sweet corn, and cabbage family. Intermediate rooted plants include beans, carrots, peppers, summer squash and cucumbers.

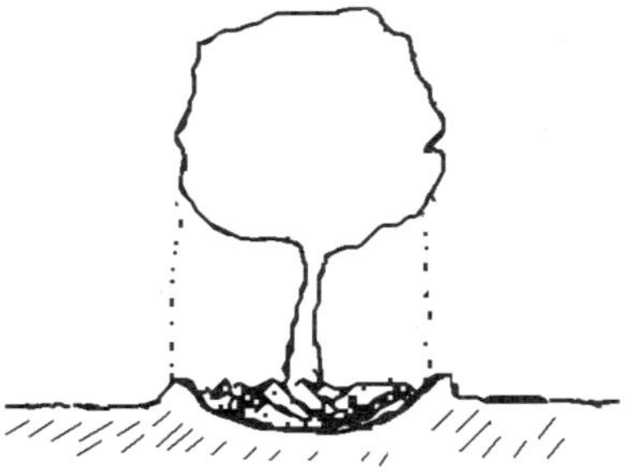

"Dripline"

Keep lawns small

Grass requires more water than other plants. A lawn only 20 feet x 40 feet is recommended for single-family homes [5]. Lawns are good for playing or lounging on, and they produce humidity that makes you feel cooler in the summer.

Lawns reduce glare and dust, absorb air pollutants, and generate oxygen. They control soil erosion while building the soil. They enhance groundwater supplies by catching rain and irrigation. Lawns provide a good habitat for birds, earthworms and other beneficial insects.

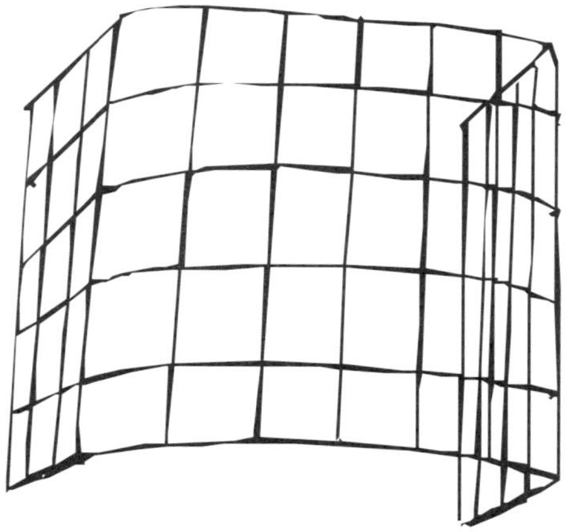

Wire frame

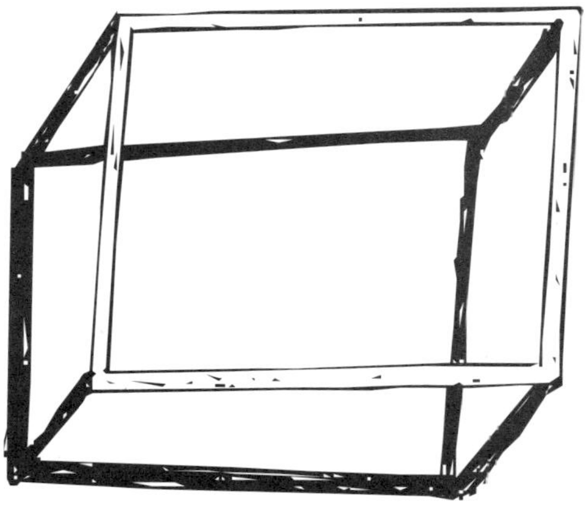

Wooden frame

Spacing is very important.

Don't put large plants too close together, because they will compete for moisture and nutrients. Instead, plant them farther apart and use thick mulch in between to keep soil cool and slow down evaporation.

Plants in containers.

Should you use large containers or smaller ones? Smaller containers dry out faster than large ones. If you have a lot of small plants in 4-6 inch pots, take them out of the pots and group them together in one large-size container, such as a half barrel [4]. Move outdoor container plants into the shade during the hot summer. Set containers on dirt or wood surface rather than cement or metal. Soil temperature is more important than air temperature. Soil temperature of a pot in the summer sun can reach well above 100°F and will severely dehydrate the plant. Such high temperatures will speed plant water use and, in extreme cases, can bake plants to death.

Pruning or thinning out

Water requirement to trees and shrubs can be reduced twenty-five percent by thinning out excessive inside growth. Thinning also allows sunlight to penetrate. But only prune lightly, because heavy pruning saps the tree's energy. Prune overgrown plants, and also prune out any dead, diseased or bug-infested branches as soon as they appear.

Fertilizer

Use only enough fertilizer to keep plants healthy. Using too much increases plant growth and requires more water (and for lawns, more mowing). Fertilize lawns in our areas only in May using a complete, balanced fertilizer like 10-10-10. For flowering plants use 5-10-5. If you use a slow-release low-nitrogen fertilizer, feed plants once in the spring and it will provide adequate food for a slower, but green growth. But if you are planning to cut down on water for a plant, don't fertilize, prune or apply pesticides, as all of these encourage growth. When plants get limited water, they slow their growth process to get by with available supplies.

Use shade cloth in heat of summer

Use cheese cloth or commercial shade cloth to shade the most sensitive plants, new transplants, and cool weather crops from hot summer sun. The cloth must not touch the plants. Set up a simple wooden frame using 4-6 wooden stakes [2], or bend a piece of stiff garden fencing [6]. Attach shade cloth to the frame with clothes pins or plastic ties. See shade protection paragraph in Planting chapter.

Maintenance

• Regularly check all irrigation systems for leaks, because even a small leak can waste hundreds of gallons of water in a single day. In drip systems, check all hose connectors, valves, and piping. On garden hoses, replace rubber washers, and repair or replace defective hoses. In sprinkler systems watch for leaks, broken pipes or broken sprinklers.

• If you're using a sprinkler system to water your lawn, check water heads for coverage and replace old heads with the new, pop-up models to ensure overlapping, complete circles, half-circles and quarter-circles.

• Keep mower blade sharp, because a ragged cut causes increased water loss, creates a brown haze on the lawn, and makes grass more susceptible to disease.

• As fall approaches and night temperatures drop to about 35°F, drain and disconnect your garden hoses at night so they don't freeze. Drip irrigation hoses are mostly self-draining, and they don't have to be opened (at the ends) until you are finished with your garden in the fall. Anytime there is a rainstorm, be prepared for a frost the first clear morning. (Yes, in the summer too !)

• Keep adjusting the timing on automatic irrigation systems along with the weather changes, and with the height of the plants as they grow.

References cited:

[1] Sunset Western Garden Book [SWGB]
[2] Surviving a drought in a CA Landsc. [Bernhardt]
[3] Drip Irrigation for the Home G & L
[4] The Water Crunch, Cal Life.
[5] "Turning over a new, dry leaf" [Hammock],
[6] Square Foot Gardening [Mel]

MULCHING

What is it? Mulch is a protective layer of material (usually organic) spread over the soil surface.

Why? To reduce weed growth, reduce evaporation, enrich the soil, prevent erosion, prevent soil (or frost) heaving in winter, increase humidity, insulates the soil against extreme temperatures, and keeps root area cool and moist.

Where? Over any bare soil, around your plants, under trees and shrubs, etc., especially over asparagus, potatoes, and strawberries.

When? In the spring after seedling are established, before hot weather, around emerging seedlings. In the fall after the ground freezes.

How Much? Cover soil with 2-3 inches of mulch. If you use rock, use 2 or 3 layers.

Types of Mulch (What is available locally):

Composted organic matter, including forest humus.
Wet peat moss.
Manure (must be aged and composted or it will burn plants).
Ground bark.
Redwood bark (attractive and durable).
Redwood chips.
Redwood shavings (they blow away).
Sawdust (robs soil of nitrogen unless it is aged, so include manure, grass clippings, or a fertilizer high in nitrogen).
Hay and cut grasses (before they go to seed).
Straw (put over potatoes with chicken wire on top to keep the straw from blowing away). Takes longer to break down.
Pine needles (plenty available free, but they have sharp tips that can poke hands !) Since longer needles break down slowly —they make great mulch.
Cotton seed hulls, cocoa bean hulls, rice hulls, etc. Decompose slowly but are beneficial to aerate the soil.
Gravel, sand, and rock cool the roots during the day, and retain heat at night.
Plastic sheeting doesn't decompose, absorbs heat, and retains moisture well, but it is VERY SLIPPERY WHEN WET so don't use it where you walk, especially on paths. White plastic is now available that absorbs less heat.
Paper and cardboard (craft or other heavy paper works when anchored with pebbles, rock, or bark).

Cover soil around plants in your garden with 2-3 inches of year-round mulch [1, 2]. If the soil is not insulated by mulch, hot summer sun can bake nitrogen from the organic matter. Mulch will moderate soil temperatures in both summer and winter. Mulch keeps the soil moist by preventing ground moisture from evaporating. It prevents winter frost heaving. It inhibits weed growth that compete with your plants for water and nutrients. It keeps strawberries clean (rainwater won't splatter mud on your plants), and strawberries won't sit on the soil (rotting where they touch soil), thus increasing productiveness.

When you want to plant some seeds or seedlings,— just pull back the mulch, plant, and then replace the mulch. If you pull back or "lift up" the mulch about two times a season to add an inch or so of compost (underneath the mulch), your neighbors will be amazed at the size and flavor of your fruits and vegetables.

Organic mulches such as compost, rice hulls, or straw are very desirable because they can be turned under at the end of the season. As the mulch decomposes, till it under and add a fresh layer of mulch as needed.

Short lawn clippings can be left on your lawn (act like a mulch), because they decompose quickly, increasing both nitrogen, potash, and organic matter without adding to thatch buildup. If you put grass clippings on your compost pile, place them in thin layers (each layer of grass covered with a thin layer of soil), or they will mat together permanently in clumps. Don't use grass clippings in your compost pile if it has been recently treated with herbicides [3]. Don't use fresh grass clippings alone as a mulch around garden plants, because they act as a shelter for breeding white flies.

WEEDING

Weedeater

A weed is an aggressive, fast growing plant that competes with your garden plants for the available sun, moisture, and soil nutrients. Plants will grow and mature faster without weed competition, so keep weeds pulled. Basically, a weed is any plant that you don't want growing there.

In the garden. If you weed well before planting, then mulch deeply around each plant after they come up, the weeds will be smothered. Don't use herbicides in your garden to kill weeds (or it will also kill the desirable plants), so the weeds have to be pulled by hand, with a trowel, weeder, or shovel. Be sure to pull all the roots. Pull weeds while they are small, before they form flowers or seeds, and you'll have fewer weed problems later. Weeding is easier the day after watering (or after a good rain), and you'll be able to get more roots up from the moist earth. If you leave pulled weeds in your garden pathways for dried mulch, be sure to leave them with their roots UP so they don't re-root themselves. Lawns, if well fertilized in spring, will grow so thickly that most weeds will be crowded out. If you keep your grass 2-3 inches long, it will shade out the weeds [4].

Outside the garden. Instead of pulling all the weeds by hand, many of them can be "mowed down" by a weedeater. Weedeaters can be a wonderful tool when used properly. They trim grass edges neatly, and work well in unlandscaped areas. DON'T use them "in" garden beds, and DON'T LET the weedeater get too close to trees or shrubs, for it can girdle the bark quickly and the plant may die. If you DO make a gash in the bark, paint it with white water-base paint, or special black pruning paint to keep bugs and disease out.

References cited:

[1] The Ruth Stout No-Work Garden Book
[2] Square Foot Gardening [Mel]
[3] Time-Life: Lawn and Garden
[4] Org Garden Mag.

SOILS & FERTILIZERS

SOILS

Soil is more than dirt on a kid's face; it is the foundation for good gardening results! Soil is usually made up of sand, clay, organic matter (living and dead), air, water, bacteria, fungi, microorganisms, and even larger living creatures. How does our mountain soil differ from other soils? How can we enrich it to grow healthy plants? This chapter discusses soil and its relationship to fertilizer, manure, air, and organic matter. It concludes with how, when, where, and even when not to apply fertilizer.

The mountains of Northern California have mostly stony, sandy, porous soil originating from volcanic activity. We are at the junction of three major geologic types (see map), so we have some of all three types. Our soils are either based on Cascade-volcanic, Sierra granitic, or Great Basin basalt [1]. Geologically speaking, Mt. Lassen lies at the south end of a line of sleeping volcanoes in the Cascade Range, it touches the southwestern corner of the great basalt flows of the Columbia Plateau, and it lies less than fifty miles from the northern edge of the Sierra Nevada Range's granitic batholith.

Different soil types influence the location of distinct types of flora. The flora of the Mt. Lassen area is very interesting as it occurs between two great mountain ranges, each of which is distinct in its geological structure and history. This flora is a mixture of types between that of the Cascade range and that of the Sierra Nevada. There are about 24 Sierran species that reach a northern limit in the Lassen area, and about 15 Cascadian or Columbian species that reach a southern limit there [1].

Mountain soils usually have fast drainage due to many rocks in the soil (half rock, half soil). To improve local soils for gardening, you must either take the rocks out (a long process) and add organic matter, or add topsoil plus organic matter on top of the native soil (i.e. in raised growing beds). Rocky soil is not as much of a problem if you are landscaping, since you just mix in organic matter and choose plants that are adapted (or can adapt) to this climate [2]. But If you have rocky soil in a vegetable garden, you can get divided carrots, and have drainage problems. Our soil here (after you take out the rocks) needs basically organic matter and nitrogen.

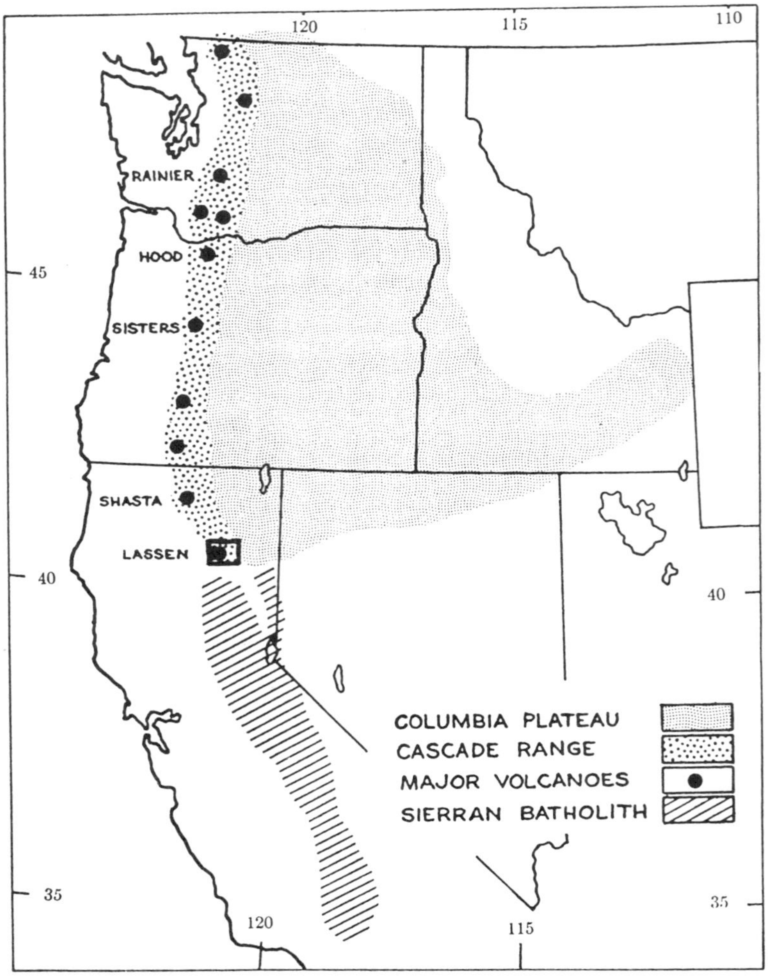

SOIL TYPES. This regional map shows the spacial relationships of Lassen Volcanic National Park, the Columbia Plateau, the Cascade Range, and the Sierra Nevada batholith. This map was reproduced with permission from Tom Howell *(A Flora of Lassen Vol. Nat. Park, CA,* and the editor of the *Wasmann Jouranl of Biology).*

In the Intensive Gardening Method, seed is planted across the whole growing bed, in contrast to the long rows of the Conventional Method. The Intensive Method uses soil more efficiently, resulting in more vegetables than in Conventional gardens. By adding massive amounts of organic matter (which will decay into humus), and organic and/or inorganic fertilizers, you can create a "supersoil" that will support maximum growth.

Is your soil deep, friable (crumbly), fertile, well-drained, and high in organic matter? Don't be disappointed if it isn't. However, before you rush out and start making changes, find out what kind of soil you have. When you understand the characteristics of your soil — you will know better how to water and fertilize your plants. What are the physical and chemical characteristics of your soil?

Physical characteristics of soil

These include the structure, composition, texture, depth, and drainage. Structure is a result of the soil's texture, organic matter, chemical composition, and how the soil has been worked (be careful not to work a clay soil when it is too wet, or it will become compacted). Your soil has good structure if it is crumbly (friable), somewhat porous, but not too lumpy. Adding organic matter (humus-making materials) to any soil can improve the structure.

Soil is <u>composed</u> of four types of materials: sand, clay, silt, and organic matter. The relative proportions of these four materials determine your type of soil and its characteristics like the texture, degree of drainage, aeration (air circulation), and nutrient retention.

<u>Soil texture</u> has to do with size of soil particles. Clay soil is fine textured with many tiny particles, while sandy soil is coarse with predominately large particles. Soils with too much sand or too much clay are at opposite ends of a range of possible soil textures. Clay is very sticky, heavy, and holds water; while sand is light but lets water and nutrients run right through. Sandy soil dries out at least three times as fast as clay soil. Sandy loams have 50-70% sand. Soils with more than 50% clay may have a drainage problem. Both clay and sandy soils will produce better if they are enriched with organic matter. The most versatile soils are loams, which contain an even mixture of sand, clay and silt; however, the ideal garden soil is a sandy loam.

How do you analyze your soil's texture? Add water to a quart jar until it is about 2/3 full. Then add a tablespoon of dishwasher detergent that contains water softener (i.e. Cascade). Add soil from your garden until jar is almost full. Put lid on, shake vigorously, and then let it settle. In a couple hours, the sand and silt particles will settle into distinct layers, but clay may take 24 hours. The layers will be: sand on the bottom, silt in the middle, and clay on top; and you can see at a glance what the proportions are in your soil.

<u>Depth</u> of soil is important because roots grow better in topsoil than in rocks, and the soil should be as rock-free as possible to 18 inches depth for best gardening results.

<u>Drainage</u> is critical to good plant growth, since soils often receive more water than they need. If a soil's pores are filled with water, then there is no room for air and the plants will suffocate or drown. The water must be able to drain through the soil.

Chemical characteristics of soil

These include the pH and overall fertility level. The <u>pH scale</u> measures soil acidity or alkalinity based on a scale of 1-14 where 7 is neutral. Most plants can tolerate a fairly wide range of pH values, but do best between pH 6-7. <u>Fertility</u> refers to amount of nutrients available to the plants. The only sure way to determine pH and fertility of your soil is with a soil test, because color, soil texture, and other physical characteristics are not reliable indicators of pH. If your soil has a problem, consider four possibilities:

- lack of some essential plant nutrient
- excessive acidity or alkalinity
- poor physical properties like texture, drainage, etc., or
- too much or too little water.

How do you test the soil?

Soil can be tested with inexpensive and easy-to-use testing kits available at most garden centers or through catalogs, or you can send a soil sample to your nearest County Agricultural Cooperative Extension Office, who will do it for a fee (see telephone book for their number). Standard soil tests tell you the pH of the soil, plus the amount of phosphorous, potassium, and organic matter your soil contains. In most cases elaborate testing is not necessary.

How can you improve the soil?

Our local mountain soils tend to be acidic (pH 4-6), but this is not a problem [2], if you add fireplace ashes or lime (both alkaline) to counteract the acid. (Don't put ashes or lime directly on germinating seeds or new plant roots as it will burn them.) If your soil is too alkaline (pH 8-9)—such as is common near Reno —add pine needles, leaves, or ferrous sulfate. <u>Organic Gardening magazine</u> [3] says not to use charcoal ashes from your briquette barbecue in your garden, because they contain high amounts of sulfur and/or metal residues

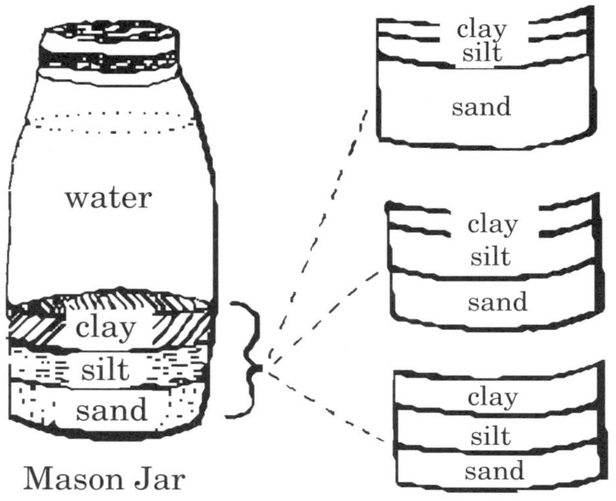

<20% clay >50% sand, or more than 75% silt.	"Sandy Loam"
No more than 27% clay >28% silt <50% sand.	"Loam"
<40%clay <50% sand and/or 60% silt.	"Clay Loam"

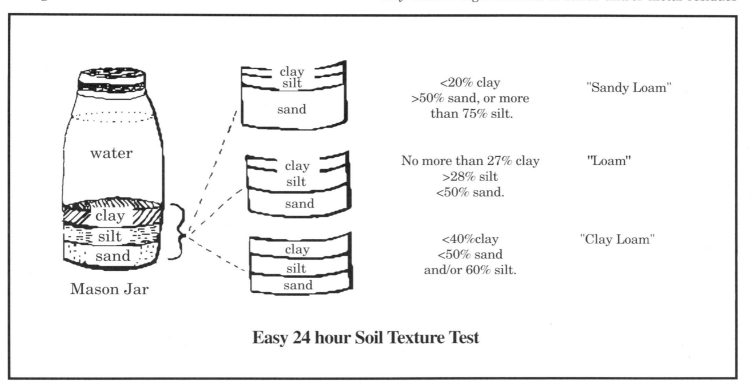

Easy 24 hour Soil Texture Test

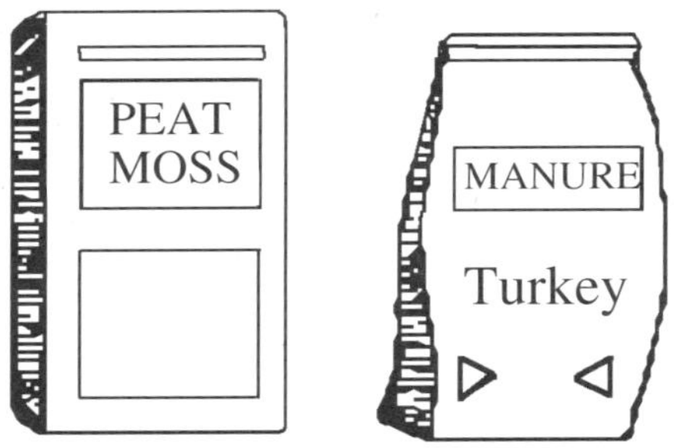

Add organic matter to the soil.

(particularly lead and cadmium). These residues can be taken up by the plants, and the high sulfur content can produce sulfuric acid when plants are watered. If you add woodstove ashes, be careful not to burn colored paper, adds, comics, magazines, etc. as they also have a higher metal content, because of the dyes in colored inks.

Over a period of several years your soil should improve if you add fertilizer as recommended; do a simple soil test for pH; work in lots of organic matter; and make sure you are watering properly. If your plants look green and healthy, and your strawberries are producing plump, delicious berries, then your garden is doing just fine.

Rototilling can improve soil structure, but if you rototill when the soil is too wet you can actually harm the soil by making it too compacted and lumpy. The goal of tilling is to break up the clods and level the surface. Rototilling should be done after fall harvest, and in the spring before planting (every year), unless you have raised gardening beds in which case you turn the soil with a shovel at these times.

If you have a heavy, clay soil you can add some sand to improve drainage. If you have a light, sandy soil you might add some clay to improve the texture. But people usually just add organic matter to most soils. Organic matter decays to form humus, and humus is often called a "magic" cure-all for every soil problem. If you add humus to clay soil, the soil will become more friable (crumbly), more easily worked, and have better drainage. If you add humus to sandy soil, you'll get better water retention. Over a period of years, adding humus to any kind of soil, will improve general soil fertility. Some humus sources are: manure, compost, peat moss, sewage sludge, sawdust, and straw. These will provide your plants with some plant nutrients, but should NOT be substituted for fertilizer.

FERTILIZERS

"Fertilizer" is used as a general term for plant food, soil enricher, organic and inorganic (chemical) materials. Fertilizers are added to improve soil fertility or to correct a specific soil nutrient deficiency, but be careful not to add too much because an overdose can kill your plants! The best way to know how much fertilizer to add, and in what proportion, is with a soil test. There are sixteen nutrient elements essential for healthy plant growth. Only four of them are commonly included in garden fertilizers: **nitrogen, phosphorous, potassium, and calcium.** The first three are included in commercial fertilizers in various proportions, whereas calcium is sold separately in the form of limestone. When the first three elements are all present it is called a "complete" or "balanced" fertilizer. The three number notation on fertilizer tells you the amount of nitrogen, phosphorous and potassium in it; for example, 10-10-5 means 10% nitrogen, 10% phosphorous, and 5% potassium by weight. The N-P-K nutrients are always listed in this same order on fertilizer labels. The rest of the fertilizer percentage is made up of inert ingredients. Plants also get **carbon, hydrogen, oxygen, sulfur, iron, and magnesium** from air, water and soil. "Micronutrients" or trace elements that are needed by plants in smaller quantities include: **manganese, copper, zinc, molybdenum, boron, and chlorine.** Don't apply micronutrients unless your soil test indicates a <u>serious</u> deficiency.

Inorganic and Organic fertilizers.

Inorganic fertilizers are soil enrichers that are either mined or manufactured and have quite different characteristics from organic fertilizers. Some examples of inorganic fertilizers are <u>charcoal, perlite, Dolomite limestone powder, egg shells, Limestone chips, sand, and vermiculite</u> [4]. Their nutrients are readily dissolved by water to be quickly available to plants, but they are not long lasting. Because they are so easily available to plants and so concentrated, they can kill plants if too much is applied, or if they directly contact leaves or roots. How and where to place fertilizer will be discussed later in this chapter.

<u>Charcoal</u> helps keep potting mixtures "sweet" by absorbing excess mineral salts and products of decay. Charcoal is most often used where there is no drainage such as in bottle or dish gardens, and terrariums. Larger pieces can also be used at the bottom of pots, tiny fragments can be mixed into the potting soil, or a small piece can be added to a jar of water where you are rooting a plant.

<u>Perlite</u> is made from sterile volcanic rock (pumice) that has been ground fine, medium, or coarse. It is used in potting mixtures or in the garden to improve soil texture, and to help absorb water and minerals. It is expensive, and not recommended because it can be inhaled into your lungs.

<u>Vermiculite</u> is made from mica rock that has been heated until it explodes (like popcorn) and forms flakes [5]. It absorbs and retains water and nutrients (like magnesium and potassium) much better than perlite, and is commonly used in rooting, potting, and garden soil mixtures. Buy a large bag because it is a much "better buy" than the tiny bag. It improves friability and water holding capacity of any soil. It decays very slowly—since it is made of rock— and may be one of the best investments you ever make.

Organic fertilizers are soil enrichers such as <u>compost, manure, sewage sludge, leaf mold, sphagnum or peat moss, tree bark, bone meal, tankage, blood meal, cottonseed meal, soybean meal, and partially decayed pine needles</u>. However these are low in the major three elements, so when you are comparing costs, you may be spending more on these than if you bought an inorganic fertilizer. Organic plant foods have nitrogen as the major ingredient with the excep-

HOW "HOT" IS MANURE?

Animal	% Nitrogen	% Phosphorous	% Potash
rabbit	2.4	1.4	0.6
sheep, goat, & cattle	1-2	1-2	2-3
poultry	5	2-3	1-2

Reprinted with permission from Rodale, the editor of "How to Grow Fruits & Vegetables by the Organic Method" [8].

tion of bone meal which contains mostly phosphorous. These nutrients are not available until the material decays in the soil. That makes them slow-acting but long-lasting. Since *organic fertilizers alone are not usually a complete source of nutrients,* many gardeners use a combination of both organic and inorganic fertilizers for best results [6]. The organic ones should be the majority as they are eventually broken down to humus to provide nourishment for soil microorganisms. Cost and available supplies also influence your choice. If organic fertilizers are so good, then why doesn't everyone use them? They aren't always easy to find in convenient size packages, and are often more expensive than chemical fertilizers [5].

Pine needles that haven't been completely burned in your burn pile, or pine needles (or other leaves) under trees that have started to break down, are both excellent sources of organic matter, and they are free!

Peat moss loosens heavy clay soils and adds body to light sandy soils. It improves soil's ability to hold moisture near the roots. In the garden, add one part peat moss to three parts garden soil. It has little nutritive value, but is an excellent soil conditioner that can be used any time of year. To improve an existing lawn — every spring, mix 3 parts peat moss with one part vermiculite and spread evenly over your lawn. (Then add a light application of chicken or steer manure.) This enrichment will improve the organic content of the soil, will reduce the amount of watering necessary during hot weather, and will help prevent soil surface from getting too hot. Use a metal rake to work it down to the grass roots, or use your power mower set at 2 inches. Peat moss is great when starting new lawns to help keep seeds moist during germination. It makes a great garden mulch 1-2 inches deep. Use peat moss or vermiculite in planting holes to aid drainage and to keep roots moist [7].

Manure (well-rotted) is an excellent source of organic (animal) matter, plant nutrients, relatively high in nitrogen, many minerals, and trace elements, but it is also high in salts. Some manures are "hotter" than others. Rabbit, horse, and hen manures have high nitrogen content, while cow, and hog manures are relatively low in nitrogen. Poultry is the hottest, so be sure it is well decomposed and apply sparingly so you don't "burn" your plants. All manures are excellent for garden use and they are commercially available in dried form. Most have been heat treated to kill the weed seeds (read the label).

The yearly rates of manure application suggested here may still not provide enough nitrogen for some crops requiring high nitrogen like corn, tomatoes, or potatoes. You may need to add more organic and/or inorganic fertilizers like those listed in the chart below.

Fall is the time to spread organic matter, fresh manure, leaves, fertilizer, bone meal, potash, etc. on your garden, since this gives the soil microorganisms a chance to decompose the material before spring planting time. Use a complete fertilizer like 10-10-10. The microorganisms that decompose organic materials to humus get some of their energy from the nutrients in the fertilizer. Spread the enrichment materials evenly over the soil surface in a thin sheet, and then rototill or turn it under with a shovel. If you apply manure in the spring be sure it is well "aged" (composted) for at least six months, or buy a bag of commercially processed manure. (If you apply fresh manure in the spring, you will "burn" the plants, and create a terrible weed problem.)

HOW MUCH FERTILIZER TO USE

Rates of Manure to use:	Type	How much
Manure:	barnyard (contains straw)	1 lb./sq ft.
	steer	1 lb./3 sq ft.
	sheep	1 lb./3 sq ft.
	chicken & rabbit	1 lb./5 sq ft.
Compost, leaf:	same	1 lb./3 sq ft.
Some Organic Fertilizers:	**Rating**	**How much**
Cottonseed meal	7-3-2	4 lbs./100 sq ft.
Dried blood	13-2-0	2 lbs./100 sq ft.
Fish meal	10-6-0	3 lbs./100 sq ft.
Tankage	7-9-2	4 lbs./100 sq ft.
Some Inorganic Fertilizers:	**Rating**	**How much**
Complete	10-10-5	3 lbs./100 sq ft.
Ammonium phosphate	16-20-0	2 lbs./100 sq ft.
Ammonium sulfate	21-0-0	2 lbs./100 sq ft.
Ammonium nitrate	33-0-0	1 lb. /100 sq ft.

Statistics in this chart were reprinted with permission from Home Vegetable Garden [9].

Three major ingredients in fertilizer:

Nitrogen promotes prolific vegetative growth in plants. Lack of nitrogen causes plants to grow small and have yellowish leaves. An excess of nitrogen causes rapid growth, which delays maturity, and makes plants more susceptible to disease and insects. Nitrogen fertilizers are derived from natural and man-made products. In nature the plant roots of the legume family produce nitrogen, while man produces nitrogen as a by-product of making coke. Nitrogen is readily lost by leaching action of heavy rains or watering especially on sandy or rocky soils, by high temperatures, and by constant use. That is why nitrogen needs to be added more often than the other nutrients.

Phosphates (phosphorus) stimulate root growth, promote flowering, and improve seedling vigor. A phosphorous deficiency is shown by a red or purple discoloring of leaves. Be sure to place phosphates close to the root zone of the plants you want to feed. Good sources are: bone meal (ground bones), rock phosphate, basic slag (by-product of the process of steel from iron ores), and lime. Steamed bone meal is very high in phosphates in the form of phosphoric acid, and it acts quickly. Phosphates reduce the acidity of soils. Most of the phosphoric acid used for fertilizer in the United States comes from superphosphates.

Potash (potassium) promotes plant vigor and disease resistance. It helps plants to synthesize sugar, is necessary for deep flower color, and is essential for strong stems and roots —especially in vegetables. Deficiency symptons are chlorosis (a yellowing and browning of leaves at their tips and edges), a curling of the leaves, and plants with weak stems. The main sources of potash are: wood ashes, hay, leaves, grass clippings, plant residues, manures, compost, and natural mineral sources like: granite dust, greensand, and basalt rock. Wood ashes provide potash, phosphates (small amount) and calcium. Use both organic and mineral potash fertilizer: organic for short term potash, and mineral for longer lasting ones.

Air and organic matter

Air is also important to plants and soil. Air is a complete fertilizer, because it contains all of the nutrients necessary for plant growth [8]. It is composed of 78% nitrogen, 21% oxygen, and 1% other gases. Air also carries pulverized nutrient material which can be dissolved and absorbed directly by the plant with the aid of dew or high humidity. It costs nothing, is easy to use, and it makes soil more fertile. Better aeration in your soil provides bigger root systems and higher yield crops. The University of Illinois at Urbana found that adding air to soil increased yields of corn from 94 to 144 bushels per acre [8].

Soil aeration can be increased by adding organic matter or manure, by earthworms, and by cultivation (rototilling, spading, turning over with shovel or plow), —but most effective of all is to add "decayed" organic matter (humus or compost). Surprised? The more organic matter in soil, the more air it contains. But don't add "fresh" organic matter directly to the soil unless you also add some form of nitrogen, because, if the decomposers can't get enough nitrogen they will take it from the soil [10]. Put the "fresh" stuff in the compost pile first. See Composting chapter. Adding decayed organic matter to soil automatically multiplies the earthworm population, and reacts with air to form more fertilizer (humus, carbon dioxide, and nitrogen).

Rain washes nutrients from air and leaves down to the soil, where the nutrients are held by decayed organic matter (humus is a slightly better nutrient "holder" than compost.) Decayed organic matter weakens clods by keeping soil porous and open: this allows water and air to enter, helping to make soil moist and fertile. The organic matter helps bind soil together to prevent erosion. It slows soil nutrient leaching. It absorbs and holds extra water like a sponge until the plant needs it, and can help to raise humidity around plants. Plants are often starving for air, so for goodness sake add organic matter to your soil and give them some air! In short, make them happy with humus!!

Whatever the need, use GOOD, ROTTEN organic material. Whatever is lacking in the soil, adding decayed organic matter will tend to correct it. Add ANY amount. It also corrects soil deficiencies and pH problems [11]. Plants will usually show you when they are lacking in some nutrient; like, when leaves turn yellow —the plant usually needs nitrogen.

HOW TO APPLY FERTILIZER

To fertilize properly you have to know HOW QUICKLY the plant nutrients become available, WHERE and HOW to place the fertilizer (plant food), and WHEN your plants need the nutrients.

HOW QUICKLY the plant nutrients become available:
PHOSPHATES (phosphorous) and POTASH (potassium) are immobile once they are placed in the soil, so if you want them near the roots, you have to place them near the root zone. NITROGEN moves quickly through the soil and needs to be replenished more often.

WHERE and HOW to place the fertilizer:

- "Broadcasting" (spreading evenly) with a mechanical spreader is the best way to spread fertilizer evenly over large areas like your garden. This should be done in fall and spring. Rototill or work it well into the top 2-3 inches of the soil.
- "Starter" solutions like B1 are best when transplanting plants like tomatoes, small shrubs, trees, or house plants.
- "Top dressing" is a way to work fertilizer into the soil around the plant.
- "Side dressing" is a good way to add nutrients after plants start growing i.e. strawberry plants and vegetables. Spread fertilizer in a long furrow at least six inches from base of the plants.
- "Base feeding" works great for roses, shrubs and most trees. Start fertilizing 6-12 inches from plant and continue until circle of plant food extends about 12 inches beyond the imaginary line beneath the branch tips. Rake fertilizer into soil carefully, while avoiding damage to the shallow roots.
- Don't put any manure or fertilizer within one foot of the base of a tree; and don't let any weeds, plants, or grass grow within a foot of tree trunks, to reduce the risk of disease.

WHEN your plants need nutrients:

There is a correct and incorrect time to fertilize plants [12, 13, 14]:

Annuals are best fertilized before planting. Spread fertilizer before turning the soil, and feed a second time when plants are thinned.

Bulbs and tubers are best fertilized in early spring or fall. Add complete fertilizer or superphosphate to planting hole, and bone meal after blooming.

Evergreens are best fed in early spring. Feed sheared ones again in fall. Use "acid" foods for azaleas and rhododendrons. Use a 7-7-7 fertilizer that also contains iron (acid-loving plants often need iron). Our local mountain soil is already acid, so using high acid fertilizers isn't so critical as it would be in Reno, Susanville, or in the Valley where soils are alkaline or neutral. But acid-loving plants do like acid peat moss, rotted oak leaf mold, and humus. Don't use lime or wood ashes (alkaline) on soil that is growing acid-loving plants. Fertilizers with nitrogen as high as 30% are too acid to use on our already acid soils (so read the labels).

Hedges are fed in spring, and sheared hedges are fed a second time in fall.

House plants can be fertilized any time (follow directions on package). But in winter when plant growth slows down, feed with dilute solutions like fish emulsion or VF-ll or not at all depending on type of plant.

Lawns need a complete fertilizer in May, and mid-June.

Perennials are best fed in early spring, and a second time when flower buds appear.

Roses are usually fed spring and summer. Fall feeding forces new growth that frost will kill.

Shrubs (young) should be fertilized in spring or late summer, but one feeding a year is usually enough for mature plants.

Small fruits and berries are usually fertilized with 5-10-5 in early spring and fall (when you rototil), and an extra summer feedings (just before blooming, plus in mid-summer) can increase the fruit crop. If you use only Ammonium sulfate (21-0-0) on strawberries you will get healthy green leaves, lots of runners, but no luscious plump strawberries, because high nitrogen stimulates <u>green leafy growth</u> and <u>not berries</u>.

Trees (fruit) are fed in early spring and "early" fall with 5-10-5. Feed at least three weeks prior to blooming and it will help set fruit, improve color, and encourage bloom. Don't fertilize fruit trees in late fall, as it can stimulate overproduction of new growth and can result in winter injury of the tree.

Trees (shade or ornamental) are usually fertilized in early spring; but if tree is weak, injured by drought, disease, or insects, then feed again in late summer. Use 10-8-6 or 10-6-4 special fertilizer for shade trees.

Vegetables are fed at planting time and again using "side dressing" when plants are thinned.

Vines are fertilized in both spring and fall, and only once a year after plants get well established.

What kind of fertilizer (plant food)?

The best all-around food for **green leafy plants** is 5-10-5 (high phosphorus). **Flowering plants** need low nitrogen, and even higher phosphorus 5-20-5 or 7-14-7 or one labeled "African violet food". Use the numbering system as a guide. If you're growing African violets and you find that a plain box of 5-20-5 plant food is cheaper than a box of 5-20-5 marked "African violet food", —then buy the cheaper plain box but be sure to read the numbers correctly [13].

There is much controversy about how much nitrogen to add to fruit trees. Some specialists say it doesn't matter how much nitrogen, while others say too much can cause injury to the tree. But they do agree on one point, that a complete fertilizer (containing all three critical elements) must be used —like 5-10-5 or 10-10-10. After reading many sources, I concluded that 5-10-5 appears to be a multi-purpose fertilizer for vegetable gardens, flowers, lawns, and fruit trees, and house plants.

Use fertilizers wisely. Some fertilizers leave an acid residue, and some leave an alkaline residue. Most fertilizers tend to burn up soil humus, even though they benefit crops. This loss of humus may leave the soil poorer than before treatment. <u>Overdoses of fertilizer can kill plants</u>, damage your soil, and kill beneficial microorganisms like earthworms. Organic gardeners prefer to use only organic materials that don't harm soil or earthworms. Good long-term soil conditioning requires more than occasional doses of fertilizer (plant food). Other beneficial measures include the importance of crop rotation, addition of lots of organic matter, an occasional season of fallow (not used) land, and use of a variety of fertilizer types over the years.

When NOT fertilize a plant

1) When you first buy a plant,—the grower has probably added enough food to feed it for six months.
2) Just <u>before</u>, or just <u>after</u> transplanting (unless it's a weak solution like fish emulsion or B1). Transplanting is enough of a shock by itself.
3) When a plant has a disease or bug infestation, —it is already sick, and fertilizer might kill it.
4) During winter months when most plants "rest", use weak fertilizers like VF-ll, fish emulsion, or no plant food depending on the type of plant.
5) Many flowering plants need food all year such as African violets. Non-flowering foliage plants indicate when they need fertilizer in the spring by starting new growth.

<u>References cited:</u>

[1] A Flora of Lassen Vol. Nat. Park, CA, HOWELL
[2] Landscaping your mountain home,
[3] Organic Gardening mag
[4] Readers Digest: SWHP
[5] Square foot Gard, [MEL]
[6] "Compost Preparation
[7] "Good gardeners know the many benefits of peat moss"
[8] How to Grow Fruits & Veg BTOM
[9] Home Veg. Garden
[10] Sunset Western Garden Book [SWGB}
[11] The Ruth Stout No Work Garden Book
[12] Better Homes & Gardens
[13] Fam Circle Great Ideas: (Vol 9, no 2)
[14] Karen Watson (Greenville Nursery Owner).

COMPOSTING

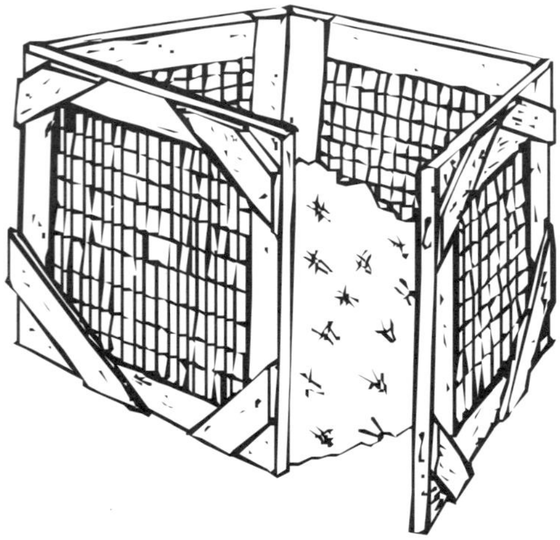

Do you have a compost pile? What do you do with the plant refuse when you harvest your garden? Where do you put your kitchen scraps? Do you haul them all to the dump? In this age of recycling, I hope that you aren't throwing away all that great organic matter that your garden so desperately needs. Why not start a compost pile and enrich your garden soil. Save the healthy plant material but destroy any diseased or bug-infested plants. Cold weather may prevent insects from surviving the winter, but old plant material like fallen leaves can protect and house them. See also Soils and Insect pests chapters.

A compost pile can solve many garden problems. It can reduce disease and insect problems, reduce watering needs, and reduce weeds (when compost is used as a mulch, it suffocates weed seeds). Compost can change the pH, improve drainage and fertility [1]. Are you ready to try a compost pile?

Difference between compost and humus?

"Compost" is decayed organic (vegetable) matter that has been broken down by soil fauna (i.e. earthworms, spiders, beetles, ants). and digested by microorganisms (bacteria). "Humus" is organic matter in a more advanced stage of decay, usually broken down into very small particles. Compost and humus are both defined as well decomposed organic matter, but the difference is that compost also contains manure and fertilizer, so that it is perfect for fertilizing and conditioning your garden soil. The contents of compost varies with the type of materials added to it. The more varied the ingredients, the more balanced the nutrients will be in the final compost. Nutrients released by composting come from all parts of the plant, especially the leaves.

What is a compost pile?

A "compost pile" is made up of one or more organic materials like grass clippings or leaves that have been piled in layers alternating with soil, and allowed to decompose (with the help of soil microorganisms, soil fauna and added nitrogen from manures or fertilizer). The final product, compost or humus, is a uniformly dark color, is sweet smelling, breaks up readily, and can be easily worked into the garden soil. This natural process called "composting" occurs in a compost pile, or in the woods when a tree falls, decays, and enriches the soil.

Why is organic matter important?

Adding decayed organic matter (compost or humus) to your garden soil will improve its physical structure, water holding capacity, and aeration, besides adding many needed nutrients. This composted organic matter can change a heavy, light colored soil into a dark, loose fertile soil. "Organic gardening" is a method based on using compost and other natural ingredients, rather than chemical (inorganic) sprays and fertilizers. Even if you use some chemical fertilizers, compost can enrich and improve your soil.

Choose a good site for the compost pile

The location must be: fairly level with a reasonably good drainage, close to a water supply (so you can sprinkle it when it becomes dry), close to your garden, accessible to a wheelbarrow, and preferably not close to houses.

Build an enclosure

An enclosure around the compost pile makes the pile much easier to make and maintain. It is not absolutely necessary, but does prevent loose material like leaves from blowing all over the yard. The bin can be made of bricks, concrete blocks, wire, snow fencing, or wood [2]. Wood will rot along with the compost unless you use decay-resistant redwood, cedar or cypress. The enclosure needs three sides with the fourth side having removable slats, boards, or wire, so you can reach the pile to turn it or to add more materials. Don't build a bin next to a building since the building's wall could also decay (unless it is concrete block).

Cinder block (containing holes)

Air is important to consider while constructing the bin, so leave some horizontal air space (about one inch) between the boards, bricks, etc.. The most common bin size is 4 x 4 and at least 3-4 feet tall. If the pile is less than 3 feet tall, it will dry out faster and the pile temperature won't be hot enough. If over 4

Log Fence

Wire bin

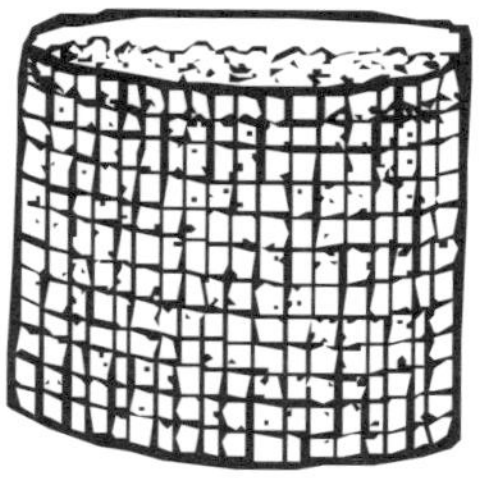

Snow fencing

feet tall, the pile will be too hard to turn. Don't add a floor to the enclosure as you need the microorganisms and earthworms that will be coming up from the soil under your pile, and you also need this way out for drainage.

It's handy having two compost bins side by side. While compost is being made in one bin, the finished compost from last year can be stored in the other bin for a constant supply. A third bin (empty) is very convenient when turning the pile, as you just move compost from one bin to the other with a pitch

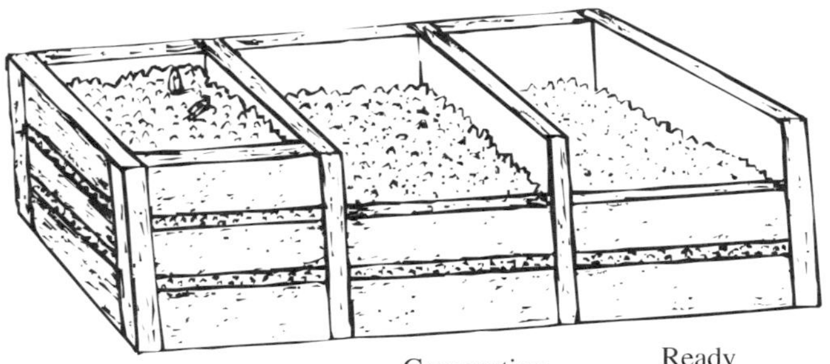

Fresh Composting Ready

Boards

fork, and presto the pile is turned. Be sure when adding a refuse layer that you always follow up with a soil-manure-fertilizer layer on the top.

What do you put in the compost pile?

After the site is selected and the enclosure built, you are ready to start the compost pile. It can be as simple or as elaborate as you like, depending on the materials available and how much time you have. Save healthy plant material from your garden, collect leaves from neighbors, and save kitchen scraps (in a large peanut butter jar or milk carton until you have enough to make a trip to the compost pile). The season of year doesn't matter, though in fall after harvest is an excellent time because all the garden refuse needs to be cleaned up anyway.

Add almost any plant or animal material such as: grass clippings, vegetable and fruit peelings, discarded flower and vegetable plants, weeds, animal manures of all kinds, leaves, straw, spoiled hay, old mulches, sawdust, brewery wastes, ground bark, seaweed, water plants, nutshells, fish wastes, used tobacco, tea and coffee grounds, paper scraps, ashes, feathers, pine needles (partially decomposed), peat moss, old grass sod, shredded cardboard or paper, bone meal, blood meal, ground limestone, rock phosphate, and potash rock. When adding a lot of leaves (acid), also add wood ashes (alkaline) to balance the pH.

Avoid using whole bones, grease, animal fat, chunks of meat, fresh pine needles, large sticks and branches as these decompose VERY slowly. Also avoid any diseased plant material, or weeds that have gone to seed. However, if you wish to use coarse or bulky plant material such as large sticks, large leaves, pine needles, or cornstalks, they should be shredded to pieces one inch or smaller.

Shredded materials will decompose faster. Use a rotary lawn mower, special compost shredder, or mill, to chop plant material. Aim the rotary mower at a wall or two vertical flat boards in a V-shape to catch the material, or the shredded material will be scattered all over the yard. Grind kitchen wastes in a blender or hand grinder. The smaller the pieces, the faster the decomposers can break down the compost!

Decomposers consis of fungi, bacteria, earthworms and other microorganisms that break down, digest and return organic matter to soil in a form plants can use. To do their job, the microorganisms need nitrogen as a source of energy, a certain amount of moisture, and air. Some catalogs sell microorganism inoculations and other "special preparations" to speed up the action of the compost pile. These preparations are helpful (and expensive), but are not necessary for a good final product[3] because microorganisms are already present in the soil, manure, and other composting materials [4].

How does the compost pile work?

Spread the material to be composted in a 5 to 12 inch layer in the bin. Over this first layer, place about a 1/4 inch dirt layer which contains a mixture of soil, manure or complete fertilizer (10-10-10), and wood ashes or lime. Then moisten thoroughly using a fan sprayer attachment on your hose, and repeat the layering process until pile is about 4 feet tall, always ending with a thin dirt layer on top. When you moisten each layer, make it thoroughly moist but not soggy —as a soggy pile slows the decay process, produces objectionable odors, and decomposers can drown. When the heap is "cooking" properly there is no bad odor. To add kitchen scraps just dig one or more holes about six inches deep in the compost pile and cover well (and don't turn pile this time).

The dirt (soil) layer is important as it contains the microorganisms, keeps the leaves from blowing away, and prevents insects from laying eggs on the kitchen scraps and grass clippings. The dirt layer acts like a lid. Some authors suggest one to two inches of dirt, but if you put too much dirt in the compost pile, you increase work for yourself both in constructing the pile and handling the compost. And the final product is less effective in improving the soil structure. What you want is compost that you can add to soil either in your garden or in pots [3].

Ideally your pile should be a 50:50 balance of wet and dry ingredients. The more variety of materials you add, the better your product. Try to mix different kinds of ingredients (wet & dry) as you assemble each layer, because single ingredient layers like grass clippings or fresh leaves will mat together. The dry materials absorb excess moisture from wet ones and both will benefit. Some authors suggest adding rock phosphate (phosphorus) to the compost pile to reduce nitrogen loss (in the form of ammonia) caused by manure fermentation.

The more often he pile is turned, the sooner it will be decomposed (finished). Turn the pile every 2-3 weeks (or sooner if you add something to the pile). Turning the pile mixes wet and dry ingredients, adds air, and more uniformly distributes the available moisture. Add more water whenever the pile seems dry. Since the center of the pile is hotter, turn the top and sides of the pile in toward the center [3].

High temperatures between 150-170°F are essential in composting to kill weed seeds, insects, and disease organisms; to keep microorganisms active; and to help break down plant material. To maintain this heat two things are necessary: fresh manure and/or high nitrogen fertilizer (a complete fertilizer like 12-12-12 gives a more balanced final product), and the compost pile has to be a minimum of 3 feet tall (having sides on the bin helps maintain proper depth). Cover the compost with black plastic if you have long wet winters, and let it "work" right through the winter. Black plastic adds heat to the pile and speeds up composting as does hot summer temperatures.

Lack of nitrogen is the most common cause of compost pile failure! A nitrogen source such as hot, fresh manure or Ammonium Sulfate (chemical high nitrogen fertilizer) is needed by the decomposers. If you don't have either of these, add bone meal, garbage compost, grass clippings, cottonseed meal, or dried blood. If you use fresh manure, wait six months before applying the compost to your garden or it will "burn" your plants (start your compost pile in fall, and by spring it will be ready to apply). Be sure any compost is fully decomposed before applying it! It should be soft, crumbly, sweet-smelling, and dark colored.

How long does it take to make compost?

The time period depends on the temperature of the pile, the temperature outside, the amount of water and air in the pile, the size of the pieces of shredded material in the pile, and the amount of nitrogen (the energy source for the decomposers). Drier materials take longer than wet fleshy ones. Compost piles (in summer) with mostly wet ingredients may only take 3-6 weeks, while piles with drier ingredients take 2-4 months, and even drier woody materials may take a year or longer.

Finished compost is a concentrated fertilizer as well as a soil conditioner and excellent mulch. It can be worked into the soil, used in potting mixtures, or used as mulch. You can spread it a half inch deep all over your garden, lawn, or around trees and shrubs [5]. Compost alone is too rich for many plants, but if you accidentally drop a seed of sunflower, squash, or tomato on your compost pile you may be surprised at the tremendous results. If the compost is finished before you are ready to use it, cover with plastic to keep the nutrients from being leached away. Compost, mulch, and earthworms solve most any soil problem as long as drainage, and soil pH are under control. Earthworms are a sign of a healthy soil. Heavy applications of fertilizers upset the soils, the ecological balance, and kill the earthworms. So be careful not to overdo your use of any fertilizer. Experiment with different ways of composting and find the best method for you.

Methods where turning of pile is not necessary:

"Sheet composting" is spreading an organic matter layer (including hot manure or other nitrogen source) like a sheet over the entire garden in the fall and then rototilling it under —to at least a depth of twelve inches. The organic matter will have decomposed and be ready to use by spring planting time.

In the "Air tube" method you place large branches, pipes or thick stakes through the pile as it is being built, and then pull them out when the pile is about five feet tall. Lightly press the outside surface to prevent blowing away, form a shallow basin in the top to catch rain water (in dry season), cover entire pile with a thin layer of dirt, and wait for it to decay. For details on an "air tube" method tried by Russ Wold, send $2.50 to Russ Wold, 2025 Westover Drive, Pleasant Hill, CA 94523 for his booklet "Compost with Ease".

Composting under plastic prevents problems from odor, insects, and rodents. For a simple and inexpensive way of composting WITHOUT AIR, simply cover the pile with black plastic. It is finished in a shorter time than exposed piles. No turning, no watering, no extra work of any kind—except maybe keeping the plastic from blowing away. First loosen the soil by rototiller or shovel, then build pile in usual manner, water well once, then cover with plastic, and wait [5].

Another no-turning method is using earthworms. Add earthworms just after the highest temperatures of the pile have subsided. There will be sufficient moisture, nitrogen, and aeration without turning. Earthworms can be amazingly good helpers for finishing your pile [5].

If you prefer one easy composting operation, just dump all your kitchen scraps into a hole in your garden, sprinkle with about one cup of lime, and cover the deposit with enough loose dirt to eliminate any odors. When the first hole is full, start filling a second. This doesn't work in raised gardening beds that are being fully used, but it works great in a conventional garden. An alternative would be to build an extra raised bed, so you can use a different "idle" bed each year for composting. Another possibility is to make a first hole at the end of a pathway (in a conventional garden) and go all over the garden working your way up the pathways. By the time you rototil your garden at the end of season, most of the waste material has been decomposed to good compost.

If you like the simplicity of the pit composting technique, but want a neater system, make an underground composter with a lid. Bury two bottomless, galvanized-steel trash cans upright in the ground, with only the tops left visible. As soon as you've filled one can, start putting your waste organic matter into the second. Then, by the time that container is full, the material in the first will be ready to use.

References cited:
[1] Rodales's Garden Problem Solver
[2] Better Homes & Gardens
[3] Compost Preparation
[4] Rodale's Guide to Composting
[5] How to Grow Vegetables & Fruits BTOM

PRUNING of Trees and Shrubs

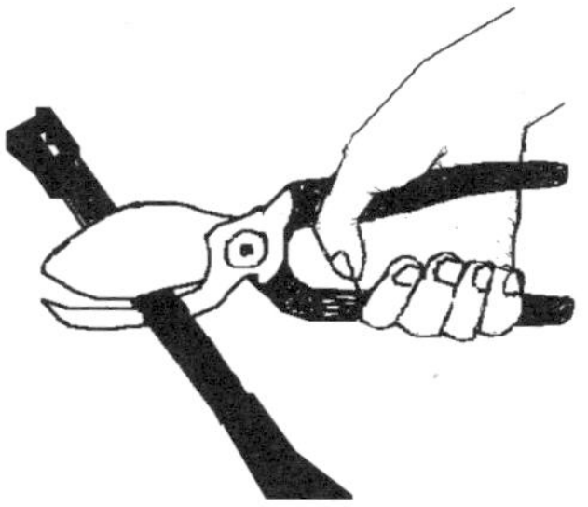

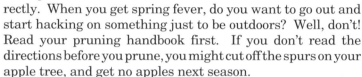

Pruning actually improves the condition and appearance of the plants in your garden, besides stimulating flower and fruit production if done correctly. When you get spring fever, do you want to go out and start hacking on something just to be outdoors? Well, don't! Read your pruning handbook first. If you don't read the directions before you prune, you might cut off the spurs on your apple tree, and get no apples next season.

No tree or shrub, or anything, should be pruned until you know WHY you are pruning WHAT. You should have a good reason for removing any branch. You might want to trim a shrub to a particular size or shape, or to cut the top of an apple tree down to size, so next year you can reach the apples. WHEN is the proper time? If you prune in the fall on spring-flowering shrubs, you will be cutting off the buds that will make next seasons flowers. Know which plants to prune in spring, and which to prune in fall (see end of chapter). HOW do you prune? In this chapter are many pruning tips with illustrated examples.

What TOOLS are needed for pruning?

Use the proper tools and keep them sharp to make "clean" cuts (see illustration). "Pruning shears" work best for branches less than one inch diameter. "Lopping shears" will cut branches to 1 1/2 inches. A "pruning saw" is necessary for larger branches. Apply wound dressing using pruning tar or WHITE latex paint to cuts over an inch in diameter.

Keep your shears clean. Wash the shears after each use and spray them with WD-40 to prevent rust. This makes pruning easier for you, and there is less chance of disease if there is a nice clean cut.

Things to know before you start.

It is neither desirable nor necessary to prune every woody plant in your garden. Most trees and shrubs need only minimum corrective pruning for plant maintenance. But some plants do need regular pruning for best performance such as flowering shrubs, fruit trees, and fruiting vines like grape, and raspberry. You need to know the variety of the plant you are working with, not just its genus and species, because each variety has its own growth pattern. Keep the center of all fruit trees OPEN enough to let light through to the lower branches to stimulate growth of the new fruiting wood or spurs.

Are flower and fruit buds located on spurs or shoots (where does the fruit grow)? First of all, a "spur" is a short shoot usually of less than four inches growth in a season and usually arises from a lateral (or side bud). *Cherry, apple, and pear trees produce their fruit on "spurs", which are located on the lower (older) branches of the tree.* These spurs often look like extra, useless "twigs" to the inexperienced gardener, but if you cut off the spurs, you will get no fruit next season. For these trees, cut away the suckers, but leave twiggy growth (fruiting spurs) along the branches [1]. Cherry, apple, and pear trees should only be pruned for shape and health (and to keep them low enough to be able pick the fruit).

Where on the branch do the spurs or shoots grow (lower or higher on branch)? In contrast to cherry, apple and pear trees,—*peach and plum trees produce fruit on the new growth, toward the base of each year's shoot.* To stimulate new growth on these trees each year, it is necessary to prune back 1/2 to 2/3 the growth of this year's growth —the new shoots [1].

For balanced growth you need a combination of heading back and thinning-out. How will your plant react to "heading-back"? "Heading-back" is cutting back the tip of a shoot (the terminal bud), twig or branch, usually to a lateral (side bud) to stimulate denser growth. "Thinning-out" involves removing an entire shoot, twig, or branch back to the

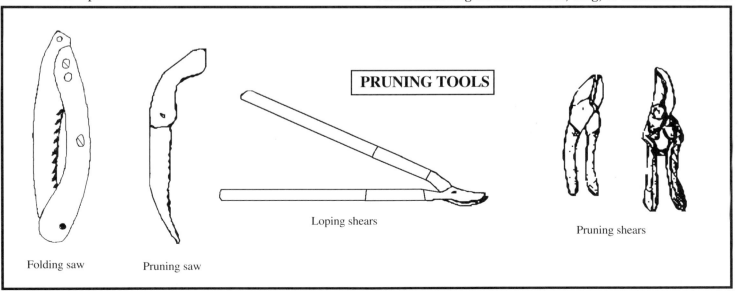

PRUNING TOOLS

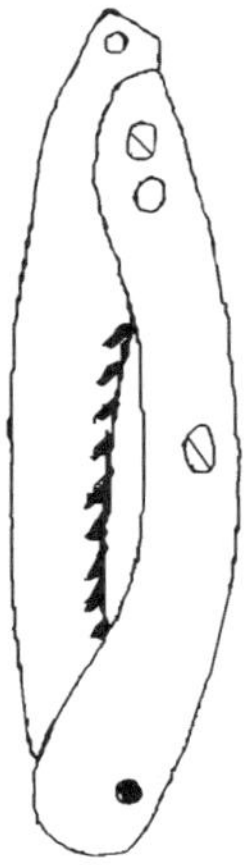

Folding saw

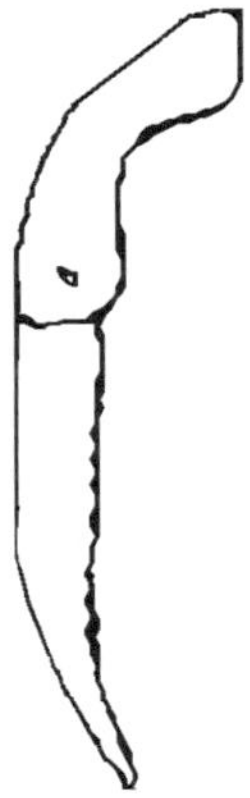

Pruning saw

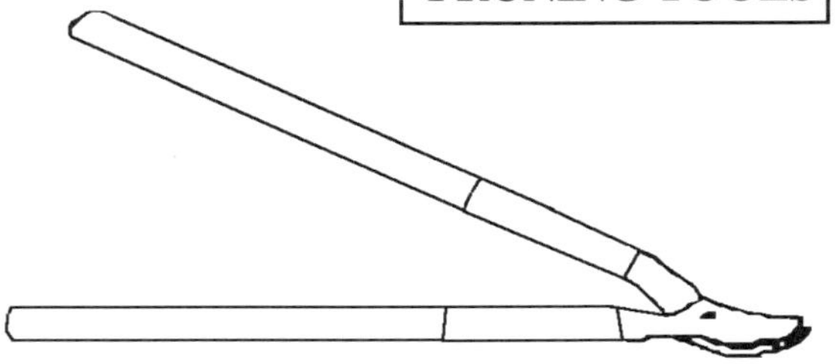

Loping shears

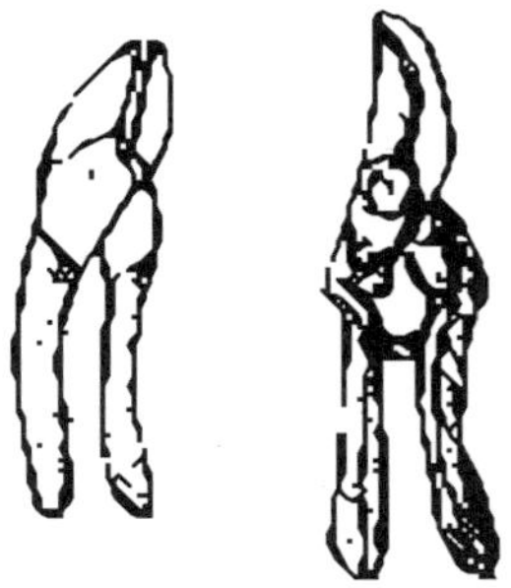

Pruning shears

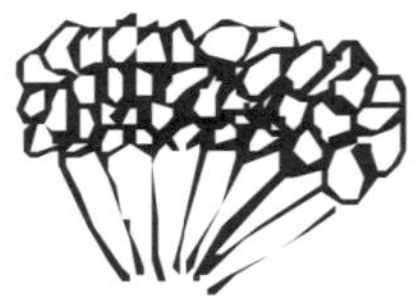
"heading back"

"thinning"

trunk or to the ground,—when thinning a shrub. Repeated heading-back with no thinning creates dense top growth that shades the lower branches (no light gets in). Continued thinning-out with no heading-back causes scraggly-looking plants with long drooping branches which can be easily broken by wind and snow, or even by their own weight.

Reasons why you prune shrubs and trees:

1) To remove diseased, damaged or dead wood as soon as possible. Remove diseased wood by cutting back into healthy wood and then dipping shears in a disinfectant (alcohol, kerosene, or 10% chlorox solution) *after each cut*. Be as careful as in a surgery room. If tree is damaged by storm (or truck, etc.) don't use wire or string (as they cut off the circulation). Use instead nails, an old sheet, rubber bicycle tubes, an old garden hose, or masking tape. If your tree is sick, pick up all the leaves in the fall, cut off branches where a whole branch is diseased and *burn* the leaves and branches.

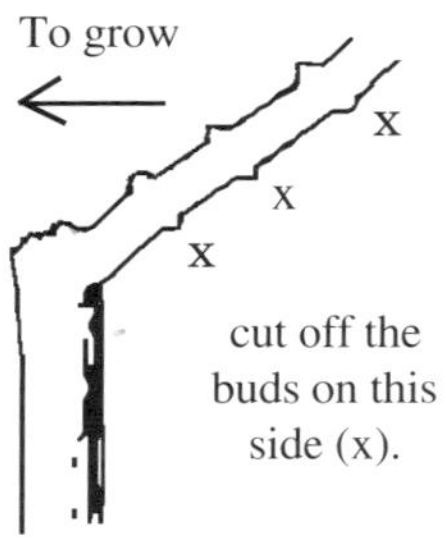

TO REPAIR DAMAGE

2) To thin dense, vegetative growth. Cut away any branches growing toward center of tree to keep center OPEN. Can you look up through the center of the branches in summer and see light? This is important basic maintenance as it lets in air, pollinators, and light necessary for leaves on the inside and lower parts of plant to function properly. In harsh winter areas, thinning is vital to reduce the number of weak branches liable to breakage by heavy snow. Pruning also provides more light and air to adjacent plants, reduces a tree's fire hazard, and lessens its water use.

3) To renew old plants. Old trees may be stimulated to fruiting again by cutting back terminal branches into wood that is 2-3 years old. This is best done in successive stages, with part of the wood being removed each year over 2 to 3 years. Heavy pruning at one time on a tree may cause it to grow too rapidly and weaken its' disease resistance, besides causing it to put out many root suckers.

4) To shape, direct, or control growth. Every time you cut, you stop growth in one direction and encourage it in another. (See discussion later in this chapter on terminal and lateral buds.) Decide the final size and shape you want for your tree,—and prune accordingly.

5) To remove branches that will become weak or hazardous as they grow older or unnecessary growth that can weaken a tree. *Low branches* on a young tree will remain at the same height as the tree matures; later, such low branches on older trees can bump heads, shade your lawn, and make mowing difficult. The lowest branch should be six feet from the ground. A tree should have only one main trunk. Horizontal forks of equal thickness create a *weak V-shaped crotch* that is easily split by heavy snow or strong winds as the branches themselves grow larger and heavier. It is better for the tree's health to choose one branch now and remove the other. U-shaped crotches are structurally stronger. Take out any *crossed or crowded* branches and any branches growing directly above each other. Take out any unattractive ones like those growing up from under a branch *("under" branches), or branches growing downward. Crowded branches* can't develop to full size. Large branches compete with small ones, and smaller branches are more susceptible to disease and breakage. *Rubbing* branches can create wounds that are open to insects and disease. Remove the weakest branch involved, and paint the rubbed wound. Some people feel that painting of wounds is no longer necessary, however, I paint all wounds and cuts over one inch diameter.

Both water sprouts and suckers, though small, are unnecessary growth, and they take strength from the tree. *Water sprouts* are soft, fast-growing branches that usually grow straight up from the trunk or large branches. They originate from latent (dormant) buds. Cut them off flush with the trunk or branch. *Suckers* are fast-growing branches that grow from base of trunk or from roots. Dig down and cut it flush where it is attached to root or trunk. If any of the sucker remains, pruning can make it produce more sucker shoots.

6) To encourage flower and fruit production. If you don't prune, the plant will spend energy making unwanted wood before producing fruit. (See fruit tree training and fruit thinning discussed later in this chapter.)

7) To train for special effect or artificial form. *Espalier* is a special effect where a plant like holly, apple tree or berry is trained along a support such as a wall or fence (both 2-dimensional & 2-directional) by cutting off lateral branching. Other examples are Cotoneaster, Pyracantha and fruit trees. *Shearing* uses shrubs having buds close together like juniper, arborvitae, or boxwood to make an artificial form like an animal hedge or a conical, "full" Christmas tree. Shearing a little year after year, not just in one summer, results in a nicer effect. Trees can also be sheared to look like shrubs.

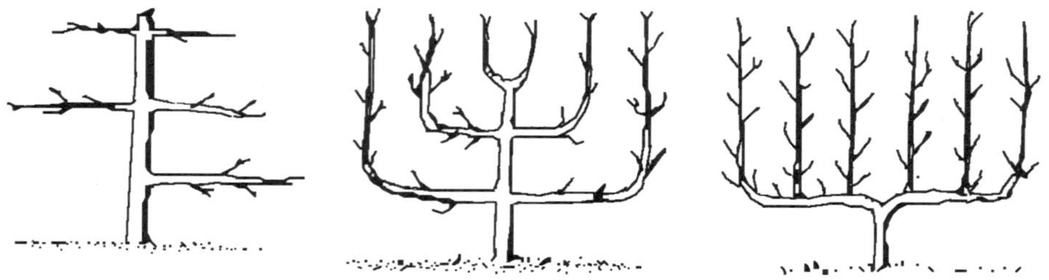
"Espalier" —To train a plant along a wall or fence for special effect.

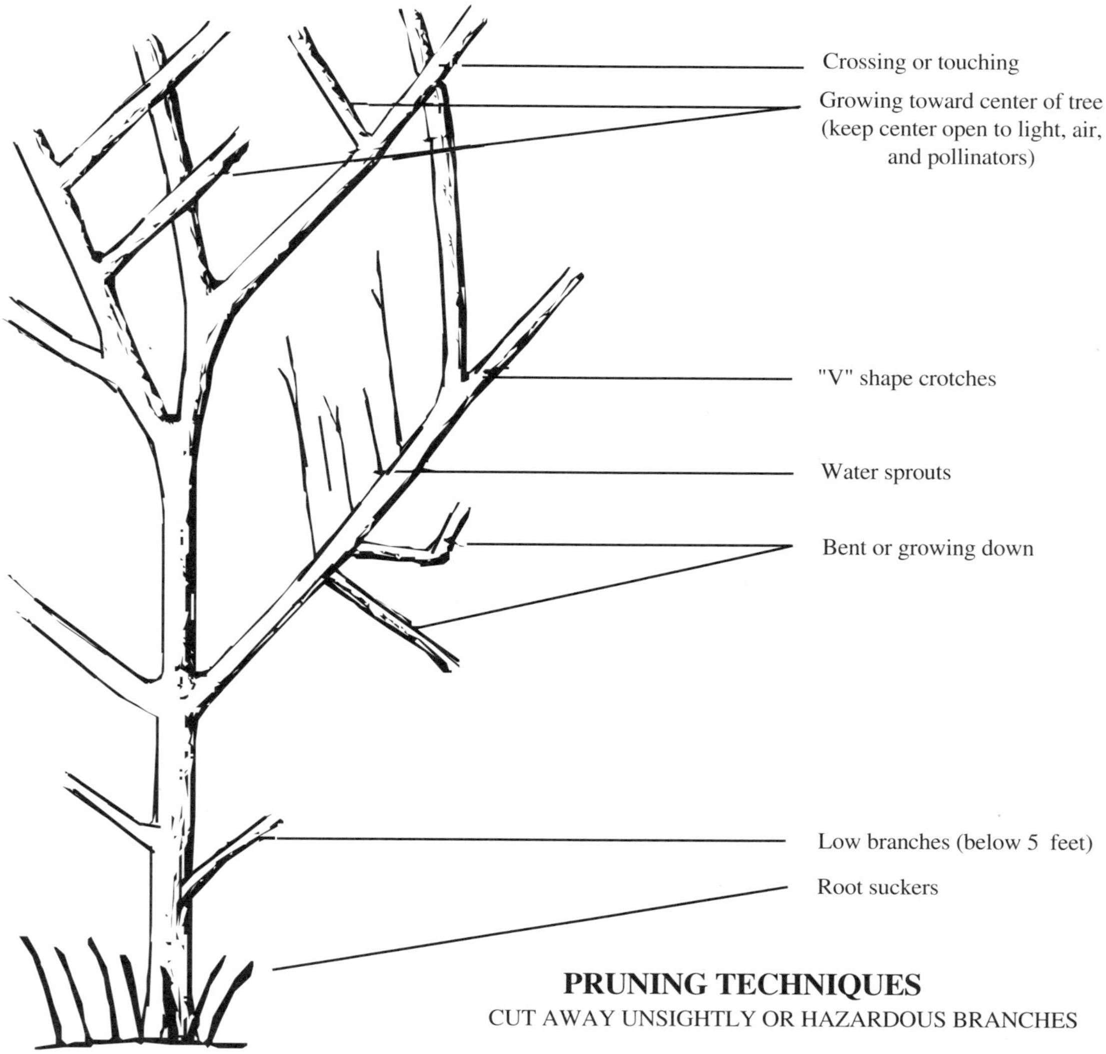

PRUNING TECHNIQUES
CUT AWAY UNSIGHTLY OR HAZARDOUS BRANCHES

<u>8) To compensate for transplanting</u>. Under normal conditions roots and leaves are about the same in mass. There are just enough leaves to manufacture food, and enough roots to take up water and minerals to keep the leaves working. But when a plant is transplanted, many roots are broken, and the delicate balance between roots and leaves is upset. To get the plant back in balance, the crown (leaves) of the shrub or tree must be pruned. Both young ornamental and bareroot fruit trees should be pruned, as the early training of the tree is important for a sturdy framework, but type of pruning varies.

Pruning techniques after transplanting young trees.

<u>If you are transplanting a young tree that is to produce fruit, you should do two things:</u> 1) Cut back the trunk of the tree to within 2-3 feet of the ground; and 2) Cut off all side branches without damaging any buds remaining on pruned tree, as some of these will form new side branches [2].

<u>If you are transplanting a young shade or ornamental tree and you want higher branches, then you</u>: 1) Cut off at least the top third of the trunk; and 2) Cut off all side branches except for the top 3 or 4. Shorten these to 3-5 inches, making each cut just above a healthy outside-facing bud [2].

How plants respond to pruning cuts.

In order to prune effectively, it is important to understand how plants respond to pruning cuts. In pruning, the most important plant parts are the buds. You can direct plant growth by removing (or deliberately keeping) selected buds. You should understand the difference between the ***three types of buds: terminal, lateral, and latent.*** The "<u>terminal</u>" bud is the one at the end of a stem or branch that extends the plants growth upward. Some trees, such as conifers, have only one terminal bud, while some fruit trees have a terminal bud at the end of several major branches. "<u>Lateral</u>" buds occur on the side of stems and branches, and they develop into leaves or side branches.

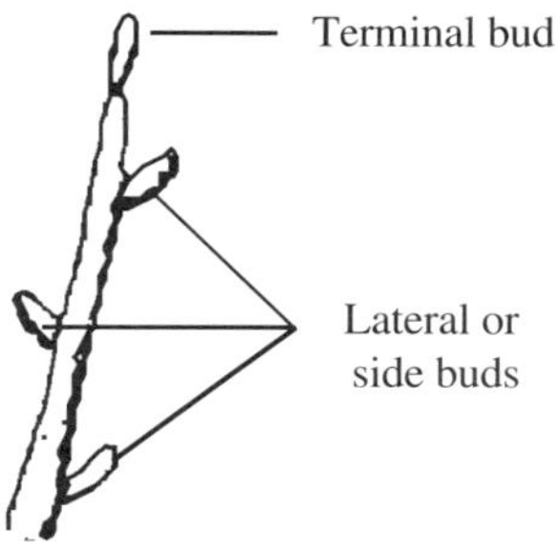

When a terminal bud is cut or injured, the closest lateral bud will usually become the terminal bud, and it will generally grow in the direction that it was pointed. You usually have a choice of

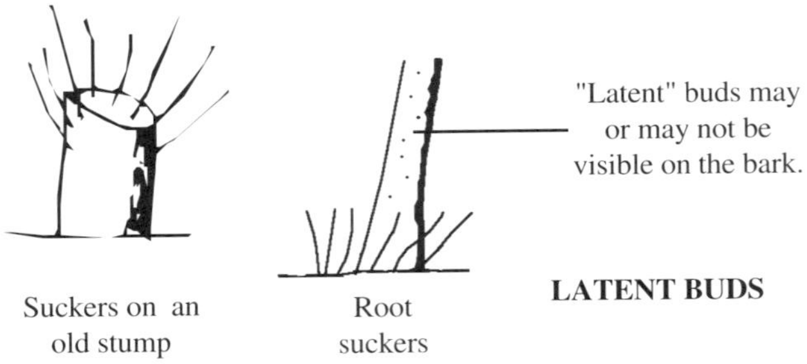

LATENT BUDS

lateral buds to cut above. You should normally pick a lateral bud pointing away from the center of the tree, but if you want more upward or inward growth, choose an inside bud. When you remove terminal buds you encourage growth in lateral buds which makes the plant denser and bushier. Commonly, the first year you remove the terminal bud, so the tree will stay within reach for picking fruit. The second year you pick 3 or 4 laterals you want to keep, and cut away the rest.

"Latent" buds lie dormant in the stem or bark for many years and start growth only after pruning or injury removes growth above them. Latent buds are where root sprouts originate, and account for sprouting of shrubs and trees from stumps.

HOW To make pruning cuts.

Pruning is removing plant parts for a purpose. This includes everything from pinching off a small branch or bud with your fingers, to removing large limbs with a saw. "Pinching off" is a technique where the growing tips on young plants are pinched or snipped off, to force side branching or bushiness [3]. Cutting with a knife or pruning shears is less harmful to the plant than pinching. All of these cuts should be made just above a bud. If you remember this, and you know little else about pruning, you can't go too far wrong. When making pruning cuts, remember these rules: DO NOT leave too much cut surface exposed. DO NOT cut so far from the bud that you leave a stub, but DO NOT cut so close to the bud that you damage the very bud you want to encourage. A proper cut looks better, heals faster, and is less likely to develop disease than jagged, torn or improper cuts.

"Pinching off" is a technique of cutting off the terminal bud to encourage bushiness.

The relationship between pruning and disease.

Practice preventive medicine. Make proper pruning cuts, apply wound dressing where needed, and spray all plants with dormant spray every fall and spring (see Insect pest chapter.) An irregular hole, jagged cut, or a long stub can become an opening for bugs and disease to enter. Wound dressing protects the plant until the cambium layer can grow over the cut surface and seal it. Exposed conifer stumps should be lightly sprinkled with Boraxo to prevent airborne fungus from settling on the stump and spreading to neighboring conifers. The "*Cambium*" is the active layer of tissue that keeps building new wood (xylem) to the inside and new bark (phloem) toward the outside of a trunk. The cambium layer makes the annual rings of wood. Damage to the cambium may kill the plant. Inspect the larger cuts regularly and see if they need to have more protective material applied until the wound is completely healed. If you don't periodically check plant wounds, disease and bugs can enter unnoticed and you will have an unexpected problem on your hands.

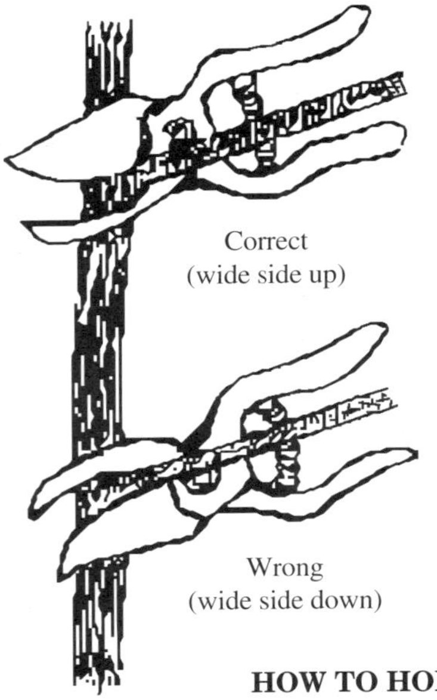

Hold the sharp blade close to the trunk or you will leave a stub.

HOW TO HOLD THE SHEARS

If you prune BEFORE you spray in the fall,—-you will have only HALF as many branches to spray! (Spray is expensive, and you don't need any longer exposure to chemicals than is necessary.) There is less chance of broken branches, because there will be no long, weak branches to catch heavy wet snow. Planned pruning every year builds a strong scaffolding of branches. Then, when heavy snows come, the remaining, strengthened branches rarely break.

Thinning fruit crops:

Most fruit crops should be thinned to give the remaining fruit enough space and nutrition to mature fully. Sunset [2] says to "leave 6-8 inches between apples, and about 4 inches between peaches." You may hate to thin out fruits when there are only a few, but if you don't, your fruits will be smaller and of lesser quality.

The wrong way:

HOW TO MAKE PRUNING CUTS

DO NOT leave too much surface exposed. (Too much slant excposes heartwood)

DO NOT cut so far from the bud that you leave a stub. (Too long a stub causes die-back, and disease & bugs can enter.)

But DO NOT cut so close to the bud that you damage the bud you are trying to encourage. (Too short a stub interferes with bud growth).

The correct way:

A proper cut looks better, heals faster and is less likely to develop disease —compared to a jagged, torn or improper cut. (In a proper cut there is no interference with the bud, so it won't be injured.) Cut 1/8 to 1/4 inch above a bud and cut at a 45°angle.

WHEN do you prune?

Most plants are pruned in winter when the plant is dormant. The food energy of the plant is being stored in the roots, so their above ground inactivity makes them less sensitive to pruning. So, if your plant is to be pruned during the dormant period, do you prune in fall or spring? If the plant is dormant, does it really matter? There are different opinions on this. I prefer pruning in early winter, because we can have heavy snow that breaks the longer branches, and there are half as many branches to spray. It is up to you, but don't try doing all your pruning in one day.

Pruning too much on one tree in one day is one of the greatest faults in pruning, other than pruning at the wrong time. If you have lots of pruning to do, don't try to do it all in one day. Do it over 3-4 days if you have to, over days or weeks if necessary. A few people prefer to do some pruning in the fall after the leaves drop, some pruning in January, and some pruning in early spring (before the new leaves or buds open, around March). Pruning times can be done about the same times you apply dormant spray. Each time you cut off some branches, you have less area to spray. Doing all the pruning in one day (on a large tree) shocks the plant and stimulates the growth of suckers, besides exposing too much area to infection all at once.

Can you prune in the summer? If you pruned only in summer, you could cause dwarfing, because in summer most of the plant's stored energy has moved into the leaves, stems, and branches, to start this years food production. When young fruit trees are severely pruned, fruit bearing can be delayed for several years. Some minor pruning such as unsightly crossing branches, root suckers, water sprouts, or diseased branches should be done in summer, but it's best to delay major pruning to the winter dormant period.

Not all plants should be pruned when dormant. Some flowering shrubs and trees that bloom in spring should be pruned right after blooming. If you prune them in the fall, you can reduce or even eliminate next year's bloom. In most cases the plant itself will give you a clue. Most flowering shrubs either *bloom in spring on last seasons' wood*, or *bloom in summer and fall on new wood formed during the current spring*. But some exceptions to this, are the shrubs that bloom twice, first on year-old wood in spring, and again on new wood later (Clematis), and shrubs that bloom on wood that is one or more years old (Flowering Quince).

Spring flowering shrubs (i.e. Lilac, Forcythia, Flowering Quince, and Spirea) should be pruned right after blooming. If you wait till fall to prune, you won't get any blooms next year. This is because it is on this summer growth that the next seasons flower buds are produced. *Don't prune after blooming if the fruit is ornamental; in this case, you would prune as soon as the fruit withers or falls.*

Lilac (shrub)

Pear (tree)

Fruit trees, if carefully pruned and trimmed, will give bigger yields and live longer. *Prune in winter* or early spring, cutting out bad crotches and enough branches to allow sunlight in. Don't cut off short spurs from the main limbs, as these bear next seasons fruit. Examples are: Pear, apple and peach.

Hydrangea (shrub)

Summer and fall blooming shrubs should be pruned either right after they bloom or next spring, just before new growth begins, but after danger of frost is past. These shrubs bloom on wood formed during the current spring. Some examples are: Hydrangeas, Chrysanthemum, Pyracantha, Winged Eunoymus, Tamarisk, and Honeysuckle.

Pyrcantha (shrub)

Evergreen, broad-leaved plants are usually pruned very little, but removal of dead or weak wood is always desirable. Some examples are: Barberry, Andromeda, Boxwood, Rock Cotoneaster, Heath, Holly (Ilex), Oregon Grape, Rhododendron and Leatherleaf Viburnum.

Holly (shrub)

Rhododendron (shrub)

Pine tree

Evergreens with needles (Conifers) cannot be pruned drastically at any time as they usually do not have live buds on the old growth. Some do have live (at least latent) buds on their trunk or main stem. They shed old needles all year, and every third to fourth year they shed more. Examples are pine and fir trees.

Non-flowering deciduous trees, shrubs and vines are pruned in winter or early spring before foliage buds swell. Examples are maple or oak.

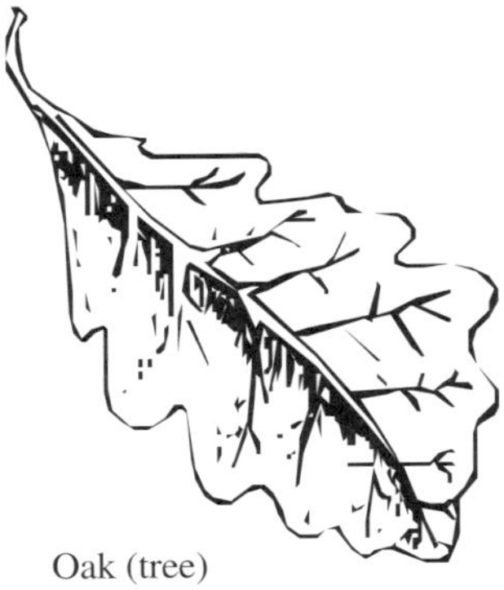

Oak (tree)

Shade tree

Shade trees can be pruned anytime if they are smaller around than your thumb. If larger, trim only in late winter when the sap is dormant. Some examples are the ornamental Sarvis tree, maple, or oak.

References cited:
[1] How to Grow Fruits & Veg BTOM
[2] Sunset: Pruning handbook
[3] Sunset Western Garden Book p 68-70

INVITING BIRDS TO YOUR YARD

Chickadee

One of the most successful and cheapest ways to control <u>insects</u> in your yard is to get birds to do most of the work for you. They can help you rid your garden of caterpillars, beetles, aphids, assorted bugs and insect larva. Birds also provide entertainment with their antics, and pleasure with their song. Many species of birds can be attracted to a garden and all have different appetites. You may have learned to identify birds by their size, coloring and bird calls —but in order to attract birds, you need to identify them by their bills. There are two main bird types: the vegetarians and the meat eaters.

What do birds eat?

The **vegetarians** have short, fairly fine bills and they eat an "all-seed" (or other plant life) diet. These birds include the English sparrows, Pigeons, Quail, Mourning doves and a few others.

We are more concerned with the **meat-eater** birds because they prefer to eat insect life. Some of these birds preferring an <u>all insect diet</u> include Barn swallows, House wrens, Chickadees, Nuthatches, Gnatcatchers, Flycatchers, Brown creepers, and some of the Warblers. They can be identified by bills which are either long and straight; long and curved; or short and whiskered.

Birds eating a <u>mixed diet of insects, seeds and other plant life</u> —have a fine sharp bill. The finer and sharper the bill —the smaller the insect, the insect egg, or aphids that they can eat.

Birds <u>eating harmful insects and insect eggs</u> have long, strong, sharp, "boring" bills that can reach into dark deep bark. Examples of these are: Flickers, Red headed woodpeckers, and Downy woodpeckers. Plant lice are eaten by Kinglets, Warblers and some of the Finches [1].

Insect Menu

Find out which are the harmful insects, and which birds will eat them.

• <u>Ants</u> are loved by Kinglets, Flickers, Tanagers, Wood thrush, Brown Creepers, Nuthatches, and others.
• <u>Spiders</u> are loved by Downy Woodpeckers.
• <u>Grasshoppers</u> are eaten by Flycatchers, Bluebirds, Mockingbirds, Brown thrashers, Meadowlarks, and some larger birds.
• <u>Crickets</u> are relished by Blackbirds.
• <u>Mosquitos</u> are loved by "Least" Flycatchers, and Chimney Swifts.
• <u>Ground insects</u> are eaten by Towhees and Juncos.
• <u>Gnats, mosquitoes, and moths</u> are eaten by bats!

What will the birds need?

<u>Provide nesting materials and/or bird boxes</u> in spring and summer. Put out some string, rags, hair, grass, and feathers. Many insect-eating birds such as Bluebirds, Flickers, House wrens, and Purple martins will use bird boxes. The size of the opening and the elevation of the bird box determines the type of bird attracted. Place bird boxes at the appropriate height: 4 feet for Bluebirds, 6 feet for House wrens, 6-20 feet for Flickers, and 15-20 feet for Purple martins—on poles, trees, or sides of buildings near the garden [1].

Bird box

Bird bath

<u>Provide water</u>. Small natural looking pools about two feet wide and one inch deep are excellent. They can be made of garbage can lids (take handle off), plastic wash tubs (sunk into ground), saucers, half barrels, or elaborate fountains, water falls, and bird baths (see Water gardens chapter). Ideally the water should be clear, cold, fresh, and slowly moving. Water dripping slowly from a faucet into a bowl, etc works fine. Most all species of birds will make use of bird baths. Small pools look great but they hatch out lots of mosquitos. Mosquito-eating fish (Gambusia) can be purchased for larger pools, and they may still be free from some Central Valley mosquito control districts. Check also with local Fish and Game Dept. See also Water Garden chapter.

Bird feeder

<u>Use simple feeding supplements in bird feeders</u> to <u>attract</u> birds such as: bread crumbs, beef suet, cracked corn, sunflower seeds, millet & hemp seeds, bird seed, bread crumbs, melon & pumpkin seeds, crumbs of dried baked goods, rolled oats, crushed egg shells, orange & apple slices, and red sugar water for humming birds. These supplements will act as a decoy to distract birds from eating your newly planted seeds (and young sprouts).

Suet holder

<u>Grow plants that attract birds</u>. Try adding birdbaths, birdhouses, feeders, hang suet,—or attract birds just by plants alone.

Plant annuals such as sunflowers, Cosmos, Marigolds, asters, or California Poppies. Plant a hedge of multiflora or Rosa Rugosa Rose. Try some Junipers, hollies, Japanese Barberry, Bush Cherry, Bittersweet, Winterberry, Highbush Cranberry, Bush Honeysuckle, Snowberry, or mulberry trees. Your landscaping trees will provide nesting sites and food. Try Flowering Crabapple, nut trees, Chinese Chestnut, Russian Olive, Wild Plum, and Mountain Ash. The birds will eat the berries on these plants instead of your strawberries and peaches, etc. Select plants that will have berries or fruit bearing at the same time as the plants you're trying to protect.

Birds can become a pest

Birds can be helpful in a garden by eating harmful insects, but they also like to eat young pea and been seedlings as soon as they poke up above ground. A pine needle mulch over the seeds doesn't slow their growth, and protects them from birds until seedlings are a few inches high and less tasty (to a bird). Or you might try a substitute food to distract birds from the new crops. Offer seed in a bird feeder or hang suet in a tree near the garden.

Some birds such as **Robins** prefer wild fruit, so strawberry beds and cherry trees need to be covered when fruits ripen. Or plant twice as much and plan on sharing it with the birds, and the birds will reciprocate by eating the worms and slugs from your strawberry bed. I highly recommend Ross Garden Net to put over strawberry patches and over fruit trees —though if your strawberry plants are healthy, they will grow a dense leaf cover that hides the berries from birds (and you).

Steller Jay

Sapsuckers or woodpeckers can be a problem too. Some people wrap the pecked tree trunks with burlap or chicken wire. Some hang shiny can lids or milk cartons on strings in the branches to scare off the birds. Paint the pecked holes with white-latex, water-base paint, or tree pruning paint. **Steller Jays** peck off the young, opening leaf buds on your trees. Try also a large plastic owl to scare off pesty birds, but move it frequently so they think it is real. Better yet, of course, is a real owl.

References cited:
How to Grow Veg. & Fruits B.T.O.M.

ANIMAL PESTS

Deer, rabbits, squirrels, chipmunks, gophers, raccoons, mice, birds, and grasshoppers are cute or charming in their natural settings —but not when they raid your garden. You basically have two choices, either you set up a barrier like a fence that will keep the pest out, or trap the pest and kill it.

A 10-12 foot chicken wire fence ("Poultry netting" comes in 1", 1 1/2", and 2" mesh) around the garden, or each shrub or tree, is the most effective, and least expensive way to keep animals out that you don't want. It keeps out everything but small animals that tunnel under, and birds that fly over.

Grey squirrel

To prevent animals from digging under, sink the fencing one foot into the ground (two feet deep for gophers). To prevent gophers from eating the vegetables' roots, make raised beds and attach smaller chicken wire ("Aviary" netting" with 1/2 inch mesh) across the bottom of the bed.

"Live" traps catch an animal without killing it; but then you have to kill it or release it somewhere else, which is not a good idea [1]. Pet dogs and cats freely roaming your yard help to deter animal pests. To keep birds out (if garden is small), put fencing over the top of the garden, or use "Ross Garden net" which is a fine-mesh, nylon netting thrown over the specific problem strawberry patch or peach tree, etc. I don't find that necessary though, as I plant enough to share some with the birds (so they can eat the bad insects).

Gold-Mantled ground squirrel

The real secret of pest control is learning to identify the presence of pests and eliminating them immediately, because one animal can wipe out an entire garden in a day. How to get rid of them is the question. In pest control, one method will work for some people some of the time for some plants, so try all the methods and see what works for you. For **bird** problems see "Inviting birds to your yard" chapter. For a **deer** problem see "Deer-resistant Plants" chapter. In the new book Wildlife in your Garden, Gene Logsdon tells of ways to attract wild animals you can enjoy on your property, without having them devastate your vegetables, fruit and other plantings.

Chipmunk

If **rabbits, squirrels, chipmunks, or mice** are a problem, try dusting the plants with talcum powder, or get a dog or cat that likes to chase (or eat) them. I had a terrible problem until I got a cat. Other rabbit repellents are garlic spray, onions, rubber snakes, blood meal, wood ashes, ground cayenne pepper, and Horsetail Tea. For mice, try planting some daffodils, narcissi, scilla, grape hyacinth, or mint. Mice and rabbits eat the bark of trees (especially apple), so if you have a problem, protect the bark of young trees with a wire cylinder of hardware cloth (3-4 wires to the inch), or 1/2 inch Aviary netting [2]. Rabbits and squirrels can be repelled by hot pepper sprinkled around plants.

Cottontail rabbit

Gophers and moles are attracted to lawns and gardens (free lunch). Their natural predators in the wild are owls, hawks, badgers, eagles, snakes, weasels, and cats. Gophers are the biggest problem. Don't confuse them with moles. Moles make tunnels under the garden too, but they don't eat your vegetables —they eat insects. You can mix garlic, Red Chile Peppers, and water in your blender to make a solution. Pour it down the gopher hole, and then squirt water from the hose into the hole.

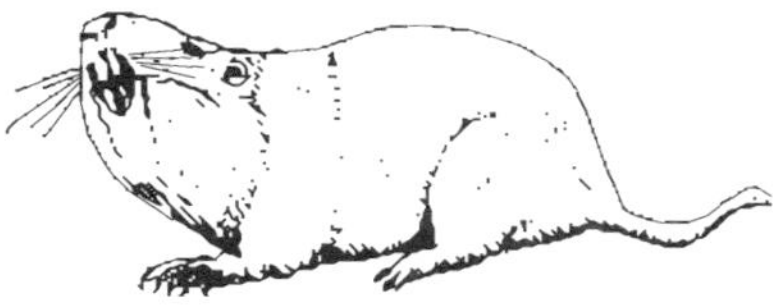

Pocket gopher

Some gardeners use two spring-loaded Macabee gopher traps [3]. Find a fresh mound of dirt. Dig down till you find the gopher run (a tunnel going in both directions 2-8" below the surface), and place traps at either side of the run. Put some carrot tops or other fresh greens to attract the gophers. Lay a board over the hole, and fill with dirt. Another method is a box trap, but dig a much larger hole so the whole trap can be lowered down into the gopher run. Gopher-repellent plants are scilla bulbs, Imperial Lily (Fritillaria), and gopher plant. Castor bean plants and meal, repel moles. Or try using rubber gloves (so they don't get the human scent) and drop two sticks (rolled up like a cigarette) of Juicy Fruit chewing gum into their hole. They eat the gum but can't digest it, so it kills them. For moles use a harpoon-type trap (set above the soil) or one that has scissors action (set in moles run), or use poison bait [3]. Expensive vibrating sticks, some even battery powered, can repel moles and rodents over as much as 1/3 acre depending on soil type [1].

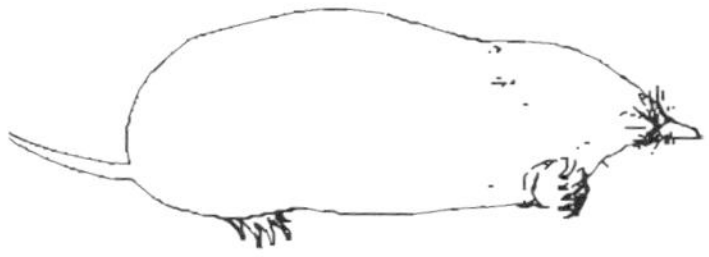

Mole

Some other pests hard to keep out of gardens are **raccoons and grasshoppers.** For grasshoppers:—plow after harvesting, or raise chickens (to eat them). For grasshoppers, snails, slugs, sowbugs: buy commercial baits or use organic methods (see Insect pests chapter). For raccoons: plant melons, squash, pumpkins, or cucumber around plants you want protected, and put hot pepper on the tassles of corn plants. Raccoons prefer darkness, so they can be deterred by lights, especially flashing or moving ones at night. The best references for all garden pests is Garden Problem Solver.

References cited:

[1] Rodale's Garden Problem Solver
[2] The Encycl. of Nat.Insect & Disease Control
[3] Sunset Western Garden Book [SWGB]

INSECT PESTS & DISEASE

Prevention techniques

The primary method of controlling disease and insect pests in your garden should be prevention. So plan carefully! Use companion planting techniques, select varieties resistant to diseases found in your area, keep your garden clean, observe your garden daily, use drip irrigation wherever possible, water plants before noon, rotate your crops, build a healthy soil, use mulch, don't spread disease, invite birds to help you rid your yard of insects, and be tolerant of some insect damage

Use companion planting techniques.

"Companion species" are plants that enjoy each others company and actually benefit from each other (see Companion Plant Chart). They enhance growth and foil pests for each other such as beans with potatoes. Some plants discourage other plants, as they can slow down or inhibit growth of other plants such as beans with onions. "Ecology" is the study of interrelations between living organisms and their environment. "Organic Gardening" is a method in which non-toxic, natural elements are used rather than chemical (inorganic) sprays to repel bugs.

Colorado Potato Beetle

Marigolds have the reputation of being the most effective and well known companion plant. Marigolds repel nematodes and Japanese beetles from strawberries, potatoes, roses, and various bulbs, as well as discouraging rabbits from nibbling almost everything. All marigold species are aromatic; their foliage and flowers have a strong odor that discourages many kinds of insects. Other flowers and herbs that repel bugs are: Aster, Anise, Artemesia, Dahlia, Feverfew, Hyssop, Horseradish, Lavender, Savory, Tarragon, Yarrow, and Rue [1].

Corn, beans, and cucumber are companion plants that benefit from each other. Corn is a heavy feeder (uses lots of soil nutrients), while beans are a soil enricher (builds up the soil nitrogen). Corn protects the beans against cinch bugs. Some sources suggest pole beans use corn plants for support. However pole beans are more susceptible to frost than bush beans in this area, so I recommend bush beans. Bush beans can resprout after being hit by frost, while pole beans are killed outright.

A method I like for planting corn is as follows: plant corn seeds in a circle about 4 feet wide with 2-3 feet between circles. Put the circles in a line. Next interplant beans between corn seeds. Then plant cucumber seeds on hills of compost or manure (aged, of course!) in the middle of each circle. You can plant either seeds or seedlings. The mature cucumber plant will act as mulch to shade out weeds. You may prefer to plant in blocks instead of circles, but don't use rows. These methods (circles, or blocks) are designed to insure pollination, as this can be a problem in home gardens. Some people take off a mature tassle and "dust" all of the corn ears to assist in pollination. If you can obtain fresh trash fish from a local lake (sometimes available from Fish and Game Dept.), they are great fertilizer to put under your corn circles.

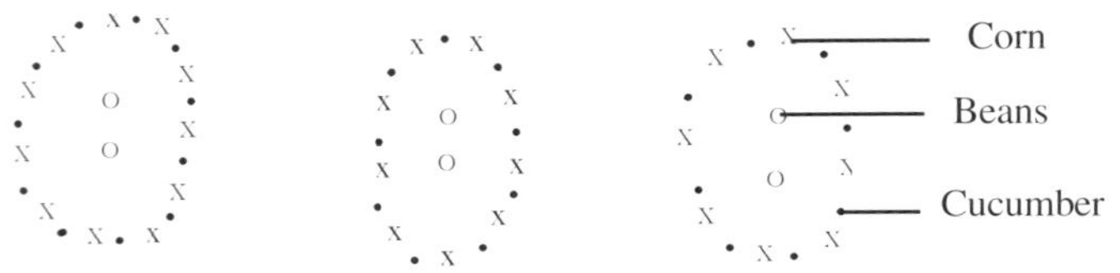

Planting corn in circles or blocks.

Many bug problems can be avoided by not planting members of the cabbage family together. They all have the same insect enemies (mostly aphids and cabbage worm) and they zero in on the odor of that family. Members of the cabbage family include: broccoli, cabbage, cauliflower, radish, rutabaga, brussel sprouts, kale, kohlrabi, and turnip. You need to confuse the bugs by planting some strong-smelling plants amongst them. Interplant with shallots, garlic, marigold, onions, sage, or mints (Apple mint, Peppermint, Spearmint, Lemon, or Orange mint). And sprinkle the ground around the problem plants (of the cabbage family) with flour and/or wood ashes. Or place each plant (especially cabbage) in a tin can with both ends cut out that is buried in the ground with just some of the rim exposed [2].

Some companion plants not mentioned on the chart are: Vines do well with Oregano, Nasturtium and Garlic. Eggplant compliments Beans and Potatoes. Turnips do not like other members of the cabbage family. Basil "likes" Tomatoes, Asparagus, and "dislikes" Rue. Chives do not like cucumber, but do like carrots and tomato. Potatoes do not like raspberries. Oregano likes broccoli and vines. Cucumbers prefer some shade and like to grow under corn and young trees. Parsley accumulates iron so it is good for your diet.

Plants grown near their friends (companion plants), make complimentary demands on the environment, and usually are healthier. Insects typically pass by healthy plants, preferring to chew on weak or sick plants. For example—above the ground, the bushy celery plant enjoys the company of the upright-growing leek, and the leek gets plenty of room and light near the celery plant. While at the root level, two friendly plants such as Swiss chard and Beans, may occupy different levels of the soil [3].

Some plants act like insecticides, exuding substances that make other plants and insects keep their distance. In some cases just growing certain plants such as Marigolds, Zinnias, Asters, Chrysanthemums, Cosmos, Coreopsis, and many of the herbs in your garden is enough to repel insects. Marigolds' exudate keep nematodes away, so plant marigolds near a plant that is susceptible to nematodes. The Mustard oil given off by the roots of the mustard plant family, can sweeten an acid soil and helps adjacent plants that suffer from too acid a soil, —pH too low [3].

COMPANION PLANT Chart

X= Likes
O= Dislikes

	Asparagus	Beans	Beets & Sw. Chard	Cabbage family*	Carrots	Corn	Cucumbers	Lettuce	Onion Family**	Peas	Potato	Radish	Spinach	Squash	Strawberry	Tomato
Basil	X				X		O									X
Beans						X	X		O	X	X	X			X	
Beets				X					X			X				
Cabbage fam.*		X	X						X	X	X				O	
Carrots		X						X	X	X		X				X
Celery		X		X					X			X				X
Corn		X					X			X	X			X		O
Cucumber		X				X		X	O	X	O	X				
Dill				X	O		O									X
Lettuce			X		X				X			X			X	
Marigold		X							X		X					X
Mint				X	X	X	O		X							
Nasturtium							X					X		X		X
Onion fam.**		O	X	X	X			X		O		X	X		X	X
Parsley	X			X	X											X
Peas					X	X	X		O			X				
Potato		X		X		X	O									O
Radish							X	X		X				X		X
Rosemary				X	X		O									
Sage				X	X	X	O		X							
Savory		X			X		O									
Spinach												X			X	
Squash						X					O					
Strawberries		X		O				X	X				X			
Sunflower		O					X				O					
Tomatoes	X	X		O	X	O			X		O	X				

* Cabbage family includes cabbage, broccoli, cauliflower, Brussels sprouts, kale, kohlrabi, turnips, rutabage, and radish. All are in genus <u>Brassica</u>, except radish, which is in <u>Raphanus</u>.
** Onion family--the genus <u>Allium</u> includes onion, leek, garlic, chives, and shallots.

Select only the most disease-resistant varieties.

Select seeds and plants in suppliers' catalogs (see special chapter), and then check with your County Agricultural agent (find number in your telephone book) to see what diseases and problems occur in your area. Buy only healthy plants from nurseries and stores; check plants over carefully for bugs and disease.

Keep your garden clean.

When you leave rotted fruit, dying plants, weeds, brush cuttings, crop residues, and other organic material in and around the garden, you're providing a place for insects and diseases to multiply and hibernate during the winter.

What you don't use in your compost pile, get rid of. If you have diseased plants, don't put them in your compost pile because the problem will find its way back to your garden. Take diseased plants to the dump right away or burn them.

Observe your garden daily.

Find, hand pick, and eliminate insects at an early stage, and you may have stopped the problem. Remove bugs and caterpillars from the leaves, and step on them or crush them with a board or rock. Check under leaves and on stems for eggs and destroy by crushing.

Use drip irrigation wherever possible.

Mildew and other diseases frequently occur when leaves stay wet over long periods of time —especially overnight. Avoid overhead watering in your garden. Instead, do hand-watering under the leaves, or use an on-the-ground drip irrigation system (see Watering chapter).

Water plants before noon.

You can reduce the mildew problem by watering in the morning so the sun dries the foliage quickly. Diseases thrive in moist, cool temperatures.

Rotate your crops.

This makes the soil nutrient level more balanced and keeps down disease. If the same type of vegetables are grown in the same spot year after year, certain diseases will build up and then spread rapidly (like wireworm on potatoes). Growing cabbage, broccoli, and cauliflower in the same bed repeatedly, for example, promotes club rot. Rotate your vegetables within the bed and between beds. Plant radishes where the cabbages were, and carrots instead of the broccoli, etc.

Rotate "heavy" feeders (corn and cabbage) with "light" feeders and soil enrichers (peas and beans). The heavy feeders quickly use up the basic soil nutrients, while others actually enrich the soil. Heavy feeders include: artichokes, cabbage, celery, potatoes, tomatoes, and corn. Medium feeders are: asparagus, broccoli, cantaloupes, cucumbers, eggplant, herbs, kale, mustard, okra, onions, pumpkins, rhubarb, squash, swiss chard, and watermelon. Light feeders are: beets, carrots, radishes, rutabagas, and turnips.

Soil enrichers are beans, peas and other legumes. Beans and peas help improve soil fertility because they have nitrogen-fixing bacteria in the nodules on their roots. This bacteria takes soil nitrogen in unusable forms and combines it with sugars from the legumes to produce ammonia, a nitrogen compound that plants can use.

Build a healthy soil

One of the benefits of a healthy soil is disease control. Recent research by Safer has shown that compost produces fatty acids that kill fungal diseases and some bacterial disease on plants. Try to use soil that is at least 10% humus or compost [4]. Earthworms indicate a healthy soil. (Earthworms are killed by chemical fertilizers).

Use mulch

Organic mulches such as chopped leaves seem to create a chemical environment that either repels or kills some soil fungi and nematodes. Straw can reduce root rot in some peas and beans [4].

Paint tree trunks.

Insects and disease seem to pick on plants not native to the area, since they are less resistant than natives. Painting the trunks of all trees you plant prevents sun scald (hardwoods are particularly sensitive to sun scald), insect infestation, borers, and nibbling by rabbits, rodents, and deer. Weedeaters and lawn mowers are also hard on tree trunks, so don't use them too close to the trunk. There are two kinds of latex paint: a kind that "seals" which you can use for pruning cuts, and a kind that "breathes", which you use for painting the tree trunks. Use white latex paint because it reflects the sun's heat; too much heat encourages fruit trees to bloom too early.

Don't spread disease.

Eliminate transmission of fungal spores and bacteria by getting rid of ways they can be spread. Use drip irrigation and cover the plastic hoses with black plastic or mulch to prevent splashing of water carrying spores, etc. And avoid handling wet leaves since you can transfer spores from one plant to another [4].

Invite birds to your yard

Refer to special chapter by that name.

Be tolerant of some insect damage.

What looks like an aphid invasion one day may be nothing the next day. Almost any change like rain, temperature, change in an insect's life cycle —can send the bugs into or out of your garden. Bugs will almost destroy broccoli when it is planted in early summer, but if you plant it a few weeks earlier, the bugs will hardly bother it. Damage varies with different plants and with different insect life cycles. Try experimenting.

Control Techniques

First identify the pest

Observe your garden daily, and soon you will learn to recognize symptoms of insect damage or disease. Check top and underside of leaves, the leaf axils, along the stem, young buds, and shoots. Are there holes in the leaves? Do they have webs or a shiny coating? Did the plant suddenly change color? Did the leaves begin to curl or wilt? Are the buds developing properly? Get out your 10x magnifying glass. Identify the symptoms first before you take action, because many of the insects you see are harmless.

Identification can become more complicated if an ailing plant has more than one problem. Symptoms may be caused by insects, disease, bugs feeding out of sight, or tiny insects that you need a microscope to see. Diseases can be caused by organisms (fungus, bacteria or viral), by environmental problems (weather or pollution), by deficiencies, or by overdoses of nutrients.

The most common insect pests are spider mite, aphid, mealy bug, scale, and white fly. Spider mites come during the hot summer forming fine webs on undersides of leaves. Mealy bugs look like small blobs of cotton in the leaf axils, growing tips, and backsides of leaves. Aphids (visible with the naked eye) are tiny green bugs that come in spring, dripping sticky honey dew, while chewing the new shoots and buds. White flies are tiny white specks on undersides of leaves, while other leaves on the plants are yellowing and drying up. Mature scale insects have a shell-like appearance; they get attached along stems and the back veins of leaves, and excrete a sugary, sticky honeydew. Scale insects and mealy bugs are closely related, and they attack the same kinds of plants.

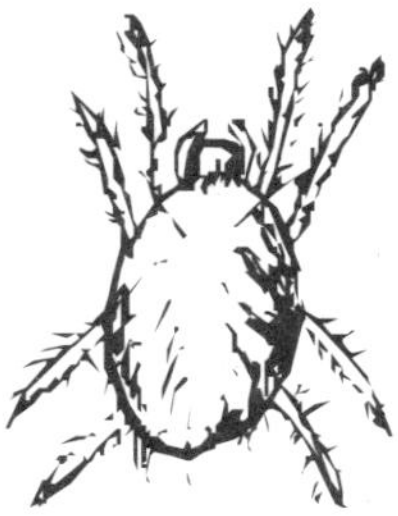

Spider mite

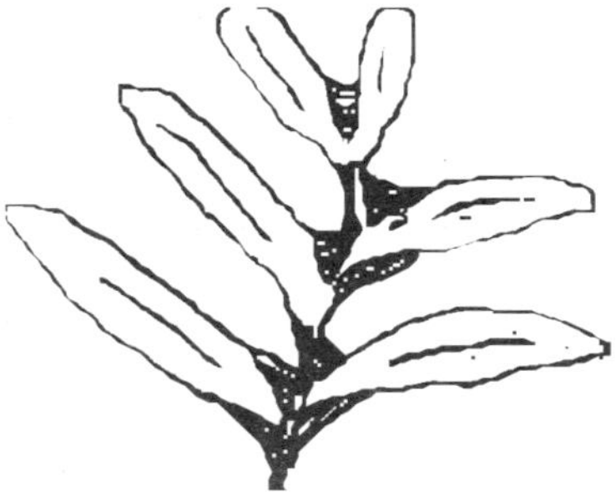

Spider mite forming webs.

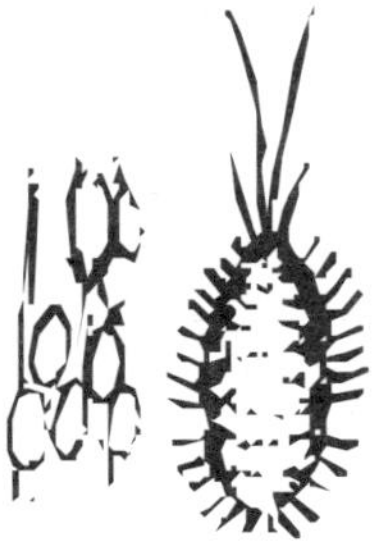

Soft scale

Mealy bug

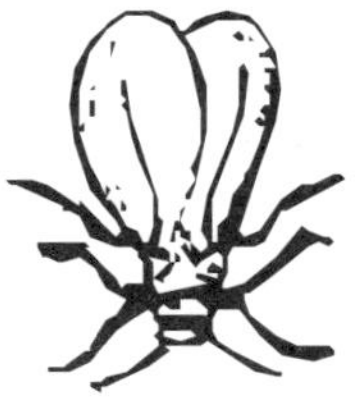

White fly

After identifying the problem, find out how to get rid of it and prevent it from recurring the next year. Many pest problems can be simply washed off with water, so don't grab for the chemicals yet. First wash all the leaves and stems thoroughly, then wait and see if the problem comes back. If it comes back, try spraying with a detergent or garlic spray, use sticky traps, cover traps, hand picking, spray water forcefully on the infected plant, dab leaves with Q-tips soaked in alcohol, or merely break off the infected branch. Destroy badly infected plants before the problem spreads to other plants. Many more eradication ideas are suggested in this chapter.

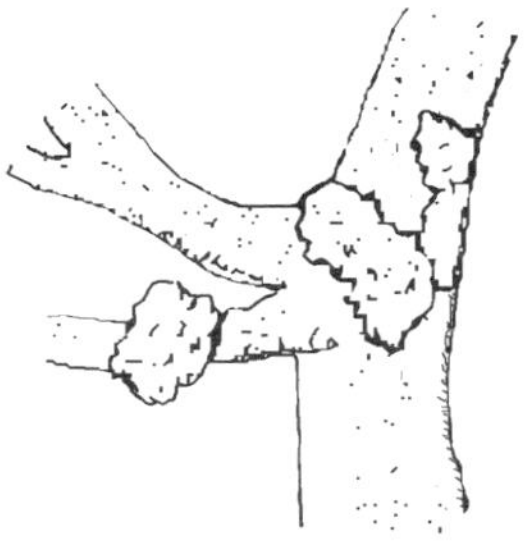

Mealy bug "cotton"

However, if you can't identify or can't get rid of the pest problem —consult your county agricultural agent. For example, in Lassen County he is at the Memorial Building in Susanville (257-5505). For your number refer to your local telephone directory. (He has informative pamphlets on many topics, and many are FREE.) Send him some sample leaves in a sealed plastic baggie in an envelope. He will identify the disease or bug and tell you how to treat it. Use chemical insecticides and fungicides only as a last resort.

Homemade Bug Sprays

If planting smelly plants doesn't discourage bugs, try a homemade bug spray. These smell and taste terrible, and often do the job so you can avoid using chemical sprays.

• Detergent spray: Fill the quart (hand) sprayer with water and add a few drops of Basic H (A Shaklee product), or your popular dish detergent. It deters all bugs, especially aphids. (Shaklee's Basic H is similar to Amway's LOC.) Spray this every ten days starting when leaves start to open.

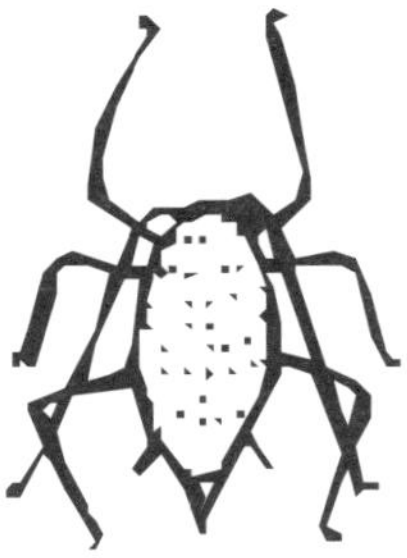

Aphid

• Basic Garlic spray: Select cloves of garlic, onion, chives, or parts of plants that have a BAD odor such as marigold, hot peppers, and/or peppercorns or anything else you think that might drive an insect away. Put the cloves, petals, leaves, etc, into a saucepan, then add water to cover and bring to a boil. Dilute the remaining liquid with 4-5 parts water, and let sit until cool. Then mix in blender. Strain, saving only the liquid. Then, to make this stuff stick to the leaves —add a couple drops of dish detergent to the saved liquid. Use a half cup of this brew to one quart water and then spray it on the plants. This spray repels aphids, cabbage worm and cutworms, and it is non-toxic to people and the environment!

• Milk and/or egg spray repels deer and many insects besides making leaves shiny. Reapply milk when washed off by rain or sprinkler.

• Bug juice spray. One year we had a particularly bad infestation of carpenter ants. They come by the hundreds every spring the first day the temperature reaches 70°F. They have wings, they mate, the wings fall off, and then they enter your house looking for a nest site. They are a nuisance to say the least. Organic Gardening magazine [5] suggested catching the problem bugs (plenty of them around), and putting them in the blender just like you would make a spray from plants or plant parts. You say, oh, what a horrible thing to put in my blender!! Well, I did it, and then I applied it all around my door sills, and it worked!!! Of course I washed my blender very thoroughly afterward.

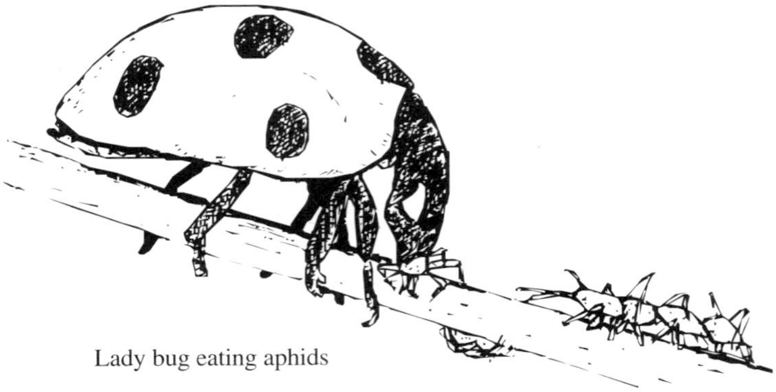

Lady bug eating aphids

Biological controls

The best known biological controls are the predatory and parasitic insects such as lady bug, lacewing, praying mantid, parasitic wasps, bacteria, viruses, and other microscopic creatures. Like the natural sprays, these controls attack and destroy the pest insects but do not harm the environment. The controls can be purchased commercially and let loose in your yard. However, they are expensive, and if you don't know what you're doing, they'll fly to your neighbor's yard or the next town before they do the job in your yard [4].

Botanical poisons

If all the other methods fail to solve the pest problem, try botanical poisons. These are plant-derived insecticides such as Pyrethrum, Nicotine Extract, Ryania, Rotenone, and Sabadilla. Even though botanical poisons are wholly natural —they still can kill the good bugs as well as the bad bugs (and can kill humans & pets too). If a botanical poison must be used while bees are around —choose Pyrethrum and spray at dusk when bees are least active, because Pyrethrum breaks down within six hours at temperatures of 55°F or higher. But don't spray at all if you expect a heavy dew, because Pyrethrum won't be able to break down before the bees start to feed the next morning [4]. Pyrethrum is a natural extract from the Pyrethrum Daisy, and it can kill most aphids and spider mites.

Nicotine Extract, another botanical poison, is effective against aphids, spider mites and caterpillars. Both Pyrethrum and Nicotine Extract are available at many nurseries. You can make your own Nicotine spray by using your blender to mix 10 cigarette butts, a little alcohol, 1-2 drops of dish soap, in a pint of water [6]. Foliar sprays of Pyrethrum and Ryania are less toxic to bees than the dusts [4].

Systemic granules

These granules (poison) are a recent, effective, chemical way to kill sap-sucking insects when they feed on plants. The granules are worked into the soil, and watered well. The chemical is absorbed through the roots, and distributed by sap throughout the plant, protecting plants for 2-3 months. They are great for ornamentals and roses, but they are not recommended for fruit trees, seeds, or vegetables, because the poison also goes into the fruit. Insecticides only affect the larva stage, but systemics can kill insects in all their life stages.

Yellow jacket

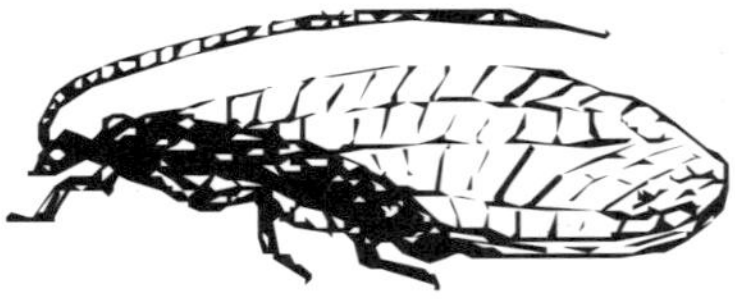

Lacewing fly

Praying Mantis

THE "GOOD" BUGS

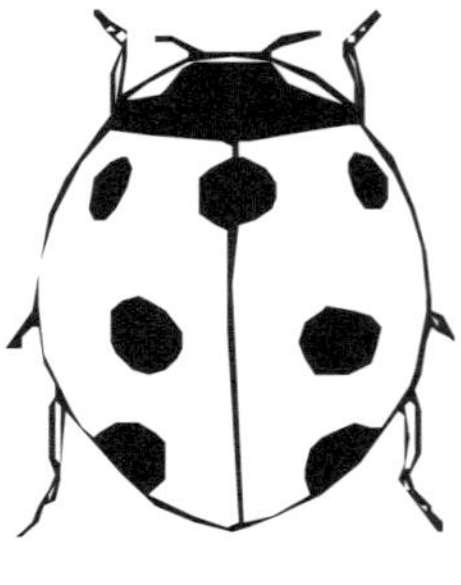

Lady bug

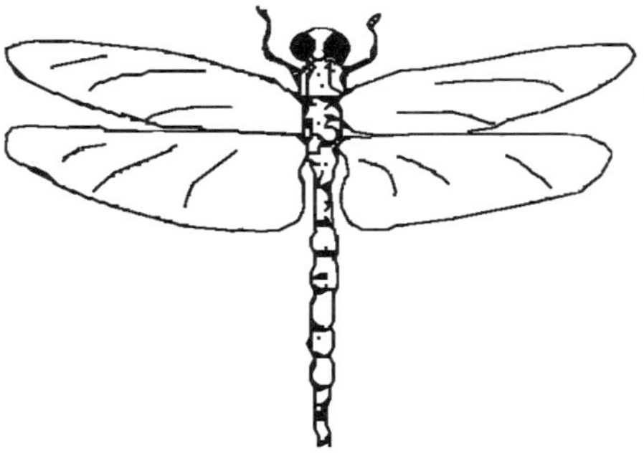

Dragon fly

Systemic granules can kill aphids, white flies, spider mites, leaf miners, and lacebugs; but don't work against chewing insects such as beetles, caterpillars, bagworms, and scale insects. One brand is Cooke's Systemic Rose, Shrub, and Flower Care which is a combination insecticide and fertilizer, effective 6-8 weeks. Don't apply after Aug 1 in cold winter areas. Another brand is Ortho which is a three in one: has fertilizer, insecticide and weed inhibitor.

Dusts and Chemical sprays

Use only as the last resort. Chemical sprays that kill pests can harm you, the sprayer as well as the good bugs like ladybugs, lacewings, and bees. Using chemical sprays to kill bugs often kills the pest and the predator. If mosquitos hatch faster than dragonflies, and your spray kills them both, then you end up with lots of mosquitoes and no dragonflies to eat them. You may become mosquito bait.

For your vegetable garden, an all purpose vegetable dust may provide the simplest insect and disease control [7]. Spray Basic H or an onion-garlic mix on minor bug problems in the garden, but if they get out of hand use Ortho Fruit & Vegetable Insect Control (spray). For lawns use Ortho Lawn Insect Spray or Diazinon. Sprays recommended in several books were: Carbaryl (Sevin) for chewing insects, such as bean leaf beetles, Mexican bean beetles, cabbage worms, and cucumber beetles. Malathion for sucking insects such as aphids and scale. Diazinon for controlling cutworms, grubs, ants, root maggots, wireworms, and many other insects.

Since chemical insecticides are extremely poisonous, it is EXTREMELY important you read all of the label very carefully. Don't use more than it says, and don't use it on crops not included on label. Store out of childrens' reach, and NOT NEAR FOOD. Keep out of lakes, streams, and ponds. Dispose of these empty containers wisely in the trash. Many local areas require special disposal methods for pesticide containers, since they are environmentally hazardous materials. As mentioned earlier, it is important to keep spray from getting on you, or from being inhaled. Use rubber gloves, long sleeves, long pants, shoes and socks, and a safety (breathing) mask or you can get very sick.

Organic insect control

With intensive insect attacks or long-term, chronic insects problems—you may need specific chemical sprays (or you might need to improve soil fertility or drainage). However, since general use of chemicals is unwise for many reasons, here are some non-chemical, popular, "organic" methods of pest control for specific insects:

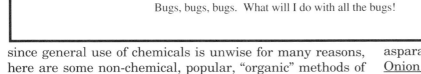

Bugs, bugs, bugs. What will I do with all the bugs!

Ants- use mulch, wood ashes, garlic, onion, cucumbers, nasturtiums, pyrethrum, lacewings and ladybugs. Plant cucumbers around base of young orchard trees to repel ants.

Aphids -Nasturtiums, wood ashes, hot pepper, garlic or soap spray. If the garlic odor of a spray wipes out the smell of rose for you, plant some onions, shallots (a mild cross between onion and garlic), garlic, or chives around the base of the bush.

Army worms- plant sunflowers.

Asparagus beetle - plant tomatoes.

Black fly - plant garlic, nasturtium, spearmint, or use Diatomaceous earth or ladybugs. (Diatomaceous earth contains diatoms or their fossils.)

Cabbage worm (of the white cabbage butterfly) plant thyme, hyssop, rosemary, peppermint, celery, sage, tomatoes, or use ashes around base of plant.

Carrot fly - plant leeks, rosemary, wormwood, parsley, or sage.

Cinch bugs (on beans) - plant some corn.

Codling moths - use diatomaceous earth.

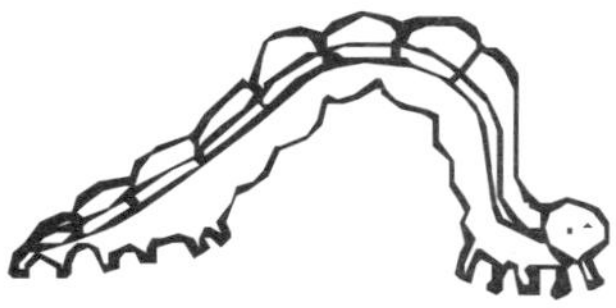

Cabbage worm

Corn worms - use diatomaceous earth.

Cucumber beetle - plant 1-2 radishes in each hill and let grow to flower and seed, or use spray of a half cup wood ashes plus a half cup hydrated lime in 2 gallons water.

Cucumber wilt - plant cucumbers with corn plants.

Cutworm -use wood ashes, tar paper, oak leaf mulch, or a 3" collar (tin can with both ends removed) around young plants extending 1" into the soil and 2" above.

Downy mildew -plant chives, or spray with Horsetail Tea (2-3 teaspoons dried horsetail into 1 cup water, boil 20 minutes, cool, and spray).

Earwigs use diatomaceous earth, hand strips of rags on stakes or in trees, or place cans filled with beer in the vegetable row (they will climb in and drown).

Gypsy moth - use diatomaceous earth.

Japanese beetle - plant Tansy, geranium, marigolds. Try blasting the insects off the plant with a hose. Garlic cloves shoved into the ground also puts off most climbing insects such as Japanese beetle.

Mealy bugs - Dip cotton swab in rubbing alcohol, apply swab on infected leaves, then rinse leaves with warm water.

Mexican bean beetle - plant cosmos, aster, chrysanthemum, rosemary, potatoes, petunias, marigolds, savory, or use wood ashes.

Mosquitoes - for adult stage: use diatomaceous earth, for the larvae: spray garlic oil over the water surface.

Nematodes -plant marigolds for 2-3 years throughout your garden. Try also planting asparagus, dahlias, or use diatomaceous earth.

Onion fly - plant carrots.

Peach leaf curl - spray with Horsetail Tea (For instructions on how to make it, see Downy Mildew, as mentioned above in this

list). Also works for rabbits.
Potato beetle - plant beans or horseradish.
Potato-tomato blight use this garlic spray: chop 2-3 garlic bulbs, soak in 2 teaspoons of mineral oil for 24 hours, add 1 pint water and 1 teaspoon fish emulsion fertilizer. Stir and strain, then dilute to 1 part to 20 parts water and store in glass container. Also good for rabbits and insects.
Rose beetle - plant some parsley.
Rose black spot - Make a spray with Rhubarb tea (leaves); plant a member of onion family; or use a tomato spray (blend tomato leaves, add 4-5 parts water and one tablespoon cornstarch, strain and spray). Refrigerate any remaining spray.
Root maggot - use oak leaf mulch, or wood ashes.
Slugs - spread wood ashes, diatomaceous earth, tar paper squares on the soil around the plant, or use lacewings.
Snails and slugs - fill pie pan with 1 1/2 inches of beer, bury pan to ground level, and the pests will drown in the beer.
Squash bugs - plant nasturtiums, or use cigarette ashes.
Spider mites - Make a Buttermilk spray: Mix together 6 tbsp. buttermilk, 4 cups wheat flour, and 5 gallons water. Try also wood ashes, diatomaceous earth, or plant radishes or rhubarb. When weather turns hot and dry, spider mites are attracted to dust on leaves. Forcefully spray water on top and underside of leaves several times a week. Natural predators are spiders, lady bugs, and lacewings [8].
Tomato hookworm - use diatomaceous earth or hot pepper-soap spray.
Tree borers - plant nasturtium, garlic, onions, chives, or use wood ash paste painted on trunks. Check the crotch of each branch with your penknife and may have to dig out the borer.
White fly - plant nasturtium, tansy, basil, mint, or use smoke from burning oak leaves. White flies tend to attack tomato plants deficient in phosphorous and magnesium. To deter flies in general in your house, plant tansy or basil near your front and back door. Bright yellow painted boards or tins covered with vaseline and hung here and there around the garden works the best for me. The bugs are attracted to the color and they stick to it like to fly paper.

Medicinal plants

The following quote about medicinal properties of plants was reprinted with permission from Nichols Garden Nursery [9], Albany, Oregon:

> "Scientists are now discovering that many plants produce actual plant medicines which are natural bactericides and fungicides. For instance, a few drops of an extract from cauliflower seeds has been found to inactivate the bacteria causing black rot, and radish seeds also contain an anti-bacterial substance. In Helsinki, Prof. A.I. Virtanen, testing nearly 1300 plants, found that 305 of them contained antibiotic substances which were especially high in the mustard family (Cruciferae).
>
> Folklore has credited garlic and onions with medicinal properties which are now being established experimentally. Researchers, using garlic juice or commercial liquid and powdered extracts, and disguising the odor with a deodorizing agent, found it to contain a powerful antibacterial agent. It is an effective destroyer of diseases that damage stone fruits, cucumbers, radishes, spinach, beans, tomatoes, and nuts.
>
> T.A. Tovstoles, a Russian biologist, experimented with a water solution of onion skin. Used as a spray 3x daily at 5-day intervals, the solution gave an almost complete kill of hemiptera (squash bugs, stink bugs), a parasite which attacks more than 100 different species of plants."

A Compressed Air Sprayer is useful for many liquid sprays, and it has an adjustible spray nozzle so you don't have to bend or stoop.

Prevention & Control in FRUIT TREES

Prune fruit trees every fall and paint any cuts that are over half inch in diameter. Use dilute WHITE latex paint. I don't recommend Tree Seal (like tar) or Grafting Wax. I prefer the white paint as it is MUCH easier to use. Also paint the tree trunks white to help protect against sunburn, bug infestation, and disease. Some people put Tanglefoot around the base of the trunk (like fly paper) to catch the bugs. Pick up any rotten fruit. And keep the mulch and other plants pulled away a couple inches from the base of the tree.

Don't move fruit trees or ornamentals once established in your garden, since moving them reduces their disease resistance and generally weakens the tree. Plan ahead.

Use Dormant foliage spray in winter —to maintain trees health and fruit production (preventative maintenance). Spray fruit trees every winter with Dormant Spray in the fall just after the leaves fall off, and just before the leaves start opening in the spring. If you have a

In winter, spray fruit trees with Dormant spray.

severe problem (like Peal leaf curl) spray three times in winter: around Halloween, Christmas, and Valentines. day. One year my friend's apple trees were bothered by one type of bug. She didn't spray. The next year there were two kinds of bugs. She didn't spray. The third year her trees were very sick with about five different kinds of bugs and fungus, and they died. Dormant spray destroys disease-carrying organisms and insect eggs that normally overwintered to reinfect plants in spring.

Use Chemical sprays in summer —if you have insect problems. Use Malathion or Ortho Fruit & Vegetable Insect Control spray at "prebloom", "petal fall" and again at the end of the summer. "Prebloom" means when blossom buds begin to show color, but before petals begin to unfold. "Bloom" is when blossoms are open. *Never apply any insecticide during blooming period, though fungicides which will not kill pollen-carrying bees, may be used.* "Petal fall" is when last petals have fallen from the blossoms. If your trees or fruit tend to get bad bug problems every summer, then spray every 10-14 days after blossoms fall until 30 days before harvest. Spray more often only if you have a terrible problem. If you add a squirt of Basic H (a Shaklee product) or dish detergent to Malathion and Dormant spray solutions, it acts as a bug repellent besides helping the spray stick. When spraying, be sure to soak thoroughly every crevice, twig, the trunk, and surrounding soil area.

In the spring of 1986, the leaves on my fruit trees looked so healthy that I didn't spray right away with detergent spray when the leaves opened. Then I got a deluge of aphids, followed by other bugs and disease, that almost killed my plum trees. I should have sprayed at the first sign of aphids (Malathion + Shaklee Basic H), but I had the excuse that my sprayer was clogged up. That excuse almost lost me my plum trees that year. I soon sprayed with Malathion and gave them some systemic insecticide granules (I use it on my house plants). I wouldn't be able to eat the fruit that year, but it was worth it to save the trees.

When spraying fruit trees remember four things: Water the plants thoroughly before spraying, and then no rain or watering for 48 hours afterwards. There must be no wind (to blow spray on you, and on the wrong plants). Wear protective clothing. Shower immediately afterwards, and wash all the contaminated clothes.

Keep tools clean. If you have a tree with any disease be sure to clean your pruning shears or saw every time you go from a diseased limb to a healthy limb on the same tree, or from a diseased tree to a healthy tree. Dip shears in a 10% Clorox solution (1 part Clorox to 9 parts water). If you don't disinfect the shears each time, every tree that is cut after the diseased tree will become infected. After pruning, be sure to wash and dry the tools thoroughly and spray with W-D 40,—or the Clorox will cause rapid rusting!

Peach leaf curl is a common disease in fruit trees especially apple trees. There are brown spots on the leaves and on the apples. If one branch has a real bad case of it, cut off the branch. Pull off the infected leaves if there are only a few. Be sure to do a good clean up of ALL the leaves that fall to the ground, as the spores from the fungus go into the ground when it rains, and are taken back up into the tree again through the roots. Cleanup and spraying can't be stressed enough.

References cited:
[1] Secrets of Companion Planting
[2] How to Grow Veg & Fruits BTOM
[3] The Encycl. of Nat. Insect & Disease Control
[4] Rodale's Garden Problem Solver
[5] Org. Gardening Magazine
[6] Success with house plants packet #69,3.
[7] "Insects & Diseases of veg. in the Home Garden"
[8] "Dry is beautiful": by Dick Tracy, Cal Life, Sac Bee, 6-2-90.
[9] Nichols Garden Nursery (quote)

VEGETABLES FOR VITAMINS

Vegetables are a good source of nourishment! You can eat as much of them as you like because they have no cholesterol, hardly any fat or sodium, and they add the much needed fiber to the diet.

Vitamins are organic food substances that exist only in living things, plant or animal. Although they occur only in minute quantities in foods, they are absolutely necessary for proper growth and maintenance of health. Plants manufacture their own vitamins. Animals obtain theirs from plants, or from other animals that eat plants. Vegetables—the edible parts of plants (except the fruits)—are an especially valuable source of many vitamins.

How vegetables are grown affects how much nutritive value they will contain. Proper use of fertilizers and other gardening or growing practices can provide foods from plants and animals of better-than-average nutritive value for human beings. Fresh vegetables offer higher overall nutrient values than either canned or frozen vegetables, and are usually cheaper "in season". Of course, the sooner they are eaten after picking or purchase, the more vitamins and other food values they have. Careful storing and refrigeration are essential to keep vitamins.

For a better, healthier life, eat more vegetables, along with legumes, nuts and seeds, plus dairy foods in moderation. Quality of protein is most important. Raw protein such as avocados, nuts, and seeds—when eaten with green, leafy vegetables—is doubly useful to the body. Legumes are a good source of complete protein when combined with grains and/or greens. Legumes include: lentils, mung beans, garbanzo beans, soybeans, lima beans, fava beans, navy beans, and peas. A small amount of RAW protein of highest quality is more valuable than many times the amount of a COOKED protein of low quality.

Know Your Vitamins and Stay Healthy:

Vitamin A is found in whole milk, butter, egg yolks, liver, dark greens, and deep yellow vegetables, keeps your skin healthy.
Vitamin B gives your blood a taste mosquitos don't like. It is found in whole grains, meat, fish, poultry, Brewers yeast, eggs, dried beans and peas.
Vitamin C is found in citrus fruits (eat the white part under the skin too), tomatoes, green peppers, raw fruits & vegetables, potatoes, strawberries, and cantaloupes.
Vitamin D is found in fish liver oils, sunshine, and enriched milk. Synthetic is less desirable than natural.
Vitamin E is found in seeds, whole grains (grind just before using), and liver. Liver is full of all vitamins but must be from a safe source (no growth hormones, or sprayed hay or feed). Liver, however, is also high in cholesterol.
Vitamin B 17 is found in pits of some fruit seeds (be careful as some pits are poisonous), whole grains and some grasses.

Some Helpful Hints About Vegetables:

Cook corn as soon as possible after picking. After buying or picking corn, the most important thing is to remove the husks immediately, or sever the husks at the base to detach them from the ears. Never leave the husks on, as the sugar in the kernels goes into the husk within 20 minutes! Keep them wrapped in (but not attached to) the husks to prevent drying out in your refrigerator. Corn can be cooked still wrapped in the husks, or add the husks to the cooking water for extra vitamins and flavor.

A method of drying corn in an iron skillet was described by Mary Shepston. Cut the corn off the cob and put in oven about 160°F. Stir occasionally. It takes all day or until completely dried. A little chewier when cooked, but absolutely delicious. (Large corn dryers are available but are expensive).

To make a delicious coleslaw, combine apple, cucumber, American cheese, cabbage, and mayonnaise (or yogurt!).

Do not eat the sprouts of potatoes as they contain solanin which is poisonous. Green potatoes (sunburned) are not harmful to humans after they are cooked. Keep potatoes well covered with straw, pine needles, or dirt while they are growing so they don't get sunburned.

One great cause of lost nutrients is the peeling of vegetables. The minerals in most root vegetables are concentrated under the skin and are discarded when the vegetables are peeled. A good rule to remember is to peel vegetables only when the skin is tough, bitter, waxed, or too uneven to be thoroughly cleaned. I put unpeeled apples (sliced thin) into apple pie, and use unpeeled potatoes for mashed potatoes (use electric mixer).

Methods of Cooking Vegetables:

Don't destroy vitamins by over-cooking the vegetables. Try steaming them or microwaving with a little moisture until they are tender. Most people cook vegetables by boiling where 50-90% of the nutrients and most of the flavor is lost before they reach the table. Nothing is less appealing than water-logged, overcooked, tasteless, boiled vegetables.

According to Rodale [1], a good cooking method should meet the following requirements: Initial heating must be rapid to destroy enzymes, but only for the shortest time necessary. It must prevent loss of vitamin C by avoiding direct contact with air. (Leave peeling on the vegetable and cover any cut surfaces with oil, or by displacing the air in the pot with steam.) Save the nutrient-rich liquid that was used to cook the vegetables, and use it in soups, to reheat leftovers, etc.

Some methods of cooking vegetables are as follows: boiling, waterless method (steaming), pressure cooker (steaming), double boiler, baking, stir fry, shish-kabob, and microwaving.

There is no objection to boiling vegetables: If the water is rapidly boiling before the vegetable is dropped in. If it is quickly reheated to boiling. If vegetable is not overcooked, and If ALL the cooking liquid is used. But how often is all the liquid used? Flavor is lost when nutritive value is lost. If you want your vegetables to be delicious, as well as nutritious, don't let them soak during washing, and cook them by methods other than boiling.

The best method of cooking vegetables is probably the waterless method or "steaming". Fresh vegetables have a high percentage of water which is sufficient for cooking them if the heat is controlled so no steam escapes. The utensil must have a tight fitting lid. Vegetables can be cooked by this method without any added water, but a tablespoon or two should be put into the preheated utensil to replace air with steam. Be sure to keep the heat low after the first few minutes so that no steam escapes.

BLANCHING VEGETABLES
By Boiling or Steaming

VEGETABLES	MINUTES WATER	MINUTES STEAM
Asparagus	2-3	4
Beans, green snap	2-3	3
Beans, wax	2-3	3
Beans, lima	2	3
Beets (until tender)	25-50	—
Broccoli (split stalks)	3	5
Brussels sprouts	3-4	5
Carrots (small, whole)	4-5	5
Carrots (diced or sliced)	2	4
Cauliflower	3	4
Corn on the cob	7-11	—
Corn (cut after blanching & cooling)	4	—
Kale	2	—
Peas, green	1 1/2	1 1/2
Spinach	2	—
Squash, summer	3	4

Reprinted from How to Grow Vegetables & Fruits By the Organic Method [1], copyright 1961 by J.I. Rodale. Permission was granted by Rodale Press, Inc., Emmaus, PA, 18049.

Some other methods are steaming in the pressure cooker (be sure to watch the cooking time), double boiler, baking, stir frying in a wok, or shisk-kabobs on a barbecue When vegetables are baked in a casserole, the liquid used should already be hot, the casserole and oven preheated, and a lid put on to hold in steam and prevent contact with air. Before the vegetables are put into the casserole, quickly steam the vegetables or put them under the broiler until they are heated through so that the enzymes will be destroyed before baking.

Many people say that they prefer the flavor and texture of vegetables that have been cooked in the microwave, as opposed to the other methods. If you don't have a microwave, then the next best is probably the waterless cooking method. Some people buy a microwave just to cook their vegetables because they are so good that way!

Blanching Vegetables for Home Freezing

The microwave oven is a great help when you like to freeze fresh vegetables while they are in season, highest in quality and lowest in price. It's especially helpful to home gardeners, since vegetable crops don't ripen all at the same time. If you use the microwave you can pick vegetables at their peak of flavor, even if you have only a few servings. Minutes after they are picked, you can have them blanched and ready to freeze, without spending all day in a steamy kitchen, handling heavy pots of boiling water. Microwaving is the easiest way to blanch, but if you don't have a microwave, you could steam or boil the vegetables.

What is blanching? Steaming, boiling and microwaving are some of the same ways you would normally "cook" vegetables, but "blanching" cooks them for less time (only long enough to stop enzyme action). Blanching kills the enzymes which would otherwise cause unnatural colors, textures, flavors, and odors to develop while foods are frozen. So, the blanching process helps frozen produce "keep" better and retain more food value, especially Vitamin C. Two to four times more Vitamin C is retained in blanched vegetables than in those frozen without blanching [1]. Another advantage is that blanched foods are somewhat softened and can be packed more solidly into freezer containers.

How To Blanch Vegetables In The Microwave [1]:

1) Prepare vegetables (wash, peel, slice or dice) as in regular cooking. Then see Microwave Blanching chart for blanching times of individual vegetables. Measure one quart or one pound of vegetables into the recommended casserole. Add water, as given in the chart. DO NOT ADD SALT. Cover.

2) Set power on high (10). Microwave for half the minimum time and stir. Cover casserole and microwave for rest of the minimum time. Stir again.

3) Check for doneness. Vegetables should have an evenly bright color throughout. If all the vegetables are not evenly bright, re-cover the casserole and microwave for maximum time. Drain the vegetables.

4) Plunge vegetables into ice water immediately, to prevent further cooking. Spread them on paper towels and blot with additional towels to absorb excess moisture.

5) Package (same way as for fruit) in freezer containers,

boil-in-bag pouches, or Ziploc bags. Label packages with type of vegetables, amount, and date. Freeze. To loose-pack vegetables (like chopped carrots) in larger containers or bags, spread the individual pieces on cookie sheet. Put a layer of Saran wrap or wax paper on cookie sheet first to prevent vegetable from sticking to cookie sheet. Place cookie sheet in freezer until vegetables are frozen, then place loose pieces in desired containers. Seal, label (use permanent ink) and freeze. Large Ziploc bags stack nicely in a freezer, and when the vegetable is loose-packed you can shake out exactly the amount of carrots you need for one meal.

When you are ready to eat the frozen vegetables — remove them from freezer, thaw, finish cooking them, and enjoy. When microwaving frozen, blanched vegetables to eat, remember that a one pint container holds about the same amount of vegetables as a ten ounce package of commercially frozen vegetables. Follow directions on a commercial package or look up in a microwave cookbook following directions for FROZEN vegetables. Most commercial packages say to start cooking them in the frozen state, and the same applies to home frozen vegetables, etc. If you package vegetables in smaller or larger amounts than a one pint container or bag, adjust the casserole size, amount of water, and microwaving time proportionately. But whatever you do, DO NOT OVER-COOK! Home-frozen vegetables taste best when cooked to crisp-tender. Microwave for minimum time, then let stand, covered, an additional 5-10 minutes to finish softening and develop flavor.

To blanch vegetables not mentioned in the following Microwave Chart, follow the directions for fresh vegetables in a microwave cookbook, but DO NOT ADD SALT and remember that the blanching time will be 1/4 to 1/3 the regular cooking time. Stir, test, and cool as directed in blanching steps (listed previously).

Storage techniques

Next to eating produce fresh from the garden, freezing is the best way to store vegetables for future use. Vegetables best adapted for freezing are those that normally are cooked before serving. Vegetables usually eaten raw, such as celery, lettuce, etc. are least suited for freezing. Onions that will be later used in cooking can be chopped and then frozen, or freeze them whole and slice while still frozen (so your eyes won't water). Tomatoes also can be frozen whole if you plan to use them later in cooking chili, etc. After freezing vegetables or fruit on a tray, seal them in a Ziploc bag, double plastic bags (one inside another, and sealed with masking tape), or Tupperware-like plastic container. Be sure to label with item name & date (for example, Onions 10-92), and use permanent ink! No food should be exposed to air in the refrigerator or freezer, or it will get freezer-burn and become tasteless.

Vitamin/mineral content fades over time in storage. The longer food stays in the freezer, the less nutrients it has when you eat it. Rotate all the food in your freezer so that you eat the oldest things first. Most foods taste best when eaten within a year. Frozen foods should not be kept long at room temperature as they loose flavor and texture; so whenever possible, thaw frozen foods in the refrigerator, or in a microwave oven that has a defrost cycle. See Vegetable chapter.

To store in pantry, basement, or root cellar, —handle the vegetables as little as possible, and as gently as you can. Any bruised spot or cut will be the first spot to spoil. Don't pile vegetables on top of one another, instead lay each one separately in a box with sawdust or crumpled newspaper. Don't wash any vegetables before storing or they will mildew. Don't cut off roots on root crops (just shake off the dirt), and leave at least an inch of the tops remaining. On other crops, leave as much of the stem as possible. Select only the unblemished vegetables for storage, and eat the others now [3].

References cited:

[1] How to Cook Vegetables and Fruits By The Org. Method
[2] The Microwave Guide and Cookbook, General Electric.
[3] Square Foot Gardening [MEL]

BLANCHING VEGETABLES
By The Microwave Method

Vegetable	Amount	Casserole size	Water	Minutes
Asparagus	1-lb., cut into 1-2 "pieces	2-quart	1/4 cup	3 - 4
Beans, green or wax	1-lb.	1 1/2-qt	1/2 cup	4 - 6
Broccoli (1" cuts)	1 bunch, 1 1/4 to 1 1/2-lb.	2-quart	1/2 cup	4 - 5 1/2
Carrots	1-lb., sliced	1 1/2-qt	1/4 cup	4 - 6
Cauliflower	I head, cut into flowerets	2-quart	1/2 cup	4 - 5 1/2
Corn	corn cut from 4 ears	1-quart	1/4 cup	4 - 5
Onions	4 medium, quartered	1-quart	1/2 cup	3 - 4 1/2
Parsnips	1-lb. cubed	1 1/2-qt	1/4 cup	2 1/2 - 4
Peas	2-lb. shelled	1-quart	1/4 cup	3 1/2 - 5
Spinach	1-lb. washed	2-quart	none	2 1/2 - 3 1/2
Squash, summer	1-lb., sliced or cubed	1 1/2-qt	1/4 cup	3 - 4 1/2
Turnips	1-lb. cubed	1 1/2-qt	1/4 cup	3 - 4 1/2
Zucchini	1-lb. sliced or cubed	1 1/2-qt	1/4 cup	3 - 4 1/2

This chart was reprinted from "The Microwave Guide and Cookbook" with permission from General Electric Company [2].

DEHYDRATE, FREEZE, OR CAN?

Sometimes we have more produce from our garden than we can use, or a friend may have just given us a bag of apples, or kiwis. You might want to make some special desserts for the holidays, to use as gifts, or just to eat for a healthy snack. Make them ahead and put them in the freezer.

There are three basic ways to preserve foods: freezing, dehydrating, and canning. Foods can be preserved either whole (raspberries) or sliced (carrots, bananas), precooked (applesauce) or raw (zucchini),—depending on the type of food, and whether it tends to turn brown. Only dehydrating and freezing will be discussed here.

DEHYDRATING METHODS

Fruit and vegetables that are firm/ripe can be cut up in dices, slices, or halves, but overripe foods are recommended for fruit leather. Dehydrated fruits and vegetables are delicious as a snack, trail mix, or in home-made granola. I will discuss making fruit leather and granola here.

HOW TO MAKE FRUIT LEATHERS:

Fruit leather is one way of preserving fruit by pureeing it in a blender, spreading it on a flat tray, and dehydrating it until dry. Usually a little applesauce (contains pectin) is added to each batch (regardless of the main fruit) to give the leather a smooth consistency. Add ascorbic acid in some form (like ascorbic acid powder, Ever Fresh, or Fruit Fresh) to prevent browning. Sugar or honey is not necessary. You can use a commercial dehydrator or make trays to dry in the sun, to use over your wood stove, or in your oven. Be sure to try apple, strawberry-banana, peach, pineapple-apricot, or apple-berry. My favorite recipe uses 3 cups applesauce, and 1 cup raspberries.

General Recipe for Fruit Leather
3 cups fruit (strawberries, cherries, raspberries, peaches, etc.)
1 cup applesauce
1 T. Powdered Ascorbic Acid.
1 T. water (or as little as possible. Just enough to make the blender work).

Prepare dehydrator tray by placing Stretch-tight wrap on the tray and attaching it with masking tape at the corners and in the middle. Do Not use Wax paper, Saran Wrap, or Handi-Wrap as they stick permanently to the fruit leather. Stretch Tight Plastic Wrap is available at Price Club and Cosco. Place about one cup of fruit in your blender. Add just enough water to blend. Add another cup of fruit and blend. Then add rest of the ingredients and blend well.

Pour some fruit puree onto a dehydrator tray and spread level with a spatula. To finish leveling, tap tray on edge of table. Place the trays in the dehydrator, and rotate the trays every hour (depending on the type of dehydrator). When the leather is evenly dry, take the masking tape off the tray and stick it to the edge of your table. Roll up the leather (including the plastic wrap!), and stick your saved masking tape pieces onto the leather roll, to keep it from unrolling. Cut the resulting leather tube into four sections. One piece of masking tape will hold each fruit leather section from unrolling. Then place the sections in a Ziploc plastic bag, burp the air out of the bag, and seal it. Store in a cool, dark place, like a pantry, or in the freezer.

Tray with fruit leather

Fruit roll

HOW TO MAKE GRANOLA:

Try granola for breakfast or snack. Use 1-6 types of rolled or flaked grains, and add any dehydrated fruit or vegetables. When you eat it, add fresh fruit on top. It is not over-processed like many commercial cereals, so it gives you natural fiber and vitamins for good health.

Lianne's Granola
6 cups raw rolled oats
1 cup raw wheat germ
1 cup flaked coconut
1/2-1 cup sunflower seeds
1/2-1 cup nuts
1/2-1 cup pumpkin seeds
1/2 cup vegetable oil
1/2 cup honey
1/3 cup hot water
1/2 tsp salt
1 tsp vanilla
1 cup raisins, dates, currants, etc.

Preheat oven to 350°F. In large bowl mix oats, flour, wheat germ, coconut, seeds, and nuts. In separate container, mix together rest of ingredients except raisins. Pour wet ingredients over dry; mix thoroughly until well blended. Spread mixture onto two well-greased baking sheets (I spray with Pam). Bake 30 minutes or until golden, stirring regularly. Store in airtight container, like a regular grind, coffee can. Add raisins, after cooking.

FREEZER METHODS

Food can be frozen individually (like raspberries), in combination with others of its kind (more raspberries), a mixture (raspberries and peaches, or a fruit salad), or in a recipe (Berry-Banana Bread). Some foods can be cooked before or after freezing (Banana Bread), while some are cooked after they come out of the freezer (pumpkin pie).

THE INDIVIDUAL, QUICK- FREEZE METHOD

Try this quick, easy method whenever you have extra fruit like strawberries or raspberries from your garden or grocery store, and you want to freeze them for future use. Wash and take the stems off. Lay a piece of plastic or waxed paper on a cookie sheet with an edge. Place the washed fruit on the cookie sheet. Blot off any excess water from pooling on the cookie sheet. Place in freezer overnight. The next day place the frozen fruit in ziploc bags labeled with date and contents, and return it to the freezer. The advantage of this method is that the fruit is frozen in individual pieces, and whether you want 1 or 2 cups out of the bag,— you can take out the amount you want. No liquid, preservative, or cooking is necessary. This also works well for chopped carrots, broccoli, and whole tomatoes. Nuts, and grated cheese can also be stored in ziploc bags in your freezer for your convenience.

Berries on a cookie sheet

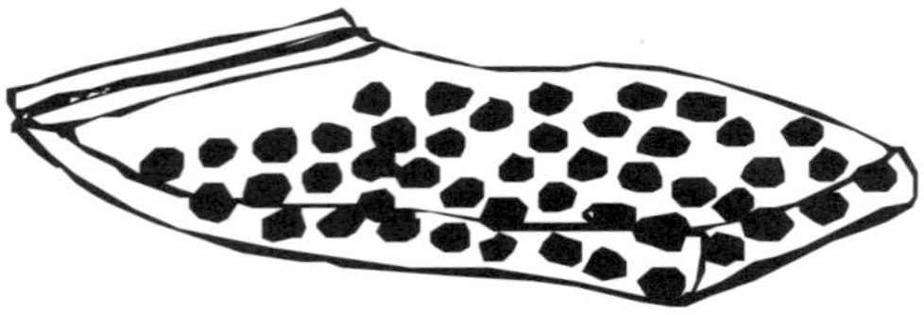

Berries in ziploc freezer bag

FRESH-FROZEN PEACHES

There are few ways to preserve peaches so they still have that special fresh taste. To one large Dutch oven add: 1 heaping T. powdered Ascorbic Acid (or 4 T. Everfresh), 1/4 cup sugar, and 1/4 cup honey. Stir well. Add peeled sliced peaches until the pot is almost full. Then add 1 cup raspberries (optional) and stir. Makes 5 quarts. Use a large funnel to put the fruit into ziploc freezer bags and place in freezer. Since peaches are sweet and berries are tart, the combination is delicious. Try on your favorite cereal or on vanilla ice cream!

TO FREEZE PLUMS —add some orange juice, lemon juice, and pumpkin pie spice. then add sugar to taste.

KIWI TEA CAKE (my favorite way to eat kiwis)

An average size kiwi has more vitamin C than an orange, as much potassium as a banana, and the same calories as an apple (only 66). It also has more fiber and iron than an apple; and it helps lower cholesterol.

6 medium (1 1/2 lb, or 2 cups) kiwi fruit
(a good way to use up "ripe" kiwis)
1 cup granulated sugar
1 teaspoon grated lemon peel
1 large egg
1/2 cup salad oil
1 1/2 cups flour
1/2 teaspoon baking powder
1/2 teaspoon salt
1/2 teaspoon baking soda

1) Either pare off the skin of the kiwi fruit with a knife, or cut kiwi in half and spoon out the kiwi fruit from the skin. Chop the fruit (about 1 1/2 cups) and place in a 2- or 3-quart-size pan. Add to the pan the granulated sugar and lemon peel. Bring to a boil on high heat, stirring. Cook until fruit turns a paler green color (about 15 minutes). Set aside to cool.
2) In a large bowl, beat egg and oil until well mixed, and set aside.
3) Stir together flour, baking powder, and salt, and set aside.
4) When cooked kiwi fruit has cooled, add the baking soda and stir until small bubbles form, then pour into egg mixture. Add flour mixture and stir until dry ingredients are moistened. Spoon batter into well-greased 5 x 9 inch loaf pan. Bake in a 350°F oven until cake just begins to pull away from pan sides and a slender wooden toothpick inserted in center comes out clean, about 55 minutes. (If you use two small loaf pans instead, cook about 40 minutes.) Let cool in pan 10 minutes, then invert onto a rack to cool completely. Keep refrigerated. Can be refrigerated one week; freeze to store longer. Keep wrapped while thawing. Makes 8 to 10 servings. Enjoy!

ZUCCHINI BREAD —2 LOAVES (or 3 small loaves)

Beat: 3 eggs till light & creamy.

Mix together:
- 1 cup vegetable oil
- 2 cups sugar
- 2 teaspoons vanilla
- 2 cups peeled & grated zucchini

Mix together:
- 3 cups flour
- 1 teaspoon baking soda
- 1 1/4 teaspoon baking powder
- 1 teaspoon salt
- 1 teaspoon cinnamon
- and 1 cup chopped nuts.

Beat eggs till light and creamy. Add next four ingredients and mix well. Add flour mixture and blend. Stir in the nuts. Grease and flour the pans! Bake at 325°F for 1 hour or till done (if use 3 small loaf pans, takes 45 minutes). Remove from pans at once. When you have extra zucchini from the garden, chop it up in amounts needed for recipe (2 cups), and freeze it in ziploc bag until needed (you don't need to blanch the Zucchini).

EASY APPLESAUCE

Into one large (1 gal) kettle or large pot add:

1 Tablespoon Everfresh or Fruit Fresh (to prevent discoloring)
1 cup sugar (or less to taste)
1 cup water
1 Tablespoon cinnamon or 1 Tablespoon Baking Blend (contains cinnamon, coriander, nutmeg, allspice, cloves, ginger, and mace)

Then prepare apples and fill the pot. To prepare apples: wash, take out bad spots, (leave skins on), cut up into quarters, core, and add to pot. Bring pot to boil and simmer at low heat until tender and slightly transparent. Stir every 5 minutes to prevent sticking and to make it cook more evenly. Let cool. Put in blender till smooth and then place in a container (like Tupperware or cottage cheese). After using blender you should see no sign of apple skins, and you have their nutrition besides saving hours of peeling. Put label on freezer container with name of contents and date. Use masking tape and Rub-a-dub laundry marker pen. Applesauce lasts one year in freezer without losing flavor or texture. Applesauce is a good thickener for drinks like milkshake so you don't have to use ice cream. Call it a Fruit Shake.

Other ways to use apples are apple cidar, apple butter, applesauce muffins, cookies, applesauce bread, apple granola, apple pancakes or waffles.

FRUIT -YOGURT DESSERT

1 ready-made graham cracker crust
1 envelope unflavored gelatin
1 package (10 ounces) frozen strawberries, thawed and drained (reserve liquid). Or use 10 ounces of fresh strawberries, or any other kind of fruit.
2/3 cup boiling water
2 containers (8 ounces each) vanilla-flavored yogurt (2 cups)
1 teaspoon vanilla.

Sprinkle gelatin over reserved strawberry liquid (or use 1/4 cup cold water); let stand 1 minute. Pour boiling water over gelatin. Stir until gelatin is dissolved, then cool completely.

Place strawberries in blender or food processor that has a steel blade. Cover and blend on high speed until smooth. Mix gelatin mixture, yogurt and vanilla until smooth. Stir in strawberries until well blended. Pour into crust. Refrigerate uncovered until set, at least 4 hours. Keep refrigerated. Makes 9 servings.

CARROT CAKE

4 eggs
2 cups sugar
1 cup vegetable oil
2 cups flour
2 teaspoons baking soda
1 teaspoon cinnamon
1/2 teaspoon salt
3 cups grated carrots

Beat eggs and sugar together well, add the oil and set aside. Sift dry ingredients together. Then add dry mixture to egg mixture. Then add carrots and mix well. Grease and flour 9" x 13" pan, or 3 small loaf pans, or use muffin tins. Bake at 350°F for 30 minutes, or till done. It's so good it doesn't need frosting. Double the recipe and put some in the freezer!

BANANA BREAD —Makes one loaf

Very ripe bananas are often discounted at your local grocer. The riper the banana, the moister the bread. If you can't make bread the day you get the "ripe" bananas, stick them in your freezer till you have time to bake. If you bake 4x the recipe you can put some baked loaves in the freezer.

1 1/3 cups flour
2 1/2 teaspoons baking powder
1/4 teaspoon salt
1 cup mashed ripe bananas (2 average bananas)
2/3 cup brown sugar (packed)
1/3 cup orange juice
1 egg beaten
1/3 cup vegetable oil
2 cups (bran flakes, oat bran, or oatmeal, or a combination totaling 2 cups)
1/2 cup chopped nuts (optional), or can use berries, or raisins and cinnamon.

Mix flour, baking powder, and salt. Add bananas, sugar, orange juice, egg, and vegetable oil. Stir until flour is moistened. Mix in cereal and nuts. Bake at 350°F in greased 9" x 5" loaf pan for 50 minutes, or in two small loaf pans for about 40 minutes. Cook until toothpick comes out clean. Cool 10 minutes. Then remove from pan. Delicious and good for you.

PUMPKIN BREAD (1 loaf)

1 2/3 cup flour
1/4 t. baking powder
1 t. baking soda
3/4 t. salt
1/2 t. cinnamon
1/2 t. nutmeg
1/3 cup melted margarine
1 1/2 cup sugar
1/2 t. vanilla
2 eggs
1 cup pumpkin (canned or fresh cooked)
1/3 cup water
1/2 cup walnuts

Mix together all dry ingredients and set aside. Mix together all wet ingredients. Then add wet to dry mixture and stir well. Then stir in walnuts. Use a 9x3x5 inch loaf pan at 350°F and cook for 45-55 minutes.

Suggested References:

Stocking Up
How to Grow Fruits & Veg.
The Green Thumb Cookbook
Dr York at U.C. Davis

FORCING SPRING BULBS INDOORS

In the wintertime you can make your home come alive with color when you "force bulbs". **Forcing** is a process that causes plants to grow and flower before their natural time by artificial means [1]. Some bulbs that can be forced to bloom indoors are daffodils, hyacinths, narcissus, crocus, lily of the valley, Gloxinia, and tulips. Their bright colors will give you some relief from the winter "blues".

Hardy bulbs require a cold winter in order to bloom the next spring (outdoors). If you want to grow these bulbs indoors, and trick them into blooming during snowy January and February, then you must give them the cold temperatures required before blooming, but don't let them freeze. There is a secret to this, however, and it differs with the type of bulb. Most of them need a cold, dark period of 8-10 weeks. Then the plant is brought out into the light in a warm room, and given water — and in a few days it will start to bloom. When it blooms depends on WHEN you start the dark period.

Bulbs may be grown in water, gravel, sand or soil. Crocus and hyacinth are favorites for water culture, while Narcissus (Paper Whites) do best in a sand or gravel bed. Those not grown in soil will use up all their stored food and should be thrown away after they finish blooming. Only the soil culture method will be discussed in detail here.

Soil Culture of Forced Bulbs:

1) Cover drainage hole in pot with gravel, pieces of broken clay pot, or a piece of kleenex.

2) Put a level layer of soil in bottom of pot about one inch deep.

3) Place bulbs as close together as possible on top of soil without touching each other.

TOP VIEW

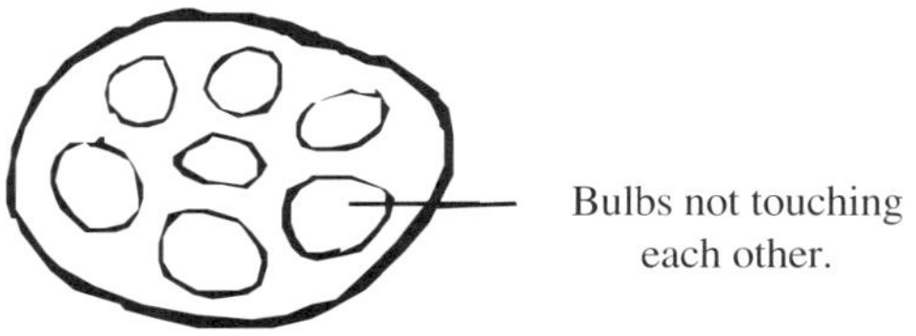

4) Cover with more soil so that only the tips are exposed. If there is more room in the pot, you can put more layers of bulbs on top of them.

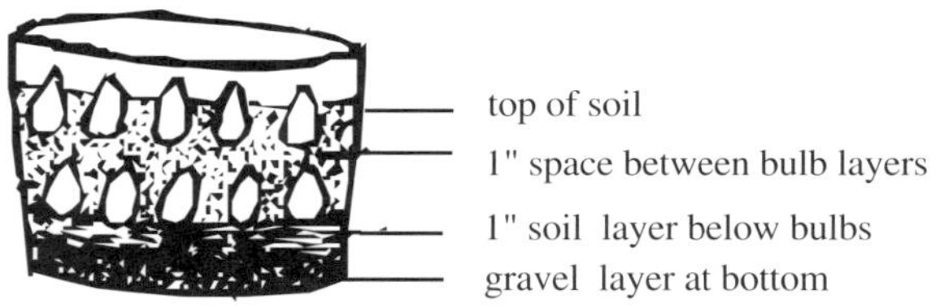

SIDE VIEW

5) Firm soil around bulbs, and water thoroughly so that water comes out the drainage hole.

6) The dark, cold treatment must last 10-12 weeks. The flower bud cannot develop without this cold. I place my bulbs in a closed cardboard box in a closet. There are four types of places you can store bulbs to accomplish this cold treatment: One, — In your refrigerator (in a dark place: either inside a cardboard box or in vegetable bin). Two, —In a glass-covered cold frame. Put inverted flower pot over the bulb pot and then cover with hay, dry leaves, peat moss, or pine needles. Three, —In a trench eight inches deep. Place pots in trench and cover them with ten inches soil, then six inches hay or pine needles to prevent heaving of the soil. And four, —In an unheated garage, porch, or closet. Put bulb pot in a box with packing excelsior, styrofoam chips, etc. [2].

Don't let the bulbs dry out! Put them in a plastic or dry-cleaning bag before covering them. Don't worry if you get

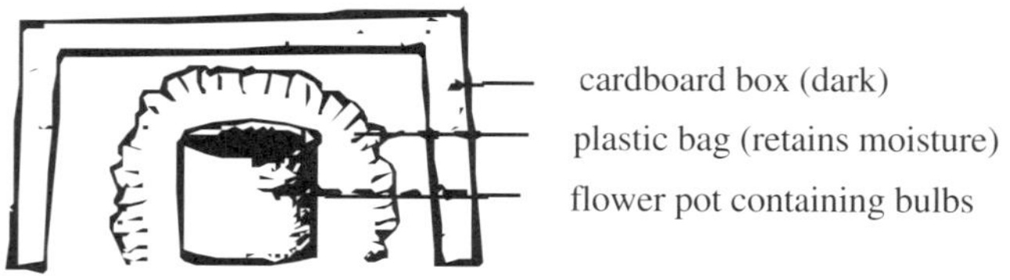

SIDE VIEW

a fuzzy layer of mold on the soil surface, as it will disappear when the pot is placed in the sun. Or if you wish, you can scrape it off with a spoon. The bulbs are ready to remove from the cold treatment when they have definite white sprouts at the bulb tips. I usually take them out around Christmas time—an easy date to remember. But this depends on the temperature where you have kept them, and how long they have been stored there.

7) <u>Put bulb pot in cool place</u> (not in direct sun) 50-55°F. Add water if necessary.

8) <u>Move bulb pot into sunny window 60-65°F</u> (when white growing tip turns green).

9) <u>Bring bulb pot into the room where you wish it to bloom 68-70°F</u> (when flower buds begin to open). Keeping blossoms out of direct sunlight will prolong the blooms, and preserve color and fragrance. If you can put the pot in a cooler place at night, it will also prolong the bloom. Tall plants may require staking. Too much water can rot the bulbs, and too little will cause the plant to wilt.

10) <u>Don't throw the bulb away</u> after it finishes blooming. Cut off the dead blossom and put the pot back in a sunny, cool window, watering regularly until the leaves die back. After the weather outdoors warms up, you can replant the bulbs in your garden with a generous helping of bone meal. They may not bloom the following spring as "forcing" is a rough experience for them. But with bone meal and time they will be producing flowers by the following spring. Use a different set of bulbs for "forcing" next winter.

Summary: Plant bulbs in a pot (in 1-3 layers) not touching each other. Water thoroughly until water comes out the bottom of the pot. <u>Store 10-12 weeks wrapped in a plastic bag in a *dark, cool* place</u> until definite white sprouts show at bulb tips. Unwrap and place in light, cool place until shoots turn green. Then place in a sunny window till flower buds start to open. Take them out of sun and put where you want them to bloom. Save the bulb, but don't use it again for "forcing" as it is too hard on it.

<u>References cited:</u>
[1] Reader's Digest: Success with House Plants,
[2] Gardening Indoors with House Plants

<u>Narcissus</u>. Many varieties, many shapes

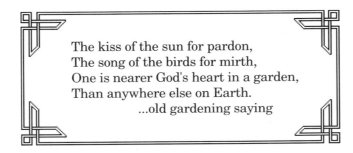

The kiss of the sun for pardon,
The song of the birds for mirth,
One is nearer God's heart in a garden,
Than anywhere else on Earth.
...old gardening saying

ENCOURAGING CHILDREN TO GARDEN

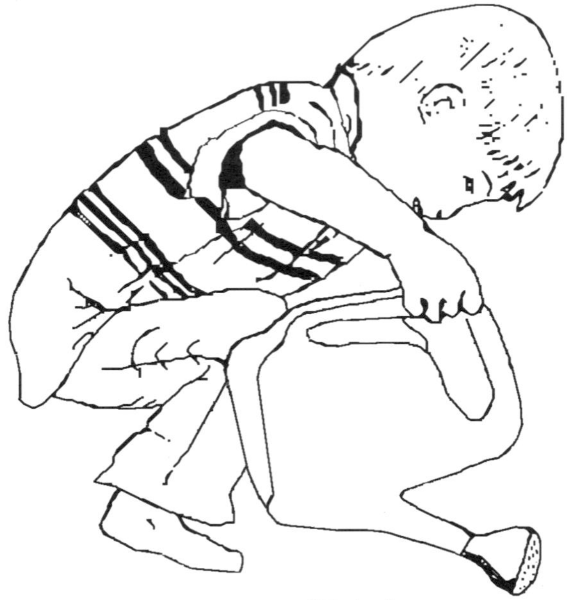

"Caring"

Help your children enjoy gardening early. Try to be encouraging, and not too critical. A child's garden is not a place to say "no" to your child. It is a place for them to explore and experiment, and to do what they want to do. Gardening is a satisfying and profitable use of time, and it offers fresh air and exercise for all ages. Gardens help alleviate the stress of modern day life, and they keep us in touch with the wonders of nature. Gardening can be creative, educational, imaginative, and a good way for families to spend time together.

Children enjoy company

Children enjoy spending time with you in the garden. The younger the child, the simpler and shorter the task should be. Keep their help sessions short (maybe 15 minutes, depending on age), so it can be a special time and a special place. "One on one" time is special "quality" time. Once the fun of gardening catches on they'll want to spend more time there [1].

Group gardening at a School, YWCA, Scout, 4-H, Church, or Day camp includes friends and is an activity children can share. They don't like to garden alone but enjoy the companionship of friends and parents. The most common age of a child interested in gardening is age 4-10, with the majority between 7-8. You can start them helping you in the garden as early as 1 1/2 or 2 years old.

Start them at a young age

Ask the youngest children be your helpers. Introduce them to the soil, the outdoors, and the fact that you can plant a seed, water it, and a few months later eat something yummy that you grew in the ground. Most all children love playing in the mud, digging in the dirt, watering, and watching seeds sprout. To them it is just having a good time, so they see soil and seed preparation as play, not work. Make gardening fun now, and emphasize gardening techniques later.

Let them help with planting. Child-size rakes, hoes and shovels are available in some hardware stores, and can be useful for adults too. They like to help you mark a row, or dig a furrow and drop in the seeds.

They love to water the garden, but don't count on them to water on a regular basis, as they may be more concerned about how wet they can get, or how funny it is when they squirt the dog. Watering is more fun if they are allowed to get wet.

Have a "treasure hunt" for potatoes in your potato patch when it's time to harvest. Let them help you find the hidden strawberries in a forest of strawberry leaves. See who can pull the biggest bucket of weeds. Ask them to help you add a lily pond with fish to your garden. Encourage them to eat the snow peas and carrots fresh from the garden anytime.

Give them their own garden plot

When they get a little older, you can share your love of gardening by giving them a garden plot of their very own to nurture. Remember, they will want to do as much as they can for themselves, but under the age of about eight years, they still need some help from adults. You need to guide them so that their first gardening experience is a positive one. Start them with only a small plot so you won't overwhelm them with too much work. 6 x 6 feet should be maximum size and can be enlarged later as their interest and ability grows [2]. They usually don't like to weed, so mulch their plot with plenty of hay, straw, or black plastic to cut down on the weeding. Weeding should be done only after a rain when the weeds come up easily because the ground is soft. Help them make a special sign or a scarecrow for their garden, to add to their enjoyment.

"Little helper"

Work together side by side.

Remember, it is okay for the child to make mistakes. The best way to learn about gardening and about growing things is by experience, and we learn from our mistakes. It should be a time when children can work, play, explore, and satisfy their curiosity by interacting with the great outdoors.

What should they plant?

Children will enjoy the garden more if you let them make some of the decisions themselves. They love to choose their own seeds. A good rule is that the smaller the child, the larger the seed should be for ease of handling [1]. A two-year-old can plant the seeds of sugar snap peas, beets, beans, sunflowers, turnips, pumpkin (warmest areas only), radishes, corn, and flowers. Children like plants that grow quickly (because they have little patience), and they seem most impressed with the tallest and biggest plants. Broccoli, tomato, and marigold seedlings can be purchased at a nursery and easily planted by the child under your supervision. Transplants give instant gratification. They transform bare ground into a real garden in minutes [3].

Children seem particularly to enjoy root vegetables. Maybe it is the surprise element, since they can't see them under the ground. Cut a potato into several pieces each with one eye, and let child plant the pieces in a mound of soil. When the potatoes are ready to harvest, they can have an exciting treasure hunt.

Even encourage children to grow some things they may prefer not to eat, but grow it for mother or aunty because they like it. When it is grown in their own garden and they watch it grow and mature, they may want to taste it because they grew it and it looks good. Because they grew it themselves, they are more apt to eat it.

Save planting of smaller seeds such as carrots, lettuce, spinach, and broccoli until the children are older and more coordinated. Use hybrid corn as it only grows 3 feet tall, and matures several weeks earlier than regular corn. My children like spinach and broccoli because they grew it in the garden. For more information see Vegetable chapter.

Planting a garden

Let them work on their garden under your watchful eye. If child and parent have a plot next to each other in the garden, the child can learn by observation. You can work together side by side and enjoy each others company, and the child can get the important "hands on experience" needed for learning. Demonstrate how to level the soil with the back of the metal rake, and then let them do it. Let them mark where the rows will go. Show them how you dump a few seeds into your left hand, and then take one at a time with the fingers of the right hand and place the seed exactly where you want it. Only plant one seed per hole, so thinning is not required (See Propagation chapter). If you have some Marigold or Petunia seedlings to plant, show them how and then let them do it (see Planting chapter). Tell them the difference between the good plants and the weeds, and help them keep their plot weed-free.

Harvesting

Show children pictures of what the plant and fruit will look like, and tell them how long it has to grow before harvest. After watching plants grow and caring for them, children are interested in tasting them at least once. Harvest is the most fun of all for them (they get very impatient). Make a fuss over the things they grew in their plot and use it in a special meal saying "we are serving Joey's carrots with our dinner tonight." Have them help harvest, cook, and eat it. The raw vegetables or slightly cooked ones are most appealing, rather than mushy overcooked ones. When they are personally involved in creating their own garden, it triggers enthusiasm.

Children can become enthusiastic easily about gardening, and are just as easily "turned off." Refrain from taking over and dominating the experience. If they want to pick all of their carrots and feed them to their pet rabbit or the neighbor's horse, let them. If they want to pick all the flowers in their garden and give them to grandma, let them. Remember it is their special garden, and this is part of ownership.

Insects can be fascinating creatures.

Insects in the garden can be fascinating to a young child, and most children like to play with them. Help them to observe what the bugs eat and why. A magnifying glass can be a educational tool to watch "action" in the garden. Ask if they would like to make a bug collection and mount their specimens on styrofoam. Put some beer in an empty (clean) tuna can and let the child watch slugs be attracted to it. Tell them about companion planting; how the beans keep the bugs off the potatoes, etc. (see Insect Pests chapter). Grow some raspberries to attract birds, and the children can observe birds eating berries and insects. Lady bugs eat aphids.

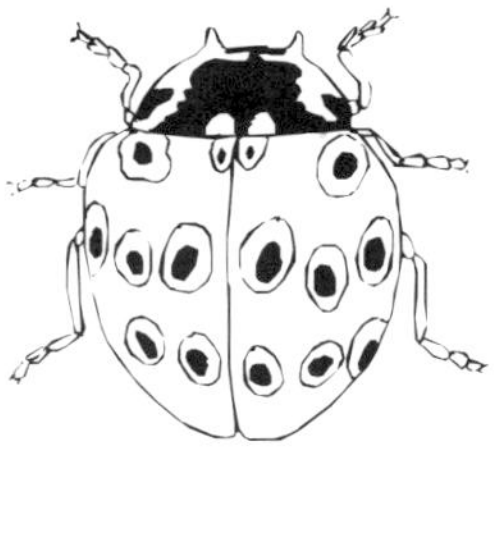

Ladybug

Planting seeds indoors.

Planting seeds indoors is a good way to spark a child's interest in gardening. We all enjoy witnessing the "birth" of a new plant. In planting a seed and watching it grow, we see the miracle of life. Show children different kinds of seeds. Then let them sprout the seeds in various ways: in jars, between paper towels, in petri dishes, or in upright viewer boxes with glass on one side so they can watch the roots and shoot grow.

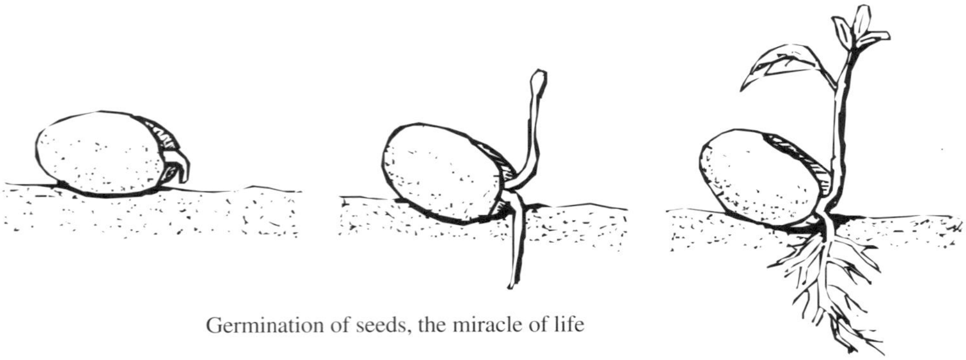

Germination of seeds, the miracle of life

Fruits, vegetables and nuts can be bought in grocery stores, or you can collect seeds from your garden. Some fruits and vegetables that will grow from seed planted in pots are: papaya, peach, pear, plums, persimmon, mango, date, orange, lemon, lime grapefruit, apples, avocados, melons, squash, beans, and yellow or red pepper.

The seeds of deciduous fruits and nuts in order to sprout, need a period of moist winter chilling to break their natural dormancy. So store them in refrigerator at 40°F in a plastic bag with wet vermiculite. Length of chilling time needed: Almonds: 4 weeks, Apple: 2-3 months, Apricot: 3-4 weeks, Grape: 3 months, Peach: 3 months, Pear: 2-3 months, Walnuts: 3 months, and Grapefruit: no chilling time required, plant anytime. Plant walnuts 4-6 inches deep, and all others about 3 inches deep [4].

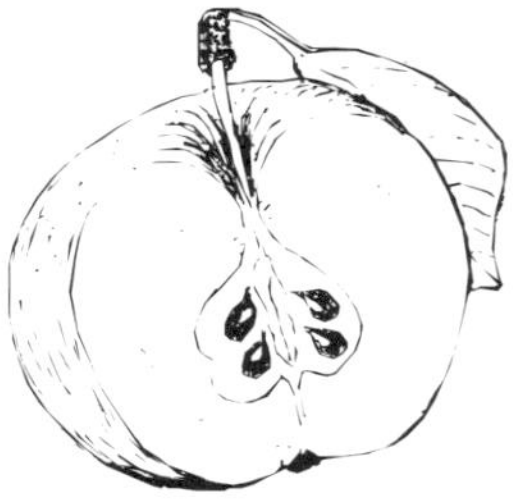

Apple seeds

Some of the largest seeds need to be nicked with a sharp knife to promote germination. Before planting, soak the smaller seeds overnight in hot water and larger ones for several days. After soaking, dry the surface of the seed and plant them immediately.

Seeds and kernels with remains of fruit clinging to them should be cleaned thoroughly. Papaya seeds, which look like small fish eggs in jelly, should be washed in lukewarm water, dried on a paper towel, and planted immediately. Tropical plants need high temperatures to germinate. Don't give up! Some seeds take weeks, even months, to germinate.

Some experiments to try indoors:

• Children can fill a glass jar full of paper towels and stick some bean or pea seeds between the paper towels and the glass. Several drops of water each day keeps the towels damp but not wet. As the seeds develop roots and leaves, the child gets a good idea what is happening below the ground. (see illustration of germination). Then plant seeds in soil in a pot, and watch them grow.

• Goodyear [5] says that making a lentil garden gives quick results. Line a shallow bowl with small pebbles, scatter a handful of lentil seeds, and fill with water. In about 2-4 days, the child has the beginning of an interesting cluster of green leaves.

• Try sprouting seeds in aluminum pie pans, each with a different type of seed: snow peas, pinto beans, alfalfa, and fava beans. Sprinkle the seeds on one paper towel placed in pie pan, and cover with another. The children need to keep the towels damp, watch for sprouting (or rotting), and they can dissect the seeds in all stages.

Growing vegetables indoors.

• Plant potatoes in a large pot, wastebasket (make holes in bottom), or planter, and you will have a beautiful flowering plant (and you can get many potatoes too). Plant carrots, the foliage will look like fern, and you can eat them when they get big enough. Spinach can begrown in the house for a foliage plant, and you can nibble on the thinnings to keep it bushy.

Avocado pit

Avocado mature plant

• A large sweet onion, avocado pit or sweet potato may either be planted in a pot of soil or suspended in a jar of water. Put the pointed half down, and use toothpicks at several places around the vegetable to keep the upper part out of the water. The avocado pit (only) should be presoaked in water for a day, then peel the outer skin. Soon it can have beautiful foliage. When the plant gets too big for the jar, plant it in a pot [4].

Sweet potato

• Cut off the top 1-2 inches of a carrot, pineapple, beet, parsnip, or turnip. Then either place the top in a shallow dish of water in a sunny window, or plant in a shallow pot of soil. Within a few days the tops will begin to grow [4, 6].

• Try growing "hair" on a white potato. Scoop some pulp from one end of a large potato and fill the hollow with wet cotton. Slice off the other end of the potato, and put sliced end down in a shallow dish lined with gravel or pebbles, and filled with water. Sprinkle grass seed over the wet cotton and poke the seeds gently into the cotton with a pencil point. Keep the water level constant, and soon the potato will be growing hair. Colored rocks can be used for eyes and mouth. The children can give haircuts with scissors [5]. Doing this is really fun!

Carrot

Other indoor projects:

• Make seed pictures using wood, glue, and many kinds of seeds. Make a mosaic of any simple picture the child chooses like a duck, kitten, owl, puppy, flower. Have some coloring book pictures for suggestions. It is a fun way to get children familiar with the names of the different seeds. Include some pine cone scales for interest, like for the plumage of an owl.

Pineapple

• Place some seedlings near a bright light for about a week; what happens? And then turn the pot in the opposite direction; what happens? Put a healthy seedling in the shade (in a closet) for a week. What happens?

• Have a plant sale of baby plants that the kids started themselves from cuttings or seed. Use milk cartons or styrofoam cups, and punch holes in the bottom for drainage. Use half vermiculite, and half potting soil. The kids will have a lot of pride selling plants that they grew.

• Forcing bulbs to sprout indoors in winter (see special chapter), is full of bright surprises during a dreary season.

Children can be delightful creatures. Love them. Enjoy them. Spend time with them and you won't feel it was time wasted. They thrive on love.

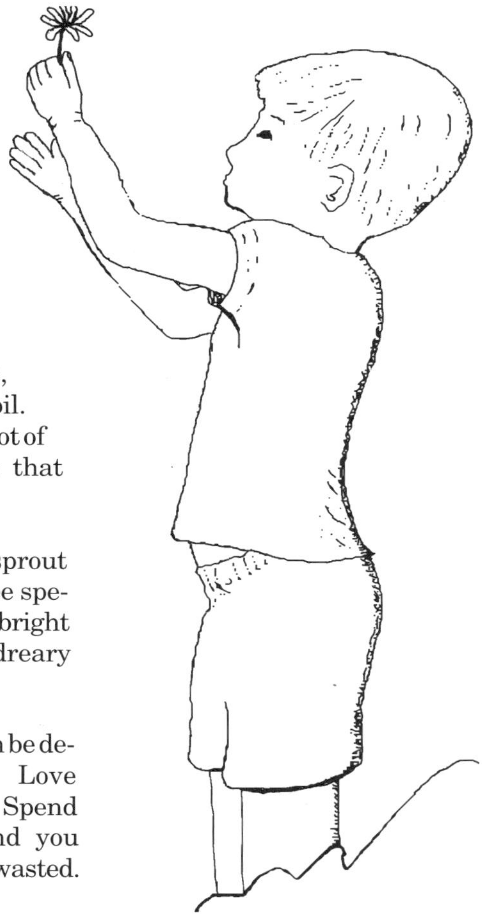

"The wonder years"

References cited:
[1] "Gardening with Children"
[2] "Gardens just for kids"
[3] "How does your garden grow?
[4] A Child's Garden, A Guide—
[5] "Indoor gardening ideas for kids"
[6] Readers Digest: [Basic]

Suggested references:
A Garden for Children
Earthly Delights
Youth Gardening
A Video Kit: Get Ready, Get Set, Grow

WONDERS OF NATURE

Did you ever wonder how water is able to go up so high in a tall tree? If you have lifted a pail of water you know that water is heavy. What makes it go up? Gravity would be pulling it down. Some trees are 300 feet tall. There are strong forces at work here. What are they? Where do they come from?

Tall tree

Life is a fascinating web of miracles. Daisies turn their faces toward the sun. Plants have been observed to grow better to the tune of soothing music, than to rock music. Plants are said to be happier when people talk to them. How can this be —do plants have ears? If plants are alive but don't have a heart, how is sap pumped through the plant? How does the green plant make its own food? Man can't make his own food. These are just a few of the many wonders of nature. People often say "Isn't Mother Nature grand!" Mother Nature is really an expression of God.

You can see God's handiwork in the wonderful complexity of life on earth. There is a complicated food chain where every living thing plays a part in the balance of nature. Many animals are dependent on each other for food. Many insects and animals are dependent on plants for food. Man is dependent on plants for food and oxygen. Nature has a very delicate balance where everything fits intricately together, and if you take out one cog in the wheel everything can be upset. Butterflies feed on specific plants, while moths are not as particular. Butterflies don't like windy areas, are attracted to native plants, and prefer tube-shaped flowers (color not so important).

Daisy facing the sun

Whether one is religious or not, man will never really be in complete control. No people or animals can survive without plants. They are our partners that we need in order to live. Even if we could live on some artificial food without depending on plants, it would be a dreary existence without them. People need plants more than plants need people. Even astronauts need plants, and any lengthy space voyages will require expert gardener-farmers to keep the inhabitants of their world happy and healthy by sharing their lives with those of plants.

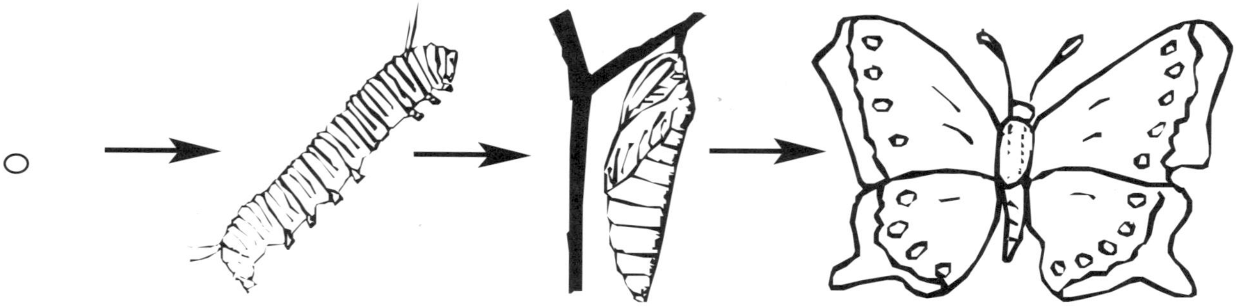

Egg — Caterpillar (larval stage) — Chrysalid (pupal stage) — Butterfly (adult stage)

WHAT CAUSES FALL COLOR ?

What makes the leaves of trees and shrubs turn deep scarlet, amber, gold, red, orange, or just fade from green to brown each fall? Not all plant species react the same, and the weather varies from year to year, causing fall color to vary. Fall foliage color depends on plant species, intensity of sun, night temperature, and amount of moisture in the soil that year. The most vibrant colors appear after a warm dry summer with early fall rains, after night temperatures drop below 45°F [1].

Big Leaf Maple (yellow)

All spring and summer the leaves act as factories to manufacture food for plants in a process called "photosynthesis". Chlorophyll absorbs the sun's energy to transform carbon dioxide and water to make carbohydrates (sugar and starch), and it gives leaves their green color. Green leaves also contain yellow or orange carotenoides, but most of the year yellowish colors are hidden by the greater amount of green pigment [2].

In fall, the drop in soil temperature, shorter days, and lack of moisture slow the plant's food manufacturing process. The sap flows more slowly as it dries and becomes more concentrated. The chlorophyll disappears, the green color disappears, and the yellowish colors become visible. Since the chemical composition of the sap residue varies, plants can have quite a variation of fall colors [3]. Other chemical changes occur in some plants to produce more pigments varying from yellow to red to blue and even purple [2].

Red Maple (scarlet)

Red maples and sumacs have acidic sap which causes the leaves to turn bright red! Ash trees growing on limestone can turn a royal-purplish-blue [3]. Hawthorn, Scarlet Oak, Amur maple and Pin Oak turn scarlet. Ginko turns a clear yellow, and drops all of its leaves at once. Sugar maple and Witch hazel turn gold. Dogwood turn orange, pink, through scarlet. Sumac turns orange-red. Euonymus turns pink or red. Sweet gum turns red, crimson, yellow, or bronze [1]. Stony mountain soils often dry earlier in the fall, and hardwoods growing on such soils often have the most dramatic color changes.

Another change takes place as the plants prepare for dormancy. A special layers of cells is produced that weakens the connection between leaves and their twigs, and the leaves flutter to the ground when disturbed by wind. Fallen leaves decompose, enriching the soil and providing nutrients for future generations of trees [3].

Calif. Black Oak (red)

Not all trees lose their leaves in fall. In the North, most broad-leaved trees shed their leaves, but some species like oak retain their brown leaves until spring. In the South, where winters are mild, some broad-leaved trees are evergreen (leaves stay green on tree all winter). In the Tropics, the broad-leaved evergreens shed their leaves continually, one at a time turning yellow and then falling, making way for new leaves. Because of climatic factors, only a few regions of the world have exceptional fall displays. Most conifers (pines, spruces, firs, hemlocks, cedars, etc) are evergreen both in the North and South. Their needles or scale-like leaves stay green all year, though some become brownish where winters are very cold. In conifers, the needle-like leaves may stay on the tree for 2-4 or more years, with some being shed each year [2].

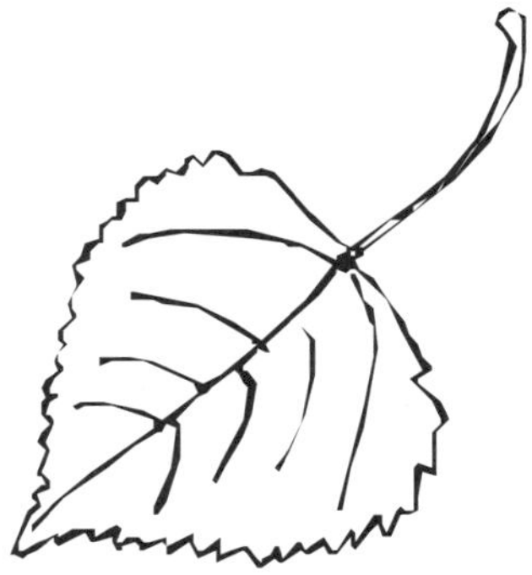

Aspen (yellow)

The first leaves to turn color are the water-loving, frost or drought-sensitive plants such as willow, aspen, wild plum and bracken fern. Next are the choke cherries, maples, and roses. And last to change are the more drought-resistant plants like oaks, buckthorn and elderberry. The change may occur anytime from September until November but most often occurs mid-October, and the fall color lasts usually 2-4 weeks. Warm wet fall weather can make the color change occur later, while cold dry weather can cause it to occur earlier [4].

References:

[1] Better Homes & Gardens
[2] Why Leaves Change Color USFS
[3] "Chemicals, not frost, create fall colors."
[4] "Chemical reaction causes leaf color change"

HEALTHY HOUSE PLANTS

Impatiens

Favorite plants not able to survive cold winters outdoors are often kept in the house year round as house plants. In Los Angeles geraniums, ivy, and wandering jew are grown outdoors, but in areas with cold winters, such as Lake Almanor, they may be grown as house plants. There are two types of house plants: those grown as foliage plants and those grown for flowers. Foliage plants can be green-leaved or variegated (different colors in stripes or patterns), often including splashes of reds and purples. Healthy plants require proper watering, feeding, light, humidity, temperature, and soil. Plants differ in their requirements, and some even require special conditions to bloom. For propagation of house plants see Propagation chapter. Here are some tips to keep house plants healthy and happy.

Winter, a forced rest period

Spring and summer are the active growth time for most plants. In fall their growth starts to slow down, except for fall-blooming plants. In winter the duration (number of hours), intensity (quality), and frequency (number of days) of sunshine are all less, and there may not be enough light for efficient photosynthesis. Encouraging house plants to grow actively during periods of low light on shorter winter days, can make them spindly and pale or promote rot, —even if other factors such as temperature, humidity, watering, and feeding are satisfactory. So, instead of encouraging them to grow in winter, most indoor plants should be forced to rest (except those under artificial lights). Restrict watering and stop application of fertilizer. A few house plants that drop their leaves in winter need cold temperature (above freezing) and even less water during their rest period [1].

Watering.

Plants, people, and animals all depend on water for life. A plant's roots act like a pipeline, pumping minerals and nutrients from the soil to its leaves. The water then evaporates from the leaves, and eventually falls back to the earth as rain, to supply the cycle all over again. Without water, there would be no way to transport food and waste products in the plant, and it could not live. That's what happens outdoors, and the same rules apply to indoor plants, only on a smaller scale. House plants contribute to a healthy indoor climate because plants raise humidity when they give off water, and they absorb carbon dioxide and indoor air pollutants to give us oxygen in return! (Without plants on earth to raise humidity and give us oxygen, people and animals could not exist.)

When air around a plant is too hot, the plant transpires more water. Large shade trees in your yard give off a lot of moisture on a hot day, which raises humidity and makes the local microclimate more comfortable for the plants and people! When the plant doesn't have enough water, it dries out and withers [2]. Remember, house plants depend completely on us for their water, since it doesn't usually rain indoors.

<u>Use only lukewarm water</u>! You can warm water inexpensively by placing gallon-size plastic milk jugs filled with tap water near your wood stove (but not so close that the jugs melt), or place the jugs in the sun on a hot day. Or heat water on top of your wood stove in a pot or kettle. Fish tank and sprout-growing water is also good for watering house plants. If your water is chlorinated it is beneficial to let it stand for a day in containers before using it on your plants (or to fill your fish tank).

Use warm water when watering house plants.

<u>There are several ways to apply water.</u> Use a lightweight watering can with a long, thin spout that can aim the water directly onto a soil surface under dense foliage. Or put warm water in a portable compressed air sprayer (holds more water). You can use an indoor hose with a narrow nozzle controlled by an on-off valve which is attached to a faucet (that

can give warm water). Plants can either be watered from the top, applying water directly on the soil; or from the bottom, standing the pot in a saucer of water for about half an hour and then pouring off the remaining water. I prefer careful watering from the top (except for African Violets).

Only use pots with drainage holes, and don't leave water in the saucer after watering. Without a drain hole (or if water is left in the saucer), the water fills the soil's pore spaces, displacing needed air, and most plants will rot [3]. Water a plant, wait about 5-10 minutes, then dump its saucer. Don't pour the saucer water into another plant! Dump all the saucers into a jug or pan and then use it outdoors (on your lawn is fine). This prevents the spread of disease from one house plant to another.

The ideal situation would be to water all your plants the same day, but some plants use more water than others. How often to water a plant depends on many factors like room temperature, type of plant, time of year. Put plants requiring less water in one room, and those requiring more water in a cooler room where their water demand will be reduced; then you could water all your plants the same day. A tomato plant uses much more water than a cactus plant, because thin-leaved plants require more water than thick-leaved succulents that store water. It is very difficult to underwater a succulent. Plants need more water during the growing season than when resting; too much water during the rest period can cause some plants to rot, while others may have abnormal growth. Plants need more water under higher temperatures, in such cases as hot dry summer weather, in hot dry rooms (winter), when hot sun shines directly into their window sill pot, or in a room with a wood stove. If you use plastic pots rather than clay pots, you won't have to water as often because plastic pots evaporate less water through the pot's sides and bottom. Some conditions require more frequent plant watering: a potting mixture that has sand or perlite added, a larger plant, a root-bound plant, or a plant in a room where the humidity is low [1].

How can you tell if a plant needs water? If a plant is dropping many leaves, it may be a sign of overwatering. Watering too often is more apt to kill a plant, than letting the plant get too dry. Wait until the soil drys somewhat, but never let it dry out completely or the plant will die. A generous watering once or twice a week is better than a light watering every day. With some experience you will soon be able to determine when your plants are thirsty. Don't try to judge water content of the potting soil from appearance of the plant alone, because by the time a plant is drooping or has wilted leaves, it may be too late. The soil is usually a better indicator of moisture content. Potting soil is usually dark brown when freshly watered and very light colored when dry. Pots also weigh a lot less when they are dry. Use a finger to test the soil an inch or two down, but use a pencil or a thin wooden stake to go farther down. If the soil is moist, it will stick to the stake and discolor it slightly [1]. If the soil is too dry before watering, water will either puddle on the surface a while before soaking in or it will run too quickly to the drainage hole (actually around the outside of the shrunken, dried soil ball) without wetting the soil. If this happens, set the pot in a tub of WARM water to soak until bubbles stop rising up in the soil. If the plant hasn't reached its "permanent wilting point", it will recover. Sometimes when the water sits on the surface too long, the soil has become compacted and needs to be loosened or replaced.

Give the right amount of water. Water plants thoroughly, but only often enough to prevent wilting. What type of house plant do you have? Does it need to be kept evenly moist or allowed to go dry between waterings? There are three categories to recommend for quantity and frequency of watering: plentifully, moderately, or sparingly. Plentifully— keep the soil moist throughout all the time, not permitting even the surface to dry out. Give enough at each watering to let some water flow through the drainage hole, then dump saucer. Moderately— water when the top half inch of the soil feels dry to your finger. Pour water onto the soil until a few drops appear from the drainage hole into the saucer. The soil will be thoroughly moistened but not saturated. Sparingly— when 2/3 of the soil has dried out. Test with a wooden stake. Cover the surface with water, so that it seeps down, but doesn't appear in the saucer. Test with stake again to see that the entire mixture is barely moist, but with no dry patches. Add more water if needed.

As you can see, *when* to water depends on many variables. I water an average of once a week —more often in summer and less often in winter (depending on the variables). When in doubt as to *how much* to give the plant, water until some water comes out the drainage hole. Wait 5-10 minutes and then dump the saucer.

Feeding (fertilizer).

Feeding house plants is something easily put off or forgotten. Learn to observe your plants. Note when each type of plant has its bloom period, produces new growth, or has a dormant season. Give fertilizer only when a plant needs it for growth and bloom, not during its winter rest period. With most fertilizers, except for the slow-release types, light (dilute) and frequent application give best results [3]. In general, fertilize every time you water during the active growing or blooming season (follow directions on the package). Time-release fertilizers release nutrients slowly over a long period of time, so they don't need to be applied as often as other types of fertilizer. Feed ferns only twice a year: in early spring and late summer, Asparagus fern and Boston fern should be fed only every 3-4 months [4]. Before feeding, be sure potting soil is thoroughly damp (if not using dilute fertilizer). If you thoroughly wash or mist their leaves using a compressed air sprayer or hand sprayer before you feed your plants, the soil will already be wet.

Hand sprayer

Use food designed for house plants, and follow the directions on the label. There are liquid types you dilute, and time release types (small round, or plant sticks) which you apply or feed every three or six months. You can spray the foliage of acid-loving plants with very dilute tea (it feeds them while washing the leaves), and it also helps those that are dehydrated from dry air (becoming brown at the tips).

There are different "recipes" for fertilizer. If you feed all your plants with a high nitrogen fertilizer (12-6-6) or Rapid Grow (23-19-17) then flowering plants won't bloom, because high nitrogen only encourages green leafy growth. For flowering plants use a fertilizer where the second number (Potassium) is higher than the first (like 5-10-5), and it will encourage both healthy root growth and blooming. I recommend **VF-11** (very dilute, but excellent) for all house plants. If you use **Miracle Grow** (15-30-15) for all house plants both foliage and flowering, or **Rapid Grow** (23-19-17) only for foliage plants that need a dose of high nitrogen —use a very dilute solution. Add these plant foods to warm water each time you water plants during the growing season. After planting or transplanting use warm water containing **B1 solution** to encourage healthy root growth and lessen transplant shock. See also Soils chapter.

Light requirements.

All plants require light 12-16 hours a day in order to maintain active growth, but vary in the duration of light needed. Plants with variegated or purple leaves, cacti, and flowering plants need the most light [1]. Some plants actually prefer less light i.e. Philodendron, Diffenbauchia, Dracena, Sansevieria, Pandanus, and Nephrthytis (Syngonium) [5].

Most house plants receive their light from a window, so be careful where you put them. Give them good light, but not hot, direct sunlight. In hot south and west windows, set the plants back from the window or use thin curtains. East windows are excellent for most plants, while those needing less light prefer a north window. Try to give plants light as it was in their native habitat: Cacti (desert) need full sun, but tropical plants that live near the ground, need shade. Plants grow towards the light, so rotate them a half turn each time you water them (if needed), so they won't grow lopsided.

Indoor plants located away from windows, can be given needed light by illuminating them 12-16 hours a day with high intensity fluorescent lights. Use two 40-watt fluorescent bulbs, one with cool white (blues) and one warm white (reds), or get the more expensive, specially formulated "grow light" bulbs for your plants [6]. Put the lights on a timer. The lights can be mounted under a shelf, hung over the plants, or enclosed in a special canopy held over the plants. Paint the surface behind the grow lights white to reflect the light better over a large area. Plants grown under artificial lights usually have more light, so they grow faster than other indoor plants, and thus require more water and fertilizer.

Planter boxes.

Planter boxes can be used effectively both inside your home and outdoors. One technique is to hold potting soil directly in the planter, or arrange individual potted plants inside the planter on medium-size gravel or wood blocks.

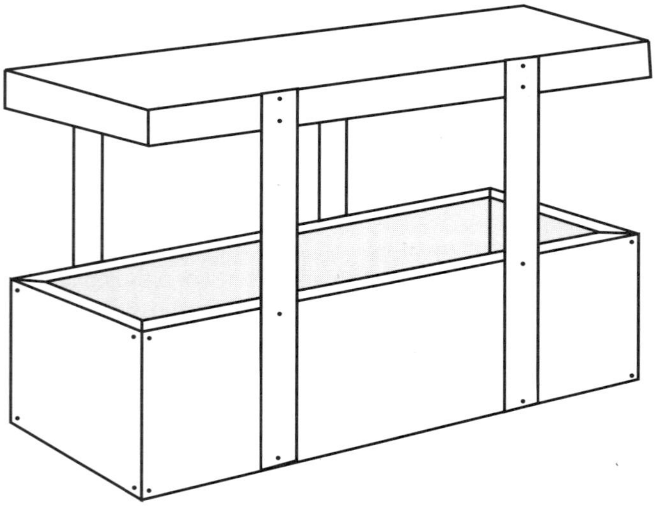

A planter box

Indoors. Boxes need a water-tight liner best made of galvanized metal, and painted with asphalt to prevent leaks [5]. For a temporary liner, staple two layers of polyethylene inside the planter. Place potted plants in the planter box, using the same size pots. Fill the rest of the box around the potted plants with unmilled sphagnum moss, pea-size gravel, or marble chips. This technique is popular in restaurants too! Take individual pots ***out*** of the planter box to water them.

Outdoors. Design the planter so it is raised up off the soil or cement at least one inch for good drainage. Drill many holes in the bottom of the planter about 3-4 inches apart. Make the holes at least 1/4 inch (or better 1/2 inch) in diameter so they won't swell shut or plug up with soil. Then stain or paint the outside for looks, but seal the wood on the inside with Thompson's water seal. Then either place individual potted plants in the planter, or use it like a big pot and fill it with soil. If filling it with soil, place hardware cloth, fiberglass, or burlap fabric layer across bottom of planter to keep soil from falling out of the drain holes. If the planter box is sheltered under the roof overhang, it won't get watered by rain in winter, so perennials planted there will depend on you for water all year.

Location and temperature.

House plants prefer temperatures of 75° days and 65° nights. African violets are the most fussy, but most plants can generally do well with cooler temperatures. Higher summertime temperatures of 80-90°F will not harm most indoor plants as long as humidity is kept high [1]. Avoid such indoor desert spots as near heaters, heating ducts, and wood stoves. Also *don't* put hanging plants, or plants on shelves near the ceiling in a room with a wood stove! Keep your plants away from exhaust fans, doorways, or open windows, as blasts of cold winter air may chill or freeze the plants. Avoid having them near heavy traffic areas in the house, since they can be in the way and may be damaged by passing people and pets.

A plant on a window sill on a cold winter night (and hot summer days), is trapped in an indoor "freezer" between the window and a heavy curtain. It is not able to get warmth from the room, and chilling can harm the plant. On extremely cold nights (or hot summer days) move the plants away from the windows, or put cardboard or layers of newspapers between the glass and the plants [1].

Humidity.

House plants do best at a humidity of 70-75% (kitchens and bathrooms generally have the highest humidity). We expect our house plants to live in conditions as dry as a desert, but most of our house plants are from the moist tropics! With old fashioned radiators and swamp coolers our plants were very happy, but now that we have wood stoves and air conditioners, plants have a dry air problem here in the West. Dry air causes static electricity, dries human eyes, noses, and throats, and can also damage house plants. Too little or too much humidity is uncomfortable for both humans and plants. Too much humidity can be solved by opening some windows. Too little humidity can be remedied in several ways, since evaporation of water raises humidity.

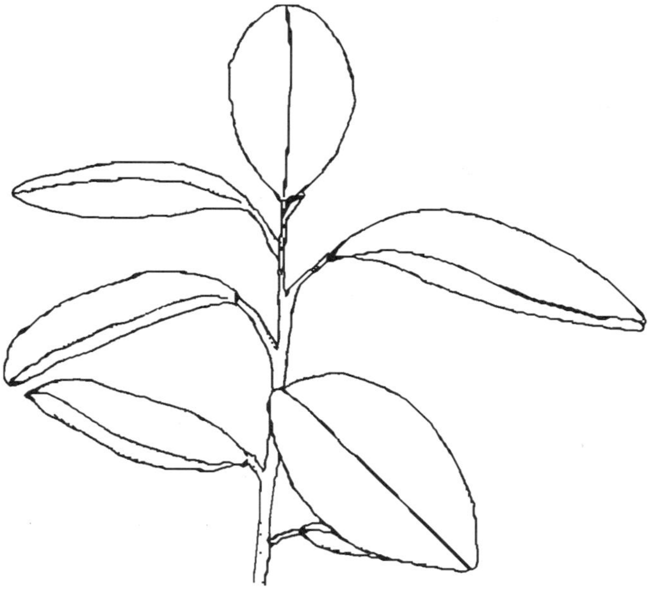

Rubber Plant,
a typical house plant

One way to raise humidity is to place an open pot of water on top of your wood stove. Select a pot with no seams, or it will eventually leak if it steams itself dry. I use a heavy aluminum milk bucket that was ordered through a catalog. Commercial humidifiers work fine, but a pot of water works free.

Place pot over pebbles.

Many foliage plants in an area can raise a room's humidity. A greenhouse is very humid because so many plants are transpiring there. Humidity there is usually regulated by how often you water or mist. To raise humidity between waterings, you can splash water on the floor. If humidity or temperature get too high, open a window or turn on fans.

Several plants together create their own microclimate. Group plants together on a window sill, in a tray, in the corner of a room, in a mini-garden, or planter box. Space the plants so they get enough light and air to circulate between them. Large or small trays can be filled with pebbles and water, but keep pot bottoms above the water level so roots won't rot. If pebbles are not available, use a block of wood in a saucer. Put plants together that need similar growing conditions. For example cactus and succulents could be clustered in a dry, warm area; while ferns could be grouped in a moister, warm area.

If you only have a few plants in your house, here are some ways to raise humidity. Try placing a glass (or pan) of water between (or near) plants. Fish tanks evaporate water too! Or place a pie pan of water filled with colored stones (aquarium type) or pebbles under a solitary house plant. One pot can be set inside a larger pot, and the space between can be filled with wet sphagnum moss or peat moss, but the plant still needs regular watering [6]. Misting your plants regularly every morning (so the leaves dry and don't get mildew) can raise humidity temporarily, but often it leaves mineral spots or dust spatters on the foliage. Don't mist your plants just before strong sunlight will shine on them, or the small drops of water will act like magnifying glasses and may burn spots on the leaves.

Place glass of water between plants.

Water quality

Usually tap water is satisfactory for watering and misting house plants, but many areas have hard water that contains harmful salts or minerals, or it is artificially softened with sodium. Every time you water or mist plants with hard water, whitish mineral deposits are left on leaves and stem (causing spots), in the soil, and on the pot. In the natural habitat of house plants, rain leaches away some of the minerals and others are neutralized by acid from organic matter. Since it doesn't rain often in houses, we need to <u>rinse off the foliage</u>, <u>water plants with plenty of water so it runs through the soil (at least once a month)</u>, and <u>change the soil at least once a year</u> to maintain healthy plants! Frequent washing of leaves, especially the undersides, cleans off mineral deposits before they get a chance to build up. Washing helps leaves to breathe better, besides making it harder for pests and disease to become established.

Try using a sponge to wash the leaves. Support the underside of large leaves with one hand, while you gently wipe the upperside.

Wash leaves with a hand spray bottle and gently wipe off the dust with a soft cloth or sponge, use a compressed air sprayer in a greenhouse, a shower extension nozzle on a bathtub filled with potted plants, or spray them outdoors with a fan nozzle on a garden hose. Avoid getting spray, mist, or water on fuzzy leaves (African Violet or Fuzzy Charlies).

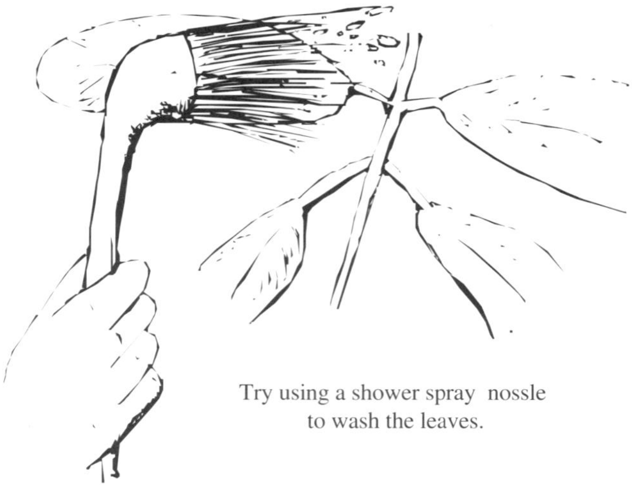

Try using a shower spray nossle to wash the leaves.

White fuzzy or hairy-leaved plants should be brushed with a soft camel hair brush [7]. When a white crust or a mold layer forms on the soil surface, use a spoon and just lift the crust off and throw it away. However if white deposits penetrate below the surface, gently remove the plant from the pot, wash the pot, and repot the plant with new soil.

If you have very hard water you can collect rainwater, boil the water (letting the minerals settle out), buy demineralized water, or filter the minerals out before using it to water or mist your plants. Demineralization filters are commercially available (the easiest and best way), or make your own filter using peat moss [9], or agricultural charcoal [8]. Punch holes in the bottom of a half-gallon milk carton, then fill 3/4 full with agricultural charcoal or peat moss. If your house tap water is artificially softened with sodium, use an outside faucet to water your house plants [3]. Don't buy a water softener just for watering your plants, as it is more apt to damage your plants instead of help them [1].

Make a homemade filter.

"Leaf Shine" is a commercial product used to make leaves shiny. Use only on top leaf surface and read directions, because it can kill some plants. I don't recommend the use of such chemicals, when spraying plants with demineralized water or just washing them can give you shiny leaves, free!

When buying a house plant.

The best time of year to purchase a house plant is spring or fall, as the outside temperature then is closer to that of their "home" environment, and doesn't present a drastic shock for the plant. Plants are very sensitive to drafts and chills. If you have to move plants in cold weather, wrap them individually in paper, pack plants together in a cardboard box, and place a hot-water bottle filled with hot (not boiling) water in the box [1].

Check over the new plant carefully for signs of bugs and disease before you buy it. Quarantine the new plant at home by isolating it from your other house plants for a while. Keep it under observation, until you are sure it is healthy.

Insect pests and disease in house plants.

Avoid overcrowding. House plants lacking good air circulation are more subject to spreading diseases or pests — especially mildew and spider mite— because these pests thrive in still, dry air. That's why greenhouses often use fans to move the air.

Watch for first signs of insects or disease and treat the plant immediately (try washing plant first with water). Separate infected plant from other house plants while it is under observation. It may take several washings. If that doesn't work, change the soil. If that doesn't work, dab off leaves with Q-tips soaked in alcohol, or spray with a solution of slightly soapy water. As a last resort, identify the disease and apply appropriate chemical. Never spray fungicides or insecticides in your house (take plant outdoors to spray it). Destroy badly infected plants before disease can spread. Sometimes breaking off the infected branch solves the problem. See Insect pests chapter for more details.

A succulent plant

Indoor air pollution? Get a plant!

We have pollutants in our home from wood smoke, fumes from carpet adhesives, paneling, furniture, drapes, wood stains, paint, and cooking. To help clean indoor air, open doors and windows when weather permits and use exhaust fans vented to the outside in your bathroom, near your cooking stove, and clothes dryer. Plants can help, too! According to National Aeronautics and Space Administration (NASA) scientists, some indoor plants absorb many home pollutants. Use at least one 10-12 inch potted plant per 100 square feet of floor space. In a test, plants in sealed chamber removed as much as 87% of toxic indoor air pollutants in 24 hours. Scientists think pollutants are absorbed through plant leaves, roots, and bacteria that live on the foliage. Recommended plants to remove formaldehyde fumes are: philodendrons, spider plants, golden pothos and snake plants. For Benezene fumes use: gerba daisies, chrysanthemums, and other flowering plants. For general air purification try: reed, palm, English ivy, peach lily, mother-in-law's tongue, Chinese evergreen, dracena, aloe and banana tree [10].

Special soil for container plants

Container plants need a porus, well drained soil, yet hold just enough moisture. Roots must be able to penetrate the soil easily. Drainage must be fast enough so that the roots don't rot in soggy soil, but still retain enough moisture so you don't have to water the plants constantly. Commercial potting soils vary slightly from brand to brand, but they all are specially designed for container plants. Commercial potting soils are highly recommended, are available in nurseries and garden centers, and you can use them right out of the bag.

Whether you are potting a lot of house plants or just wish to make your own potting soil, remember that any soil mix used in the house must be sterile (commercially sold products are already sterilized). Soil-borne pests, diseases and weed seeds present in garden soils, when brought in the house with warm, moist, low light conditions, can cause health problems for your house plants [3]. Four ways to make your homemade potting soil:

- a mixture of 1/3 commercial potting soil, 1/3 peat moss, and 1/3 perlite (for roses).
- a mixture of 1/3 commercial potting soil, 1/3 peat moss, and 1/3 sterile sand.
- a mixture of 3 parts commercial potting soil to 1 part vermiculite (I prefer this).
- a mixture of sterilized garden soil, peat moss, and perlite or sterile sand.

Then add one tablespoon rock phosphate and one tablespoon limestone to each gallon of soil mixture. Before using the soil mixture, mix thoroughly together, and then add WARM water until the mixture is crumbly moist. I use my kitchen plastic dishpan to mix the soil and water. ("Just playin' in the mud" can bring back childhood memories.) Whatever soil you use, wet it thoroughly before placing a plant in it, or the dry soil will kill the fine root hairs instantly!

Some plants have more specific soil needs. Cactus (and succulents) require very good soil drainage so they need a soil mix of 1/2 sand or perlite, 1/4 potting soil, and 1/4 peat moss. They need less watering, and more sunlight. Ferns need a soil mix high in organic matter: 1/2 peat moss, to 1/4 potting soil, and 1/4 sand. Ferns like soil that is moist but not waterlogged. Put an inch of pebbles or other drainage material in the bottom of a pot. Never allow ferns to stand in water! Fern fronds appreciate daily misting, but mist them in the morning so foliage can dry off. Ferns require bright, indirect light (no direct sunlight), and they like north-facing windows.

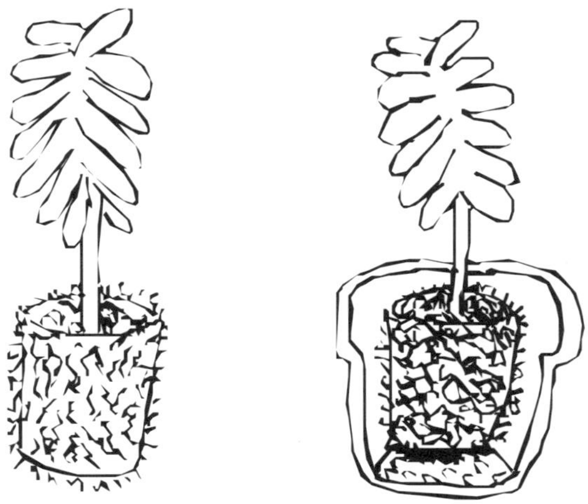

Rootbound plant moved to a larger pot.

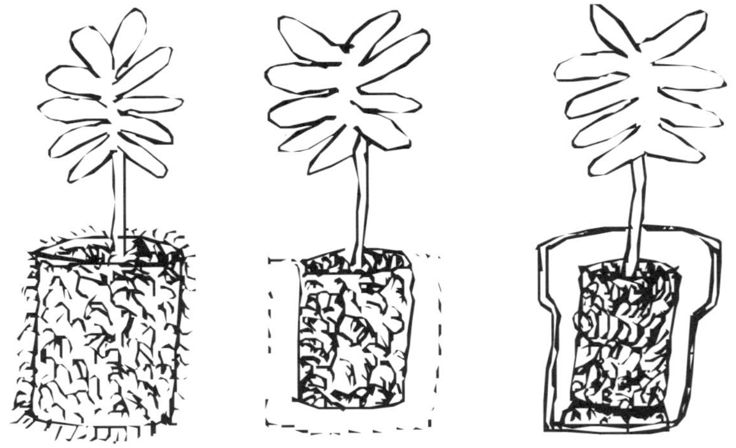

Rootbound plant with its' roots trimmed, so it can be put back in the same size pot.

Transplanting (repotting)

Roots can become quite crowded in a pot, and soil deteriorates over time. When roots are coming out the drainage hole or appear at the soil surface, it is rootbound and time to transplant. This is also a good time to change the soil, get a new or cleaned pot, wash the plant, divide or prune plants that too large, and to trim off brown tips on leaves. Young plants should be transplanted into the next size **larger pot** once a year, usually in spring. Older plants need to be repotted less frequently (every 2-3 years), usually back into the **same size pot**, but trim the roots and tops equally, wash the pot, wash the leaves and stem, and then place plant back in the cleaned (or new) pot. Or a plant might have been placed in too large a pot to start with, so transplant it into **a smaller pot**.

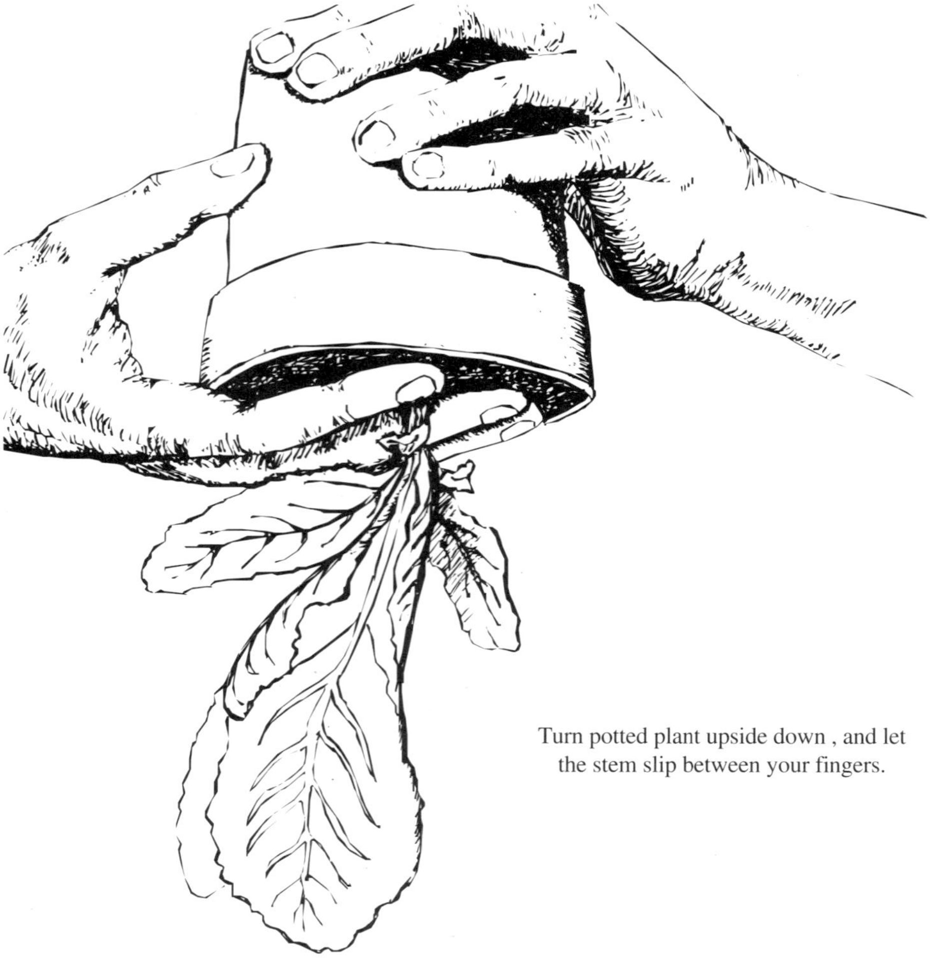

Turn potted plant upside down , and let the stem slip between your fingers.

Use clean supplies. When transplanting plants, use sterile soil mix, cleaned or new pots, and washed plants. Wash the leaves and stem of the plants with only warm water. Soak the used pots in hot water containing Chlorox and dish soap (use 1 part Chlorox in 10 parts water), and then scrape off any whitish material (alkali and minerals) with a table knife and scouring pad. When it is clean, rinse and dry the pot.

Get equipment together before you start. I place a big piece of polyethylene plastic on my kitchen table. Then I put on the table, the plastic dishpan of wet soil, a gallon plastic milk jug full of warm water containing one cap full of B1 solution, the plants to be transplanted, the clean pot, table knife, spoon, pruning shears, and scissors. I wear rubber gloves because frequent contact with soil and water causes my hands and fingernails to dry out and crack. (Shake some baby powder or baking soda into the rubber gloves before putting them on to keep them dry inside.)

Select the right pot. The new pot should be 1 inch larger all around the root mass (sides and bottom), and allow 1 inch top space for watering. Moving from a 3-inch to a 10-inch pot is called "overpotting". If you use too large a pot relative to the size of plant, unused water is held in the pot too long, and the roots will rot [2]. A plant can be up to two times taller than the height of the pot, but if it is taller —repot it to a larger pot. Use only pots that have a drainage hole. **Clay pots** need gravel, a piece of hardware cloth, or a pot shard (broken piece of clay pot) placed convex side up over the hole to keep soil in the pot. Clay pots have to be soaked in water for a few hours before potting, or they will absorb water from the soil and dry out the plant roots. Plants don't dry out as fast in **plastic pots** and they are easier to get out of the pot. In plastic pots, I use one-ply kleenex (it decomposes) cut in squares slightly larger than the bottom of the pot to stop soil erosion.

Ready to transplant. Turn potted plant upside down allowing plant stem to slip between your fingers. Slightly squeeze the plastic pot and tap its' bottom with your hand or a stick to loosen the root ball. If it still sticks to the pot, run your knife inside pot all around the edge where soil and pot meet. When plant is out of the pot, remove as much of the old soil as possible. If half the roots are dead or sick, cut them off. Put some new soil on bottom of the clean pot. Place cleaned plant in center of the pot, and fill in around it with new potting soil to within one inch of rim. Tap or jiggle the pot as you add soil to help eliminate air pockets. Pack soil firmly with your fingers, and then water well with WARM water containing B1 solution. Do not feed plants (fertilizer) for two weeks after planting as roots are very sensitive. When you begin to fertilize, gradually increase the dosage up to normal concentrations. This transplanting procedure also applies to outdoor container plants.

Clean the area. After transplanting house plants into clean pots with clean soil, put them in a fairly sterile area while you clean up the rest of your plants. Don't set a clean plant down next to one that has spider mite, and don't put the clean plant right back where it was, (yet). Clean and sterilize the area where you will be putting the clean plants. Use hot water, detergent and Chlorox and wash all surfaces; floor, wall, window sill, window etc, and vacuum the rug.

The best time to transplant is spring, but do repot root-bound plants and those with other problems when they need it during the year. If you repot with clean soil at least once a year, and keep leaves washed, you can avoid many problems.

House plants vs pets and children.

Since many plants are poisonous, read the chapter on poisonous plants so you will be informed, and keep children or pets from harm. Keep poisonous sprays out of reach of pets and children, and keep them from brushing against or eating plants that have just been sprayed. Don't leave fertilizer or poison in a bucket or open container where an animal or child might drink.

Cats often use large house plant pots as their potty. Discourage them by mulching with "sharp" decorative rock. Use wide, sturdy pots that cats can't easily knock over.

Cats like to nibble grass-like leaves, so plant some grass or catnip in flower pots just for them, and they will probably leave your other plants alone. If there is one of your plants that the cat particularly likes to nibble —put powdered ginger on the leaf tips. First mist the plant, and then put the powder on the leaves with your fingers. Add more as needed to reinforce the point for the cat (11).

Talk to your plants?

When you talk to your plants you breathe carbon dioxide on them, increasing the amount of carbon dioxide in the air, and your plant will grow faster. Some people believe that plants also respond to speech, music, or psychic vibrations, but these claims are not conclusively proven. However, talking to a plant may be as healthy for people as it is for the plant, since it makes some people feel good and plants can't talk back!

Bring house plants outdoors in the summer?

If you bring tender house plants outdoors in the summer, they can get sunburn, and can also pick up diseases and bugs from outside. Then, when you bring them in the house, they will spread their bugs to other plants. Container plants shouldn't be left in the hot sun on a concrete porch in summer, especially in clay or dark-colored pots, because soil temperature in the pots can reach well over 100°F and that heat will not only dry out the plant, but cook it. Soil temperature is much more critical to a plant's survival than air temperature. Plants can usually survive hot air temperatures if they are properly watered, but direct sunlight can damage or "burn" plants that grew up in indoor shade.

While you are away.

Many house plants die while the owner is away from home on a vacation or business trip. If you can't get someone to care for your plants, there are some things you can do. If you will be gone only 1-2 weeks, you may not have a problem. Room temperatures less than 50°F are too cold for house plants. You can leave the heat set at 50°F in one room and close the doors to save money (if you have electric heat or a heater with a thermostat). The best room for this is the bathroom for two reasons. First, you need to keep the pipes from freezing anyway; and second, you can raise the room humidity by putting about one inch of water in the tub. If you want to put the plants <u>in</u> the tub, first lay a piece of plastic (so the bricks won't scratch the tub), then place bricks over the plastic, add about one inch of water, and then set the plants on the bricks. This is to keep the plants from sitting in the water (and rotting). Water the plants thoroughly just before you leave. The plants won't have to be watered as often because of the high humidity. African Violets seem to be the most sensitive plant to changes of temperature and light, so find a warmer location for them or ask a special friend to "keep" them while you are gone.

If you will be gone longer than two weeks, you can expect that some of your plants will die. You can keep the moisture in better by covering the plants with a polyethylene sheet. Anchor the sheet but don't seal it, so there will be some air movement. Prop up the sheet so it doesn't touch the plants. Or you can cover each plant with a plastic bag (not touching the leaves), sealing it around the pot with a rubber band. You have already reduced the air temperature, so also reduce the lighting to eight hours/day (don't have them near a sunny window!), so the plants don't grow too fast, and they will need less water [5]. Removing all flowers and flower buds will also reduce water use [6].

There are special plant boxes and pots designed for long-term watering. They have a water container from which plants can draw the water they need. They don't have to be used just for vacations, but they are expensive especially if you have a lot of indoor plants [5].

Some other methods are: Pack the plants in a deep box, surrounding them with crumpled, wet newspapers or wet peat moss. Or use an elaborate capillary system using a wick, where water is seeped from a large central container of water down to the individual potted plants surrounding it [6].

Pruning and Staking

Little pruning is needed on house plants. Plants can be made bushier by frequent "pinching back" of the tip growth —both the growing tip and side branch tips. Instead of a geranium three feet tall on one stem, you'll have ten blooms on a nicely shaped, one foot high bushy plant. Prune overgrown plants to the shape you want by cutting long branches off just above a node. Train climbers to a bamboo stake or trellis frame, tying the shoots loosely with inconspicuous plant ties. Climbing plants with aerial roots are best trained on moss-wrapped poles or on wire frames filled with sphagnum moss, kept moist.

<u>References cited:</u>

[1] Readers Digest: Success with House Plants
[2] "House plant care"——
[3] Sunset Western Garden Book p 80.
[4] Better Homes & Gardens
[5] Indoor Gardens for Decorative Plants
[6] Readers Digest: Basic
[7] Gardening indoors with house plants (Poincelot)
[8] "Plant-Growing Magic
[9] Success with House Plants, Packet #69, p 3.
[10] General Wellness & Health Related, USFS
[11] "Some tips for keeping cats from house plants"

POISONOUS PLANTS

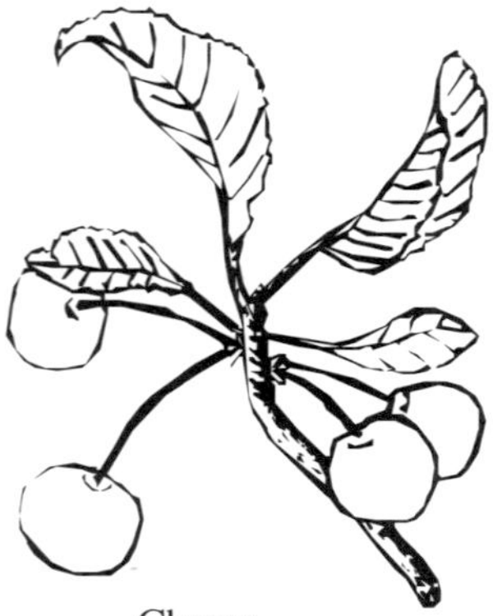

Cherry

Plants listed in this chapter are not limited to just the ones that grow here (where there are cold winters). Permission was granted by the editor of The Sacramento Bee, and Patricia Sullivan to print this quote from her article, "Poisonings, 26 plants cause most problems" [1]:

"Nine of ten plant poisonings reported nation wide each year can be traced to just 26 plants. You probably have one in your home or garden. And 88 percent of poisonings occur with children under 5 years of age.

This information has been gathered by Joe M. DiTomaso, a Weed Scientist at the University of California at Davis who surveyed poison control centers in 81 major metropolitan areas. DiTomaso estimates there are between 150,000 and 750,000 accidental poisonings annually throughout the country. The recent rise in reported poisonings is because reporting methods have improved, DiTomaso says, and also because gardening and keeping house plants have become so popular.

Poisonous plants frequently are the most colorful. Poinsettias, oleanders and azaleas are examples. So are some plants with colorful fruit, such as holly.

DiTomaso's definition of poisonous is 'any plant that disrupts the normal bodily function. It doesn't necessarily have to kill.' The disruption will vary in severity, depending on the plant, amount ingested and size of the person. **It can be a very small amount.** Half an oleander leaf can kill a child; one oleander leaf can kill an adult, and two will kill any animal, DiTomaso observes. But few plant poisonings are fatal.

His warnings, particularly for parents of small children include knowing what is poisonous, keeping such plants out of the reach of children, marking poisonous plants and teaching children not to eat them, knowing what to do in case of poisoning and having handy the phone number of the nearest poison control center.

A toll-free number for U.C. Davis Poison Control Center is 1-800-342-9293. For accidental poisoning of any kind, give the victim water, call the center for instructions, and always have on hand syrup of Ipecac, (to induce vomiting), but don't use it unless the Poison Control says to.

The aroid plant family is most frequently involved in poisonings. Easily recognizable by common names, some are among the most popular house plants: philodendron, dieffenbachia (dumbcane), anthurium, pothos, syngonium, and calla lily. Some common house plants are frequently reported to have caused poisonings but are not actually toxic. They include jade plant, schefflera, African violets, spider plant, and Swedish Ivy.

Poinsettias, Jerusalem cherry and mistletoe make the list because of the Christmas season when they are brought indoors. Poinsettia and all the members of the spurge family have a caustic sap—a milky, white latex —which burns the throat.

Food such as potatoes and tomatoes, members of the deadly nightshade family, have poisonous leaves and green fruit (cooking destroys the toxins). Rhubarb is another food that has poisonous parts. Only its stalk is edible.

'So few people know anything about mushrooms.' DiTomaso observes. *'They're difficult to identify. Certain mushrooms that are considered poisonous in one country are edible in another. Toxicity varies from ecological condition or from geographical location.'*

The most toxic substance in plants is ricin, found in castor beans. A minuscule amount injected in an adult is fatal. One of the most poisonous plants in North America is Poison Hemlock. Children are (commonly) poisoned by making flutes out of hemlock's hollow stems."

Steve Young, a U.S. Forest Service Hydrologist, has this to say about mushrooms: Some mushrooms contain extremely powerful toxins. Would you bet your life on your ability to identify which ones are safe? Every year, newspapers carry items about unknowing people trying to enjoy wild mushrooms, and about the often tragic consequences of their mistake. If you have **ANY** doubts about wild mushrooms, pass them by and treat yourself to some store-bought, safe ones. Some of the bigger supermarkets, deli's, and gourmet food stores in larger towns and cities now carry several kinds of mushrooms for a diverse choice of flavors.

The following tables summarize the results of Joe M. DiTomaso's research (reprinted here with his permission).

PLANTS REPORTED MOST POISONOUS TO HUMANS IN U.S. (in descending order of occurrence)

COMMON NAME	GENUS & SPECIES	FAMILY
1) Philodendrons*	Philodendron spp.	Araceae
2) Dumbcane	Dieffenbachia spp.	Araceae
3) Mushrooms	———	———
4) Holly	Ilex spp.	Aquifoliaceae
5) Poinsettia	Euphorbia pulcherrima	Euphorbiaceae
6) Nightshades	Solanum spp.	Solanaceae
7) Jerusalem cherry	Solanum pseudocapsicum	Solanaceae
8) English ivy	Hedera helix	Araliaceae
9) Rhubarb	Rheum rhaponticum	Polygonaceae
10) Azalea & Rhododendron	Rhododendron spp.	Ericaceae
11) Daffodil, jonquil	Narcissus spp.	Amaryllidaceae
12) Caladium	Caladium spp.	Araceae
13) Mistletoe	Phoradendron spp.	Viscaceae
14) Lily-of-the-valley	Convallaria majalis	Liliaceae
15) Oleander	Nerium oleander	Apocynaceae
16) Wisteria	Wisteria spp.	Leguminosae
17) Yew	Taxus spp.	Taxaceae
18) Buckeye, horsechestnut	Aesculus spp.	Hippocastanaceae
19) Pokewood, pokeberry	Phytolacca americana	Phytolaccaceae
20) Pyracantha, firethorn	Pyracantha spp.	Rosaceae
21) Iris	Iris spp.	Iridaceae
22) Datura, jimsonweed	Datura spp.	Solanaceae
23) Castor bean	Ricinus communis	Euphorbiaceae
24) Honeysuckle	Lonicera spp.	Caprifoliaceae
25) Poison oak, ivy, & sumac	Toxicodendron spp.	Anacardiaceae
26) Poison hemlock	Conium maculatum	Umbelliferae

*Philodendrons includes: calocasia, pothos, calla lilies, alocasia, jack-in-the-pulpit, and split-leaved philodendron.

PLANTS FREQUENTLY REPORTED TO CAUSE SKIN RASHES, IRRITATION, OR ALLERGIC REACTIONS (NOT TOXIC)

COMMON NAME	GENUS & SPECIES	FAMILY
1) Jade plant	Crassula argentea	Crassulaceae
2) Schefflera, Umbrella tree	Brassaia actinophylla	Araliaceae
3) Begonia	Begonia spp.	Begoniaceae
4) Spider plant	Chlorophytum comosum	Lilaceae
5) Wandering Jew	Tradescantia spp.	Commelinaceae
6) Swedish ivy	Plectranthus spp.	Labiatae
7) African violet	Saintpaulia ionantha	Gesneriaceae
8) Wandering Jew	Zebrina pendula	Commelinaceae
9) Creeping charlie	Pilea nummularifolia	Urticaceae
10) Rubber plant	Ficus elastica	Moraceae
11) Snake plant	Sansevieria spp.	Agavaceae

In the following chart, Joe DiTomaso lists 26 plants, marked with a *, which are most commonly reported as causing poisoning. Those with (*) were mentioned with one of the 26 on original list. Additional sources were [2,3,4].

Poisonous Parts of Common House & Garden Plants:

FLOWER GARDEN PLANTS

Plant	Toxic part
Autumn Crocus (Colchicum), Meadow Crocus	all parts
Azalea*	all parts
Bleeding Heart, Dutchman's Breeches	foliage, roots
Christmas Rose	rootstocks, leaves
Daffodil (Narcissus spp.)*	bulb
Delphinium (Delphinium spp.)	seeds, young plants
English ivy (Hedera)*	berries, leaves
Four-O'Clock (Mirabilis)	roots, seeds
Foxglove (Digitalis)	leaves, seeds, flowers
Hyacinth	bulbs
Hydrangea	bud, leaves
Impatiens	Don't eat any parts
Iris, Blue Flag*	underground stems
Jonquil (*)	bulbs
Larkspur (Delphinium spp.)	seeds, and entire plant
Lily-of-the-valley (Convallaria)*	leaves, flowers, (entire plant)
Monkshood (Aconitum)	roots, seeds, leaves
Morning Glory (Ipomoea)	seeds
Narcissus	bulb
Oleander (Nerium)*	leaves, branches (entire plant)
Opium poppy (Papaver)	unripe seed pod
Peony	roots
Star-of-Bethlehem (Ornithogalum)	bulbs
Violet, pansy	seeds

HOUSE PLANTS

Plant	Toxic part
Caladium (Caladium spp.)*	entire plant
Castor Bean (Ricinus)*	seeds
Dieffenbachia (Dieffenbachia), dumbcane*	all parts
Jequirity Bean	seeds, esp. orange spot
Mistletoe (Viscum)*	berries
Mother-in-laws-tongue	leaves
Poinsettia*	leaves, (skin rash)
Rosary Pea	seeds
Philodendron*	leaves
Wandering Jew	leaves

ORNAMENTAL PLANTS

Plant	Toxic Part
Daphne	berries, bark, leaves
English Holly (Ilex)*	berries
Golden Chain	bean-like capsules in which seeds are suspended.
Jerusalem cherry (Solanum)*	fruits
Lantana, Red or wild sage(Lantana)	green berries
Magnolia	flower
Mock Orange	berries, leaves, & bark
Oleander	No cut flowers in house; don't use for hot dog sticks
Pyracantha, firethorn*	?
Rhododendron (Rhododendron spp.), Western Azalea.*	all parts
Wisteria (Wisteria)*	seeds, pods

Yellow Jessamine (Cestrum)	berries (causes skin rashes)
Yew (Taxus)*	all parts, esp. seeds, except the red pulp of the fruit.

TREES AND SHRUBS

Plant	Toxic Part
Apple	seeds
Black Locust	bark, sprouts, foliage, seeds
Buckeye (Aesculus), horse chestnut*	leaves, flowers, seeds
Cherry	leaves, twigs, seeds
Elderberry	all parts, esp. roots
Oak	foliage, acorns
Peach	leaves, twigs, esp. seeds.

VEGETABLE GARDEN PLANTS

Plant	Toxic part
Potato (Solanum) (*)	all green parts, and sprouts
Rhubarb (Rheum)*	leaves
Tomato (Lycopersicum)	green parts

WILD PLANTS

Amanita (deadly)

Plant	Toxic part
Carolina Yellow Jasmine (Gelsemium)	flowers
Baneberry	all parts
Buttercup	all parts
Honeysuckle (Lonicera spp.)	?
Jack-in-the-pulpit	all parts
Jimson Weed, (Datura), Thornapple*	all parts, esp. seeds
Marsh Marigold (cowslip)	all parts
Moonseed	berries
Mushrooms (Fly Agaric, Death cap, and several Amanita)*	all parts
Nightshades (Solanum)*	all parts
Poison Hemlock (Conium)*	all parts
Poison Ivy, Oak, & Sumac*	all parts
Phytolacca (Pokeweed)	berries, roots.
Skunk cabbage	leaves, rhizomes
Water Hemlock (Cowbane)	all parts

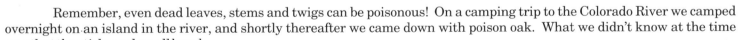

Remember, even dead leaves, stems and twigs can be poisonous! On a camping trip to the Colorado River we camped overnight on an island in the river, and shortly thereafter we came down with poison oak. What we didn't know at the time was that the sticks and small brush we slept on were poison oak. When we broke the sticks we exposed ourselves to the oil.

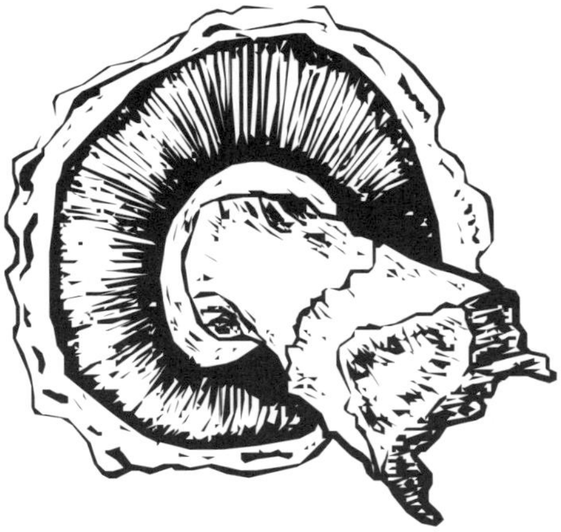

References cited:
[1] "Poisonings, 26 plants cause most problems."
[2] "Poisonous Parts of Common H & Garden Pl.
[3] Family Circle: Great Ideas (Vol 10, No.2)
[4] The Garden Dictionary [Taylor]

DRYING PLANTS FOR ARRANGEMENTS

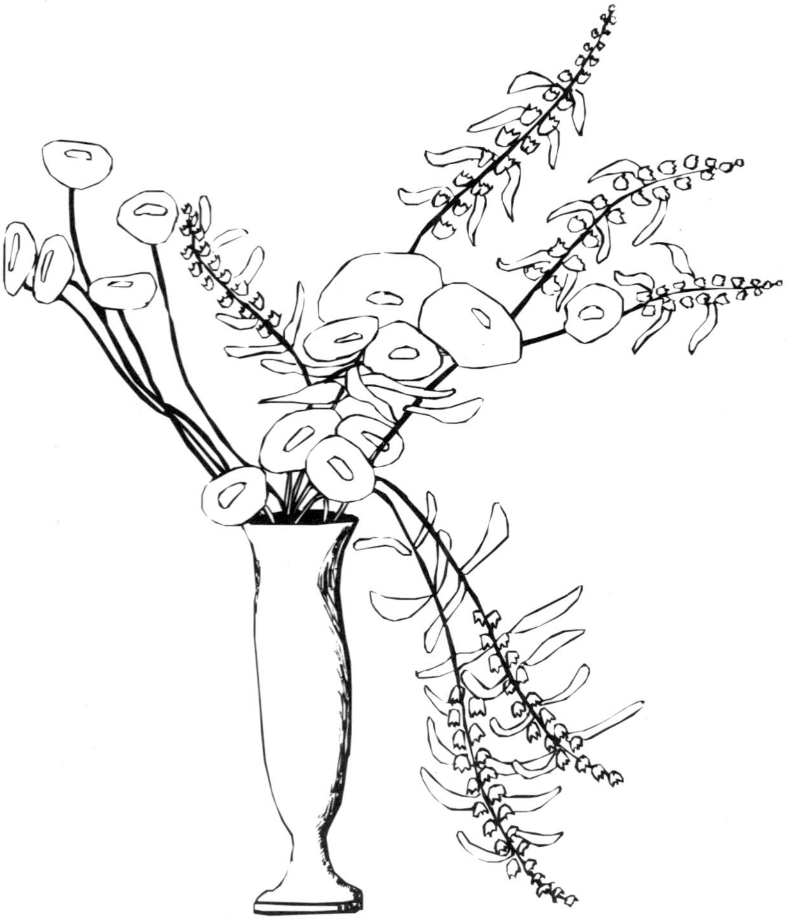

Fresh flowers bring a feeling of life and vitality into the home that is hard to match with even the best plastic flowers. However, buying store-bought fresh arrangements weekly is very expensive. If you have a garden you can provide your own fresh arrangements for summer and fall. What about also making some beautiful dried floral arrangements that are color coordinated with wall, carpet, drapes, furniture, and add to your interior decor. Dried flowers can be used all year round.

Late summer and fall are good times to gather materials for dried flower and plant arrangements. Along roadsides, in the fields, as well as in your garden, you have abundant material for processing into long lasting, colorful bouquets. Pick healthy flowers at different stages of development and this will add that "natural" look in your arrangements.

Several basic methods of preserving flowers are: using desiccants, air drying, solution treating (i.e. with glycerin or tertiary butyl alcohol), pressing or microwaving.

Desiccants:

Desiccants are drying agents that absorb moisture from the plant. Some desiccants are: sawdust, sand, borax, silica gel, kitty litter, cornmeal, cornstarch, sugar, talcum powder, and activated alumina. Desiccants must be used with care or the petals may be burned.

A good example of desiccant drying is using clean, dry ***SAND.*** Place several thicknesses of newspapers in the bottom of a sturdy cardboard box and add four inches of sand. Remove foliage from flower stems and trim stems to desired length. Stand flowers upside down on the sand, making sure flower heads don't touch. Pour sand gently over flowers, making sure sand is between all petals and in trumpets. Dry 1-2 weeks. When flowers are dry, brush sand off with soft brush or tissue, pack flowers in boxes, label and store in dry place until ready to use. Stems and leaves can be treated in this manner also.

Drying plants with ***SILICA GEL*** is like sand-drying but faster, and flowers retain their colors better.

Drying times using silica gel:

2-3 days for coralbells, lantana, miniature rose, myosotis, and viola.

3-4 days for dwarf dahlia, dwarf marigold, feverfew, larkspur, pansy, small zinnia, and tea rose.

4-5 days for buttercup, delphinium, hydrangea, large zinnia, peony, and shasta daisy.

5-6 days for aster, calendula, large dahlia, lilac, marigold, and snapdragon.

To use ***BORAX or KITTY LITTER,*** you double the drying times indicated for silica gel. Any plants recommended for silica gel will also work in Borax or kitty litter. Kitty litter is much cheaper and does just as well as silica gel [1].

ACTIVATED ALUMINA is a very powerful desiccant and is used only when humidity is high. Cover blossoms with sand and push a few of these crystals into the sand carefully so that they don't touch the flower.

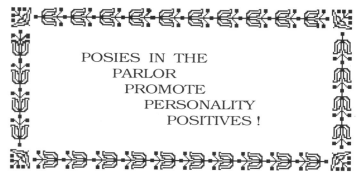

POSIES IN THE
PARLOR
PROMOTE
PERSONALITY
POSITIVES !

Air drying

The Air Drying method is an easy way to dry flowers, but it doesn't work for all species. Earl Aronson [2] gave me permission to print his list of plants best adapted to the air drying method: baby's breath, strawflowers, milkweed pods, thistles, seed heads of sumac, ornamental grasses, hibiscus seed pods, fern fronds, bayberry, rose hips, cattails, bittersweet, lilac seedheads, tansy, Queen Anne's lace, bells of Ireland, cockscomb or celosia, statice, spirea, zinnias, oats, bee-balm, butterfly weed, calendula, castor bean pods, Chinese lantern, chives, dusty miller, everlasting, gaillardia, globe amaranth, honesty, annual larkspur, lavender, lemon verbena, marigold, okra, plume poppy, sage, blue salvia, and yarrow.

These additional plants have been suggested for air drying by other people: goldenrod, sedum, heather, chives, pussywillow, tamarisk (salt cedar), artemisia, delphinium, peegee hydrangea, pampas grass, teasel, dock, Achillea, Acroclinium, Ageratum, Amobium, Echinops, Liatris, starflower, Xeranthemum, and Astilbe.

How do you air dry plants? Choose a dry, dark place with good air circulation like an attic or pantry, because it is important to keep the flowers dry. If the air is too damp the flowers will mildew. Harvest before the flowers are fully open and strip foliage from stems. Tie small flowers in bunches so their heads do not touch, and hang upside down. Most will dry in two to three weeks.

Dried bouquets can be placed on wooden or stone slabs, in baskets, and in bowls and vases. Floral clay, oasis (like styrofoam), marbles, or sand may be used to hold the plants in place. Floral clay and oasis are available in florist or craft shops. Keep dried arrangements out of direct sun, away from drafts —and definitely out of reach of cats.

DRYING FLOWERS IN THE MICROWAVE

Flower	Number in container	Microwave on High	Rotate Position	Let Stand in Drying agent
Azaleas	Several clusters	2-min.	Every 1//2 minute	10 hours
Carnations (2 containers at once)	1	3-min.	Every minute	12 hours
Dogwood cluster	2-3	3-min.	Every minute	8 hours
Rose (Medium) in full bloom	1	2 1/2-min.	Every 1/2 minute	12 hours
Rose (Miniature). Use cardboard platter.	Several	1 1/2-min.	Every 1/2 minute	5 hours
Pansy (Use cardboard platter).	5-8	2-min.	Every 1/2 minute	4 hours
Chrysanthemum (Large). Use Pyrex bowl.	1	3-min.	Every minute	12 hours
Chrysanthemum (Single bloom). Use cardboard platter.	3-5	2 1/2-min	Every 1/2 minute	10 hours
Zinnia (Large)	1	2 1/2-min.	None	10 hours

Reprinted with permission from the publisher of "The New Magic of Microwave Cookbook" (Magic Chef).

Glycerin:

Glycerin solution when applied to plants makes them more supple and usable such as oak or maple leaves, besides making them last indefinitely. In an algae course in college, my teacher had treated his red and brown algae specimens with glycerin. The specimens were soft and pliable, and very life-like though they had been dead for years. This is a great technique for teachers. Other foliage that can be used are: aspidistra, beech, crab apple, eucalyptus, holly, laurel, magnolia peony, pear, yew, pyracantha, sycamore, forsythia, spirea, and weigelia.

Collect the foliage while it is still tender (before mid-August). Cut branches no longer than 24 inches. At the end of the branch, first scrape off the outside covering of the lower three inches, and then pound the scraped part. Make up a solution of one part glycerin to two parts hot water. This should be put in a jar and shaken well. Place the pounded end of the branch in a container with 2-3 inches of the solution. Let stand 1-2 weeks or until most of the solution is absorbed. When it is done the leaves should be soft and pliable. Hang upside down until ready to use. Include these glycerin-treated branches in dried arrangements or even fresh floral arrangements as water will not damage this material. This glycerin solution can be used again and again if kept stored in a tightly covered jar.

Pressing plants

Pressing plants between two absorbent pieces of paper is an easy technique that you can use outdoors. Good plants to press are: buttercup, daisy, delphinium, dusty-miller, fern, lobelia, pansy, hydrangea florets, sweet alyssum, verbena, and viola. You can use an old thick telephone book or magazine, or bring two rectangle lightweight boards (the size of a newspaper folded in half) plus a pile of cardboard sheets and newspapers. This latter system is called a "plant press" and is commonly used by botanists. I carried my plant press all over Colorado, Arizona, California and Hawaii. And they are easy to make.

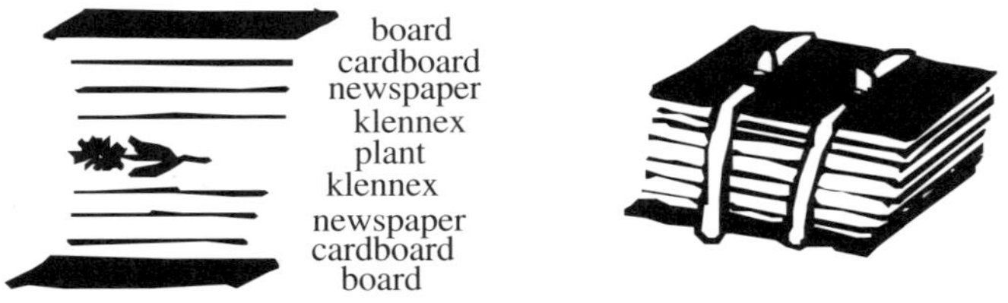

PLANT PRESS

To use a book for pressing plants: place a layer of newspaper, with a layer of kleenex on top, at intervals throughout the book. Then place a flower on the kleenex, another kleenex on top, ad then another newspaper—like a sandwich. If you forget the kleenex, the ink from the newsprint will be printed on the flower. After you have a whole book full of flowers, put a weight on the book (like a rock or more books), and store for 3-4 weeks in a dark, dry place.

Both systems of pressing use the same basic technique, except the plant press uses cardboard instead of book pages, and a plant press is designed to be tied by two straps instead of using weights. If you need to dry the plants more quickly, then place the book or press near a heater or stove (but not too close, as dry paper is flammable).

Pressed flowers obviously can't be used for standard type arrangements, but they are great for pictures for your wall, stationery, or your own local plant herbarium. Buds, stems and leaves also can be pressed with the flowers to make an attractive picture. Use tweezers and white glue to attach flower to background material. Insert picture in a frame with glass. Then tape the back of the picture to the frame so the picture is air tight and dust-free. Instead of using a frame with glass, you could cover your plant (mounted on cardboard) with Saran wrap, but be sure it is sealed well at the back.

The microwave oven

The Microwave Oven can dry flowers in minutes with a fresher appearance and color than flowers dried by traditional methods, and its flowers are also less perishable. This technique requires a drying agent to absorb moisture and hold the flower in its natural shape. Three different agents may be used: Silica gel (available in most hobby shops), a 50:50 mix of Borax and cornmeal, or kitty litter (inexpensive and easiest to use). Silica gel is best for drying smooth petals such as orchids. All three agents can be used over again. Rubber or plastic gloves will protect your hands from the drying agents.

Drying flowers in the microwave is described here with permission from the publisher of The New Magic of Microwave Cookbook [1]:

Step 1. Select fresh flowers or leaves. Flowers should be just at the peak of bloom. Flowers which have past their prime will continue to turn brown. Clip flower stem to a half inch long.

Step 2. Select a glass or paper container large enough to hold the flower and deep enough so that the drying agent covers the entire bloom. Small flowers may be dried individually in small bowls; up to three may be dried in the oven at once. Use a casserole dish for large flowers.

Step 3. Spread a half inch layer of drying agent in bottom of selected container. Place flower in container, bloom up. With a spoon, carefully sprinkle drying agent between and over the petals, making sure that each petal is covered, but not bent out of shape by the weight of the agent.

Step 4. Place a 1-cup measuring cup full of water next to the flower container in the microwave oven. The separate container of water provides moisture, and keeps the flowers from becoming too dry.

Microwave on HIGH. The time length depends on the size and type of flower (see Chart: Drying Flowers in the Microwave).

Let flower stand in the agent 4-12 hours, or when container is cool to the touch. When removing flower from the agent, tap flower gently until all granules of the drying agent are removed. Tape wires or floral sticks to the remaining half -inch of flower stem.

Fall leaves also may be dried in the microwave oven to retain their beautiful color. Select a branch of three leaves, with the largest leaf about four inches wide. Clean leaves carefully. Invert a 12 x 8-inch baking dish on the oven floor. Cover with a paper towel. Place the branch on the towel. Cover with another paper towel. Microwave 1 minute and 30 seconds on HIGH. Turn branch over and cover with towel. Microwave again 1 minute and 30 seconds on HIGH. To dry larger branches, increase the oven time.

Some warnings when using the microwave. When you put dried flowers with paper towels in the microwave, WATCH VERY CLOSELY as they are quite dry and can catch on fire! And DO NOT USE recyclable paper towels in the microwave anytime, as they contain metal chips {1}.

References cited:

[1] The New Magic of Microwave Cookbook.
[2] "It's time to gather good-looking dry plants"

Suggested reference:

Everlastings, the complete book of dried flowers

DEER-RESISTANT PLANTS

If you live in the mountains where frost can occur any day of the year, you need to select either native plants or hardy plants able to withstand cold winters and summer occasional frosts. If you have a deer problem, you will soon see which plants are deer-resistant! Though deer are entertaining to watch, they surely can ruin the looks of a garden, and you can enjoy deer more when you know your favorite plants are safe within a fence.

The following **remedies** only work temporarily until the deer get used to them: noise makers, plastic owls and snakes, scarecrows, odor repellents (mothballs, raw egg sprays, deodorant soap, lion manure, milk, cougar urine, blood meal, sprays of hot sauce and cayenne pepper, human hair hung in panty hose or in piles around the garden), or hanging bright can lids or milk cartons on a string extending across an area. A three-foot-wide chicken wire fencing laid flat on ground all around garden edge has worked for some, because deer don't like to step on it.

The Herb Society of America has been successful in deterring deer by putting **strongly scented soap** in burlap sachets hung at a deer's "nose level" in the new trees and shrubs. Unlike the chemical repellents, rain only makes the soap scent stronger for the deer. Try also plants with gray leaves (not botanically related) such as Artemisia, Santolina, and lavender, as they have highly volatile oils which often repel animals and bugs [1].

Fencing is the only sure way to keep deer from nibbling your plants. High fences are expensive, not beautiful, but often necessary for large gardens. To fence a large area, use enough chicken wire to make an 8-10 foot fence, but it must be stretched tight. Use a piece of heavy bailing wire the full length of the fence, across the top and the bottom. This keeps the deer from going under the fence, and prevents sagging from the snow load. For fence posts you can use old pipe, metal fence posts, or 4x4 inch Cedar posts. Buy them two feet longer than the fence will be tall, and sink them two feet into the ground. If you use cedar posts, paint the bottom two feet with creosote before inserting into hole. Post hole diggers are available from friends, hardware stores, or some rental shops. Corner posts must either be very heavy and deeply placed, or they must be braced using angled posts or guy wires to keep them upright.

To fence individual areas or single plants, use stiff green fence, chicken wire fences, or Ross Garden Net around and over young plants, and these cages can keep out other nibblers too. Chicken wire around individual plants is ugly, bends under the deer's weight, and needs lots of support stakes. The stiff green fencing is excellent and it needs stakes about 6-8 feet apart. Use a five foot fence until the plants outgrow their protection; then remove the fence (i.e. lilacs, and apple trees). Ross Garden Net is ideal for covering strawberry patches, petunia planters, fruit on fruit trees. Build a "T" out of small sticks or wood to keep the Ross net from touching the plants, and anchor around the edges if rodents or birds tend to creep under.

One year we tried a four-wire **electric fence** using eight foot metal fence posts sunk two feet in the ground to keep deer out of our apple trees. The sound of gentle beeping from the fence, plus white strips of cloth hung on second from top (the non-electrified wire), were supposed to show deer the presence of the fence. However, they still ran into it and knocked the wires down. Electric fencing can keep wildlife out, but high amp chargers have to be connected to several strongly mounted wires.

Choosing **deer resistant plants** is one answer. Deer, like most animals, have some foods they prefer, while they dislike others. Use plants that deer dislike in your landscaping to lessen browsing damage. However, the resistance of ornamental plants also depends on availability of other nearby deer foods. When there is plenty of preferred browse plants for the deer, there is no danger to your ornamental plants, although they will still taste the young growing tips. If the deer's natural food supply is low, no plant is totally safe from deer. Also, the more deer using an area, the more they compete for limited food supplies [2]. So, how "deer-proof" a plant is depends on how hungry the deer are. Deer become more of a problem in late summer and fall when the wild plants they forage on dry out, and the ones in your garden are still moist, tender and green. Deer aren't supposed to like Iris, but one fall they ate mine to the ground and even pulled out the roots.

Don't plant anything on a deer trail; if the deer don't eat it, they'll trample it. If you want to test some plants to see if they are deer proof, get a one gallon can of each type of plant and set them alongside a known deer trail. The deer are most interested in the tender leaves, and they usually ignore plants with sharp thorns and tough or leathery leaves. Water the plants well, and wait a week or two. If the deer don't eat them, then you can plant more. But the plants you really want to protect from deer should be fenced. Deer will mow your lawn for you (not destroy it), and save you some work—especially if your lawn has clover.

This list of deer-resistant plants should be considered as a general guide only because under the conditions already discussed, deer will sometimes eat these plants, while avoiding other plants. You might also plant a patch of clover nearby so the deer will eat it instead of your favorite plants. Deer love clover, it makes an excellent ground cover, and it feeds the soil some nitrogen.

Abbreviations used in this plant list are: Tree (**T**), Shrub (**S**), Ground Cover (**GC**), Annual (**A**), Biennial (**B**), Bulb (**BB**), Perennial (**P**), Kitchen Herb (**H**), Perennial Vine (**PV**), Vegetable (**VEG**), <u>all</u> species (**spp.**), and very deer-resistant (*).

Deer-Resistant Plants That Grow Here:

AARON'S BEARD (Hypericum calycinum), GC.
AGERATUM (Ageratum spp.), P
AJUGA (Bugleweed, Ajuga spp.), GC.
ARALIA (Acanthopanax), S.
ARTEMISIA (sagebrush, Artemisia), P.*
BARBERRY (Berberis spp.), S.
BEARDED TONGUE (Penstemon), P.
BELLS OF IRELAND (Molucella), A.
BLACK LOCUST (Robinia pseudoacacia), T.*
BLEEDING HEART (Dicentra spectabilis), P.
BOX ELDER (Acer negundo), T.
BOXWOOD (Buxus spp.), S*.
BUTTERFLY BUSH (Buddleia davidii), S.*
BUCKTHORN (Rhamnus), S.
CACTUS (cactus family). Many species*.
CALIFORNIA POPPY (Eschscholzia), A.
CANTERBURY BELLS (Campanula), B.
CATALPA (Catalpa), T.
CEDAR (Cedrus spp.), T.
CHIVES (onion family), H.
CLEMATIS (Clematis spp.), PV.*
COLUMBINE (Aquilegia spp.), P.*
COREOPSIS (Coreopsis), P.
CORNFLOWER (Centaurea), P.
COTONEASTER (Cotoneaster spp.), S.
CREEPING CHARLIE (Lysimachia) not house plant, GC.
CREEPING THYME (Thymus), groundcover.
DAFFODIL, NARCISSUS, JONQUIL (Narcissus spp.), BB.*
DAPHNE (Daphne spp.), S.
DELPHINIUM (Delphinium spp.), P.*
DAY LILLIES (Hemerocallis), P.
ELDERBERRY (Sambucus), S.*
ENGLISH IVY (Hedera helix), PV.*
EUONYMUS (Euonymus), S.
EUROPEAN LARCH (Larix), T.
FALSE CYPRESS (Chamaecyparis), S.
FERNS
FIR (Abies spp.), T.
FLOWERING QUINCE (Chaenomeles), S.
FORGET-ME-NOT (Myosotis spp.), B.
FOXGLOVE (Digitalis spp.), B.*
GAILLARDIA (Blanket flower, Gaillardia spp.), P.*
GERMANDER (Teucrium), GC.*
GLORIOSA DAISY (Black-eyed Susan, Rudbeckia hirta), B.*
HAWTHORN (Crataegus spp.), T.
HELLEBORE (Helleborus spp.), P.*
HOLLY (Ilex spp.—except thornless), S.*
HOLLYHOCK (Alcea), B.
HYPERICUM, GC.
INCENSE CEDAR (Calocedrus decurrens), T.
IRIS (Iris spp.), BB.
JAPANESE DOGWOOD (Cornus kousa), S.
JAPANESE MAPLE (Acer palmatum), T.
JAPANESE ROSE (Kerria japonica), S.*
JAPANESE SPURGE (Pachysandra), GC.
JUNIPER (Juniperus spp — all green, not variegated), S.
LAVENDER (Lavandula spp.), GC.
LAVENDER COTTON (Santolina), GC.
LUPINE (Lupinus spp.), P.*
MAGNOLIA (Magnolia spp.), T.
MANZANITA (Arctostaphylos uva-ursi), S.
MAPLE (Acer spp.), T.
MARIGOLD (Tagetes spp.), A.
MINTS. (mint family), H.
MOCK STRAWBERRY (Duchesnea indica), GC.
MONKEY FLOWER (Mimulus spp.), P.
MONKSHOOD (Aconitum spp.), P.
MUGHO PINE (Pinus mugo), S.*
OREGON GRAPE (Mahonia spp.), S.*
ORIENTAL POPPY (Papaver orientale), P.
PENSTEMON (Penstemon spp.), P.
PERIWINKLE (Vinca spp.), GC.
PINE (Pinus spp.), T.
POT MARIGOLD (Calendula), A.
RED-HOT POKER (Kniphofia uvaria), P.*
RHODODENDRON (Rhododendron spp...except azalea-leaved varieties), S.*
RHUBARB, VEG.
ROSEMARY (Rosmarinus), H.*
SAGE (Salvia), H.
SEDUM ('Utah' variety), GC.
SCOTCH BROOM (Cytisus scoparius), S.*
SHASTA DAISY (Chrysanthemum maximum), P.*
SHRUBBY CINQUEFOIL (Potentilla), S.
SILK TREE (Albizia spp.), T.
SMOKE TREE (Cotinus coggygria), T.*
SNOWFLAKE (Leucojum spp.), BB.*
SNOWBERRY (Symphoricarpos albus), S.
SPANISH BROOM (Spartium junceum), S.*
SPIRAEA (Spirea spp.), S.
SPRUCE (Picea spp.), T.
SQUASH. a vegetable.
STRAWFLOWER (Helichrysum spp.), A.
SUNFLOWER (Helianthus spp.), P.*
TREE PEONY (Paeonia suffruticosa), S.
TULIP (Tulipa spp.), BB.*
VIBURNUM (Viburnum), S.
WESTERN RED BUD (Cercis occidentalis), S.
WILD STRAWBERRY (Fragaria), GC.
YARROW (Achillea spp.), P.
YEW (Taxus spp.), S.
ZINNIA (Zinnia), A*.

References cited:
[1] "Soap and Herbs Limit Deer Diets
[2] Deer-Resistant Plants for Ornamental Use

Other References:
Sunset Western Garden Book
Karen Watson, and local residents.
"Here are a few ways to control deer in garden"
"Uninvited guests, how do you tell a deer that the landscaping isn't lunch".

DROUGHT-TOLERANT PLANTS

When we have drought conditions year after year and water is rationed or non-existent, there may be little water allowed for gardens. We must sometimes choose plants (like wildflowers and native plants) that thrive on little or no water, once they're established. Consolidate lawn into one small area (about 20'x 40'), either in front or in back of your house, and plant drought-resistant trees, shrubs, and ground covers for the rest of the yard. Many drought-tolerant species can be (unfortunately) a fire hazard and should be more than thirty feet away from your house (i.e. Manzanita). If you are in an area where you would want drought-tolerant plants, you may also need fire-resistant plants. See also chapter on fire-resistant plants.

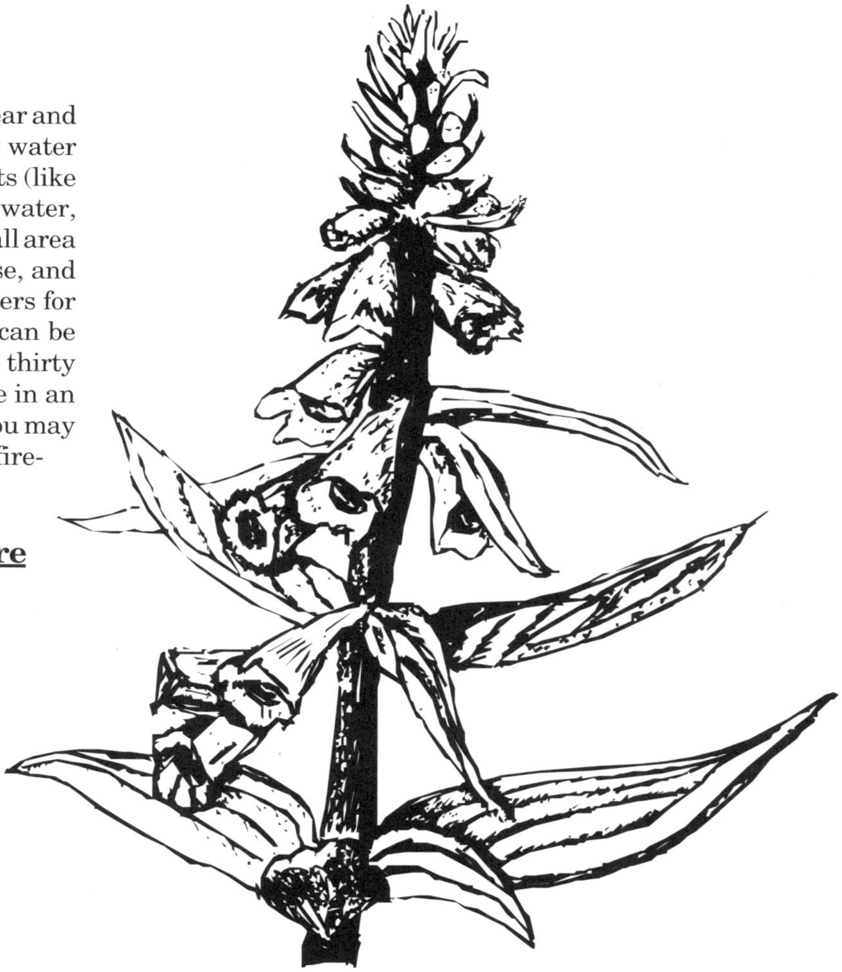

Foxglove

Drought-Tolerant Plants That Grow Here

Trees:

Black Locust (Robina), all zones
Deodar Cedar (Cedrus deodara), Zone 6
Golden Rain Tree (Koelreuleria), Zone 6
Hackberry (Celtis occidentalis), Zone 4.
Incense Cedar (Calocedrus), native
Linden (Tilia tomentosa), zones 5
Maidenhair (Ginkgo)
Oak (Quercus spp.), varies.
Osage orange (Maclura pomifera), all zones
Pine trees (Pinus spp.), varies.
Sequoia (mt), (Sequoia dendron giganteum) zone 7
Siberian Elm (Ulmus pumilla), zones 5
Silk tree (Albizia), Zones 6
Tree of Heaven (Ailanthus), All zones.

Shrubs:

Apache Plume (Fallugia parodoxa), Zones 6
Broom (Cytisus), varies
Ceanothus (Ceanothus), varies
Cotoneaster (Cotoneaster), varies
Fremontodendron (Fremontia californicum) zone 7
Germander (Teucrium) varies —ground cover.
Lavender (Lavendula), varies, ground cover.
Lavender cotton (Santolina), all zones, ground cover.
Manzanita (Arctostaphylos), varies
Mt. Mahogany (Cercocarpus),all zones
Oregon grape (Mahonia), varies
Pyracantha (Pyracantha) varies
Redbud (Cercis occidentalis), zones 6
Rose (Rosa rugosa)
Russian Olive (Elaeagnus), varies.
Sagebrush (Artemisia), all zones, ground cover.
Siberian Pea Tree (Caragana), zones 5
Smoke tree (Cotinus coggygria), all zones
Spanish Broom (Genista),zone 6
Tamarisk (Tamarix), varies
Toyon (Heteromeles californica) zone 7
Yew (Taxus) zone 7

Vegetables, herbs:

Jerusalem artichoke
Beans (frost tender)
Beets
Chamomile
Chard
Chicory
New Zealand Spinach
Rhubarb
Thyme
Allium (onion family)
Spaghetti squash (frost tender)
Horehound (Marrubium vulgare) all zones
Sage (Salvia)

Perennials, bulbs, annuals, vines, ground covers:

African Daisy (Dimorphotheca)A.
Alyssum (Aurinia), zone 3, P.
Arrowleaf Balsamroot, P.
Aster, Wild (Aster) A.
Baby's Breath (Gypsophila) A.
Baptisia australis, all zones, P.

Batchelor's button (Centaurea) A.
Bishop's flower (Ammi) A.
Black-eyed Susan (Rudbeckia hirta) B.
Blue Bells, California (Phacelia)A.
Calif. poppy (Eschscholzia), A.
California Poppy, Dwarf, A.
Catchfly (Silene)A.
Cat claw (Pithecolobium), P. vine
Cleome (Cleome), all zones, A.
Clover, Red (Trifolium) P.
Clover, Yellow (Trifolium) P.
Cockscomb, (Celosia), A.
Coneflower, Purple (Echinaceae) P.
Coneflower, California (Rudbeckia) P.
Coral bells, (Heuchera) P.
Coreopsis (Coreopsis), varies, P.
Cosmos (Cosmos) A.
Daffodil etc. (Narcissus), all zones, Bulbs
Day lily (Hemerocallis), Bulb
Euphorbia (most), varies, P.
Evening Primrose (Oenothera), all zones, B.
Flax, Lewis (Linum), all zones, P.
Fleabane daisy (Erigeron), P.
Fountain Grass (Pennisetum setaceum), all zones, P. grass
Four O'Clock (Mirabilis), A.
Foxglove (Digitalis), zone 4, B.
Gayfeather (Liatris), zone 5, P.
Gazania (Gazania), A.
Geranium, Wild (Geranium) P.
Globemallow, Orange (Sphaeralcea) P.
Hardenbergia, zone 7, P. vine
Hollyhock (Athaea), B.
Hypericum spp. G.C. & P.
Indian Blanket (Gaillardia), all zones, P & A.
Indian Paintbrush (Castilleja) P.
Indian Strawberry (Duchesnea), G.C.
Iris, bearded (Iris), all zones, Bulb
Jerusalem sage (Phlomis fruticosa), all zones, P.
Juniper (Juniperus) Shrub
Knotweed (Polygonum cuspidatum compactum), all zones, P.
Lambs ear (Stachys), G.C.
Lily (Lilium), Bulbs
Lupine, Silky (Lupinus) P.
Marigold (Tagetes), A.
Milkweed or Butterfly weed, P.
Monkey flower (Mimulus), P.
Morning glory (Convolvulus), G.C.
Nicotiana (Nicotiana), A.
Penstemon (Penstemon), P.
Periwinkle (Vinca), G.C.
Petunia (Petunia), A.
Poker plant (Kniphofia), zones 5, P.
Portulaca grandiflora, all zones, A.
Scarlet Gilia (Gilia) B.
Sea Lavender (Limonium), A.
Shasta daisy (Chrysanthemum) P.
Snow in summer (Cerastium), G.C.
Stonecrop (Sedum) many, varies, P.
Strawflower (Helichrysum), A.
Sunflower (Helianthus), P.
Sunflower, Mexican (Tithonia rotundifolia), all zones, A.
Sunflower, Wild (Helianthus) A.
Thrift (Statice, or Armeria), G.C.
Tidy Tips (Layia) A.
Valerian (Valeriana capitata ssp. californica), P.
Verbena (Verbena), A.
Windflower (Anemone), Bulb
Wisteria (Wisteria), all zones, P. vine
Yarrow (Achillea), all zones, P
Yucca (Yucca), varies, P.
Zinnia (Zinnia), A.

References used:

Sunset Western Garden Book p 149.
The Water Crunch
Surviving a Drought in a California Landscape
The Garden Dictionary [Taylor]
A California Flora [Munz]
"Turning over a new, dry leaf"
High Altitude Gardens Catalog.

FIRE-RESISTANT PLANTS, landscaping that reduces fire hazard.

When buying drought tolerant plants, find out if they are a fire hazard. There is no such thing as a fireproof plant. All plants will burn if there is enough heat and if other environmental conditions are right. However, some plants burn more slowly than others because of reduced oil content, moist leaves, or the minimal amount of litter they produce [1]. How can we live safely in the fire-prone hills of California? Fire hazards at higher elevations aren't as dangerous as those in the chaparral zone, but we still need to minimize the risk of losing our homes [2]. Proper spacing, what you plant, and how you maintain it, really can make a difference.

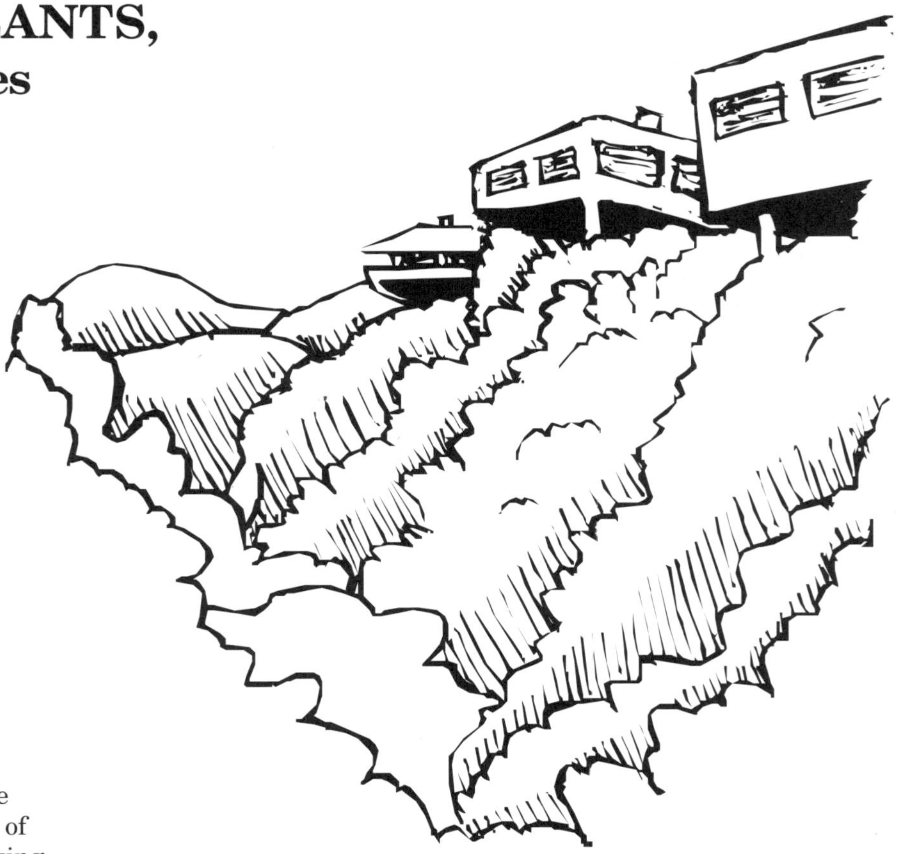
Don't build wooden decks over bushy canyons.

Create natural fire breaks

Sparse, low growing plants provide little fuel to burn, but dense, uninterrupted areas of bushy shrubs and trees are a fire hazard just asking for trouble. Build fire breaks into your garden design such as a circular driveway near your house, a wide walkway, or a rock garden. Mulch near your buildings with gravel or small rocks instead of flammable wood chips. Don't build wooden decks over bushy canyons. Use concrete, stucco, or chain-link fence rather than wood [1].

The biggest problems

Flammable roofs and inadequate brush clearance are the biggest fire hazards. Shake or shingled roof can be like kindling, to catch fire from windborne sparks (even from your chimney). Convert from wood or shake roofs to painted metal, fake shakes, fiberglass shingles, tile or gravel. California state law requires a complete brush clearance for a minimum of 30' around all structures [2], but that does not require that lawns or <u>all</u> ornamental shrubs be removed. They are most concerned with the flammable native vegetation, because <u>unwatered</u> plants become highly flammable under drought conditions.

Do I have to remove native vegetation?

Total vegetation removal around your house for a specific distance is neither necessary nor practical. It would be unsightly, and it would create other problems such as dust and erosion. Instead, plant lawn and iris, etc. (well-watered), near your house, and have native plants (less-watered) <u>farther away</u> from your house.

Plan the landscaping <u>near your house</u> to include a **lawn**; or carefully selected **fire-resistant plants**; or a **low or discontinuous ground cover** [3]. An irrigated and shaded <u>lawn</u> is the most effective and easiest landscaping to maintain.

Many of the **fire resistant plants** recommended are frost-sensitive succulents such as Ice Plants, Capeweed, Oleander, Aloe, and Catalina Cherry which do not grow here. Those that grow here are: Quaking Aspen, <u>Senecio cineraria</u>, Yucca (trunkless kinds), Spring Cinquefoil, Trumpet Vine, Saltbush (some), Germander, Yarrow, <u>Artemisia</u> (the low-growing kind) [4], Creeping Sage (<u>Salvia sonomensis</u>), Oaks (<u>Quercus</u>), <u>Pyracantha</u>, <u>Armeria</u>, Daylilies, Red-hot poker, Indian mock strawberry, <u>Bearberry cotoneaster</u>, <u>Coreopsis</u>, <u>Penstemon</u>, <u>Limonium</u>, <u>Lavandula</u>, <u>Santolina</u>, Wild lilac, Toyon, and White Alder. Avoid growing <u>Juniper</u> (all species) and <u>Manzanita</u> near buildings because they have high volatile oil content which is highly flammable.

If you don't have fire resistant plants, choose <u>ground covers</u>, trees, shrubs, and herbaceous flowering plants having low fuel volume and height, so they will either burn cooler or smolder. The goal is to reduce fuel volume while achieving the desired protective (against dust and erosion) and aesthetic effects. Select both introduced and native plants. Whenever possible, replace Manzanita and Chaparral with a low or discontinuous ground cover that will produce less fuel. Manzanita and chaparral are particularly dangerous in a canyon or on a slope below your house, because fire tends to race uphill faster than it does on level terrain. Topography and wind patterns can make a big difference. But even more important than <u>what</u> you plant, is <u>how you maintain it</u>.

Trees should not overhang the house.

Watering.

You might think that instead of removing the native (flammable) vegetation, that you could just water it more to make it fireproof. However, it takes a lot of water to raise the moisture content of the soil and plants even a little, and watering stimulates the growth rate which increases the amount of fuel [3].

Full-time residents can keep a well maintained and watered lawn and yard, so it it not necessarily a fire hazard, but the part-time resident may have a problem —so they need to invest in a good sprinkler system. Use pop-up sprinklers for lawn and ground covers, with drip irrigation for flowers, shrubs and trees. A watered landscape is safer than an unwatered one. If drought tolerant plants are watered, they will do better but be careful not to overwater them.

Roger Evans —a U.S. Forest Service, Fire Specialist in Chester, CA — suggests you keep your yard cleaned up of flammable debris all year round. Brush can be a fire hazard even in fall and winter, especially in the foothills. You don't normally water shrubs in winter while they are dormant, but the fuel is dry and can be a fire hazard —especially during a drought winter. Cold winter weather and higher humidity reduce fire hazard but they still happen. Winter fires usually start from a controlled burn (of trash or pine needles) that gets away. Using a shredder or chipper is better than burning pine needles; it is less polluting and less fire hazard. Summer fires usually start from lightning, a careless match, or cigarette.

Hosing down the roof from a ladder.

Leave some space between plants!

Trees and shrubs should be spaced far enough apart that their crowns will still be separated when fully mature (especially the flammable Manzanita, chaparral and Juniper), and trees should not overhang the house [3]. Proper spacing prevents the direct spread of fire from one tree or bush to another and on to your house. It is better to vary the heights of the clumps and the distances between shrubs, rather than taking out every other plant or every third plant [1].

Proper maintenance

Take out plants where necessary, and prune and remove dead material in the bushes that remain, so they won't spread fire easily. Keep the area cleared of pine needles and leaves, but don't rake down to bare soil; leave the "duff" (older, discolored pine needles that have started to decompose in the layer just above the soil). Prune out lower branches (dead and alive) up to six feet high on the trees. Don't stack firewood near your house during the summer (highest fire danger). Don't plant trees under power lines.

Roger Evans says young Manzanita plants (twenty years or younger) in the wild are not very susceptible to fire, but after twenty years they will have accumulated lots of dead material. In your yard, keep them trimmed, spaced a safe distance from the house and each other, and keep leaf litter picked up.

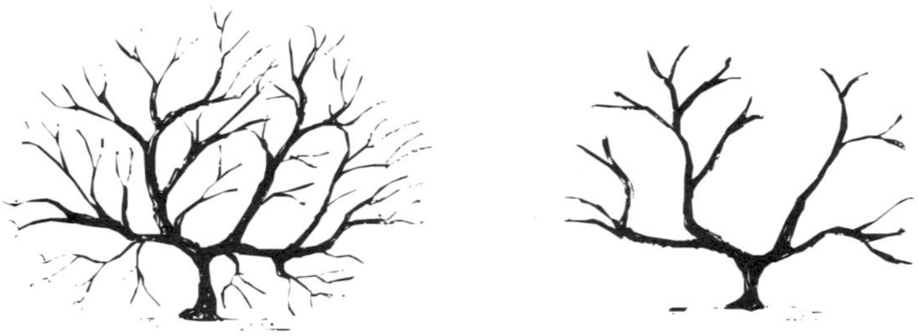

Unpruned shrub vs pruned shrub

If a wildfire is coming your way

Turn on the sprinklers and soak the landscape. If you have a flammable roof, wet it down using a garden hose from a ladder located on the side of the house opposite the flames. Move outdoor furniture made of wood (i.e. lawn furniture) into the house or garage. Move your car into the garage and close the door. Put all important papers into the car and prepare to leave if necessary [1].

If you have planted appropriate plants, used proper spacing, incorporated fuel breaks into your garden design, and provided regular maintenance of pruning, raking, weeding, and watering—your house will probably still be standing after a wildfire passes [1].

References cited:
[1] "Firescaping"
[2] "Landscape for Fire Protection"
[3] "Protecting residences from wildfires"
[4] SWGB

SHADE-TOLERANT PLANTS

Shade can be provided by trees, shrubs, north-facing walls, an overhanging roof, or a fence; creating a different micro-climate for plants. Light intensities are lower and temperatures are cooler in the shade, in contrast to sunny locations. Some plants do well in both sun or shade; some prefer only sun; and some prefer only shade. Sun-loving plants will not do well in the shade and vice versa. I have listed plants that tolerate shade, and some even prefer it. These are trees, shrubs, vines, perennials and annuals, but NOT most bulbs (they usually prefer sun). If bulbs are planted in shade they will bloom the first year but not after that. They need sun to make food to store in their bulb.

Abbreviations used in plant list: Tree (T), Shrub (S), Ground cover (GC), Perennial (P), Biennial (B), Annual (A), Fern (F), Perennial Vine (PV), and Bulb (Bulb).

Plants growing in shade of the fence

Shade-Tolerant Plants That Grow Here:

Aaron's Beard (Hypericum calycinum), GC
Amethyst flower (Browallia), all zones, A
Andromeda (Pieris), zone 4+, S
Anemone hybrids (Anemone), all zones, Bulb
Balloon flower (Platycodon), P
Barrenwort (Epimedium), zone 4+, GC
Bee Balm (Monarda), all zones, P
Beetleweed (Galax urceolata), zone 4+, GC
Bergenia (Bergenia), zone 4+, light shade, GC
Bishop's Weed (Aegopodium podagraria), zone 4+, GC
Bleeding Heart (Dicentra), zone 4+, P
Bluebells, English (Endymion non-scriptus), all zones, Bulb
Bloodroot (Sanguinaria canadensis), zone 4+, P
Boxwood (Buxus sempervirens), zone 6+, S
Buckthorn (Rhamnus purshiana), zone 4+, S
Bugleweed (Ajuga), all zones, GC
Buttercup, Creeping (Ranunculus repens), GC
Butterfly Flower (Schizanthus pinnatus), zone 4+, A
Calceolaria (Calceolaria 'John Innes'), all zones, P
Candytuft (Iberis), GC
Canterbury Bells (Campanula), varies, B
Christmas Rose (Helleborus niger), P
Cineraria (Senecio hybridus), all zones, A
Columbine (Aquilegia), all zones, P
Comphrey (Symphytum), P
Coralbells (Heuchera), P
Cardinal Flower (Lobelia), P
Creeping Charlie (Lysimachia nummularia), zone 4+, GC
Daffodils, etc. (Narcissus), all zones, Bulb
Dead Nettle (Lamium), many varieties, P
False Dragonhead (Physostegia), P
Dogwood, Canadian (Cornus canadensis), S
Euonymus (Euonymus fortunei), zone 4+, S
Ferns, many
Fern, Alaska (Polystichum setiferum), F
Fern, Deer (Blechnum spicant), F
Fern, Male (Dryopteris filix-mas), F
Fern, N.E. Maidenhair (Dryopteris cristata), F
Fern, Royal (Osmunda regalis), F
Forget me not, Woodland (Myosotis), all zones, P
Foxglove (Digitalis), all zones, B
Gas plant (Dictamnus), P
Globeflower (Trollius), all zones, P
Helleobore (Helleborus spp.), P
Holly (Ilex), varies, S
Holly, English (Ilex aquifolium), S
Hydrangea (Hydrangea spp.), varies, S
Impatiens (Impatiens wallerana), all zones, A
Iris, Crested (Iris), varies, Bulb
Iris, Gladwin (Iris foetidissima), all zones, Bulb
Iris (Iris spp.), Bulb
Ivy, Boston (Parthenocissus), all zones, PV
Ivy, English (Hedera helix), GC
Jacob's ladder (Polemonium), zone 4+, P
Juniper (Juniperus), all zones, S
Lemon Balm (Melissa officinalis), all zones, P
Leopard's Bane (Doronicum), zone 4+, P
Leucothoe (Leucothoe), varies, S
Lillies (Lilium), all zones, Bulb
Lily, Alpine, etc (Erythronium), zone 4+, P
Lily of the valley (Convallaria majalis), zone 4+, GC
London Pride (Saxifraga umbrosa), zone 4+, P
Loosestrife (Lythrum), zone 3+, P
Lungwort (Pulmonaria), zone 4+, P
Maltese-cross (Lychnis chalcedonica), P
Maple, Japanese (Acer palmatum), zone 4+,T
Monkey Flower (Mimulus hybridus), all zones, P
Monkshood (Aconitum), zone 4+, P
Mt. Laurel (Kalmia), zone 4+, S
Maple, Vine (Acer circinatum), zone 4+, T

Meadow Rue (Thalictrum), all zones, P
Oregon Grape (Mahonia aquifolium), S
Penstemon (Penstemon), P
Periwinkle, Greater (Vinca major), GC
Periwinkle, Lesser (Vinca minor), GC
Phlox, Creeping (Phlox stolonifera), GC
Plantain Lily (Hosta spp.), zone 4+, P
Poppy, Himalayan (Meconopsis betonicifolia), zone 4+, P
Primrose (Primula), varies, P
Privet, California (Ligustrum ovalifolium), S
Ramondia (Ramondia myconi), P
Raspberry (Rubus), zone 4+, light shade, Berry
Rhododendron (Rhododendron), hardy hybrids, S
Shortia (Shortia), zone 4+, P
Siberian Forget me not (Brunnera macrophylla), P
Silver dollar plant (Lunaria annua), P
Solomon's Seal (Polygonatum multiflorum), zone 4+, P
Solomon's Seal, False (Smilacina racemosa), zone 4+, P
Spiderwort (Tradescantia andersoniana) all zones, GCor P
Spirea, False (Astilbe), zone 4+, P
Spurge, Japanese (Pachysandra terminalis), zone 4+, GC
Strawberry-like (Waldsteinia), partial shade, GC
Strawberry, Indian Mock (Duchesnea indica), all zones, P
Sweet William Phlox (Phlox divaricata), zone 4+, P
Sweet Shrub (Calycanthus), varies, S
Symphoricarpos (Symphoricarpos), native, all zones, S
Trailing Arbutus (Epigaea repens), zone 4+, GC
(Vaccinium spp.), cow, blue & cranberry, S
Violet (Viola), all zones, A
Virginia Bluebells (Mertensia), zone 4+, P
Wake Robin (Trillium), varies, P
Wintergreen, Creeping (Gaultheria procumbens), GC
Weigela (Weigela), light shade, S
Yew, Spreading English (Taxus baccata), S

References used;

Sunset Western Garden Book
Right Plant, Right Place [Ferguson]
Better Homes & Gardens
The Garden Dictionary [Taylor]
A California Flora [Munz]

SUPPLIERS' CATALOGS

Breck's Garden Catalog, Peoria, IL (Excellent selection of bulbs, seeds, flowers, & plants) www.brecks.com/catalog

Brookstone Hard-to Find Tools, Peterborough, NH (Tools for garden & greenhouse) www.brookstone.com

Burpees Harvest Catalog, Warminster, PA (Aids for picking, preparing, & preserving home-grown harvest) www.burpee.com

Burpee Seeds, Warminster, PA (Excellent selection of flowers, seeds, vegetables and bulbs) Includes also some hardy seeds!!! www.burpees.com

Clyde Robin Seed Co., Castro Valley, CA (Native CA plants, seeds, wildflowers & mixes; garden supplies & tools; bird supplies) www.clyderobin.com

Dutch Gardens Inc. Lisse-Holland (They send Holland's finest bulbs and plants to beautify gardens throughout the US. The bulbs are half the price of Breck's and shipping is free over $15) www.dutchgardens.com

Ed Hume Seed Inc, Kent, WA (Specializes in seeds for short seasons & cool climates) www.humeseeds.com

Environmental Seed Producers, El Monte, CA (Native plants! Large scale distributor and producers of garden flower seeds, native grass seeds and native forbs) www.espseeds.com

Forestfarm Plant Nursery, Williams, OR (Extensive selection of plants, including hard-to-find native CA plants and seeds) www.forestfarm.com

Gardener's Eden Home Décor, Williams-Sonoma & San Francisco. (Has plants, home gadgets, ornaments, gifts, yard furniture) www.gardenerseden.com

Gardener's Supply, Burlington, VT (Practical gardening tools, supplies, and solutions including composters, seed starting equipment, greenhouses, and fertilizers) www.gardeners.com

Gardens Alive! Sunman, IN (Researches and sells biological controls for pests in lawns, soil, plants, animals and home, i.e. yellow sticky traps) www.gardensalive.com

Gurney's Seed & Nursery Co., Yankton, SD (Excellent source of all kinds of plants: bulbs, perennials, flower, vegetable, and wildflower) www.mailordergardening.com

Henry Field's Seed & Nursery Catalog, Shenandoah, IA (Outstanding selection of all plants) www.henryfields.com

High Altitude Gardens, Ketchum, ID (Specializes in foothill & mountain short season varieties; includes wildflower seeds) Excellent!! www.seedstrust.com

Jackson & Perkins Roses, Medford, OR (Excellent! Roses, flowers, vegetables, berries, & dwarf fruit trees, garden décor, & more) www.jacksonandperkins.com

Johnny's Seeds Co, Albion, ME (Specializes in foothill and mountain plants with short growing season. Offers vegetable, flower & herb seeds; flower bulbs; raspberry, strawberry & blueberry plants; garden tools & accessories) www.johnnyseeds.com

Larner Seeds, Bolinas, CA (Excellent source of CA natives: wildflowers, bunchgrasses, shrubs, vines, & trees) www.larnerseeds.com

Las Pilitas Nursery, Santa Margarita, CA (Specializes in CA native plants; also their photos, descriptions, and information) www.laspilitas.com

Michigan Bulb Co, Grand Rapids, MI (Excellent trees, shrubs, vines, perennials, bulbs, herbs, fruits, and vegetables) www.michiganbulb.com

Native Plant Information Network, Your Online Resource for Native Plant Information in North America. www.wildflower2.org/NPIN/Suppliers

Nichols Garden Nursery, Albany, OR (New and unusual herbs, vegetables, flower, & rare seeds. Emphasizing short season varieties, flavor and performance. Excellent!!!!
www.nicholsgardennursery.com

Park Seed Catalog, Greenwood, SC (Wild & domestic flower seed and vegetables) Excellent!!!!
www.parkseed.com

Peaceful Valley Farm & Garden Supply, Grass Valley, CA (Tools and supplies for serious organic gardeners and farmers in cold climates!)
www.groworganic.com

Petals Catalog (Quality silk flowers & home accessories) Excellent!! www.petals.com

Richters Herbs Catalog---Medicinal, Culinary, Aromatic herbs---plants & seeds. (Hundreds of different herb seeds, and it lists the medicinal properties) Goodwood, Ontario.
www.richter.com

Roses of Yesterday & Today, Watsonville, CA (Excellent for roses!!)
www.rosesofyesterday.com

S&S Seeds LLC, (Highest quality California wildflowers) www.wildflowerseed.com

Shepherd's Garden Seeds are now back at Renee's Garden Seeds. (Excellent vegetables, flowers, herbs, unusual varieties)
https://www.reneesgarden.com

Siskyou Rare Plant Nursery, Medford, OR (Hard-to-find hardy perennials, shrubs and smaller conifers, alpine and rock garden plants)
www.wave.net/upg/srpn/

Springhill Nurseries, Tipp City, OH (flowers, perennials, bulbs, roses, wildflowers, vines, shrubs, ferns) Excellent! www.springhillnursery.com

Stark Bros. Nurseries, Louisiana, MO (Outstanding, quality grower of fruit trees)
www.starkbros.com

Territorial Seed Co., Lorane, OR (Vegetable, herb, annual flower seeds, transplants, and growing guides -- for foothill and mountain plants with short growing seasons) www.territorialseed.com

Theodore Payne Foundation, Sun Valley, CA (California native plants and seeds)
www.theodorepayne.org

Thompson & Morgan Seeds, Jackson, NJ (Large illustrated seed catalog with quality flowers, vegetables, herbs) Excellent!!
www.seeds.thompson-morgan.com

Van Ness Water Gardens, Upland, CA (Everything you need to start a water garden!!!!) Excellent!! www.vnwg.com

Wayside Gardens, Hodges, SC (Outstanding source for trees, shrubs, and perennials)
www.waysidegardens.com

Yerba Buena Nursery, Woodside, CA (Specializing in Native Plants & ferns)
www.yerbabuenanursery.com

REFERENCES

A Calif. Flora [Munz}. By Munz & Keck. UC Press, Berkeley, CA, (1963) 1681p. (plant lists).

A Checklist of Ferns & Seed Plants of Plumas County, CA. By Wayne Dakan, U.S. Forest Service, Chester, CA (1978) 73p. (plant lists)

A Child's Garden, A Guide for Parents & Teachers. 1974. By Chevron Chemical Co., Ortho Div., Public Relations, 200 Bush St., S. F., CA. Pamphlet.

A Dictionary of The Flowering Plants & Ferns. By J.C. Willis. Cambridge U. Press, NY & London (1966) 1214p. (plant lists).

A Flora of Lassen Vol. Nat. Park, CA. By G. W. Gillett, J. T. Howell, & H. Leschke. The Univ. S. F., Filmer Brothers Press, Taylor & Taylor, San Francisco, CA (1961) 185p.

A Garden for Children. By Felicity Bryans. Contains info on how & what to plant, and sample garden layouts. Call Smith & Hawkins (415) 383-4050, cost $19.95.

Alpine Wildflowers of Rocky Mt. Nat. Park, flowers that grow in the land of no trees. By B.E. Willard & C.O. Harris. Rocky Mt. Nature Assoc., Vivid Color Printing, Estes Park, CO (1963) 23p.

Am. Hort. Soc. Illust. Encyclopedia of Gardening: Vegetables. The Am. Hort. Soc., Mt. Vernon, VA, (1980) 144p.

A Vegetation Survey of the Butterfly Botanical Area, CA. By W. and I. Knight, & J. T. Howell. U of S.F., S. F., CA (1970) 46p.

A Video Kit: Get Ready, Get Set, Grow. For children aged 9-14, cost $29.95. Kit includes two booklets: "Ideas for parents & teachers", and "Kid's guide to good gardening." Order from Brooklyn Botanic Garden, 1000 Washington Ave., Brooklyn, NY 11225 or call (718) 622-4433, Ext. 339.

Basic Herb Cookery & Herb Recipies. A handout sheet by N.P. Nichols of Nichols Garden Nursery, Albany, OR.

Best Methods for Growing Fruits & Berries. By editors of Org. Gard. Mag. Rodale Press, Emmaus, PA (1963) 48p.

Better Homes & Gardens [BH&G]: Complete Guide to Gardening. By Meredith Corp., Des Moines, IA, (1983) Landscaping, house plants, general gardening, greenhouses, and plant lists. 551p.

Botany, an introduction to plant science. By Robbins, Weier, Stocking. Wiley & Sons, Inc., NY (1959) 578p.

California Mountain Wildflowers. By Philip A. Munz. UC Press, Berkeley, Los Angeles, & London (1972) 122p.

"Chemical reaction causes leaf color changes." Chester Progressive, Chester, CA, p 1B, 10-24-89.

"Chemicals, not frost, create fall colors." Chester Progressive, Chester, CA, p 7B, 12-6-88.

Compost Preparation. By J.P. Martin & B.A. Krantz. Div. of Agric. Sci., U of C, Leaflet #2559 Coop. Ext. Serv., Agric. college, U of C (1978).

Deer-Resistant Plants for Ornamental Use. By Cummings, Kimball, & Longhurst. CA Agric. Expt. Stat. Ext. Serv. Leaflet #167 (1980).

Draft Environmental Impact Statement, Gallatin Marina, Future Development Policy. By Steve Young, U.S. Forest Service, Susanville, CA (1987) 85p.

Drip Irrigation for the Home Garden & Landscape. Div. of Agric. Sci., U of C, Leaflet #21025 (1978).

"Dry is beautiful. "By Dick Tracy. Cal Life Mag., Sac. Bee 6-2-90.

Earthly Delights. By Rosalind Creasy. Presents ideas for twelve different theme gardens, including one for children. Call Random House (800) 638-6460.

Everlastings, the complete book of dried flowers. By Patricia Thorpe. $17.95. Rodale Press, Emmaus, PA.

Family Circle Great Ideas: Gardening & Houseplants. Vol 10, No 2 (Feb 1984 issue). The Family Circle, Inc., 488 Madison Ave, NY 10022. 128p.

Family Circle Great Ideas: Gardening & Houseplants. Vol 9, No. 2 (Feb 1983 issue). The Family Circle, Inc., 488 Madison Ave, NY 10022. 128p.

Field Guide to Edible Wild plants, a quick all-in-color identifier of more than 100 edible wild foods growing free in the U.S. & Canada. By Bradford Angier. Stackpole Books, Harrisburg, PA (1986) 255p.

'Firescaping." By Joan Bolton. In Horticulture, The Magazine of American Gardening, October 1991, pp 54-60.

Gardening Indoors with House Plants. By Raymond P. Poincelot. Rodale Press, Emmaus, PA (1974) 266p.

"Gardening with Children." By Anne S. Cunningham. The Workbasket, April 1990, pp 52-53.

"Gardens just for kids." By Charlotte Hagood. Creative Ideas for Living pp 24-26.

General Wellness & Health Related Information for Forest Service Employees, WOP & CR, S&H Branch, April 1991. Handout.

Getting the Most from your Garden, using advanced intensive gardening techniques. By editors of Org. Gard. & Farming Mag. Rodale Press, Emmaus, PA (1980) 482p.

"Good gardeners know the many benefits of peat moss." By Ed Hutchison, Cal Life Mag., Sac. Bee, p 10., 6-15-91.

Grafter's Handbook. By R.J. Garner. Oxford Univ. Press, NY (1967).

Greenhouse Gardening. By Miranda Smith. Rodale Press, Emmaus, PA (1985) 278p.

Green Thumb Cook book. By the editors of Org. Gard. & Farming Mag. Edited by A. Moyer. Rodale Press, Emmaus, PA (1977). Over 350 natural ways to prepare 61 different fresh vegetables. 316p.

Ground Covers in the Landscape. By Emile L. Labadie. Sierra City Press, Sierra City, CA 96125 (1983) 314p.

Growing Berries and Grapes at Home. By J. Harold Clarke. Dover Pub., NY, (1976) 372p.

Growing Food in Solar Green houses, a monthly guide to raising vegetables, fruits, and herbs under glass. By Delores Wolfe. Dolphin Books, Doubleday & Co., Garden City, NY (1981) 192p.

Growing Fruits & Nuts in Lassen, Plumas, and Sierra Counties. Coop. Ext. Serv., Quincy Fairgrounds, Quincy, CA (1978) 12p.

Gurney's Grow It Guide. By Gurney's Seed & Nursery Co. (1984).

"Here are a few ways to control deer in the garden." By Richard Post (Area Horticulture Specialist), The Record-Courier, Gardnerville, NV. 10-9-86.

High Altitude Gardening (catalog) Written & Published by Leslie McBride & Mary Street, Tahoe City, CA (1985) 51p.

High Altitude Gardens (catalog) by Bill McDorman. Ketchum, Idaho. (at 6,000 ft).
(800)-874-7333 (1992) 47p.

Home Garden Guide, J&P (A) By Jackson & Perkins Co. Pamphlet 29p. No date. $1.

Home Vegetable Garden, Lassen, Plumas, Sierra Counties. Coop. Ext. Service, U of C (1977) 35p.

Home Vegetable Gardening. Calif. Agric. Exp. Station, Extension Serv. Circular #499, U of C, Davis (1968).

"House plant care, water is both a blessing and a curse." By Don Horton. Cal Life Mag., Sac. Bee, no date.

"How does your garden grow?, Six Steps: how to help your children get started on the road to gardening." By G. Brennan. Cal Life Mag., Sac. Bee, Fall Gard. Guide, 9-29-90, pp 6 & 8.

How to Grow Vegetables and Fruits by the Organic Method. By the editors of Organic Gard. and Farming Mag., Rodale Press, Emmaus, PA (1973) 926p.

"Indoor gard. ideas for kids,—from seeds and pits to plants in pots". By Lucille J. Goodyear. 1977. OFA. pp 149-150.

Indoor Gardens for Decorative Plants. Home & Garden Bulletin No. 133, USDA 1967.

"Insects & Diseases of Vegetables in the Home Garden." A handout from county agricultural agent.

Invite Birds to Your Home. Sup.of Documents, U.S. Gov. Printing Office, USDA pamphlet # PA-982. (1971) 16p.

"It's time to gather good-looking dry plants." Article by Earl Aronson. Cal Life Mag., Sac Bee, (Sept. '84).

Keys for Identification of Wild Flowers, Ferns, Trees, Shrubs, Woody Vines of N. CA By Vesta Holt. Mayfield Pub. Co., Palo Alto, CA, (1964).

"Landscape for Fire Protection." 1967. By UC Agric. Ext. Service, AXT-254.

Landscaping With Roses, J&P (B). By Jackson & Perkins Co., Pamphlet w/ pictures. Medford, OR 97501. No date.

Landscaping Your Mountain Home (Tahoe plant list). Coop. Ext., Quincy Fairgrounds, Quincy, CA (1963) 12 p.

Let's Live Mag. (January '74). Edited by P. Mac Donald. Article (p. 6) by B. Rateaver on seeds. L.A., CA 90004.

Native Edible Fruits, Nuts, Vegetables, Herbs, Spices, & Grasses of CA, II. Small or Bush Fruits. Div. of Agric. Sci., UC Leaflet #2278 (1979) 26p.

Native Edible Fruits, Nuts, Vegetables, Herbs, Spices, & Grasses of CA III —Vegetables. Div. of Agric. Sci., UC Leaflet #2705 (1978) 19p.

Native Edible Fruits, Nuts, Vegetables, Herbs, Spices, and Grasses of CA, I. Fruit Trees and Nuts. Div. of Agric. Sci., UC Leaflet #2226 (1975) 14 p.

Native Plants for use in the CA Landscape. By E. L. Labadie. Sierra City Press, Sierra City, CA 96125 (1978) 248p.

Nature's Design. By Carol A. Smyser. Rodale Press, Emmaus, PA, (1982). (Excellent on Landscaping).

Organic Gardening & Farming Magazine. By Rodale Press, 33 East Minor St., Emmaus, PA 18049 (1981).

Ornamental Shrubs for use in the Western Landscape. By Emile Labadie. Sierra City Press, Sierra City, CA 96125 (1980) 308p.

Plumas County Selected Socio-Economic Data. Compiled by Cooperative Extension Service., UC Davis and Plumas County Chamber of Commerce, (1984). (Climate charts).

"Plant-Growing Magic: Jerry Baker's 10 Most Startling 'Tricks' to Brighten Up Your House." By Jerry Baker. Family Weekly Magazine. Feb 10, 1974, p4.

"Poisonings, 26 plants cause most problems." Article by Pat Sullivan. Cal Life Mag., Sac. Bee, (May '84).

"Poisonous Parts of Common House & Garden Plants." By Nat. Assoc. of Retail Druggists, One East Wacker Dr., Chicago, IL 60601. Pamphlet.

"Protecting residences from wildfires, a guide for homeowners, lawnmakers, and planners." By Howard E. Moore. 1978+ USDA, Forest Service, Pacific SWF & R Exp. Sta., General Technical Report PSW-50.

Put Color, Form & Excitement in Your Garden. By Dr. R.E. Atkinson, Rainbird Sprinkler Mfg. Corp, Glendora, CA (1969). (plant lists)

Reader's Digest: Practical Guide to Home Lands. By Reader's Digest Assoc., Inc., Pleasantville, NY (1972). 479p.

Reader's Digest: Success with House Plants. By Reader's Digest Assoc., Inc., Pleasantville, NY (1983). Best complete house plant book on the market !!! 480p.

Reader's Digest: [Basic] Illustrated Guide to Gardening. By the Reader's Digest Assoc., Inc., Pleasantville, NY. (1978) 672 p. (plant lists). Excellent!!

Right Plant, Right Place, The Indispensable Guide to the Successful Garden. By Nicola Ferguson. Summit Books, NY (1984) 292p. (plant lists).

Rodale's Garden Problem Solver: Vegetables, Fruits, & Herbs. By Jeff Ball, Rodale Press, Emmaus, PA (1988) 550p.

Rodale's Guide to Composting. By Jerry Minnich, Marjorie Hunt, & editors of Org. Gard. & Farming Mag. Rodale Press, Emmaus, PA (1979). Pamphlet.

Roses for the Home. USDA Home & Garden Bull. # 25 (1978). Available at Quincy Fairgrounds, CA. Pamphlet. 25p.

Roses of Today and Yesterday (A catalog of old timers by the Watsonville Nursery.) Old fashioned roses.

Secrets of Companion Planting for Successful Gardening. By L.Riotte. Gardenway Pub., Charlotte, VT (1976).

Secrets of Plant Propagation, Starting your own flowers, vegetables, fruits, berries, shrubs, trees, and house plants. By Lewis Hill. A Garden Way Publishing Book. Storey Communications, Inc., Pownal, VT 05261 (1987) 168p. Excellent.

Selected Western Native Plants. A 1984 handout pamphlet by Forest Farm, 990 Tetherow Rd., Williams, OR 97544.

Selection and Care of Fruit Trees, Plumas-Sierra-Lassen Co.'s. By D.C. Alderman and C.W. Rimbey. Agric Ext. Serv., UC, and Plumas-Sierra-Lassen Counties Cooperating, Quincy, CA 95971 (1975) 8p.

Sierra Nevada Natural History, An Illus. Handbook. By T. Storer and R.Usinger. UC Press, Berkeley, CA (1974) 374p.

Sierra Wildflowers, Mt. Lassen to Kern Canyon. By T.F. Niehaus. UC Press, Berkeley, L. A. & London (1974) 223p.

Simon & Schuster's Guide to Trees, field guide to Conifers, Palms, Broadleafs, Fruits, Flowering Trees, and Trees of Economic Importance (with over 650 illus. —350 in full color —showing tree shapes, leaves, flowers, and fruit). A Fireside Book Publ. by Simon & Schuster (1978) 299+p. (plant lists).

"Soap & Herbs Limit Deer Diets, Herb Society plants what animals dislike." By Susan Mc Clure (of the New York Times). San Francisco Chronicle, Home & Garden Section (no date).

"Some tips for keeping cats from house plants." By Gina Spadafori. Sac. Bee 6-15-91, p Scene 2.

Square Foot Gardening. By Mel Bartholomew. Rodale Press, Emmaus,PA (1981) 347p.

Stocking Up, how to preserve the foods you grow, naturally. By editors of Org. Gard. and Farming Mag. Edited by Carol Stoner, Rodale Press, Emmaus, PA (1974) 351p.

Suburban and Farm Vegetable Gardens. USDA Home & Garden Bulletin No. 9 (1970) 46p.

Success with House Plants Packet #69, 3. By International Masters Publishers, USA.

Sunset: Basic Gardening Illustrated. By Editors of Sunset Books & Mag. Lane Publ. Co., Menlo Park, CA (1990) 160p.

Sunset: Garden Pools, Fountains & Waterfalls. By editors of Sunset Books and Mag. Lane Publ. Co., Menlo Park, CA (1976). 80p.

Sunset: House Plants, How to choose, grow and display. Lane Publ.Co., Menlo Park, CA (1968) 112p.

Sunset: How to Plan, Estab., & Maint. Rock Gardens. By George Schenk. Lane Publ. Co., Menlo Park, CA (1967) 112p.

Sunset: Pruning Handbook. By Editors of Sunset Books & Mag,. Lane Publ, Co., Menlo Park, CA (1978) 96p.

Sunset: Roses. By Editors of Sunset Books & Mag. Lane Publ. Co., Menlo Park, CA (1990) 96p. Excellent!

Sunset: Vegetable Gardening. By editors of Sunset Books & Mag., Lane Publ. Co., Menlo Park, CA (1972) 72p.

Sunset Ideas for Landscaping & Garden Remodeling. By editors of Sunset Books & Mag., Lane Publ. Co., Menlo Park, CA (1979) 80p. (plant lists)

Sunset Western Garden Book [SWGB]. By editors of Sunset Books & Mag., Lane Publ. Co., Menlo Park, CA (1984) 512p. (plant lists). Excellent.

Surviving a Drought in a Calif. Landscape. By Roger K. Bernhardt. Groundskeeper Publications, Petaluma, CA 1989.

The Audubon Society Field Guide to N. Am. Wildflowers. By R. Spellenberg. A. A. Knopf Inc., NY (1979) 862p.

The Dictionary of Shrubs (in color). By S.M. Gault. The Royal Hort. Soc. & Exeter Books, NY (1983) 208p. (plant lists).

The Encyclopedia of Natural Insect & Disease Control. Edited by Roger B. Yepsen, Jr. Guide to protecting plants and crops against disease, fungus, insects, and pests on vegetables, fruit, flowers, trees, & lawns—without toxic chemicals. Lists proven remedies and controls. Rodale Press, Emmaus, PA (1984) 490p.

The Garden Dictionary [Taylor], An Encyclopedia of Practical Horticulture Garden Management and Landscape Design. Edited by Norman Taylor. Houghton-Mifflin Co., Boston and NY (1938) 888p. (plant lists)

The Green Thumb Book of Fruit & Vegetable Gardening. By George Abraham. Prentice-Hall, Inc., Englewood Cliffs, NJ (1970).

The Green Thumb Cookbook. By the editors of Org. Gard. Mag. Edited by Anne Moyer. $12.95 hardcover. Rodale Press, Emmaus, PA (1977) 316p.

The Microwave Guide & Cookbook. By General Electric. USA 1980.

The National Gardening Book of Tomatoes. Published by National Gardening Assoc., 180 Flynn Ave. Burlington, VT 05401 (1985).

The New Magic of Microwave Cookbook. By Magic Chef Inc., Microwave Div., Anniston, AL (1978). (dried plants).

The Principles of Gardening [Johnson], a guide to the art, history, science and practice of gardening. By Hugh Johnson. Simon and Schuster, NY (1979) 272p. $30. (plant lists)

The Rodale Guide to Composting. By J. Minnich, M. Hunt, & the editors of Org. Gard. Mag. Rodale Press, Emmaus, PA (1979) 405p.

The Ruth Stout No-Work Garden Book, secrets of the famous year-round mulch method. By Ruth Stout & Richard Clemence. Rodale Press, Emmaus, PA (1973). (use mulch instead of rototilling) 218p.

The Solar Greenhouse Book. Edited by James C. McCullagh. Rodale Press, Emmaus, PA (1978) 328p.

"The Water Crunch" Cal Life Mag., Sac. Bee, 6-2-90.

Time-Life: Fix it Yourself, Lawn & Garden. Time-Life Books, Alexandria, VA (1987) 144p.

Trees & Shrubs of Lassen. By Raymond L. Nelson. Loomis Museum Assoc., Lassen Vol. Nat. Park, Mineral, CA (1971) 35p. (plant lists).

"Turning over a new, dry leaf." By Marie Hammock, S. F. Examiner & Chronicle 4-17-88, p E-6.

"Uninvited guests, how do you tell a deer that the landscaping isn't lunch." By Dick Tracy, Cal Life Mag., Sac. Bee, 9-1-90, p 11.

USDA Plant Hardiness Zone Map. ARS Misc. Publ. No. 1475. (1990)

Water '85 Visions, The Complete Guide to Water Gardening. By Van Ness Water Gardens, 2460 North Euclid Ave, Upland, CA 91786. (714) 982-2425. Complete instructions on how to build waterfalls, fountains, and fish ponds with catalog of plants, pumps, lights, and all accessories. (1985) 48p.

"What's Bugging You." (in the Water Crunch special article) By Dan Pratt, Cal Life Mag., Sac. Bee, 6-2-90.

"Where plants can be happy. Gardening. Your shrubbery is suffering? You may live in a 'plant hardiness' zone that is simply too far north." By Charles Fenyvesi. U.S. News & World Report, March 26, 1990.

"Why Leaves Change Color." U.S. F. S., FS-012, GPO 1983.

Youth Gardening is a soft cover book filled with tips, info, and projects. Price $8.95. Write to Nat. Gardening Assoc., 180 Flynn Ave., Burlington VT 05401.

KINDS OF PLANTS LISTED

WOODY PLANTS:

- Trees
- Shrubs
- Roses
- Perennial vines
- Fruits, Nuts, & Berries
- Hardy ferns

HERBACEOUS PLANTS:

- Annuals
- Biennials
- Perennials
- Bulbs
- Ground covers
- Vegetables & Kitchen herbs

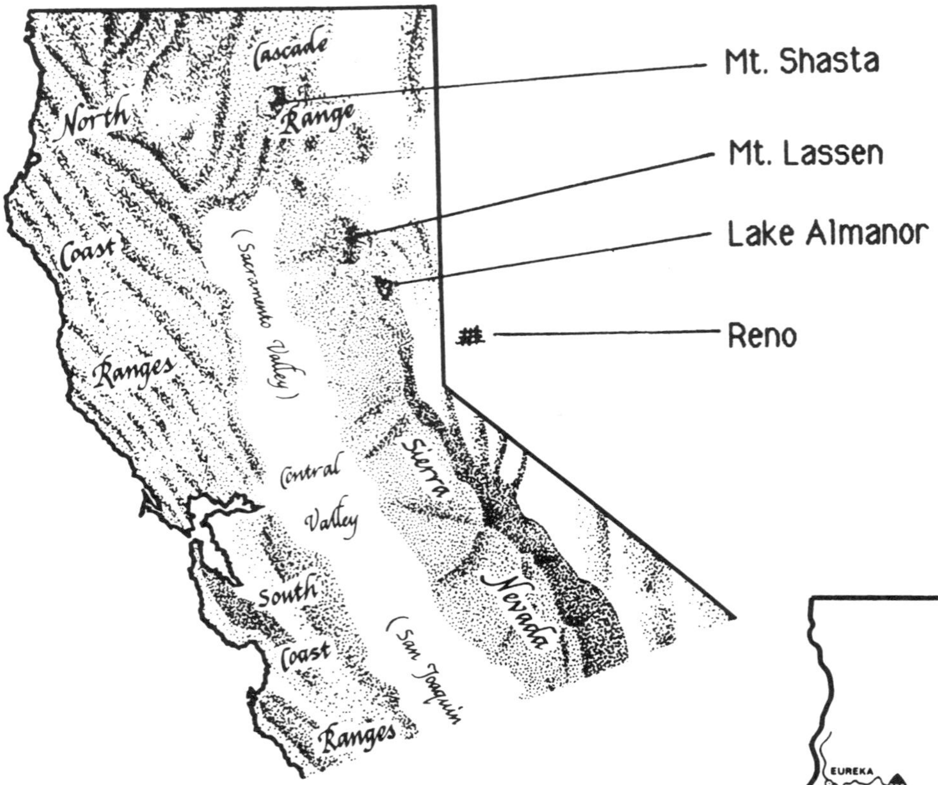

TOPOGRAPHIC MAP OF CALIFORNIA

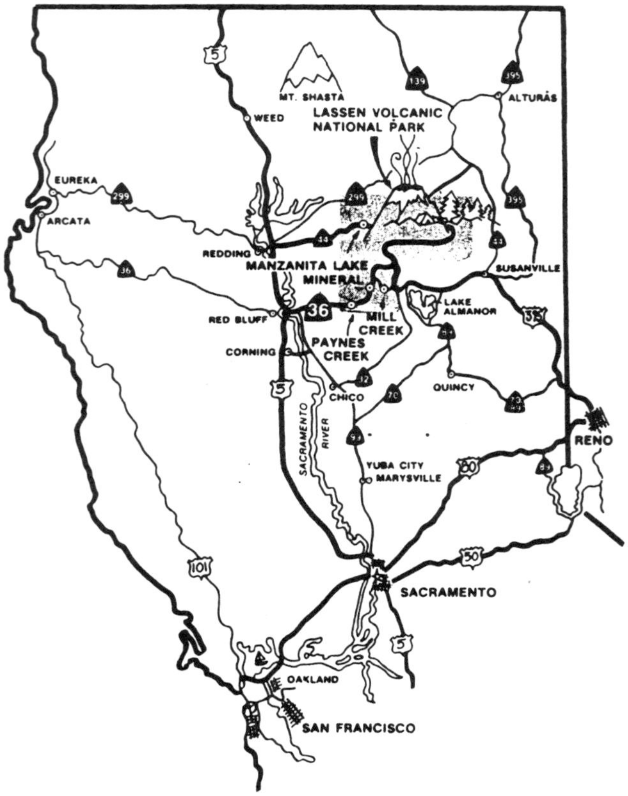

ROAD MAP OF CALIFORNIA

COUNTY MAP OF CALIFORNIA

Index to Scientific and Common Names

USDA CLIMATE ZONES

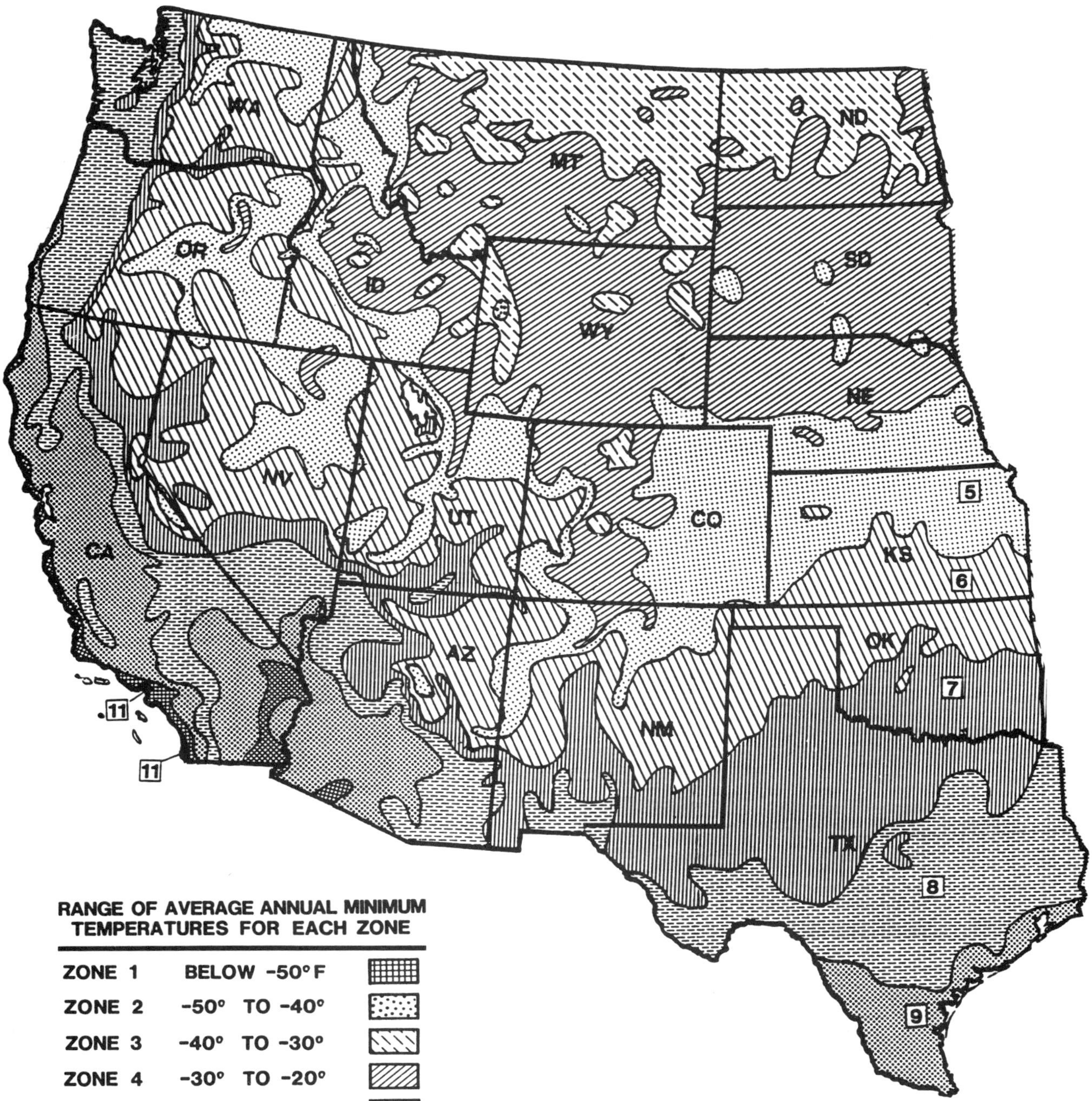

RANGE OF AVERAGE ANNUAL MINIMUM TEMPERATURES FOR EACH ZONE

ZONE 1	BELOW -50°F		
ZONE 2	-50°	TO	-40°
ZONE 3	-40°	TO	-30°
ZONE 4	-30°	TO	-20°
ZONE 5	-20°	TO	-10°
ZONE 6	-10°	TO	0°
ZONE 7	0°	TO	10°
ZONE 8	10°	TO	20°
ZONE 9	20°	TO	30°
ZONE 10	30°	TO	40°
ZONE 11	ABOVE 40°		

These **USDA Climate Zones** are based on only one factor: minimum average annual temperature (data from selected weather stations). They can be used only as a "general" guide due to the many local microclimates present in our irregular mountain terrain. Reprinted from USDA Agric. Research Service Misc. Pub. #814: Plant Hardiness Zone Map (1990).

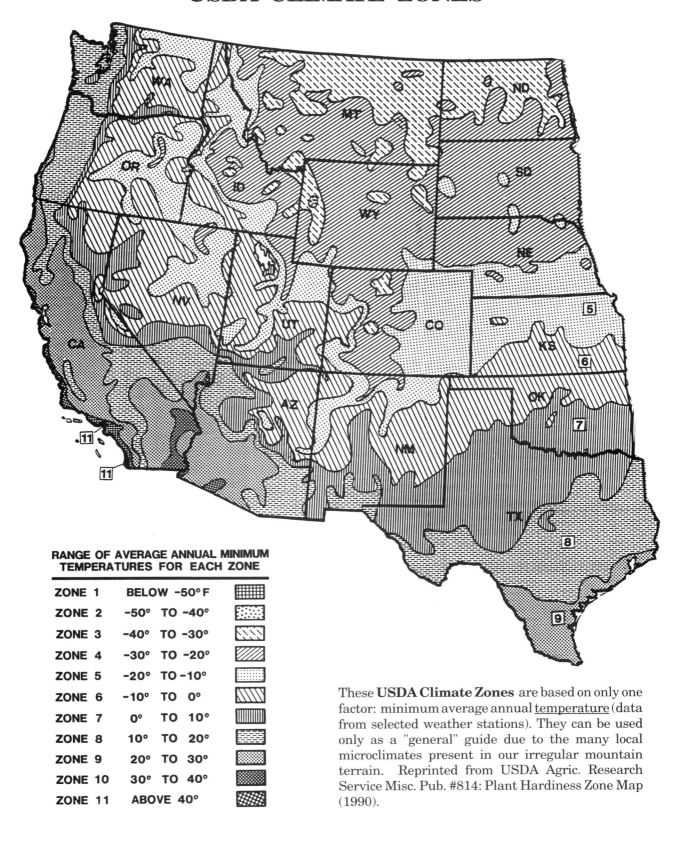